Elijah
The Lonely Zealot

מגיד

MAGGID

Elchanan Samet

ELIJAH
THE LONELY ZEALOT

Translated by Kaeren Fish

Maggid Books

Elijah
The Lonely Zealot

First Edition, 2021

Maggid Books
An imprint of Koren Publishers Jerusalem Ltd.

POB 8531, New Milford, CT 06776-8531, USA
& POB 4044, Jerusalem 9104001, Israel
www.maggidbooks.com

The publication of this book was made possible
through the generous support of *The Jewish Book Trust*.

ISBN 978-1-59264-533-6, *hardcover*

Printed and bound in the United States

In honor of our parents

Miriam and Bernard Hochstein

*whose commitment to learning Torah
and generosity of mind and spirit
inspired us*
להגדיל תורה ולהאדיר

In memory of

Mr. and Mrs. Phillip Braun

and

Mr. and Mrs. Norman Liberman

Contents

Preface to the English Edition .... *xiii*

Introduction .... *xv*

THE DROUGHT

1. *Elijah's Appearance* 3

2. *Elijah's Oath: Commanded by God or at the Prophet's Initiative?* 9

3. *Elijah's Experiences During the Drought: Why Are They Recorded?*.. 14

4. *Wadi Cherith (I Kings 17:2–7)* 20

5. *The Widow in Zarephath (I Kings 17:8–16)* 29

6. *Elijah Revives the Widow's Son (I Kings 17:17–24)* 51

7. *Elijah on His Way to Appear Before Ahab (I Kings 18:1–16)* 96

8. *The Second Encounter Between Elijah and Ahab (I Kings 18:16–18)* ... 121

9. *Structure of the Drought Narrative (I Kings 17:1–18:18)* 133

*Appendix: The Complete Narrative of I Kings
Chapters 17–19 and Its Components* 139

CARMEL

10. *Was Elijah Commanded to Act as He Does?* 153

11. *Elijah Addresses the Nation (I Kings 18:21–24)* 161

12. Elijah Addresses the Prophets of Baal (I Kings 18:25–29) 167

13. Elijah's Preparations for Descent of God's Fire (I Kings 18:30–35)...... 181

14. Elijah's Prayer (I Kings 18:36–37) 195

15. God's Fire 213

16. "To Whom Shall You Compare Me, That I Shall Equal
    Him? – Says the Holy One" (Isaiah 40:25) 218

17. The Nation's Response (I Kings 18:39–40)....................... 225

18. Ahab's Return to the Scene (I Kings 18:41–42).................. 232

19. "Go Up, Eat and Drink, for There Is the Sound of Rumbling
    Rain" (I Kings 18:41) 237

20. Why Is Elijah's Prayer Not Answered
    Immediately? (I Kings 18:42–44) 243

21. "God's Hand Was Upon Elijah... and He Ran Before Ahab"
    (I Kings 18:45–46) 251

Appendix: Elijah the Prophet and Ḥoni HaMe'agel 259

HOREB

22. Structure of the Story (I Kings 19:1–21) 269

23. Elijah's Flight (I Kings 19:1–4) 272

24. God's Angel's Two Revelations to Elijah
    (I Kings 19:5–8)... 287

25. "He Announced Rebuke at Sinai, and Judgments of
    Vengeance at Horeb" (Sefer Ben Sira) 299

26. Revelation in a "Small, Silent Voice" (I Kings 19:11–14).......... 307

27. "They Seek My Life, to Take It" (I Kings 19:14) 314

28. The Mission (I Kings 19:15–18)................................. 318

29. Was the Mission Fulfilled? 334

30. Elijah and Elisha's First Encounter (I Kings 19:19–21) 349

Appendix I: Comparison Between Elijah's and Jonah's
Flight and Move East of Nineveh 372

Appendix II: Haftara of Parashat Pinḥas........................... 378

NABOTH

31. *The Episode of Naboth and the King's Rights* 383

32. *"Have You Murdered and Also Inherited?" – Ahab's Responsibility* 388

33. *Naboth's Refusal and His Motives* 395

34. *Ahab's Punishment and That of His Household* 401

35. *"Have You Found Me, My Enemy?" (I Kings 21:20)* 409

36. *The Significance of Ahab's Submission (I Kings 21:27–29)* 413

37. *Ahab's Two Responses: A Comparison* 420

38. *Conclusion: Structure of the Narrative* 426

AHAZIAH

39. *Ahaziah Son of Ahab: Overview* 441

40. *Ahaziah's Messengers: King vs. Prophet* 444

41. *Ahaziah's Messengers: "Go, Inquire" vs. "Go, Return"*
   (II Kings 1:2–6) 447

42. *"A Hairy Man with a Girdle of Leather About His Loins"*
   (II Kings 1:7–8) 454

43. *The Consumption by Fire of the Two Captains of Fifty and*
   Their Fifty Men (II Kings 1:9–12) 458

44. *The First Captain of Fifty vs. the Second (II Kings 1:9–12)* 471

45. *The Third Captain of Fifty (II Kings 1:13–14)* 476

46. *"Who Has Ascended to Heaven and Descended Again?"*
   (Proverbs 30:4) 484

47. *Structure of the Narrative* 495

48. *God and His Prophet's Word vs. the King's Word: Summary* 501

THE STORM

49. *Preface* 509

50. *Elijah's Journey to His Place of Ascent* 519

51. *Elijah and Elisha on Their Way to the Jordan* 538

52. *The Dialogue on the Other Side of the Jordan (II Kings 2:9–10)* 544

53. *Elijah's Ascent (II Kings 2:11–12)* 555

54. *After Elijah's Ascent*... 561

55. *Elijah Lives On* 570

Preface to the English Edition

*E*lijah: *The Lonely Zealot* presents a systematic literary commentary on the chapters in the book of Kings in which the prophet Elijah appears.

Elijah first makes an appearance in chapter 17 of I Kings, and he continues to be at the center of events until chapter 2 of II Kings (excluding chapters 20 and 22 of I Kings). There are six different episodes in these chapters, and we have devoted a series of studies to each of them, with the titles: (1) The Drought, (2) Carmel, (3) Horeb, (4) Naboth, (5) Ahaziah, and (6) The Storm.

For each episode, the series of studies constitutes a "close reading" of that episode. However, each study deals with a separate topic and can be read independently.

Elijah's powerful character is at the core of the six episodes discussed in this book, some of which are among the most turbulent of the biblical narratives. Is there a central theme that links these stories, other than Elijah's appearance as the main character in each of them? Do the chapters attempt to deal with, and perhaps even answer, a focal question that lies in the background of the Elijah narratives?

The answer to these questions seems to be yes. The prophet's policy of action often aroused opposition and protest among the people with whom he came into contact. The main question facing the reader is: To what extent is a prophet's policy of action, inasmuch as it is the product of his own initiative, accepted by the One who sent him?

This book was first published in Hebrew in 2003 with the title *Pirkei Eliyahu*, by Ma'aliyot Publishers of Yeshivat Birkat Moshe, Maale Adumim; it was republished as a new edition in 2009, by Yedi'ot Sefarim.

This English translation has been made possible thanks to the generosity of Susan and Barnet Liberman and Suzanne and Michael Hochstein. I owe them my deepest gratitude.

Kaeren Fish, whose translations of my writings have accompanied me for many years, translated this volume. I am delighted that her translation of this work is the first of my writings to appear in English as a book, thus opening the door for many more readers. May Ms. Fish see blessing in all her endeavors.

I am most grateful to Rabbi Reuven Ziegler, editors Rachelle Emanuel, Debbie Ismailoff, and Ita Olesker, and the entire staff at Maggid Books, who have worked hard to publish this book in its current format.

Elijah: The Lonely Zealot is complemented by the Hebrew book *Pirkei Elisha* (Tel Aviv: Miskal Publishing, 2009), which goes on to explain, by means of the same literary methods that I use in this volume, the sections in the book of Kings that focus on the prophet Elisha, Elijah's disciple and successor. In that book we examine, among other issues, the emotional and practical bond between the mentor and his disciple, a bond that we begin to see and discuss in the present volume. In *Pirkei Elisha*, additional light is shed on the character of Elijah. It is possible that at some time in the future, it too will be translated into English.

I thank God for granting me the privilege of seeing this book, the first of my books to be published in English translation, in print. Now those who are unable to read *Pirkei Eliyahu* in the original Hebrew will be able to become acquainted with the ideas, interpretations, and analytical methods proposed in *Elijah: The Lonely Zealot*.

Elchanan Samet
Kfar Etzion, July 2021

Introduction

THE ELIJAH AND ELISHA NARRATIVES: UNIQUE ASPECTS

Starting with Elijah's appearance in chapter 17 of I Kings, the book of Kings devotes several chapters to the personality and actions of this great prophet and, later, to those of his disciple and successor, Elisha. This extended focus on the two prophets – even where they do not directly affect the history of the Kingdom of Israel – is a phenomenon unparalleled in Tanakh. (Moses and Samuel are also at the center of the books describing their activities, but in addition to being prophets they are also leaders of the nation, while Elijah and Elisha serve only as prophets.)

The stories of Elijah and Elisha share a number of special characteristics:

1. *Multiplicity of miracles:* This is particularly noticeable in comparison with the paucity of miracles performed both before the appearance of Elijah and after Elisha leaves the scene. For the most part these miracles seem to be performed at the initiative of Elijah or Elisha alone; only very rarely is a miracle based on an explicit divine command. There are even miracles where there is no mention whatsoever of God's name. In addition, some of the miracles are performed for the prophets' own benefit or for the benefit of a single individual, rather than in response to any national need.

2. *Continuity:* Elisha, who is Elijah's disciple and attendant, is also his heir and successor as a prophet of Israel. This phenomenon has no

parallel in all the history of prophecy. Admittedly, it is somewhat reminiscent of the relationship between Moses and Joshua, but the latter serves as Moses's successor as national leader, not as a prophet. The unique relationship between Elijah and Elisha demands that we pay close attention to the link between the two sets of narratives, especially to those stories in which the two prophets are described together. Similarly, this unique relationship calls for a constant comparison between the deeds of the disciple and those of his mentor.

3. *Literary framework:* This comprises individual narratives, at the center of which stands the prophet. From the collection of narratives as a whole, we gain understanding of the prophet's character and his unique prophetic approach.

The singular nature of the stories of Elijah and Elisha raises several questions, which we shall address later on.

ELIJAH'S APPEARANCE IN KING AHAB'S GENERATION

Few prophets are mentioned in the book of Kings prior to the arrival of Elijah. So why does Elijah appear in the Kingdom of Israel at this specific time, leading to intensified prophetic activity from this period onward?

The Kingdom of Israel, ever since its establishment under the reign of Jeroboam son of Nebat, deteriorated steadily. It is easy to see how the religious sins went hand in hand with the internal political disintegration of the kingdom. Rapid degeneration characterized the kingdom, especially during the period prior to the rise of Omri, as described in I Kings, chapter 16.

A significant change occurred with the rise of the House of Omri to power. With the stabilization of the kingdom, the political assassinations that had been frequent occurrences until then ceased, and the internal regime in Israel became secure. Omri and his son, Ahab, also made efforts to fortify their kingdom through large-scale construction, reinforcement of the army, and a foreign policy based upon treaties with neighboring countries. The relations between the Kingdom of Israel and the Kingdom of Judah changed completely, and they became allies to the extent that marriages were forged between the two royal houses. The treaty with the kingdom of Tyre and Sidon was renewed, and here too, marriages cemented the bonds between the two royal houses, with Ahab marrying Jezebel, the daughter of Ethbaal, king of Sidon. This period was one of promising political ascendancy for the Kingdom of Israel. These processes did not happen spontaneously; the vision and efforts of Omri and of his son Ahab brought about this progress, and both the biblical text and *Hazal* give them credit for this.

However, alongside this process of political revival, the Kingdom of Israel underwent an inverse process of religious decline. The contrast between these two developments is described already during the reign of Omri, founder of the dynasty:

> He bought the Samaria mountain from Shemer for two talents of silver, and he built up the mountain and called the name of the city which he built after Shemer, the owner of the Samaria mountain. But Omri did evil in the eyes of God, and he did worse than all those who had preceded him. He walked in all the ways of Jeroboam … to anger God, the Lord of Israel. … The rest of the things that Omri did, and the valor that he performed, are they not written. … (I Kings 16:24–27)

On one hand, Omri built up a new capital city, thereby symbolizing, like David before him, his intention to introduce a new national era. On the other hand, he "did evil in the eyes of God … worse than all those who had preceded him." On one hand, he angered God; on the other hand, he performed mighty acts of valor in Israel's wars against its enemies.

This dissonance becomes even more acute in the days of Ahab, his son. Here we discover that there is a connection between the two processes:

> Ahab, the son of Omri, did worse in God's eyes than all those who preceded him. It was an easy thing for him to walk in the sins of Jeroboam son of Nebat: *He took as a wife Jezebel the daughter of Ethbaal, king of the Sidonites, and he went and served Baal and bowed down to him.* He established an altar to Baal in the house of Baal which he had built in the Samaria. And Ahab made an

ashera, and Ahab did more to anger God, the Lord of Israel, than all the kings of Israel who had preceded him." (16:30–33)

Within the framework of the political covenant with the kingdom of Sidon (a covenant dating back to the days of David and Solomon), Omri married his son to Jezebel, daughter of the king of Sidon. Thus, for the first time, the stage was set for institutionalized idolatry in Israel, supported by the royal family.[1]

It quickly becomes apparent that Jezebel was a forceful woman – both in relation to Ahab, her husband, and to the kingdom which she had entered. While the wives of King Solomon had exploited his old age in order to build altars to their gods, apparently for personal worship, Jezebel tried to import idolatrous worship into Israel on a grand scale. She brought hundreds of prophets of Baal with her from her birthplace, and it seems that it was on her initiative that the altar to Baal was established in the city of Samaria. These steps aroused the opposition of the prophets of God, and therefore Jezebel instituted a campaign of persecution in order to eliminate them from the kingdom; it is possible that this campaign even included destruction of God's altars. Such deeds had never before been perpetrated in Israel.

Jezebel also interfered in other aspects of the administration of the kingdom; the story of the vineyard of Naboth illustrates the corrupt norms that she introduced into the regime.

Despite all this, Ahab was a great king, promoting the benefit of his nation, as he understood it, fighting Israel's wars selflessly when necessary, doing much to build up the kingdom and its army, and implementing a foreign policy of great scope and vision.

Such a generation and such a king required a prophet of great stature, who had no fear of persecution and would not hesitate to make his voice heard, to berate and rebuke the nation and its king, and even to punish when necessary. The success of the House of Omri in those public spheres in which the kings were active contrasts starkly with their very grave actions in the religious sphere. This contradiction demanded

---

1. According to some commentators, Jeroboam's act of placing golden calves in Beit El and in Dan was not true idol worship but rather an inappropriate way of serving God.

the appearance of a prophet who was able to warn of the results of such sins. In these historical circumstances, there was a need for a prophet with sufficient personality to draw both king and nation after him.

PERFORMING MIRACLES WITHOUT A DIVINE COMMAND

It is clear that miracles were the main "tools" that Elijah and Elisha employed to fulfill their prophetic mission. Their miraculous acts might be compared to the prophetic monologues delivered by prophets of later generations (Hosea, etc.). But while these oral prophecies generally emphasize that the prophets were conveying God's word (and even when this is not stated explicitly, it is implicit in what they say), the miracles performed by Elijah and Elisha were not, for the most part, commanded by God. In most cases the prophet did not even offer a prayer. We may therefore assume that these prophets operated on their own initiative and at their own discretion and, nevertheless, God answered them and fulfilled their wishes. Indeed, this is the situation as Maimonides describes it in his Introduction to the Mishna (R. Shilat edition, p. 29):

> All that Elijah and Elisha and the other prophets did in the realm of wonders was not done in order to establish their prophecy, for their prophecy had already been confirmed previously. Rather, they performed these wonders because they needed them, and owing to their closeness to God He fulfilled their wishes, as it is written concerning the righteous, "You shall utter a decree and it shall be fulfilled for you" (Job 22:28).

Rabbi Joseph Albo, in the fourth article of his *Sefer HaIkarim*, condenses this idea into a principle of faith:

> It is a great principle of the Torah, and a root of faith…that the blessed God bends nature under the feet of the believers…and certainly by the word of the prophets, who could perform as many miracles as they decreed. Elijah said, "As God lives…if there will be dew and rain for these years, except by my word" (I Kings 17:1); he also said, "If I am a man of God, let fire descend from heaven and consume you and your fifty men" (II Kings 1:10) – and it was

so. Likewise, Elisha said, "At this time tomorrow, a *se'a* of fine flour will be sold for a shekel" (II Kings 7:1), and it was so; also, the iron floated (II Kings 6:6), in addition to the rest of the miracles that he performed without any preceding prophecy or divine command.

However, not all the commentators agree. Some assume the existence of a divine command or a prayer offered by the prophet concerning each individual miracle. Rabbi Yitzḥak Arama, for instance, differs sharply with Rabbi Albo; in the eighth chapter of *Akedat Yitzḥak* he writes:

> I am certain, concerning all of the prophets and righteous men that [Rabbi Albo] mentions, that if there had been no divine command concerning each instance, they would not have performed [the wonders] on their own accord."

Other commentators deliberate on this question in several places in their commentaries. See, for example, below, "The Drought," chapter 2.

> Straightforward reading of the text would seem to support the view of Maimonides and Rabbi Albo. If we examine the rare cases in which there is a divine command or a prayer to God offered by the prophet prior to the performance of the miracle, we see that these instances are the exception, implying that where no command or prayer is mentioned, the miracle took place without them, on the initiative and by decree of the prophet alone.

One of the commentators who adopts the opinion of Maimonides and Rabbi Albo is Abrabanel, and he raises the following question:

> As to the stature of [Elisha] as a prophet, there is no doubt that the text attests to it and to that of Elijah.... It appears from their actions that most of what they performed in wondrous ways was done on their own initiative: They made decrees concerning natural phenomena, and their word was fulfilled. We must then ask: *How did these prophets merit... to perform the miracles without a divine command?* (Abrabanel, commentary on II Kings 8:1–6)

The answer that we propose to this question represents, in our view, the necessary background for understanding the status of Elijah and Elisha in Tanakh and for an understanding of their activity in general. It is also the key to the exegetical study of their actions, as the end of this introduction will show.

THE PROPHET'S PART IN THE DIVINE MISSION

Is the prophet merely a vehicle to convey God's word to his listeners (a sort of recording and broadcasting device which receives a frequency that is inaudible to others, which he "translates" into audible speech), or is he an active partner in the effort to achieve the aims of his prophetic mission? It would seem that the second description is more accurate: The prophet is required to place all his talents and ability, his very personality, and even his personal lifestyle at the disposal of his mission.

The Talmud (Sanhedrin 89a) states: "No two prophets prophesy in the same style." God's word, then, appears in a verbal garb suited to the style – the personality and traits – of the prophet who declares it. The prophet must couch God's word in the most suitable terms and concepts he can find in his vocabulary, using the literary and rhetorical devices that will best succeed in conveying the content of the message to the listener. The prophet's unique style is what creates the literary form in which the prophetic message, or substance, manifests itself. This substance is like a soul that gives life to the body, but it is also dependent on it. A change in style, a change in the form in which God's word appears, will necessarily affect the image of the inner substance. This intimate relationship between substance and form makes the prophet a partner in the prophetic mission, in the full sense of the word.

This is true of prophetic *speech*. However, the early prophets, who preceded the oratory prophets, are characterized by the *acts* that they performed in the various spheres of their prophetic activity. What is the nature of the partnership between the prophet and his Sender in these acts? Does any such partnership exist here?

Sometimes the prophet is commanded by God, "Go and do such and such." Even then, the fulfillment of God's command within the conditions of a dynamic and changing reality requires resourcefulness on the part of the prophet. He must enlist his own originality and initiative, and adapt himself to the prevailing conditions, as he perceives them.

However, sometimes the divine command indicates to the prophet only the long-term aim of his mission. Then the prophet must bridge the gap between the present situation and the future when the purpose of his mission will be achieved. He must create all the intermediate stages himself, with no explicit instructions. How is he to do this? Obviously, by enlisting all of his human resources, placing all his abilities at the disposal of his mission, and exerting maximum physical and spiritual effort. Clearly, the choice of strategy to achieve the aim of his mission is left to the prophet's discretion. This discretion, and the way he chooses to implement his strategy, will depend on his personality, on his personal style. This individual style of operating corresponds to the verbal style of the oratory prophet. We may paraphrase the words of the Talmud and add that "no two prophets *operate* in the same style."

All of the above is equally applicable to a scenario in which an agent represents a human dispatcher: To the extent that the agent is loyal to his handler or supervisor, he will exert every effort to fulfill his mission successfully, even when he lacks precise instructions for every stage of the mission and every possible situation that may arise. Some situations may help him and he should take advantage of them, while others are likely to harm his mission and he must overcome them. We learn what is expected of a loyal emissary from the detailed and repeated description in the Torah of the way in which Abraham's servant went about fulfilling the mission entrusted to him by his master in very few words (Gen. 24). In the book of Proverbs, too, we find some insightful adages concerning loyal agents (see, for example, 13:17 and 25:13). If all of this is true concerning a mission on behalf of a mortal, how much more so concerning a mission that God entrusts to His prophets.

PROPHETIC ACTS WITHOUT AN EXPLICIT COMMAND

What is the prophet's part within his partnership with God in the actions that he performs as part of his prophetic mission? We have already stated that his role changes in accordance with the nature of his mission and the command that he is given. We may add that the greater the prophet, the greater is his human part in the fulfillment of his mission as a prophet. To clarify this point, let us return to our metaphor of a mortal dispatcher.

A person who sends his messenger on a highly important, complex mission will formulate his instructions in accordance with the agent's personality and level. If the agent is inexperienced, and his loyalty has not yet been proven, or if he is not very intelligent, the dispatcher will take care to make his instructions as detailed as possible. He will enumerate several possible situations that the agent may encounter, and will guide him how to respond in each instance. If possible, he will request that the agent maintain continuous contact with him, in order to receive ongoing guidance as he progresses. In this scenario, where the dispatcher has little confidence in his agent, the latter is left with not much room for independent action. He is certainly a loyal emissary, following his instructions with great precision, but ultimately, he is not a very effective one.

The picture is quite different if the agent is experienced, wise and intelligent, and completely loyal to his dispatcher. In such a case, the dispatcher can entrust him with the mission with just the briefest mention of the final aim. The dispatcher will be quite confident that the agent will achieve the aim in the best possible way, using his own initiative and drawing on his rich experience, altogether focused on the wishes of his dispatcher to whom he is close and whom he understands well.

Let us now return to the prophet participating in the fulfillment of his mission, and ask: How are we to relate to and evaluate those actions which he performs on his own initiative? Are they actions that are performed "by God's word," to be considered as though they had been explicitly commanded? On one hand, it is difficult to make such an assertion, since God does not in fact command these actions; they are based on the prophet's own discretion, on his "style," and hence their source is mortal. On the other hand, the prophet is apparently required to perform these acts; they are required by virtue of the divine command that indicates only the final aim. These acts express the partnership discussed above, between God and His prophet. For this reason, we frequently find clear expressions – either by the prophet or in the text – indicating that these actions are performed "by God's word." The prophet's actions bear a divine seal of approval, for his intention is directed toward his Dispatcher; he aims to fulfill His wishes and achieve His aims.

ELIJAH'S AND ELISHA'S PROPHETIC MISSION

Let us now return to agents of mortal dispatchers. In days gone by, it was quite common for wealthy landowners to leave the administration and operation of their estate in the hands of a representative whom they would appoint. This steward would be left alone to operate at his discretion, the general aim being to run the estate in optimal fashion for the benefit of its owner. Only once in a long while would the steward present himself before the landowner and report on his actions and his plans.

It was rare for a landowner to find a steward so loyal, so aware of his preferences, and so capable in his job that it was possible to leave the running of the estate completely in his hands, such that he would operate in place of the owner, with almost total freedom.

A superficial observation would mislead one to identify the steward (who would usually reside in the landowner's castle) as the landowner himself. Only someone who knew the steward to be less well-to-do than his surroundings would suggest, or who saw him performing all manner of labor around the estate that was not appropriate for someone of the owner's apparent means, would realize that he was operating as the agent of the wealthy landowner.

The same relationship can exist in the realm of prophecy. To the extent that the prophet appears to act independently within the framework of his prophetic mission, not requiring explicit commands from God telling him what to do, we may conclude that he is a great and responsible prophet, loyal to God. A proper perception of his actions shows them to be undertaken with their Dispatcher's approval and with the intention of fulfilling His will; thus these, too, are performed "by God's word."

This is the key to understanding most of the acts that Elijah and Elisha performed of their own accord and at their own discretion, as part of their mission to serve as prophets for their generation. They were entrusted with the general task of guiding Israel, God's inheritance. They were loyal stewards to the "Landowner"; God handed them the keys, as it were, and relied on their judgment to do everything necessary for God's "estate" to flourish and produce abundant fruit.

We can now understand the multiplicity of miracles that characterize the respective careers of these two prophets. They performed them, in general, at their own discretion and without any command, in order to combat the mistaken impression that their messages were not inspired by God's word. The miracle was proof that their actions were performed by God's word, for no mortal could generate such wonders without God acceding to the prophet's will in initiating them. The miracle served as a divine stamp of approval, certifying that the "Landowner" approved of what His prophet-agent was doing.

THREE LEVELS OF PROPHETIC ACTS

We have mentioned that the prophet may act based on his own judgment and his human understanding as part of his partnership in the prophetic mission. We must then ask: Is it possible that the prophet might be mistaken in his judgment and his desire to perform some act that is not suited to, or will not have any value in relation to, the aim of his mission, such that his actions will be undesirable in God's eyes?

When God gives the prophet explicit instructions as to what he must do, it would seem that there is no room for error. Our question concerns those actions performed by the prophet as part of his mission without any explicit divine command.

Our answer must be that it is indeed possible for errors to occur, for the source of the prophet's action is within himself. Since he is mortal, he is not immune to human weaknesses. Therefore, when it comes to actions that are undertaken based on personal judgment, it is possible for the prophet to be mistaken, or for there to be some deviation from the divine will.

We may mention here three examples of prophets who tried to act in a certain way, as part of their prophetic mission, without any divine command – and were mistaken:

1. Samuel is sent by God to anoint one of Jesse's sons as the future king of Israel in place of Saul. Upon setting eyes on Eliab, the eldest, he is certain that this is the chosen son. He proclaims, "Surely God's anointed one is before Him!" (I Sam. 16:6). But God rebukes him

for his mistake: "Do not pay attention to his outward appearance ... for it is not as man sees it: Man sees [only] with his eyes, but God looks into the heart" (v. 7).

2. David approaches Nathan the prophet, expressing a desire to build an edifice to house the Ark of the Covenant. Nathan tells him, "All that is in your heart, go and do, for God is with you" (II Sam. 7:3). But the same night Nathan receives a prophetic message telling him that God does not want David to build the Temple.

3. Elisha responds to the Shunammite woman whose son has died: He sends his attendant, Gehazi, armed with the prophet's staff and with instructions as to how to revive the boy. But the attempt at resuscitation fails (II Kings 4:29–31). It is only when Elisha himself comes to the home of the Shunammite woman, prays to God, and performs a series of actions, that the boy opens his eyes.

Obviously, we must seek the reason for the prophet's mistake in every such instance. But whatever it may have been, it is clear that the prophet's word, based on his own judgment, does not become God's word except where God's view accords with his. In the above examples, God does not agree with the prophets' word, and He even reveals Himself to Samuel and Nathan, ordering them to correct their mistake.

Here we must raise a different question: Is it possible that a prophet may act in a way that is not desirable in God's eyes, but that God will still permit his actions and fulfill his word? There may be different reasons for such a situation – perhaps because divine opposition to what the prophet is doing is not absolute, or because the prophet is acting in public (unlike the three examples above), and a lack of response on God's part would harm the prophet's status in the eyes of the nation as well as the institution of prophecy in general. In situations such as these, once again, it is difficult to say that the prophet's actions are performed "by God's word." God admittedly responds to him, even acceding to the miracle that he wishes to perform, but this is no proof that God in fact agrees with the prophet's view.

It seems that we can divide actions of the prophets based upon their own human judgment into three levels. The lowest is when his action is defined as a mistake (either explicitly, in the text, or by inference), and the prophet is required to cancel his act or to correct it. Such instances are extremely rare, but they are not difficult to identify, for the text attests to the mistake. We must explore the reason for the mistake, and what we may learn from it.

The next level is where the prophet's action is not in accordance with God's will, but nevertheless, God fulfills his word for some reason. Such instances are more complicated to identify, since the prophet's action appears to be rewarded with success – why should we think that God did not desire it? A very sensitive reading is required for this purpose, with attention paid to the *way* in which God fulfills his word, as well as to what transpires afterward both in the actual situation and in the relationship between God and the prophet. All of this should expose the criticism of the act and lead the prophet himself to recognize his mistake. We will discuss such a case in depth in the first part of the book – in the chapters on the drought.

The highest level, fundamentally different from the others, is when the prophet's action reflects the divine will and achieves the objective of his mission. Such an act is performed "by God's word" even where there is no explicit command. There is no doubt that the great majority of the actions by all the prophets in Tanakh fall into this category.

The chapters concerning Elijah and Elisha in the book of Kings tell us about two great prophets, most of whose actions as prophets are not performed by divine command but rather on the basis of their own judgment. This fact alone speaks in praise of these prophets and teaches us something about their greatness and their loyalty to God. We need not necessarily conclude from this that every one of the narratives is meant to praise the prophet. A reading of these chapters requires a degree of sensitivity that is constantly questioning whether the narrative includes criticism of the prophet or whether it describes his actions as bearing a resounding divine stamp of approval.

The Drought

אִם יִהְיֶה הַשָּׁנִים הָאֵלֶּה טַל וּמָטָר

There shall be no dew or rain during these years.

I Kings 17:1

Chapter 1

Elijah's Appearance

> Elijah the Tishbite, one of the residents of Gilead, said to Ahab: "As the Lord God of Israel lives, before whom I have stood, there shall be no dew or rain during these years, except by my word." (I Kings 17:1)

With no background or introduction – as we would expect when an important character is about to appear for the first time – Elijah bursts onto the scene, right into the midst of the action. A reading of the above verse would certainly not give the impression that we have reached the beginning of a new and great narrative, the introduction to a series of chapters; rather, we feel that we are in the middle of a plot with familiar characters. But the reader has no prior information. Who is this Elijah? And what is the meaning of his fearsome oath?

ELIJAH: NOVICE OR EXPERIENCED PROPHET?

In lieu of an introduction to the character of Elijah, we are given a phrase that describes him, and is meant to satisfy our curiosity: Elijah is a "Tishbite, one of the residents of Gilead." These words give rise to extensive speculation and much commentary, which we shall not discuss here. Suffice it to say that Elijah arrives at the center of the kingdom having hailed from Gilead, on the eastern side of the Jordan River. Is his visit to Ahab (apparently in Samaria) his first appearance as a prophet, or is he an established prophet whose words and actions are being recorded for the first time in Tanakh?

It is difficult to arrive at an unequivocal answer to this question, but the reader's impression is that Elijah is not a prophet who is just beginning his career and role. This impression is created firstly by the power of his appearance, in which he swears that the rainfall will depend on his word, and secondly, by the formulation of his declaration, which would seem to bear out his veteran status: "As the Lord God of Israel lives, *before whom I have stood.*"

What is the significance of these words? Radak (Rabbi David Kimḥi) interprets the "standing before God" as standing in *prayer*. Abrabanel, on the other hand, maintains that this expression indicates that Elijah is a prophet who stands ready to *serve God* at all times:

> He says, "Before whom I have stood" – meaning, before whom he prophesies and from whom he receives the spirit of prophecy. This may be compared with what Jeremiah says (Jer. 23:18), "For who has *stood* in God's counsel, and seen and heard His word." (Abrabanel, commentary on I Kings 17:1)

It would seem that Abrabanel's interpretation fits the verse better, since the first part of his oath, "As the Lord God of Israel lives … before whom I have stood," appears to represent the justification for the second part, "there shall be no dew or rain … except by my word." This makes sense only if we assume that Elijah's "standing" before God expresses a special relationship on God's part *toward him* – his appointment as a prophet, and not a relationship on Elijah's part toward God, i.e., the fact that he stands in prayer before Him.

In addition, the wording of his oath, "as the Lord God of Israel lives … before whom I have stood," appears only another three times in the book of Kings (and in the whole of Tanakh).[1] An examination of these sources reveals that all three are uttered in the context of the prophets' prophetic activity, and so it is reasonable to assume that the expression "before whom I have stood" here is meant in the same context.

---

1. See I Kings 18:15; II Kings 3:14, 5:16.

Moreover, a review of the expression "standing before" (*amida lifnei*) in Tanakh reveals that it refers to a slave or servant standing before his master to serve him.[2]

It seems that Radak's interpretation, suggesting that Elijah stands before God in prayer, arises from the fact that we have not met Elijah as a prophet prior to his appearance here. Radak therefore chooses to interpret the expression in a more limited way. However, the wording of the oath, as well as its content, may specifically testify that Elijah is not a novice. Only by virtue of being a prophet who constantly stands before God and who is ready to serve Him at all times, can he have the audacity to swear as he does.

ELIJAH'S OATH: BACKGROUND

Why does Elijah utter such a severe oath? And we must also ask: Does his confrontation with Ahab begin and end with this oath, or does this verse represent the conclusion of a longer speech or dialogue that is not recorded in the text?

The reason for Elijah's oath is clear from the text preceding his appearance, in the description of Ahab's kingdom at the end of chapter 16:

> Ahab, the son of Omri, did worse in God's eyes than all those who preceded him. It was an easy thing for him to walk in the sins of Jeroboam son of Nebat: He took as a wife Jezebel the daughter of Ethbaal, king of the Sidonites, and he went and served Baal and bowed down to him. He established an altar to Baal in the house of Baal, which he had built in the Samaria. And Ahab made an *ashera*, and Ahab did more to anger God, the Lord of Israel, than all the kings of Israel who had preceded him. (I Kings 16:30–33)

Later, we hear a belated justification for the decree of drought in the words of Elijah to Ahab. When Ahab accuses the prophet of being a "troubler of Israel," since he has brought famine upon them, Elijah answers:

---

2. The expression has this meaning both in the context of one person standing before another (see I Sam. 16:21–22; I Kings 1:2) and in the context of a person standing before God (see Jer. 15:19).

> I have not troubled Israel, but [rather] you and your father's house, by abandoning the commandments of God and going after the Baal gods. (18:18)

This accusation against Ahab, king of Israel, for having officially introduced idolatrous worship (inspired by his gentile wife) in a city of his kingdom appears here for the first time in Tanakh and in the history of Israel.[3] Concerning such actions the Torah warns:

> Guard yourselves lest your hearts tempt you, and you turn aside and worship other gods and bow down to them. Then God's anger will burn against you and He will close the heavens, and there will be no rain, nor will the ground give its produce. (Deut. 11:16–17)

Thus, Elijah's oath is simply the realization of the Torah's warning. But did Elijah make this clear when he spoke to Ahab, or did he rely on his listener's understanding of the background to his oath? In the Midrash, Elijah's oath is depicted as the climactic conclusion of a heated and dramatic dialogue between Elijah and Ahab:

> Ahab, king of Israel, asked Elijah the Tishbite; he said to him: "It is written in the Torah, 'Guard yourselves lest your hearts tempt you … God's anger will burn against you and He will shut the heavens. …' Here I am, worshipping all the idolatry in the world, and see what good is coming about in my time. …" Elijah was immediately filled with great anger against him. He said: "Worthless man! You have despised Him who created all the world for His glory, Him who gave the words of Torah for His glory. By your life, I judge you only on the basis of your own words." As it is written, "Elijah the Tishbite, one of the residents of Gilead, said to Ahab: As the Lord God of Israel lives … there will be no dew or rain during these years except by my word." Elijah took the

---

3. See above, p. xviii, for reference to the gods of King Solomon's wives and Jeroboam's act of placing golden calves in Beit El and in Dan.

keys of rainfall and left, and there was great famine throughout the whole world. (*Eliyahu Zuta* 8)

According to this midrash, there is no doubt that Elijah's oath followed a dispute between the prophet and Ahab, the king.

This conclusion is also borne out by the literal text. Even if no verbal dialogue actually took place, the midrash still reflects our impression that the verse recorded in the text is not an introduction to the events, but rather a vehicle to bring us into the midst of the action to start the narrative concerning Elijah.

We understand from here that Elijah, who appears in Tanakh for the first time in our verse, is an experienced, veteran prophet, but the Tanakh has told us nothing about him until now. From the present discussion, we see that even his first appearance as a prophet is a somewhat fragmented one, since the text fails to offer a proper introduction.

THE FRAGMENTED INTRODUCTION

If we assume that Elijah is an experienced prophet, our question concerning the fragmented nature of his introduction is intensified, since we are faced with an exceptional literary phenomenon: A central character, who will stand at center stage for the next several chapters and who will be the focus of all the reader's attention from this point onward, enters the scene with none of the background that would usually be presented in Tanakh. Not only do we sense a lack of some general introduction as to the identity of Elijah as a prophet, but the text even fails to provide background to the specific incident that triggers his oath.

It seems that Elijah's surprising, sudden, and mysterious appearance at the beginning of his role mirrors his disappearance at the end, which is even more surprising and mysterious, although in a different sense. What is common to both is the unexpectedness and suddenness of his arrival and departure. In the Midrash the verse from the book of Nahum (1:3), "God's way is in the tempest and in the storm; the clouds are the dust of His feet," is interpreted as follows: "'In the storm': This refers to Elijah, as it is written, 'Elijah ascended in a storm to the heavens'" (Deuteronomy Rabba 3).

Indeed, this characterizes Elijah's path in general: He proceeds in a storm. He appears in a storm, he acts in a storm, and he leaves the scene in a storm, leaving a cloud of dust behind him. The mystery surrounding him is one of his most distinctive characteristics, both as described in the text itself and as perceived by the people of his generation (to the extent that this is expressed in the Tanakh).[4]

This, then, is the answer to our question: Elijah's sudden appearance at the beginning of chapter 17, without our knowing who he is or what circumstances provoke his adamant oath, is an intentional literary device calculated to create a mood and to prompt an attitude toward him on the part of the reader that will match that of the nation of Israel at the time.

---

4. This aspect of Elijah's character is seen when, after suddenly appearing here, Elijah disappears from the sight of the people for a long time in a most unexpected way. (The reader, however, follows his actions.) From Obadiah's words to Elijah (18:1), we understand that Ahab has failed in his desperate searches for him. When Elijah asks Obadiah to tell Ahab that he will appear before the king, Obadiah responds in a way that demonstrates how the people perceive Elijah: "It shall be, when I go from you, that *God's spirit will take you* I know not where, and I will come to tell Ahab, but he will not find you" (v. 12).

After the events at Mount Carmel, Elijah again vanishes from the eyes of the people and goes to Mount Horeb. Upon his return, he unexpectedly appears in the fields of Abel Meholah and takes Elisha with him without any advanced notice. He then again vanishes for an extended period, during which significant battles occur, but the prophet connected to these events is not Elijah. He suddenly appears in Naboth's vineyard, and later, completely unexpectedly, meets Ahaziah's messengers who have gone to inquire of Baal-Zebub, the god of Ekron. After meeting Ahaziah, he again suddenly disappears, and we, the readers, see him once more when he ascends to heaven in a storm. In this last narrative, we indeed follow his disappearance, but it is all beyond our comprehension. At the end of this narrative we read of the request that the "sons of the prophets" make of Elisha – a request that can summarize our review of Elijah as being a prophet who acts in a storm: "Let them go and seek your master, lest *God's spirit has taken him* and cast him upon one of the mountains or in one of the valleys" (II Kings 2:16). In this request they use similar words to those of Obadiah: "*God's spirit will take you* I know not where." Here again we can learn how Elijah is perceived by the people, even by those of the highest caliber.

Chapter 2

Elijah's Oath: Commanded by God or at the Prophet's Initiative?

Elijah the Tishbite, one of the residents of Gilead, said to Ahab: "As the Lord God of Israel lives, before whom I have stood, there shall be no dew or rain during these years, except by my word." (I Kings 17:1)

Does Elijah issue this decree, halting the dew and rain, because God has commanded him to appear before Ahab and speak in this way, or does he act on his own initiative? This question, as we shall see in future chapters, is of critical importance for an understanding of the rest of his story.

In the Midrash and in most of the commentaries we find the unequivocal position that Elijah acts on his own initiative. Let us examine, in this regard, two midrashim and the opinions of two commentators:

Ahab, king of Israel, asked Elijah the Tishbite … Elijah was immediately filled with great anger against him. He said to him, "… By your life, *I judge you* on the basis of your own words. …" *Elijah took the keys of rainfall and left. (Eliyahu Zuta 8,* quoted in full on pp. 6–7 above)

God created winter such that it would be winter, and summer such that it would be summer. *Elijah came and turned* the winter into summer, as it is written, "As the Lord God of Israel lives … there shall be no dew or rain during these years except by my word." … What is the meaning of the verse "a righteous man rules in the fear of God" (II Sam. 23:3)? The righteous rule, as it were, over that which God rules. How? Everything that God does, the righteous do. How? … God halts the rain, *and Elijah halted the rain*. (Deuteronomy Rabba 10:2)

Radak comments on our verse as follows:

Here *Elijah made a decree concerning the rainfall in his zealousness for God* because of the idolaters. As it is written in the Torah, "Lest … you turn aside and worship other gods and bow down to them. Then God's anger will burn against you and He will shut the heavens, and there will be no rain" (Deut. 11:16–17). *He trusts God to keep his word.* And concerning him and others like him it is written, "You shall utter a decree and it shall be fulfilled for you" (Job 22:28),[1] as Samuel the prophet said, "I will call out to God and He will give thunder and rain" (I Sam. 12:17). And since [Ahab] did more evil than anyone who had preceded him, Elijah decreed and announced to him that there would neither be dew nor rain, [so that] perhaps he would change his ways. And God, who is slow to anger, demonstrated patience with him as He did to those who preceded him. The words "except by my word" mean: Until he would see that everyone, or at least some, had returned from the path of idolatry.

Abrabanel (commenting on I Kings 17:3) writes: "Elijah did this without a divine command and without permission, but rather by his own will and choice, in pursuit of his zealousness for God."

---

1. Here Radak alludes to the teaching in the Talmud (Taanit 23a) concerning Ḥoni HaMe'agel: "'You shall utter a decree' – you decree it down below, and the Holy One, blessed be He, fulfills it from above."

Among the earlier commentators, a clear exception is Ralbag (Gersonides), who expresses his dissenting opinion only incidentally:

> Elijah exaggerated, *by God's command*, in withholding dew and rain from them altogether for all those years, until the time Elijah would order it, *by God's command*.

Ralbag is preceded in this view by a great many years, by Josephus in his *Antiquities of the Jews*:[2]

> There was one prophet to the Great God from the city of Teshev in the land of Gilead; he came to Ahab and told him *that God had notified him* that He would not give rain in those years, nor would dew descend upon the earth, except for when he [the prophet] would appear [before the king].

Are these two exegetical views of equal weight, or can we bring proof from the verse to support one of them over the other?

The fact that there is no description of a divine revelation to Elijah preceding his appearance before Ahab is no proof. It is quite common for prophets to be described as fulfilling a mission from God without any previous mention of having received a divine revelation. From the mission itself the reader deduces, in such instances, that the prophet's actions are performed as a divine mission. A record of the actual command would create unnecessary repetition.

More significant is the fact that Elijah himself makes no mention of the divine source of his mission. He does not introduce his declaration with the words, "So says the Lord," nor does he formulate his oath in such a way that we may understand that he is speaking God's words.[3] Such a formulation would be particularly important in a case such as ours, where there is no mention of a divine revelation. The lack of any

---

2. Josephus, *Antiquities of the Jews*, ed. and trans. A. Shalit, Book VIII, par. 319, p. 300.
3. If, for example, Elijah had said: "Behold, I am shutting the heavens and will not give you of My blessings," it would have been clear that he was not speaking his own words but those of God.

description of a revelation, coupled with the formulation of an oath that makes no reference to its divine source, are enough to attest to the prophet's independence of action.

But it is not only that which Elijah does not say to Ahab that strengthens this view; more importantly, we reach the same conclusion from what he does say: The very need to swear, together with the personal formulation of the oath, demonstrate that withholding rainfall is the prophet's independent initiative. A regular prophetic mission in God's name, in which the prophet foretells the punishment that will come upon Israel, requires no oath. But when the prophet makes a decree of his own volition, and his listeners understand his words correctly, then his oath comes to strengthen their faith in the fulfillment of his decree; it states: Even though I am the one who is making this decree, it should not be taken lightly. I am certain that my decree will be fulfilled, and I am ready to swear by God's name.

When we come to the conclusion of Elijah's oath, there would seem to be no further room for doubt concerning what we have said above: "Except by *my word*."

This conclusion comes to limit the decree: The cessation of the dew and rainfall during "these years" was not irreversible; it depended on the discretion of the prophet, "until he would see that everyone, or at least some, had returned from the path of idolatry" (Radak). This limitation emphasizes the power of human action in Elijah's oath. It leaves the prophet the option of changing his decree in accordance with changing circumstances. The midrash presents us with an incisive "paraphrase" of this oath: "Elijah took *the keys of rainfall*, and left" (*Eliyahu Zuta* 8). The keeper of the keys will sometimes lock the door and at other times open it, in accordance with the circumstances and at his discretion.

Our discussion thus far has led us to agree with the midrashic conclusion – and that of most of the commentators – that Elijah was not commanded to announce the halting of the rain; he makes this oath of his own volition. As an experienced prophet, accustomed to standing before God and serving Him, Elijah sees that what his generation and his prophetic mission require was a grandiose act, an act that will halt the situation in which Ahab stubbornly upholds idol worship throughout the country, in light of the plentiful rainfall that has blessed the land.

God, who includes His prophets in His counsel and entrusts to the greatest among them the role of leading the generation in accordance with their discretion and the needs of the hour, performs the will of those who fear Him, such that "there was no rain in the land" (17:7).

Chapter 3

Elijah's Experiences During the Drought: Why Are They Recorded?

> *Many days* passed and God's word came to Elijah *in the third year,* saying: "Go and appear before Ahab, and I will give rain upon the face of the earth." (I Kings 18:1)

What happens in the meantime, during these "many days" that last more than two years, while severe drought prevails throughout the country?

As regards Elijah, although he is out of Ahab's sight, he has not disappeared from the reader's consciousness. A chain of three literary units describes what he does during these years, thereby filling in the void between his first appearance before Ahab (17:1) and God's command that he appear before him a second time (18:1).

As regards the events in Samaria during this time, we learn what has happened only incidentally, in retrospect, from what we are told in the first half of chapter 18 (until verse 18). Let us gather the details from those verses and try to organize them more or less chronologically:

- Ahab undertakes intensive searches to try and discover Elijah's hideout. He even goes so far as to send messengers to neighboring nations and kingdoms to seek him, making them swear that Elijah has not been offered asylum within their borders (18:10).

- As a result of the failure of these search missions, Elijah's disappearance is perceived as miraculous: It is God's spirit that has carried him off to an unknown place, thereby leading Ahab and his men astray (based on 18:12).

- Jezebel has attempted to destroy the prophets of God, and Obadiah, who is in charge of the royal household, has saved one hundred of them (18:4). Although this is not stated explicitly, it seems that Jezebel's act was meant as a vengeful response to Elijah's oath and his disappearance.

- In "the third year" of Elijah's oath, "the famine was severe in Samaria" (18:1–2).

- At the end of this period, Ahab and Obadiah divide the land (around Samaria) between them in search of a little fodder for their livestock, so that they will not starve to death (18:5–6). This is a graphic description of the situation in the land following two years of drought.

- Elijah is perceived by Ahab, in light of the severe national crisis, as a "troubler of Israel" (18:17). However, inwardly Ahab is planning to cooperate with Elijah to change the religious situation (18:20ff.).

Let us now return to the chain of units describing Elijah. They parallel, chronologically, the period described above in the environs of Samaria. The continuation of chapter 17 may be divided as follows:

1. Elijah at Wadi Cherith (vv. 2–7)
2. Elijah's meeting with the widow at the gates of Zarephath, and his stay in her home (vv. 8–16)
3. Elijah's miraculous revival of the widow's son (vv. 17–24)

What is the thread that binds these events into a single entity – if such an entity exists – and how do all three connect to the story that serves as their framework, namely, Elijah's two meetings with Ahab, one to announce the imminent drought and the other to end it?

These three episodes are in fact connected to each other as well as to the literary framework surrounding them on several different levels.

TIME FRAME

First, the dimension of time in the story unites all that we read in chapter 17 and the beginning of chapter 18. The three brief events occur between Elijah's two appearances before Ahab, thereby updating us as to what Elijah has been occupied with during this time. This significance of the events, in terms of time, features prominently in the description of the events themselves, in the emphasis placed on when they took place, or on their duration: "It was *after some time* that the wadi dried up, for there was no rain in the land" (17:7). This indicates the conclusion of the period of a year[1] during which Elijah has resided at Wadi Cherith.

At the end of the second unit, we read: "He and she and her household ate *for some time*" (17:15). The third unit begins: "It was, after these things …" (17:17). In other words, it is only after "some time" that Elijah spends at Wadi Cherith and "some time" that he spends in the home of the widow that we find a more specific indication of time: "*Many days* passed, and God's word came to Elijah *in the third year*, saying: Go and appear before Ahab, for I shall give rain upon the land" (18:1).

PLOT

Second, all the events narrated in chapter 17 are units that lead from one to the other from the point of view of the plot. After Elijah swears before Ahab that the rain will cease and will return only by his word, it is reasonable to expect that Ahab and Jezebel will plot against him in some way. For this reason, God commands him to go to Wadi Cherith. But about a year later the wadi dries up because of the drought, and so Elijah is forced to wander to some place of habitation outside the boundaries of the Kingdom of Israel – to the home of the widow in

---

1. The word *yamim*, translated here as "time," is used in the sense of "year" in a few other places in Tanakh. See, for example, Genesis 24:55; Leviticus 25:29–30; I Samuel 27:7. This interpretation is logical in this context because a flowing river dries up only after a year without rain.

"Zarephath of Sidon." This widow's son takes ill and dies, and by means of a most wondrous miracle, Elijah restores him to life.

But this perception of the narration in our chapter, as a continuous plot whose only purpose is to describe Elijah's activities, fails to provide a satisfying answer to the questions posed above. We are left with the following difficulties:

- The concept of the story's circumstantial development from one unit to the next does not apply to the connection between the three units describing Elijah's activities and the divine command to appear before Ahab that follows them. The group of three units is connected properly to its framework at the beginning, but not at the end.
- Even where the circumstantial connection between links in the story is clear and logical, this does not answer the question of *why* the text tells us what happens to Elijah during this time. In what way does the description of these events contribute to the main narrative, which begins with Elijah's oath as to the cessation of rain and continues in chapter 18 with his second encounter with Ahab?

If the story intended simply to fill us in on events that took place during the period between Elijah's two appearances before Ahab, would it not be more appropriate to describe what was taking place in Samaria at the time? The events there are directly related to the central plot, for they relate to the influence of the drought on Samaria and its king, both materially and psychologically. Elijah's doings could be summarized in a single verse, indicating that he hid for two years. But instead, the text adopts the opposite approach: We hear about what is happening in Samaria only incidentally, while Elijah's activities are described at great length, covering twenty-three verses whose contribution to the main subject of the story is not clear.

- The third unit of the revival of the widow's son is entirely unrelated to the subject of Elijah's *hiding*. Even in the first two units, this is not the main subject, neither in terms of subject nor style. Although God's command to Elijah in verse 3 is: "*Hide* at Wadi Cherith which faces the Jordan," the description of his fulfillment of this command tells us something else: "He went and did according to God's word; he went and *sojourned* at Wadi Cherith which faces the Jordan" (v. 5). In the second unit, the concept of "hiding" vanishes even from God's command: "Arise, go to Zarephath of Sidon, and *sojourn* there" (v. 9). Anyone reading this verse in isolation from its context would never imagine that the situation involves a person hiding from someone else.

Thus it can be said that the central subject of these two units is the problem of Elijah's physical survival during the drought, rather than the matter of his hiding. An examination of the words common to these two episodes confirms this view: the expression "I have commanded…to sustain you" appears in both, as does the word "bread," the verb "to drink," and the word "rain."

We may say, in summary, that neither the dimension of time which links the narrative in chapter 17 with the beginning of chapter 18, nor the narrative that connects some of the events with causal links, can explain why these three episodes are included, let alone answer our questions.

AN INTRODUCTION TO ELIJAH

We could explain the purpose of describing these events as being to introduce us to Elijah. Elijah bursts onto the scene without any previous background, and the reader has no idea who he is and what is special about him. It is true that there is a reason, which we discussed at the end of chapter 1, for this "storming in." However, the reason given does not compensate the reader for what he was deprived of in the presentation. Therefore, these three episodes come to retroactively complete the picture of the character of Elijah, so that we will assess him correctly. Their purpose is to introduce us to Elijah as a prophet who is privileged to have a special relationship with the One who sends him, a relationship which finds expression in the miracles he experiences and performs wherever he turns.

According to this approach, there is no need to look for a substantive link between the three episodes and their framework of Elijah's two appearances before Ahab. The connection between them in the dimension of time and their circumstantial progression, which we discussed above, serve only as an excuse for portraying the character of Elijah.

The main connection between the episodes lies in the *miracle* that occurs in each one, with each miracle being more wondrous than the previous one. In the first episode, the miracle is initiated by God for Elijah's survival in Wadi Cherith. Here the prophet himself takes no part in the miracle. In the second episode, Elijah decrees the miracle according to God's word, and God sustains him during the entire year of his stay at the widow's home. In the third episode, the most phenomenal miracle of them all, Elijah prays to God to revive the widow's son, and God accedes to his request. The increasing wonder of each miracle is expressed through the extent that they depart from the laws of nature.

This approach to explaining the significance of the three units does answer some of the questions we raised, and obviates the need to deal with others, but this is also its weakness: It assumes that there is no direct connection between the three units and their framework and that their contribution to the main plot is secondary. Hence, we cannot adopt this approach as the resolution to our main question.

We conclude this chapter, then, with a question mark. We have attempted to suggest three answers to the question posed at the outset, yet none of them has proven satisfactory. The next three chapters, each of which will be devoted to one of the episodes, will ultimately lead us to the answer to our question here.

Chapter 4

Wadi Cherith
(I Kings 17:2–7)

The brief unit describing Elijah's stay at Wadi Cherith (17:2–7) is composed of three parts: (1) God's command to Elijah (vv. 2–4); (2) Elijah's fulfillment of the command (vv. 5–6); and (3) the drying up of the wadi (v. 7).

In this chapter we shall devote a detailed discussion to each of these parts, seeking at each stage the answer to one of the questions we posed above.

GOD'S COMMAND TO ELIJAH

> God's word came to him, saying: Go from here; take yourself eastward, and hide at Wadi Cherith, which faces the Jordan. And it shall be that you will drink from the wadi, and I have commanded the ravens to sustain you there. (vv. 2–4)

What is the reason for this divine command to Elijah, and why do we need the precise specification of Elijah's destination? If the main reason for Elijah leaving the place where he made his oath is to hide from Ahab and Jezebel (as Abrabanel and other commentators maintain), is it not obvious that he must go? And if so, what is the point of God's command? And if the essence of God's command is the promise of sustenance for Elijah in his hiding place, then the second part of God's words would be sufficient; why do we need an indication of the exact place where he must stay?[1]

Rabbi Samuel Laniado, in his commentary *Keli Yakar* on the Early Prophets, explains that this command came to him from God because Elijah's oath was undertaken on his own initiative:

> Although Elijah's intention [in his oath] was for the sake of heaven, for the glory of God and His service, nevertheless it was cruel to withhold from them even the dew, which does not cease.... *And in response to this* God says to him, "Go from here" – *that He drove him away from there*, or possibly, "Go from this (*mizeh*)" – in other words, [separate yourself] from this cruelty that you have shown in withholding dew from the blessing.

These words reveal a revolutionary attitude in the perception of Elijah's oath: Elijah's decree meets with divine criticism, even though God Himself actually fulfills it. The rest of the story comes to highlight this criticism.

Rabbi Laniado detects a note of rebuke in the command, "Go from here." It is a sort of expulsion order to Elijah, aiming to "drive him away from there," from the center of the kingdom, from the company of his people. Elijah is banished from his people, and therefore he is not told, "Go eastward (*lekh lekha kedma*)," but rather "go *from here* (*lekh mizeh*)."

This bold interpretation continues:

> Go – *wandering and roaming* – and head eastward, and hide at Wadi Cherith, for that is the [appropriate] place of your dwelling. [Your dwelling place] must be cut off, like the name of the place where you will dwell: Wadi Cherith – derived from the word *kerita* (cutting off).

---

1. God's command in that case would have taken the form of notification, along the lines of "I have commanded the ravens to sustain you in the hiding place of your choice."

It is not only the command to "go from here" that hints at rebuke of Elijah. The *Keli Yakar* also detects a rebuke in the direction in which God points him: "Go, wandering and roaming, and head eastward." The indication of his intended destination, Wadi Cherith, likewise hints, through its name, at a criticism of Elijah, whose words would cause the water of that wadi to be cut off – as indeed happened later on – and would cause food to be cut off from his people.

The *Keli Yakar* continues: "Thus we can understand why his sustenance came by means of the cruel ravens, rather than any other animal, because he acted in a cruel manner."

Thus, even in what seems to be a gesture of concern for the prophet's well-being, a miracle to keep him alive in a place where he was to spend a whole year, far from any human company, this commentator senses a reproach of Elijah. And indeed, why is it specifically the ravens that are commanded to supply his food? Based on the literal text we could answer that these birds will grab and eat anything, and hence they are suited to the task of obtaining meat and bread for Elijah. But considering that the raven is a highly symbolic creature,[2] it is reasonable to seek some additional, symbolic significance to their selection as the agents to keep Elijah alive.

The source for the *Keli Yakar*'s depiction of ravens as cruel birds is to be found in several teachings of Ḥazal, who deduce from two verses in Tanakh that the raven is cruel toward its offspring:

> "He gives the beast its bread; and to the ravens that cry out."
> (Ps. 147:9)

> "Who prepares provisions for the raven, while its young cry out to God, wandering for lack of food?" (Job 38:41)

In light of these verses, we find the following teaching: "'Black as a raven' (Song. 5:11): In whom do we find this borne out? ... Rava said: In someone who treats his children and the members of his household with cruelty, like a raven" (Eiruvin 21b–22a).

---

2.   In many cultures of the past and present, the raven is used as a negative symbol.

The fact that the birds chosen to be sent to Elijah are symbolic of cruelty (toward their own young) may be interpreted in different ways. The *Keli Yakar* perceives the ravens as symbolic of Elijah himself. Elijah demonstrates cruelty toward his people, like the ravens toward their young, and therefore it is they that are chosen to bring him sustenance.

Malbim offers a similar interpretation:

[God] arranged for his sustenance by means of ravens, which are cruel by nature, in order that [Elijah] would remember that he acted in a similarly cruel way toward the nation, to have them die of starvation.

Baal HaMetzudot, on the other hand, sees the lesson intended for Elijah in the fact that the ravens changed their nature in relation to him:

"I have commanded the ravens": In order to make him conscious that *he should not be cruel* toward Israel. When he would see that the cruel ravens had mercy on him and sustained him, how could he then not have mercy on Israel?

Perhaps the symbolic significance of the ravens can be understood in a third way: The ravens, which withhold food from their young, bring that food to Elijah, who is then nourished, as it were, from the food of the young ravens that cry out to God. Is the prophet prepared to survive miraculously at the expense of others? This food, which Elijah receives by means of the ravens, has been snatched from his people, who are desperate in the wake of the absence of rain. Will Elijah be prepared to eat "bread and meat in the morning, and bread and meat in the evening," when the food in question is in fact the bread and meat of his suffering brethren?

ELIJAH'S FULFILLMENT OF THE COMMAND

So he went and did as God had said; he went and sojourned at Wadi Cherith which faces the Jordan. And the ravens would bring him bread and meat in the morning and bread and meat in the evening, and he would drink from the wadi. (I Kings 17:5–6)

There is an overall parallel between God's command in the preceding verses (2–3) and its fulfillment by Elijah in these following verses, as we see from the following comparison:

God's command	Elijah's actions
v. 2: *God's word* came to him, saying:	v. 5: So he went and did *according to God's word.*
v. 3: *Go from here* and head eastward, and hide at *Wadi Cherith, which faces the Jordan.*	v. 5: *He went* and sojourned at *Wadi Cherith, which faces the Jordan.*
v. 4: And it shall be that *you will drink from the wadi,* and I have commanded *the ravens* to sustain you there.	v. 6: And *the ravens* would bring him bread and meat…*and he would drink from the wadi.*

Attention should be paid to the three differences between these corresponding elements:

1. As opposed to God's command, "*hide* at Wadi Cherith," we are told that Elijah "*sojourned* at Wadi Cherith." This slight difference suggests that hiding was not the main purpose of his actions.
2. The order of food and drink is exchanged: In God's command the water is mentioned first, while the description of Elijah's actions mentions the food first. The reason for this is simple: God mentions water first, for this is a more fundamental need than food. When it comes to Elijah's actions, the text postpones the water in order to juxtapose his drinking from the wadi with the crisis that concludes this episode: The drinking arrangement cannot continue; "It was *after some time* that the wadi dried up."
3. God's offhand mention of His "command to the ravens to sustain him" turns into a reality that is quite different from what we would have expected, and this is perhaps the biggest surprise of the story: Twice a day, morning and evening (the ancient custom was to eat two meals a day), the ravens bring Elijah bread *and meat.* Elijah is thus living a life of luxury at Wadi Cherith. Does Elijah's situation justify such a lifestyle?

> When the Lord your God expands your borders as He told
> you, and you say, "I shall eat meat," because your soul desires
> to eat meat, then you shall eat meat to your heart's content."
> (Deut. 12:20)

From this verse *Ḥazal* deduce that it is proper to eat meat only in conditions of plenty and with appetite, not at times of distress or famine.[3]
To this we may add the words of Mishna Taanit (1:4–7), describing
the communal lifestyle that is appropriate during a dry winter, like the
one experienced that year, characterized by fasting and curtailment of
celebration.

Thus, while the Israelites are engaged in fasting over the harsh
drought, Elijah – the cause of the drought – is served regular, daily meals
of "bread and meat in the morning, and bread and meat in the evening"!

What is the nature of the criticism hinted at here?

Elijah has to separate himself from his people and from the suffering that he has brought upon them. His isolation becomes a test to see
whether he is capable of living alone for a year and experiencing, twice
a day, how he is different – his separation from them and their fate. This
yearlong stay at Wadi Cherith hints at a rebuke aimed at the prophet:
In his decision to withhold rain he has brought suffering on his people,
but he fails to sense their distress. The divine command therefore forces
him to leave them, to go and try to live a lifestyle of stubborn disregard
for their suffering, a lifestyle that expresses his lack of involvement in
their fate. Perhaps this lifestyle at Wadi Cherith will lead him back to
his people, to feel their pain, and to share their fate. Such a step – were
he to take it – would be a first step toward the cancellation of his oath.[4]

---

3. See Ḥullin 84a; Rashi on Deuteronomy 12:20; Maimonides, *Laws of Beliefs and
   Character Traits* 5:10.
4. This manner of "argument" between God and man, conducted not through words
   but rather through actions, appears elsewhere in Tanakh, where God attempts to
   convince man to change his ways and his mind. For instance, a dispute of this type
   is maintained throughout the book of Jonah, and to some extent in God's dialogue
   with Job, including God's speech at the end of the book. Apparently, a direct appeal
   to man's reason, in the abstract, theoretical realm, lacks the power to convince him
   to change his mind. In that type of exchange, a person might come to believe that his

Elijah appears to respond to this veiled criticism. In the description of his sustenance, the lack of symmetry between his food and drink is pronounced: "And the ravens would bring him bread and meat in the morning and bread and meat in the evening – and he would drink from the wadi." We are not told that Elijah eats of the food that the ravens brought; the verse describes him only drinking from the wadi. Perhaps this is meant to hint at his anguish over the meat that is delivered to him twice a day. But has the covert criticism achieved anything beyond this?

THE WADI DRIES UP

"And it was after some time that the wadi dried up, for there was no rain in the land." (v. 7)

A whole year, with its entire cycle of seasons, passes by while Elijah lives at Wadi Cherith. He does not experience the results of his oath – the drying up of the wadi – all at once. Following the dry winter, the water is less abundant, and during the summer months the supply steadily decreases. The wadi that was a green ribbon of life in the heart of the parched wilderness slowly evaporates. As the supply and force of the water diminish, the green banks of the wadi begin to dry up and the vegetation yellows. As the water retreats, the surrounding desert takes over, and Elijah, who lives off this wadi, feels himself slowly perishing. He senses how his stubborn persistence in his oath is cutting off life and giving reign to the blazing heat of the summer and the desolation of the desert until the logical conclusion of the process: "the wadi dried up." And why? "For there was no rain in the land."

Elijah remains steadfast. He is not prepared to retract his oath, to restore the rainfall with a word. Hence, God's "dispute" with him continues. But it will not take place here, at Wadi Cherith, nor will it continue through these "pressure tactics" of having ravens, full of symbolic meaning, bringing bread and meat morning and evening to the prophet who dwells in isolation at Wadi Cherith (a name that is also symbolic). This strategy has not brought results. The prophet must be moved somewhere

---

arguments are no less valid than God's, as it were. For this reason, God's pedagogical methods must appeal to a deeper level of man's nature. This increases the chances that man will eventually agree that God is right, although there is still no guarantee.

else and a new strategy of persuasion must be adopted. A new experiential test will be presented to the prophet; perhaps this will soften him and change his stance.

It is for this purpose that the yearlong stay at Wadi Cherith ends in crisis: The drying up of the wadi, the inevitable result of Elijah's oath, forces the prophet to seek a different place in which to live out this difficult time. God's command will lead him to his new home and to a new mode of existence there, in order to continue the dispute.

Attention should be paid to the fact that although God takes care of Elijah's sustenance through miraculous means, only his food is provided in this manner, while his water supply is natural (both at Wadi Cherith and in the next episode, in Zarephath). When the water in the wadi is gone, God does not help Elijah to find water through some miraculous procedure – neither in the wadi nor elsewhere. Malbim explains this as follows:

> "It shall be that you will drink from the wadi": The outpouring of divine providence descends upon a person according to the measure of his preparation. Since Elijah prepared himself, through this act [his oath], to stop the supreme blessing from descending, it was also prevented from descending to him as well. Therefore, it was impossible for him to subsist through…blessing on the water that he drank, for this would run counter to his own preparation…. [God] showed him that it was impossible for him to draw a new outpouring from the source of life; he would therefore drink from the wadi that already contained water, and which would ultimately dry up – just as he had stopped [the blessing of rain] from the nation, such that they would have to live only from the food and water that was in existence prior to his curse.

Rashi likewise states explicitly that the drying up of the wadi represents an element in the "argument" between God and Elijah, but in his view it is not the drying up itself that represents the "claim" but rather its result: The fact that Elijah must move to a new place in order for the argument to continue:

> "The wadi dried up" – so that he would recognize the need for rain and *would have the trouble of uprooting himself from his place*. For it was cruel, in God's eyes, that Israel was experiencing famine.

Rashi is already hinting here at the direction that becomes characteristic of the argument with Elijah during his stay in Zarephath, and it is the opposite of what we have demonstrated in the description of his stay at Wadi Cherith. Now Elijah's stance will be tested through an unmediated encounter with the suffering caused by his oath. He will experience firsthand the hardship that people must undergo during famine: The need to uproot themselves from their place and seek somewhere else where they can survive. He will be forced to go among the famine-struck people and witness their suffering.

Chapter 5

The Widow in Zarephath (I Kings 17:8–16)

COMPARISON WITH THE PREVIOUS EPISODE

This section of Elijah's stay in Zarephath has two parts, corresponding to the first two parts of the previous episode: Verses 8–9 contain God's command to Elijah (corresponding to vv. 2–4); verses 10–16 describe its fulfillment (paralleling vv. 5–7). The third part of the previous section, the drying up of the wadi (v. 7) – representing the crisis that concludes the stay at Wadi Cherith and the preparation for God's new directive – has no parallel in the episode of Zarephath, which would appear to conclude on a positive note: The widow and her son are saved from death by starvation thanks to Elijah, who finds in her home a safe haven where his sustenance is provided for. Only the Israelites continue to suffer from the increasingly oppressive drought. However, at the end of this episode the text hints that this situation, too, will end in crisis and the solution that has been found will not last indefinitely: "So he [to be read 'she'] and she [to be read 'he'] and her household ate *for some time*" (17:15).

As in the previous unit, here too the expression "for some time" (*yamim*) refers to a year. Thus, Elijah's stay in the widow's home lasted a year, like his stay in Wadi Cherith. The reader asks himself: Why only a year? What happened at the end of that year that brought this seemingly ideal situation to an end? What is the parallel, in our unit, to the words in the previous unit, "It was after *some time* that the wadi dried up" (v. 7)? The answers to these questions are to be found in the third episode. There we find the crisis, the death of the widow's son, that brings Elijah's stay in her house to an end. But this "crisis" will be discussed at greater length in the next chapter, and its resolution leads us, and the entire story, in a new direction.

There is a striking similarity between the previous episode at Wadi Cherith and our episode. Both share the same subject: the possibility of Elijah's continued existence during a drought, far away from his people. In both cases God directs Elijah where to go, and in both He informs him how he will receive his sustenance in his new location. Let us compare these two divine commands:

First command	Second command
v. 2: *God's word came to him, saying:*	v. 8: *God's word came to him, saying:*
v. 3: *Go* from here and head eastward, and hide at *Wadi Cherith which faces the Jordan.*	v. 9: Arise, *go* to *Zarephath of Sidon*, and sojourn there.
v. 4: And it shall be that you will drink from the wadi, and *I have commanded the ravens to sustain you there.*	v. 9: Behold, *I have commanded there* a widowed woman *to sustain you.*

There is also some similarity in what transpires following God's command: In both cases Elijah obeys God's command, and God fulfills His promise.

The general similarity between the descriptions of the two events is expressed in a series of key words that appear in both. These phrases serve to sketch the outline of each of the events, with the problems that each contains:

1. "God's word" appears twice in each episode (vv. 2 and 5 with regard to Wadi Cherith, and vv. 8 and 16 with regard to Zarephath).
2. The verb "to go" (*heh-lamed-khaf*) appears three times in the first episode (vv. 3, 5) and four times in the second: twice with regard to Elijah (vv. 9, 10) and twice with regard to the widow (vv. 11, 15).

3. The verb "to drink" (*sh-t-h*) appears in both cases (vv. 4, 6, 10).

4. The word "bread" appears twice in the first episode (v. 6) and once in the second (v. 11), but further on we find also "baked goods" (*ma'og*) (v. 12) and "a small cake" (v. 13).

5. The expression "I have commanded...to sustain you there" appears in both episodes: first concerning the ravens (v. 4), and then concerning the widow (v. 9).

6. Elijah's stay in each case lasts "some time" (*yamim*), namely, a year (vv. 7, 15).

7. The word "rain" appears once in each episode (vv. 7, 14).

To all of the above we may add that in both episodes Elijah drinks water in a natural way, while his food comes to him miraculously, by means of an agent sent by God's command.

Aside from all of these parallels, we must also examine the differences between the two units, for it is the unique aspects of each that define its specific subject.

ELIJAH IN ZAREPHATH: SIGNIFICANCE OF THE LENGTHY DESCRIPTION

The reader is struck by the lack of symmetry in length between the two episodes: The description at Wadi Cherith covers only *two* verses (vv. 5–6), while his actions in Zarephath occupy *seven* verses (vv. 10–16).[1] What is the reason for this discrepancy?

It stems from the difference between the agents appointed to feed Elijah in each case. At Wadi Cherith the ravens are commanded to feed him, and the text reports them as doing so, without any further comment. This mission embodies the miracle presented in the first episode, for it is not natural for ravens to forgo the food that they have stolen, all the more so, to do it with such

---

1. It should be noted that while the two verses in the previous section describe the cycle of an entire year, Elijah's actions recorded in these seven verses all take place at the gates of Zarephath, and describe his first encounter with the widow. This is true of verses 15 and 16 as well. Although the text states there that Elijah's decree at the gates of Zarephath was fulfilled over the course of a whole year, the essence of those verses describes what happened at the first meeting with the widow.

regularity – twice every day. Elijah is not involved in the miracle; he simply enjoys its benefits.

The situation in the second episode is different: Here a widow is commanded to take care of Elijah's sustenance,[2] and matters are more complex. First of all, Elijah must identify the woman whom God has appointed for this purpose.[3] After he ascertains who she is, it transpires that she does not have enough food even for herself. Elijah encounters this difficulty in understanding God's command to the woman immediately upon asking for some bread:

> She said: As the Lord your God lives, I have nothing baked but a handful of flour in a jar and a little oil in the bottle; and behold, I am gathering two sticks so I may come and prepare it for myself and for my son, that we may eat it and die. (v. 12)

How is God's promise with regard to this woman – "Behold, I have commanded there a widowed woman to sustain you" – to be fulfilled? Radak explains as follows:

> When Elijah saw that the widow lacked food even to sustain herself – how much more so to sustain him – he knew that what God had told him, "I have commanded there …," was meant to be fulfilled miraculously. For He promised that *His commanding word and His blessing* would be upon the widow's house, that she would be able to sustain him. Therefore he tells her, "For *so says the Lord* God of Israel: The jar of flour will not finish, nor will the bottle of oil be lacking." (v. 14)

---

2. The phrase "I have commanded to sustain you" in both units does not indicate an explicit command. Commenting on verse 4, Radak explains that God inspired the ravens to bring food to Elijah, but even this is impossible to propose with regard to the widow. Radak therefore understands this phrase as an allusion to the miracle that would happen in the widow's home. See his commentary as cited below.

3. According to Malbim, the very fact that upon arriving at the city gates he encounters a widow preparing a meal indicates to Elijah that this is the woman he is looking for. According to Rashi, however, Elijah does not know that this is the woman, and his request for some water is meant as a test, in the same manner that Abraham's servant had once tested Rebecca (Gen. 24).

Thus, elaboration of Elijah's actions in Zarephath (about five verses out of the total of seven) are related to the need to first identify the human agent, the widow, and to become familiar with the problem that prevents her from being able to fulfill her mission. Thereafter Elijah must solve this problem both on the subjective level (to motivate the widow to accede to his request) and on the objective level (by means of the actual miracle).

This difference between the two types of agents – the ravens and the widow – affects not only the length of the description of Elijah's actions, but also the nature of the miracle. Although in both cases the miracle concerns Elijah's sustenance, what transpires in the widow's home is very different from the miracle that is recounted in the previous episode. There, the miracle is *the actual agent*; namely, the fact that ravens supply Elijah's food. The food itself, on the other hand, is in no way miraculous. It is snatched by the ravens in their usual manner, from whatever source they happen to find. As we have said above, Elijah is not party to the miracle of the ravens. By contrast, in the second episode the mission is carried out in a natural way, with the destitute widow agreeing to share the little food she has with the stranger. In order to allow the widow to agree to this, and in order that her readiness will have some practical expression, Elijah is forced to call for a miracle with regard to *the food* that is destined to sustain him, the widow, and her son.

Another difference between the two miracles is that in the first episode Elijah is provided with plentiful food, "bread and meat in the morning and bread and meat in the evening." In the second, a "small cake," made from a spoonful of flour and a little oil, which hardly suffices for two, is meant to suffice as a miserly meal for three, once a day, throughout that year.

What is the meaning of these differences in terms of what the story is teaching us? In what way do they contribute to its special meaning?

In order to answer these questions we must first ask a different one: Is it imperative that the divine plan concerning Elijah's stay in Zarephath be fulfilled in this particular way? Are the difficulties that arise in Zarephath an indispensable function of the transition that Elijah makes from Wadi Cherith where the ravens sustain him, to an inhabited place like Zarephath and the widow? Not necessarily. If the main subject of our story were the way a solution is found for Elijah's sustenance, for him to be able to dwell far from the center of the kingdom and still survive during the drought, we would expect a different chain of events in our section – a simpler arrangement. God would send Elijah to Zarephath and inform him that He has appointed a widow to take care of his provisions (as we are told in verses 8–9). Upon reaching Zarephath, he could be welcomed by a wealthy widow who would invite him to dine with her at her home. Elijah would accept the invitation and remain in her home for a whole year; she would take care of his meals. Such a description would be much shorter and would parallel almost perfectly what happened at Wadi Cherith. The lack of an apparent miracle in this scenario could be compensated for by having Elijah bless the widow that she would not lack anything even during the drought, and the widow would indeed remain wealthy, with the expansive hospitality that she extends to Elijah not affecting her wealth and comfort in any way.

Thus the problems that Elijah addresses in our section – the need to identify the widow and to persuade her to fulfill her mission – are not a direct consequence of the transition from reliance on birds who bring food to reliance on a human source of sustenance. They arise, rather, from the fact that the agent sent to Elijah appears unsuited for the task, and therefore there is a need to act differently in order to adapt the agent's conditions to the task.

The meaning of the story would seem to hinge on the following question: Why is it specifically this poverty-stricken widow who is chosen to fulfill the mission of feeding Elijah? It seems almost as though divine providence has selected the wrong person solely with the purpose of making the story longer and more complicated. We must therefore attempt to define precisely the theme of the episode describing Elijah's stay in Zarephath.

CONTINUATION OF GOD'S DISPUTE WITH ELIJAH

In our discussion of Elijah's stay at Wadi Cherith, we saw how the commentators view the events recounted there as a dispute concerning Elijah's oath, aimed at causing the prophet to retract his promise. The most important among these is Rashi, who views the drying up of Wadi

Cherith and God's command to Elijah to move to Zarephath as a lesson to him: "So that he would recognize the need for rain and would be forced to move himself, for it was cruel in God's eyes that Israel was suffering from drought."

Rashi regards the very fact that Elijah is forced to move from Wadi Cherith to Zarephath as a hardship for him; it is banishment to a distant, foreign place, and hence an expression of God's dissatisfaction and an attempt to make Elijah retract his vow. Do the events in Zarephath itself also support this exegetical approach, suggesting that God is conducting an "argument" with Elijah, and all that happens to him is meant to illustrate God's "claims" against him?

In this sense, too, our unit resembles the previous one: The commentators who understand Elijah's experiences in the previous episode as a dispute between God and His prophet regard our unit as a continuation of the same dispute. However, this time the claims are different and God's tactic in dealing with Elijah also changes.

In the commentary *Marot HaTzovot*, Rabbi Moses Alsheikh, a contemporary of Rabbi Samuel Laniado, author of *Keli Yakar*, writes concerning the previous episode that through the details of the story "God hints to Elijah... of claims that he [Elijah] should be patient, even though his intention was to sanctify the name of God."

Concerning the conclusion of the stay at Wadi Cherith, Alsheikh writes:

> Here God wanted to uphold the word of His servant and not to give rain except by his word, but God wanted Elijah not to wait any longer in asking for rain, and He hinted this to him... through his being sustained by the ravens at Wadi Cherith. But out of zeal for God's honor, Elijah did not ask [for rain]. Therefore, God hinted to him further by drying up the wadi, such that he had no water to drink and was forced to move, *in order that he would notice that many destitute people were seeking water and there was none.*

Alsheikh views the crisis that concludes the previous episode as teaching Elijah a lesson about the poor and destitute who, like him, were forced to uproot themselves and wander in their search for water. He hints at the words of Isaiah:

> The poor and the destitute seek water and there is none; their tongue is parched for thirst. I, God, shall answer them; [I,] the God of Israel, shall not abandon them. I shall open rivers on high places and fountains amid the valleys; I shall make the wilderness into a pool of water and parched land into springs of water. (Is. 41:17–18)

Will the prophet identify with the view of his Creator, and agree to "turn the parched land into springs of water"? Alsheikh continues:

> Despite all this, he does not abandon his zealousness, for his zealousness for God is great. Therefore, our merciful God commands him to go to Zarephath, of Sidon. Through this, He means to hint to him that Israel has already been purified (*nitzrefu*) in the matter of the food (*tzeida*) that they have lacked thus far. But the essence of the matter is that he should see, in that place, the suffering of a widow and orphan, upon whom God Himself has mercy and concerning whom He warns against causing them suffering (Ex. 21:22). For were it not for him, both of them would die, as she says to him: "That I may come and prepare it for myself and for my son, that we may eat it and die." *From them he will see that a great many like them, among the masses of Israel, will die of hunger,* and it would be good were he to pray for mercy for them, that there should be rain and dew by his word. And there he will see that if he, in the widow's merit, is sustained in a miraculous way, what are others to do? This is the meaning of "I have commanded there *a widowed woman* to sustain you."

Now it is clear that the true subject of the events in Zarephath is a new strategy in God's dispute with Elijah. The "technical" solution aimed at finding Elijah a new dwelling place in which he will have food to eat is no more than a framework in which to lead him to an unmediated encounter with the suffering and hunger of the weakest strata of society – a widow and orphan. Perhaps this encounter will teach Elijah the magnitude of the anguish that he has brought upon his people, and from this individual example he may understand the general situation, in which "a great many like them" – widows, orphans, and the other downtrodden poor – "will die of hunger." Perhaps this encounter will lead him to soften his heart, and he will "pray for mercy upon them, that there should be rain and dew by his word."

The question that we posed concerning the purpose of the lengthy description of events in Zarephath now finds a simple solution. The continuation of the dispute between God and Elijah that began at Wadi Cherith requires Elijah to come into contact with a poor widow who, together with her son, is about to die of hunger. It is specifically they who are appointed by divine providence to sustain Elijah, so that he will be exposed to their misery, which will affect him directly.

Hence, the move from Wadi Cherith to Zarephath involves a change in the way that God conducts His argument with Elijah. At Wadi Cherith the prophet's stance was tested as to whether he was prepared to separate himself from his people and from the bitter fate that he had brought upon them. But when this tactic did not achieve the desired effect, and Elijah was not moved to retract his oath and rethink his zealousness for God, and as the drought entered its second year, with its signs showing clearly among the weak elements of society, the tactic moves to the opposite extreme. Now Elijah will experience the opposite of his lifestyle at Wadi Cherith. He is sent to live among people, in a town whose poor are hard-hit by the drought. He will be forced to live in the home of a widow who can hardly support her own orphan child, such that both of them are in constant danger of starving to death. Elijah will join them once a day in their meager meal, hardly sufficient for themselves, and together with his hosts he too will suffer pangs of hunger. The lives of all three of them will hover on the brink; for tomorrow's pitiful meal they will depend daily on a miracle that will keep their supply of a spoonful of flour and a little oil steady.

According to what we have said, the purpose of having Elijah move to Zarephath is not only for him to meet the widow, but to cause him to participate in the experience of hunger. Elijah himself lives the experience of lacking food during his yearlong stay in the widow's home. This is the meaning of the drastic decline in his "standard of living" – the sharp transition from Wadi Cherith, with his twice-daily feasts of bread and meat, to Zarephath and the meager, once-daily morsel that Elijah must share with his widow hostess and her son.

ELIJAH'S REQUEST OF THE WIDOW AND HER REFUSAL: SHAME AND REBUKE

Let us now sketch a more detailed picture of the new dual experience that awaits Elijah at the gates of Zarephath: The experience of *personal* hunger, which he senses for the first time, and the unmediated encounter with the widow and orphan who are about to die of starvation.

At first glance, considering the woman's actions as they appear to Elijah upon arriving at the city, it is not unreasonable for him to deduce that she does actually have some food: Were this not so, why would she be gathering wood? Surely it must be in order to bake bread. Nevertheless, he refrains from asking for "a morsel of bread" right away; rather, he first asks: "Fetch me, I pray you, a little *water* in a vessel, that I may drink" (17:10)

Only after she accedes to this request (even before she is actually able to fulfill it) does he request a more substantial favor – a morsel of bread. Why does he do this? Alsheikh explains:

> Elijah was embarrassed to begin by asking for food, since food was dear at that time. Therefore, he began by asking for water to drink, and even that – only "a little." When she was going to fetch the water, "he called to her and said: Bring me, I pray you, a morsel of bread in your hand" (v. 11). In other words, since [drinking] water without first [eating] bread is harmful for the heart, therefore: "First please bring me a morsel of bread in your hand" – before I drink.

According to this interpretation, in ordering his requests the way he does, Elijah reveals his own hunger pangs and the humiliation that they cause him. He now experiences the feelings of anyone who has lost his possessions and is forced to beg. Even greater is the shame of being forced to beg from a poor widow, who will not necessarily be able to give him what he requests. Therefore, reluctantly, he begins by asking for something that he is certain that she is able to give him: a little water in a vessel.

Elijah's embarrassment and careful attempt not to ask the widow outright for something as valuable as a morsel of bread are in vain. When he finally dares to express explicitly what he wants: "Bring me, I pray you, a morsel of bread in your hand," he is met with an emotional refusal; words that he is certainly not expecting:

> She said: As the Lord your God lives, I have nothing baked, but a handful of flour in the jar and a little oil in the bottle; and behold, I am gathering two sticks so I may come and prepare it for myself and for my son, that we may eat it, and die. (17:12)

The woman is unaware of the identity of the man in front of her; not for a moment does she imagine that this is the very the person who is responsible for her terrible hunger and suffering. But Elijah, aware of his responsibility for her state, hears in her words a most severe accusation. What contributes to this in particular is the widow's introductory oath. The sensitive reader is reminded – undoubtedly like Elijah himself – of Elijah's own oath before Ahab:

Widow's oath	Elijah's oath
v. 12: *As the Lord your God lives*, I have nothing (*im yesh li*) baked but (*ki im*) a handful of meal.	v. 1: *As the Lord God of Israel lives*, there shall be no (*im yihye*) rain or dew in these years but (*ki im*) by my word.

Just as Elijah expresses his special closeness to God, in whose name he takes his oath, so the widow expresses in her oath Elijah's special closeness to God, in whose name she is now speaking. She obviously does this out of recognition that Elijah is a man of God. The continuation of her words is likewise similar in structure to the continuation of Elijah's original vow. This linguistic connection between the two declarations hints to Elijah – and to the readers – that it is his oath that has led to the widow's words. Elijah's oath, barring rain and dew from the land, has brought about the dire situation of this destitute woman: "That we may eat it, and die."

Elijah now faces a dual conflict: On the external level, he is in conflict with the widow. His request has been met with a justified refusal. Her life and the life of her son take precedence over the life of this stranger, even if he, too, is destitute and hungry for bread. She explains her refusal with in emotional and bitter words, thereby unconsciously serving as God's mouthpiece. Her mission here is not just to sustain Elijah as he has been promised, but rather to hint to him, unknowingly, that the responsibility for her situation rests with him.

Then there is the second, hidden conflict: between Elijah and God. How is the contradiction between God's promise upon sending him here – "Behold, I have commanded there a widowed woman to sustain you" – and the woman's justified refusal to fulfill her mission, to be resolved? We might formulate this conflict as follows: The widow is meant to fulfill a double-edged, self-contradictory mission. On one hand, she is meant to provide Elijah with food (although she does not know this), thereby sustaining him and allowing him to maintain his zealous stance concerning the drought. On the other hand, she comes to rebuke him for this very stubbornness concerning his oath and his zealousness for God (this too, unknowingly), but to achieve this she should in fact refrain from sustaining him.

God means this to be a test for Elijah. The simple solution to this complicated situation would be for him to restore, with a single word, rain and dew to the land. This would alleviate the suffering of the widow and her son, and Elijah would no longer depend on the mercies of various divine agents to sustain him. But he is not yet ready to do this, and the situation will continue for a long time before being resolved.

ELIJAH'S MIRACLE LEADS TO THE CONTINUATION OF THE DISPUTE

Earlier in the chapter, we noted that in Elijah's move from Wadi Cherith to Zarephath there is a change God's tactic in His argument against him. At Wadi Cherith, Elijah was tested when isolated from the fate of his people and the suffering of the drought, while in Zarephath he is tested as a participant in this suffering. But this distinction, with its two components, is not quite accurate, as we shall see below. Already at Wadi Cherith, Elijah begins to witness scenes of drought, as the wadi gradually shrinks and dries up before his eyes. He encounters the ramifications of the drought as manifested on the land itself – its wadis, its plants, and animal life. This affects Elijah personally, not just as an observer: He is forced to leave his place and move somewhere far away, in order to have access to water (see Rashi, v. 7). However, neither the suffering of the land on account of the drought, nor his own personal suffering as a refugee who must roam about as a result, causes Elijah to budge from his stance. Now he will have a more shocking encounter with the effects of the drought – the suffering of two unfortunate individuals, a widow and her orphan son, who represent many more like themselves: people on the brink of starvation. Perhaps being in the company of such people will soften the prophet's position.

Elijah's journey to Zarephath and his meeting with the widow, including his mortifying request that she give him bread and her refusal, turns him into a partner in the suffering – but only for a moment. At the gates of Zarephath, and likewise throughout the year that he dwells there in the woman's house, Elijah is still being tested (as he was during his year at Wadi Cherith) as to his ability to separate himself from the fate of his people, the fate of human beings who are wasting away from hunger. Thus, the argument that characterized his year at Wadi Cherith continues. His test concerns the way in which he will resolve the conflict in which he is now embroiled.

> For so says the Lord God of Israel: The jar of meal will not fin-
> ish, nor will the bottle of oil be lacking…. She went and did as
> Elijah had spoken, and he [read: she] and she [read: he] and her
> household ate for some time. The jar of meal did not finish, nor
> did the bottle of oil lack. (17:14–16)

Thus, it is not by nullifying his decree and restoring the rain that Elijah resolves the contradiction, but rather by means of a local, personalized miracle that is meant to allow this widow to fulfill her mission to sustain him. It is not with a view to saving her and her son that Elijah acts, for in what way are they more important or more worthy than the many other widows and orphans living throughout the drought-stricken land, who are equally hungry? Rather, he acts for the sake of his own survival, so that God's command may be fulfilled: "Behold, I have commanded there a widowed woman to sustain you." For Elijah, the widow is no more than a device through which he will receive food. Since this reality involves unforeseen objective difficulties, Elijah goes about resolving them through miraculous means.

We saw above that in Radak's view, the very fact that God tells Elijah that he will be sustained by the widow includes within it the instruction that, if necessary, he should perform a miracle in her home. Indeed, the miracle that Elijah decrees is fulfilled "as God's word that He spoke, by Elijah's hand" (v. 16). But this very word of God itself, hinting at the possibility of Elijah performing a miracle that will facilitate his survival, is meant only to test Elijah's readiness to make use of this device. Will the prophet choose a lifestyle that will constantly emphasize his superiority over all those in his environment? From this perspective, it appears that this divine command to Elijah resembles the command that led him to Wadi Cherith and his unique and isolated existence there, but the difference between the two commands is clear. In the second command, God does not tell him *explicitly* to create a framework for his existence that is dependent on a miracle that distinguishes him from his surroundings; rather, it is a matter of choice. In choosing to solve the problem by miraculous means, Elijah reveals his concern for himself. This is hinted at by Alsheikh at the end of the same excerpt that we quoted above: "There [in Zarephath] he will see that even he, in the merit of a widowed woman, is sustained [only] by virtue of a miracle; what, then, is everyone else to do?" (17:11).

In other words, what should regular people do, those who have no miracle to protect them from hunger and thus are threatened with starvation?

The egocentric basis of the miracle that Elijah performs for the widow may be discerned in his directions to her: "Elijah said to her: Do not fear; come, do as you have said, but *make me* a small cake of it *first*, and bring it *to me, and then afterward make for you and for your son*" (v. 13). Why does Elijah ask that he be given preference over the owners of the meal and the oil – the widow and her son? Ralbag seems to best answer our question:

> Elijah commanded her thus because it is *owing to* [her act of] *sustaining him* that the blessed God would bring blessing upon that meal and the oil; if she were to first prepare for herself and her son, the meal and the oil would be finished.

In other words, the widow herself is not worthy of a miracle. Only on account of Elijah are her and her son's lives saved. She merits having her provisions miraculously provided only so that she will be able to sustain the prophet.

This order, in which Elijah receives his portion first and only afterward do the widow and her son eat of the remains, is maintained throughout that year. According to Ralbag, the continuity of the miracle depends on this order, and since the miracle does indeed continue throughout that year, its condition must also have been maintained. This is hinted at in the *ketiv* (the literal wording of the written text) in verse 15: "He [to be read: she] and she [to be read: he] and her household ate for some time."

Concerning this textual formulation, the Midrash (Song of Songs Rabba 2:16) teaches:

> R. Yehuda bar Shimon said: Did he then eat of her [food]? Was it not the case that both she and he ate of what was actually his? As it is said, "She and he ate," but it is written, "He and she."

The verb in this verse is in the feminine form, corresponding to the way the verse is to be read with the subject "she" first. Radak (ad loc.), bringing more examples, writes: "The grammatical rule is that when a male and female are mentioned together, the verb follows whichever of them is mentioned first, whether male or female, for the first one is the more important and is therefore mentioned first." But it appears that even according to the way the verse is *written* ("he ate, and she"), we must conclude that the verb in its feminine form, referring specifically to the widow, comes to emphasize the widow's reward. Since she believed what the prophet told her and did as he said ("she went and did as Elijah had spoken"), she merits to eat food that lasts that entire year by means of a miracle. The way the verse is read, with her being mentioned before Elijah, strongly emphasizes this idea.

In the widow's home, Elijah is tested as to his ability to accustom himself to a privilege that distinguishes him – to his benefit – from all the other people living in the same city and that ensures his survival. Even within the limited circle in which he is living, in the widow's house, this privilege is constantly emphasized: Elijah demands that at every meal held in the house and prepared from the provisions upon which he invokes the miracle, his portion should be served first, before the widow and before her son.

Can Elijah maintain such a problematic situation, witnessing around him people who are collapsing from hunger, while ensuring his own survival by means of constant emphasis on his own preferential status? The situation continues for an entire year.

THE ENCOUNTER WITH THE WIDOW: ITS EFFECT ON ELIJAH

Neither stage in the ongoing dispute, neither at Wadi Cherith nor in Zarephath, succeeds in altering Elijah's rigid stance. But can we perhaps identify, in his deeds and words, any sort of response to the tests that he faces? Perhaps there is some kind of objection to the "claims" that are made against him, with a hardening of his intransigence, or perhaps the opposite – hesitation and a rethinking of his unequivocal position.

We have noted previously that the text conspicuously avoids any description of Elijah actually eating the bread and meat delivered to him by the ravens twice a day at Wadi Cherith. Our assumption was that Elijah did indeed react to this hinted criticism by refusing to "cooperate" and partake of the peculiar lifestyle forced upon him during the first year of the drought.

What about his stay in Zarephath? Can we point here, too, to some reaction on Elijah's part to the complex pressures that are being applied to him? There can be no doubt as to the answer to this question: Elijah does display signs of softening. While not retracting his oath, he cannot remain indifferent to the widow's suffering. This predicament finds expression several times in Elijah's words:

1. At the very outset of his encounter with the widow, Elijah hesitates in asking for a morsel of bread, preferring first to request some water, since "Elijah was embarrassed to start off by asking for food, since food was dear at that time," as Alsheikh explains. We note something of a lack of confidence in his stance, faced with the hunger that he has encountered and for which he is responsible.

2. We highlighted above Elijah's difficult request of the woman in verse 12 that he first be served his portion of the sparse meal. This request is admittedly necessary, since the miracle depends on it, as Ralbag explains, but this in no way softens the shocking impression that it makes. What does somewhat mitigate the tone of his request are Elijah's introductory words: "Elijah said to her: *Do not fear*; come, do *as you have said*, but make me…" (v. 13).

These reassuring words in response to the widow's despairing monologue testify to Elijah's sensitivity toward her torment and his attempt to present what he wants in the gentlest possible way. To this we must add the modesty of his request, "a *small* cake," likewise indicating that the widow's words had an effect on him.

3. In order to persuade the widow to do as he has asked, Elijah attaches a forceful declaration in God's name:

> For so says the Lord God of Israel: "The jar of flour will not finish, nor will the bottle of oil be lacking, until the day when God gives [written *titen*, read *tet*] rain upon the face of the land." (v. 14)

The final clause here is most surprising: Why does Elijah mention this "target date"? Baal HaMetzudot's answer – "For then there will be no need for a miracle" – fails to explain this phrase adequately. How can Elijah be so certain that his stay in the widow's home will continue until the end of the drought? And why does he make the rainfall dependent on God? Is it not Elijah himself who holds the "key to the rainfall"? Did he not swear that the rain would return only "by my word"?

As in many other instances in Tanakh, the *written* form reveals an important level of significance in understanding the story. The written form in our verse exposes what lies hidden in the heart of the speaker: "Give [or "You will give"], O God, rain upon the face of the land." Elijah expresses a covert plea: "Please, O God, may it be Your will to give rain upon the face of the land." In other words: "Take back the responsibility for the rainfall; release me from [the task of] holding the key to the rain."

In this sentence Elijah reveals, for the first time, some hesitation in his position. Anyone who is unfamiliar with Elijah and the background to the story (as is the widow) hears in these words a clear expression of his wish that God should soon send rain.

The suffering of the widow and Elijah's need to share her food in a way that causes him discomfort lead the prophet, for the first time, to express in words a new attitude. Nevertheless, he is not yet ready to retract his vow. The words, "until the day when God will give rain upon the face of the land" are uttered immediately after his invocation of the miracle, whose entire purpose is to facilitate Elijah's existence in Zarephath as the drought continues.

When the conditions become ripe for a nullification of the decree of the drought, as a result of a change in Elijah's stance (following the next episode), God will eventually repeat Elijah's words here, entrusting him with the task:

> Go and appear before Ahab, and *I will give rain upon the face of the earth.* (18:1)

Here Elijah tells the widow:

> Until the day when *God will give rain upon the face of the land.* (17:16)

STRUCTURE OF THIS UNIT AND ITS SIGNIFICANCE

As we noted previously, in terms of content, this unit comprises two unequal parts: God's command to Elijah in verses 8–9, and its fulfillment in verses 10–16. But in terms of literary form, it is structured as a single unit of nine verses, with the fifth verse (v. 12) serving as the central axis, while the other sections form pairs of verses around this central axis in a developing chiastic structure, as follows:

A: God's word came to him, saying: (v. 8)

Arise, go to Zarephath of Sidon, and sojourn there; and behold, I have commanded there a widowed woman to sustain you. (v. 9)

B: So he arose and went to Zarephath, and when he came to the entrance of the city... he called to her and said: Bring me, I pray you, a little water in a vessel, that I may drink. (v. 10)

So she went to bring it, and he called to her and said: Bring me, I pray you, a morsel of bread in your hand. (v. 11)

C (*Central Axis*): She said: As the Lord your God lives, I have nothing baked but a handful of flour in a jar, and a little oil in the bottle; and behold, I am gathering two sticks so I may come and prepare it for myself and for my son, that we may eat it, and die. (v. 12)

B': Elijah said to her: Do not fear; come, do as you have said, but make me a small cake of it first, and bring it to me, and then afterward make for you and for your son. (v. 13)

For so says the Lord God of Israel: the jar of flour will not finish, nor will the bottle of oil be lacking, until the day when God gives rain upon the face of the land. (v. 14)

A': She went and did as Elijah had spoken, and she and he and her household ate for some time. (v. 15)

The jar of meal did not finish, nor did the bottle of oil lack, as God's word that He had spoken by Elijah's hand. (v. 16)

The first pair of verses, part A (vv. 8–9), contains God's command to Elijah and the promise of the possibility of his survival in the widow's house in Zarephath. This pair corresponds to the final pair of verses, part A' (vv. 15–16), in which we discover how this divine word was fulfilled. "*She and he* and her household ate *for some time*" corresponds to "*Sojourn there;* and behold I have commanded there *a widowed woman to sustain you*." The new idea in the second pair is that "the jar of meal did not finish, nor did the bottle of oil lack," but even though this was not mentioned explicitly at the beginning of the story, it certainly happens by virtue of that command: "as God's word that He had spoken by Elijah's hand."

Thus, the section opens with the words "*God's word* came to him," followed by details of this divine word, and it concludes with a description of the miracle that represents a fulfillment of "*God's word* that He had spoken by Elijah's hand."

The next pair of verses, part B (vv. 10–11), corresponds to B' (vv. 13–14). In both pairs Elijah speaks to the widow, and in each instance there is a double statement. In the first pair he presents two requests. In verse 10 he asks for a little water – a not unreasonable request, which is accordingly answered in the affirmative. In verse 11 Elijah requests a little bread – a request which is impossible to fulfill in the prevailing circumstances. In the corresponding pair, Elijah first repeats his request for food from verse 11. Corresponding to "*Bring me, I pray you, a morsel of bread,*" he promises the widow, in verse 14, a miracle upon her jar of flour and bottle of oil; he thereby turns his request into one that may be fulfilled. He concludes this promise with a mention of rain, corresponding to his original request for water upon his first encounter with her. There, in the first pair of verses, Elijah first spoke about water and then about bread; in the corresponding pair he starts with food and concludes with water – rain. The water and the bread in the first pair are requested from the widow's hand, while in the corresponding verses they are given from God's hand: "*For so says the Lord God of Israel: the jar of flour* will not finish…until the day *when God gives rain* upon the face of the land."

In between these two sections, with their chiastic parallel, we find the widow's emotional outburst, declaring her situation desperate – hence her inability to accede to his request. This monologue is the most dramatic in the story, as well as the most surprising. We, the readers, do not expect such an outburst; nor does Elijah. Until verse 11 events move along more or less predictably. Then, suddenly, along comes the widow's oath and upsets the orderly progress. It confronts both Elijah and the plot of this unit with a crisis. The part of the unit that follows her outburst (parts A and B) comes to resolve this crisis. The resolution lies not in a withdrawal of Elijah's original request of the widow, but rather the opposite: A repetition of the same request, accompanied by a promise that what she currently lacks will be provided by God. At this point, the woman agrees to Elijah's demand, as we expected her to do at the start, and God fulfills Elijah's word.

What molds the structure of the unit as we have described it above? The answer is simple: The heart of this unit, verse 12, stands out prominently in the central axis. This represents the dramatic climax of the section and the key to all its developments. All that precedes it is meant to build up to the climactic outburst and to become irrelevant as a result of it. All that follows is an attempt to make all that preceded it relevant and possible once again, despite what she has said.[4] The chiastic

---

4. Indeed, in terms of both form and content the last part of the unit is influenced by the language used by the widow. This is expressed in each verse as follows:
   Verse 13:
   (1) Elijah's words to the widow, "Do not fear," are a response to her statement: "That we may eat it *and die*." Elijah is reassuring her that she will not die.
   (2) His next words to her: "Come, do (*bo'i asi*) as you have said," are a reference to her words: "So I may come and prepare (*bati ve'asitihu*) it for myself and my son." Elijah is encouraging the woman to act as she had planned, but he adds his own request:
   (3) "But make (*asi*) me a small *cake* of it first." This is a repetition of his first request (in v. 11), but here Elijah replaces the phrase "Bring me, I pray you" with the phrase "make me," and the word "bread" with the word "cake" [*uga*]. Thus he echoes the widow's use of the terms "flour" [*ma'og*], from the same Hebrew root as *uga*, and "prepare it."
   (4) "And prepare (*taasi*) for yourself and for your son afterward." This parallels her statement "That I may prepare (*asitihu*) it for myself and my son."
   Verse 14:
   (5) The existence of the jar of flour and bottle of oil, with which Elijah promises that a miracle will occur, is known owing to the widow's reference to them in her speech, in which she tells Elijah that she has "a handful of flour in a jar and a little oil in the bottle."

structure around the central axis, as we have demonstrated it here, represents an artistic structural rendering of this idea.

Thus, the essence of this unit is not the description of the solution that is found for Elijah during the drought – a solution that will allow him to live in an inhabited area and survive without difficulty – but rather *the considerable difficulty involved in realizing and implementing this solution*. This difficulty finds painful expression in the widow's monologue, which is located precisely at the center of the unit, drawing all of the reader's attention. This outburst is also the focus of the plot. It transpires that Elijah is sent to Zarephath not in order to live there in tranquility, but rather in order to hear the widow's words, to be forced to deal with the challenge that her outburst presents. At the gates of Zarephath Elijah is presented with the question of *whether* he will be able to "live there peacefully," and following the widow's oath, *how* he will do this – as we have explained.

Verse 15:

(6) "She went and did as Elijah had spoken." Elijah had told her: "Come, do as you have said." The term "doing," which is repeated five times in this section, was first used by the widow: "That I may go in and do [prepare] it."

Verse 16:

(7) "The jar of meal did not finish, nor was the bottle of oil lacking, as God's word that He had spoken by Elijah's hand"; yet Elijah's words, as is clear from the above, are actually based on the widow's own speech, in which she mentions her two vessels and the substances they hold.

It should be noted that none of the terms discussed here – "go in," "do" (or "prepare," "make"), "son," *ma'og/uga*, "jar," "bottle," and "oil" – appears anywhere in the first part of the section, prior to the widow's speech. Only the root *dalet-bet-resh* appears both in the first verse, "And God's word (*devar*) came…," and another four times in the last part of this section, in different contexts. Indeed, it would seem that this root, meaning "speak" or "word," which is nowhere to be found in the widow's speech, is the key word connecting the two parts of this unit, before and after the speech.

Chapter 6

Elijah Revives the Widow's Son (I Kings 17:17–24)

COMPARISON WITH PREVIOUS UNITS

Despite the obvious continuity of this unit with the previous ones in terms of characters, time, and place – all of which are common to both – it is difficult to define this episode in the more general context of the story as a whole. Unlike the episodes of Wadi Cherith and Zarephath, it does not address the problem of Elijah's survival and sustenance during the drought. The subject here appears to be something altogether extraneous: The death and resuscitation of the Zarephath widow's son, a boy whom we shall not meet again in the text (his mother, too, plays no further role). The appearance of the boy and his mother in the story in the previous unit was only for the purposes of describing the actions and character of Elijah, who is at center stage. In this section, the text does not even hint at the drought and famine. It is no wonder, therefore, that most of the key words that link the two preceding units are absent in our section: The verb "to drink" is absent here, as is the expression "I have commanded … to sustain you"; we find no mention of the nouns "bread" or "rain." In short, all the terms related to the drought and to the problem that it presents to the people in general and Elijah in particular are nowhere to be found in this unit.

Two further differences between these verses and the previous ones should be noted, and they will serve as a bridge to our discussion of their theme:

1. The two preceding sections are each constructed in similar form: They begin with God's word to Elijah (2–4; 8–9), and then go on to describe the way in which this divine word is fulfilled both by Elijah, who does as he is commanded, and by God, who fulfills what He has promised to the prophet. Our unit is not built on this pattern at all. On the contrary, its central event, the boy's death, appears to contradict God's word at the beginning of the previous unit, telling Elijah to remain in the Zarephath widow's house and to be sustained by her. This is because the widow's claims against Elijah (v. 18) bring their relationship to a turning point, threatening his continued stay in her home, as we shall explain below.

   In our section, God does not instruct Elijah as to what he should do; rather, Elijah prays to God to perform his request. It is not Elijah who performs God's word, but rather God who listens to Elijah and fulfills his request (v. 23).

2. Each of the two preceding episodes covers a period of one year. The event described in our section, by contrast, is a onetime occurrence.

These two differences between our unit and the previous ones lead us to deduce that our unit serves as the conclusion of the previous one in the form of a crisis, which actually creates a similarity between the events of Elijah's stay in the widow's house and the events of his stay at Wadi Cherith. The crisis at the end of the first episode, "Wadi Cherith," is expressed in the verse "It was *after some time* that the wadi dried up, for there was no rain in the land" (v. 7).

This conclusion is not part of the (general) structure that is common to Elijah's stay at Wadi Cherith and his stay in Zarephath, for the latter ends with the fulfillment of God's word without any problem or hindrance: "He [to be read 'she'] and she [to be read 'he'] and her household ate *for some time* … according to God's word which He spoke by the hand of Elijah" (vv. 15–16).

This "happy ending" could have facilitated the continuation of the situation indefinitely. Everyone, it seems, is now satisfied: The widow and her son have been saved from starvation, Elijah has found a suitable place to stay and a source of sustenance, albeit meager, but in no danger of drying up. But this, of course, is an illusion: The subject of the story as a whole is not finding a satisfactory arrangement for Elijah, but rather the drought which the prophet has brought upon his nation. From the perspective of this main subject, everything here is temporary and must change. Elijah's "comfortable" conditions in the widow's home are not a solution in the context of the broader story but rather the opposite: His sustainable situation is actually an obstacle to its flow and progression. It must therefore reach a crisis point that will not allow for Elijah's continued peaceful stay; it must involve a continuation of the main theme of the drought. The end of the previous section hints at the need for such a device, and its imminent appearance: "She and he, and her household, ate *for some time*" (v. 15).

Why does the verse stipulate this time frame for Elijah's peaceful stay at the widow's home? What happens at the end of that time (year)? The reader remembers that Elijah's stay at Wadi Cherith also lasted a year, ending with a crisis that forced him to move to a new place and adopt a new lifestyle. We now expect a similar crisis to bring Elijah's stay in Zarephath to an end. The third episode comes to fulfill this expectation. However, in contrast to the crisis that concluded the period at Wadi Cherith, described in a single verse, the crisis that concludes Elijah's stay in the widow's house represents the subject of a brief independent unit. This is because of Elijah's reaction to the crisis, as opposed to his lack of reaction to the previous crisis.

THE BOY'S REVIVAL: "CRISIS CONCLUSION" OF THE PREVIOUS EPISODE

Is our perception of the episode here as being the conclusion of the previous one hinted at in any way in the text itself? Let us pay close attention to the verses.

First, the opening words of our unit, "It came to pass after these things," raises the question: After what things? Namely, to which previous event (or which detail of a previous event) is our section related? This question is justified here, since our unit is closely related to the previous one (in terms of the characters, the time, and the place, as noted above), and both together are part of the greater story. So, after which "things" did "the son of the woman fall ill"? It would seem that the key to this question rests with the last notation of time at the end of the previous unit (v. 15) – "some time," i.e., a year. It is after that year that "the son of the woman … fell ill." Clearly, then, the introduction to our unit intends to hint to the termination of that "idyllic" period described in the previous unit.

Second, it sometimes happens that the way a character is referred to changes during the course of a narrative, generally reflecting different views of that character. Sometimes the change of perspective arises from a change in the people who interact with that character, and sometimes from a change in circumstances. Let us pay close attention to the ways in which the text refers to the widow, one of the leading characters in both of the units under discussion.

Twice in the previous unit (at the beginning, in verses 9 and 10), the woman is referred to as the "widowed woman" (*isha almana*). This title describes her low socioeconomic status, thereby preparing us for the great difficulty that is about to be revealed: As a widow with a child to care for, she is incapable of feeding even herself and her son adequately during the famine, and certainly lacks the ability to take care of a stranger.

In our unit the woman is referred to four times: three times in the narration and once by Elijah. In each instance her title is different:

1. "The son of the *woman, mistress of the house* fell ill" (v. 17)
2. "Have You also brought evil upon *the widow with whom I lodge*?" (v. 20)
3. "He gave him to *his mother*" (v. 23)
4. "*The woman* said to Elijah" (v. 24)

Interestingly, the title used in the previous unit, "widowed woman," does not appear in that exact form anywhere in our unit. This shows that the fact of her widowhood, as an expression of her low socioeconomic status, is not of importance at this stage. It is easy to understand why the text refers to her as "[the boy's] mother" in verse 23: Her joy upon receiving her child back, alive, from Elijah is principally the joy of a woman who is once again the mother of her child. Her title at the end of the section, "the woman," is likewise understandable: It is not as the mother of her son that she utters her final words to Elijah, nor as a widow, but rather as a "woman" (*isha*). In other words, as a human subject (*ishiyut*) expressing her conclusion regarding all that has happened: That the divine word that Elijah speaks is true. We shall address the lengthy title that Elijah uses for her in his first prayer – "the widow with whom I lodge" – when we discuss the prayer in detail.

The first title used for the woman in this unit, "the woman, [who is] mistress of the house," is somewhat surprising. Why does the text choose to emphasize the fact that she is the "mistress of the house"? Would it not be more suitable to emphasize the fact of her widowhood? This would surely amplify the tragedy of the death of her son. What has the death of the boy to do with his mother being the "mistress of the house"?

The answer appears to be that when describing the son's illness and his death, the text seems to be more concerned with their practical ramifications regarding Elijah than in the personal, family relationship between the son and his widowed mother. When the text tells us that the woman is the "mistress of the house," it means that she is the *mistress of the house in which Elijah dwells* as a secondary tenant, and therefore the death of the boy is significant also for Elijah. This becomes clear in Elijah's prayer, when he describes the woman as "the widow with whom I lodge."

But why does the text indirectly link the boy's illness and death to Elijah? The answer is clear: The illness and death represent a turning point in the relationship between Elijah and the mistress of the house. The boy's death threatens the continuation of Elijah's stay, as we shall explain below.

Third, what does the woman mean when she says to Elijah, "What have I to do with you, O man of God" (v. 18)? "What have I to do with you" is an expression that appears in five other places in Tanakh.[1] A study of these sources and their contexts reveals its exact meaning. In all instances, it is a call to cut off contact. A person who utters these words

---

1. Judges 11:12; II Samuel 16:10, 19:23; II Kings 3:13; II Chronicles 35:21.

to someone else means, "Let me be; leave me in peace; there is nothing between us." In most of the cases, it is addressed toward someone who intends to *harm* the speaker (either intentionally or unintentionally).

We may explain the widow's words in our unit accordingly: In telling Elijah, "You have come to me to recall my sin and to put my son to death" (v. 18), she is accusing him of being responsible for the death of her son. She does not mean to ask Elijah to revive him. It appears that such a thought never entered her mind; it is Elijah who initiates the idea. On the other hand, her words are not without practical implications. These are expressed in the introduction to her accusation: "What have I to do with you, O man of God?" The intention behind this rhetorical question is as in all its other appearances in Tanakh: "Please, leave me alone. Why have you come to me to cause me harm?" Or: "Since you have 'come to me to recall my sin and to put my son to death,' get out of my house!"

Clearly, then, the son's death represents a crisis that ends Elijah's stay in the woman's house, for in response she asks him to leave.

CONNECTION BETWEEN THE BOY'S DEATH AND THE DROUGHT

Let us now compare the crisis that ends his stay at Wadi Cherith with the crisis that ends his stay in the widow's house.

At Wadi Cherith	At the widow's house
v. 7: It was *after some time* that the wadi dried up, for there was *no* rain in the land.	v. 17: *And it was*, after these things [after "she and he and her household ate *for some time*"] that the son of the woman who was mistress of the house fell ill, and his illness was exceedingly grave, such that *no* breath was left in him.

In both instances, the crisis itself does not stand in the way of a continuation of the miracle by means of which Elijah is fed in each place. The ravens could have continued to bring Elijah bread and meat twice daily even after the wadi dried up; and the jar of meal and the bottle of oil were not diminished even after the boy's death. It is rather the continuation of that part of his stay in each place that is "natural," which is cut short by the respective crisis: his drinking from the water of the wadi, and the continuation of civil relations with the widow hosting him in her home in Zarephath. We could say that in both places, the lodging "rebels" against its guest, preventing him from continuing to dwell there. The wadi – Elijah's lodging place in the first section – ceases to exist, thereby no longer serving as his lodging. In Zarephath, Elijah's human hostess, the widowed woman, "attacks" her guest verbally: "What have I to do with you, O man of God?"

In both cases, the crisis that arises is not a sudden one. It is the outcome of a prolonged process which is noted in both of the verses quoted above in the table of comparison. The reason for the drying up of Wadi Cherith is that "there was no rain in the land." The drought, which has continued throughout that year, has slowly weakened the flow of the wadi; by the end of the year, it dries up completely. The death of the widow's son is preceded by an illness that becomes increasingly acute: First he "fell ill," then "his illness was exceedingly grave," and eventually "such that no breath was left in him."

What is the meaning of these parallels between the two crises that cut short Elijah's stays at his two lodgings? It would seem that they lead to the unavoidable parallel between the wadi being *cut off* from water, and the boy being *cut off* from life.

The drying up of a wadi is not like stopping the flow of water in a closed pipe. It is a process of slow death for the plant and animal life on its banks. Therefore, the process of the water being cut off from the wadi represents a process of perishing and death. Water is the source of life in the world. When its regular supply ceases, it is as though the living soul is cut off from existence: from plants, from animals, and from man.

It therefore becomes apparent that the episode of the death of the widow's son is tightly bound up with the subject of the story as a whole: the drought. Through this episode, Elijah comes to realize that the cessation of rain from the land by his own word has cut off life from the land. And when the drought reaches its most severe stage, even human life is cut off. The way of the world is such that the first victims are those from the weakest sectors of society, such as orphaned children.

The fact that the boy's death is a direct or indirect result of the drought arises not only from the parallel between the water being cut off from the wadi and his life being cut off, but also from the information that the story provides. The woman and her son were indeed saved from immediate death by starvation by the miracle that Elijah invokes on the jar of meal and the bottle of oil. However, throughout that year in Elijah's company, they remain constantly on the brink of starvation, sharing their meager, monotonous rations with a third party. A young child cannot grow healthy and strong under such conditions. Where there is drought and famine, weakness prevails and outbreaks of disease and plague are common. It comes as no surprise, then, that the widow's weak and hungry child also falls ill: "His illness was exceedingly grave, such that no breath was left in him."

Previously we noted that the words linking the first two episodes, indicating the drought and the problems that it creates, are absent here. But we have just argued that this unit is nevertheless likewise connected to the drought. Are there words linking our unit to the previous one that would support this claim?

The words we are looking for are "death" and "life." This pair appears for the first time in the previous unit, in the widow's words (v. 12). She starts with an oath: "As the Lord your God *lives*, I have nothing baked," and concludes with the words "I...prepare it for myself and for my son, that we may eat it *and die*."

The contrast between her first words, "As...God lives," and her closing words, "and die," hints that only He who lives eternally and holds in His hand the lives of all can save the starving from death.

In this unit, each of these two key words appears twice. At the start of the unit we find the root *mem-vav-tav* (death) twice:

You have come to me to recall my sin and to *put my son to death.* (v. 18)

Have You also done evil to the widow with whom I dwell, to *put her son to death*? (v. 20)

These two questions, which are actually protests, are eventually answered (following a complex process which we shall discuss later) in inverse order:

> God heard the voice of Elijah and restored the boy's soul within him, *and he lived.* (v. 22)

> He gave him to his mother, and Elijah said: Behold, your son *lives.* (v. 23)

This linguistic connection between the two units goes beyond the syntax. The widow's fear, in the previous unit, expressed in the word *vamatnu* (that we may die), is half realized in this unit. She feared that starvation would lead to their death, and the partial realization of this scenario here tells us that it is indeed the famine that ultimately leads to the boy's death, as his mother had predicted. This is not a sudden, chance disease that attacks the boy, but rather a death that was foretold, based on a realistic evaluation of the terrible situation. The miracle that Elijah performed with the oil and flour allowed himself and the widow to survive, but ultimately did not save her son from death.

This death, which has occurred because of the drought, must be healed and erased. The world needs life!

THE THREE-STAGE DISPUTE BETWEEN GOD AND PROPHET: HOW CAN IT BE AT ISRAEL'S EXPENSE?

During the course of the three units describing Elijah's existence throughout the drought, he has encountered three very serious results of the drought in the world. These increasingly acute phenomena affect Elijah himself in that they oblige him to act and react in different ways.

Elijah's first encounter with the results of the drought takes place at Wadi Cherith, which dries up, "for there was no rain in the land." There he watched the wadi's gradual shrinking until it dries up altogether at the end of the year. He is shown the destructive results of the cessation of rain with regard to *the land*, its streams, and its plant and animal life. But the drying up of the wadi is also significant *for Elijah himself,* since he is dependent on its water. Nevertheless, this does not cause him to retract his oath. And so he has to move somewhere else, where he will be able stay alive. God's command sends him to Zarephath, where further encounters with the results of his drought await him.

The second encounter takes place at the gates of Zarephath. Here Elijah views the significance of the drought on the *human level*, specifically what it means to the weakest sectors of society: a widow and an orphan. But here again, the suffering of the woman and her child because of drought and famine, although *affecting Elijah himself* – since his sustenance depends on them – does not cause him to retract his oath. In order to overcome the problem that has presented itself, he invokes a miracle allowing him to continue living for a whole year in the widow's home in Zarephath.

Elijah's third encounter with the results of the drought takes place at the end of the year of lodging with "the woman who was mistress of the house," with the death of her son. Now Elijah is forced to contemplate the most tragic consequences of the famine: The death of a poor, orphaned child, illustrating the fate of many more like him. Once again, the event has an effect on Elijah's personal fate: The child's mother accuses him of responsibility for the death and asks him to leave.

These three encounters are all part of the ongoing argument between God and His prophet. We find ourselves asking, if "it was grave in the eyes of the Holy One that Israel was mired in famine" (Rashi, v. 7), why does He not unilaterally bring an end to the famine? So long as the dispute with the prophet goes on, the famine continues, causing the deaths of innocent children! Is it proper that the boy's death in the wake of three years of famine serve as a "claim" in the dispute?

This question brings us back to the issue of the extent of the prophet's independence in choosing his policy of action (see introduction). Elijah is one of the greatest prophets whom Tanakh describes as attempting to lead Israel to repentance. He is entrusted with the task of being the prophet whose mission is to correct his generation in accordance with his own understanding.

This broad authority vested by God in the greatest among the prophets turns his actions into those performed by God's word, even when they are not explicitly commanded. However, as we noted at the end of the introduction, this freedom of action enjoyed by the prophet may lead to a situation in which he performs a deed that does not correspond with God's intentions; in this case, we cannot say that his actions are performed in God's name.

In extreme cases, where the prophet's action is absolutely opposed to God's will, he is explicitly instructed to undo what he has done (see introduction). But where the prophet's action is neither altogether mistaken nor altogether desirable in God's eyes, there may be a situation in which God will fulfill the prophet's word, but still try to cause him to change his view and his actions, so that they will be better aligned with those of his Sender.

Had Elijah uttered his oath to bring a drought upon Israel at a time when the nation had not degenerated into the grave sin of idolatry, at a time when they were altogether not deserving of such a harsh punishment, God would certainly have commanded him to retract his oath, or at least He would not have fulfilled it. But the situation in our case is different: Elijah's decree of drought is not unjustified. After all, the Torah warns that as a punishment for idolatry God "will close up the heavens and there will be no rain, nor will the ground give its produce" (Deut. 11:17). In his oath, Elijah simply realizes this warning. Obviously, a heavy drought, such as described in the Torah, affects not only those who have sinned and engaged in idolatry, but everyone, including innocent widows and orphans.

Hence, Elijah's oath represents the measure of justice of which the Torah warns. Nevertheless, for reasons that are not made explicit in the story, this act of Elijah does not reflect God's will, for "it was grave in the eyes of the Holy One that Israel was mired in famine." The longer the drought goes on, the worse it is in God's eyes. We may propose various hypotheses as to why God had mercy on this sinful generation and why the ongoing suffering of Israel because of the famine was so grave in His eyes, but none of this makes the path that Elijah has chosen a completely mistaken one.

We may express this idea more explicitly, as follows: The power given to a prophet to act in rebuking and guiding his generation may indeed entail a situation whereby his policy brings suffering to his people. And in cases where this suffering is not unjustified, God will not prevent it, for it is He who gives the prophet the authority to guide the nation.

This explains the situation in our story. Elijah utters the oath which creates the drought on his own initiative, not as a result of a divine command. Nevertheless, it is just, and is based on Elijah's calculation that the destruction wrought by the drought will bring Israel back to God. It appears that this does not happen as Elijah expected, and God is not pleased that Israel was suffering from famine. However, God does not force Elijah to retract his oath until the prophet himself agrees to it, until it becomes difficult for *him* to see Israel suffering from famine.

THE WIDOW'S ACCUSATION: THE DISPUTE WITH ELIJAH REACHES ITS CLIMAX

What is the meaning of the widow's allegation, "You have come to me to recall my sin and to put my son to death"? Has Elijah not saved her and her son from death by starvation for the past year?

The nature of Elijah's stay in the widow's home throughout the year ("Make *me* a small cake of it *first* and bring it *to me*, and then afterward make for you and for your son") is ample proof for the woman that it is not out of compassion for her and her son that Elijah performs the miracle of the jar of meal and the bottle of oil. She and her son are serving merely as vehicles for Elijah's sustenance; the miracle is meant not for them, but for himself. It appears that the woman intuitively senses that the power of Elijah's personality, with the heavy demand that he makes of society, brings with it punishment and suffering for those around him. She makes no mention of what "sin" she has committed which has caused her son to die; perhaps she herself does not know what it was. Nevertheless, she feels that his death is somehow connected with the introverted personality of the strange, foreign man of God in her home.

Apparently, the woman has no knowledge of Elijah's identity or the extent of his responsibility for the famine, which is causing her and her son and all the inhabitants of their city so much suffering. However, without her knowing it, she is correct in what she says: Elijah is indeed the reason for her son's death. It is his oath concerning the cessation of rain that has caused, directly or indirectly, the famine and death. Her intuition is not far from the truth. This being the case, the widow's words in this section, like those in the previous section, serve as an accusation against Elijah. At the gates of Zarephath, on the surface, she was apologizing over her inability to fulfill this stranger's request. Only to Elijah, who recognizes his responsibility for the situation that arises from her words (and to us, the readers), does her speech sound like an accusation. But in this section, the woman really means what she says as an accusation. The difference between what she means to say and what Elijah (and we) are meant to hear in her words is merely the difference between someone who accuses based on intuition and someone who knows how justified the accusation really is – even more than the accuser believes it to be.

The widow's second outburst resembles the first in another aspect, too. Here again, Elijah is faced with a practical problem: How is he going to continue living in this woman's house?

Elijah has encountered this problem of survival already twice before. Faced with the dried-up wadi, he was exiled by God's word to Zarephath, and at the gates of Zarephath he invoked a miracle to maintain the jar of meal and the bottle of oil, in light of his understanding of God's command to him. Now, Elijah is faced for a third time with the crisis of the drought, threatening his own survival. This time the crisis is particularly severe, and it seems that Elijah has no escape, no way of solving it. This time God's word does not lead him to a new place where he may continue to exist, as was the case at Wadi Cherith. Neither does he have any possibility of decreeing a miracle that will solve his troubles, as was the case at the gates of Zarephath. There, God had promised that the widow would sustain him, and therefore Elijah could conclude that in order to overcome her inability to do this, he must perform a miracle that would make it possible. But the death of the widow's son is not a direct contradiction of that divine word; it is also entirely unreasonable to imagine that Elijah would decree, on his own initiative, the resuscitation of the boy, as he decreed the preservation of the meal and the oil.

At this stage of the story, with the severity of the drought and famine in the third year, the claims against Elijah also become more acute. The new "claim" in this dispute – the death of an orphan child because of the famine – pushes Elijah into a corner from which there is no escape. What is Elijah going to do? Will he forgo his oath and thereby bring the dispute to its conclusion, or will he maintain his stance despite the boy's death and despite the mother's demand that he leave her home? Where can he go and how will he survive the famine, with no word from God nor any promise as to his continued sustenance?

ELIJAH'S RESPONSE

> He said to her: Give me your son. He took him from her bosom and took him up to the attic where he lodged, and he lay him down upon his bed. (v. 19)

This verse and the next describe Elijah's surprising reaction to the crisis. Elijah attempts to repair the injustice through a new miracle, even greater than the previous ones, and to return the dead child to life. This act, as yet unparalleled in Tanakh, is as unexpected for us, the readers, as it is for the mother. It was not with this in mind that she brought her complaint to Elijah after her son died in her arms. Even after he instructs her, "Give me your son," she does not cooperate, and so *"He took him from her bosom."* It is Elijah who initiates this audacious endeavor; he performs the necessary actions himself, intent and decisive: "He took … he took him up … he lay him down."

This intensive activity demonstrates that the prophet has a clear interest in solving the problem. But what could that interest be? Does it arise from his knowledge that the woman is correct in her accusation that he is responsible for the death of her son; do his pangs of conscience prompt him to want to appease her? This is a difficult claim to maintain, since the son is not to be perceived as an individual phenomenon, but rather as representative of many other unfortunate children who are wasting away and even dying of starvation and the diseases associated with the famine. The resuscitation of this boy will not appease all the other heartbroken mothers, for whom the widow of Zarephath is a mouthpiece when she accuses Elijah of causing her son's death.

Perhaps Elijah's interest is to restore the previous status quo that allowed him to live in the widow's home. Perhaps he seeks a miracle similar to the one that maintained the meal and the oil, which would allow him to return to his previous calm by means of a "technical" solution to the problem. If this is so, then it is not for the sake of the mother and her son that Elijah is acting, but rather, once again, for his own sake.

Does Elijah really believe that God will answer his plea for such a great miracle, allowing him once again to find refuge from the drought and from the ongoing argument concerning his approach?

The fact that God ultimately answers Elijah's prayer, such that the child is restored, alive, to his mother, does not necessarily answer our question. This outcome is achieved only after Elijah has undergone a complex development in his relationship with God. Only after a clarification of this process, with all its various stages, will we arrive at the answer to the question of Elijah's motives.

WHY IS ELIJAH'S FIRST PRAYER NOT ANSWERED?

> He called out to God and said: Lord, my God! Have You also done evil to the widow with whom I lodge, to put her son to death? (v. 20)

In order to understand Elijah's intention in this address to God, and perhaps even in order to understand God's lack of response to it (until Elijah calls a second time), we must first examine the meaning of a single, small word: "[Have You] also" (*hagam*). In general, in most of the places where this word appears in Tanakh, it is used in the cumulative sense. If we interpret it here in the same way (and we have no linguistic nor substantive reason to interpret it in some other, rare, sense), then what Elijah means is something like: "I can deal somehow with the fact that You have done evil to so-and-so, but that You have done evil to the widow with whom I dwell, to put her son to death – this I cannot accept without questioning and objecting." The expositor is left with the task of supplying the missing variable: who is the "so-and-so" to whose loss Elijah now adds the loss of the widow's son? This is the key to the nature of the entire sentence; this will help us understand why his prayer is not answered, as we shall see reflected in the various commentaries.

1.   Radak comments:

> "Have You also…to the widow" – meaning: "Have You punished the sin even of the widow, just as You have punished Israel's sin today in holding back the rains? And even if You have punished

the sin of this widow by putting her son to death, will You not restore his life in my merit, since I dwell with her?"

Radak's answer, then, is: "Have You done to the widow... *as You have done to Israel.*" It is not the personal sins of the widow that have led to the death of her son (as she believes), but rather the sins of Israel, which are being punished by drought. Since the sin and the punishment are shared by all, even young children like the widow's son are affected by the famine. But here, Elijah claims, there should be a different way of doing justice. In Elijah's view, God is not taking him into consideration, in including the widow in the collective punishment. Elijah, according to Radak, refuses to accept the boy's death, because it affects him personally. Radak deduces this from the "extra" words that Elijah utters in describing the widow, since they seem superfluous, adding no new information: "The widow *with whom I dwell.*" From this Radak deduces Elijah's claim: "Will You not restore his life *in my merit*, since I dwell with her?"

Elijah feels that the widow who is providing him with lodgings should be excluded from the rules of reward and punishment as they apply to the rest of the nation. This should happen in Elijah's merit and for his sake, so that he will have a dwelling place and a means of subsistence. Indeed, his claim has a solid precedent: Through the miracle of the flour and the oil, Elijah excluded the widow and her son from the nation as a whole and from the suffering that would have been their portion during the drought. He did this, not because of the widow's righteousness, but rather in order that there would be someone to provide him with sustenance during the drought. Elijah therefore expects a continuation of this preferential treatment toward himself, and, in his merit, toward whomever is meant to serve him.

According to this explanation, Elijah is hinting at the apparent contradiction between the miracle that happened for this widow and her son, "by God's word which he spoke by the hand of Elijah," with regard to the jar of meal and the bottle of oil, and the death of the boy from starvation.

In what way have the circumstances changed from what they were throughout the year? Why did God save the widow and her son from starvation for Elijah's sake then, but no longer takes him into consideration now?

What has changed is that the ongoing drought is becoming increasingly oppressive, and the world is no longer able to bear it. Therefore, the dispute with Elijah over his oath continues and even intensifies. A situation in which Elijah dwells peacefully in the widow's home can no longer be tolerated. The preferential conditions that he has enjoyed for the last year have now expired, and therefore the widow and her son are likewise no longer different from anyone else suffering the effects of the drought. Now the events and the widow's outburst push Elijah into an inescapable corner. Against his will, Elijah is becoming party to the suffering of the drought.

But Elijah's call to God testifies (according to Radak) that he is not ready to recognize the "claim" represented by the death of the widow's son as a continuation of God's argument with him. He maintains his position, requesting for himself and those around him, even now, the right to preferential treatment. It is not surprising, then, that God does not accede to his request, and the widow's son is not revived.

2. Rabbi Samuel Laniado, in his commentary *Keli Yakar*, explains Elijah's call to God differently:

> The word "also" refers to what has already been mentioned: Wadi Cherith was cut off in order to cause sorrow to Elijah, so that he would also be distressed together with everyone else. And this is the meaning of "also": "As You did to the wadi, which dried up *because I was there*, will You likewise do evil also to the widow, to put her son to death *on account of my lodging with her*? Such an act seems strange, for the opposite should be the case: It would seem proper [for You] to do good to all those who provided me with lodgings, for they were close to me when I fled from before Ahab, on my divine mission."

This commentator's perception of the boy's death as a clear parallel to the drying up of the wadi, and both events as stages in God's dispute with Elijah concerning his approach, matches what we have said above. The *Keli Yakar* finds a source substantiating this parallel in the words of Elijah himself: "Have You *also* done evil to the widow with whom I lodge [*as You did evil to the wadi* where I dwelled previously]?"

Elijah is made to suffer two types of evil so that he will "be distressed together with everyone else": He accepted the drying up of the wadi in silence, firstly because no human victim had to pay the price of God's dispute with him (only the wadi dried up), and secondly, because God's command guided him to a new place where he would find a way to survive. However, when it comes to the new "evil" that God has done – bringing death to the son of the widow – he is no longer prepared to remain silent. He calls out to God and presents two grievances. First his own: Why should he have to suffer while he is trying to fulfill his divinely imposed duty? But he also presents the grievance of the widow, who has paid such a terrible price for the hospitality that she has offered him: "On account of my lodging with her, You have done this evil, to put her son to death!" In truth, she deserves a reward for her actions: "It would seem proper [for You] to do good to all those who provided me with lodgings."

The fact is that Elijah's claim is not justified. Wadi Cherith did not dry up because Elijah lived on its banks, but rather, as the text testifies, "because there was no rain in the land." Likewise, the widow's son did not die because Elijah was lodging with them. He, too, died because of the drought, which in turn brought about weakness and disease that eventually took his life. Thus, God is not directing any particular evil at Elijah; rather, He is showing him the results of the drought that he brought upon the land. It is clear, then, why God does not answer this prayer.

3. Certain commentators interpret the inclusion in Elijah's prayer ("also") differently from the ways we have discussed above. Alsheikh, in his *Marot HaTzovot*, writes:

> "He called out to God and said: Lord my God ..." If it is because of my zealousness against Israel for Your honor that I am exiled and am troubled [to move] from place to place, because I have punished Your nation Israel, does it justify that You have done evil "to the widow with whom I lodge" – because she is my hostess? For even if it is justified [that You should punish me for my zealousness], it is unacceptable that she is dealt a greater evil than mine. For "to put her son to death" is an evil greater

than mine, despite the fact that I am the principal [object of punishment].

In Alsheikh's view, "also" is intended to include Elijah himself, for God desires to make him suffer for his oath. It must be admitted that this interpretation seems the most likely, both linguistically and thematically. In terms of theme and content, this interpretation is not far from that of the *Keli Yakar*, quoted above. According to both commentators, Elijah refers here almost explicitly to his experiences since Wadi Cherith, all of which express God's displeasure with his approach and his oath. According to Alsheikh (and others), that which we have tried to prove from hints in the text starting with the story of Wadi Cherith, is expressed here explicitly, in Elijah's own words.

As opposed to the interpretation of Radak, who regards Elijah's speech as a complaint, the essence of which concerns the fact that he himself has been affected, the *Keli Yakar* and Alsheikh maintain that what really troubles Elijah is the lack of justice toward the woman from Zarephath. This explanation appears to be correct, for the following reason: Elijah refers to the woman as "*the widow* with whom I lodge." This is the only time in the unit that the woman is referred to as a "widow" (in contrast to the previous section, where this was her only title). This stands out particularly starkly against the background of her first title in our unit: "*The woman* who was the mistress of the house." In keeping with this title, Elijah could have said, "Have You also done evil to *the woman* with whom I lodge" – and it seems that this is indeed what he would have said, had the point of his argument been his own suffering. In referring to her as "the widow," Elijah means to complain about the injustice done to a widowed woman whose only child has died.

On the other hand, even according to the *Keli Yakar* and Alsheikh, there remains an element of personal benefit in Elijah's prayer: He wants to clear his conscience of responsibility for the calamity that has befallen the widow. We suggest this because the linguistic and thematic basis of Elijah's call to God is the hostility between himself and the woman that precedes his prayer. The parallel between her words and his, in terms of both general structure and key words, bears this out quite clearly:

The widow's words to Elijah	Elijah's call to God
v. 18: Man of God! *You have come to me* to recall my sin *and to put my son to death*.	v. 20: Lord my God! Have You also done evil to the widow with whom *I lodge, to put her son to death*?

What is the meaning of this parallel? At the heart of Elijah's call to God is his discomfort in the face of the harsh accusation that the widow directs at him. He "passes on" her complaint, addressing it to God in similar words. In this way, he tries to remove the burden of responsibility from his own shoulders.

In any event, it is clear that at this stage Elijah is still defending his position; he insists on maintaining it even now, and so his implied request that the widow's son be resuscitated is not answered.

"HE STRETCHED OUT OVER THE CHILD THREE TIMES" (I KINGS 17:21)

Chronologically, how are we to regard this action of Elijah? Is it the conclusion of his first cry to God, which was not answered, or is it the introduction to his second cry, which was answered? In other words: At which point did Elijah sense that God was not responding to his efforts to revive the child and that he must change his direction? Was it before he stretched out over the boy or afterward? Does Elijah sense the lack of response before his stretching out, in which case we must regard the stretching itself, and not only the second prayer, as the conclusion he draws from the failure of his first prayer? Or does he sense it only afterward, in which case his stretching over the child is a superfluous act that does nothing to make his first prayer effective, and is entirely unnecessary for his second prayer?

In what way is the second prayer different from the first? We shall provide a detailed answer to this question in the following section. Here we shall highlight only one point, which will help us clarify our view of Elijah's action. At the center of Elijah's consciousness in his first prayer are two elements: the widow and himself. "Have You done evil also *to the widow* with whom *I lodge*?" The implied request in this prayer that the dead boy be revived is that it will bring benefit to both parties and repair the ruptured relationship between them. (We conclude this based on all the commentaries quoted in the previous section.) In the second prayer, by contrast, there is no consideration of anything other than "this boy" himself. There is no benefit for the mother or for Elijah himself, nor the relationship between them; only "restore, I pray, the soul of *this boy* within him," because it would be better for the child to be alive than dead.

When does this transition take place? At what point does Elijah begin focusing on the child alone, rather than anything extraneous? It is when he stretches out over him three times. In the first prayer, Elijah thinks only of the boy's mother and his own obligation toward her ("with whom I dwell"); his cry is not accompanied by any act that is related to the child. When his first cry is not answered, Elijah turns toward the boy, to stretch out over him; this signifies the change in perception. He now senses responsibility for the dead boy; he wishes to transpose life forces from his own body into the boy. Radak, in his first commentary, interprets the stretching out in this way:

> "He stretched out" (*vayitmoded*), derived from the word *midda*...
> meaning, he placed himself in the child's measure when he
> stretched out over him, as it is said of Elisha (II Kings 4:34): "He
> lay over the boy and placed his mouth over his mouth, and his
> eyes over his eyes, and his hands over his hands."

Hence, this stretching out over the boy should be viewed as an act that takes place *after* the failure of the first cry to God, as a conclusion drawn from the lack of divine response. The act serves, then, as an introduction to the second prayer. Radak continues:

> The meaning of this matter is that his prayer would be better
> focused upon the boy while he is lying upon him, stretched out
> over him. Similarly (Gen. 25:21), "Isaac pleaded to God in the
> presence of his wife," meaning that his wife was before him at
> the time of his prayer, so that he would be concentrating on her
> in his prayer, "for she was barren."

Let us attempt to support our claim in terms of style. We discussed above how the change in the way a character is referred to during the course of a biblical story has significance. In general, the various titles testify to different perspectives or different relationships toward the object of the title among the other characters in the story. However, sometimes a change in title testifies to a change in *attitude* toward the object of the title on the part of just one character in the story.

In the previous unit, the boy was twice referred to as the woman's "son." Once he is referred to thus by the mother herself: "[I shall] prepare it for myself and for *my son*" (v. 12), and once by Elijah: "Afterwards make for you and for *your son*" (v. 13). (There is also an allusion to the boy in the narration: "She and he and *her household* ate" [v. 15].) At the beginning of this unit, he is referred to another four times as the woman's son:

1. In the narrative: "*The son of the woman* ... fell ill" (v. 17)
2. By the mother: "To put *my son* to death" (v. 18)
3. By Elijah: "Give me *your son*" (v. 19)
4. By Elijah: "Have You done evil ... to put *her son* to death" (v. 20)

Following these four references, in which the mother, Elijah, and the text all refer to the boy as her son in an altogether natural manner, there is a change, and he is then referred to as "the child" (or "the boy" – in Hebrew, *hayeled*) four times:

1. In the narrative: "He stretched out over *the child*" (v. 21)
2. By Elijah: "Restore ... the soul of *this child* within him" (v. 21)
3. In the narrative: "The soul of *the child* was restored within him, and he lived " (v. 22)
4. In the narrative: "Elijah took *the child*" (v. 23)

It seems that what the text is doing here is more than simply introducing literary variation. The change is a deliberate, systematic phenomenon, and the reason for it is clear: It expresses a change in the attitude of the main character, Elijah, toward the child. Elijah ceases to relate to him as just "the son" of the mistress of the house where he lodges, and begins to relate to him as a person in his own right, a young "child" whose life has been cut short before his time, and this arouses his sorrow. And just as Elijah now refers to him as "this child," the text refers to him in the same way in the description of the actions that bind Elijah and this boy.[2] When does the change in title take place? Not in Elijah's second prayer, but in the action that precedes it: "He stretched out over *the child* three times." In the continuation of this chapter we shall substantiate this point more fully, in the analysis of these words and their place in the structure of the literary unit.

THE SECOND PRAYER'S SIGNIFICANCE AND ACCEPTANCE

> He called out to God and said: Lord my God; restore, I pray You, the soul of this child within him. God heard the voice of Elijah; the soul of the child was restored within him, and he lived. (vv. 21–22)

In what way is Elijah's second prayer different from the first, and why is he answered this time? Furthermore, what is its significance in terms of the ongoing dispute between God and His prophet?

No great effort is required to discern the profound differences between the two prayers. Their introduction, "He called out to God and said: Lord my God…," is the same, inviting us to compare them in order to emphasize the contrast between them.

Elijah's first cry to God – "Have You also done evil to the widow…" – is not a prayer of supplication, except by inference. On the literal level, it is Elijah's complaint against the evil that God has done in putting the widow's son to death. For this reason, it is formulated as a rhetorical question: to express lack of comprehension at God's actions.

The second call to God is formulated quite clearly as an insistent plea, even on the simplest, literal level. It does not conclude with a

---

2. Only when he is mentioned for the last time in the story is the son referred to once again as the mother's "son": "And Elijah said, Behold, your son lives" (v. 23). This makes sense in view of the fact that Elijah now addresses the mother and describes the episode as it relates to her perspective: She is once again a mother to her child.

question mark, like its predecessor; the tone of supplication is apparent: "Lord my God; restore, *I pray you*…"

However we interpret Elijah's previous call, it is clear that the prophet places himself, to some extent, at the focus of the prayer. Earlier in this chapter, we saw that some commentators view the focus of the prayer as concerning himself,[3] while others understand the prayer as being offered principally on behalf of the widow, asking that she be spared an injustice of which he, Elijah, would be the cause.

The situation in the second prayer is entirely different. Here, Elijah makes no mention of himself at all. He does not even mention the mother, whose accusation against him echoes in the first prayer. At the center of his prayer there is only "this child." Elijah's request that the soul of the boy be restored to him is not justified on the basis of any external factor. The meaning of this prayer, then, is simply that it is better that "this child" live than that he die, and so Elijah asks that his life be restored. The exclusive focus on "this child" is expressed in the change in his title, as explained in the previous unit.

What is the meaning of this request for life on behalf of the dead child? We have noted previously that the death of this particular child is meant to represent those who are suffering and dying from the famine and all its attendant distress. It represents a more severe version of the drying up of Wadi Cherith. The transition that Elijah makes from an implied request to revive the child for Elijah's own sake and the sake of the mother, who is connected to the prophet in various ways, and a request for revival only for the sake of "this boy" himself, is a drastic one in terms of the ongoing argument with the prophet. The moment that the request to revive the child no longer falls into the category of a request for privileges for the prophet, it becomes an implied request for an end to the drought! For now, any child that dies of starvation is presumably going to cause the prophet to offer an identical prayer. And what is the meaning of a prayer to restore life to the world, if not a request for rain?

---

3. Radak, as cited above, pp. 65–67. See also the Baal HaMetzudot.

In this prayer, and in God's favorable response ("God heard the voice of Elijah"), we find the turning point of the story: The argument with the prophet reaches its conclusion after the prophet has been prepared, step by step, for a nullification of the decree of drought. Now he will not need to be coerced from the outside; rather, the change will arise from his new view of the tragic reality that has occurred as a result of his oath. Obviously, despite the fact that the woman is appeased by having her son restored to life, Elijah will not continue to lodge in her home. The woman's new recognition of Elijah: "Now I know that you are a man of God, *and God's word in your mouth is true*" (v. 24), requires Elijah to leave her home and return to the place that he originally left, in order to allow the rain to return.

Admittedly, the change that has come over Elijah is only implied. He is in a *process* of change that already began at Wadi Cherith. The impressions slowly accumulate in his consciousness, gradually influencing him to change his mind. More time will pass, and great acts will be performed, before Elijah will reach the point of *pleading* with God to restore the rain. Meanwhile, his prayer that the boy's life be restored to him reveals that Elijah is ready to *agree* for the rain to return. But he still needs an external command to push him in this direction. This command follows on immediately in the text: "Many days passed,[4] and God's word came to Elijah in the third year, saying: Go and appear before Ahab, and I will give rain upon the face of the earth. So Elijah went…" (18:1–2)

Our reading of the account of the revival of the child follows the interpretation of Ḥazal; it is simply an attempt to translate their pictorial, exegetical language into a commentary following the literal text. Let us now examine Ḥazal's interpretation as it appears in an aggada in Sanhedrin 113a, the first part of which has been mentioned more than once in previous chapters:

> "Elijah the Tishbite, one of the residents of Gilead, said to Ahab: As the Lord God of Israel lives…there shall be no dew or rain during these years.…" He asked for [divine] mercy and the keys

---

4. These "many days" are counted from the beginning of the drought, although it seems that God's command here comes immediately after the child's revival.

of rainfall were given to him; he stood up and left. "God's word came to him, saying: Go from here, and head eastward, and hide at Wadi Cherith.... And the ravens would bring him bread and meat in the morning.... It was, after some time, that the wadi dried up, for there was no rain in the land." Since he [the subject here is ambiguous – it may refer either to God or to Elijah] saw that there was suffering in the world, it is written, "God's word came to him saying: Arise, go to Zarephath," and it is written, "And it was after these things, that the son of the woman who was mistress of the house fell ill." He asked for mercy, that the key to resurrection be given to him. They told him: There are three keys that are not given to any agent [God alone holds them]: that of childbirth, that of rain, and that of resurrection. People will say: Two are in the hands of the disciple [Elijah] while only one remains in the hand of the Mentor [God] [and such a situation is unacceptable]. Give back the one [of rain] and take the other [of resurrection]. As it is written, "Go, appear before Ahab, and I will give rain."

The "three keys" are the keys to life in its different manifestations in the life cycle of man: his birth, his existence on the earth (his sustenance by means of rain, which makes it possible for him to cultivate the earth), and his return to life after death (which includes, in our situation, the healing of the sick). A person who takes one of the keys and prevents its use to open the treasure houses of life, brings death to the world, not only in the specific area of that "key," but also in other spheres. Therefore, whoever desires life for himself and for the world in general, cannot prevent the use of any one of the keys for an extended time. The deposit of one of the keys in the hands of God's prophet, in order to lock the doors to God's abundant gifts, cannot continue for too long. When it becomes apparent that Elijah does not seek evil and suffering for the world, that he wants life to be restored to the dead child, then the key that he holds is exchanged: He is given the key of resurrection, and, quite naturally, the key that *locks away* the rain is taken from him. The concept of life cannot be divided: Wanting life for the dead child means wanting life for every person, and this will be possible only if rain returns to the land.

In conclusion, let us quote the commentary of Malbim on the above teaching of *Ḥazal*:

> "Many days passed, and God's word came to Elijah" (18:1): The teaching of the Sages is well known – that when [Elijah] needed the key of resurrection, he had to return the key of rain. And my explanation is … that at the time when he revived the child, he had to renounce his [previous] way of closing up and stopping the [divine] abundance. On the contrary, he needed to bring down an abundance of vitality and life upon the boy, and thereby all the sources of life were opened after having been closed up by the lack of rain which brings life to the world, upon the animals, the herbs of the field. And therefore God told [Elijah] that He would now give rain [in addition to giving life to the boy], for He has already said, "To those that are bound up – an opening of the prison" (Is. 61:1).

THE WOMAN'S REACTION

> The woman said to Elijah: Now I know that you are a man of God, and God's word in your mouth is true. (I Kings 17:24)

Is it really only now that the woman discovers that Elijah is a man of God? Did she not already declare in her complaint, before he revived her son, "What have I to do with you, O *man of God*" (v. 18)? Has she only just now realized that God's word in Elijah's mouth is true? Did she not witness how, throughout the whole year, "the jar of flour did not finish, nor did the bottle of oil lack, *as God's word that He had spoken by Elijah's hand*" (v. 16)? As a result of the realization of God's word as spoken by Elijah, she and her son survived the entire year!

Indeed, the woman knew that Elijah was a man of God and that his decree in God's name was being fulfilled. But in all of this she did not sense "truth," not in the sense of fulfilling that which one has spoken, but in the wider sense of the term. She did not see in Elijah a person who radiates "truth" as the stamp of God (see Shabbat 55a). God directs the world through a combination of two traits that are mutually contradictory: that of strict justice and that of mercy. But God, who makes peace in the heavens, also makes peace between these traits and combines them in His running of the world. It is the combination of both these traits that represents God's seal of truth.

Elijah has indeed been revealed to the woman of Zarephath as a "man of God," but only as a representative of the divine trait of strict justice. His presence at the gates of Zarephath, like his year's stay in her home, has been a demanding one: "Make *me* a small cake of it *first* and bring it *to me*, and *afterward* make for you and for your son" (v. 13). His decree that the jar of meal and the bottle of oil would not run out was admittedly fulfilled, thereby proving without any doubt that Elijah was a man of God, and that God's word in his mouth was realized. Nevertheless, Elijah decrees this miracle not out of mercy and compassion for the starving widow and her son, but rather to facilitate the fulfillment of his demands. And these demands concern the man of God himself.

This sense of Elijah as a man of God representing only the trait of strict and demanding justice is expressed quite clearly by the widow when she tells him: "What have I to do with you, O man of God? You have come to me *to recall my sin and to put my son to death*" (v. 18).

Thus far, Elijah has not represented God fully. He has represented Him in only one dimension, and therefore the stamp of "truth" does not emanate from God's word in his mouth; his representation is not complete.

However, now, after Elijah resurrects the woman's dead son for the child's own sake ("Restore, I pray, *the soul of this child* within him"), with no thought about any other benefit (as in the miracle of the jar of flour and the bottle of oil) and without presenting any demands, the man of God is revealed to her in a new light. He represents God's trait of compassion in the world, and he performs miracles through this trait. The fact that his decree on the jar of flour and bottle of oil was fulfilled proved that God's word in Elijah's mouth was indeed realized (and that he was indeed a "man of God"). The miracle of the child's resurrection proves that he is a man of God in whose mouth God's word is *truth*. Elijah's personality is now revealed to the woman, through this miracle, as a genuine representation of his Sender, rather than a one-dimensional reflection of Him.

We may conclude this unit by stating that the woman's reaction here also relates to the ongoing dispute between Elijah and God. We saw above that both of the widow's outbursts – at the gates of Zarephath and in her bitter recriminations over the death of her son, before Elijah restores him to life – are harsh criticisms of Elijah. Without knowing it, the woman voices God's concealed accusation against Elijah for maintaining his oath that has brought hunger and devastation to the world. We must also address this dimension of her final words to him. Her praise for Elijah as bearing God's word *in truth*, rather than in a one-dimensional form, is a sort of divine assent to what seems to be Elijah's new path – a path in which he represents his Sender both in strict justice and in mercy and compassion.

STRUCTURE OF THIS UNIT

This unit consists of eight verses, divided into two equal parts of four verses each. The separation between the two parts, as in many other biblical narratives structured in similar fashion, is to be found in the dramatic turning point. This is not the resuscitation of the boy, in verse 23, as the reader might have assumed, but rather in Elijah's second prayer, which is preceded by his lying on top of the boy three times. It is not God's wonders that represent the essence of this unit, and therefore it is not the miracle that serves as its focus. Rather, the subject concerns the prophet's path and his relationships with his human environment, on one hand, and with God, on the other. For this reason Elijah's own actions are the focus. The transition between his first call to God, representing an argument with himself at the center, and the second call, which focuses exclusively on improving the fate of "this child," expresses a dramatic change in Elijah's path. This change (which we have discussed at length above) is what divides the two sections of the unit.[5]

---

5. This is true not only in the narrow context of this section of the story, but also in relation to the broader narrative (as explained above in the discussion of Elijah's second prayer). Indeed, the change that Elijah undergoes in this unit brings about a shift in the direction of the entire narrative. The prophet who had sworn that there

Let us note the contrast between the two halves of the unit. There is no phrase in the first half without a contrasting element in the second half. We present the two halves below; for the sake of contrasting them we record the first half in its proper order, each phrase with its corresponding contrast from the second half:

First half (vv. 17–20)	Second half (vv. 21–24)
v. 17: The son of the woman who was mistress of the house fell ill, and his illness was exceedingly grave, such that no breath was left in him.	v. 22: The boy's soul was restored within him.
v. 18: She said to Elijah: What have I to do with you, O man of God? You have come to me to recall my sin and to put my son to death.	v. 24: The woman said to Elijah: Now I know that you are a man of God, and that God's word in your mouth is truth.
v. 19 (1st clause): He said to her: Give me your son.	v. 23 (2nd clause): He gave him to his mother, and Elijah said: Behold, your son lives.
v. 19 (2nd clause): He took him from her bosom and took him up to the attic where he lodged, and he lay him down upon his bed.	v. 23 (1st clause): Elijah took the child and brought him down from the attic.
v. 20: He called out to God and said: Lord my God! Have You also done evil to the widow with whom I dwell, to put her son to death?	v. 21: He stretched out over the boy three times, and he called to God and said: Lord my God, restore, I pray you, the soul of this child within him.

The contrasts between the two halves of the unit exist on several different levels of the story, all complementing one another. On the level of plot, the first half presents us with a death which is irreversible, a prayer that is not answered, bitterness and accusation on all sides; in the second half we have God's response and accession to the voice of the prophet, life that is restored, joy and appeasement on all sides.

---

would be no rain, and who had distanced himself from his people and from the center of the kingdom in Samaria, is now at a turning point: He returns to Samaria and to Ahab, its ruler, with the aim of restoring the rain.

On the literal level the contrast between the two halves is expressed in the fact that twice in the first half we find the root *mem-vav-tav* (death – "to put my son to death," "to put her son to death"), while the second half makes mention twice of the root *ḥet-yod-heh* ("he lived," "see, your son lives"). Moreover, the child is referred to four times in the first half as his mother's "son," and four times in the second half as "the child" (as discussed above).

The difference between the terms used to describe the woman in the two halves points to the contrast between them. In the first half: "The woman who was *mistress of the house*" (v. 17), "The widow *with whom I lodge*" (v. 20). In the second half: "his mother" (v. 23), "the woman" (v. 24).

These references indicate a transition from the perception of the woman solely in relation to Elijah and his distress, in the first half, to a perception of her as an independent personality, whose situation as a *mother* and whose independent recognition as a *woman* are the subject of the second half (as discussed previously).

On the broader stylistic level, the first half is characterized by two rhetorical questions that express unresolved tension. The widow's address to Elijah and Elijah's address to God both conclude with the same question: "To put my son to death?" and "To put her son to death?" The second half, in contrast, is characterized by two calls, each in fact an exclamation. There is Elijah's call to God: "Restore, I pray, the child's soul within him!" and his address to the mother: "See, your son lives!" Each of these exclamations is a stylistic and thematic contrast to one of the two rhetorical questions in the first half, in chiastic order:

A: "You have come to me…to put my son to death?"

B: "Have You also…to put her son to death?"

B': "Please restore the soul of this boy within him!"

A': "See, your son lives!"

Moreover, there is a significant difference between the respective endings of the two halves. The second half concludes with a statement that is neither a question nor an exclamation ("and God's word in your mouth is truth"). This relaxed mood is a sharp contrast to the tension that concludes that first half ("Have You also done evil…to put her son to death?")

All of these contrasts between the two halves, on the level of plot, the appearance of key words, and style, are functions of a single phenomenon: The change that takes place in Elijah's thinking when faced with the dead child lying on the bed, realizing who and what has caused this death.

An examination of the comparison between the two halves of the unit, as set out above, reveals that other than the first corresponding pair in the table, the order of correspondence of verses is actually inverse. In other words, an earlier verse in the first half corresponds to a later verse in the second half, while a later verse in the first half corresponds to an earlier verse in the second half. This raises the possibility that perhaps this episode, too – like its predecessor (see p. 47) – is built as a system of symmetrical parallels around a central axis. The presentation below demonstrates that this is, in fact, the case (except that the symmetrical structure is imperfect):

A: *She said to Elijah*: What have I to do with you, *O man of God*? You have come to me to recall my sin and to put my son to death. (v. 18)

B: He said to her: Give me your son;

C: he *took him* from her bosom and *took him up to the attic*, where he lodged, and lay him down upon his bed. (v. 19)

D: *He called out to God and said: Lord my God,* have You also done evil to the widow with whom I lodge, to put her son to death? (v. 20)

E: He stretched out over the boy three times,

D': *and he called out to God, and said: Lord my God* restore, I pray, the soul of this child within him. (v. 21)

God heard the voice of Elijah; the soul of the child was restored within him, so that he lived. (v. 22)

C': Elijah took the child and brought him down from the attic to the house

B': and gave him to his mother, and Elijah said: See, your son lives. (v. 23)

A': *The woman said to Elijah*: Now I know that you are *a man of God*, and God's word in your mouth is truth. (v. 24)

This symmetrical structure addresses four contrasting pairs:

A. The woman's complaint to Elijah at the beginning of the unit, while holding her dead son, and correspondingly her words to him at the end of the unit, expressing her new appreciation for him after her son is returned to her alive.

B. Elijah's words to the woman while she is still holding her dead son ("Give me your son"), and correspondingly, his words to her when he returns her son alive ("Behold, your son lives!"). The root *nun-tav-nun* (to give) has a diametrically opposite meaning in these two places: "*Give me* your (dead) son" as opposed to "*He gave him* (alive) to his mother."

C. Elijah's actions leading up to the resurrection of the boy, and correspondingly, his actions leading up to returning him to his mother: "*He took him* (dead) from her bosom," "Elijah *took* the boy (alive, from the bed)," "*He brought him up* (dead) to the attic," "*He took him down* (alive) from the attic."

D. Elijah's first call to God, which was not answered, and correspondingly the second call, which is answered (both introduced with the same words: "He called out to God and said: Lord my God").

What does our discovery of this symmetrical structure add to what we already know about the structure of the unit? It highlights the inverse order of the events in the second half as compared to the first half. The crises that appear in the first half are gradually repaired and solved in the second half in the wake of the change that takes place within Elijah himself – but in inverse order. When the crises appear, they are listed from the most innocuous to the most grave: From the crisis in Elijah's relations with the widow to the crisis in his relations with God, who refuses to accept his first call. The second half, with the solutions, is listed from the most significant down to the least significant: First, there is a repairing of the severe rift between the prophet and God, who now accepts his prayer and answers him. As a result, even the painful lack of confidence that the widow expresses toward Elijah is now repaired; it is replaced with a clear declaration of assurance.

Another significant contribution offered by the structure of the unit presented above is the highlighting of the central axis, giving it extra importance. We discover, then, that the five words (in Hebrew) – "He stretched out over the boy three times" – represent the climax of this unit. Why is this so? Because, as explained above, this phrase testifies to the dramatic change that has taken place in Elijah's approach. This change is the key to the whole reversal that unfolds in the second half of the unit, as we have explained above.

STRUCTURE OF THIS UNIT VS. STRUCTURE OF PREVIOUS UNIT

The symmetrical structure of this unit is important for yet another reason. It creates an interesting connection with the previous unit, which describes Elijah at the gates of Zarephath. This connection goes beyond the fact that these adjacent units are structured in a similar, symmetrical way, each around its central axis. This fact is of little importance in itself, relative to the broader elements common to both – the dimensions of time, space, and characters. But if we compare the symmetrical structure of these two units, we discover that they represent an interesting inversion: That which forms the core of the first unit becomes the outer framework in the second unit, while that which forms the outer structure in the first unit moves inward, close to the nucleus of the second unit. The following table clarifies this:

Elijah at the gates of Zarephath	Revival of the widow's son
A. *God's* words to Elijah	A. The *widow's* words to Elijah
B. Elijah's demands of the *widow*	B. Elijah takes the child from his mother
	C. Elijah's first cry *to God*
C. The *widow's* words of refusal	**D. "He stretched out over the boy three times"**
	C'. Elijah's second cry *to God* and God's accession
B'. Elijah's demands of the *widow*	B'. Elijah restores the child to his mother
A'. The fulfillment of God's words to Elijah	A'. The *widow's* words to Elijah

God's speech to Elijah, introducing the unit about the gates of Zarephath (together with Elijah's demands to the widow), corresponds to Elijah's first call to God, while standing over the widow's dead son. The widow's refusal, which represents the central axis of the first section, is echoed in the second unit in its introduction (her first speech to Elijah) and in its conclusion (her declaration of confidence and faith in him after her son is restored to life and returned to her). In the end, Eliyahu once again demands food from the widow, with his promise that the jar of meal and bottle of oil will not run out, and God's word to Elijah is realized (he is now able to be sustained by the widow, as God promised); this corresponds to Elijah's second call to God, and God's accession to his prayer.

The widow's adamant refusal, forming the central axis of the first unit (and representing her only opportunity to speak in that unit), is "transformed," in the second unit, into her two speeches that form its external framework. At first she speaks harshly to Elijah; ultimately she is appeased.

Elijah's demands of the widow in the first unit are paralleled in the second unit by his actions in taking her son from her and later returning him to her. But in the first unit Elijah's demands give rise to the widow's speech (which in turn gives rise to a reformulation of his demands). In the second unit, the widow's introductory speech leads to Elijah's actions. When Elijah says, "Give me your son," he is not "asking" for something from her; rather, he is reacting to her complaints against him. While Elijah is the "plaintiff" in the first unit, making his demands, he is the "defendant" in the second unit, reacting to the widow's accusations.

The outer framework of the first unit consists of God's opening words to Elijah, which are fulfilled without any further complication by the end of the unit. In the second unit, the relationship between Elijah and God "moves inward" toward the nucleus of the unit; it surrounds the central axis (Elijah stretching out three times over the child) on both sides. But here, too, there is an internal difference. It is not God speaking to Elijah and fulfilling His promises to him, but rather Elijah who turns to God in prayer, and God eventually accedes to his request.

What is the meaning of these "inversions" between the two adjacent units? The answer is that the structural inversions hint at the fact that these two units are indeed inversions of one another, in terms of their common subject: the drought and the dispute with Elijah as to its continuation.

The *means* for maintaining this dispute are the same in both units: In both cases, the widow serves as God's agent to accuse Elijah of responsibility for her distress (even though she does this unknowingly, without understanding the profound truth of her accusation). The distress that reveals itself in both cases is a result of the ongoing drought, and the widow presents Elijah with a dual challenge: a moral challenge, by pointing to him as the party responsible for bringing the suffering, and a personal challenge, by obstructing Elijah's way of finding for himself a means of subsistence during the drought.

But despite this great similarity, the two units are diametrically opposed to one another in the most important sense: the *result* of the dispute in both of them. In the first unit, it is Elijah who "wins," as it were. The unit is arranged around the widow's refusal of his demand for food, and it demonstrates how Elijah *overcomes* the "obstacle" of her outburst, how he acts to achieve, for the duration of the year, a balanced coexistence with the widow and with God's word that has presented him with the test. For this reason, in this unit it is Elijah who makes demands of the widow and maintains his demands even after her adamant refusal and accusation. Elijah exploits his special merit before God, decreeing a miracle that will allow him to live through the drought and to continue evading the argument over his approach.

In the second unit, Elijah can no longer evade the argument. This time the unit *opens* with the widow's accusation, and we see how Elijah, who is now on the receiving end of her demands, gradually retreats from his unflinching position in the first unit, leading up to his stretching out over the child and his second prayer to God. The central axis this time is not the accusation aimed at Elijah, but rather *his response to this accusation.* And the framework of the unit this time is not how Elijah manages to overcome the accusation against him, as in the previous unit, but rather *what leads him to change his position*, and the *results* of this change.

Once again, we see how the structure of the narrative faithfully represents its themes and ideas. Whether the reader tackles the details of the story first and then moves on to its structural framework or first considers the form in which it is presented and then the content itself, either way he is led to the same conclusion.

SUPPLEMENT: COMPARISON BETWEEN ELIJAH'S AND ELISHA'S "RESURRECTION" STORIES

In this supplement we shall undertake a detailed comparison between the two stories of resurrection recorded in the book of Kings – the one in which Elijah revives the son of the woman of Zarephath, and the parallel narrative (II Kings 4) in which Elisha, his disciple, revives the son of the Shunammite woman.

Relationship between Woman and Prophet in Each of the Stories

Both the woman of Zarephath and the Shunammite woman accuse the men of God who lodge in their attics, and to whom they have shown hospitality, of responsibility for their anguish upon the death of their respective sons. But the obvious similarity between the narratives does not blur the fundamental differences between them.

The women's view of the prophets

The Shunammite woman accuses Elisha not of responsibility for her son's death, but rather for giving him to her without her asking, thereby leading indirectly to the cruel disappointment of his death: "She said: Did I ask a son from God? Did I not say: Do not delude me!" (II Kings 4:28).

The woman of Zarephath, by contrast, accuses Elijah quite explicitly of responsibility for her son's death: "You have come to me to recall my sin and to put my son to death!" (I Kings 17:18).

The story of the Shunammite woman, from beginning to end, is a story of great faith in the man of God, in his holiness and his ability to bring about miracles. Her complaint to Elisha is not an expression of disappointment or a challenge, but rather a push for the man of God to feel some responsibility and act to repair the situation. Therefore she comes to him at Mount Carmel in order to bring him back to her home, so that he can act to restore her son's life: "The mother of the boy said: 'As God lives and as your soul lives, I shall not leave you.' So he arose and went after her" (II Kings 4:30).

The woman of Zarephath, on the other hand, expresses, in her accusation of Elijah for her son's death, a lack of faith in him. We learn this from her final words, when Elijah restores her son to her, alive, and she declares: "*Now* I know that you are a man of God and God's word in your mouth is truth" (I Kings 17:24), meaning that previously, when she complained, she did not believe that God's word in his mouth was truth (as discussed earlier).

The complaint-rebellion of the woman of Zarephath against Elijah, who lodges in her home, is truly the opposite of the Shunammite woman's aim in her complaint. The former, as explained above, is meant to substantiate her demand that Elijah leave her house: "What have I to do with you, O man of God?" (v. 18).

In other words, these two stories present fundamentally opposite relationships between the bereaved mother and the prophet whom she addresses.

The mothers' actions

Let us now address the actions of the two mothers. The Shunammite woman, who anticipates Elisha's ability to restore her son to life and who directs her actions accordingly, reveals this at the very outset: "She went up and lay him upon the bed of the man of God, and shut the door for him and went out" (II Kings 4:21).

The woman of Zarephath, who comes to Elijah to ask that he leave her house, never imagines that this severe man of God is either able to or interested in reviving her son. She takes her dead son in her arms as incontrovertible support for her complaint against the man of God as being responsible for his death.

Not only does she not ask Elijah to try to restore the boy to life; even when he wants to do so, his efforts are apparently met with mistrust on her part, perhaps even a refusal to cooperate: "He said to her: '*Give me* your son.' *He* took him from her bosom" (I Kings 17:19).

We are told not that she gave her son to the prophet, but rather that he took him, meaning that the woman did not believe in Elijah and was in no hurry to hand over her son's dead body. Verse 19 continues: "*He* took him up to the attic where he lodged, and *he* lay him upon his bed."

The contrast with the story of the Shunammite woman, who performs these actions herself, is striking: "*She* went up and lay him upon the bed of the man of God" (II Kings 4:21).

The prophets' attitudes and the mothers' reactions after the miracle
In keeping with the difference that we saw in the attitude of the two women toward the prophets, there is a corresponding difference in the attitude of the two prophets toward the women, both prior to the resurrection and afterward.

In the case of Elijah, we notice a great effort to appease the widow and to regain her trust. We have already discussed the actions that Elijah undertakes on his own initiative: He takes the dead boy from his mother's arms, brings him up himself to the attic, and lies him down upon the bed. After he revives him through his prayer and actions, Elijah performs the reverse actions, once again on his own: "Elijah *took* the boy *and brought him down* from the attic into the house, *and gave him* to his mother." (I Kings 17:23)

The continuation of this verse records Elijah's words as he hands the boy to his mother, clear evidence of his great joy, or participation in her own joy: "Elijah said: See, your son lives!" Indeed, his efforts have borne fruit, and the woman rewards him with a response that expresses her renewed trust and a change in attitude toward him.

Elisha, who returns to the Shunammite woman's house because she has committed him to doing so (after his attempt to help her through Gehazi, in his own absence), enters the attic of the house "And behold, the boy was dead, *laid out* upon the bed" (II Kings 4:32). After reviving the boy, Elisha does not rush to restore him to his mother; in fact, he does not perform this action himself at all. The mother, who took her son up to the attic of the man of God, comes to take him down. Elisha does not descend from the attic into the house; rather, the Shunammite ascends to him: "He called to Gehazi and said: 'Call out to this Shunammite.' So he called, and she came to him" (v. 36).

The continuation of this verse also records the prophet's words, but in contrast to Elijah's joyful shout – "Behold, your son lives!" (I Kings 17:23), Elisha's chilly instruction stands out starkly: "He said: Take up your son" (II Kings 4:36). And unlike the woman of Zarephath, who expresses her newfound recognition of Elijah after he returns her son to her alive, the Shunammite says not a word when she receives her son: "She came and fell upon his feet and prostrated herself to the ground, and she took up her son and went out" (II Kings 4:37). This reaction is because nothing has changed in her basic attitude toward Elisha. She expected in advance that this would happen, and so she suffices with this silent show of thanks. (Elisha's attitude toward her may also explain some of her behavior.)

These contrasting elements of the respective relationships in the two stories arise from the fundamental difference between them: In our story, the woman serves unknowingly as God's agent in criticizing Elijah and attempting to change his position concerning the prolonged drought – hence the tension that characterizes the relationship between her and the prophet, and hence the change in her attitude toward him after the change indeed takes place within him. The Shunammite woman, on the other hand, is a central character in the story when she confronts Elisha. Her role is not to effect change in the prophet or to criticize his actions; on the contrary, she is a great admirer and she believes in his wondrous abilities. Her role in the story is to change herself as regards her maternal relationship with her son.

Revival of the Sons by Elijah and by Elisha:
The Differences and Their Significance

In order to compare the relationships between the two prophets and the two women involved, we must examine the framework of the two revival stories. At this point, we shall complete our task by comparing the nucleus of the two stories, namely, the description of the actual resuscitation (vv. 19–22 in our chapter, and vv. 29–35 in II Kings, ch. 4). In both places the prophet secludes himself in the attic with the dead child who is lying upon his bed, while the mother remains in the house below. In addition, both descriptions include three elements: the prophet's prayer to God, a physical act of contact with the dead child, and the resuscitation of the child. Another aspect that both stories have in common is that in both cases the prophet's initial attempt to restore the child to life fails. Let us now turn our attention to the differences between the two occurrences.

The two descriptions present opposite relations between the prophet's prayer to God and his practical actions to resuscitate the boy. As a result of this inversion, the nature of the third element – the description of the resurrection – is different in each case. In fact, this inversion determines the completely different nature of each of the two descriptions of resurrection in its entirety. Before discussing this idea, let us present it in the form of a comparative table:

Elijah (I Kings, ch. 17)		Elisha (II Kings, ch. 4)	
Prayer	v. 20: *"He called out to God and said:* Lord my God! Have You also done evil to the widow with whom I lodge, to put her son to death?"	Action	v. 31: *"Gehazi passed over before them and placed the staff upon the boy's face,* but there was no voice and no sound.... He told him, saying: The child did not awaken."

91

Elijah (I Kings, ch. 17)		Elisha (II Kings, ch. 4)	
Action	v. 21: "*He stretched out over the child* three times."	Prayer	vv. 32–33: "Elisha came to the house.... He went in and closed the door behind both of them, *and he prayed to God.*"
Prayer	v. 21: "*He called out to God and said*: Lord my God; restore, I pray, the soul of this child within him."	Action	vv. 34–35: "He went up and *lay upon the child.* He placed his mouth over his mouth and his eyes over his eyes, and his hands over his hands, *and he stretched himself over him,* and the boy's flesh was warmed. *Then he returned* and walked about in the house, to and fro, and he went up and stretched himself over him, and the boy sneezed – all seven times over."
Resurrection	v. 22: "God heard the voice of Elijah and restored the child's soul within him, and he lived."	Resurrection	v. 35: "The boy opened his eyes."

Admittedly, both prophets prayed to God. But in the description of Elisha, the text suffices with merely noting the fact that he prayed, devoting only three words to convey this information, with no mention of the content of his prayer. And from this point onward the story does not come back to this issue. Apparently, Elisha's prayer is not a central element at all in the miracle of the resurrection; he offers it only as an introduction to the act of resuscitation – since such an extraordinary miracle certainly requires an introductory prayer. (This, perhaps, is one of the lessons of Gehazi's failure.)

How different is the situation in the story of the resurrection by Elijah! His call to God is the focal point of the entire miracle. Elijah offers not one prayer, but *two*. The first does not achieve its aim, and the child remains dead; for this reason Elijah formulates his second prayer differently. The text describes the two prayers as *"calling out to God"* (*keria*); this expression indicates a prayer that is not formal in character, but rather expresses the anguish of the supplicant. The text does not suffice with a record of the fact that Elijah prayed, as it does in the case of Elisha; it records the wording of both prayers, in full. Thus, in contrast to the *three* words that the text devotes to Elisha's prayer, we find *thirty* words devoted to the two prayers offered by Elijah.

We find the situation reversed in the description of the actions that the two prophets perform. Elijah's actions with regard to the child are summed up in *five* words (in the Hebrew): "He stretched over the child three times." By contrast, in the story of Elisha, the text describes in great detail *two* actions with regard to the child. The first is the act that Gehazi performs, at his master's orders: He places Elisha's staff over the boy's face. This action does not achieve its aim: "The child did not awaken." Therefore, Elisha performs this act himself (after offering a prayer); this parallels Elijah's act in stretching himself over the child. But Elisha's action is described in the minutest detail, and it is described not once but twice:

> "He went up and lay over the child ... and stretched himself over him" (II Kings 4:34).

> "He returned ... and went up ... and stretched himself over him" (v. 35).

This repetition is a contrasting parallel to the duality of Elijah's prayer:

> "He called out to God and said: Lord my God" (I Kings 17:20).

> "He called out to God and said: Lord my God" (v. 21).

Elijah, in fact, performs his action *three times*, but the text suffices with noting this number, omitting any detailed description of even one of the times that Elijah stretches himself over the child. Elisha's stretching over the child is described twice, in detail, along with the gradual results: First, "the boy's flesh was warmed" (II Kings 4:34), then "the boy sneezed" (v. 35). The number of times that Elisha stretches is, as noted in the text, "*seven times,*" and here again the number is striking in comparison with Elijah's threefold stretching.

In light of these differences, we understand the reason for the discrepancy in the third element in the two stories – the resurrection of the child. Since, in Elijah's story, the prayer is the dominant element in the miracle, the resurrection of the child is described as *God's answer to Elijah's prayer*: "God heard Elijah's voice" (I Kings 17:22).

The actual description of the resurrection is likewise directed, linguistically, toward the prophet's (second) prayer:

Prayer: "Restore, I pray, the soul of this child within him" (v. 21).

Answer: "God...restored the child's soul within him, and he lived" (v. 22).

By contrast, in Elisha's resurrection of the boy there is no connection between the actual revival and Elisha's prayer, which introduced the process. On the other hand, the description here emphasizes the physical, practical element of the resurrection: "The boy opened *his eyes*" (II Kings 4:35).

Thus, the text clearly relates the resurrection to Elisha's *actions* in stretching out over the child: "He placed... *his eyes over his eyes.*" The opening of the boy's eyes, as the final stage of his resurrection, relates back to the earlier stages of Elisha's *actions*: his first stretching over the boy brings about that "the flesh of the boy was warmed." His later stretches bring about that "the boy sneezed," and after the seventh time the process of resurrection is complete: "The boy opened his eyes."

What is the significance of such clear differences between the two descriptions of resurrection that exist within a similar general framework? The answer seems quite simple: Each description is built around a challenge which the prophet must address by mobilizing all his energies. The difference between them concerns the question of *who* is challenging the prophet: Elijah is in conflict with God; Elisha is in conflict with the dead child himself.

The story of the resurrection performed by Elisha is not connected with any sort of tension between the prophet and God. Therefore, Elisha's prayer to God is not highlighted at all in the story. On the other hand, it is clear that Elisha bears a certain responsibility for the death of this boy, who was born at his decree and whose death was hidden from him by God (II Kings 4:27). The description of Elisha resurrecting him is the description of the prophet dealing with his responsibility toward the boy. When Elisha sends Gehazi to revive him, the servant has no success because he lacks the prophet's acceptance of responsibility for the child and for his existence. Elisha's *actions* in stretching over the child come to express his renewed attitude toward the child; they express an assumption of responsibility, a spreading of the prophet's patronage over the child. When he places "his mouth over his mouth and his eyes over his eyes and his hands over his hands," the prophet gives of his own living soul into the boy's body (as is written in *Sefer HaKaneh*, an early kabbalistic work, "When one exhales, he exhales his own breath"). Therefore, this description specifically emphasizes the prophet's actions, requiring considerable and prolonged effort on his part, because they express the confrontation with the problem of the story: The death of the child, arising, *inter alia*, from Elisha's deficient attitude toward this child and his mother.

The story of the resurrection by Elijah represents a confrontation between the prophet and God. Therefore, the description of the resurrection centers on the prophet's *prayers* to God. The problem in this situation is not between Elijah and the dead child, nor between Elijah and the child's mother (even though Elijah demonstrates a strong desire to appease her); the tension is clearly between Elijah and God. Therefore, Elijah requires a second prayer after the first goes unanswered. Only the second prayer merits the desired response: "God heard the voice of Elijah."

Chapter 7

Elijah on His Way to Appear Before Ahab (I Kings 18:1–16)

> Much time passed, and God's word came to Elijah in the third year, saying: *Go and appear before Ahab, and I will give rain upon the face of the earth.* So Elijah went to appear before Ahab. (18:1–2)

The text offers no explanation for God's announcement to Elijah that He will cancel the decree of the drought. If Ahab and the nation had repented, it seems certain that this would have been reported either in the narrative as a fact, or in God's words, as a reason for the announcement to Elijah. And if they did not repent, why is the decree of the drought being canceled?

According to Radak's view, God's notification of the end of the drought may be explained in terms of a change: "'And I will give rain' – since, owing to the famine, many had repented and mended their ways." However, this is neither written nor even hinted at in the text, and, if anything, the rest of chapter 18 would seem to give the opposite impression: Jezebel continues her attempts to dispose of God's prophets who are hiding from her in caves (v. 4), and no one voices any objection.

When Elijah rebukes the nation, attempting to stop them from serving Baal, he is greeted with silence (v. 21).

Radak's assumption is based not on what we read in our story, but rather on the very fact that God announces that the drought will come to an end. But further on in chapter 18 we discover that the cloudburst that ends the drought comes only with the repentance of the nation at Mount Carmel, meaning that when God commanded Elijah to go to Ahab, the nation was not yet worthy of having the rain restored. Why, then, is the announcement of the end of the drought presented as being unconditional, seemingly independent of the nation's repentance?

If we read the story from the perspective presented in the previous chapters, we may understand God's announcement better. It is not Elijah's conflict with Ahab or with Israel's Baal worship that is the subject of the story of the drought. This conflict is no more than the background to the action which is the true focus of the story: The behind-the-scenes dispute between God and Elijah concerning the prophet's strategy in the battle that he wages against the nation and against its king.

The three previous episodes describing Elijah (discussed in chapters 4–6 above) are the framework within which the existence of this struggle is hinted at. In each of the three episodes a new claim (or claims) is presented against Elijah. The event that Elijah experiences in each case is supposed to make him aware of the damage wrought by the drought, and its injustice.

Although all three units are meant to prepare Elijah for the divine message that follows immediately after them – to change the decree of the drought – this notification is related to and arises *directly* from the third episode, the resurrection of the widow's son. God's announcement is simply a mirror reflection of the change that has taken place within Elijah himself; it represents a direct continuation of God's response to his prayer to revive "this child." In Ḥazal's terminology, what we have here is an "exchange of keys": The key to resurrection is given to Elijah in exchange for the key to rainfall, which he must now relinquish.

Thus, it is not the events in Samaria (as Radak supposes) that lead to God's announcement at the beginning of chapter 18, but rather Elijah's readiness to retract his oath. From the perspective of Ahab and Israel, it is possible that no change has taken place which would merit a restoration of the rain, but they are not the focus of the discussion in our narrative, and a change in the decree does not depend on them.

Indeed, *Midrash Tehillim* (psalm 117) explains the basis for God's command to Elijah not as Radak teaches, as a result of repentance, but rather the very opposite:

> God *seduced* Elijah into going and appearing before Ahab, as it is written, "Go, appear before Ahab." Elijah said to Him: "How can I go; thus far he has not yet repented?!" God answered him: "Once, when I watered My world, there was one single man in the world, and I watered the world for his sake, as it is written (Gen. 2:6), 'A mist arose from the earth.'... Likewise now: Go, appear before Ahab, and I will give rain."

According to this midrash, the nullification of the decree of drought arose from the need experienced by the world and by man, rather than from any change that the drought had brought about in the actions of Ahab.

What is the basis for the assertion in the midrash that God "seduced" Elijah into going and appearing before Ahab? The verse that the midrash brings to prove this, "As it is written, 'Go, appear before Ahab,'" contains no proof of any seduction; on the contrary, it is formulated as an absolute command. It would seem that the midrash is referring to the dispute that was maintained in the story preceding this divine command. This midrash relies upon other midrashim, which regard God's command as resulting from Elijah's agreement to "exchange the keys."

However, a reading of the introduction to God's command in verse 1 raises a difficulty regarding our assertion that this divine command is the obvious conclusion drawn from the previous three episodes, and especially from the third one: "*Much time passed*, and God's word came to Elijah in the third year, saying."

The style of the introduction creates the impression that the text is now starting a new story, unrelated to the previous one. It is possible that this introduction hints at the reason for God's imminent command, although this reason is not a change that has taken place in Elijah and which was described in the previous sections, but rather a change in divine policy. The introduction here is reminiscent of a similar instance of a change in divine policy toward Israel:

> It happened, *in the course of those many days*, that the king of Egypt died. The children of Israel sighed as a result of their labor, and cried out, and their cry rose up to God, as a result of the labor. And God heard their groaning, and God remembered His covenant…and God knew. (Ex. 2:23–25)

In our narrative, verse 1 seems to have the same intention: "Much time passed, during which time the heavy drought continued, and the suffering of the nation grew, until in the third year their suffering reached God and He commanded Elijah to restore rain to the earth." The highlighting of the dimension of time, the continuation of the drought, through the use of two different expressions, "many days" and "in the third year," hints that God's command is His own initiative, similar to, "His [God's] soul grieved for Israel's suffering" (Judges 10:16).

Is God's command the outcome of the three preceding units, describing the change that takes place in Elijah's thinking, as we concluded from our previous analysis, or is it a new element in the development of the story, arising from a change in divine policy? In order to answer this question, let us go back and reexamine the *Midrash Tehillim* quoted above.

According to the description in the midrash, Elijah does not yet identify with the cancellation of the decree of drought; he claims, "How can I go?" Therefore, a counterargument is required in response to his claim. Indeed, this is exactly the situation in the verse upon which the midrash is based. First of all, it is God who commands Elijah to go and appear before Ahab; Elijah does not undertake this mission on his own initiative, as was the case when he made the oath that started the drought. Secondly, in God's command he is told, "*I will give* rain" – not "give rain." Meaning, the rain will come not when Elijah decrees it will (as we may have expected, based on his oath – "except by my word"), but rather by His word: He will be the one to announce the end of the drought. Thus it appears that Elijah will carry out his mission as one who is commanded, but not with a sense of full identification with it.

Elijah, according to the midrash, is *not yet reconciled* to the cancellation of his oath, but he is *ready* for it, and therefore a divine command, sending him to Ahab, is required; he will not go of his own accord. For this same reason the text obscures the special connection between Elijah's resurrection of the widow's son and this divine command. If the text were to highlight the connection, the reader would be led to think that the resurrection caused Elijah to be reconciled to the restoration of rain. Instead, the text emphasizes the dimension of time accumulated over the course of the preceding events. This conveys to the reader the unbearable length of the drought, and hints at the reason for God's command. This is expressed in the midrash in God's response to Elijah's protest: "Once, when I watered My world, there was only one person in the world.... Likewise now."

Thus, the formulation of the introduction to God's command in verse 1 is indeed meant to emphasize the novel aspect of this command; this new direction does not necessarily arise from any change in Elijah. His way of thinking has not completely been revised; he is still in the stages of readjustment.

Nevertheless, this introduction itself, appearing as the opening to a new narrative, hints at the definite continuation of this section from the preceding one. A closer examination of the text reveals a clear connection between the beginning of verse 1 and the entire preceding story. The drying up of Wadi Cherith took place "after *some time*" (I Kings 17:7), namely, after Elijah had lived there for a year. His stay in the widow's house likewise lasts "*some time*" (v. 15), again, a whole year. The addition of these two periods together leads us to the introduction to God's command: "*Much time* passed" – the time during which Elijah lived at Wadi Cherith, together with the time when he lodged with the widow. The widow's son died "after these things" (v. 17), after Elijah had dwelled in the widow's home throughout the second year of the drought, in other words, in the third year of the drought. And "in the third year" of the drought God's word comes to him (18:1). Thus, the demarcations of time in verse 1 are explained by what preceded them; they thereby point to the direct connection between God's command and the preceding narrative.

Verse 1 expresses the ambivalence of Elijah's position. On one hand, the verse hints that God's command comes as a result of the events described in the three preceding episodes. In this sense, the command is related to a change that has taken place within Elijah, and especially the change that took place in "the third year" of the drought. On the other hand, the style highlights the independence of God's command from Elijah and that the change that he has undergone is only partial.

Despite all that we learn from the midrash and from close analysis of the verse concerning Elijah's lack of full identification with God's command, we must also consider the opposite aspect. Elijah expresses no reservation, nor does he attempt to argue with his Sender (in contrast to the midrash, which, in its usual manner, gives verbal expression to internal doubts). Hence, we conclude that Elijah is prepared to carry out this mission; he recognizes its justness.

In summary, we may say that Elijah sets off to fulfill his mission with mixed feelings. His experiences over the past two years at Wadi Cherith and, especially, in Zarephath lead him to recognize the unconditional necessity of rain for the world. On the other hand, he knows that "thus far [Ahab] has not repented." This ambivalence in his journey to Samaria is the key to the continued development both of this story (until 18:18) and of the following one (the test at Carmel). Our narrative will see a continuation of the process of "seducing" and convincing Elijah of the justness of restoring rain to the land that needs it so desperately, because his strategy thus far has been ineffective. In the next episode, Elijah acts on his own to change the religious state of the nation (and of its king, Ahab) so that the problem of "thus far he has not repented" will no longer present an obstacle.

ELIJAH'S ENCOUNTER WITH OBADIAH: QUESTIONS

On Elijah's way to appear before Ahab, as he was commanded (18:1), there is a slight delay. Before he reaches Ahab, he first meets Ahab's officer, Obadiah, who is "governor of the house."[1] This brief stop on Elijah's way presents a textual problem: No less than fourteen verses

---

1. It would appear that the most senior minister (at the time of the split kingdom) was the "governor of the house" who functioned as the minister of finance and economy for the kings of Israel and Judah (S. Yavin, s.v. *"pekidut," Encyclopedia Mikra'it*, vol. 6, p. 547).

(3–16) cover this encounter. This part of the story seems very strange. First of all, why does the text record every detail of the meeting at such painstaking length? Secondly, it is also strange in terms of various specific details of the story, which we shall discuss below.

The direct continuation of verse 2, "Elijah went *to appear* before Ahab, and the famine was severe in Samaria," would seem to be verse 17: "And it was, when Ahab *saw* Elijah, Ahab said to him: Is that you, O troubler of Israel?" What would be lacking if the intervening fourteen verses were removed? Is there, perhaps, some matter further on in the story that requires these fourteen verses for its proper understanding? Seemingly not, and therefore the significance of these verses must be sought within themselves.

An examination of the section under discussion reveals that it is comprised of two main parts. Verses 3–6 represent the "setting." Here we become acquainted with the new character who has just appeared in the story, Obadiah, and we are given the circumstances in which Elijah finds him as well as Ahab. This prepares us for the action in verses 7–15: the encounter between Elijah and Obadiah, and the dialogue between them. Verse 16 then describes the result of their meeting.

What is the content of the dialogue between Elijah and Obadiah? When they meet, Obadiah recognizes Elijah and takes pains to emphasize his subjugation to him: he falls upon his face before him (v. 7), calls him "my master" (vv. 7, 13), and refers to himself as "your servant" (vv. 9, 12). Elijah's words in this encounter are brief: He affirms his identity with a single word, "*anokhi*" ("it is I," v. 8), and immediately attaches a command, consisting of only five words: "Go, tell your master: Elijah is here!" Obadiah, by contrast, gives a long and emotional speech that continues over six verses (vv. 9–14). Elijah's reaction to this speech is, once again, brief and forceful. In verse 15 he swears an oath, to ease Obadiah's fears, and the latter then goes off to do as he has been instructed (v. 16).

There are many instances of repetition in this section:

1. The description of Obadiah's fear of God, and his act of saving the prophets, which is noted in the introductory setting (vv. 3–4), are repeated in his own speech (vv. 12–13).

2. Elijah's command to Obadiah (v. 8), "Go, tell your master: Elijah is here!" is quoted another *two times* in Obadiah's speech (vv. 11, 14).
3. Obadiah's fear of the outcome of his mission – being put to death by Ahab – is expressed *three times* in his speech (v. 9, "to put me to death"; vv. 12, 14, "he will kill me").

All of these seemingly redundant repetitions are included in Obadiah's speech.

Beyond the multiple repetitions, there are even more troubling questions of content:

1. Why does Elijah need Obadiah in order to announce his arrival to Ahab? Can he not appear before Ahab unannounced, as he does later, in Naboth's vineyard (I Kings 21:20)? If we want to assume that he prefers to use the opportunity afforded him by Obadiah's appearance, could he not forgo it the moment it appears that his request of Obadiah is going to cause problems? His continued insistence on his previous command, to the extent that he is ready to swear to Obadiah (18:15), reveals that he attaches great importance to Obadiah's agency. But the text seems to present Obadiah as crossing Elijah's path by chance.
2. How can Obadiah fear that Elijah will disappear after commanding him explicitly to go and tell Ahab, "Elijah is here"? Obadiah himself explains (v. 12): "God's spirit will carry you I know not where," but on what basis does he imagine that this will happen? Does he not trust Elijah?
3. Why does Obadiah think that Ahab will kill him because Elijah has disappeared? What accusation can be made against Obadiah, rendering him deserving of the death penalty?
4. A final question, most perplexing of all: Whatever the subjective reason for Obadiah's fear, we know in advance that it is not justified. Elijah has been commanded explicitly to go and appear before Ahab (v. 1), and he indeed does so (v. 2). Even Obadiah is eventually convinced of the seriousness of Elijah's intent, after the latter swears by God's name that "today *I shall appear* to him" (v. 15, using the same verb as the original command in v. 1, "Go and *appear*," and the start of its fulfillment in v. 2, "He went to *appear*"). Obadiah's entire lengthy

and emotional speech, then, is based on a mistake. His fear for his life is based on a mistaken evaluation of Elijah's intentions. Even though we still do not understand the reasons for this fear, we know that he is mistaken. Why, then, does the text record the speech? A person is allowed to make a mistake, but why perpetuate his mistake and its correction in seven whole verses? The text could simply move from verse 8 directly to verse 16.

We shall try to address all of these questions below.

ELIJAH'S MEETING WITH OBADIAH BEFORE MEETING AHAB

We shall start our attempt to answer the questions posed above by examining verse 7 more closely. Do Elijah and Obadiah really meet each other by chance? For Obadiah it is certainly a complete surprise, as the language of the verse indicates: "Obadiah was on the way, and *behold*, Elijah was coming toward him."

In many instances in Tanakh, the word "behold" (*hinei*) indicates surprise. Obadiah's reaction, further on in the same verse, when he asks, "Is that you, my lord Elijah?" likewise testifies to his surprise, as we shall discuss below.

But is it a surprise for Elijah, too?[2] The text gives us no reason to think so. The factual background preceding their meeting makes it more likely that Elijah initiated their encounter. It is he, after all, who is coming to surprise Ahab with an unexpected visit. He decides on the time and place of his appearance, as well as *the person* to whom he will appear first.

Why does Elijah first want to meet Obadiah? Undoubtedly, in order to send him to Ahab. Elijah does not want to make a sudden appearance before Ahab, for several possible reasons:

1. Elijah wants Ahab to come to him, rather than vice versa, so that Elijah's appearance before him will not be interpreted as capitulation. The strategy that Elijah chooses makes it look as though he happened

---

2. Were the order of the verse inverted – "Elijah was on the way, and behold, Obadiah was coming toward him" – we would infer that both parties were surprised at this unexpected encounter.

to meet Obadiah by chance, and since the opportunity has arisen, he is also prepared to meet Ahab. It should be emphasized that this is not a matter of personal prestige. Rather, Elijah has in mind the goal of ensuring Ahab's agreement to cooperate with him in staging the contest at Mount Carmel.

2. Obadiah is a righteous, God-fearing man, and Elijah initiates his meeting with Ahab specifically through him to hint that it is only in Obadiah's merit that he is prepared to speak with Ahab.

3. What is Obadiah, a God-fearing man, doing in Ahab's service? It would seem that Ahab seeks his services, perhaps to counterbalance the influence of Jezebel. It is difficult to imagine that Obadiah hid a hundred prophets for a prolonged period, providing them with regular sustenance, without Ahab's knowledge. In any event, his service in the royal palace is a point of merit for Ahab. In appearing before Ahab, with Obadiah as mediator, Elijah wants to hint at this merit that the king has, resulting in Elijah's appearance.

Whatever the explanation (or combination of them, since they do not contradict one another in any way), there is fundamental importance in Elijah's plan to meet Ahab specifically through the agency and invitation of Obadiah. What is common to all of the possible explanations listed above is that Obadiah's mediation will serve to "soften" Ahab before Elijah's appearance, and will prepare him to cooperate with the prophet in facilitating the event at Mount Carmel and the consequent renewal of rain upon the earth. It is for this reason that Elijah decides to meet Obadiah first, and that he maintains his insistence (to the extent that he is ready to swear) that Obadiah call for Ahab, even though this request is met with strong protest.

OBADIAH'S FEAR

Having clarified Elijah's intentions, we must now try to understand Obadiah. First, let us try to answer our question concerning the source of his fear that Elijah is going to disappear. We may suggest three possible reasons to explain this fear; only a combination of all of them produces an acceptable answer.

1. Obadiah asks himself, with justification, what has changed in the Kingdom of Israel and in the palace of Ahab that has brought Elijah back. Is Elijah's sudden appearance to be understood as a sign of his intention to change his decree of drought? This seems unlikely, since Ahab has not repented; and Obadiah, savior of the prophets from the hand of Jezebel, knows this better than anyone. Obadiah is unaware of what we, the readers, are privy to: God's command to Elijah.

2. The language of the instruction that Elijah gives to Obadiah – "Go, tell your master: Elijah is here!" – does not testify to any desire on the prophet's part to maintain a dialogue with the king for any constructive purpose. Had he had any such intention, Elijah would have formulated his command differently: "Go, tell your master that I wish to see him and speak with him," or something similar.

The combination of both of the above points leads us to the possibility that Obadiah perceived Elijah's intention to simply provoke Ahab and mock him. Against the backdrop of Ahab's desperate searches for Elijah (as revealed to us in Obadiah's words in verse 10), Elijah obviously intends to appear somewhere in Ahab's close environs, only to irritatingly disappear immediately afterward, as if to say, "See Ahab, I'm still alive and active. All your searching for me is of no avail. I still stand by my oath; only a change in you and in Israel will cause me to change it. No violent attempt to force me will have any effect." If this is indeed Elijah's intention, the purpose of his appearance before Obadiah here and now fits well with the feud that Elijah embarked upon "many days" ago, when he announced his oath of drought before Ahab and then disappeared immediately afterward in a most wondrous manner. This intention would also explain the style of Elijah's instruction, which actually means nothing more than "Tell your master: Elijah is here, in town; we must quickly try to catch him."

We, the readers, obviously know that it is incorrect to attribute this intention to Elijah. Elijah has been commanded by God to appear before Ahab, with the positive intention of acting in cooperation with him. The formulation of his instruction to Obadiah, to tell Ahab only that "Elijah is here," is intended only to prevent the possibility of Ahab thinking that Elijah has capitulated and has come to withdraw his oath for no apparent reason. The formulation of the instruction is meant as a reserved expression of readiness to meet Ahab "incidentally," since Elijah happens to be in the area.

3. Here we come to the third point that explains Obadiah's concern: If, indeed, Obadiah attributes the intention described above to Elijah, we must explain on what basis he thinks that Elijah's plan to appear and then immediately to suddenly and completely disappear is realistically possible. Without such an explanation, there is no point in our whole reconstruction of Obadiah's thinking. After all, the king could easily instruct his forces to block all possible escape routes, such that Elijah will ultimately be caught.

The answer to this is provided by Obadiah himself: "It shall be, when I go from you, that *God's spirit will take you I know not where*, and I will come to tell Ahab, but he will not find you." (v. 12)

This doubt in Obadiah's mind, which seems altogether fantastic to us, illustrates the way the people of that generation perceive the figure of Elijah and his activities. Not only the common people, who tend toward exaggerated and wondrous folktales, but even important people like Obadiah, a respected officer of the kingdom and a God-fearing man, and even the children of the prophets in Jericho (II Kings 2:16–18), perceive Elijah in this way. This is the result of him being a figure shrouded in mystery, living outside of society, and particularly as a result of the prophet's custom of making unexpected appearances and sudden disappearances. The years that passed since Elijah vanished, after declaring his oath of drought, only strengthened this perception of him. What rational explanation could be offered for Ahab's failure to find Elijah, despite having sent search parties throughout the entire geographic region surrounding the Kingdom of Israel?

> As the Lord your God lives, there is no nation or kingdom to which my master has not sent to seek you, and they said, "He is not here," and he made the kingdom and the nation swear that they had not found you. (18:10)

Indeed, we know that it is only thanks to great and revealed miracles that Elijah has been able to maintain his secrecy and hide from human society. This deep-rooted perception of Elijah's disappearances is what leads Obadiah to mistakenly attribute to him the intention of mocking Ahab.

Malbim interprets Obadiah's speech (v. 12) in a manner similar to the approach we have taken above:

> "It shall be, when I go from you, that God's spirit will take you." We must conclude that you do not wish to appear before him; you wish only to show that he seeks you in vain in other lands, since you are here. But nevertheless, "It shall be, when I go from you, that God's spirit will take you I know not where" – this is what you intend to show him!

OBADIAH'S MONOLOGUE

Everything that we have said thus far has not yet explained Obadiah's emotional outburst. What is the connection between Elijah's plan, as Obadiah estimates it, and Obadiah's own fate? Why will Elijah's mockery of Ahab lead to the king slaying Obadiah?

Obadiah believes that Elijah is using him as a pawn in his mockery of Ahab. He believes that on his way to provoke Ahab, Elijah is exploiting the mediation of an innocent bystander who will fulfill his mission specifically because of his faithful obedience to the prophet. But this innocent messenger will be the one to pay the price of this "game" between the prophet and the king. Ahab's anger at Elijah's provocation will fall on the head of Obadiah, the scapegoat.

We may imagine the sort of claims that Ahab will make against Obadiah: Why did he not capture Elijah before the latter disappeared? Why did he not bring him before the king? Either he was negligent, or he intentionally refrained from doing so out of honor for the prophet. Ahab is aware that Obadiah is a God-fearing man. This being the case, it will be apparent that Obadiah favors the prophet over the king. Either way, he is deserving of punishment, and Ahab, in a rage, is quite likely to kill him.

Thus, Obadiah ponders the fate that awaits him as a result of becoming involved in the conflict between the prophet and the king. He objects to what he perceives as an injustice in the form of the prophet's request of him. It is this sense of injustice that gives rise to his impassioned speech.[3]

Why does Obadiah believe that Elijah would want to do an injustice to a righteous man? Obviously, we need not necessarily know the reason. Perhaps this is the meaning of Obadiah's cry, that the injustice is being done unintentionally, and he is going to be obliterated in a battle of the mighty in which he has no part. But a close reading of the beginning of the dialogue between the two may reveal a different answer:

Obadiah asks an obviously rhetorical question: "*Is it you*, my master Elijah?" (v. 7). In the first half of that verse we just read: "*He recognized him*, and fell upon his face." What, then, is the meaning of the question: "Is it you?" What Obadiah is saying is: "Are my eyes seeing correctly, that you – the prophet who has kept himself hidden for so long – have finally decided to appear?" The question is formulated in respectful language, but it still contains a note of covert criticism. When Ahab finally meets with Elijah, he addresses a similar rhetorical question, but there the criticism is overt and clear, and the style lacks any sign of respect or subjugation: "And it was, when Ahab saw Elijah, Ahab said to him: *Is it you*, O troubler of Israel?" (v. 17).

The words "my master Elijah" are absent from Ahab's question; in their place we find a reference to the prophet as the "troubler of Israel." But the intention of the question is the same: To express grievance over the prophet's prolonged absence, the results of which are being played out at that very moment, with the king and his ministers searching all over to "find grass to save the horses and mules."

Elijah ignores the critical tone hinted at in Obadiah's question (unlike his encounter with Ahab, where there is no possibility of ignoring the furious criticism). He treats it as though it was an informative question, answering laconically, "It is I." But he attaches an order, clarifying the meaning of his surprising appearance: "Go tell your master, Elijah is here!"

---

3. Other monologues by characters who feel that someone in a position of greater power has done them an injustice include Jacob, speaking to Laban (Gen. 31:36–42); Judah, speaking to the viceroy of Egypt, whom he fails to identify as Joseph (Gen. 44:18–34); David, speaking to Saul, who is pursuing him (I Sam. 24:9–15), among others.

Attention should be paid to the dual use of the word "master," as spoken by Obadiah and by Elijah. In both cases the word "master" refers to Obadiah's master, and the question is: Who is Obadiah's true master? Obadiah calls *Elijah* "my master" (as he does once again, in v. 13; he also refers to himself twice as "your servant," in vv. 9 and 12). Elijah, however, refers to *Ahab* as Obadiah's master (and Obadiah refers to him the same way himself in verse 10). Thus Obadiah is the servant of two masters. This is, indeed, his objective situation. And from Obadiah's perspective, it is this situation that has led him into the tragic crisis in which he now finds himself.

In our scrutiny of the dialogue between Elijah and Obadiah, we may perhaps guess that Obadiah hears a hint of countercriticism in Elijah's response, as if to say: "You call me '*my master*,' but you are actually a servant of Ahab, his confidant; it is not I who am your master but rather Ahab, with whom you cooperate. *Therefore* I tell you: Go tell *your master*, Elijah is here." Obadiah surmises that it is perhaps no coincidence that Elijah turns him into a messenger to Ahab; it is meant as a punishment for being Ahab's trusted servant and confidant.

Thus, Obadiah's cry of unfairness and injustice becomes more focused. It concerns the presumed accusation that Elijah is directing at him. He answers this accusation specifically: "How have I sinned?" (v. 9). If you mean that I have sinned by being Ahab's servant, "the governor of the house," does this say anything about me? "Your servant fears God since my youth!" (v. 12). If that is precisely your point – if you mean that a God-fearing person should not cooperate with Ahab – "Has my master not been told of what I did when Jezebel killed God's prophets, and I hid a hundred of God's prophets, fifty to a cave, and I fed them bread and water?" (v. 13).

In other words: This cooperation brings blessing and salvation to God's prophets; it is maintained for the sake of heaven! Is Obadiah deserving of punishment for having risked his life, by using his respected status in Ahab's house to save the prophets?

Perhaps there is another element in Obadiah's cry against the injustice he feels. His fearful hesitation to fulfill Elijah's command (expressed in the threefold repetition of his fear of being killed by Ahab) may make him appear cowardly to Elijah. Therefore, he tries to defend his refusal. It is not out of fear that Obadiah is refusing to fulfill Elijah's demand; after all, "has my master not been told of what I did?" Obadiah, then, is a man of courage who is prepared to risk his status and even his life to save a hundred prophets from Jezebel. However, this is a case of risking his life for true benefit: Saving a great many prophets who would certainly have died had it not been for Obadiah's assistance. But why should he forfeit his life for the prophet's wish to provoke and anger Ahab, his master, with no real benefit? Should he endanger himself for this purpose?

STRUCTURE OF OBADIAH'S SPEECH

Following our attempt to reconstruct Obadiah's line of thinking, let us now analyze the structure of his speech. A monologue delivered by a character during the course of a biblical narrative is usually a polished literary gem, and Obadiah's speech here is no exception. The thought behind his words, and their careful composition, explain the many repetitions that characterize this speech, as noted previously.

Obadiah's speech begins with a surprising introduction, formulated as a stinging rhetorical question and meant as a harsh moral claim against Elijah, whose command to Obadiah will cause him to be killed by Ahab: "How have I sinned, that you are giving your servant into the hand of Ahab, to put me to death?" (v. 9).

The reader finds it difficult to understand what Obadiah means. There is no apparent logical connection between Elijah's preceding command and this claim. Obadiah's next words, therefore, are meant to justify and clarify this opening statement. This clarification happens in two stages: In the first, including verses 10–11 and most of verse 12, Obadiah explains the *second* part of his introductory statement: "You are giving your servant into the hand of Ahab, to put me to death." Why is this so, and how will Elijah's instruction bring about such far-reaching results – the execution of Obadiah by Ahab? This claim must be substantiated in terms of realistic probability, before the first part of the initial claim – the moral argument, "How have I sinned?" – can be addressed. The moral argument rests upon the probability of the scenario that Obadiah predicts. If the scenario is not convincing, there is no further point to the moral clarification.

On the other hand, there is reason to start the introductory statement with the sharp rhetorical question, "How have I sinned?" in order to give the question its due weight and dramatic significance, right at the start. Thus the relationship between the opening statement and its dual clarification is chiastic in form. Let us attempt to analyze the speech according to the structure that we have described:

Argument part I: (v. 9) How have I sinned?

> Argument part II: (v. 9) That you are giving your servant into the hand of Ahab, to put me to death.

> Clarification of part II:

>> PAST (v. 10) As the Lord your God lives, there is no nation or kingdom to which my master has not sent to seek you, and they [all] said, "He is not here," and he made the kingdom and the nation swear that they had not found you.

>> PRESENT (v. 11) *And now you say, "Go tell your master, Elijah is here."*

>> FUTURE (v. 12) And it shall be when I go from you, that God's spirit will take you I know not where, and I will come to tell Ahab but he will not find you, *and he will kill me.*

Clarification of part I:

> PAST (vv. 12–13) Your servant has feared God from my youth. Was it not told to my master what I did when Jezebel killed the prophets of God, and I hid a hundred of the prophets of God, fifty to a cave, and I fed them bread and water?

> PRESENT (v. 14) *And now you say: "Go tell your master, Elijah is here,"*

> FUTURE (v. 14) *and he will kill me.*

As we can see from the above, each of the two clarifications that is given for the two parts of the opening statement comprises three stages. Stage 1 relates to the past, with a review of the facts and actions that substantiate the claim made in the opening statement. Stage 2 relates to the present (introduced with the expression "and now"), which will lead to the expected outcome in stage 3: the future. Stage 2, the "present" stage is of necessity identical in both clarifications: This is the stage of Elijah's command to Obadiah. Stage 3, the "future," is likewise identical in both clarifications, but its purpose differs. The first clarification (of part II, the second part of the argument) explains the expected *practical* outcome of Elijah's command. Therefore there is a detailed description of the process that will lead to that result. In the second clarification (of part I, the first part of the argument), the "future" stage consists entirely of one word: *veharagani* (he will kill me). Here there is no need for elaboration, not only because the process that will lead to this result has already been presented, but also for another reason. The function of the description of the future here is to present a stark moral contrast to the lengthy description in stage 1 of the clarification, which presents as a background a description of Obadiah's righteousness in *saving the lives* of a hundred prophets. It is specifically the terrible brevity of the single word *veharagani* that has the effect of creating this dramatic contrast.

We can now understand the repetitions that previously presented a problem: They arise from the dual clarification. The same phrases appear twice because they play a different role in each of the two parts of the speech. The quotation of Elijah's command and its result, "He will kill me," in the first part of the speech (clarification of part II) is meant to explain *how* this will happen, while in the other part of the clarification (part I) they function as a moral contrast to the description of Obadiah's God-fearing stance and good deeds, thereby substantiating the claim, "How have I sinned?"

The repetition of the description of his act of saving the prophets can now also be explained. The function of this description in Obadiah's speech is entirely clear. Its omission from the speech would detract greatly from the power of his moral argument and thereby nullify the contrast between his act of *saving lives* and his expectation of imminently being *put to death* by Ahab.[4] But in the narration itself, it is also important that this heroic episode be recorded, as an illustration of the assertion in verse 3: "Obadiah had great fear of God." This ensures that we, the readers, develop the appropriate attitude toward this man, and a proper appreciation of his personality. It helps us understand the conflict that faces him. We also better understand Elijah's decision to appear first before Obadiah and to turn him into his messenger to Ahab.

Finally, two comments concerning the first part of the speech:

1. What is the purpose of the lifelike, dramatic description of Ahab's searches for Elijah? It serves a dual purpose. First, Elijah's total disappearance during these years is the background to Obadiah's fear, expressed later on, that "God's spirit will take you [again] I know not where." Second, the description of Ahab's desperate searches serves as the psychological background to the expected furious response: "He will kill me." Ahab is frustrated by his continued failure to locate Elijah, and yet another disappearance, compounding this failure, will cause an outburst directed against Obadiah.

2. Obadiah introduces his first clarification (clarification of part II) with an oath: "As the Lord your God lives." Why does he make this oath before describing Ahab's search missions? Does he fear that Elijah may not believe his completely credible story? It seems that his oath is meant to apply to the entire clarification. In other words, he swears that the situation is so grave that when Elijah disappears (as Obadiah is certain that he intends to do), Ahab will immediately have him executed. In fact, the oath may even be meant to apply to the description of his righteous act, as well, in the second part of the speech. Elijah responds to Obadiah's oath with an oath of his own,

---

4. The purpose of Obadiah's testimony about himself is not only to support his previous assertion – "I, your servant, have feared God since my youth," but also much more: He seeks to justify his presence in Ahab's house and his cooperation with him, as well as demonstrating his willingness to risk his own life for a positive and real goal such as saving the prophets (which proves in turn that his opposition to Elijah's command is not motivated by fear), as explained above.

nullifying the speculative stage of Obadiah's prediction of another "disappearing act" by Elijah, which he fears so greatly: "As the Lord of Hosts, before whom I stand, lives – today I shall appear before him" (v. 15).

Once this stage is removed from Obadiah's "scenario," the entire edifice collapses, and his fear of being put to death by Ahab turns out to be baseless. At this point, he fulfills the prophet's command without further argument: "Obadiah went to meet Ahab, and he told him" (v. 16).

OBADIAH'S MISTAKE: PART OF THE POLEMICS OVER ELIJAH'S APPROACH

To conclude our study of this section, we must still answer the most difficult question of all: Why does the text perpetuate Obadiah's mistake and record his speech in such detail, occupying an entire six verses? The fact that he has misunderstood Elijah's intention is clear to Elijah himself, as well as to us, the readers, from the outset. The text could therefore move from verse 8 to verse 16, and dispense with the intervening seven verses. What is their contribution?

The answer is that the text intends to include the confrontation between Obadiah and Elijah within the framework of the literary units that comprise chapter 17, and adapts it to this purpose. A mistake such as the one under discussion, although altogether insignificant in the actual plot of the story and not serving in any way to further its development, is sometimes of great importance in another sphere of the story: the molding of the characters and creating the authentic situation in which the action takes place.

Obadiah will not appear again in this story or in any other biblical narrative, and therefore it is not so much his own personality as such that the incident comes to illuminate, but rather his personality as representative of many others like him in Israel: people who are loyal to God and His prophets. Obadiah's speech comes to teach us (as well as Elijah) how this great prophet is perceived in the eyes of the people. Obadiah's mistake is of marginal importance in the story, but the practical and psychological background that makes such a mistake possible – the attitude toward the figure of Elijah on the part of Obadiah and others like him – is of critical significance.

The fact that Obadiah attributes to Elijah the type of intentions that he does, tells us that, as Obadiah saw it, it was quite reasonable to assume that the prophet who was familiar to him from the beginning of his conflict with Ahab would indeed act in this way. He would display hard-heartedness, a lack of consideration, for the distinction between those deserving of punishment and those not deserving, to the point of causing the death of a righteous man. Obadiah's emotional speech is a genuine condemnation of Elijah and his approach, even though its factual basis is mistaken. Ultimately, the reason for Obadiah's mistake is that he does not know that which we do know – that Elijah is now acting on God's command; he has been sent to appear before Ahab. This lack of information opens a window for us to understand how Elijah was perceived by the righteous people of his generation. It allows us to understand the great importance of God's command that brings Elijah back to his people.

In our studies of the three units in chapter 17, we saw how the narrative serves to mold the divine criticism of Elijah's stance concerning his oath, and how God arranges events and experiences that are calculated to cause him to renounce it. We also saw how, at the end of the third episode, in the description of the resuscitation of the widow's son, there is a turning point in Elijah's position, and he is ready for the decree of drought to be changed. This turning point leads to God's command to Elijah at the beginning of chapter 18. Why, then, is there still a need to continue the dispute within the framework of the present confrontation between him and Obadiah? At the end of the previous paragraph, we hinted that this represents a retrospective comment on the importance of God's command that causes Elijah to return to his people. But we should not suffice with this answer.

At the beginning of this chapter, we noted that Elijah's heart is torn as he sets off on his mission; he still needs some additional persuasion that what he is about to do is indeed the right thing. Obadiah, in his speech, becomes part of the previous criticism of Elijah, and his confrontation with him adds a human dimension to the divine criticism. It is not only in the heavens, but also on earth, among the select individuals and the loyal servants of God, that criticism is being voiced over the prophet's approach.[5] With all due recognition of Elijah's greatness ("He recognized him, and he fell upon his face"), what we see here is a clear expression of disagreement with the harshness that Elijah has displayed toward his people.

Support for this view of the story about Obadiah (vv. 3–15) being another instance of confrontation and having the same intention as the episodes in chapter 17, arises from a comparison between them, from various perspectives:

Comparison with the First Episode at Wadi Cherith

The description of the severe drought in the Samaria region (18:5) connects us to what we were told in the previous chapter (17:7), "The wadi dried up, for there was no rain in the land." In Samaria, too (where "the famine was severe"), the familiar wadis and streams have dried up, and Ahab and Obadiah divide the land between them and go off "to all the springs of water and to all the wadis; *perhaps* we shall find grass to save the horses and mules" (18:5). Just as the drying up of Wadi Cherith brings Elijah face-to-face with the meaning of the drought in terms of the ecosystem in the area, the drying up of the wadis and streams in Samaria is likewise affecting the animal life and killing it off. And just as the drying up of Wadi Cherith causes Elijah to leave his place and to wander in order to find the place where he will be able to live, so the drying up of the springs in Samaria causes Ahab and Obadiah to have to leave their place and travel all over to find a place that offers some grass for their livestock.

This connection between the two sections also finds expression in vocabulary that is common to both: The noun "wadi" appears in both, and, more importantly, the root *khaf-resh-tav* (cut off, kill off) appears

---

5. Human criticism of Elijah has already been voiced by the widow of Zarephath (17:12, 18), but this was an intuitive reproach that was not based on familiarity with Elijah's relations with his people, nor any identification of Elijah as the party responsible for causing the drought with his oath. Obadiah's criticism, by contrast, is focused and deliberate, taking into account the prophet's oath, followed by his disappearance, as well as the totality of the elements of Elijah's personality as known to all.

both in the name of the wadi where Elijah hides and which eventually dries up, and in 18:5: "so that all our livestock will not die off."

In the description of the famine and drought in Samaria and the surrounding areas we find interwoven the figure and righteous acts of Obadiah (18: 3–4). This, again, connects back to the events at Wadi Cherith: Like Elijah, who is forced to hide at Wadi *Cherith* because of his oath, the hundred prophets hid in caves "when Jezebel killed (*behakhrit*) the prophets of God" – apparently an indirect result of Elijah's oath before Ahab. Just as the ravens *fed* Elijah while he hid at the wadi, bringing him bread and meat, so Obadiah *feeds* the hundred prophets, bringing them bread and water.

The significance of all these parallels is that Elijah now relives his experience at Wadi Cherith – but this time multiplied by a hundred, both in terms of the scope of its influence (a hundred prophets as opposed to a single one; many wadis as opposed to a single wadi; a whole city as opposed to a single person), and in terms of the severity of the drought in its third year.

Comparison with the Second Episode at the Gates of Zarephath

The description of the confrontation between Elijah and Obadiah (18:7–16) is built in a manner that is most reminiscent of the confrontation between Elijah and the widow at the gates of Zarephath (17:9–16). In both places Elijah reaches the environs of the cities to which he has been sent by God's command, and there he unexpectedly (" ehold" – 17:10, 18:7) encounters the person that he wanted to meet. In both instances he presents his partner in dialogue with a demand, which is met with refusal, explained in an emotional monologue. Both monologues begin with a similar oath: "As the Lord your God lives" (17:12, 18:10). Then the prophet clarifies his request, formulating it in such a way as to neutralize the opposition, and in both cases his partner is appeased. Following the prophet's clarification and explicit commitment that his request will not cause the other person any harm, his request is acceded to and is performed ("*She went* and did as Elijah had spoken" [17:15]; "Obadiah *went* to Ahab and told him" [18:16]).

In terms of the vocabulary that is common to both places, we discover the following: (1) *Water and bread* are what Elijah asks of the widow at the beginning of his encounter with her, and *bread and water* are what Obadiah supplied to the hundred prophets, as he testifies himself in his monologue. (2) The widow and Obadiah introduce their oaths with the same expression, as noted above. (3) The widow concludes her speech with the word *vamatnu* (we shall die); Obadiah starts with *lehamiteni* (to put me to death) and ends with *veharagani* (he will kill me).

This aspect of the corresponding sections again hints to us that Elijah is reliving an experience similar to the one at the gates of Zarephath: His person and his request of his partner in conversation gives rise to recoiling and resistance. Here again, as in the previous parallel, Obadiah's resistance is stronger than that of the widow. The latter does not blame Elijah for the fact that she and her son are about to die of starvation (although to Elijah and to ourselves, the readers, she appears to do so, because we know something that she does not). But Obadiah explicitly accuses Elijah of being responsible for his anticipated death at the hands of Ahab.

Comparison with the Third Episode: Resuscitation of the Widow's Son

In both cases, Elijah's partner in conversation accuses him unjustly. The widow claims that he has come to her to "make remembrance of my sin and to put my son to death" (17:18). On the literal level of the story, this accusation has no basis. Likewise, Obadiah claims that Elijah is handing him over to Ahab to be put to death without having sinned. In both cases the monologue starts with the word *mah* (what) – "What have I to do with you?" (17:18); What is my sin?" (18:9). In both cases Elijah refutes the claims against him, although in very different ways: In chapter 17 he revives the boy and restores him to his mother; in chapter 18 he commits himself with an oath to appear the same day before Ahab.

The words that are common to both sections are "sin" and "death": "Have you come to me to make remembrance of *my sin* and to *put* my son *to death*?" (17:18); "What is *my sin*, that you are giving your servant... *to put me to death*?" (18:9). This parallel links with the previous ones to show that Elijah's confrontation with Obadiah is merely a continuation of the preceding confrontations at the beginning of the story.

The situation in which Obadiah confronts Elijah so sharply presents us with two worldviews that differ over the question of how God-fearing people of the generation are meant to deal with the House of Ahab. Elijah, the prophet of the generation, has chosen thus far the path of headstrong, fiery confrontation and conflict, followed by cutting off contact. Obadiah, a man who is "exceedingly God-fearing," has chosen precisely the opposite path: that of brave cooperation with the wicked king with an attempt to influence from within. It is with this approach that he exerts himself to save whatever can be saved, placing himself on the front lines against the influence of Jezebel and her evil deeds.

From a personal point of view, Obadiah nullifies himself before Elijah, the great prophet of the generation. He falls upon his face when meeting him, and he calls Elijah "my master" and himself "your servant," thereby expressing his subjugation to him. But despite his recognition of Elijah's greatness, he will not relinquish his contrasting position to that of Elijah. He even emphasizes its tangible achievements in front of the prophet, who negates it completely: "*Has my master not been told* of what I did when Jezebel killed the prophets of God, when I hid a hundred of God's prophets, fifty to a cave, and I fed them bread and water?" (v. 13).

Obadiah's recriminatory speech in response to Elijah's demand of him, as he mistakenly understands it, is the speech of a person who is defending and justifying his approach before someone whom he believes to be strongly opposed to it.

Chapter 8

The Second Encounter Between Elijah and Ahab (I Kings 18:16–18)

> And *Ahab went* to meet Elijah. And it was, *when Ahab saw* Elijah, *Ahab said* to him: Is that you, O troubler of Israel? He said: I have not troubled Israel, but rather you and your father's house, by abandoning God's commandments and going after the Baal gods. (18:16–18)

ELIJAH'S TWO MEETINGS WITH AHAB: THE DIFFERENCES

The present altercation between the prophet and the king closes a circle, which started with the prophet's first appearance before Ahab, when he made his oath to stop the rain: "Elijah the Tishbite, one of the inhabitants of Gilead, said to Ahab: As the Lord of Israel lives, before whom I stand, there will be no rain or dew during these years, except by my word" (17:1).

There are so many differences between the original confrontation and the present one that they may in fact be regarded as inversions of one another:

1. Inversion of role: In the original confrontation, with which the story begins, Elijah appears to be the one who initiated the meeting with Ahab; he appears before him as a prosecutor, bringing punishment. In the present confrontation, the situation is reversed. Although we, the readers, know that Elijah has come in order to appear before Ahab as God commanded him to do, Ahab is unaware of this. From his point of view, it seems that he finally happens to have an opportunity to meet the prophet whom he has sought so desperately.[1] Therefore he goes to meet Elijah; it is he who initiates the encounter, and his address is, astonishingly, a rebuke of the prophet and an indictment for the suffering he has brought upon the nation of Israel.[2]

2. Reciprocity: In the first confrontation between them, Elijah's oath is met with no reaction on Ahab's part – or, if there was one, it is not recorded in the text. Thus the description of that meeting is one-sided; it is the description of Elijah's one-man show. From a certain perspective, the second encounter between the king and the prophet contains Ahab's delayed reaction to Elijah's oath, following years of drought and suffering, during which the severity of the oath has become apparent.

   The present confrontation is of an entirely different nature. It is a dialogue; admittedly tense, but attention is given to both sides. Elijah responds to Ahab's accusation and explains his position. Moreover, this dialogue serves as the introduction to the cooperation that Elijah demands of Ahab, and to which Ahab agrees (vv. 19–20).

3. Circumstances and results: The most important difference, of course, concerns the circumstances that have brought each of the parties to the meeting and, consequently, the results that each reaps from it. The first meeting is initiated by Elijah himself, with no preceding divine command. Elijah's initiative of making an oath to stop the

---

1. We have discussed above how Elijah acted deliberately to create this impression in Ahab's mind, and the reason for doing so.
2. Ahab's role as the initiator and active party in this encounter is highlighted in our presentation of verses 16–18 above.

rain led to a period of severe drought in the land and terrible hunger in Samaria.

Elijah's second appearance before Ahab takes place not on his own initiative, but rather as a result of God's command. Ahab, unlike the reader, is unaware of both this divine command and the purpose of the meeting with Elijah: a renewal of the rains. Indeed, the rest of this second encounter between the king and the prophet is conducted with cooperation, with an eventual return of the rain and an end to the drought.

Thus, from almost every possible angle, the two altercations between the king and the prophet are opposites of one another.

The present meeting represents the conclusion of the first narrative within the larger story of chapters 17–19. Our story begins (apparently) in Ahab's royal palace in Samaria with a confrontation between the prophet and the king; it concludes close to Samaria with another confrontation between them. What separates these two confrontations in the text (some forty verses) is the description of the events and circumstances that Elijah has experienced during the course of his wanderings from his starting point until his return (and, to some extent, also the events that have been experienced by Ahab and Israel during the same period). These trials and tribulations are what have facilitated the change in the respective stances of both characters. In other words, the story essentially comes to show how the two confrontations, at the bookends of the narrative, come to be the opposite of one another.

ELIJAH AND AHAB'S CONFRONTATION: A LINK BETWEEN THE DROUGHT NARRATIVE AND THAT OF THE TEST AT CARMEL

The meeting with Ahab that now awaits Elijah has a dual purpose. On one hand, this event is another of all the encounters that Elijah has experienced throughout the story, all of which were aimed at softening the prophet's stance and preparing him to agree to the renewal of rain, as we shall clarify below. On the other hand, the ultimate purpose of this encounter is spelled out at the end of God's command to him: "And I will give rain upon the land." The appearance before Ahab is a preparatory stage on the way to this objective. The road from this encounter until the actual rainfall is still long. Although in chronological terms it may not have taken more than a few days, it includes many events which are described in the following narrative, covering twenty-eight verses.

Thus, the altercation between Elijah and Ahab serves as the link between the two stories. It concludes the chain of events that were aimed at bringing about a change in the prophet's view (which appears to be the subject of the story of the drought), and in this respect it forms part of that collection. From this perspective, the aim of the meeting is to bring the prophet closer to the experience of the king (who is the representative of the nation). However, the meeting also serves as the first in a series of actions by Elijah, described principally in the next narrative, aimed at changing the national reality such that Israel will be worthy of having God restore the rain. From this perspective, its aim is to bring the king closer to the position of the prophet. Thus, the encounter between the two is meant to lead them to the point of consensus which will ultimately facilitate the restoration of the rainfall.

Let us now examine the encounter itself and see how it, like Elijah's previous encounters, promotes the conclusion that the policy undertaken by the prophet thus far should not be pursued any longer, and how Elijah directs matters, by means of the encounter, so as to lead to the rainfall with which the next story concludes.

AHAB'S "REBUKE"

When Obadiah comes to Ahab and tells him, in accordance with Elijah's command, "Elijah is here," Ahab is faced with two possibilities. One would be to try to capture Elijah by calling for reinforcements from nearby Samaria. For this purpose, Ahab could even make use of Obadiah who, at Ahab's command, would call for the king's forces to block all escape routes, while the king spoke with the prophet. Ahab has several reasons to choose this course of action:

1. He has desperately sought Elijah in every possible location, as Obadiah testifies in his speech (v. 10). Now he has an opportunity to catch the elusive prophet. Can he allow him to get away again?

2. If Obadiah feared Elijah's sudden disappearance in order to irritate Ahab, Ahab himself must certainly be entertaining the same possibility.

3. Preservation of his own honor as king would likely have prevented Ahab from going to Elijah. The sense of power invested in him by virtue of his office could easily lead him to seek a forceful conflict with Elijah.

However, Ahab chooses to avoid this path. Trusting the prophet's serious intentions, he chooses the opposite course: "Ahab went to meet Elijah" (v. 16).

Close attention should be paid to these simple words, because they skim lightly over a most remarkable picture: The king of Israel forgoes his honor and proceeds, alone and on foot, with no entourage and no trappings of royalty, to meet the prophet. This is the downcast step of a leader who understands the gravity of the situation and who, in his search for some grass to keep the horses alive, is prepared to hold a dialogue with the prophet and to recognize the supremacy of his path. It would seem that it is with a sense of submission that Ahab approaches Elijah. The prophet's plan to appear before Ahab in this mood appears to have been met with success, and we expect the flow of events to continue unchallenged in accordance with Elijah's plan.

But then we are surprised: The lowly spirit with which Ahab approaches Elijah suddenly turns into an outpouring of anger: "Is that you, O troubler of Israel?" (v. 17).

Did Ahab go to Elijah just to say these words? Were we wrong in our description of his mood? Apparently not. The text uses a great many words to lead up to Ahab giving vent to his anger: "And it was, when Ahab saw Elijah, that Ahab said to him ..." (v. 17).

This introduction could be written in considerably fewer words; the end of verse 16, "Ahab went to meet Elijah," could be followed immediately by "He said to him." Had the text been formulated in this way, we would have reason to think that it was for the purpose of this declaration that Ahab went to meet Elijah. But the unusual pause in the text, postponing Ahab's attack, conveys a clear message: This is a spontaneous outburst that erupts at the sight of Elijah: "It was, when Ahab saw

Elijah...." It is at that moment that Ahab's anger flares up at the thought of what the prophet has caused his nation, by means of his oath, and Ahab's previous mood of submission is suddenly replaced by a rage that finds expression in his invective: "Is that you, O troubler of Israel?"

This change in Ahab takes place before the prophet's eyes. At first, Elijah sees Ahab coming toward him alone, and he understands Ahab's submission correctly. But he also sees how, as the king comes closer and recognizes the prophet, standing firm in his stance, his facial expression changes; he becomes angry, and then bursts forth with his rebuke.

Applying the title "troubler of Israel" to Elijah is harsh criticism. This expression appears in only one other place in all of Tanakh: "The children of Karmi: Akhar, *the troubler of Israel*, who stole from the consecrated property" (I Chr. 2:7). Akhar is a pseudonym for Akhan, who took from the consecrated loot after the fall of Jericho (see Josh. 7).

What is the meaning of the inescapable comparison to the deed of Akhan, who is repeatedly described as having troubled Israel (Josh. 7:25–26)? It would seem that what Ahab means to say is that, like Akhan, Elijah too has brought catastrophe upon his nation out of personal interests. It is specifically this emphasis on the human independence of Elijah's oath – the pretension of complete control over the rainfall, "except by my word," followed by the prophet's mysterious disappearance while his nation collapses with weakness from the "severe famine in Samaria" – that lead Ahab to accuse him of "troubling Israel." Ahab views Elijah as someone who insists on his view being upheld at any price, for the sake of preserving his own pride and honor, even at the expense of national disaster.

This title for Elijah, "troubler of Israel," is expressed as part of a penetrating rhetorical question: "Is it you, O troubler of Israel?" It is just like Obadiah's question asked after he recognizes Elijah and falls prostrate before him: "Is that you, my lord Elijah?" (v. 7).

While Obadiah expresses an outward display of honor toward Elijah, with the criticism only hinted at in the rhetorical question, Ahab dispenses with any form of polite veneer, leaving only the harsh, glaring criticism. However, both questions have the same intention: To criticize Elijah for his prolonged absence and for waiting so long to return.

Attention should be paid to the fact that Elijah responds to this rebuke neither when it is presented by Obadiah (when he answers simply, "It is I," as though it were an informative question) nor when it is posed by Ahab. He responds only to Ahab's title for him, "troubler of Israel," with no comment on the reproach for how long it took him to appear.

In the supplement to this chapter, we shall compare the encounter between Elijah and Ahab in our story to their encounter in the story of Naboth's vineyard (ch. 21). One of the most significant differences between the two is the title that Ahab uses for Elijah when he sees him. In our story he calls him "troubler of Israel," while in Naboth's vineyard he asks, "Have you found me, *my enemy*?" (21:20). In Naboth's vineyard Elijah comes to rebuke Ahab for his personal sin, and this rebuke is interpreted by Ahab as an expression of personal aversion. In their encounter here, Ahab emphasizes the damage that Elijah has caused to the entire nation of Israel, righteous and wicked alike, through his oath of drought.

As regards our story, this comparison is instructive concerning Ahab's conviction of the justice of his moral cause as the representative of the nation of Israel. That which has only been hinted to Elijah in various ways during the course of the story thus far, by God and His agents – Obadiah and the widow of Zarephath – is now presented most directly by Ahab.

However, Ahab is not the right person to accuse the prophet in this way. The fact that it comes from him allows Elijah to defend himself by placing the responsibility squarely upon the shoulders of his attacker: "I have not troubled Israel, but rather you and your father's house, by abandoning God's commandments and going after the Baal gods!" (18:18).

EFFECT OF CONFRONTATION ON ELIJAH'S APPROACH

What effect do Ahab's words and actions have on Elijah, who is making his way to Samaria at God's command but with distinctly mixed feelings? In order to answer this question, we must ask ourselves how Elijah imagines the effects of the famine and drought on the nation of Israel. How does he gauge the success of the punishment with regard to Ahab – the principal cause of this punishment? How does he imagine the reaction of those who fear God to this punishment that has been meted out to the entire nation in equal measure? Obviously, the answers to these questions are speculative; the text gives us no information regarding Elijah's thoughts on these matters. But it seems that we may guess his thoughts based on the very fact that Elijah initiated this punishment, as well as the fact that he has insisted on maintaining it for such a lengthy period. We may assume that Elijah expected that his initiative would be received with understanding and support by the God-fearing people (even though they, too, suffered as a result, both from the famine and from the decrees of Jezebel, which may have been a vengeful reaction to Elijah's oath). Likewise, Elijah expected his approach to help break Ahab's pride, and generate in him a readiness to change his path.

The encounter with Obadiah reveals to Elijah that his path is not acceptable to the God-fearing public, and they do not identify with his decision to bring a drought upon Israel; rather, they share in the national suffering and the sense of responsibility that Ahab displays toward the people.

The meeting with Ahab, although at first promising from Elijah's perspective, shows him that the king not only fails to justify the prophet's course of action or to regret his own actions, but – on the contrary – holds the prophet responsible for the suffering of the nation, and is full of anger toward him.

Thus, these two encounters prove to Elijah that the way he has chosen to lead the nation to repentance has failed. He must therefore seek a new path to repentance and to the restoration of rain. His statement, "except by my word" (17:1), in its simplest meaning – "unless he sees that they all, or at least some of them, repent and cease their idolatrous worship" (in the words of Radak, ad loc.) – is no longer tenable.

Ahab's rebuke of Elijah, then, serves as another important stage in the process leading Elijah to the conclusion that his approach thus far has not led to success, nor will it do so in the future. A different and more constructive approach is needed in order to cause the nation to repent and to fulfill God's intention of giving "rain upon the land." Thus, Ahab himself joins all the other characters who have expressed opposition to Elijah's oath. Despite his direct responsibility for the prophet taking this drastic step in the first place, his words represent real proof of its failure. Clearly, one of the most obvious disadvantages of Elijah's approach was that it allowed the party that was truly guilty – the king – to bring serious moral claims against the prophet, and thereby to remove the burden of responsibility from himself.

Despite what we have said above, Elijah could have detected in Ahab signs of readiness to cooperate from this point onward. Firstly, the situation in which the prophet finds the king going to extraordinary lengths to find fodder for his animals reveals something of Ahab's psychological state. Moreover, Ahab's readiness to come to the prophet alone (after the latter has summoned him through the agency of Obadiah), forgoing the opportunity to capture Elijah, is clear proof of his agreement to speak with the prophet and even an expression of submission to him. His angry outburst, "Is it you, O troubler of Israel?" ultimately reveals the extent to which the suffering of his people as a result of the drought has troubled him, and how greatly he yearns to bring this unbearable situation to an end.

Therefore, Elijah is wise enough, in response to Ahab's offensive words, not to increase the tension between them and cause an explosion. Rather than seethe with anger over Ahab's words, he defends himself against them. Instead of dwelling on the past, he turns Ahab's comment, an expression of genuine pain over Israel's suffering, in a constructive direction: toward the present and the future. "And now" let us have a useful discussion aimed at ending the "troubling" of Israel. Since it is your and Israel's Baal worship that is the reason for the drought that is troubling Israel, let us deal with the root of the problem: "And now send forth [messengers] and gather all of Israel to me at Mount Carmel, as well as the four hundred and fifty prophets of Baal" (v. 19). Ahab, without adding a word to their exchange thus far, listens and accepts the instruction: "Ahab sent [messengers] among all of the children of Israel, and he gathered the prophets to Mount Carmel" (v. 20).

Thus Elijah redirects the confrontation between himself and Ahab from the painful and controversial past to a somewhat opaque future situation in which there will be cooperation between them, with a view to a positive solution to the suffering of the famine. The next narrative in the greater anthology of stories – the ceremony at Mount Carmel – is now ready to begin.

SUPPLEMENT: THE CONFRONTATIONS BETWEEN KING AND PROPHET IN CHAPTERS 17 AND 21 – A COMPARISON

We noted previously the need to compare the confrontation between Ahab and Elijah in our story to the next and final confrontation between them: the dramatic meeting at Naboth's vineyard (I Kings 21:17–24). This comparison will allow us to appreciate the full significance of the dialogue between the two characters in our story, and of the moral position that each of them adopts here for himself and for his opponent.

> God's word came to Elijah the Tishbite, saying: Arise, go down to meet Ahab, king of Israel who is in Samaria; behold, he is in the vineyard of Naboth, where he has gone down, to take possession of it. Speak to him, saying… Ahab said to Elijah: Have you found me, my enemy? And he said: I have found you, because you have devoted yourself to performing evil in the eyes of God. Behold, I shall bring evil upon you. (I Kings 21:17–21)

The external framework is similar in both meetings: In both cases God commands Elijah to meet Ahab. In both cases Ahab reacts to Elijah's appearance (or to his opening words) with a rhetorical question aimed at offending the prophet ("troubler of Israel"/"my enemy"), and in both cases Elijah's response to the king includes an accusation of the king concerning severe transgressions.

But, as in many other instances in Tanakh, the external similarity between the two situations conceals a fundamental contrast between them, and merely serves as a convenient opportunity for the reader to examine the contrast in greater depth.

First, the reason for the command to Elijah in each case is quite different. In chapter 18, God's command arises from His mercy: "And I will give rain upon the face of the earth"; Elijah is therefore sent to cancel his previous oath. Ahab, in this case, serves as the vehicle for the realization of this divine mercy, by virtue of the fact that he helps Elijah to guide the nation toward repentance. But in chapter 21, it is divine justice that lets its voice be heard. Elijah is sent to Ahab to tell him of the terrible punishment that will befall him and his household.

Second, Ahab's situation is quite different in each of the two occasions. In both cases the meeting takes place in a field outside the city, but the circumstances are entirely diverse. In our chapter, Ahab arouses our pity – perhaps even identification – as he forgoes his royal honor and goes out alone "in the land, to all the springs of water and to all the wadis; perhaps we shall find grass to save the horses and mules so that all our livestock will not die off" (18:5). It seems that his sense of royal responsibility for the lives of the animals that are needed for the army and for the kingdom causes him to do this.

In chapter 21, by contrast, the appearance of Ahab in the vineyard of Naboth, "to which he has gone down in order to possess it" following the murder of its owner, arouses anger and hatred toward the king who has so abused his power.

Third, and here we come to the essence of the comparison, we must examine Ahab's offensive, rhetorical question in each story. Once again we find that the questions are in fact the inverse of each other in every respect, and their inversion arises from the other differences between the two situations. In chapter 18, it is Ahab who seeks Elijah, as Obadiah testifies (v. 10); Ahab approaches Elijah (v. 17). In chapter 21, the prophet seeks out the king. Ahab certainly has no interest in meeting Elijah at that place and at that time. If, by his question in our chapter, "Is it you?" Ahab means to say, "Here, I've finally managed to find you!" his question in chapter 21, "Have you found me, my enemy?" means exactly the opposite: "You have finally managed to find me." This indicates the respective positions of Ahab and Elijah in each situation. In Naboth's vineyard it is clear to all that Ahab is the accused, while Elijah is the stern accuser. Ahab speaks strictly for himself when he calls Elijah "my enemy." He is well aware of the weakness of his position before the prophet, and his question-declaration means, "Have you finally managed to catch me in my sinfulness, O prophet who lies in wait for me, preparing for my downfall?" Elijah's decisive response is accordingly: "I have found you!" – "Indeed, you have been caught red-handed, at the height of your sinfulness, and in the very place of the sin." At that point, the prophet foretells Ahab's demise.

In our chapter, Ahab seeks Elijah and goes toward him, armed with a moral position which *he perceives* to be superior to that of the prophet; for this reason, he perceives himself as the prophet's accuser.

He, the king, is concerned for the fate of his people, collapsing under the suffering of the drought, while the "cruel" prophet who brought the drought upon them and then disappeared is the "troubler of Israel"! What his rhetorical question here means, as we have said, is: "Have you finally been good enough to appear – you, the prophet who has troubled Israel with your severe decrees, and whom I have pursued for so long?" Accordingly, Elijah's response is almost apologetic: He does not thunder against the king who has shown such disrespect, nor does he speak of any punishment. He suffices with pointing out that the actions of Ahab are the true reason for the troubling of Israel, "by your abandonment of God's commandments, and going after the Baal gods!" (18:19). The prophet then immediately moves on to propose productive cooperation between them: "And now, send and gather to me all of Israel, at Mount Carmel" (v. 20).

Chapter 9

Structure of the Drought Narrative (I Kings 17:1–18:18)

T he "drought" narrative is the first of three semi-independent
narratives that are different from one another in their literary nature and
subject, but which lead on to each other in terms of plot. These narratives stretch over chapters 17, 18 and 19. We shall address the nature of
this group of narratives and of each of its elements, as well as the flow
between each of the constituent stories, later on, in the appendix that
follows this chapter. For now, we shall suffice with a discussion concerning the dividing line between the first two stories in the collection, and
we shall accept as a given that the first story, that of the drought, concludes in chapter 18, verse 18.

One of the characteristics of the story of the drought (distinguishing it from the other two) is the fact that it is composed of "closed," well-
defined sections, to the extent that they may mistakenly be regarded as
independent literary units. In these circumstances, can we still speak of
the "structure of the story"? Can we show, in this lengthy and complex

story, that its various parts are built in a harmonious manner according to a guiding principle? In two of the episodes – Elijah at the gates of Zarephath and Elijah's revival of the widow's son, we noted that there is a common principle upon which their composition is based: Each episode is divided into two equal parts, in terms of the number of verses, with a verse or verse fragment situated in between them and serving as a central axis for that episode, with the elements symmetrically arranged around the central axis (see p. 82). Can we detect the same pattern in the story of the drought as a whole?

The story of the drought contains forty-two verses (17:1–18:18). At the center of the story, in verses 21–22 of chapter 17, we find the essential turning point of the entire story: Elijah stretching himself out over the child. His second prayer to God, as described in verse 21, indicates the turning point in his approach, leading him to be ready to cancel his oath and restore life to the famine-stricken land. God's response to Elijah's prayer and the resurrection of the dead child, as described in verse 22, are the first signs of the cancellation of the decree of drought in reality. From the beginning of the story until this turning point there are twenty verses, and from after the central verses (21–22) to the end of the story there are another twenty verses. Verses 21–22 themselves serve as the central axis of the story. The first part describes the various unsuccessful attempts to cause Elijah to retract his vow. Verse 21 reveals a turning point in the prophet's position both regarding the reality around him, which is collapsing under the hardships of the drought and which is embodied in the dead child lying on his bed, and regarding his relationship with God, to whom Elijah prays with humility to restore the child's soul.

God's response to Elijah in verse 22 opens the door to the tidings of rain, which follow soon after, in God's command to Elijah (18:1–2). In the second part of the story, the tension that characterized the first part is somewhat relieved. Already in verses 21–22, in the central axis of the plot, the tension between the prophet and God relaxes, and immediately following this the tension between the prophet and the widow is alleviated. Then comes God's command to Elijah to go to Ahab and restore the rain, thereby relieving the remaining tension between the prophet and his nation and its king. Still, the second half of the story is not altogether without tension. On his way to fulfilling God's word,

Elijah experiences some tense encounters – first with Obadiah, governor of Ahab's house, and then with Ahab himself. The function of these confrontations has been explained in the preceding chapter as being aimed at a final softening of Elijah, making him recognize the failure of his approach to date and readying him for a change in policy toward Israel from this point onward. Indeed, the measure of tension that characterizes these encounters is different from that characterizing the first half of the story. In the meeting with Obadiah, the tension dissolves immediately as Obadiah realizes that his evaluation of Elijah's intentions was mistaken, and the confrontation with Ahab quickly turns to productive cooperation, which is already the beginning of the next narrative.

Having established that the story of the drought consists of two halves of equal length straddling a central axis, we need to investigate whether a parallel exists between the secondary sections of each half and the nature of that parallel. In previous chapters we noted several such parallels; here we shall complete our discussion from the perspective of the story as a whole. The following is a schematic presentation of the structure of the story, followed by an explanation.

A: Elijah's oath before Ahab concerning the onset of drought (17:1)

   B: God's words to Elijah: "*Go from here*, head eastward, and *hide*." (vv. 2–3)

      C: The stay at Wadi Cherith until it dries up (vv. 4–7)

         D: Elijah and the widow of Zarephath (vv. 8–17)

            E: She said to Elijah: "What have I to do with you, O man of God; you have come to me to recall my sin and to put my son to death." (v. 18)
            Elijah takes the child from his mother (vv. 19–20)

               Axis: "He stretched over the boy three times, and called to God, saying: Lord my God, restore, I pray you, the soul of this boy within him." (v. 21)

"God heard the voice of Elijah; the soul of the boy
was restored within him, and he lived." (v. 22)

E': Elijah returns the boy to his mother (v. 23)
"The woman said to Elijah: Now I know that you
are a man of God, and God's word in your mouth
is true." (v. 24)

B': God's word to Elijah: "*Go and appear* before Ahab,
and I will give rain upon the face of the earth." (18:1–2)

C': Ahab and Obadiah set off to find fodder in the dried-up
wadis (vv. 3–6)

D': Elijah and Obadiah (vv. 7–15)

A': Encounter between Elijah and Ahab, aimed at ending the drought
(vv. 16–18)

On either side of the central axis we find the inverse parallel between the
woman's accusation of Elijah and his taking the child from her arms in
order to nullify her claim against him, on the one hand, and the restoration of the live boy to his mother with her monologue acknowledging
the truth of God's word in his mouth, on the other.

Surrounding the central axis as the outer framework, at the
beginning and end of the story, we find another inverse parallel
between the two meetings between Elijah and Ahab. The first meeting
is characterized by a unilateral rebuke of the king by the prophet; it
is a declaration of imminent punishment for Israel. The second meeting, although also tense, is an open dialogue between the king and the
prophet, aimed at restoring the rain to the earth; its immediate result
is cooperation between the king and Elijah. The nature of the contrast
between these two encounters resembles the nature of the previous
contrast between the two monologues delivered by the widow. But
Ahab, unlike the widow, does not change his attitude toward Elijah. A
slight change in the king's attitude may be induced only from the fact

that he walks alone toward the prophet and that he agrees to cooperate with him.

In between the sections whose parallels we have discussed above, we find several more parallels, this time direct rather than chiastic:

B-B': God's word to Elijah immediately after his oath is inversely parallel to God's command to him after he restores the boy to his mother and she expresses her acknowledgment:

> God's word came to him, saying: *Go from here*, head eastward, and *hide* at *Wadi Cherith* which faces the Jordan. (17:2–3)

> God's word came to Elijah in the third year, saying: *Go and appear* before Ahab, and I will give *rain upon the face of the earth*. (18:1)

In chapter 17 God commands Elijah to hide from Ahab; in chapter 18 He commands him to appear before Ahab. In chapter 17 the command facilitates the fulfillment of the prophet's oath concerning the drought; in chapter 18 the command comes to end the drought and annul his vow. In chapter 17 the prophet is banished – "Go from here" – to Samaria; he leaves his people for Wadi Cherith, whose name hints at the fact that it is destined to dry up. In chapter 18, God's command returns the prophet to his nation and to the capital of the kingdom, to the dried-up wadis and riverbeds that are about to be showered again with rain.

C-C': The story of the drying up of Wadi Cherith (17:4–7), following immediately after God's command to Elijah, parallels the description of the journey undertaken by Ahab and Obadiah "to all the springs of water and to all the wadis" in the Samaria vicinity, in search of grass to feed the horses and mules. This description, in turn, immediately follows God's command to Elijah to appear before Ahab. This parallel is not an inverse one: The second account is meant to intensify and broaden Elijah's own personal experience in the first, at Wadi Cherith. This teaches us that God's commands to Elijah also share the same purpose, despite their contrast. Both aim to lead Elijah to an encounter with the horrific effects of the drought and cause him to change his approach toward the Israelites. However, while at Wadi Cherith this aim was not attained, when Elijah returns to Samaria he is basically psychologically ready for this; all he needs is a little persuasion and reinforcement.

D-D': The description of Elijah's encounter with the widow at the gates of Zarephath (17:9–16) parallels the description of his encounter with Obadiah in the second half of the story (18:7–15). This parallel, once again, is not inverse. Both confrontations share the same purpose, with the second complementing the first and reinforcing the conclusion that Elijah has reached in the meantime.

Thus, the order of the parallels this time is B, C, D/B', C', D'. This is a direct order, unlike the outer parallels which create a chiasm: A, E/E', A'. These two compositional principles in the structure of the story of the drought (the chiastic parallel between the two halves in the outer sections, with the direct parallel between them in the internal sections) reflect an ambivalent relationship between the two halves of the story. On one hand, there is a relationship of contrast: In the first half, Elijah steadfastly maintains his oath, while in the second half he withdraws from this position and is prepared to change the decree. This contrast is expressed specifically in the chiastic structure. The definitive change in Elijah's position takes place at the central axis, and this is expressed in the contrast between the elements surrounding the central axis and the contrast between the beginning of the story and its conclusion.

On the other hand, the withdrawal in Elijah's position in the second half of the story is not absolute. Elijah still needs further arguments to reinforce those that he faced in the first half; these include his encounter with the God-fearing Obadiah. This characteristic of the second half is matched by its direct parallel to the first half.

Thus, both the direct parallel, illustrating the partial and gradual change that has taken place in Elijah's consciousness, and the chiastic parallel, illustrating the reversal in his position (as reflected in the widow's attitude toward him, and in the relationship between him and Ahab), pave the way for Elijah's second appearance before Ahab when they will cooperate to restore rain to the land.

Appendix – The Drought

The Complete Narrative of I Kings Chapters 17–19 and Its Components

Elijah appears for the first time at the beginning of chapter 17 in the book of Kings.[1] The story of this prophet is told in unbroken continuity over chapters 17, 18, and 19. The events develop from one to the next, and they follow a continuum of time and place. This turns these three chapters into a single narrative body. The other three stories featuring Elijah in the main role (I Kings, ch. 21: Naboth's vineyard; II Kings, ch. 1: his confrontation with Ahaziah and his emissaries; and II Kings, ch. 2: Elijah's ascent) are independent narratives, whose connection with

---

1. This appendix is really an introduction to the whole collection of stories in chapters 17–19. The reason for its placement here is that it is only in the transition from the story of the drought to the story of the test at Carmel that the reader addresses, for the first time, the question of the relationship between the different elements of the complete narrative.

one another (as well as with chapters 17–19) and with the surrounding events, is not immediately apparent.

Despite what we have said about chapters 17–19, it is difficult to regard them as truly a single story. They are more accurately described as a narrative body composed of three semi-independent units, which lead on from and complement one another. Each of the three units has its own unique subject, its own special literary nature, and its own structure. These elements give each unit an internal integrity and wholeness, but this is slightly marred by the impossibility of understanding any single unit properly without viewing it in the context of the literary body as a whole.

In light of the above, we have devoted a series of chapters to each of the three stories in chapters 17–19, as we shall do for the remaining independent narratives.

The three stories comprising the whole are:

1. The drought   17:1–18:18   (42 verses)
2. The test at Carmel   18:19–46   (28 verses)
3. The revelation at Horeb   19:1–21   (21 verses)

One of the elements common to all three is the sudden and unexpected opening. The first story starts with the sudden appearance of this unknown prophet, and the astounding oath that catches Ahab, and the readers, by surprise. The second story starts in an equally unexpected way. Once Elijah has finally met Ahab face-to-face again, we expect a speedy realization of the point of that meeting: "I will give rain upon the face of the earth" (18:1). But Elijah presents Ahab with a demand that at first makes no sense – to gather the entire nation, along with the prophets of Baal, at Carmel. This at first seems unrelated to the matter of rain. Elijah's plan will gradually unfold, over the course of the narrative, with the connection between his plan and the rain becoming clear only at the end. The third story also starts with a surprise: Jezebel's threat to Elijah's life, and his flight from her to the desert. These developments are unexpected against the background of his preceding success at Carmel.

Since we have now completed our study of the first story, let us note the following introductory comments concerning each of the three stories, both as pertains to the boundaries that we draw between them and to their connection to each other.

THE DROUGHT (17:1–18:18)

This narrative – the longest in the collection – has a dynamic nature. Elijah, the central character, is continually moving from place to place. The story appears to begin in Samaria, with Elijah's appearance before Ahab; it ends, once again close to Samaria, with another encounter between Elijah and Ahab. In between the first meeting and the second, Elijah is located at Wadi Cherith, which faces the Jordan, and in Zarephath, which is part of Sidon.

Just as the dimension of space in this story extends over great distances, the dimension of time is likewise characterized by the expression "many days" (years): The end of the story takes place in the third year after it starts (18:1). Alongside the various geographical units in which the action takes place, we can also trace the larger units of time that parallel them: Elijah spends a year at Wadi Cherith (17:7) and a year in the home of the widow of Zarephath (17:15). In the third year (18:1) he returns to Samaria, where he meets Obadiah and Ahab.

One of the most striking characteristics of the story of the drought is the clear distinction between its various composite sections. These sections are separated by more than just the dimensions of time and space; the stages of the plot and the secondary characters also play an important role in defining these boundaries.

Another characteristic of this narrative, one which pertains directly to its unique subject, is the relationship between Elijah and each of the other characters. Following his solo appearance, when he declares his oath before Ahab, the story addresses the responses of the other participants. These express their attitude toward Elijah either covertly or overtly, and their attitude is either a direct or an indirect result of his oath. In his first appearance, when he declares his oath, Elijah is the initiator; he is active. However, for most of the remainder of the story, Elijah is activated either by explicit divine commands or by the events themselves, requiring him to act as he does. The people who encounter him make various accusations, and there is considerable misunderstanding between them and him. We may summarize all of these relationships as follows:

Elijah's oath (17:1)

God	→	Elijah (17:2–9)
The widow of Zarephath	→	Elijah (17:12)
The widow of Zarephath	→	Elijah (17:18)
God	→	Elijah (18:1)
Obadiah	→	Elijah (18:9–15)
Ahab	→	Elijah (18:17)

The characteristics of the first story serve as an appropriate background for a distinction between it and the narrative of the test at Carmel – a story whose characteristics are different from, and even the opposite of, those of its predecessor.

THE TEST AT CARMEL (18:19–46)

The boundary between the first story and the second is not very sharp. Clearly, in verse 21: "Elijah approached the entire nation and said," we are already involved in the scene at Carmel. Verses 19–20 belong to the same subject, since they describe the preparations for the event: Elijah commands Ahab to gather everyone to Mount Carmel (v. 19), and Ahab does so (v. 20). On the other hand, Elijah's speech in verse 19 is a continuation of his speech in verse 18, which in turn is part of the dialogue between the prophet and the king that began in verse 17.

Between the two parts of this dialogue, we find a gentle formal distinction, which would seem to justify the "break" that we insert here: Verse 19 opens with the words, "And now." This expression indicates a halt to the fruitless discussion that preceded it, relating to the past, and a transition to a purposeful discussion oriented toward the future. Were verse 19 to begin with the words "Elijah said to Ahab: Send forth [messengers] and gather," we would have no trouble at all asserting that this verse represented the beginning of a new story. The difficulty, then, arises from the intentional insertion of the beginning of the new story in the midst of the conclusion of the previous one. This reflects a facet of the collection of stories that we are currently discussing: There is continuity and flow among the constituent stories, to the point where the boundaries between them become blurred. Nevertheless, a reader who wishes to engage in literary analysis must determine the boundaries of each story in the collection. Attention should also be paid to the fact that the structure of the story of the drought represents further proof of the proposed boundaries.

What characterizes the second story in the collection is the opposite of what characterizes the first: its geographical stability. The story starts, admittedly, with Elijah speaking to Ahab somewhere in the region of Samaria (18:19), and it ends with Elijah running in front of Ahab's chariot from Carmel to Jezreel (v. 46), but the majority of the story is bound up with Mount Carmel and with Wadi Kishon, at its foot. It is there that all of the major events take place, and even the beginning and the end of the story are related to Mount Carmel as a destination (vv. 19–20) or as a starting point (vv. 45–46).

The dimension of time, too, is contracted into a single day (assuming that we leave out the preparations described in verse 20, which apparently took a few days, but this period is not mentioned in the text), unlike the lengthy time frame of the previous story.

It is easy to see how this story may be divided into two parts. But, in contrast to the story of the drought, whose constituent units are clearly distinguished from one another in every respect, the two parts of the story at Carmel are a single continuum. The first part of the story, consisting of verses 19–29, has as its subject Elijah's proposed test and the failure of the prophets of Baal. The second part consists of verses 30–46, and its subject is the miraculous descent of the fire and its consequences.

The relationships between Elijah and the other participants in the story are different in nature from the relationships in the story of the drought. In the Carmel story, the prophet addresses his proposals, in most cases, to whomever is facing him, and they answer him with speech and, generally, with action. Only on one occasion is he met with unwillingness and silence. This contrasts with the nature of the relationships in the drought story, in which Elijah is generally on the receiving end of demands and complaints, such that he is required to defend and justify himself. In the Carmel story, Elijah becomes active; he initiates and he makes demands of others:

Elijah (v. 19) → Ahab (v. 20)	Response: action
Elijah (v. 21) → nation (v. 21)	Silent unwillingness
Elijah (vv. 22–24) → nation (v. 24)	Verbal agreement: "It is good"
Elijah (v. 25) → prophets of Baal (v. 26)	Response: action
Elijah (v. 27) → prophets of Baal (v. 28)	Response: action
Elijah (v. 30) → nation (v. 30)	Response: action
Elijah (v. 34) → nation (v. 34)	Response: action
Elijah (vv. 36–37) → God (v. 38)	Response: action
Elijah (v. 40) → nation (v. 40)	Response: action
Elijah (v. 41) → Ahab (v. 42)	Response: action
Elijah (v. 43) → his attendant (vv. 43–44)	Response: action
Elijah (v. 44) → Ahab (v. 45)	Response: action

It should be noted that the nature of the first verses, 19–20, in which Elijah makes demands of Ahab and the king responds not with words but with action, proves that they belong to the second story rather than to the first. The two preceding verses (17–18), also containing dialogue between Elijah and Ahab, are characterized by inverse relations: There Ahab "attacks," while Elijah is the defendant. This determines that verses 17–18 belong to the first story, in which the prophet is continually on the defensive.

All of these differences between the characteristics of the two stories arise, obviously, from their differing subjects. The subject of the first narrative is the debate over Elijah's path and his prolonged, stubborn upholding of his oath. The prophet's unwillingness to revoke his decree of drought is what causes the story to drag on over "many days," and also requires Elijah to move to distant places where the polemics can continue. The relationship between the prophet and those around him, in the story, is the result of that same debate. In each relationship in which Elijah is attacked or accused, we hear an additional claim in the argument against him. Elijah is forced to defend himself all the time and to find solutions that will facilitate his survival during the drought, while maintaining his stance – hence the nature of the story as a whole.

The subject of the second narrative, by contrast, is how Elijah brings Israel back to faith in God. This becomes possible only after a change in the prophet's policy (the way in which Elijah arrives at that change is the subject of the first story). In contrast to the non-uniform nature, in terms of time and space, of the ongoing debate in the first story, in the second story he brings Israel back to God through a great concentration of effort in one place and within a short time, generating a dramatic change in consciousness. Hence the "concentrated" nature of the second story. In this story Elijah is no longer attacked; he has no more reason to defend his position, neither before God nor before man, for now his prophetical policy toward Israel has changed. Now it is Elijah who makes demands, who initiates; everyone is required to obey him. Thus, the nature of the relationships between Elijah and the other characters here is the opposite of what it was in the first story.

THE REVELATION AT MOUNT HOREB (19:1–21)

In the series of chapters devoted to this episode, we shall address its structure, its unique content, and the problems regarding how it relates to the previous narrative. Here, we shall address only two issues: the transition from the second narrative (the revelation at Mount Carmel) to the third (Elijah's experiences at Horeb), and the connections between the third and each of the preceding narratives.

The boundary dividing the third story from the second is clearer than the one marking the previous transition: The harmony achieved at the end of the previous story is instantly shattered at the beginning of this story, by Ahab's report to Jezebel concerning Elijah's actions (19:1) and her threat to Elijah (v. 2).

As in the previous transition, here, too, we find both geographic and thematic continuity between the two stories. The city of Jezreel, where the previous story concludes (18:35), serves as the point of departure for this story. Likewise, the events at Carmel, and especially the elimination of the prophets of Baal at Wadi Kishon, represent the background driving the events at the beginning of our story.

The story of Elijah at Mount Horeb is closely related to the two preceding narratives, but its connection to the story of the test at Carmel differs from its connection to the story of the drought. The connection with the story of the test at Carmel is anchored mainly on the level of plot; from this perspective, it represents a direct continuation of the previous story. We cannot start at verse 1 and understand properly what transpires unless we are already familiar with the previous episode. Both Ahab's report to Jezebel and her vehement response make sense only against the background of the events described at the end of chapter 18 (from v. 40 onward).

The connection between this story and the story of the drought is mainly literary. A broad parallel exists between them:

1. Both open with an antagonistic confrontation between Elijah and the royal house. At the beginning of chapter 17, this confrontation occurs as a result of Elijah's determined oath, while in the third story, the confrontation results from a vehement oath on the part of Jezebel. But the underlying reason common to both clashes is Elijah's activity opposing Baal worship.

2. In both stories, the confrontation leads to Elijah's flight from habitation; at this point, each story focuses on what happens to Elijah during his period of solitude. Chapter 17 describes what happens to him in three distinct sections. The overt theme there is how God cares for him during the drought, so that he finds sustenance in the places where he hides. For this purpose, various miracles are performed in relation to Elijah's food. In the story in chapter 19, God once against ensures Elijah's sustenance in the wilderness to which he flees: He sends an angel to place before Elijah "a cake baked on the coals and a container of water" (19:6). The appearance of these provisions in the heart of the wilderness is not only a onetime miracle; like the parallel miracles in chapter 17, it allows Elijah an extended existence in desert conditions: "He ate and drank, and went on the strength of that meal for forty days and forty nights" (19:8).

3. In both stories, the section focusing on what happens to Elijah ends in the same way: God instructs His prophet to return to the "battlefield" and to act as a prophet. In the first story we read, "*Go* and appear before Ahab, and I will give rain upon the face of the earth" (18:1); in the third story, "*Go*, return on your way... and when you arrive, anoint Hazael... and Jehu... and Elisha" (19:15–16). Indeed,

in both cases Elijah returns to within the borders of the Kingdom of Israel and begins to act as he has been commanded, even though his method of fulfilling God's word raises exegetical questions in both cases.

Thus, both stories are characterized by a similar general progression, and this generalized parallel is at times also expressed in the details.[2] Admittedly, there are differences in the nature of the transitions between one part of the story and another: In the narrative of the drought, the transitions between the outermost, "framework" story and the events surrounding Elijah are extremely sharp, and even the episodes surrounding Elijah himself are composed of three well-defined sections. In chapter 19, by contrast, there is a continuous flow of events which develop from one to another without any clear demarcation between them.

The parallel discussed above demonstrates that, thematically, the story in chapter 19 is related to the story of the drought, despite it clearly continuing after the story of the test at Carmel in terms of plot. The similar literary form hints at a similarity of subject between the two stories: In both cases, the relationship between Elijah and God stands at the heart of the story (even though this is not always immediately apparent), and the subject under discussion is the prophet's policy concerning the nation.

THE CONNECTION BETWEEN THE THREE STORIES

Having discussed the independent and unique nature of each of the three stories comprising the narrative collection in chapters 17–19, we

---

2. It should further be noted that the two stories are also similar in terms of the geographic dimension: In both stories Elijah is constantly on the move, and in both cases he makes an almost complete circle. In the first story, he journeys from the center of the kingdom far northward, and then returns; in the third story he journeys from the center of the kingdom far southward, and then returns.

At this point, we might point out that in terms of geography, the collection of stories as a whole covers enormous distances, encompassing the entire Land of Israel. Elijah is active everywhere from Zarephath, near Sidon in the north, to Beer Sheba and Mount Horeb, in the south; and from Wadi Cherith, at the Jordan, to Mount Carmel in the west.

shall now point out what prevents each story from standing entirely alone, requiring that all three be treated as a whole.

1. The first story cannot stand independently because of its open ending. The purpose for which Elijah goes to appear before Ahab, "and I will give rain upon the face of the earth," has not yet been achieved, nor even begun. Therefore, it is impossible for a reading of this story to end with chapter 18, verse 18; we must continue to the next story to read of the realization of this goal.

2. The drought is not addressed at the occasion on Mount Carmel, nor is it mentioned explicitly even at the end of that story, when the rainfall is renewed. Nevertheless, it would seem that the second story cannot be read as an independent unit: First, the circumstances surrounding the gathering at Carmel, and the demand that Ahab bring about this gathering, are not clear to someone who begins reading only from the opening of this narrative. Second, the circumstances surrounding the rainfall at the end of the story, and the significance of this event, are likewise concealed from anyone reading this story separately from its preceding narratives. Only as a continuation of the previous story does the rain represent the end of the drought that was described there, and as a fulfillment of God's word to Elijah in the first verse of chapter 18. Third, the image of Elijah running before Ahab at the end of this story assumes its full significance only against the background of the previous harsh confrontation between them.

3. One could perhaps claim that the end of the second story represents the end of an independent unit (chapters 17–18), with no need to continue further to the third story. But here, too, the end of chapter 18 is left somewhat open. One of the characteristics of the formal conclusion of a narrative in Tanakh is the "dispersion" of the characters: "So-and-so returned to his place, and so-and-so went to his place," or "All of Israel returned to their tents," etc. Here, the story of the test at Carmel concludes, instead, by bringing together the central characters, Elijah and Ahab: "He ran before Ahab until the entrance to Jezreel" (v. 46). This unification is surprising and unnatural, even in light of the cooperation that prevailed previously between the king and the prophet. This situation arouses expectations on the

part of the reader. Clearly, the story cannot conclude here, because the factors that led to the crisis described in chapters 17–18, Jezebel, the wife of Ahab, and the house of Baal in Samaria, are still in place. Therefore, Elijah's running to Jezreel, Ahab's city, is interpreted not only as showing honor to the king and as a sign of appeasement, but also as a continuation of Elijah's prophetic supervision over him and his demand for complete amendment and repentance. How, then, does the story end? Here we embark on the third story, which unexpectedly dashes the reader's expectations.

4. The third story cannot be understood alone, for the reasons already discussed. Elijah's flight at the beginning of the story makes sense only against the background of the two previous stories, and particularly in light of the events at Mount Carmel. Elijah's despairing response, fleeing to the wilderness of Beer Sheba and seeking death, can likewise be understood only in light of the preceding narrative.

The conclusion of the third story is also open, to some extent. It fails to answer many of the reader's questions; several issues treated in the body of the story do not reach closure. But there is no continuation from here – neither in the following chapter nor in any future chapter. Therefore, the conclusion of chapter 19 should be regarded as the conclusion of the collection as a whole.

It would seem, then, that chapters 17–19 should be regarded as a single, lengthy, literary whole. At the same time, though, we should not ignore the fact that this whole is composed of three semi-independent units which differ from one another. The special nature of each unit justifies the need for a separate series of studies on each.

Carmel

וְיֵדְעוּ הָעָם הַזֶּה כִּי אַתָּה ה׳ הָאֱלֹהִים

Let this nation know that You are Lord, the God.

I Kings 18:37

Chapter 10

Was Elijah Commanded to Act as He Does?

> "Now, send forth and gather to me all of Israel, to Mount Carmel, as well as the four hundred and fifty prophets of Baal, and the four hundred prophets of the Ashera, who eat at Jezebel's table." So Ahab sent [messengers] among all the Israelites, and he gathered the prophets to Mount Carmel. (I Kings 18:19–20)

As in the opening of the story of the drought, with Elijah's first appearance (17:1), the reader is once again taken by surprise: Elijah is commanded to appear before Ahab (18:1), and this he does.[1] The meeting between the king and the prophet initially leads to a sharp, brief altercation between them: "Is that you, O troubler of Israel?" "I have not troubled Israel, but [rather] you " (vv. 17–18). Now it seems that the time has come for the remainder of God's command,

---

1. Much of this section on Carmel is based on Professor Uriel Simon's article, "Milḥemet Eliyahu BeAvodat HaBaal (Melakhim I 17–18)," first published in *Iyyunei Mikra UParshanut* (Ramat Gan, 5740), 51–118, and appearing also in his book *Keria Sifrutit BaMikra: Sippurei Nevi'im* (Jerusalem-Ramat Gan, 5757), 189–278. Where we have quoted him here, the page references are to the book.

"And I will give rain upon the face of the earth" (v. 1), to be fulfilled. We expect Elijah to announce the imminent rainfall, or at the very least, to issue some pronouncement regarding it. However, to our surprise, we hear Elijah presenting a demand to Ahab that has nothing to do with rain.

At first glance, we do not even understand the point of this demand. We can only guess at the general direction of his intentions in light of Elijah's accusation of Ahab for going after the Baal gods (v. 18), and his mention of the prophets of Baal and Ashera as being invited to the gathering at Carmel. The purpose of Elijah's initiative of gathering everyone at Carmel soon becomes apparent, when Elijah addresses the people in the following verses (21–24). But the connection between this and God's words, "And I will give rain upon the face of the earth," is not yet clear. Only at the end of the story, from verse 41 onward, does the reader understand that the point of all the preceding action was, in fact, to bring about the renewal of the rainfall. Thus, as we have noted previously, the story begins with a surprise, and only during the course of the story, stage by stage, does the reader discover the intention behind the actions performed at the beginning.

Here we must ask: Does Elijah's intention to postpone the rain, making it dependent on Israel's repentance at Carmel, conform with God's command? It would appear that not only does God's command contain no hint of the actions that the prophet proceeds to undertake, but that his actions actually contradict what God tells him. God sends him to Ahab in order to tell him that God is about to bring rain, but Elijah makes no mention of this news, nor does he even reveal to the king that he was sent by God. Instead, he turns his encounter with Ahab into a means of assembling the nation and the prophets of Baal for a test that he plans to hold at Carmel. We must therefore ask: What would Elijah do if the nation, or the prophets of Baal, were to refuse the test that he proposes, or if the nation did not engage in repentance at the sight of the fire descending from heaven? Would the rain then be withheld? What, then, would happen to God's words, "And I will give rain upon the face of the earth"? How can Elijah make the rainfall dependent on the behavior of the nation, thereby placing God's promise of the rain's renewal in question?

A deeper and more precise analysis of God's words reveals that we have understood them inaccurately. Elijah is not told to "Go and appear before Ahab and *tell him*, 'So says the Lord: I will give rain upon the face of the earth.'" Rather, "Go and appear before Ahab and I will give rain upon the face of the earth." (v. 1)

The implied connection between the two parts of this instruction, turning the second part, "and I will give rain," into an announcement that is supposed to be passed on to Ahab, has no basis in the actual language of the text. Admittedly, it is clear that God's promise to give rain is the ultimate purpose of the appearance before Ahab, but the act of appearing before him and the achievement of its purpose, rain, may be separated by several intermediate stages. Moreover, there may be different ways of connecting them.

On the question of the relationship between the two parts of God's command, Abrabanel comments: "Go, appear before Ahab in such a way that he will entreat you, and you will pray, *in order that the rain may be brought about by you.*" What is the point of this? Why can the rain not be brought immediately? Abrabanel answers: "Because I wish to give rain upon the land, *but out of honor to you I do not wish to give it except by your hand and by your word.*"

Thus, God's command reflects consideration for the prophet's dignity; God is careful to honor Elijah's oath concerning the drought. Although God wants to restore the rain immediately, He wants Elijah to be a full and active partner in that process, in order that the rain will come about by the prophet's word, as he had decreed, "Except by my word" (17:1).

Malbim, on the other hand, relates the two parts of the command differently:

> He commanded him to appear before Ahab *and to try to cause Israel to repent*, such that they would recognize God's power, as in fact happened afterward, when they said, "God is Lord," as it is written (Jer. 14:22): "Are there any, among the worthless gods of the nations, who can bring rain? [Or can the heavens bring showers? Are You not the One, O Lord our God; so we put our hope in You, for You have done all these things"] and thereby, "I will give rain."

It would seem that Malbim's interpretation is the more compelling approach. First, the continuation of the story supports his explanation, as Malbim himself points out ("as in fact happened afterward"). Second, according to Malbim, God's command does not take the prophet's dignity into consideration, but rather the possibility of using the drought, which has already undoubtedly had some effect on the national psyche, to prepare the nation's heart for the prophet's new initiative to lead them toward repentance. Why not exploit this situation before restoring the rain? Is it proper that the rain be restored while the nation remains mired in its deplorable religious and moral state?[2]

Ralbag discusses this last consideration in his explanation of Elijah's actions in our story as not having been carried out by divine command:

> "And by Your word I have done all of these things" (v. 36): Even if our understanding is that God did not command him concerning this, he may still claim that he did it by God's word, because He told him to appear before Ahab and that He would give rain upon the face of the earth. *But it would not be right for rain to be given upon the face of the earth while [the people] still maintained their wickedness,* for then the cessation of rain would lose the whole purpose for which it had come about, that is, so they would return from their evil ways. If this were to be [that the rain would commence while they were still wicked], they would say that [the drought] just happened, coincidentally, not because of their sins. *Thus it was necessary that he first do something that would cause them to repent, to whatever degree possible, and then they would acknowledge that it was their sins that had brought about the drought.*

According to this view, God's command to Elijah was meant not only to overturn the prophet's oath and to make him change his own course,

---

2. This explanation of God's command at the beginning of chapter 18 allows us to understand Elijah's actions in our story, aimed at leading the nation toward repentance, as his own initiative, but with the aim of realizing God's command and all that is alluded to in it. Indeed, Radak, Ralbag, and Abrabanel all tend toward the view that Elijah acts here at his own discretion.

but also as a hint to Elijah regarding the *new path* that he was to adopt toward that purpose: to bring Israel to repentance. This was not to be a complete nullification of Elijah's previous approach, but rather a command regarding a new tactic that would employ the achievements of the past for the purpose of the same ultimate aim.

Hence, Elijah was not commanded to perform the specific actions that he undertook. On the other hand, not only did his actions not contradict God's word, but they represent the realization of what was hinted at in the command: That the situation that had been created be used for a positive effect, and that Elijah cooperate with Ahab, in order that God could give rain, as appropriate once Israel had repented. According to this conclusion, Elijah's actions in our story are similar to his actions at the gates of Zarephath. Although Elijah acts on his own initiative in invoking a miracle concerning the jar of flour and the bottle of oil, he remains within the framework of the divine command, which gives him a wide berth for independent action in order to fulfill that command.

However, there is an important difference between these two incidents. The purpose of Elijah's act of invoking the miracle at the gates of Zarephath was to facilitate his own survival during the famine (as God promised him). His actions here are aimed at fulfilling his prophetic mission for the benefit of Israel: To bring them back to God, and thereby restore the rain.

Elijah's actions as described in our story are therefore the most important of all his prophetic endeavors thus far. On the one hand, they reflect something of the prophet's own initiative; on the other hand, they are aimed at realizing God's word and fulfilling His aim of "And I will give rain upon the face of the earth." Thus, these actions represent a partnership between God and His prophet, sharing the same purpose: To restore Israel to God and to restore God's kindness to Israel.

"BY YOUR WORD I HAVE DONE ALL OF THESE THINGS"

The conclusion that Elijah's actions were undertaken on his own initiative, but as an active partner in realizing the divine plan, depends, to a great extent, on our interpretation of a verse that appears later in the

story: a clause from Elijah's prayer for fire to descend from heaven onto
the altar that he has built:

> Lord God of Abraham, Isaac, and Israel: today let it be known
> that You are God in Israel, and I am Your servant, *and by your*
> *word I have done all of these things.* (v. 36)

"These things" to which Elijah refers apparently include not only the
present act – offering a sacrifice upon the altar at Mount Carmel,
with the expectation that God's fire will descend from heaven and
consume it – but undoubtedly all of Elijah's activities in our story:
the gathering of the nation and the prophets of Baal at Carmel; his
proposal of the test; his goading of the prophets of Baal, causing them
to intensify their call to their god; and the series of actions aimed
at bringing about the fire's descent. However, given the absence of
any record of a command, since we have already concluded that all
these actions were performed at Elijah's own initiative, how are we
now to interpret this declaration: "*And by your word* I have done all
of these things"?

Radak comments as follows:

> The meaning of the expression "by Your word" is: Let them not
> say that I did all that I did on my own account, and that all the
> times when I performed miracles, they were instances of witch-
> craft or magic. If You answer me with fire descending from the
> heavens, they will know that all that I do is *with Your approval,*
> *and out of my faith in You.*

Thus Radak understands "by Your word" as referring not to an explicit
divine command, but rather to divine approbation.

Abrabanel provides a different interpretation:

> When [Elijah] says, "By Your word," he does not mean that he
> did it by divine command, but rather that he did it *for the glory of*
> *God's name, and for the sake of the Torah, which is His word.* And
> thus we learn in the Midrash (*Tanḥuma, Naso* 28), that Elijah did

what he did for the sake of God's name, as it is written, "By Your word [namely, *for* Your word] I have done it."

The Baal HaMetzudot adopts Abrabanel's approach (as he usually does), but clarifies it somewhat: "'By Your word,'" meaning… Are not all the things that I did… *in order that they will observe Your word*? I did not do them for my own sake."

The latter two commentators (in contrast to Radak) agree that "Your word" means "Your commandments," or "Your Torah," and both alter the meaning of the letter *bet* that prefixes the word *devarekha* (Your word) so that it means not *by* Your word, but rather *for the sake of* Your word. This interpretation changes the entire meaning of Elijah's remark. Elijah here speaks not about the source of authority for his actions, but rather about their purpose: To bring Israel to observance of God's commandments, which are "His word."[3]

Finally, let us return to the beginning of Ralbag's explanation, which we addressed above:

> "And by Your word I have done all of these things" (v. 36): Even if our understanding is that God did not command him concerning this, he may still claim that he did it by God's word, *because He told him to appear before Ahab and that He would give rain upon the face of the earth*. But it would not be right for rain to be given upon the face of the earth while [the people] still maintained their wickedness.

Unlike the other commentators we have cited here, Ralbag understands Elijah's statement on its simplest and most literal level: "By Your word" – "by Your command," and this "even if our understanding is that God did not command him concerning this." Since the prophet's actions, undertaken on his own initiative, are aimed at fulfilling God's command *in the spirit in which it was intended*, we may say that they are done "by God's

---

3. This interpretation is well suited to the written form (the *ketiv*) of Elijah's formulation, which is in the plural form: literally "Your words," Your commandments, written in the Torah.

word," even if not all this is explicit in the command. Interpretation of God's command "Go and appear before Ahab, and I will give rain upon the face of the earth" (v. 1) on a profound level, requires that several actions be inserted between appearing before Ahab and the giving of rain, all aimed at bringing Israel to repentance. The choice of these actions is left to the prophet; it is up to him to decide upon the most effective way to achieve the nation's repentance in these circumstances.

This is the source of the prophet's power, and hence his glory: He is a partner with God in bringing Israel to repentance. But this is also the source of his weakness: When it comes to actions that lack a clear divine stamp, actions which even the prophet himself will not claim to have been commanded to perform, the people can easily argue that they are not performed by God's word and do not reflect His will, having rather been contrived by the prophet. Only God's response to the prophet's initiative in a clearly miraculous revelation that astounds and terrifies all who see it can negate such a claim against the prophet. Elijah therefore prays, "Today let it be known that You are God in Israel, *and I am Your servant."*

In other words: Let it be known that all my actions are performed by "Your servant" – not for my honor or the honor of my father's house, but rather as part of my role as a servant of God, always ready to perform Your will. And since this is the definition of the prophetic role, "*By Your word* I have done all of these things."

Elijah is like a servant whose master relies on his judgment, leaving him in charge of running his affairs. Therefore, all the servant's actions performed within the framework of his role are meant only to perform his master's will and to fulfill his word, even if he decides upon specific courses of action independently, without explicit instruction.

Chapter 11

Elijah Addresses the Nation (I Kings 18:21–24)

REBUKE AND SILENCE

Elijah's address to the people gathered at Mount Carmel consists of two stages. First, he issues a brief, harsh condemnation:

> Elijah came near to all the people and said: How long will you go on lurching between two opinions (*se'ipim*)? If the Lord is God, follow Him; if Baal, follow him. And the people answered him not a word. (v. 21)

Many commentators address the question with which Elijah's rebuke opens. We shall follow the opinion of Rashi, Radak, and others who interpret the word *se'ipim* as "opinions" (or views).[1] "Lurching between two opinions" means jumping from one to the other and back, believing

---

1. There are other places in Tanakh where we find the word *se'ipim* appearing in different forms. In most cases, the word is used in the sense of "thoughts" – see Psalms 94:19, 119:113, 139:23; Job 20:2.

     In biblical Hebrew, the root *samekh-ayin-peh* denotes the branch of a tree: "All the birds of the sky made their nests in its boughs (*bise'apotav*)" (Ezek. 31:6). The

alternately in God and in Baal. This would mean that Elijah's audience had not abandoned the service of God, but do not serve Him faithfully and exclusively. They have attached elements of Baal worship to their worship of God, oblivious to the contradiction inherent in maintaining both forms of worship simultaneously.

Elijah demands that the nation choose between these two contradictory modes of worship. As Ḥazal explain (*Midrash Tehillim* 119:113): "He said: *You cannot hold the rope at both ends*; decide today whom you want to worship."

Attention should be paid to Elijah's careful choice of language: The two alternatives that he presents are not formulated in precisely parallel terms. Only concerning God does Elijah mention the word "Lord." He mentions no term of divinity when he speaks of Baal, even though the syntax of his sentence suggests the parallel. From this we can learn that if a person is going to say something that is not true, even if the circumstances require that the words be uttered, he should still endeavor, to whatever extent possible, not to actually verbalize a false statement.

Helping the nation to make this decision is Elijah's task at Carmel, as the continuation of the story demonstrates. Meanwhile, his words of condemnation so far are not powerful enough to lead them to that decision, and Elijah is certainly aware of this. He is met with silence: "The people answered him not a word." Because, in all honesty, what can they say? Are these words alone enough to trigger a revolution in their thinking?

SUGGESTION OF THE TEST AND ITS ACCEPTANCE

Elijah's first monologue is merely an introduction to the test, which he proposes, in the second stage of his speech:

> Elijah said to the people: "I alone remain a prophet to God, while the prophets of Baal number four hundred and fifty men. Let two bulls be given to us. They shall choose one bull for themselves

---

Baal HaMetzudot, commenting on our verse, writes that the term *se'ipim* here is "a metaphor borrowed from the branch of a tree, for the opinions (thoughts) are to the heart as a branch is to the tree."

and cut it into pieces and place it upon the wood, without placing
any fire. I shall prepare the other bull, placing it upon the wood,
without placing any fire. Then you will call out in the name of your
god, and I shall call out in the name of the Lord. And the God
who will answer with fire, He is God." All the nation answered
and said, "It is good." (vv. 22–24)

The people who have been alternating between the two options, unable
to decide on their position, are now being called upon to judge the contest that Elijah proposes between himself, the sole representative of the
prophets of God and those who have remained completely faithful to
Him, and the four hundred and fifty prophets of Baal, representing the
opposite view. The nation is called upon to accept the results in advance,
whichever way the matter will be decided.[2]

In the midst of his remarks to the nation, Elijah addresses the
prophets of Baal directly for the first time, telling them, "You will call
out in the name of your god." Clearly, these words cannot be understood
as an appeal to the nation: Elijah does not claim that the nation has
exchanged God for other deities. He addresses the prophets of Baal in
the midst of his speech to the nation in order not to appear to be forcing the challenge and its conditions upon his opponents by not discussing it with them first. He does not want to be perceived as making an
agreement with the nation while ignoring the prophets of Baal, and he
therefore addresses them directly.

But in truth, this appeal to the false prophets is merely lip service.
Elijah has no intention of endangering his plan with a possible refusal

---

2. We might compare the test proposed by Elijah to the one that Moses proposes to
Korah and his company (Num. 16:5–7). This test, too, is proposed at Moses's own
initiative rather than at God's command (see Nahmanides, Num. 16:5). There, too,
the test entails fire either descending from heaven or not descending, but the situation there is reversed: the fire that comes down strikes the sinners and consumes
them, while Aaron is left unharmed. The main difference between the two scenes
lies in the purpose of the test: Moses seeks to establish, by means of the test, who
has been chosen by God and who are the unlawful pretenders to the role of high
priest, and who should be punished. Elijah, by contrast, seeks to prove who is God
and who is not. The other discrepancies between the two episodes stem from this
fundamental difference.

to cooperate on the prophets' part. Therefore, he makes a dual appeal: to the nation (vv. 22–23), and, as a direct continuation, to the prophets of Baal (v. 24). He foresees the nation's positive response, and indeed it comes quickly: "All the nation answered and said, 'It is good.'"

Following the nation's positive response, the false prophets' acceptance actually becomes redundant; it is taken for granted. How could they possibly refuse? All Elijah needs to do now is to arrange with them the details of the test (v. 25).

In this spirit, Abrabanel comments:

> The text does not record that the prophets of Baal gave the same response ("It is good"); [in fact,] they did not answer at all. They thought it a bad idea to accept the challenge, but the nation had already answered, "It is good."

Further on, Abrabanel continues:

> Why did the prophets of Baal agree to this test, given that it was dangerous for them? Because they were forced to. Once they saw that the entire nation had answered, "It is good," they had no way out; they could not argue and extricate themselves from the test, because the nation would stone them.

As in his opening words to the nation (v. 21), when proposing his test, Elijah is again careful not to disturb the balance between the two alternatives facing the people. But while in the first stage of his speech this is achieved through a simple rhetorical device, such that everyone understands quite clearly what Elijah means when he says, "If God is the Lord...and if Baal," here his intention is to ensure that the test remains fair. Therefore, the balance here is expressed in the emphasis on the egalitarian relationship between Elijah, who proposes the test, and the prophets of Baal, his opponents.

Moreover, in proposing his test first to the people (v. 22), and then to the false prophets themselves (v. 25), Elijah repeatedly highlights the numerical superiority of the false prophets in relation to himself. At the outset, he presents the challenge with the words, "I alone remain a prophet to God, while the prophets of Baal number four hundred and fifty." Why does he say this? We understand the reason in light of his remarks to the false prophets later on: "Choose yourselves one bull and prepare it first, *for you are the majority*" (v. 25).

This, then, is a gesture of magnanimity; it is an open recognition on the part of the individual that the majority is entitled to a certain privilege. Elijah therefore allows the false prophets to do everything first: to choose their bull, to prepare it as a sacrifice (v. 23), and to call upon their god (v. 24).

In so doing, Elijah ensures himself an image of fairness and courtesy. However, it is doubtful whether this is his only, or even his principal, aim. In inviting his opponents to perform all their actions first, Elijah actually prepares a trap for them: He needs their abysmal failure as a vital preface to his own dramatic success. His objective will be achieved by both stages, and specifically in the sequence that he arranges them. His generous offer, which he justifies based on the false prophets' constituting the majority, is simply a cover for his true intentions. We shall address this point in greater detail in future sections; here we shall pay attention only to the linguistic arrangement of Elijah's "fair presentation" to the people. He does not say, "I am the only prophet of God here, while the prophets of Baal number four hundred and fifty," which would be an accurate description of the situation. Rather, he asserts, "*I alone remain* a prophet to God." In other words, Elijah not only makes note of the numerical discrepancy, but also hints at the circumstances of this discrepancy: "I am the sole prophet of God who remains, following Jezebel's persecutions and elimination of the other true prophets in the kingdom.[3] I am a persecuted prophet representing a downtrodden sector, while the four hundred and fifty prophets of Baal are representatives of the royal establishment; they 'eat at Jezebel's table.'" A sensitive reading detects the blatant lack of equality between the two sides: between the many persecutors and the lone prey, between the complacent aggressors and the weak, isolated victim. This perspective serves only to intensify Elijah's victory and to amplify its significance.

---

3. The prophets who are hiding in the cave are not counted, since they are no longer active as prophets, and thus we might say that their prophetic activity ceased as a result of Jezebel's persecution.

WHY DOES ELIJAH NOT MENTION THE DROUGHT?

The question of why Elijah makes no mention of the drought lurks throughout the story of the test at Carmel. Even at the end of the story, when the rain finally arrives, it is not described as being explicitly connected to the drought and the suffering. This lack of mention of the drought is especially troubling in the context of the two-stage dialogue that Elijah conducts with the nation at the beginning of the gathering at Carmel. The drought and consequent famine are the background to Ahab's agreement to cooperate with Elijah in gathering the people at Carmel, and appear also to be the background to the nation's eager response to this invitation. Why, then, does Elijah not "exploit" the success achieved through the drought by mentioning it explicitly? After all, when Elijah comes to rebuke Israel for "lurching between two opinions," he could invoke the drought as proof that it was God who brought the famine, while Baal and his prophets had been unable to bring rain throughout these years.

It would seem that despite the contribution of the drought toward the softening of the nation's and particularly Ahab's stance, the subject is too sensitive for Elijah to enlist it in an attempt to draw near to the people, and to bring them closer to himself. The terrible suffering that the people have endured (and which, at this stage, shows no signs of abating), has given rise to harsh accusations and feelings of animosity toward Elijah, as being the person responsible for the dreadful situation. Elijah has inferred this state of affairs from all his encounters since the declaration of his oath, and throughout the story of the drought: with the widow of Zarephath (who, admittedly, was unaware of the fact that Elijah was responsible for the famine); with Obadiah, representing the God-fearing public; and especially with Ahab, who called Elijah the "troubler of Israel." Now, as Elijah embarks on a new path in bringing the nation to repentance, his approach is now clearly a conciliatory one: "Elijah *came near* to all the people" (v. 21).

Elijah's dual appeal to the people (vv. 21–24) contains no hint of the belligerence that characterized his attitude toward Ahab in the previous story. His approach here takes into account the spiritual level of the people. Elijah does not come to them with complaints and accusations. Mentioning the drought here, at Carmel, would boomerang and sabotage his objective: To restore the nation to belief in God in a conciliatory manner, rather than through harsh condemnation and drastic measures.

Chapter 12

Elijah Addresses the Prophets of Baal (I Kings 18:25–29)

ELIJAH'S TWO PROPOSALS: THE DIFFERENCES

Already in his address to the nation, when Elijah proposes the test between himself and the prophets of Baal (vv. 22–24), he includes an appeal to the false prophets: "You will call out in the name of your god" (v. 24). However, he does not wait for their response, and the people, who respond with enthusiasm to his proposal ("They said, 'It is good'"), obligate them to agree (as discussed in greater detail in the previous chapter).

Now, having obtained their agreement, Elijah addresses the false prophets separately:

> Elijah said to the prophets of Baal: Choose one bull for yourselves and prepare it first, for you are the majority; and call out in the name of your god, but do not apply any fire. (v. 25)

Is this proposal identical to the one previously presented to the entire nation (including the false prophets)? Let us compare them:

Proposal to the nation (vv. 23–24)	Proposal to the prophets of Baal (v. 25)
1. "Let two bulls be given to us;	
2. they shall choose one bull for themselves	1. "Choose one bull for yourselves
3. and cut it into pieces, and place it upon the wood	2. and prepare it first, for you are the majority;
4. but they shall not apply any fire.	3. and call out in the name of your god
5. And I shall prepare the other bull, and place it upon the wood	
6. and I shall apply no fire.	
7. Then you will call out in the name of your god	4. but do not apply fire."
8. and I shall call out in the name of the Lord."	

The proposal as presented to the nation includes eight stages, while the prophets of Baal are presented with only four. Even these four fundamental elements differ from their parallel counterparts. Let us list all the omissions and changes:

1. The proposal to the prophets of Baal omits the first stage as presented to the nation – "let two bulls be given to us." Perhaps because, by this stage in the events, the bulls were already before them, and they needed only to choose between them.

2. Stage 3 of the proposal to the nation corresponds to stage 2 of the proposal to the prophets, but the latter is condensed in one aspect and expanded in another. The carving of the bull and placing its limbs on the wood is condensed into a single word: *Vaasu* (you shall prepare it). On the other hand, Elijah explains why they will prepare their bull first (as well as having first choice of the bull): "For you are the majority." This elaboration has a parallel in his words to the nation, in verse 22, which precedes his detailed proposal: "I alone remain a prophet to God, while the prophets of Baal number four hundred

and fifty." This verse is a justification for requiring the false prophets to perform every stage of the proposal first. Now, in addressing the prophets themselves, Elijah includes this justification within his proposal.

3. The original order of the proposal is reversed. In the proposal to the nation (stage 4), the noting of the fact that no fire will be applied to the sacrifice, precedes the mention of the false prophets calling out to their god (stage 7). But in his address to the prophets themselves, Elijah first describes them calling out to their god, and only afterward tells them that they will apply no fire. His intention seems to be to combine the calling to Baal and the preparation of the sacrifice into a single, continuous act; only after the description of this act as a whole is it appropriate to note what will *not* be done. This discrepancy serves as preparation for the following principal and most striking difference between the two proposals.

4. Stages 5, 6, and 8 of the proposal to the nation are omitted from Elijah's proposal to the false prophets. The explanation for this would seem to be that these stages all pertain to Elijah's own actions; therefore, they have no place in his address to the prophets. But this raises a problem: Elijah's original proposal gives the impression that his own actions are meant to be combined with the actions of the false prophets, such that the "calling out" of both sides takes place simultaneously. Why, then, does Elijah omit his part in the action, corresponding to the actions of the prophets of Baal?

We may answer this question by referring to Abrabanel:

> Elijah misled them when he said, "Let two bulls be given to us … then you will call out in the name of your god, and I shall call out in the name of the Lord." *They thought that they and Elijah would offer up their sacrifices together.* … But Elijah, seeing that they were acquiescing and had no possibility of avoiding this test, then corrected what they had understood from his deception, by saying, "Choose one bull for yourselves and prepare it first." In other words, *they would not prepare their sacrifices together, for there would be no way of distinguishing the truth from falsehood*

unless each group prepared its sacrifice separately. Therefore he said, "and prepare it first."

In his first address, Elijah is careful to preserve a perfect balance between himself and his opponents. But once the latter are already irreversibly committed, he is able to diverge slightly from this strict balance. He introduces a "technical" correction into his original plan which, from the nation's point of view, seems logical – their attention should not be divided between two actions taking place simultaneously; rather, they should be able to concentrate on each separately. This "correction" fits in with Elijah's general plan, whose success requires that the false prophets be met with failure before God answers his own call.

THE FALSE PROPHETS' FIRST FAILURE

Elijah presents his proposal to the prophets of Baal, and they respond:

> They took the bull which was offered to them, and prepared it, and they called out in the name of Baal from morning until noon, saying: "Baal, answer us!" But there was no voice, nor any answer, and they capered around the altar which had been made. (v. 26)

Does their response match the original proposal in every detail? Let us compare:

Elijah's proposal (v. 25)	False prophets' action (v. 26)
"Choose for yourselves one bull	"They took the bull which was offered to them
and prepare it first...	and prepared it
and call out in the name of your god"	and they called out in the name of Baal"

The number of stages and the order of their appearance are identical, but the discrepancy in the first stage stands out starkly. Elijah emphasized, both in his words to the nation (v. 23 – "*They shall choose* one bull *for themselves*") and in his direct appeal to the false prophets (v. 25 – "*Choose* one bull *for yourselves*"), their right to choose the bull they wanted first. This has significance for the success of the test: Elijah wants to prevent any possible claim that they were given a blemished bull and that it was for this reason that their sacrifice failed. However, when it comes to the test itself, we are seemingly told exactly the opposite: "They took the bull *which was given* (or "which he gave") *to them*" – implying that Elijah selected the bull and gave it to them. This contradicts the offer that he himself made twice, as well as running counter to the attempt to preclude any after-the-fact complaints on their part!

On the literal level, Rabbi Kiel[1] appears to solve this problem by interpreting this phrase in the general sense: "'which was given to them' (by whomever gave it) – referring to the people who brought the bulls to Mount Carmel."

For half a day, "from the morning until noon," the false prophets persist in their efforts to obtain some response from Baal. They try to achieve this in two ways. First, through prayer: "They called out in the name of Baal ... saying, 'Baal, answer us!'" (v. 26); second, through bizarre worship rites: "They capered around the altar[2] which had been made."[3]

But none of this has any effect. In contrast to their cry, "Baal, answer us!" the result is that "there was no voice, *nor any answer.*"

To all those present at Mount Carmel, as well as to us, the readers, the failure of the false prophets appears to have been demonstrated beyond any doubt. Now, with noon having passed, it seems that the time has come for Elijah to prove his faith in God. But Elijah has other ideas. He conducts himself in a relaxed manner, as someone who has time on his side and is in no rush to exploit the failure of the false prophets, his opponents, and push them off the stage. With astounding and noble generosity – of the sort that expresses absolute self-confidence – he offers his opponents another opportunity.

---

1. *Daat Mikra.*
2. Rashi comments, "They danced around their altar in accordance with their rites."
3. This formulation comes to highlight the contrast between the altar of the prophets of Baal, which "had been made" by whoever had built it, and God's altar at Carmel, which was in ruins, and which Elijah now had to repair (v. 30).

"AND ELIJAH MOCKED THEM"

> It was noontime, and Elijah mocked them, saying: Call out in a
> loud voice, for he is a god! Either he is musing, or easing him-
> self, or he is on a journey; perhaps he is sleeping, and must be
> wakened! (18:27)

This offer that Elijah presents is not for a brief extension; it lasts "until
midday had passed ... until the *minḥa* offering" (v. 29). Radak explains,
"until the time of the *minḥa* sacrifice"; the Baal HaMetzudot elucidates,
"always offered at twilight." Thus, the false prophets were given an extension of several hours, until nearly nightfall.

Elijah's motives for this exceptional generosity are quite clear. It
is a continuation of the generosity he has shown throughout, starting
with the original suggestion to the nation that the test be held, followed by his proposal to the false prophets themselves with certain
changes. So long as the possibilities for failure of the false prophets
have not been completely exhausted, Elijah will continue to "give in"
to them as much as he is able. He will encourage them to be first in
everything, so they will have maximum public attention focused on
them for the longest possible time. Similarly, he encourages them to
intensify their religious efforts even beyond those they originally performed. The greater and more resounding their defeat, the greater the
victory reaped by Elijah, even before commencing his own actions.
The false prophets become Elijah's unwilling allies in proving the futil-
ity of Baal. Through his show of generosity and the "advice" that he
offers, Elijah turns them into his active partners. By constantly obeying his words, they are led, as though hypnotized, into the trap that
he has set for them.

If this is indeed Elijah's intention in all of his actions, he
seems, out of an excess of self-confidence, to reach the point of
endangering his own objectives in the type of advice that he offers
them. What is the meaning of the expression "Elijah mocked them
(*vayehatel bahem*)," and what does Elijah mean by describing Baal's
various possible occupations that might cause him to miss the cry
of his prophets?

The verb *ḥet-tav-lamed* is interpreted even by the earliest commentators as an expression of mocking and scorn.[4] *Targum Yonatan:* "Elijah *laughed at them.*"

But this interpretation raises an obvious problem. Surely the prophets of Baal, sensing the scorn in Elijah's words and seeing that he is making a mockery of them and their god in the eyes of the entire gathering at Carmel, would react in precisely the opposite manner to that intended by Elijah. They would likely abandon the test, ceasing their efforts at this noon hour, leaving Elijah without the fruits of the second half of their doomed endeavor. This would seem to be most likely, since derision and sarcasm usually have the effect of weakening the resolve of those at whom they are directed.

Furthermore, they would have good reason to give up at this point. Were they to continue in their efforts after Elijah's mockery of them, they would be seen to be following his scornful advice, thereby making themselves into objects of even more derision in the eyes of the public.

Indeed, in the text's description of the continuation of their actions, there is an emphasis on their precise adherence to his advice. He tells them, "Call out in a loud voice" (v. 27), and they "called out in a loud voice" (v. 28). Is it reasonable to posit that they would act in this way, following his scornful advice and thereby turning themselves into the laughingstock of the nation?

Abrabanel and the Baal HaMetzudot note this difficulty, but offer no solution. Ralbag, in his first interpretation of Elijah's words in verse 27, adopts a different approach. He attempts to interpret Elijah's suggestion as a reasonable one from the point of view of the Baal worshippers. As such, "The prophets of Baal believed him, and cried out in a loud voice, for this was their way in such circumstances as those suggested by Elijah.... This is a most acceptable explanation

---

4. Josephus, in his *Antiquities of the Jews*, Book VIII, par. 339, paraphrases our verse with the words "Elijah mocked them, and said that they should cry out loudly to their gods." Radak, Ralbag, and Malbim offer similar interpretations. In a similar vein, some of the commentators explain Elijah's suggestions of the possible occupations that are keeping Baal from answering his followers as jesting and ridicule.

here." In other words, Elijah spoke to the false prophets not in a derisive way, but rather in accordance with their beliefs. Indeed, the prophets believed his suggestion that perhaps Baal was sleeping or busy; they really believed that calling out in a loud voice would wake him and cause him to respond.

This exegetical approach to the verse is also to be found among some contemporary scholars, who find support for their thesis in mythological texts of the Ancient Near East, discovered in the last few generations.[5] Indeed, anyone with even the most superficial familiarity with the mythologies of ancient peoples would agree that Elijah's words would not seem unrealistic to his listeners.

If this is the case, what is the meaning of the word *vayehatel*? Uriel Simon notes that the principal meaning of the root *heh-tav-lamed* or *tav-lamed-lamed* is "to lie," not "to scorn."[6] He brings proof from all the appearances of this root in Tanakh.[7]

Thus, it is not with scorn that Elijah addresses the prophets of Baal, but rather with guile. He tells them things that from his own point of view are ludicrous, but for them these words have meaning. His listeners will act on his suggestion, never suspecting that they are making themselves a laughingstock in the eyes of the audience.

Still, we should examine this matter more closely. Were Elijah merely to mention Baal's various possible occupations, but nothing more, we could conclude that the background to his suggestion is ancient Canaanite mythology (which is known to us, to some extent, today). But Elijah prefaces his words with the phrase "for he is a god!" This must be understood as being uttered with irony. Simon[8] states:

> Elijah could not have said of Baal, "for he is a god," without the tone of his voice clearly expressing his meaning: "in your opinion." The word *vayehatel* is therefore a literary substitute for a derisive tone of voice.

---

5. See M. D. Cassuto, *HaEla Anat* (Jerusalem, 5711), 40; B. Oppenheimer, *HaNevua HaKeduma BeYisrael* (Jerusalem, 5733), 204–6.
6. *Keria Sifrutit BaMikra*, 225–26.
7. For example, "Behold, you have deceived me (*hetalta bi*) and told me lies" (Judges 16:10, 13, 15). See also Genesis 31:7; Exodus 8:25; and elsewhere.
8. *Keria Sifrutit BaMikra*, 225–26.

Simon then continues:

> Let us now try to paraphrase Elijah's words to the prophets of
> Baal: "Shout out louder to Baal ('Call out in a loud voice'), for,
> according to what you say, he has the power to answer you ('for
> he is a god'). If he has not answered you thus far, it is because
> he is busy ('he is musing, or easing himself'), or far away ('or on
> a journey'), 'or perhaps fast asleep'; but if you raise your voices,
> he may answer you ('he will awaken')." The rationality of Elijah's
> words, from an idolater's point of view, ensures that the proph-
> ets of Baal will comply: "They called out in a loud voice" (v. 28).
> At the same time, the ironical derision allows God's prophet to
> address, at the same time, the congregation standing about, pre-
> paring them for the imminent downfall of Baal, by exposing him
> for what he is. It is clearly meaningless to explain the embarrass-
> ing silence of this non-god – to whom four hundred and fifty
> of his prophets are crying out with all their strength – in terms
> of a temporary absence or sleep. The true God, who is going to
> respond with fire to His single prophet before their very eyes,
> "neither slumbers nor sleeps"; He does not travel, He is never far
> away. It is only from His hand that evil and good come to you.
> When the prophets of Baal raised their voices, in the wake of
> Elijah's encouragement, they gave their (once again unwilling)
> approval to participate in this test of their faith. The Baal who
> has not answered the great cry of his prophets at such a fateful
> hour of need – he has ears, but does not hear!

THE FALSE PROPHETS' SECOND FAILURE

> They called out in a loud voice, and cut themselves according to
> their custom, with knives and lances, until blood poured out upon
> them. And it was, when midday had passed, that they prophesied
> until the time for offering the *minha* sacrifice, but there was no
> voice, nor any answer, nor any regard. (vv. 28–29)

The second effort on the part of the false prophets to extract some
response from Baal, lasting "when midday had passed… until… the

offering of the *minḥa* evening sacrifice," comprises two types of actions: prayer and magical-ecstatic rituals that characterize their form of service. In both areas there is a noticeable intensification of their actions compared to their efforts in the morning:

	First effort (v. 26)	Second effort (v. 28)
Calling out	*They called out* in the name of Baal... saying, "Baal, answer us!"	*They called out in a loud voice.*
Actions	They capered around the altar which had been made.	They cut themselves, according to their custom, with knives and lances, until blood poured out upon them.

Following these activities, which have now gone on for several hours before a huge audience, the prophets of Baal achieve a state of ecstasy – the "prophesying" mentioned in the text in verse 29. Just as their first efforts were in vain, so their present exertions bring no results. And just as we see a development in the description of their actions from the first effort to the second, so there is a development in the description of their failure:

First failure – at noon	Second failure – at the time of the evening sacrifice
v. 26: There was no voice nor any answer.	v. 29: There was no voice, nor any answer, *nor any regard.*

This "development" requires explanation: Can there be any "progress" or "development" in the absolute lack of response on the part of an object that does not exist? It would seem that the text means to convey to us the development that takes place among *the people present* at Carmel, in the face of this twofold failure. First, the nation becomes aware of the empirical fact that the actions of the false prophets have not met with any response. But what is the meaning of this? Is this clear evidence of Baal's non-existence? Perhaps now, with the false prophets having taken into account the possibility (as suggested by Elijah) that the previous

lack of response resulted from Baal's various "occupations," and now
that they have tried to overcome this obstacle by raising their voices
and engaging in desperate rites, "until blood poured out upon them," if
even now "there is no voice and no answer," then the nation is reaching its unequivocal conclusion: The reason for this is that "there is no
regard." As Radak explains, "If there were anyone listening to them, he
would answer them."

SUPPLEMENT: "ELIJAH'S BULL"

We mentioned above the ambiguity of the formulation of verse 26:
"They took the bull *that was given to them*" (or, literally, "which he gave
to them"), implying that Elijah selected the bull that the false prophets
would sacrifice, contrary to his proposals (to them and to the nation)
that they would choose it themselves.

The Midrash offers a fascinating solution to this question which,
despite its deviance from the literal text, masterfully explains the formulation of the verse and illustrates the situation as a whole:

> The Holy One said to them: Learn from [the example of] Elijah's
> bull. When Elijah told the Baal worshippers, "Choose one bull
> for yourselves and prepare it first, for you are the majority," the
> four hundred and fifty prophets of Baal and the four hundred
> prophets of Ashera gathered together and were unable to move
> [the bull's] feet from the ground. See what is written there: "Let
> two bulls be given to us, and they shall choose one bull for them-
> selves and cut it into pieces and place it upon the wood, but they
> shall not apply any fire, I shall prepare the other bull, and place it
> on the wood, and I shall apply no fire." He said to them: Choose
> two identical bulls born of the same cow, that have been raised
> in the same pasture.… They chose for themselves one bull, and
> Elijah's bull started following him. Concerning the bull that was
> supposed to be for Baal: All the prophets of Baal and the prophets
> of Ashera gathered together, but they were unable to [get it to]
> move its feet, until Elijah addressed it and said: Go with them!
> The bull answered and said to him, before the whole
> nation: My friend and I emerged from the same stomach, from

the same cow, and we were raised in the same pasture. He is being dedicated to God, and the name of the Holy One will be sanctified through him. But I am being dedicated to Baal – to provoke my Creator!

Elijah said to him: Bull, bull, have no fear. Go with them, and they will find no pretext. For just as the name of the Holy One will be sanctified by the bull that is with me, so it will be sanctified through you.

[The bull] said to him: Is this what you advise me to do? I swear that I shall not move from here until you [personally] hand me over to them. As it is written, "'They took the bull that was given to them.' Who gave it to them? Elijah." (Numbers Rabba 23:9)

The solution that the midrash proposes for the difficulty in our verse is that the false prophets did indeed choose their own bull, but nevertheless Elijah (and not Ahab, or some anonymous "giver") was required to actually hand it over to them, thereby prevailing over the bull's (sworn!) refusal to budge. The lesson that the midrash wants us to learn from Elijah's bull (which is actually the bull selected and slaughtered by the prophets of Baal, having been handed to them by Elijah) concerns the trait of loyalty to divine service and distancing oneself from idolatry; even a bull was careful to observe this.

What does this midrash add to our story? It would seem that the story is intended to clarify for us the immense importance of Elijah's efforts to exploit to the very end the false prophets' failure. The bull, being a bull, did not understand this (and hence the question: "Is this what you advise me to do?"). But we as human beings are required to understand this from Elijah's words: "Just as the name of the Holy One will be sanctified by the bull that is with me (namely, the one upon whom fire is destined to descend from heaven), so it will be sanctified through you (when you are sacrificed by the prophets of Baal)."

Attention should be paid to the fact that God's name is sanctified equally through the failure of the false prophets and the success of Elijah. The role of both bulls in *kiddush Hashem*, the sanctification of God's name, is equal in value. This is because the failure of the false prophets will magnify the impact of the victory of God's prophet when fire descends from heaven, and hence serves as a perfect psychological preparation.

The failure of the prophets of Baal also has important religious significance in its own right. The recognition of the nullity of the gods is in itself a precondition for pure faith in God. As R. Yoḥanan teaches (Megilla 13a): "Anyone who denies idolatry is called a Jew."

It is interesting to note the way in which various commentators deal with this midrash. Rashi and the Baal HaMetzudot quote it, in a substantially abbreviated form, as the solution to the difficulty in our verse. In order to adapt it as far as possible to the literal sense of the text, they omit the dramatic dialogue between Elijah and the bull (which is so characteristic of the midrash) and retain only the basic fact:

> "Which was given to them": It ran away from them so as not to be involved in idolatrous worship; it fled and took refuge with Elijah. He said to it, "Go! God will be sanctified through both of you." (Rashi)

> "Which was given to them": Our Rabbis taught: After they chose their bull, it did not want to go with them, until Elijah handed it to them. (Baal HaMetzudot)

But Radak, after both of his more literal explanations, writes: "An aggada (midrashic narrative) contains things that are far removed from logic." Then he quotes the midrash, at length. In his opinion, this story is so far removed from logic because he understood the midrash as a literal account of events. If this is so, several questions arise concerning an event such as this, described in the midrash. Indeed, during the course of the generations, many questions have arisen, including that of Rabbi Yosef Kara:

> I question the many bulls that were slaughtered for idolatrous purposes, without any one of them any making any problems. Why did this particular bull see fit to act differently from all

of them? But one does not propose solutions concerning an aggada.

Or, the question that is answered in the Responsa of Rabbi David ben Zimra:

> You have asked of me, so I shall tell you my view concerning Elijah's act on Mount Carmel, concerning that which is explained by the Rabbis.... It is difficult for you to accept this, for what need was there for this miracle [that the bull could speak]? And if this great miracle did indeed take place, why does the text not make it explicit, as in the story of Balaam's donkey?"

But *Ḥazal* did not mean, in this midrash, to describe a real situation or to reconstruct an event that is not mentioned in the biblical text. Their intention was to illuminate the text and its profound significance in a midrashic light, with no pretense (in this case) at representing the literal sense of the story. Nevertheless, as we have noted above, this midrashic illumination hints at the profundity of the literal level of the text: The failure of the false prophets is an integral part of Elijah's success, and God's name is sanctified through it.

Chapter 13

Elijah's Preparations for Descent of God's Fire (I Kings 18:30–35)

LENGTHY PREPARATIONS: THE RATIONALE

In the last few chapters, we addressed the first part of our story: the gathering of the nation, the proposal of the test, and the failure of the prophets of Baal. Now we move on to the second part of the story (from verse 30 until the end of the chapter), discussing Elijah's actions and their results. This section is constructed in a manner with which we are already familiar: two halves that are equal in length, on either side of a central axis.

> Verses 30–37 (8 verses) – the six stages of Elijah's preparation for the descent of fire

> Verse 38 (*Central Axis*) – fire descends from heaven

> Verses 39–46 (8 verses) – the six results of the miraculous descent of the fire

The six stages of preparation in the first half of this section are: (1) repairing the broken altar for God (v. 30); (2) rebuilding it with twelve stones (vv. 31–32); (3) digging a ditch around it (v. 32); (4) preparing the wood and the bull (v. 33); (5) pouring the water (vv. 34–35); (6) prayer (vv. 36–37).

The six results described in the second half of this section are: (1) the nation's recognition of God (v. 39); (2) slaughter of the false prophets (v. 40); (3) Ahab's command to eat and its fulfillment (vv. 41–42); (4) Elijah's forecast of rain (vv. 42–44); (5) rainfall (v. 45); (6) Elijah runs before Ahab's chariot (v. 46).

In proposing the test to the nation (vv. 23–24) and to the prophets of Baal (v. 25), Elijah maintained a distinction between the two stages of the activities to be performed by each party: the stage of technical preparations, including cutting up the bull and placing its meat upon the altar, while applying no fire; and the stage of "spiritual" preparation, calling out in the name of God.

Indeed, we find both of these stages described in the actions of both the false prophets and Elijah. Attention should be paid to the length of the description of each of these stages in the text, its actual duration in the case of each party, as well as the relationship between the two parties.

The text describes the technical preparations of the false prophets with great brevity, in the first half of verse 26: "They took the bull that was given to them, *and prepared it* (in Hebrew, this is a single word: *vayaasu*)." The term *asiya* (literally, "doing," or "making") is a concise summary of the carving of the bull and all the other actions involved in preparing a sacrifice; Elijah uses the same term in verse 25, where he tells the false prophets, "and *prepare* it first."

In contrast to this surprising brevity, the text elaborates in its description of their call to Baal and the various worship rituals involved. All of this is presented in two stages: first in verse 26, and then (following the failure of their first cry) in verse 28.

It is not only in the narrative description that this stage is drawn out; even more strikingly, the actual time involved is lengthy. Both stages together last from the morning until the time of "offering the *minḥa* sacrifice," near evening.

The relationship between these two stages is reversed when Elijah's turn arrives. The stage of the "technical" preparations goes on at length, occupying six verses (vv. 30–35). His prayer, occupying a further two verses, does not last any longer than the time needed to utter the words quoted in the text. This is in sharp contrast to the call of the false prophets, which is likewise described in two verses, but actually lasted a full day. Needless to say, Elijah's prayer is not accompanied by any sort of magical or ecstatic rites.

What is the meaning of the opposite proportions between these two stages by the two parties participating in the test?

The stage of technical preparations as carried out by the false prophets holds no special interest; it contains nothing beyond the norm in offering a sacrifice or in comparison with the prior description outlined by Elijah. Therefore, the text suffices with a single word: *vayaasu* – they prepared it.

The stage of calling out to Baal, on the other hand, along with the accompanying rites and rituals, is of great significance to our story. It is at this stage that the failure of the prophets of Baal becomes clear to the nation, and the deity is thereby nullified. The detailed description in the text – like the emphasis on the actual duration of this stage – is important in and of itself; these represent a critical preparation for Elijah's own actions and the miracle of the descent of fire that is going to take place.

Elijah's actions are highlighted in the story – both the stage of his practical preparations and the stage where he offers prayer. The brief duration of his prayer and the immediate response to it are, of course, a sharp contrast to the parallel stage in the false prophets' activities. But what is the function of the many tasks that Elijah performs when preparing the sacrifice? Why are these actions described in such detail, over the course of six verses, in complete contrast to the brief description of the parallel stage in the false prophets' preparations?

As we shall see below, Elijah has several objectives, which his various actions are meant to address. But they all share the same general aim: To increase the tension and the nation's anxious anticipation of the miracle. Between the final failure of the prophets of Baal and Elijah's success in bringing down fire from heaven, some time must elapse – although it need not take the same amount of time as all the efforts of the false prophets. It would be a severe psychological mistake to allow the miraculous descent of fire to take place immediately after the failure of the false prophets; this would dampen the effect of the miracle. But this duration of time cannot be achieved by means of Elijah's prayer. The prayer must be brief, a contrast to the prolonged calling out by the prophets of Baal. Hence, Elijah "buys time," as it were, by prolonging his physical preparations.

Prolonging the stage of physical preparations also has another positive effect. In his calm attention to all the details, Elijah demonstrates his complete faith that God will answer him. He is not pressured; he is in no hurry to pray. Rather, he acts calmly, as someone who has time on his side; he can afford to slightly postpone the most important stage – that of prayer.

Obviously, the dual reason that we have presented above would not explain an artificial lengthening of the preparatory stage if these actions did not have their own intrinsic value. But each action has an additional reason, as we shall discuss later on. At this stage, we shall focus only on one of Elijah's actions, which serves to prove the general explanation that we have proposed for his lengthy arrangements: "He laid out the wood and carved the bull into pieces, and set it upon the wood" (v. 33).

These actions are the only ones that he is committed to performing based on his proposal at the beginning of the story; they are, therefore, also the only actions that have a parallel in the actions of the false prophets (*vayaasu*). Here, there is no room to question Elijah's motives in performing his actions. They arise from the necessity to prepare the sacrifice upon the altar in anticipation of the decisive test. Nevertheless, we may still comment on the *length of the description* of Elijah's actions, in contrast to the extreme brevity of the description of the parallel actions by the prophets of Baal.

There appear to be two possible explanations. One is that this discrepancy is meant to express the difference between the actions of the false prophets and those of Elijah. The prophets of Baal act hastily and impatiently, because they want to move on as quickly as possible to the more purposeful stage in their efforts – the stage of calling out to Baal, with all the accompanying rituals. The cramming of all their preparations into a single word – *vayaasu* – is meant to express this impatience. The opposite is true of Elijah: Every small action is described individually; the mood here is relaxed, the prophet has all the time he needs, and all the confidence to do what he needs to do calmly.

The other possibility is that the details in the description of Elijah's preparation of the sacrifice stem from what follows, both concerning the pouring of the water: "Pour it upon *the offering* and upon *the wood*" (v. 34), and the descent of the fire: "It consumed *the offering* and *the wood* and the stones and the dust, and licked up the water that was in the ditch" (v. 38). This order is (almost) the reverse of the order of Elijah's actions. He began at the bottom and worked his way upward (from *the dust* of the foundation of the broken altar), concluding with the wood and the sacrifice upon it. The fire consumes first the sacrifice at the top, and proceeds downward until it reaches the dust. Thus, the list of his actions comes to fix in our minds the order of the "layers," as a preparation for the description of the eventual descent of the fire.

"AND ALL THE PEOPLE CAME CLOSE TO HIM"

Elijah's first act, in preparation for the anticipated miracle, is to gather the people around him: "Elijah said to all the people: Come close to me. And all the people came close to him" (v. 30). This introduction to Elijah's actions is a stark contrast to the preamble to the event in verse 21: "Elijah came close to all the people, and said: How long...."

At the start of the day, the people had reservations about Elijah. The prophet had to approach them, and what he told them, when he approached them, was greeted with a perplexed, or uncertain, silence: "The people answered not a word." Now the nation is quick to respond to his invitation. The people draw close, and with curiosity and anticipation, they await his next words. But now is the time for action, not words, and Elijah acts silently. It is through these actions that Elijah will convey to the people what he wants to say.

Hence, this invitation to the people to approach is meant to facilitate the continuation of the halted dialogue that the prophet began when he initially approached them. The possibility of continuing this dialogue, with such a striking change in the nation's attitude toward Elijah, is the result of the ongoing failure of the prophets of Baal.

We may attribute two further objectives to Elijah's invitation to the people to approach. First, he wants to demonstrate by means of a mass action, performed by the entire nation, that they have turned their back on the prophets of Baal and the altar of Baal, left, shamed and alone, following their terrible defeat.

Elijah's second objective – and we shall elaborate on this further – is to invite the closest, most public scrutiny of himself and what he is about to do. As Abrabanel explains: "Elijah commands the entire nation to approach him, so that they will see everything that he is going to do and not suspect him of deceit."

PREPARING THE ALTAR

The next two stages in Elijah's actions are related to establishing the altar:

> He repaired God's broken altar; and Elijah took twelve stones, as the number of tribes of the children of Jacob, to whom God's word came, saying: Your name shall be Israel. And he formed the stones into an altar in God's name. (vv. 30–32)

The question that arises from these verses is: Did Elijah make use of an existing altar, which merely needed some "repair" (v. 30), or did he build a new altar from the twelve stones that he took, as verse 32 would seem to suggest?

This question perplexed earlier as well as more modern commentators, and various solutions have been proposed. Uriel Simon suggests the following:[1]

> It is more reasonable to assume that informal altars – like the altar to God on Mount Carmel and like the altar that Elijah establishes in its place – were formed from stones of the field, which had not been cut with any iron instrument and which were placed one on top of the other to form a raised surface. It appears that such a stone altar would sometimes be built upon a mound of earth ... as hinted in the description of God's fire that descends upon Elijah's altar: "It consumed the offering and the wood, and the stones, and *the earth*, and licked up the water that was in the ditch" (v. 38). The order here is from top down, from which we may

---

1. Simon, *Keria Sifrutit BaMikra*, 230.

> deduce that between the level of the altar stones and the ditch
> around it, the earth upon which the stones had been arranged
> was visible, and this was considered part of the altar. The stones
> of such an altar would have been scattered, as a result of neglect
> or destruction, and anyone who came to rebuild it would have
> had to regather suitable stones. Hence … Elijah started by repair-
> ing the earth basis of the broken altar (by raising it, packing the
> earth close, and forming its shape), and continued by gathering
> twelve stones … from which he built the body of the altar.

This represents a realistic explanation of Elijah's actions concerning the
building of the altar.

But Elijah's main objective in these actions was not the tangible achievement at the end: a finished altar ready for a sacrifice. All
of these could have been described in two words: *vayiven mizbe'aḥ* (he
built an altar). But the text devotes two full verses to the description of
his actions. We must conclude, then, that Elijah's actions are symbolic
and convey important messages. Thus, the actions themselves become
a means of communication between Elijah and the people – a silent
communication which is more effective than words. In the following
sections we shall examine each of these actions and the messages that
they are meant to convey.

REPAIRING GOD'S BROKEN ALTAR

Elijah does not build an entirely new altar. Rather, he chooses to establish
his altar upon the foundations of "God's broken altar," which he repairs.
It would seem that he means thereby to highlight the contrast between
God's altar and that of the prophets of Baal. Concerning the latter, we
are told (v. 26), "They capered about the altar *that had been made*" (literally: "which he had made"). They had no need to build an altar, for
"someone" had already made it long ago, for the purpose of worshipping
Baal on the Carmel. Therefore they made use of the altar that was ready
and waiting for them, an altar which, apparently, was still in active use.

The situation of God's altar upon the Carmel was very different.
It was broken – apparently not as a result of neglect, but rather as part
of the intentional destruction of such altars that was inspired by Jezebel.

This is what Elijah would complain about at Mount Horeb: "The children of Israel have abandoned Your covenant; *they have destroyed Your altars*, and put Your prophets to death by the sword" (19:10). By selecting this broken altar as the basis for his altar, Elijah is hinting at the real imbalance between the two competing parties: Elijah represents the service of God, suppressed by the royal house, while the false prophets represent the form of worship that is fostered by the royalty. As we have mentioned, Elijah hints at this contrast in his proposal of the test: "Elijah said to the people: I alone remain a prophet to God, while the prophets of Baal [number] four hundred and fifty men" (18:22). Just as there his intention was to hint at the grave circumstances in which the numerical superiority of the false prophets had come about ("It was, when Jezebel cut off the prophets of God" [v. 4]), here too, he means to present the contrast between the two competing sides at the time of Jezebel's domination over Israel.

Indeed, in Elijah's words at Mount Horeb, quoted above, we detect a clear reference to the connection between these two actions, concerning which Elijah expresses outrage on God's behalf: "They have destroyed *Your altars* and put *Your prophets* to death with the sword." In this verse, Elijah attributes these actions to the entire nation, rather than to Jezebel alone, but this stems from the nation's silent acquiescence to Jezebel's deed, and the fact that the people themselves are "lurching between two opinions" (namely, straddling the fence). Hence, Elijah's choice of using God's broken altar (along with his words in v. 22) is meant as a veiled rebuke: "You allow this situation in which Jezebel and the servants of Baal are obstructing the service of God in Israel, persecuting His prophets, and destroying His altars." By repairing the altar, Elijah hints at the restoration of divine service at which this entire occasion is aimed.

TWELVE STONES CORRESPONDING TO THE TRIBES OF ISRAEL

Having repaired the foundation of the broken altar to God, Elijah goes on to rebuild the upper part of the altar, using a new collection of stones. This stage, too, becomes a symbolic act: Elijah takes care to ensure that the number of stones from which the altar will be built is twelve. We may assume that the intention of the text here is to tell us that not only are we, the readers, aware of the number of stones and its significance, but that Elijah also ensures that his entire audience notices as well. How he achieves this, whether by mentioning it explicitly or by making it clear in some other way, is unknown.

What does Elijah mean by highlighting the twelve tribes of Israel, at this place and time?[2] This act reminds us of a similar act by Moses, when he built an altar at the foot of Mount Sinai and prepared to forge the covenant between the nation and God:

> Moses came and told the nation all that God had said, and all the precepts, and all the people answered with a single voice and said, "All the things of which God has spoken – we shall do." Moses wrote down all of God's words, and he arose early in the morning and *built an altar* at the foot of the mountain, *with twelve stones, corresponding to the twelve tribes of Israel....* Moses took half of the blood and put it in basins, and [the other] half of the blood he sprinkled on the altar. He took the book of the covenant and read it out to the people, and they said: "All that God has said we shall do, and we shall hear." Moses took the blood and sprinkled it over the people, and said: "Behold, the blood of the covenant which God has made with you, concerning all of these things." (Ex. 24:3–8)

In imitating Moses's actions, Elijah hints at his desire to renew the covenant between all of Israel and God. The people who are now gathered at Mount Carmel serve as the representatives of all the twelve tribes, and this altar that Elijah repairs will soon turn into the basis for the revelation of a sign of the covenant between God and the tribes of Israel. The fire that descends from God onto this altar, built from twelve stones, will be the signal that God is resting His Presence among Israel

---

2. Attention should be paid to the fact that this number is alluded to again in Elijah's actions: He commands that *four* jars of water be poured onto the sacrifice and the wood, *three* times. Thus, a total of *twelve jars* of water are poured. (See Radak on 18:34.)

and renewing the bond between the nation and God: "Today let it be known that You are God *in Israel*" (v. 36).

But we must also take note of the differences between the two events. Moses is about to forge a covenant between God and the nation concerning *the words* that he reads out to them: "Behold, the blood of the covenant which God makes with you concerning all of *these things* (or: words)." "These things" are the commandments and precepts of the Torah. There was no need to forge a covenant or to provide any special explanation concerning the fundamental faith that God is the Lord of Israel. Elijah, by contrast, is coming to renew the covenant between the nation and God on the most fundamental level: a covenant concerning recognition of His divinity and accepting it.

Another difference between the two instances is that Moses receives the response of a nation eager to enter the covenant in advance: "All the people answered with a single voice and said: All the things of which God has spoken – we shall do." Elijah, on the other hand, encounters suspicion and doubt. It is only after the descent of the fire from heaven that he receives the nation's wholehearted response.

These differences are also reflected in the different times when the action takes place. The covenant at Sinai is forged in the morning: "*He arose early in the morning* and built an altar at the foot of the mountain." The morning hour symbolizes the dawning of the nation. Elijah performs his actions "*at the time of the minḥa offering*," the evening sacrifice, offered at twilight when darkness and light intermingle in the lives of the nation that is "lurching between two opinions." But when the fire descends from heaven it will illuminate the darkness with a great light, and all the "lurching," deliberation, and doubts will vanish. Then the words of the prophet will be fulfilled:

"There shall be one day that will be known as being God's – neither day nor night, and it shall be that at evening time there will be light" (Zech. 14:7).

JACOB – ISRAEL

We have not yet exhausted the content of verse 31. The text does not suffice with noting the numerical connection between the stones that Elijah takes and the tribes of Israel, but adds: "As the number of tribes of the children of Jacob, to whom God's word came, saying: Your name shall be Israel." What is the purpose of this addition?

Mount Carmel, upon which the events in our story take place, is located in the north of the Land of Israel. As far as we know (and not only from what is hinted at in this chapter), the height and beauty of the mountain, rising up over the sea, made it a site of idolatrous worship for many different nationalities, and particularly, for the Baal worshippers from Sidon.[3] Carmel, then, was the site of bitter conflict with the world of the neighboring nations, which tempted the Israelites with their wealth and culture, drawing them toward their pagan beliefs and customs.

In this mighty battle against the world of the other nations, Elijah has to bring about a victory for monotheistic faith in the consciousness of Israel, and a renewal of the ancient covenant. In the background to Elijah's battle here stands Jezebel, daughter of Ethbaal, king of Sidon, and the congregation of prophets of Baal who enjoy her patronage, and who apparently are her fellow nationals. Elijah has to undo the faith of his fellow Israelites in the god of Sidon.

The emphasis here on the twelve tribes, children of Jacob, is meant to create a dividing line between the twelve tribes of Israel and the foreign elements that are threatening the unity and uniqueness of the people of Israel. The emphasis on the name of Jacob as the one "to whom God's word came, saying: Israel shall be your name," is meant to recall Jacob's battle against the angel – the spiritual representative of Esau ("the prince of Esau," in the words of the Sages). In this battle our forefather prevailed: "For you have striven with God and with man, and have prevailed" (Gen. 32:29). And like Jacob, so too his descendants, Elijah and the entire nation, now standing at Carmel will prevail in their spiritual battle against the four hundred and fifty alien prophets of Baal.

BUILDING IN GOD'S NAME

"He built the stones as an altar in God's name" (v. 32).

Having clarified to the nation (in a way that is not explained in the text) his intention in taking the twelve stones to build the altar, Elijah

---

3. See Z. Kalai, s.v. "Karmel, Har HaKarmel," *Encyclopedia Mikra'it* IV, 328.

uses the stones to build the main part of the altar "in God's name." What does this mean? Malbim explains: "[Elijah] said explicitly that he was building it for God's sake, so as to sanctify it with the sanctity of an altar."

Attention should be paid to the fact that God's name is mentioned in every one of Elijah's actions here: "*He* repaired *God's* broken altar. Elijah took twelve stones… to whom *God's* word had come, saying.… He built the stones into an altar in *God's* name" (vv. 30–32).

The complete and finished altar, upon which Elijah arranges the wood and the parts of the bull, is a combination of old and new. As to the old – God's name is upon it from ancient times. Everyone knows it to be "*God's altar*," but now it needs renewal; it needs to be given appropriate form, since it is "broken." The new, on the other hand, needs to be sanctified as an altar. Therefore Elijah builds it "in God's name," as Malbim explains.

A most appropriate summary of the symbolism of Elijah's actions here is to be found in the famous axiom of Rabbi Avraham Yitzḥak HaKohen Kook: "The old shall be renewed, and the new shall be sanctified."[4]

DIGGING THE TRENCH

The next stage of Elijah's preparations consists of digging the ditch around the altar: "He made a trench, such as would contain about two *se'a* of seed, around the altar" (v. 32). Following this, Elijah arranges the wood and the meat, and instructs that water be poured upon the sacrifice and upon the wood, until the trench is full of water.

These two actions, digging the trench and pouring the water, are interrelated. The digging of the trench assumes its full significance only when the great quantity of water is poured upon the altar, so that it fills the trench. Why, then, does Elijah first dig the trench and then arrange the sacrifice, rather than the other way around, such that the purpose of the trench – to contain the water – would immediately be apparent? In the order in which the text presents the events, verse 33 – describing the arranging of the sacrifice – appears to be an unnecessary separation between two actions that belong together: "He made a trench … around

---

4. *Iggerot HaRe'iya* (Jerusalem, 1985), I:214.

the altar. He laid out the wood and carved the bull into pieces, and set it upon the wood. He said: Fill four jugs with water." (vv. 32–34).

The answer would seem to be that the trench has an additional purpose: To designate the perimeter of the sanctified area of the altar. In the continuation of the story, it becomes clear that this is indeed the limitation of the sanctified area, up to which the fire reaches when it falls from the heavens: "God's fire descended and consumed the burnt offering… and licked up the water that was in the ditch" (v. 38).

The digging of the trench therefore serves a dual purpose. It is meant to collect the water that is poured upon the altar, but it also represents part of the building of the altar and *its demarcation*, in God's name. Only after preparing the altar and demarcating the *sanctified area*, is it possible to arrange the sacrifice upon it. It is for this reason that the digging of the trench is mentioned immediately after the building of the altar in God's name, and both of these actions are included within the same verse (v. 32); only thereafter does the text go on to describe the arranging of the sacrifice (v. 33).

The area demarcated by the trench – "such as would contain about two *se'a* of seed" – is considerable. It equals a hundred cubits by fifty cubits (according to Rashi), which is the area of the courtyard of the Tabernacle (Ex. 27:18). In several halakhot an area of this size is considered as being a public area. (See, for example, R. Judah's opinion in Mishna Eiruvin 2:43.)

POURING THE WATER

> He said: "Fill four jugs with water, and pour it upon the offering and upon the wood." And he said: "Do it a second time" – and they did it a second time; and he said, "Do it a third time" – and they did it a third time. The water ran around the altar, and the trench was also filled with water. (vv. 34–35)

What is the purpose of this action? Rashi, commenting on verse 34, provides a laconic explanation: "To amplify the miracle."

However, it would seem that we can detect another purpose in this action. Elijah is very concerned that the performance of the miracle might be met with skepticism, that the audience will find explanations to deny the miracle. This would nullify the entire spiritual effect of the miracle. The Baal HaMetzudot (taking his lead from Abrabanel) presents this explanation for the invitation to all the people to gather to Elijah (v. 30): "To see that there was no deceit in what he was going to do." Uriel Simon summarizes the idea as follows:

> It is appropriate that we specify and highlight the precautions that the prophet adopts with a view to preempting any possible claim against the veracity of the test.... Elijah does nothing until all the people approach him and he has hundreds of eyes watching every one of his movements.... It appears that it was for this reason that he dug the wide trench around the altar, but refrained from pouring the great quantity of water upon the sacrifice and the wood with his own hands, choosing instead to accomplish this through the agency of people among the audience. The highlighting of the punctilious fulfillment of the prophet's command is meant ... [to teach us] of the prophet's decisiveness in his efforts to remove any doubt. He does not suffice with four jugs of water, nor even with eight; he is not satisfied until everything is sodden with water.[5]

---

5.   Simon, *Keria Sifrutit BaMikra*, 228.

Chapter 14

Elijah's Prayer
(I Kings 18:36–37)

TWO PRAYERS: A CONTRAST

Our story is characterized by a duality of plot: The test that is held at Carmel is between two parties; Elijah demands a decision from the nation that is "lurching between two opinions"; two bulls are brought for the purposes of the test; the process undergone by each participant in the test involves two stages, "action" and "prayer." Twice the prophets of Baal attempt to draw down fire from the heavens. First, they call on Baal's name from the morning until noon; then, they cry out "in a loud voice" from noon until the time of offering the *minḥa* sacrifice. In both cases they are unsuccessful: "There was no voice nor any answer" (v. 26); "There was no voice, nor any answer, nor any regard" (v. 29).

Corresponding to this duality in the prayers of the false prophets, which extends throughout most of the day, we also find a duality in the prayer that Elijah offers, as well as in the nation's reaction to the great miracle. But both of these are condensed, both in real time and in the record of events in the narrative. This phenomenon is clearly noticeable both in Elijah's repetitive call: "Answer me, Lord, answer me!" (v. 37), and in the nation's repetitive cry of acknowledgment: "God is the Lord; God is the Lord!" (v. 39).

The repetition/duality in both cases may be explained against the backdrop of the fundamental duality of the story of the test at Carmel – namely, the stance of the false prophets against Elijah, and the need to side with one of the parties. This is reflected in R. Abahu's perception of Elijah's repeated call to God:

> "Answer me" – that fire will descend from the heaven … and "answer me" – that You should be the object of their attention, so that they will not say that this was an act of witchcraft. (Berakhot 9b)

The danger of the claim that "this was an act of witchcraft" undoubtedly emanates from the direction of the false prophets; this being the case, their presence is the reason for the repetition.

Malbim explains the repetition in the nation's cry of acknowledgment (v. 39) as follows:

> The first utterance is a positive assertion – that God is the Lord, which has become apparent from the descent of the fire. The second [utterance] is a negative statement – that *only* God is the Lord, and none other. This has become apparent from having seen that Baal is a false god.

Aside from these obvious repetitions, there is a less apparent level of repetition in Elijah's prayer. His prayer in its entirety occupies two parallel verses:

	Verse 36	Verse 37
Appeal to God	Lord, God of Abraham, Isaac, and Israel,	Answer me, Lord, answer me;
Expected results	today *let it be known*	let this nation *know*
	that You are God in Israel and I am Your servant,	*that You are Lord*, the God
	and by your word I have done all of these things.	and You have turned their hearts backward.

What is the purpose of this duality? Simon comments as follows:

> The text elaborates at length, relatively speaking, when quoting the prophet's words to highlight the contrast between the bloody gashes that the prophets of Baal inflict upon themselves and the verbal prayer of God's prophet. Just as the fruitless efforts of the former are described in two stages (vv. 26, 28)…so his prayer has two stages.[1]

But of course there is a difference, and Simon notes it. The two stages in the efforts of the false prophets, lasting most of the day, "are interrupted by the words of their opponent, encouraging them to make a supreme effort (v. 27)." The two parts of Elijah's prayer, which represent a very brief prayer even when joined together, "are not separated by any intermediary stage, which would emphasize the failure of the first stage."

Thus, it is specifically the similarity of the external framework – the duality – that emphasizes the fundamental difference between the prolonged cries of the false prophets and the brief, clear prayer offered by Elijah.

The difference between the prophets of Baal and Elijah is discernible in another important sphere, hinted at in Simon's words. The efforts made by the prophets of Baal to communicate with their god are composed of two elements: crying out to Baal and worship rituals. Their cry is conveyed to us in direct speech only in their first attempt, where it consists of only two words (in the Hebrew): "They called in the name of Baal from the morning until noon, saying: '*Baal, answer us!*'" (v. 26).

It appears that they repeated this cry continually for many hours during their second attempt, too – from noon until the time of the *minḥa* sacrifice. The only change was that now they called out "in a loud voice." In contrast with the meager content of their verbal prayer, its active, ritual accompaniment is rich and varied. In their first attempt, we are told, "They capered around the altar that had been made" (v. 26). In their second attempt, they introduce new and varied actions: "They cut themselves, according to their custom, with knives and lances, until

---

1. Simon, *Keria Sifrutit BaMikra*, 234–35.

blood poured out upon them.... And they prophesied until the time for offering the *minḥa* sacrifice" (vv. 28–29).

On the other hand, when it comes to Elijah, the text makes no mention of any actions that accompany his prayer. This is emphasized in the introduction to his prayer: "And it was, at the time for offering the *minḥa* sacrifice, that Elijah the Prophet approached and said" (v. 36).

Where did he "approach"? The text is opaque in this regard, and Simon explains:

> "He approached" is a common expression indicating an intensification of engagement preceding an attempt at persuasion (Gen. 44:18) or prayer (Gen. 18:23). The exceptionally brief, three-word (Hebrew) description – "Elijah the Prophet approached" – amplifies the contrast with the extreme lengths to which the prophets of Baal were required to go in order to intensify their engagement with [Baal]. In contrast to their capering and cutting [of their flesh], God's prophet needed to do no more than to approach his God; while their ecstatic cries are uttered "in a loud voice," he has confidence in the power of his words – "and said...."[2]

This contrast between Elijah and the prophets of Baal is completed by the fact that it is specifically Elijah's prayer – accompanied by no magical acts or rituals of worship – that is complex and rich in content, in contrast with the simple cry of the false prophets: "Baal, answer us!" We shall address this aspect of Elijah's prayer below.

DIFFERENCES BETWEEN CORRESPONDING PARTS OF ELIJAH'S PRAYER

Having examined, in the previous section, the deliberate contrast between the description of the fruitless efforts of the prophets of Baal and the pure prayer offered by Elijah, we now address the contents of his prayer with a view to clarifying the similarities and differences between its parallel sections. Let us once again present a comparison between the two parts of the prayer:

---

2. Ibid., 231.

	Verse 36	**Verse 37**
Appeal to God	Lord, God of Abraham, Isaac, and Israel,	Answer me, Lord, answer me;
Result A	today let it be known that You are God in Israel	let this nation know that You are Lord, the God
Result B	and I am Your servant, and by Your word I have done all of these things.	and You have turned their hearts backward.

The two sections of the prayer are different from each other in two main respects: The status of the nation as expressed in each part, and the status of Elijah as expressed in each part.

Status of the Nation:

1. In the appeal to God in verse 36, mention is made of the three forefathers: "Lord, God of *Abraham, Isaac, and Israel*" (the name Israel appears again in the prayer as the name of the nation). In verse 37, the appeal to God is direct: "Answer me, Lord."

2. In verse 37, the purpose of the descent of fire is to bring about a change in the consciousness of the *nation*: "Let *this nation* know"; the content of their knowledge is "that You are Lord, the God" (and not Baal). In verse 36, the purpose is to bring about a change in the consciousness of the entire world: "Today let it be known" – to everyone. And the content of the knowledge is "that You are God *in Israel*." The Baal HaMetzudot comments: "When the fire descends, it will be known this day that You are God in Israel – in other words, *that You rest Your Presence among Israel*."

What is common to these differences is that verse 36 emphasizes the national significance of the descent of fire; it is perceived within the framework of the historical connection between God and His nation. The knowledge by the entire world that "You are God *in Israel*" means widespread recognition that God has chosen His nation, Israel.

Status of Elijah:

1. Elijah's status as God's prophet is highlighted only in verse 36, where it represents an important part of the prayer. Alongside his aspiration that it be known that God is Lord in Israel, the prophet asks that it also be known that he is God's servant, and that it is by God's word that he has done "all of these things."

   In verse 37, this element is altogether absent. Here Elijah prays only for the nation to recognize God and His actions. A shortened presentation of the two verses highlights this difference:

Verse 36	Verse 37
Today let it be known that...	Let them know...that
You... and I...	You...
And by Your word I have done...	and You...

2. A further difference is to be found in the introduction to each of the two parts of the prayer, in the appeal to God. At the beginning of the prayer in verse 36, Elijah starts speaking without mentioning himself: "Lord God of Abraham, Isaac, and Israel." His appeal to God at the beginning of verse 37, By contrast, opens with the words, "Answer me, Lord, answer me."

   This difference does not have the effect of balancing the previous one, since his emphasis of himself in the first person at the beginning of the second section of the prayer does not in any way highlight the fact that Elijah is a prophet – a fact that is given great prominence in the first section. Rather, the significance of this difference is that it serves to create a different atmosphere in each section of the prayer. The appeal in verse 36 lends a sense of dignity and calm; it projects quiet and unshakable faith that what Elijah prays for is going to happen. The appeal in verse 37 is emotional and highly personal; it expresses a lack of certainty as to God's response. In the words of *Ḥazal*: "Answer me, Lord; answer me" – this is a cry (Taanit 15a, 17a).

We shall discuss further the meaning of the differences between the two sections of this brief prayer in the next sections.

THE TEST AT CARMEL: DUAL SIGNIFICANCE

The events at Mount Carmel have a dual significance, and Elijah has given attention to both aspects in his words and actions thus far. Accordingly, there are two messages in the descent of the fire from heaven, and Elijah's prayer, too, has double meaning.

One significance of the test at Carmel is as Elijah proposed at the beginning of his speech to the priests of Baal; we shall refer to this as the "universal-religious" meaning: "If the Lord is God – follow Him; if Baal – then follow him" (v. 21).

Elijah proposes this as a private individual: A religious test should be held to determine the true God to be followed. From the point of view of this test, there is no special significance in the fact that the adjudicator here is the nation. The decision is to be objective, and is meant to be impressed upon the consciousness of anyone present to witness the test: "The God who will answer with fire, He is God. And all the nation answered and said, 'It is good'" (v. 24).

Because of this universal aspect of the test, Elijah appears, to us and to his audience, to observe an apparently perfect balance between the two alternatives, both in his demand that they choose (v. 21) and in his proposal of the details of the test (vv. 24–25). What we seem to have before us is a neutral question requiring an experiment and an empirical conclusion; these will be conducted with no prejudice in either direction. Any overt attempt to rebuke the nation and bring it back to the service of God would harm the deliberate even-handedness of the test.

However, even at this stage, Elijah slips into his words a first hint at the national significance of his suggestion. When he declares, "I alone remain a prophet to God," he is making oblique reference to the persecution of God's prophets by Jezebel, the non-Jewish queen, and the nurturing of the foreign prophets of Baal, whom she apparently brought from her native Sidon. Here we sense for the first time, that the issue that is about to be put to the test is not so neutral after all, but rather touches on the very essence of Israel being the nation of God, and the conflict between it and its neighbors, the pagan foreign nations.

That which was only hinted at thus far, is clarified quite pointedly in the actions that Elijah chooses to perform in silence – the detailed preparations that he undertakes prior to his prayer: The repair of the altar to God that was destroyed by the worshippers of Baal, and its rebuilding "in the name of God," using twelve stones "as the number of the tribes of the children of Jacob, to whom God's word came saying: Your name shall be Israel" (v. 31).

We have previously discussed at length the significance of these symbolic actions. Their meaning is conveyed to the nation in silence. The message that they broadcast is a highly particularistic one. Elijah means to place a wedge between the Israelite nation present at Carmel and the foreign prophets of Baal, and to remind the nation that which it has forgotten: its former loyalty to the service of God, as symbolized by the broken altar; the covenant between the nation and God, forged by Moses at the foot of Mount Sinai; and Jacob, forefather of the nation, who, in his struggle with the angel, "fought and prevailed."

From this national perspective, the test at Carmel is an event that is meant to renew the covenant between Israel and God. It is not only the conclusion of the period of "lurching between two opinions"; it is the beginning of a new period in the covenantal relationship between the nation and its God. It is not only empirical proof that God is the Lord of the universe, but also a repeat of previous revelations of God through fire before His chosen nation, to have the Divine Presence dwell among them.

The descent of fire on Mount Carmel is related, in accordance with this latter aspect, to two previous events in the history of Israel. First, we recall the descent of fire at the consecration of the Tabernacle: "Fire emerged from before God and consumed upon the altar the burnt offering and the fats; and all the people were afraid, and they called out, and fell upon their faces" (Lev. 9:24).

The second related event is the descent of fire at the dedication of the Temple built by Solomon: "When Solomon was finished praying, fire descended from the heaven and consumed the burnt offering and the sacrifices, and the glory of God filled the Temple" (II Chr. 7:1).

Just as in these events, the descent of fire represented proof of the Divine Presence resting within the Tabernacle and within the Temple, so too in our context the descent of fire is a sign of the renewal of the covenant and of the Divine Presence dwelling among Israel.[3]

From this perspective, Elijah's role toward Israel also undergoes a change. He is no longer a dispassionate mediator coming to propose an objective test to clarify faith in the true God, with careful preservation of neutrality at every step of the process. Rather, he is a messenger from God, and all of his actions at Carmel are performed in God's service. His purpose is not a decision between his view and the view of the prophets of Baal, but rather the fulfillment of the classical role of the prophet in Israel: To make peace between Israel and their Father in heaven. In this context, Elijah stands before the people with no connection to the foreign prophets of Baal.

Now it is easy to see how Elijah's two parallel prayers express quite explicitly the two different meanings that the prophet attaches to the test at Carmel. The order of these prayers is the inverse order of his actions, thereby creating a chiastic structure. His first prayer, in verse 36, is a direct continuation of his actions in rebuilding the altar, which focus on the national, Israelite aspect of the test. The prayer expresses in words that which is only hinted at by his actions.

The connection between these symbolic actions and the prayer in verse 36 is obvious. By gathering the twelve stones, Elijah hints at "the number of the tribes of the children of Jacob," while in his prayer he mentions all three forefathers. The name "Israel" echoes both in his actions: "to whom the word of God came, saying: Your name shall be Israel," and in the prayer in verse 36: "that You are God in Israel."

In his prayer in verse 36 Elijah emphasizes his role as prophet in Israel, and the expression "I am Your servant" in this context means, "Your prophet," "Your messenger." "By Your word I have done all of these things" means that, despite the seemingly neutral character that Elijah attributes to the test that he initiates at Carmel, he is in fact acting "by

---

3. The difference between the two occasions is not great. Concerning the verse (Ex. 25:8), "And let them make Me a Sanctuary, that I may dwell in their midst," the author of *Tzeda LaDerekh* comments, "[God] does not say, 'That I may dwell in *its* midst', but rather 'in *their* midst' – indicating that the Divine Presence rests in the Sanctuary not in the merit of the Sanctuary but rather by virtue of Israel, for *they* are God's Sanctuary."

God's word," as a prophet who is being sent to bring Israel back to God, on one hand, and to restore the Divine Presence among them, on the other.

From the point of view of this aspect of the test at Carmel, Elijah's prayer is uttered firmly and with complete faith, for there is no doubt as to God's response. In fact, this verse is not a supplication, but rather advance notice of what is about to happen: "This day it shall be known." It is uttered as a declaration, as a direct appeal to "the Lord God of Abraham, Isaac, and Israel." The certainty expressed in the first prayer arises from the fact that Elijah acts here as God's agent, as His servant, and the descent of the fire itself is performed "by God's word." Hence, there is no room for any doubt.

Elijah's second prayer, in verse 37, is very different. This prayer goes back to the objective contest that is going on between Elijah and the prophets of Baal. In this test, Elijah is not playing the role of a prophet in God's service, but rather that of an individual who wants to put his faith in God to a test against the faith of the prophets of Baal in their idol. Hence the tone of the appeal here is personal – "Answer me, Lord, answer me" – and highly emotional and tense. As a private person acting on his own initiative, Elijah has no assurance that God will answer his prayer. He must plead with God and clearly explain his request which relates entirely to the issue of sanctifying God's name: "They shall know...that You...and You...." Elijah himself has no role here – neither in the act that is about to be performed (the descent of fire from heaven) nor in its result (faith that God, not Baal, is the true Lord).

Owing to this universal-religious nature of the test at Carmel, no mention is made of the name "Israel" in verse 37. Instead, Elijah speaks of "this nation." He himself is not referred to in this verse as a prophet. The linguistic connection between his prayer in verse 37 and the test that he proposes to the nation at the outset, as well as the cries of the prophets of Baal, is obvious. Corresponding to the call of the false prophets, "Baal, answer us!" (at two different stages), Elijah cries out, "Answer me, Lord, answer me." Corresponding to his words to the nation – "If (*im*) the Lord is God" he now prays, "Let this nation know that (*ki*) You are Lord, the God."

Now we must answer the question that arises from the above: Are these two aspects of the test at Carmel not mutually contradictory? How can two such different prayers be uttered together? If Elijah is speaking as God's messenger, certain that his prayer will be answered, then why is there a need for any further plea to God, as an individual filled with uncertainty? Furthermore, if the significance of the gathering at Carmel is a renewal of the covenant between God and His nation and the bringing down of the Divine Presence to dwell among Israel, then of what value is a test between faith in Baal and faith in God? In other words, Elijah, in his actions related to the rebuilding of the altar and in his first prayer, raises the event to such a lofty level that its first aspect – a religious test – now appears trifling and redundant, along with its corresponding, second prayer.

The answer is that not only is there no contradiction between the two aspects, but they are in fact interdependent. The dependence of the higher (national-historical) significance of the occasion upon its more basic level – a religious test – is quite clear. So long as the nation has not yet made its decision between two options, so long as the people do not yet recognize the exclusivity of belief in God and His service and the non-existence of Baal, there is no room to renew the covenant between the nation and its God, so as to merit the Divine Presence among them. Therefore, the order of events must necessarily be that first Elijah calls upon the nation to make its decision, proposing a test that will help them to recognize that the Lord is God and that Baal is worthless; only afterward does Elijah perform the actions that hint at the renewal of the covenant between the twelve tribes of Israel and the Lord God of Israel.

On the other hand, not every person and not every nation is worthy of the opportunity to set up the sort of test that Elijah proposes, and to have God respond with fire descending from heaven. It is only God's love for Israel and Elijah's status as God's faithful servant that allow him to initiate this test, with confidence that God will answer him. In other words, it is only the historical connection between Israel and their God, the covenantal relationship, that permits the actions that are performed at Carmel on the universal-religious level. Therefore, at the prayer stage, Elijah starts with the covenantal relationship between God and Israel as a basis for his confidence in God's response; only afterward does he attach his own emotional prayer that God answer him in the actual test that he faces.

The two aspects, then, are interdependent. It is the covenantal relationship between Israel and God that makes it possible for the test against the prophets of Baal to be held, while God's response to this test, initiated by Elijah, is what will bring about the renewal and reinforcement of the covenant. This explains the reversal of the order between Elijah's actions and his prayers, in the chiastic structure that we noted previously. In Elijah's words to the nation and in his actions, he charts a practical educational course: First, the indecision of the nation must be resolved; afterward it will be possible to renew the covenant with them. But in his prayer, Elijah mentions first the merit by which he dares to carry out the test: the merit of the forefathers and the covenant that God forged with them and with their descendants.

The above analysis of the dual nature of Elijah's prayer serves to explain a fascinating midrash in Exodus Rabba (44:1):

> You will thus find that Elijah offered up many supplications on Mount Carmel, for the fire to descend, as it says, "Answer me, Lord, answer me," but he was not answered. As soon, however, as he mentioned the dead, and said, "Lord God of Abraham, Isaac, and Jacob," he was immediately answered. For what does it say? "God's fire came down...."

This midrash raises an obvious problem: At first, in verse 36, Elijah prays: "Lord God of Abraham." If he was not answered (and there is nothing in the text that would indicate this), then it is specifically this prayer that was not answered. But afterward, when he prays in his own right – "Answer me, Lord, answer me!" – then, he is answered immediately!

The answer is that the midrash is not recalling the actual sequence of Elijah's prayer – for in truth there was no stage at which Elijah was not answered. What the midrash means to do is to explain the duality of the prayer: Why was it necessary for him to offer two prayers? The answer is that the second prayer alone, "Answer me," would not have been answered had Elijah not introduced it with his first prayer. It was only the mention of the forefathers of the nation, and their merit that extended to their descendants, that made it possible for Elijah to hold the test at all and to expect that his personal prayer – "Answer me, Lord, answer me" – would receive a divine response. Indeed, the mood of each of the two prayers indicates which was uttered with uncertainty and anxiety, and which was offered with complete faith and trust.

"YOU HAVE TURNED THEIR HEART BACKWARD"

We have yet to explain the final words that conclude his prayer. Let us now consider whether this concluding phrase – "And You have turned their heart backward"[4] – matches the proposed overall framework for the prayer.

In Berakhot 31b we find a teaching that serves as the basis for several of the early commentaries: "R. Elazar said: Elijah made accusations against God, as it is written, 'You turned their heart backward.'"

Many commentators regard Elijah's words here as attributing to God the responsibility for the fact that Israel has been engaged in sin: "You turned their heart backward from You, such that they did not recognize You and did not serve You until now." The interpretation of Elijah's precise intention here differs among the various commentators, but all the variations are difficult to accept.

Elijah's aim in his actions, as well as in the prayer that he offers, is to prepare the hearts of Israel for return to God in the wake of the miraculous descent of fire from heaven. But according to the above interpretation, Elijah's assertion here, "You have turned...," is likely to bring about the opposite result. By placing responsibility for Israel's grievous sin upon God, he is absolving them of responsibility and providing them with a claim that allows them to continue in their sin, even after the descent of the fire.

---

4. Reviews of the various interpretations of these words in Elijah's prayer are to be found in two articles: Professor Moshe Greenberg, "VeAta Hesavta et Libam Aḥoranit" in *Meḥkarim BeAggada, Targumim UTefillot Yisrael LeZekher Yosef Heineman* (Jerusalem, 5741), 52–66, and Professor Uriel Simon, in his article which was reprinted in his book *Keria Sifrutit BaMikra*, 232–33. Greenberg's review is thorough and comprehensive, while Simon's is brief and partial. The exegetical conclusion that we arrive at here tends toward Simon's presentation.

Let us therefore consider a different line of interpretation, which understands these words in the opposite way. In his first commentary, Radak writes: "Rabbi Saadia Gaon explained as follows: Their heart, which has been backward – You will now turn it toward You, if You answer me."

In Rabbi Saadia Gaon's words:

> "And you have turned their heart backward" – in other words: If this fire descends and consumes the sacrifice, the hearts which are backward will be rectified. All that is missing from this sentence is the letter *heh*; it should say *haahoranit*.[5]

Rabbi Saadia Gaon, then, interprets the word *ahoranit* (backward) as an adjective describing their heart: "their backward heart," meaning crooked, distorted.

What is interesting about this understanding of the verse is its perception of the tense of the verb, "You have turned." This verb (*hasibota*) appears in the past tense, and the other commentators understand it accordingly. How, then, does Rabbi Saadia Gaon turn it into a verb in the future tense: "If the fire descends…the hearts which are backward *will be turned [rectified]*"? The answer is simple. The past tense of the verb "You have turned" is in fact the "future past"; it indicates that at some certain time in the future, the action in question will already be done and completed. Thus, Rabbi Saadia Gaon's understanding of our verse is as follows: "Answer me, Lord, answer me; then, when You answer me (in the future), this nation will know, first of all, that You are God, and second, that You have turned (previously, in the past, when You answered with fire) their hearts back."

In his second commentary, Radak writes: "Some interpret: … their hearts backward *from believing in Baal*, and they shall know that it is false."

---

5. Rabbi Saadia Gaon, *HaNivhar BeEmunot UVede'ot*, at the end of the fourth article, ed. Rabbi Kapah (Jerusalem, 1970).

This interpretation follows immediately, in Radak's words, after Rabbi Saadia Gaon's interpretation, and it differs only in the understanding of the word *ahoranit* (backward). According to this understanding, the turning back of the hearts is in relation to the prior situation. Since the hearts of the nation were previously turned toward Baal, the turning backward means abandoning belief in Baal for belief in God.

Abrabanel prefers this latter interpretation:

> The interpretation, "You have turned their hearts backward" means, from worship of Baal, whom they followed; that their hearts should turn backward from that worship…this is the correct interpretation in accordance with the literal text.

In other words, God's response will cause Israel's heart to turn back from Baal worship toward worship of God. Commenting on this interpretation, Simon writes as follows:

> Concerning the possibility that "backward" is indeed meant here to indicate "back (in return)," attention should be paid to the fact that orientation in the Bible does not necessarily rely on a fixed point of observation. … Thus it is said of Shem and Japheth, "They walked *backward* [*ahoranit*] (i.e., opposite to the direction that they were facing), and covered their father's nakedness, and their faces were *backward* [*ahoranit*] (i.e., opposite to the direction in which they were walking)" (Gen. 9:23).

Simon brings further examples to substantiate his point, and then concludes:

> There is nothing stopping us from interpreting the turning of Israel's heart "backward" as meaning: in relation to the situation in which they are currently. And because they [previously] turned their faces from their God (compare II Chr. 35:22), "turning their heart backward" [now] means turning them toward Him. Thus, what the text is saying is: When the fire descends upon God's

altar, this nation will know not only that You are God, but also that You are their God who has turned their hearts toward Him.[6]

Here we may ask: If this is indeed the meaning of our verse, why is such a simple statement formulated in a way that can so easily be misleading? Indeed, many commentators are led to understand the verse in exactly the opposite way! To this, Simon answers:

> Had the text read, "You have returned their hearts to You," it would all be clear and simple; we may perhaps posit that such a formulation is not adopted because it is too far-reaching. God will sever them from following after Baal, but the matter of returning to Him is still left to them."[7]

Of all the commentaries, the explanations of Rabbi Saadia Gaon, Radak, and Abrabanel best match the formulation of the text (as we have discussed at length) and its context (Elijah's aim of bringing the nation back to God). The descent of fire from heaven not only proves to the nation "that You, Lord, are God," but also proves to them that "You have turned their heart backward," toward You. In other words, it proves not only God's existence, but also His providence over man, and His interest in them and their ways, in order to bring them back to Him.

These commentators also relieve our verse of various theological difficulties that arise in light of some of the other commentaries that are offered – such as the question of the nullification of free choice.[8]

The final consideration that we shall discuss here concerning the preference for the commentaries of Rabbi Saadia Gaon, Radak, and Abrabanel, brings us back to the structure of Elijah's prayer, which we examined above. We demonstrated that the two parts of the prayer (vv. 36–37) parallel one another, but with fundamental differences between them. We present here once again the parallel between the two parts of Elijah's prayer:

---

6. Simon, *Keria Sifrutit BaMikra*, 233.
7. Ibid., note 101.
8. See Maimonides, Introduction to Mishna Avot, ch. 8; *Laws of Repentance*, ch. 6.

	Verse 36	**Verse 37**
Appeal to God	Lord God of Abraham, Isaac, and Israel	Answer me, Lord, answer me
Result A	Today let it be known that You are God in Israel	Let this nation know that You are Lord, the God
Result B	And I am Your servant, and by Your word I have done all of these things	You have turned their hearts backward

The important difference, for the purposes of our discussion, concerns the conclusion of each verse. At the end of verse 36, Elijah highlights the fact that he is God's servant and that he acts as such, and he asks that the imminent descent of fire strengthen faith in him and in the actions that he has performed by God's word. This appeal is entirely absent from verse 37. In this section, Elijah asks only that the nation recognize God in a different way, as explained above.

Is there, despite this difference, any connection between the respective concluding components of the two parts of the prayer?

According to the commentaries that we have adopted, the answer is affirmative, since it is only according to their explanation that the words "You have turned" refer to the result – fire descending from heaven – that Elijah requests in his prayer. This being the case, what causes the "turning of the hearts" in verse 37 is what Elijah refers to more broadly in verse 36 as "all of these things." Thus, according to this interpretation, in both prayers Elijah is addressing a dual result of the descent of fire. The first, immediate result is the awareness of God's Presence (that He is "God in Israel"); the second is the awareness that God wishes to return the hearts of His children toward Him. But the description of the action to restore Israel to God is different in each section. In verse 36 God operates through His prophet-servant, who performs "all of these things" by God's word so as to bring Israel back to God, whereas in verse 37 God acts directly to turn the hearts of His children back (in verse 36, "And I... have done," while in verse 37, "You have turned"). But even in verse 36 the source of the action is God, for "I" am "Your servant," and what "I have done" is "by Your word."

What is the source of this discrepancy between the two corresponding verses? Firstly, it arises from Elijah's attitude to different events. In verse 36 Elijah is speaking about "all the things" that he has *already* done. He refers to all the actions that were performed on his own initiative at Carmel: gathering the nation, proposing the test, causing the prophets of Baal to be exposed, rebuilding the altar, and the implied promise of fire descending. All of these actions were undertaken by Elijah as God's agent, with a view to bringing Israel back to Him. In verse 37, Elijah refers only to the descent of fire *that is still to happen*; this miraculous act is an act of God alone; no human has any part in it. But this very fact – Elijah's attitude toward his own actions thus far, in verse 36, or to God's imminent revelation, in verse 37 – is itself the result of a fundamental difference between the two prayers, which we discussed previously. Each of the two prayers reflects a different significance of the test at Carmel. Verse 36 reflects the national-historical significance – and in this context Elijah's status as God's servant is highlighted. All of his actions have been performed by God's word. Verse 37, on the other hand, reflects the universal-religious significance of the event. In this context, God Himself and the sanctification of His name are the focus, while Elijah has no special role.

Thus we conclude that the analysis of the structure of Elijah's prayer and the exegetical conclusions that we draw in fact reinforce one another.

Chapter 15

God's Fire

> God's fire descended and consumed the burnt offering and the
> wood and the stones and the dust, and licked up the water that
> was in the ditch. (v. 38)

This verse brings us to the dramatic climax of the episode at Carmel.
What happens here represents the purpose of all the actions that were
performed until now as preparation, and it is the point of departure that
facilitates all the actions that are to follow. Indeed this verse is highlighted
as the climax of the story in terms of content, style, and its location
within the literary unit to which it belongs (vv. 30–46).

Climax of Content

In terms of content, this verse is exceptional in relation to the entire
story in its description of the direct action performed exclusively by
God. The opening words, "God's fire," should be understood as *Targum
Yonatan* renders them – "fire descended from God," i.e., "sent by God."[1]
Thus, this verse is reminiscent of other verses describing similar events:

---

1. In several places in Tanakh, when a noun is juxtaposed to God's name, it expresses
    the superlative. For example, *harerei El* (Ps. 37:6) means extremely high mountains;
    similarly, *arzei El* (Ps. 80:11) means massive cedar trees; and *shalhevetya* (Song.

213

> Fire emerged *from before God* and consumed the offering and the fats upon the altar. (Lev. 9:24)

> Fire descended *from the heaven* and consumed the offering and the sacrifices. (II Chr. 7:1)

Attention should be paid to the fact that even though the purpose of our story is to prove to Israel that God is the Lord, and thereby to bring them back to the faith of their forefathers, the nature of the actions undertaken here is entirely human. There is almost no mention of any direct divine involvement. Even the descent of rain at the end of the story is not described in the text as an act of God. Nevertheless, there are a few exceptions. The first is the point of departure for our story, which belongs to the previous episode of the drought:

> Many days passed, and God's word came to Elijah in the third year, saying: Go and appear before Ahab, and I will give rain upon the face of the earth. (18:1)

The second instance is our present verse:

> A fire descended from God and consumed… (v. 38)

The third is the concluding verse of the story:

> God's hand was upon Elijah, and he girded his loins and ran before Ahab until the approach to Jezreel. (v. 46)

Thus, at these three critical junctures – at the point of departure for these events, at the point of their conclusion, and at their climax – there is mention of some level of divine involvement. But it is only at the climax of

---

8:6) means a huge flame. However, here, rather than as an expression indicating a "colossal" fire, as we might have understood it in light of the above, the emphasis seems to be on the fact that the fire descends as an immediate response to Elijah's prayer ("Answer me, Lord, answer me") and as the realization of the prophet's words to the people (v. 24), "and the God that answers by fire, He is God."

the story that this involvement is overt and visible to all. God's involvement here admittedly comes in response to Elijah's prayer, but it does not come about through his agency, as it does in the other two cases.

Style

The substantial importance of our verse, as explained above, finds expression in its ceremonious, grandiose style. The detailed description of the elements consumed by the fire is reminiscent of the preceding actions undertaken by Elijah, as described in verses 30–35. This serves to emphasize the connection between these actions and their fruition; everything that was prepared has been consumed by the divine fire that descends from heavens.

Aside from this reminder, the description of the consuming fire stands out in its chiastic structure. Let us consider a literal translation of verse 38:

> … And consumed
>> the offering and the wood and the stones and the dust
>> and the water that was in the ditch
> it licked up…

The description opens and concludes with verbs, while the middle is filled with nouns – all the items that are consumed by the fire. The order of the objects that are consumed is in accordance with their location: from the highest (the offering) to the lowest (the water in the ditch that Elijah dug out). But the division of the verse, indicated by the cantillation marks (the *etnaḥta* under the word "dust"), creates two unequal groups. The first contains four items (the offering, the wood, the stones, the dust), while the second contains only one (the water in the ditch). What is the reason for this? Firstly, there is the linguistic explanation: "consumed" is not a verb that is appropriate to the evaporation of water by the fire, since water is not flammable and fire cannot burn it. Therefore the verb "licked up" is selected in relation to the water.

The second reason for the water being set apart from the other items is a thematic one: The licking up of the water by the fire demonstrates the awe of the miracle in a way that the consumption of the other items does not. This is not only because water is the element that is most opposite to fire (which is the reason why Elijah pours it over the sacrifice and the wood), but also because the water in the ditch is a considerable distance from the altar itself. In other words, by emphasizing that the fire licks up even the water in the ditch, the text gives us an idea not only of the power of the fire, but also of the extent to which it spreads throughout the area prepared for it. For this reason, the text separates between the consumption of the altar and what is on it, and the licking up of the water in the ditch.

The extent of the miracle, expressed specifically in the licking up of the water, is highlighted by means of the postponement of the second verb until the end of the sentence. This, then, is the reason for the chiastic structure of the verse.

Location of verse

We have elaborated on the location of our verse within the section of the story describing Elijah's actions, starting in verse 30 and continuing through verse 46, in "Carmel," chapter 13. We may recall here that this verse serves as the central axis of this part of the story. The preceding eight verses (vv. 30–37) describe the six stages of Elijah's preparations for the miracle, and the eight verses that follow (vv. 39–46) describe the six results of this miracle.

It is difficult to point to exact parallels between the "preparatory" verses and the "results"; nevertheless, we may point to a general framework that creates a symmetrical structure. On either side of the central axis there is a clear parallel between Elijah's prayer, in which he expresses his faith that God's response will bring about a situation in which the nation will "know that You are Lord the God" (v. 37), and the fulfillment of this prayer: "All the nation saw… and they said, 'The Lord – He is God'" (v. 39).

There is also a hidden parallel between the introduction to the unit and its conclusion. At the outset, Elijah calls upon the nation, "Come close to me," and the nation obeys. After turning their backs on the prophets of Baal and their altar, the nation finally attaches itself to its true prophet and begins to cooperate with him – increasingly so after the miracle of the fire. Thus, the nation comes to deserve complete reconciliation: Not only with the resumption of rain, but also with the return of the prophet. The story ends with Elijah running before Ahab. If Ahab here symbolizes the nation, then this act represents the prophet's rejoining the nation in return for the nation rejoining him.

The important point for our discussion here is that all that we read in this unit leading up to the verse that serves as the central axis serves to lead us to that verse, while all that follows is a result of it. For this reason, this verse is located exactly midway through the unit.

Thus content, style, and structure come together to emphasize our verse as being the climax of the gathering at Carmel.

Chapter 16

"To Whom Shall You Compare Me, That I Shall Equal Him? – Says the Holy One" (Isaiah 40:25)

KEY WORDS

After devoting the previous chapter to I Kings 18:38, the climax of the story, we must now pay attention not only to what is said in that verse, but also to what is not said in the adjacent verses.

From the very beginning of the story, there are some frequently repeated key words of thematic importance in the story. Let us list them and examine the contexts in which each of them appears, as well as the contexts where they are absent even though they would appear to belong there.

Kol (**voice, sound**)

The word *kol* appears four times in the first part of the story (I Kings 18:19–29), in four consecutive verses:

A: "No *voice* nor any answer" (v. 26)

B: "Call out in a loud *voice*" (v. 27)

B': "And they called out in a loud *voice*" (v. 28)

A': "No *voice*, nor any answer, nor any regard" (v. 29)

There are two "voices" here: the voice of man, and the hoped-for voice of Baal. The human voice here – that of the false prophets – grows stronger from the first attempt to call out to Baal to the second. However, their attempts are futile: Baal's voice does not make itself heard in response to those calling out to him, because in fact there is no one listening.

In sharp contrast to these "voices" – both of those who call out and the hoped-for response which is absent, this word is almost entirely absent from the second part of the story. Some of the technical preparations that Elijah undertakes in anticipation of the descent of fire are conducted in silence; the rest are accompanied by very few words. Elijah offers his prayer without lifting his voice: "Elijah the Prophet approached *and said*" (v. 36), and God's response of sending fire from heaven takes place in silence, with no voice at all. Even in the reaction of the nation – its verbal component – there is no mention of lifting their voices: "*They said*, The Lord is God" (v. 39).

This avoidance of using the word "voice" in everything pertaining to the descent of God's fire and the related prior and subsequent actions and utterances, is quite deliberate. The text differentiates between the pure and the impure and avoids any connection between them – not even in the form of contrast.

Nevertheless, we find that the word *kol* ("voice" or "sound") does appear once in the second part of the story: "Elijah said to Ahab: Go up, eat and drink, for there is the *sound* of gathering rain" (v. 41).

If we are correct in linking this "voice" to the voices in the first part of the story (and it would appear that there is reason to do so, since the expression "the sound of gathering rain" seems to empha-size the auditory aspect), then the veiled implication would seem to be the following: The divine response to the mortal attempts to create a connection with that which is above and beyond is manifest not in a direct divine voice (as the false prophets expected to hear from Baal), but rather within the framework of the regular workings of the world. It is within this world that divine providence – that which God does for His servants – is revealed. God's voice is audible in His beneficence toward man within the natural world, in the rain that descends from the heavens.

It is appropriate that we conclude this part of the discussion with the following verses from Psalms 29, whose subject is so close to our own:

> Ascribe to God, O mighty ones; ascribe to God glory and strength. Ascribe to God the glory of His name; worship God in the splendor of holiness. *God's voice is upon the waters*, the God of glory thunders; God is upon many waters. (vv. 1–3)

Kof-resh-alef (to call/cry out)

This root is repeated six times in the first part of the story (I Kings, ch. 18), in five consecutive verses:

1. "*You will call out* in the name of your god" (v. 24)
2. "And *I shall call out* in the name of the Lord" (v. 24)
3. "*Call out* in the name of your god" (v. 25)
4. "And *called out* in the name of Baal" (v. 26)
5. "*Call out* in a loud voice" (v. 27)
6. "*They called out* in a loud voice" (v. 28)

Here again, this root is absent in the second part of the story. Despite what Elijah says in verse 24: "I shall *call out* in the name of the Lord," the text does not use this verb in its description of his prayer. We are told only, "Elijah the Prophet approached and said…" (v. 36). Once again, the reaction of the nation that falls and prostrates itself is expressed in an utterance (*alef-mem-resh*), not a "call" (*kof-resh-alef*).

The reason for this is as we mentioned above: So as not to compare – even by means of contrast – the "call" (in a "loud voice") of the prophets of Baal with Elijah's manner of prayer before the Lord God. The frequent use of verbs based on the root *kof-resh-alef* in the first part of the story, concerning the prophets of Baal, "disqualifies" the verb for further use in the story when it comes to describing prayer to God, so as "to distinguish between the impure and the pure."

This distinction between the words "calling out" and "voice" (with respect to the prophets of Baal) and "saying" (in relation to Elijah and the nation) also has thematic significance – aside from the linguistic distinction, whose purpose lies in its very existence. "Calling out," in the context of our story, means "declaring," "appealing verbally." When, in addition to this, the "calling out" is also "in a loud voice," we have a hint of the enormous effort invested in these magic actions and ecstatic "prophesying" which are required for the service of Baal – and which ultimately bring no results. Elijah needs none of this. The Lord God of Israel neither slumbers nor sleeps; He needs no "crying out in a loud voice." He hears the prayer of every individual, even when it is uttered in a low voice or a whisper. (In fact, the Talmud in Berakhot 31a specifically teaches in connection to Hannah's prayer: "'But her voice could not be heard' [I Sam. 1:13] – from here we learn that one does not raise one's voice during prayer.")

Indeed, in the first part of the story, five out of the six appearances of the root *kof-resh-alef* relate to the prophets of Baal. Even the sole instance related to Elijah – when he says that he will "call out" in the name of God (second appearance of the root) – is uttered only when Elijah presents the conditions of the test to the nation for its approval, and is careful to formulate the conditions in an equitable fashion.

Ayin-nun-heh (to answer)

The most prominent key word in our story – both because of its ubiquitous presence (from verse 21 until verse 37) and because of its repetition in different contexts a total of seven times (characteristic of many key words in Tanakh) – is "answering," in various forms and in reference to various characters:

1. "The people *answered* him not a word" (v. 21)
2. "The God who will *answer* with fire – He is God" (v. 24)
3. "All the nation *answered* and said, 'It is good'" (v. 24)
4. "They called in the name of Baal from morning until noon, saying, 'Baal, *answer* us'" (v. 26)
5. "But there was no voice nor any *answer*" (v. 26)

6. "There was no voice, nor any *answer*, nor any regard " (v. 29)
7. "*Answer me, Lord, answer me*! Let this nation know that You are Lord the God"[1] (v. 37)

These verbs refer to four bodies, with the addressee answering in some cases and not responding in others:

- The public gathered at Carmel: They fail to answer the demand that they decide (1). They respond positively to the proposal of the test (3)
- God whose answer will serve as proof of His existence (2)
- Baal (in the appeal to him by his prophets – 4) and his lack of response (5 and 6)
- God (in Elijah's appeal to Him – 7)

A review of these uses of verbs derived from the root *ayin-nun-heh* shows that the entire development of the story, and the change of heart that transpires in it, are expressed in the progression of these verbs.

Unlike the root *kof-resh-alef* and the noun "voice/sound," which are used to characterize the actions of the false prophets and are therefore eschewed in the second part of the story, the root *ayin-nun-heh* is not associated specifically with them. Only in appearances 4, 5, and 6 is this root related to the false prophets and their failure. In appearances 1 and 3 it pertains to the nation, and in appearance 2 it speaks of "the God who will answer with fire." Therefore, Elijah does not shy away from this root in his prayer, and even repeats it: "Answer me, Lord, answer me."

Despite the above, attention should be paid to the fact that in verse 38, in the description of the fire falling from the heavens, the text does not state that "God answered." Had this been written, a parallel, or contrast, would be created vis-à-vis the "no answering" that appears

---

1. A word that appears twice in close succession for emphasis, as in our verse, is counted as a single appearance of a key word. Proof of this is to be found in several places where it is clear that there is deliberate repetition of the key word seven times, and one of these appearances – usually the last – is doubled. For instance, in the story of Jacob's flight from Laban (Gen. 31:17ff.) the root *gimel-nun-bet* is a key word that is repeated seven times, concluding with the double appearance in v. 39: "whether stolen by day (*genuvti yom*) or stolen by night (*genuvti layla*)."

twice in the description of the failure of the false prophets. Here again we are witness to the same attempt to keep God's name far from the direct, bold contest arranged by Elijah. The lack of any relationship or comparison between God and Baal – the latter being no more than the imaginary creation of his adherents – means that there is no place for God's response to be compared with the "no answering" in relation to Baal. It is only because man, in his weakness, finds himself in the contemptible situation of "lurching between two opinions," weighing up the true God against false gods, that Elijah's act of putting the inexistence of Baal to the test against the existence of God is legitimate and positive. From the objective perspective of truth, there is no place at all for such a test, and in order to demonstrate this, the text systematically avoids any comparison between the divine revelation at Carmel and that which preceded it. As the prophet says: "To whom shall you compare Me, that I should equal him? – says the Holy One" (Is. 40:25).

STRUCTURE OF THE STORY

The phenomenon we noted in our analysis of the style of the story in the use of key words also serves to explain the unusual structure of the story. The principle that we established above is that the story means to reject any relationship or comparison – even a contrast – between Baal and his ways, and God and His revelation. Therefore the description of the revelation of the Divine Presence on Carmel is almost severed from any linguistic connection to the description of the failure of the prophets of Baal that preceded it. This finds expression, as mentioned, in the structure of the story, too.

The biblical narrative usually follows a harmonious structure that is easily revealed: It is divided into two parts more or less equal in length, and they create some sort of parallel between themselves. Sometimes, at the heart of the story –between the two halves – there is a verse, or a group of verses, that serve as a central axis for the story.

This pattern is difficult to apply to our story as a whole. The episode of Carmel is certainly divided into two parts, in accordance with the development of the plot, but they are of noticeably different lengths. The first part, verses 19–29 (the proposal of the test and the first of its results – the failure of the prophets of Baal), occupies eleven verses, while the second part, verses 30–46 (preparations for God's revelation, and its results), occupies a full seventeen verses. While some sort of parallel exists between these two halves, it is very general in nature.[2]

The second half of the story, however – whose structure we have discussed above[3] – is divided into two halves of equal length (eight verses each), straddling a clear central axis, verse 38, describing the miracle of the descent of God's fire. In the previous chapter, we noted certain parallels between the two halves, creating a chiastic framework. This structure, which characterizes many biblical narratives, tends to create the impression that this is an independent story, with its own internal integrity. But clearly this cannot be the case: This part is the conclusion of a story that began previously.

The explanation for the unusual structural character of our story is to be found in its unique aim of separating and distinguishing between its two halves. They are not presented as parallels – neither in terms of equality of the number of verses[4] nor in the paucity of corresponding elements between the subsections that comprise each half. On the contrary: The second half of the story stands alone, with a clear, independent internal structure, as though cut off from the first half. This is another manifestation of the text cautioning the reader, as it were, lest he be misled by the events at Carmel and conclude that there is a qualitative parallel between the prophets of Baal and their failure, and the revelation of God that follows it.

Thus, even the curious structure of the narrative here echoes the words of Isaiah that serve as the title of this chapter: "To whom shall you compare Me, that I shall equal him? – says the Holy One."

---

2. The first part of the story begins with cooperation between Elijah and Ahab (vv. 19–20: two verses), continues with a description of Elijah's problematic relations with the nation (vv. 21–24: four verses), and concludes with the failure of the prophets of Baal (vv. 25–29: five verses). In the second part of the story the situation is reversed in terms of the order, and also, at times, in terms of substance. This part begins by Elijah succeeding where the prophets of Baal had failed (vv. 30–38: nine verses), continues with smooth and unbegrudging cooperation between Elijah and the people (vv. 39–40: two verses), and concludes with restored cooperation between Elijah and Ahab (vv. 41–46: six verses).

3. Chapter 13 and the end of chapter 15.

4. The fact that the second part is considerably longer than the first points to its greater importance.

Chapter 17

The Nation's Response (I Kings 18:39–40)

"THE LORD – HE IS GOD"

Following the description of the great miracle of the descent of God's fire, the text describes the reactions of the nation. In verses 39–40 they declare, "The Lord – He is God," and they capture the prophets of Baal. From this point onward, until the end of the chapter (v. 46), we hear nothing more about the nation.

The first reaction of the nation is described as follows:

> All the nation saw it, and they fell upon their faces, and they said: "The Lord – He is God; the Lord – He is God!" (v. 39)

The people do not react this way just because of the conditions of the test which they had accepted upon themselves in advance. Both from their actions and from their words, as described in these verses, we sense a genuine and spontaneous awe and fear of God.[1] This awe is

---

1. Indeed, we find in *Midrash Eliyahu Rabba*, ch. 17: "'Then God's fire came down ...' – at that moment Israel abandoned the idolatry that they were involved in and became genuinely God-fearing, as it is written, 'All the nation saw it, and they fell on their faces, and they said, The Lord – He is God.'"

225

demonstrated, first and foremost, by the fact that they fall upon their faces. This is a response to seeing God's fire falling from heaven to the earth. In falling before Him, the people repeat the actions of their forefathers in the desert, in similar circumstances: "Fire emerged from before God and consumed upon the altar the burnt offering and the fats, *and all the nation saw it*, and they shouted, *and fell upon their faces*" (Lev. 9:24).

In both cases, this falling to the ground is the acknowledgment of the Divine Presence – the human response to the appearance of God. The Baal HaMetzudot (following the example of Abrabanel) interprets, "They fell upon their faces – to prostrate themselves before God."

The nation's declaration, "The Lord – He is God," does indeed seem to be the required conclusion arising from the conditions of the test: "The God who will answer with fire – *He is God*" (v. 24), and as a belated response to Elijah's demand that they make a decision: "If *the Lord is God*, follow Him" (v. 21). But in their repetition of this cry, they reveal their great emotion and the independence of their conclusion, as Radak explains: "The repetition [is meant to express] the strength of the faith in their hearts. They say and repeat, 'The Lord – He is God!'"

THE CAPTURE AND SLAUGHTER OF THE PROPHETS OF BAAL

It is only after the nation has proved its true repentance and return to God in the spontaneous reaction discussed above, that Elijah turns to them and tests their readiness to translate their new awareness into practical action: "Elijah said to them: Take the prophets of Baal; let not one of them escape" (v. 40).

Amazingly, the people who that same morning were still "lurching between two opinions" and were not ready to turn their backs on Baal worship, now immediately heed Elijah's call, and do as he commands: "They took them." Thus Elijah channels the powerful, newfound religious

---

It could only be based on such an understanding of the people as genuine and complete penitents, as evident from their response, that their passionate cry was incorporated in the Yom Kippur service, at the conclusion of the Ne'ila prayer, representing the transition between the dramatic day that has passed and the night that follows. It was at a similar twilight hour that the words were first uttered at Carmel, after the offering of the sacrifices.

devotion in the nation into a decisive, practical expression of that feeling, thereby also testing its sincerity. Obviously, aside from the importance of putting the false prophets to death as a test of the nation's sincerity at this moment, it also puts a halt to these false prophets' activity.

This development is actually quite surprising: The other results arising from the miracle of the descent of fire and described in verses 39–46 are all more or less to be expected. We are not surprised by the reaction of the nation described in verse 39, nor by the description, from this point onward, of the resumption of rainfall. But the capture and slaughter of the prophets of Baal is different: Not only do we not expect this, but it actually seems to contradict the conditions of the test that Elijah proposed at the start of the chapter. The purpose of the test, as explained by Elijah, is a clarification of the question of which God is the true One, who should be followed. There was never any hint, in his words, that the clarification of this question would lead to the physical liquidation of the losing side. On the contrary, the balanced attitude toward the two sides that Elijah takes such pains to exhibit at every stage, and the generosity that he displays toward his opponents at the various stages of the buildup, create a matter-of-fact atmosphere that gives no impression of animosity between the sides. The ramifications of this test are meant to influence its adjudicators and their faith. There was no hint that the test would have such dramatic results for the participants themselves. Now, it turns out, in contrast to the tolerant tone that has been maintained, Elijah utilizes his victory to physically annihilate those who stood against him in this test and lost. What is the meaning of this sudden change?

In chapter 14 we noted the dual significance of the test at Carmel. The one message is a universal-religious one – the purpose proposed by Elijah at the beginning of his address to the nation and to the false prophets. The other message, which becomes manifest in the course of Elijah's preparations for the great miracle of the descent of fire, is the nationalist-Israelite aspect of the event: a renewal of the covenant between Israel and God. On the basis of this dual significance, we explained Elijah's two-part prayer, and we noted that he also awards dual significance to the miracle of the fire. Here it must be added that the same duality extends to the nation's reaction.

The initial spontaneous reaction of the nation, as described in verse 39, is directly related to the conditions of the test that were set out at the beginning of the story, although, as noted above, this reaction did not arise from a formal obligation to the conditions of the test, but rather from genuine awe and the nation's own, independently drawn conclusion. Still, this in no way negates the obvious linguistic connections between Elijah's words at the beginning of the story and the nation's present reaction, and hence the attachment of this reaction to the sphere of the "test" – the first message of the episode.

The people's second reaction – their response to Elijah's demand that the prophets of Baal be caught and put to death, as described in verse 40, is a reaction that arises from the higher significance of the events at Carmel: the renewal of the covenant between the nation and their God and a return to the commandments of the Torah. In this context, the prophets of Baal are not partners in a cordial attempt to establish who is God, but rather are leading Israel astray into idolatry, thereby endangering the existence of Israel as God's nation.

When Elijah proposes the test to the nation "lurching between two opinions," he creates a mood of relativist tolerance, which suits the pagan concepts with which the nation has become infected. "Idolatry is indulgent" – it tolerates the existence of a multiplicity of deities.[2] But now that the one God has revealed Himself to His nation in order to renew the covenant with them, He is revealed as a jealous God who will not abide the sin of idolatry among His nation, the members of His covenant. Now Elijah cannot suffice with the spiritual "high" of the people who are falling upon their faces and declaring, "The Lord – He is God." He must act to remove all idolatry from Israel by putting to death those who incite to it, in order that the covenant will not be violated again.

Let us now turn our attention to the second part of verse 40: "Elijah took them down to Wadi Kishon, and slaughtered them there."

---

2. Y. Avoda Zara 1:1 (39a). Despite this general assertion, Jezebel herself was not tolerant: She "cut off the prophets of God" (18:4), as Elijah hints in his opening words to the people (v. 22), "I alone remain a prophet of God." Now that Elijah has the upper hand and enjoys the enthusiastic support of the people, the tables have turned, and instead of God's prophets being "cut off," the prophets of Baal, who have Jezebel's backing, are cut off: "Let not one of them escape."

This brief account – just seven words in the Hebrew – gives rise to several questions:

1. Why does Elijah take the prophets of Baal down to Wadi Kishon, which is at the foot of the Carmel, rather than putting them to death at the top of the mountain, where they had spent the whole day?

It would seem that the descent of fire onto the altar that Elijah built, and onto the area demarcated by the trench, bestowed a sanctified status on the site; this was a place where God's Presence rested. The significance is that killing anyone – even a person legally deserving of the death penalty – could not be carried out at this holy place, because of the complete contrast between the altar and the spilling of blood.[3] The descent from the Carmel to Wadi Kishon therefore expresses a severance – not only from the specific place where God's fire came down, but from the geographic area that served as the arena for this event.

2. What is the legal basis, in the Torah, for putting the prophets of Baal to death?

Against the background of the very severe prohibitions in the Torah against idolatry, and the death sentence that it carries for all those who engage in it and influence others to engage in it, not one of our commentators raises this question. It is clear to all that these prophets were deserving of death according to Torah law, both based on their actions prior to coming to Carmel and in their actions there on this day.

Nevertheless, we must conclude that Elijah's action here represents a "prophetical ad hoc measure." He does not put the false prophets to death through the accepted procedure as commanded by the Torah,

---

3. The Torah commands: "And if you make Me an altar of stone, you shall not build it of hewn stone; for if you lift up your sword upon it, you will have defiled it" (Ex. 20:22). Likewise, we find Jehoiada the priest commanding that the wicked Athaliah be put to death as follows: "But Jehoiada the priest commanded the captains of the hundreds, the officers of the host, and said to them, 'Bring her out between the ranks, and him that follows her kill with the sword.' For the priest had said, 'Let her not be slain in the House of the Lord'" (II Kings 11:15).

on the basis of evidence by witnesses and a decision by judges. He acts on the urgent need of the moment and the necessity of acting in a quick and decisive way. In any event, the fact that the prophets of Baal are deserving of death is clear.

3. What is the meaning of the text attributing the two actions – "Elijah took them down… And he slaughtered them" – to Elijah? It would seem that what we are being told here is that Elijah did this with his own hands, without help from others. But here we must ask why, in the very same verse, we read about the capture of the false prophets by the people, who acted in accordance with Elijah's instructions – "they took them," while thereafter Elijah operates alone?

In truth, it would seem that it is difficult to imagine that Elijah single-handedly slaughtered all four hundred and fifty prophets of Baal. Realistically, the slaughter of four hundred and fifty men by one person is complicated and would have taken many hours. For one person to lead them down, live, to Wadi Kishon is almost impossible.

Therefore, the explanation of Radak seems logical: "He slaughtered them there – *he commanded* that they be slaughtered, for all the nation was on his side when they saw this great wonder."

But if this is the case, we must ask why the text changes its formulation, starting in the plural ("they caught them"), but thereafter attributing actions performed by the nation at Elijah's command, to the prophet himself? Would it not be more accurate and linguistically consistent to say, "They caught them and led them down to Wadi Kishon, and slaughtered them there"?

We may propose two answers to this question:

i. The formulation of the verse as we propose above would be misleading. The reader might conclude that the leading of the false prophets down to Wadi Kishon and their slaughter there is performed not only *by* the nation but also at their initiative, swept up in a tide of religious fervor and enthusiasm toward such radical action, without any command by Elijah. This mistake would arise because the verb "they caught them" is preceded by Elijah's command, "Take (catch) the prophets of Baal," while the two other verbs (which, in our proposed reading, refer to the nation) are not preceded by any such command. But this understanding does not suit the facts. It is Elijah who instructs the people to perform all of these actions, and this is important not only for a proper evaluation of their behavior (namely, they did not act as a crazed mob without restraint), and for our appreciation of Elijah's responsibility for their actions.

ii. It is also possible that the formulation of the verse, in the form in which it is written, hints that Elijah did not command the entire nation to kill the false prophets. He only commanded all of them to catch them, but the prophet chose to carry out the rest of the operation with a handful of faithful followers who chose to go with him, those whom "God had touched their hearts" (see I Sam. 10:26). These people admittedly acted at Elijah's command, but they were not representative of the entire nation, and therefore the text leaves off the general plural with which the verse started out ("they caught them"). This emphasizes that these actions are attributed mainly to Elijah, who acted with the help of his loyal followers. If this hypothesis is true, we learn from this that Elijah limits his demands of the nation; he does not demand their partnership in actions that lie beyond their ability or what they are prepared to do.

Chapter 18

Ahab's Return to the Scene (I Kings 18:41–42)

ELLIPTICAL NATURE OF BIBLICAL NARRATIVES[1]

Elijah said to Ahab: "Go up, eat and drink, for there is the sound of rumbling rain." So Ahab went up to eat and drink, and Elijah went up to the top of the Carmel. (vv. 41–42)

---

1. The expression "the elliptical nature of the biblical narrative" is coined by Yechezkel Kaufmann in the introduction to his commentary on the book of Joshua (Jerusalem, 1976), 74. He defines the concept as follows: "The biblical narrative contains motifs that first appear and then disappear, and other motifs that are absent at first, and appear later on in the story. The parts of the story complement each other, and the narrator relies on the imagination and understanding of the listener or reader. For this reason the biblical narrative contains 'surprises.'" He brings examples, mainly from the books of Genesis and Joshua.

   Uriel Simon, in his article "HaDemuyot HaMishniyot BeSippur HaMikra'i" in *Keria Sifrutit BaMikra*, 317–24, broadens the discussion of this literary phenomenon, especially with regard to the appearance of secondary characters. In our discussion we shall follow in the footsteps of his article "Milḥemet Eliyahu BeAvodat HaBaal" in his book, with quotes from this article forming the basis of our discussion.

Simon writes as follows:

> The narrator has not referred to or even hinted at Ahab since he
> first gathered the prophets and the representatives of the people
> to Carmel (v. 20). The reader might well conclude from this con-
> sistent silence that the king was not present at the confrontation
> between Elijah and the prophets of Baal. But now, suddenly, with
> not a word of explanation, Elijah turns to Ahab; "Go up, eat and
> drink, for there is the sound of rumbling rain" (v. 41). Is this the
> text's way of telling us that the king of Israel was not only witness to
> the failure of the prophets of Baal and the success of God's prophet,
> but was even party to the general prostration of the nation and
> their great exclamation? Moreover, if the command "go up" and its
> fulfillment – "went up" – refer back to the expression "took them
> down" in the immediately preceding verse [discussed in the pre-
> vious chapter], the indirect implication is that Ahab even joined
> those who went down to the Kishon, putting aside any hesitation
> as to the far-reaching implication of his presence there, and thus
> giving legitimacy to the slaughter of the prophets of Baal. (p. 241)

As eloquently as Simon formulates the problem of Ahab's sudden appearance toward the end of the story, having maintained a lengthy absence,
so does he answer his own question:

> The narrator's … silence as to Ahab's actions as Carmel … comes
> to teach us … [that] Ahab was passive and did not intervene in
> any meaningful way in the course of events. Since Ahab's reac-
> tion to Elijah's dramatic activity … is not part of the subject of
> the story, the narrator prefers to remain silent in this regard.
> Leaving one of the characters in the story in complete darkness
> goes against the literary norms to which we are accustomed, and
> our bewilderment is an expression of the fact that our expec-
> tations and our curiosity have not been satisfied. However, in
> this matter, the biblical story is different from what has become
> acceptable in Western stories; it should be understood only on
> its own terms.

Simon brings several proofs from our story to demonstrate this characteristic of the biblical story – that it fails to settle the reader's questions with regard to matters lying outside of the central subject:

> Just as no explanation was previously given as to who supplied the two altars and the two bulls, and where the twelve jugs of water came from, so we will find no explanation as to the "attendant" who "looks out toward the sea" (v. 43) and where he entered the picture, or when it is that he catches up with his master after the marathon run to Jezreel. Moreover… we do not hear of the attendant accompanying Elijah on his flight from Jezreel, until [we are told that] Elijah leaves him in Beer Sheba (19:3)!

In these examples, we indeed see that the narrative ignores various details along the way where they do not serve the main theme. But Simon's argument is meant to apply to Ahab – who, after all, is not an irrelevant detail or a minor character in the story. Nevertheless, Simon maintains that his contention applies even when the text ignores an important element in the narrative, and for this purpose he brings proof from the next story:

> The narrator's perplexing disinterest in Ahab is renewed at the beginning of chapter 19. … When Ahab returns to Jezreel he tells Jezebel about all of Elijah's actions at Carmel and at the Kishon (19:1), and this – unexpectedly – concludes his role in the story. Not only is the threat to the life of the prophet uttered by a messenger of the queen, but we are told nothing at all about Ahab's stand on this counterattack on the part of the Baal-worship loyalists. (p. 241)

Again, Simon (further on in his article) offers the same answer: In Jezreel, too, the narrator's silence as to Ahab's actions tells us that Ahab was passive. Although the significance of this passivity in the face of Jezebel's actions may be the very opposite of its significance in relation to the deeds of Elijah, the text nevertheless avoids elaborating on it since it adds nothing to the main subject.

Simon enlists further evidence of the narrator ignoring a central player in the story from the continuation of our episode:

> Just as the narrator ignores Ahab in the account of Elijah's confrontation with the nation, so he now ignores the nation in the description of the renewal of contact between the prophet and the king. (p. 242)

We should note that this disregard continues until the end of our narrative, in verse 46. Simon offers further comment on this:

> It cannot be denied that this silence bewilders even someone who has accustomed himself to the elliptical style of the biblical text, for it would have been sufficient to include a brief note of clarification (such as, "All the nation went back – each man to his house") within verse 46... It is simply because he [the narrator] knows that his readers will not question that which we, in fact, do – because the literary norms that they and he shared were different from ours. (note 114)

Simon is attempting, mainly, to explain the reason for the narrator's silence as to Ahab's actions during the course of the story thus far. He explains this in terms of Ahab being a secondary character in the story, such that his reaction does not belong to the main subject.

> This ellipticism [of the biblical story] is especially common in relation to the appearance of secondary characters on the scene and their disappearance from it... [The biblical story retains] the freedom...to pursue a secondary character or to ignore him.[2]

It is specifically because of this habit of the biblical narrative with regard to its secondary characters that the reader must ask himself why a secondary character who has disappeared from the stage suddenly reappears later on. In our case: Why is Ahab retrieved from the oblivion to which

---

2.   Simon, "HaDemuyot HaMishniyot BeSippur HaMikra'i," 319–20.

he was consigned, just as we are reaching the end of the story? What new role is being conferred on this secondary character at this late stage?

A full answer to this question will be given only after a clarification of Elijah's instruction to Ahab (v. 41), "Go up, eat and drink" and a discussion of the significance of Ahab's acquiescence to it,[3] as well as an exploration of the meaning of Elijah running before Ahab's chariot.[4] But without getting into the details of these actions, we may assert at the outset that Ahab's return to the scene is meant to illuminate the great change that has taken place within – paradoxically – the person of Elijah. Elijah's wholehearted return to his people (following the religious turnaround of all of the nation and its king, at Carmel) is dramatically completed with the reconciliation between the prophet and the king. This reconciliation is the big news with which the story concludes, and which – from the perspective of the process of reunion between prophet and nation – represents its climax.

From the point of view of the structure of the story, Ahab's return to functioning in relation to Elijah at the end represents a closing of a circle. The story began (v. 19, continuing the confrontation of vv. 17–18) with an encounter that was admittedly full of tension, but showed indications of a readiness for cooperation. This cooperation produced spectacular results in the continuation of the story, and it concludes with a renewed encounter between the prophet and the king. But this time the meeting is devoid of any tension; all that is left is cooperation. There is also another difference between the cooperation at the beginning and that at the end. The second time, there is no practical objective to the cooperation; it is principally symbolic. Furthermore, this time not only does the king acquiesce to the demands of the prophet, but the prophet honors the king. All of this will be further clarified in the coming chapters.

Chapter 19

"Go Up, Eat and Drink, for There Is the Sound of Rumbling Rain" (I Kings 18:41)

What is the meaning of this instruction that Elijah conveys to Ahab at Wadi Kishon – "Go up, eat and drink," and how is it related to the reason he gives – "for there is the sound of rumbling rain"?

Radak explains as follows:

> "Go up, eat and drink" – it appears that [Ahab] fasted because of the lack of rain; now [Elijah] told him that he could eat and drink, for the rain was on its way.
>
> "For there is the sound of rumbling rain" – it was not yet heard; what he meant was "now you will hear the sound of rumbling rain." For Elijah had faith in God, that He would give rain as He had told him: "And I will give rain upon the face of the earth,"

and even more so now that [Elijah] had put the Baal worshippers to death and had removed idolatry.

We may ask: How is it that there has been no mention, thus far, of the fact that this day, when the great ceremony at Carmel was held, was declared as a day of fasting? Simon answers: "This assumption, that we are being told about the nullification of a fast without anything having been said about its institution, is reasonable in and of itself, for it matches our conclusions concerning the elliptical style of the text."

Nevertheless, it is worth noting the explanation of the Baal HaMetzudot, who adopts Radak's explanation without making the assumption that the day had been declared a fast day because of the drought:

> Go up, eat and drink" – meaning, as it were: Since all have repented and declared, "The Lord – He is God," therefore arise now and "eat your bread joyfully and drink your wine with a content heart" (*Kohelet* 9:7), for the sound of rushing rain is about to be heard.

This discussion may appropriately be concluded with Simon's original interpretation of Elijah's instruction here to Ahab. First, Simon proves that the instruction is given to Ahab at Wadi Kishon – for immediately after the text notes that the king listens to the prophet ("Ahab went up to eat and drink"), it continues, "And Elijah went up to the top of Carmel." Elijah certainly ascended to the Carmel from Wadi Kishon, where he had slaughtered the prophets of Baal. Hence, the king and the prophet proceeded to ascend to the Carmel from the same starting point. If this is the case, and the prophet gave his instruction to the king down below, in the wadi, then we may propose that it was also said in relation to what had just happened there. Simon writes:

> But it seems that we may propose a different explanation for Elijah's words to Ahab, relating them more powerfully both to the immediate context and to the structure of the story as a whole. Just as we find, in Tanakh, that refraining from eating and drinking on

a day of trouble is meant to express profound identification with those who are affected by it (II Sam. 1:12, 3:35), so hard-hearted indifference to the plight of others is expressed by purposeful eating and drinking. Joseph's brothers sit down to eat after casting him into the pit (Gen. 37:24–25); King Ahasuerus and Haman sit down to drink while the city of Shushan is plunged into anxiety (Est. 3:15); and Jehu eats and drinks immediately after his horses trample Jezebel (II Kings 9:33–34). It is possible that Elijah attaches to his message of imminent rain a sort of command to the king to remove any question as to his complete identification with the killing of the prophets of Baal, by eating and drinking in public (just as David asks Joab to admit to the injustice of the killing of Abner by joining the mourning and eulogizing – II Sam. 3:31). But instead of relating this explicitly to what has just happened, the prophet connects his instruction with the reward that will come to those who have returned to worship God alone – the end of the drought. In his characteristic manner, the narrator here again emphasizes the king's acquiescence by repeating the words of the command: "Ahab went up to eat and drink" (v. 42). This emphasis would seem to reinforce the assumption that this is not a mere announcement, but rather another test of faith with which the prophet challenges the king. … Ahab is required to gather all of Israel and the idolatrous prophets at Carmel, without having this demand accompanied by any explicit promise, but now that he is required to complete the action by demonstratively rejecting the slaughtered prophets of Baal, he is promised: "*For* there is the sound of rumbling rain."

This interpretation is the opposite of the previous ones in explaining the relationship between the two parts of Elijah's statement. According to the early commentators, *ki* (for) here means "since"; "the sound of rumbling rain" is the cause, or reason, and "arise, eat, and drink" is the result. According to Simon's interpretation, the reverse is true: Ahab's eating and drinking are going to be the reason for the rain that is destined to fall. This interpretation does not necessarily contradict the previous ones (especially not the Baal HaMetzudot). The formulation of the verse may hint at its intentionally ambivalent message.

"SOUND OF RUMBLING RAIN" – FROM WHERE?

When Elijah commands Ahab to ascend from Wadi Kishon to Carmel in order to eat and drink, the sky is quite clear. There is no noticeable sign that the drought is about to be broken. What, then, is the source of Elijah's confidence that "the sound of rumbling rain" is about to be heard, within a short time, even the same day? This question is posed by Malbim: "How could he say, 'For the sound of rumbling rain,' while there was not yet any sign of the rain, as is written afterward?"[1]

Ralbag, in his customary manner with regard to our narrative, raises two possibilities (he raises two similar possibilities concerning Elijah's actions at Carmel for the purposes of bringing fire from heaven). First he writes: "Elijah trusted God that He would do this."

In other words, Elijah is issuing another decree here – this time, concerning the immediate descent of rain, even as Ahab is still at Carmel, and he trusts that God will do as he has decreed. However, Ralbag immediately goes on to propose another possibility: "Or, he knew this through prophecy."

Concerning the possibility that Elijah does everything in our story based on prophecy, we must ask: Why, then, does Elijah offer a prayer that God answer him with fire, and that He answer him with rain? After all, God Himself has told Elijah that He will bring fire from the heaven, and that He will bring rain upon the face of the earth!

There is no reason here to abandon the approach that we have followed throughout our discussions, and to attribute to Elijah an explicit prophecy that conveyed to him the message that he now tells Ahab. The text offers no hint of the existence of any such prophecy – neither in its description of the events, nor in Elijah's words to Ahab. Despite this, Radak, commenting on this verse, relates Elijah's words here to a previous prophecy:

> Elijah trusted God that He would give rain, *just as He had said to him: "And I will give rain upon the face of the earth"* (18:1). Furthermore [he expected Him to do so] since he had killed the worshippers of Baal (the prophets of Baal) and had removed idolatry.

---

1. From vv. 42–44 we see that when Elijah addressed these words to Ahab there was as yet no sign of the imminent rain.

Thus, on one hand we do have in the background an explicit prophecy as to God's intention to restore the rainfall. But this prophecy was not speaking about the specific event that we are witnessing. At the time of the prophecy, God did not tell Elijah exactly when the rain could be expected – whether it would come that same day or maybe a few days later. Elijah promises immediate rainfall on his own initiative, out of "faith in God" that He would do this. Why does Elijah believe this? Because, quite simply, there is no longer any reason to withhold the rain. God wants to give rain, and all the conditions have been fulfilled, via the actions at Carmel and at Wadi Kishon. Why, then, should rain not come immediately? Moreover, only immediate rainfall will have the effect of demonstrating the direct connection between the nation's repentance and its results. Any delay, even of a single day, may cause great educational harm in its influence on the nation and their king.

Radak's approach here actually nullifies our question as to why Elijah had to pray for rain. Since Elijah had *not* been promised that the rain would fall now, immediately, at the time when *he* felt that it would be most effective, from a religious, educational perspective, he had to pray that God would indeed send the rain at the time when, on his own initiative, he decreed so.

Once again, we witness the partnership between the prophet and his Sender. Elijah operates within the framework of an explicit prophetic mission, which defines only the final objective: "And I will give rain upon the face of the earth." The way to achieve this,[2] the exact circumstances in which the rain will come – all this God leaves to His prophet. It is Elijah who evaluates the situation and the methods best suited to the time and place. Within this framework he initiates various actions which, although they have not been specifically commanded, nevertheless fall within the scope of his prophetic mission. Nevertheless, some of these actions are meant not only for the nation, but also for God, and it is for the success of these – such as the descent of fire and the rainfall – that he prays. Indeed, *Targum Yonatan* interprets his

---

2. In other words, all the actions that Elijah undertakes with a view to making the people worthy of a renewal of the rain: the gathering at Carmel and the proposal of the test.

first prayer (v. 37) in such a way as to reflect both aspects: "'Answer me, Lord, answer me' – Accept my prayer, God, with fire; accept my prayer, God, with water."

Now while Ahab is busy eating and drinking, by command of the prophet, Elijah stands atop Carmel, removed from everyone: "He bent to the ground and placed his face between his knees" (v. 42). He offers a prayer for God's *immediate* response – for the final purpose to which all of his actions thus far have been directed: restoring God's kindness toward Israel and toward the land upon which they dwell – "And I will give rain upon the face of the earth."

Chapter 20

Why Is Elijah's Prayer Not Answered Immediately? (I Kings 18:42–44)

Elijah ascended to the top of Carmel, and he crouched to the ground and placed his face between his knees. He said to his attendant, "Go up, now, look toward the sea." So he went up and he looked, and he said: "There is nothing." Then he said, "Go again, seven times." And it was, on the seventh time, that he said: "There is a small cloud, like a man's hand, ascending from the sea." And he said: "Go up, say to Ahab: Prepare your chariot and come down, that the rain not stop you." And it was, in the meanwhile, the heavens grew dark with clouds and wind, and there was great rain. (vv. 42–45)

In the previous chapter we noted that Elijah's promise to Ahab – "There is the sound of rumbling rain" (v. 41) – was admittedly uttered on his own initiative, and therefore he had to pray to God for it to be fulfilled. But the promise was made with absolute trust that God would answer him, for he had given his word on the basis of the explicit prophecy, "I will give rain upon the face of the earth" (v. 1), as well as Elijah's belief that Israel was now worthy of the divine blessing and that the immediate descent of rainfall would reinforce their repentance.

However, to our great surprise, God seems to be in no hurry to bring rain. The verses quoted above describe a drawn-out, lengthy process. This discrepancy between Elijah's promise to Ahab – "There is the sound of rumbling rain" – and its realization only after three verses full of effort and activity aimed at causing the prophet's words to be realized, demands some explanation. If the plot were to unfold according to our expectations, then immediately after Ahab and Elijah ascend once again to the top of Carmel, and as Ahab is eating and drinking (as described in the first half of verse 42), we would hear what we are in fact told only in the middle of verse 44: "There is a small cloud, like a man's hand, ascending from the sea. And he said … to Ahab, Prepare your chariot and come down.…" In other words, we would expect to find the promise fulfilled immediately, with no need for any further prayer, for any prolonged waiting, or for any attendant watching and observing.

We may postulate that Elijah's prayer has a function: To teach us that it was the prophet's own initiative to promise that the rain would come immediately, and therefore he has to pray. Still, we would expect a brief prayer that would be answered promptly, as in the case of the descent of God's fire upon the altar.

Attention should be paid to the great difference between Elijah's prayer here for rain, and the previous prayer for the descent of fire. First, the circumstances are different. At the time of the great test, Elijah prayed in front of the entire nation, while now he offers a silent, personal prayer in which he stands alone before God. Second, the text told us what the words of the previous prayer were, but offered no clue as to the manner in which Elijah presented his prayer, other than the words, "Elijah approached and said" (v. 36) – apparently because the prayer was accompanied by no outward pose. Now, the situation is reversed: We are told nothing of the content of Elijah's prayer; we have only a description of how Elijah behaved when he offered it: "He crouched to the ground and placed his face between his knees."

It appears that this was how Elijah was positioned all along, until he was informed of the small cloud ascending from the sea. Radak writes, "He did not yet want to get up from his prayer until he found out if there was some sign of rain. Therefore he told his attendant, 'Look toward the sea,' while he himself was still engaged in prayer."

What is this position, assumed by Elijah for his prayer, meant to express? Ralbag writes:

> He bent his head downward such that his face was between his knees, *and he prayed to the blessed God with this submission and humility* in order that his prayer would be better heard, and God would bring rain sooner, in His concern for the prophet *that he would not have to maintain this discomfort.*

This explanation by Ralbag brings us to the third difference between the two prayers. In contrast to the confidence expressed in the prayer that Elijah offers prior to the descent of God's fire (at least in its first part, v. 36), here there is submission and self-effacement meant as supplication to God to answer the prayer speedily and not leave the prophet in prolonged distress. In the meantime, it is to no avail. Ralbag continues:

> Elijah would not agree to move himself from this uncomfortable position until he saw some sign that God had heard his prayer – and this is why Elijah himself could not see (the direction of the sea). And so he continued to pray in this position, and when he completed his prayer he would call to his attendant to look out toward the sea, if he could see any cloud, and he would tell him, "There is nothing" until the seventh time, when he told him that he could already see "a small cloud like a man's hand ascending from the sea."

This, then, is the most obvious difference between the two prayers. Previously, there was an immediate answer as Elijah ended his prayer, while here he is answered only after he offers his prayer seven times in an uncomfortable, self-afflicting position, with his expectation of God's response being dashed time after time.

This is most surprising. We would have expected exactly the opposite: Renewal of the rainfall is precisely the purpose for which Elijah was sent to do all that he has done. But now, as the moment arrives for the realization of all these activities (and indeed, this is the only thing that is mentioned explicitly in the prophecy of the mission that is entrusted to Elijah in 18:1) – specifically now there are delays, and it appears that God barely answers the pleading supplication of His prophet. How are we to explain this, especially considering the fact that the renewal of rain is more of a realization of Elijah's mission than was the descent of fire, which was entirely his own initiative?

Fascinatingly, the commentators pay scant attention to this question.

Let us propose a way of resolving this problem. Perhaps it is not the nation which is the cause for the delay in Elijah's prayer being accepted (as Ralbag maintains), but rather Elijah himself. Elijah, after all, is the only person who is clearly aware of the delay, and thus it would seem that the message of the delay is directed toward him.

At this point in the narrative – when Elijah tells Ahab, "For there is the sound of rumbling rain" and then prays for the rain to actually descend – we find the connection between this story and the previous one, about the drought. It is through Elijah's "word," his oath, that the rain ceased, at the beginning of chapter 17, and it is by his word that it is restored, as Elijah promised at that time: "Except by my word" (17:1).

The prophet's first "word" – his oath in the name of God, "There shall be no dew or rain during these years" – has admittedly been realized, but it has created a conflict between the prophet and God, who has applied different techniques in getting the prophet to retract his oath and to change his unbending position with regard to the nation.

As explained at length in the series of studies on the drought, Elijah is not forced to change his position through external coercion. God leads him to change one step at a time. The decisive stage where the change that he has undergone becomes apparent is in his prayer for the resuscitation of the son of the widow of Zarephath. Elijah's pleading there that the soul of the boy be restored includes an implied agreement to the restoring of rain.[1] And therefore God commands him immediately thereafter, "Go and appear before Ahab, and I will give rain upon the face of the earth" (18:1). But Elijah still needs this command from

---

1. See "The Drought," chapter 6, especially pp. 73–77.

God; he is not moved, on his own initiative, to restore the rain, as he was moved to halt it.

On his way to Ahab and in his meeting with him, Elijah still encounters criticism of his position (both from Obadiah and from Ahab himself). Thereafter begins the second unit within the overall literary narrative – the story of the test at Carmel. The focus of the story shifts away from the matter of the drought and the need for the renewal of rain, but it is clear that it is for the purposes of restoring the rain (which he has been commanded to do) that Elijah carries out all of his activities at Carmel.

The dispute between the prophet and God concerning the necessity of renewing the rainfall has been forgotten in the course of the events at Carmel. After all, this was already decided, when Elijah prayed for life to be restored to the son of the woman of Zarephath, and he was commanded immediately thereafter to appear before Ahab in order that God would give rain. Nevertheless, the conclusion of the dispute was not complete and wholehearted. At the end of the previous narrative of the drought, we did not sense an enthusiastic concurrence on the part of Elijah as to the renewal of rain. He carries out God's command to go to Ahab with mixed feelings, not yet entirely reconciled to the annulling of his oath. He does not rush to cancel the drought and announce the imminent renewal of rain before orchestrating the awesome events at Carmel to lead the nation to repentance. In the first chapter in this unit of Carmel we discussed the fact that Elijah was justified in setting up this test, and that his actions were compatible with God's will. Nevertheless, the subject of the previous narrative – the dispute between God and His prophet concerning the drought – has been left somewhat undecided, for the "parties" never reached any complete and harmonious accord.

Now, following the grand success at Carmel, the time has come for the purpose of the mission entrusted to Elijah to be fulfilled; now he must announce that rain is on its way. Will Elijah still deliberate on this matter? Will he do this only because of the divine word, "I will give rain upon the face of the earth"? Were this the case, Elijah would suffice with notification to Ahab that the rain would soon be renewed, and with this he would conclude his mission and disappear from the scene. In this case, we would note that Elijah had fulfilled his mission in full, as one who is commanded and obeys, but perhaps we would be left with some lingering sense of the previous resistance, which characterized Elijah on his journey to Ahab. We might suspect that the prophet, in his zealous defense of his original position, is not able to change his view and to truly desire good for Israel even now, when they have become worthy of it, and that his promise of rain here simply reflects a situation of being forced by divine command.

However, this is not the way the events turn out. Elijah does not make a laconic announcement that there will soon be rain, but rather *decrees*, with full responsibility, that God is going to fulfill His promise, that rain is going to fall *immediately*: "For there is the sound of rumbling rain." In this he continues his prior prophetical approach, characterized by initiatives on his part meant to repair the state of the nation – initiatives in which God cooperated with him (as in his oath that rain would cease, and as in his proposal of the test at Carmel with its advance assurance that God's fire would descend from heaven and consume his sacrifice).

This already is some indication that Elijah wants to "correct" his prior oath. Just as he applied all his prophetic weight in decreeing the drought, with absolute faith that God would fulfill his word, so he now acts for the opposite objective – the renewal of rain. In this manner, Elijah expresses his *own desire* for the renewal of rain, his full personal concurrence to change his prior oath, and he does this in connection with Ahab, the king, just as his original oath of drought was announced to the king.

However, this is not enough. The dispute as to the renewal of rain was conducted mainly between Elijah and his Sender. In order for it to reach its conclusion, and in order for the complete harmony between the prophet and God in this matter to be clarified and revealed, there is a need for Elijah to appeal to God, in supplication and prayer. There is a reversal of roles here: God, who until now "pressured" Elijah, with the intention of causing him to reconsider his oath and renew the rain, is now revealed as somewhat reluctant to actually make it happen. It is not, heaven forefend, a matter of God reconsidering His intention to give rain – "God is not a man, that He changes His mind, nor a mortal that He may regret: Will He say and not perform; speak and not fulfill

His word?" (Num. 23:19). Rather, now God wants to allow Elijah to reveal his devotion to the nation and to completely retract his oath, in the wake of the nation's repentance, expressing this in heartfelt prayer to God. Thus Elijah expresses his full agreement and personal desire for the renewal of rain *before God*, and through this admission he gives a sort of *retroactive justification* to God's command, at the beginning of the current mission: "Go and appear before Ahab, and I will give rain upon the face of the earth" (v. 1).

This reversal of roles takes place in the verses that we quoted at the outset: God delays His response to Elijah's prayer for some time, thereby leading Elijah to a position of intense supplication, not moving from his earthbound crouch with his head between his knees, until there is rain. The prophet, who was being *requested* all along to change his oath, has become the one who *requests* this so passionately.

In praying for the renewal of rain, Elijah fulfills his task as prophet. He no longer assumes the one-sided role that he has played until now, as God's emissary to Israel; he changes his position and becomes *Israel's emissary before God*. This dual role – of emissary mediating between God and Israel and representing each "party" before the other – is the quintessential role of the prophet in Israel, as fulfilled by the greatest of prophets including Moses, Samuel, and Jeremiah. In his prayer here to God, Elijah is revealed as a prophet like them.

In light of all of the above, it appears that the final section of our story takes us back to the theme of the previous narrative. It is only owing to the success of the test at Carmel in our story that it is possible to bring the subject of the previous story – the dispute between the prophet and his Sender – to a true and final conclusion. In this sense, the plot of the first story is dependent on the plot of the second, just as a proper understanding of the conclusion of the second story requires the background of the first.

The situation in the previous story that is closest, thematically, to Elijah's prayer for the renewal of rain is, of course, the prayer that God restore life to the boy (17:19–24). We may say that that first prayer serves as a preface and preparation for the second. In the first prayer, Elijah asks that life be restored to a single boy; in the second – to an entire nation and its land. In the first prayer, there is an initial, implied expression of

Elijah's readiness to change his oath; in the second, this is explicit and final (as shown above). Indeed, there are several noticeable parallels between the descriptions of these two prayers, as also between God's responses to the prophet in both instances:

- In both places Elijah ascends in order to offer his prayer: there we are told, "He *took him up* to the attic" (17:19), and here: "Elijah *ascended* to the top of Carmel" (18:42).[2]
- There Elijah's prayer was accompanied by action: "He stretched out over the child" (17:21), and here too his prayer is accompanied by action: "He crouched to the ground and placed his face between his knees" (18: 42).
- God does not immediately answer Elijah's prayer for the boy: his first prayer (17:20) meets with no response; only after stretching over the boy "three times" and offering a second prayer (v. 21) does he receive God's answer. Here, too, God does not answer Elijah right away, but only after Elijah has sent his attendant to look out to sea "seven times" (18:43), while he himself remains all the while crouching and praying.
- Elijah informs the mother of the boy that God has responded to his efforts: "See, your son lives" (17:23). Here, too, he sends his attendant to tell Ahab, "Prepare your chariot and come down, that the rain not stop you" (18:44).

And just as the widow reacted to the revelation of this new aspect of Elijah with the words "Now I know that you are a man of God, and that God's word in your mouth is true" (17:24), so we may say that here, too, Elijah has been revealed to Ahab and to Israel as a prophet of Israel who walks in the footsteps of Moses and Samuel, and that God's word in his mouth is true.

---

2. Elijah's ascent to the top of the mountain is prompted by his wish to utter his prayer at the site of the great and auspicious event that made Israel deserving of an immediate renewal of the rain. Furthermore, Mount Carmel now serves Elijah (via the agency of his attendant) as an elevated lookout point, close to the sea – a sort of meteorological station. From here, he will be able to know right away when God answers his prayer, and he can pass on the message to Ahab.

Chapter 21

"God's Hand Was Upon Elijah ... and He Ran Before Ahab" (I Kings 18:45–46)

And he said: Go up, tell Ahab: Prepare your chariot and come down, that the rain not stop you. And it was, in the meanwhile, the heavens grew dark with clouds and wind, and there was a great rain. And Ahab rode and went to Jezreel. And God's hand was upon Elijah, and he girded his loins and ran before Ahab, until the approach to Jezreel. (18:44–46)

ELIJAH RUNNING BEFORE AHAB: SIGNIFICANCE

In chapter 15 we noted that only at three important points in our story do we find evidence of direct divine involvement. The first is at the beginning of this unit:

And it was after many days that *God's word* came to Elijah, in the third year, saying: Go and appear before Ahab, and I will give rain upon the face of the earth. (18:1)

The second point is at the climax of the story:

> *God's fire descended* and consumed the burnt offering and the wood. (v. 38)

And the third is in the concluding verse:

> *God's hand* was upon Elijah, and he girded his loins and ran before Ahab, until the approach to Jezreel. (v. 46)

In chapter 15 we discussed the unique nature of the divine intervention at the climax of the story, in the form of the fire that descends upon the altar built by Elijah. Here we shall discuss the conclusion of the story, which is similarly marked with the stamp of divine intervention.

Although it would seem at first that the third instance of God's involvement here is related to the second (since they both involve miracles), a thematic and linguistic comparison between the three sources reveals that God's involvement in the third is actually connected to the first:

First intervention (18:1)	Third intervention (18:45–46)
	"There was a great rain.
"*God's word came to Elijah* …	*and God's hand was upon Elijah* …
go and appear before Ahab	*and he ran before Ahab.*"
And I will give rain upon the face of the earth."	

Three elements repeat themselves in these two sources: (1) the connection between God and Elijah ("God's word" or "God's hand"); (2) the result – the connection between Elijah and Ahab (the command "Go and appear" to him, or the act of running before him); and (3) the rain (as the original purpose of the command, or as the background to the deed). But the order of these elements is not the same in both cases. When God speaks to Elijah, the giving of rain serves as the purpose of the divine command, and as the aim of his appearance before Ahab. Only after the prophet appears before the king and gets him to cooperate will the result be a renewal of the rainfall. Indeed, this is what happens. But at the end of the story, the rain that falls is what precedes Elijah running before Ahab.

The clear connection between these two points in the story and the change in their internal order (which has the effect of creating a chiastic parallel: going to Ahab, promise of rain; rain falls, running before Ahab), teach us that Elijah's appearance before Ahab at the end of the story is a sort of reconciliatory gesture of honor toward the king. Ahab, who had last met with the prophet at the height of the drought and in a situation that so eloquently illustrated it, argued with the prophet and was required by him to do things that must certainly have been difficult for him. During the course of the story, up until the end, Ahab fulfilled all of the prophet's demands, and thereby he merited seeing the renewal of the rainfall. Now, as the precious rain is falling, the prophet returns to the king, not in order to make demands, but to express – without words, his praise for him. Elijah's running before Ahab, in the pouring rain that *both* of them have so longed for, is a sort of gesture of appreciation and admiration for the king, a demonstration of respect and loyalty. Through this action, which follows on the heels of the cooperation with Ahab during the events at Carmel, Elijah gives legitimacy to Ahab's kingship.

This is the way in which Elijah's running is perceived in *Melkhilta DeRabbi Yishmael* (*Masekhta DePisḥa Bo* 13): "So Elijah demonstrates honor toward the king, as it is written, 'God's hand was upon Elijah, and he girded his loins and ran before Ahab.'"[1]

"GOD'S HAND WAS UPON ELIJAH"

This connection that we have pointed to, between Elijah's appearance before Ahab at the beginning of the story and his running before him at its conclusion, raises the need to examine the relationship between

---

1. Parallels formulated in a different style are to be found in Zevahim 102a and Menahot 98a: "R. Yanai said: The fear of the sovereign should always be upon you.… R. Yohanan deduced it from this verse: 'And God's hand was upon Elijah, and he girded his loins and ran before Ahab.'" Rashi, commenting on our verse (as well as in the above-mentioned talmudic discussions) explains that the honor that Elijah showed Ahab was that "Ahab should not travel alone." However, this prompts us to ask on what basis Rashi assumes that Ahab is alone in his chariot.

Radak seems to suggest that the actual act of running, on foot, before Ahab's chariot, is the expression of giving honor to the king. This makes sense, since both Absalom and Adonijah – both of whom merely aspire to the throne – prepare chariots and horses for themselves, along with fifty men to run before them (see II Sam. 15:1; I Kings 1:5).

"God's word" that came to Elijah at the outset and "God's hand" that was upon him at the end. Are these two instances of divine intervention to be regarded as equivalent, or are they different from one another?

It is perhaps the very connection that we are presently discussing that leads some commentators to regard "God's hand" as a regular prophetic command. Ralbag writes:

> "God's hand was upon Elijah" – this means that *God's word had already come to him*, [telling him] that he should do this; namely, gird his loins and run before Ahab until Ahab reached Jezreel.

The expression "God's hand" may, indeed, be interpreted as referring to verbal prophecy. This is the case, for example, in II Kings 3:15–16: "God's hand was upon him, and he said: So says the Lord." There are several more examples from the book of Ezekiel and from other sources in Tanakh.

However, most of the commentators reject this interpretation of the verse, preferring the approach adopted by *Targum Yonatan*: "A spirit of valor emanating from God was with Elijah."

Rashi writes similarly: "'God's hand' – a spirit of valor emanating from God. He [Elijah] was garbed in strength so as to run on foot before the chariot."

Radak explains in the same vein: "'God's hand' – …as interpreted by the *Targum*… that he was given extra strength and valor. For Ahab had already started riding in his chariot, but Elijah went after him on foot and caught up with him, and then ran before him up until Jezreel."

The same idea is echoed by Abrabanel (whom we shall quote presently), the Baal HaMetzudot, Malbim, and other commentators. Indeed, the expression "God's hand" is used frequently in Tanakh as an expression of *God's strength* as revealed in the physical reality.[2]

The difference between these two commentaries – that offered by Ralbag and the one preferred by those who disagree with him – is not limited to the understanding of the expression "hand of God" at the beginning of 18:46 (whether it refers to prophecy or to a special "spirit of valor" from

---

2. This is true of the great majority of the verses in Tanakh in which this expression appears. An example is, "Behold, *God's hand* is upon your cattle" (Ex. 9:3).

God). This exegetical controversy also gives rise to different ways of perceiving the continuation of the verse. In Ralbag's view, it would seem that Elijah's actual running before Ahab's chariot is nothing out of the ordinary; certainly not something that would usually seem impossible. This was simply Elijah's fulfillment of the instruction that he had received from God.

As the other commentators see it, Elijah's running was something altogether exceptional, a clear deviation from normal human ability. Rashi highlights the fact that Elijah ran *on foot* before a chariot drawn by horses. Radak adds to this that Elijah started running only after Ahab had already begun to ride away, and Elijah managed to catch up with him – on foot. He also adds that the prophet ran before him "up to Jezreel." His astonishment is clear when taking into account the great distance that Elijah ran (about twenty-five kilometers) through the pouring rain, which only made conditions more difficult. Were it not for the "hand of God" – in the sense of a "spirit of valor emanating from God" – Elijah could not have roused himself to such action nor succeeded in it.

Abrabanel, criticizing Ralbag's interpretation, eloquently explains the dispute between the two exegetical approaches:

> "God's hand was" – Some commentators have written that "God's hand" mentioned here was a prophecy that came to Elijah, commanding him to run before Ahab. With all due respect, what they say in this regard is not correct. For Elijah did not receive any word nor any prophecy after God told him, "Go appear before Ahab." When he was atop Mount Carmel, where he acted "with fire and water" and performed miracles and wonders, he received no prophecy about any of them. [Hence it is not logical that specifically here he would experience a prophecy.]
>
> Rather, the "hand of God" mentioned here is the strength that God gave in his heart – Elijah being an elderly Nazirite, a weakened recluse – to run before Ahab, wanting to declare "my foot before his chariot is like a deer" [see II Sam. 2:18], since Ahab was riding upon his horse, and he maintained his pace until he came to Jezreel.

Even if we do not accept Abrabanel's depiction of Elijah as elderly and weak, it is clear that even in the case of someone who is young and fit, there are some activities for which this healthy physical condition can only serve as a good basis for the special divine aid that will be required. So it was in the case of Elijah's journey to Mount Horeb where he was for forty days and forty nights, sustained by the single meal that he ate at the angel's command in the wilderness of Beer Sheba (19:7–8). And the same may be said of his running before Ahab from the top of Carmel to the city of Jezreel in the middle of a downpour. It is with regard to such instances as these that the prophet declares:

> Youths shall grow faint and weary and young men shall stumble and fall; but they who wait upon God shall renew their strength; they shall rise up with wings like eagles, they shall run and not grow weary, they shall walk and not grow faint." (Is. 40:30–31)

This ability on the part of those "who wait upon God" – to run without growing weary, faster and further than all the youths and strong young men (who do not wait upon God) – is a gift bestowed by God from His own strength, as it were. This idea arises from the verses immediately preceding those quoted above:

> The everlasting God, the Lord, Creator of the ends of the earth, does not grow faint, nor does He tire; there is no searching of His understanding. He gives power to the faint, and to the powerless he increases strength. (Is. 40:28–29)

Hence we must conclude, although this is not stated explicitly, that the "hand of God" that was upon Elijah means that a gift of divine strength was bestowed upon the prophet when he decided, of his own accord, to perform a great deed that would have required extraordinary human strength. Maimonides expresses it thus in his *Guide for the Perplexed*:

> A person is accompanied by divine aid, stirring and urging him to perform some great, valuable good ... such that he finds *within himself* a stirring and urging to action.... The purpose of this strength is to arouse that valiant person to action. (II:45)

MOMENT OF GRACE

While the pouring rain serves as the *background* to Elijah running before Ahab, we would be underestimating this act were we to assume that it results from an explicit divine command – as Ralbag suggests. At this point, the prophet is reconciled with his people and their king. Therefore, just as Elijah offered a lengthy prayer (accompanied by prolonged self-affliction) in order for the rain to fall immediately, thereby giving expression to the change in his attitude toward *the nation*, so we now expect him to give some practical expression, *through his own action*, to the change in his attitude toward the king. And this action is his running before Ahab. Abrabanel is correct in his observation that after having performed all of his actions atop Carmel without any explicit divine command, after having succeeded – at his own initiative – in causing the entire nation to repent by means of the test at Carmel, and having restored God's mercy toward His nation, Elijah has no need at this point for an explicit divine command to run before the king's chariot.

The description of the "hand of God" that was upon Elijah is meant to explain Elijah's ability to perform such an extraordinary and difficult feat. But we may add to this that at the conclusion of the story, divine intervention is mentioned as a sort of *seal of divine approval* to the reconciliation and harmony symbolized by Elijah's act. Just as the fire that descended upon Elijah's altar immediately after he offered his prayer expressed God's approval of his actions at Carmel, so the divine aid granted him in his running, and its emphasis in the text, express God's approval of Elijah's final act in this story: his gesture of honor toward the king.

Attention should be paid to this concluding picture, in which we see Elijah running before Ahab's chariot in the driving rain. This is the only image in all of the stories of Elijah in which total harmony prevails among the prophet, his nation, and their king; and between all of them and God.[3] Elijah is a prophet whose path is strewn with struggles on

---

3. The uplifting nature of the moment finds stylistic expression in the sevenfold use of verbs based on the root *ayin-lamed-heh* (ascend) in verses 41–44, indicating a key word. Analysis of the seven appearances shows that everyone "ascends" at this elevated time: Ahab is commanded to "**Go up** (*aleh*); eat and drink, for there a sound of the rumbling of the rainstorm" (v. 41), and he does so: "So Ahab **went up** (*vayaaleh*) to eat and to drink" (v. 42). Other people go up to him: "And he said, '**Go up** (*aleh*),

every front. Not only does he challenge his nation and the royalty, but he is also in conflict with his Sender. There is one sole moment of blessed rest in all of his endeavors, when his prophetic activity has succeeded in a way that is the dream of every prophet: restoring the heart of the nation of Israel to God and God's kindness toward Israel. What joy can be compared to that of a prophet who has succeeded in such a task? We may permit ourselves to imagine this wondrous running of Elijah before Ahab's chariot, his heart overflowing with satisfaction at having arrived at a situation where he is able to show the proper respect to the king of Israel. This act represents Elijah's wholehearted return to his people.

The heavy rain not only fails to halt his running and to dampen his joy; it is testimony to the divine approval of all that he has done. The rain itself is the reason for the joy and the running.

The rain coming down from heaven, the royal chariot progressing through the mud, the drenched prophet with girded loins, running joyfully and tirelessly before the chariot, God's hand replenishing his strength – all converge to create the most perfect and harmonious image that exists in all the chapters of Elijah's activity, and one of the most joyous scenes in the entire history of prophecy.[4]

We sense that this picture contains the first germ of Elijah as he is destined to be revealed in the future: As the one to restore the hearts of the fathers to their children, and the hearts of the children to their fathers; the prophet who comes to bring peace to the world. Elijah, as revealed in the book of Malachi as the bearer of tidings of redemption, and in the legends of our Sages as an old man who loves Israel, sows the seeds of this future activity in our chapter, by running before the chariot of the king of Israel in the middle of the blessed downpour of rain.

---

say to Ahab'" (v. 44). Elijah also ascends: "And Elijah **ascended** (*alah*) to the top of the Carmel" (v. 42). His attendant, too, is commanded to go up, and he does: "And he said to his servant, 'Go up now (*aleh na*), look toward the sea.' And he **went up** (*vayaal*), and looked and said, 'There is nothing'" (v. 43). Lastly, the small cloud representing God's acquiescence also ascends: "And he said, 'Behold, there is a small cloud ... **ascending** (*olah*) from the sea, like a man's hand'" (v. 44). The appearances of this key word were pointed out to me by my friend Shmuel Kedar.

4. Our appreciation of the wholeness and joy of this image is in no way marred by our knowledge that this represents but a brief and fleeting moment, soon to be replaced with bitter disappointment and the continuation of Elijah's dual struggle.

Appendix – Carmel

Elijah the Prophet and Ḥoni HaMeʾagel

I n the last part of the story of Carmel, Elijah announces the imminent arrival of the rain, and then prays for it to come, crouching for a prolonged period on the ground, with his head between his knees, until his prayer is answered and there is a great downpour. The scene is reminiscent of the well-known story of Ḥoni HaMeʾagel, which is likewise set against the background of drought. Let us consider some of the parallels between the two narratives. Our comparison will include the various versions of the story of Ḥoni.[1]

COMPARISON BETWEEN THE TWO CHARACTERS

1. Length of the period of drought before the character acts to bring rain:

---

1. The story appears in a few different tannaitic sources, with minor variations: Mishna Taanit 3:8; a *baraita* in Taanit 23a; and Megillat Taanit, ch. 12, 20 Adar.

Elijah	Ḥoni
"Many days passed and God's word came to Elijah in the third year, saying: 'Go and appear before Ahab, and I will give rain upon the face of the earth.'" (I Kings 18:1)	"Because there was a famine and a drought in the Land of Israel, and rain had not fallen for three consecutive years … until Ḥoni prayed." (Megillat Taanit, 20 Adar)

2. Advance announcement of the imminent rainfall with complete confidence, even before offering prayer:

Elijah	Ḥoni
"And Elijah said to Ahab, 'Go up, eat and drink, for there is the sound of rumbling rain.'" (I Kings 18:41)	"One day they said to Ḥoni HaMe'agel: 'Pray that rain will fall.' He said to them, 'Go out and bring in the Pesaḥ ovens, so that they will not be ruined.'" (Mishna Taanit)

3. Prayer with self-affliction on the part of the worshipper:

Elijah	Ḥoni
"And he crouched to the ground and placed his face between his knees…. Then he said, 'Go again seven times.'" (18:42–43)	"What did he do? He drew a circle and stood inside it, and said to [God]: 'I swear by Your great name that I will not move from here until You have mercy on Your children.'" (Mishna Taanit)

4. The prayer is not answered at first:

Elijah	Ḥoni
"Elijah ascended … and he crouched to the ground…. He said to his attendant … and he looked and said, 'There is nothing.' Then he said, 'Go again seven times.'" (18:42–43)	"He prayed, but no rain fell…. Rain began to drip down. He said, 'This is not what I asked for….' It began to rain hard; he said, 'This is not what I asked for.'" (Mishna Taanit)

5. Eventually there is abundant rain:

Elijah	Honi
"And there was a great rain." (18:45)	"[The rain] fell in moderation, until Israel had to go up from Jerusalem to the Temple Mount because of the rain." (Mishna Taanit)

After the story of the rain that falls in the merit of Honi's actions, the *baraita* records the message that Shimon ben Shetah sent to him, concluding with the words "You importune God and He performs your will, like a son who importunes his father, and he performs his will ... Concerning [the likes of] you the verse says, 'Let your father and mother be glad, and let she who bore you rejoice' (Prov. 23:25)."

The Talmud cites another *baraita* in which the Sanhedrin praise Honi, in a homiletical interpretation of verses in Job:

> For then you shall have your delight in the Almighty, and shall lift up your face to God; You shall make your prayer to Him, and He shall hear you, and you shall fill your vows. You shall also decree a thing, and it shall be established for you, and the light shall shine upon your ways. When men have humbled you, you shall say, There is lifting up – then He shall save him who is humble. He delivers him who is not innocent, and you shall be delivered by the pureness of your hands." (22:26–30)

The *baraita* expounds as follows:

> Our Sages taught: What was the message that the Sanhedrin sent to Honi HaMe'agel? [It was an interpretation of the verse] "You shall also decree a thing and it shall be established for you, and the light shall shine upon your ways": "You shall also decree a thing" – You have decreed [on earth] below, and the Holy One, blessed be He, fulfills your word [in heaven] above. "And the light shall shine upon your ways" – You have illuminated, through your prayer, a generation in darkness. "When men have humbled you,

you shall say, There is lifting up" – You have raised, through your prayer, a generation that has sunk low. "Then He shall save him who is humble" – You have saved, through your prayer, a generation that is humiliated with sin. "He delivers him who is not innocent" – You have delivered, through your prayer, a generation that is not innocent. "And you shall be delivered by the purity of your hands" – You have delivered [the generation] through the work of your pure hands.

All of this praise about the relationship between the *tzaddik* and God, on one hand ("you decree below, and the Holy One, blessed be He, fulfills your word above"), and between the *tzaddik* and his generation, on the other (all the other teachings) could also be said of Elijah's actions in our narrative. Indeed, the commentators sometimes use this teaching, which centers on Ḥoni, to explain how Elijah (and, later, also Elisha) makes decrees which God then fulfills.

DIFFERENCES BETWEEN THE TWO CHARACTERS

Notwithstanding all of the above, there is a great difference between the two characters. Ḥoni's original intention is to end the prolonged drought and renew the rainfall, while Elijah starts by halting the rainfall and making it dependent on his decree; only at the end of the story does he, too, pray for the rain to return. Still, there is a similarity between them even at the stage preceding Elijah's supplication for rain: Both of these characters hold the "key to rain" (although in the early stages they use it in opposite ways).

Indeed, there are fascinating parallels between Elijah's actions before he prays, and the actions of Ḥoni:

1. The vow:

Elijah	Ḥoni
"As the Lord God of Israel lives, before whom I stood; there shall be no dew or rain during these years except by my word." (17:1)	"I swear by Your great name that I will not move from here until You have mercy upon Your children." (Mishna Taanit)

2. The prayer:

Elijah	Honi
"Lord, God of Abraham, Isaac, and Israel, Today let it be known that You are Lord in Israel and I am Your servant, and by Your word I have done all of these things." (18:36)	"Lord of the universe, Your children are depending on me, for I am like a familiar and trusted servant before You.... I shall not move from here until You have mercy upon Your children." (Mishna Taanit)

3. The bull:

Elijah	Honi
"Let two bulls be given to us." (18:23) "And he carved the bull into pieces, and set it upon the wood." (18:33)	"'Bring me a bull for a thanksgiving offering.' So they brought him a bull for a thanksgiving offering. He placed both his hands upon it and said." (*Baraita*, Taanit 23a)

Both characters are distinguished by the elevated position that they occupy before God, who fulfills their decrees. But their decrees are intended for different purposes: Elijah decrees a drought for the people, and God fulfills his word; at Mount Carmel he undertakes various actions with a view to bringing the nation back to God, and here, too, his actions are awarded divine approbation. All of Honi's actions, by contrast, are meant for one single purpose: To cause God to take pity on Israel and grant them rain. Honi is single-mindedly compassionate toward Israel, with no conditions and no limitations.

The contrast that we see between the respective oaths of Honi and Elijah finds explicit expression at the beginning of the *baraita* quoting Shimon ben Shetah (cited above):

Shimon ben Shetah sent to him, saying: "Were you not Honi, I would issue a decree of excommunication against you. For if now was a time like the period of Elijah, when Elijah held the keys of rain [and he decreed a drought, but you caused it to rain], would God's name not be desecrated because of you?"

The commentary attributed to Rashi explains as follows:

> [Shimon ben Shetaḥ is telling Ḥoni:] Elijah swore, "As the Lord lives … there shall be no dew or rain during these years except by my word," while you swore that you would not move until rain fell. Thus, there would be a desecration of God's name through you – since one of you, necessarily, would be shown to have sworn in God's name in vain.

In other words, Shimon ben Shetaḥ suggests that perhaps the drought in Ḥoni's time was decreed by someone righteous like Elijah, and Ḥoni's vow would directly contradict the vow of that righteous person.

The contrast between Elijah and Ḥoni goes beyond the purpose of their prospective vows. The two narratives also differ in terms of their general atmosphere. The story of Elijah is full of tension and includes shifts in the relationship between the prophet and God, on one hand, and in the relationship between the prophet and the king and nation, on the other. The story of Ḥoni, on the other hand, is full of joy, despite the criticism of Shimon ben Shetaḥ. It is no coincidence that in terms of his relationship with God, Elijah says, "I am Your servant," while Ḥoni calls himself a "familiar and trusted servant" (*ben bayit* – meaning, someone born as a servant in his master's house).[2] Despite the fact that both terms denote servitude, the expression that Ḥoni uses connotes a closer relationship. Shimon ben Shetaḥ takes the love and intimacy a step further: "Like a son who importunes his father, and he performs his will. Concerning [the likes of] you the verse says, 'Let your father and mother be glad, and let she who bore you rejoice' (Prov. 23:25)." His words conclude with a fitting expression of the joy expressed in this story.

These differences between the two characters, who are described in surprisingly similar terms, reflect the stark difference between the circumstances of the biblical period and those of the late Second Temple

---

2. Cf. Genesis 15:2–3.

period, toward the end of the reign of the Hasmoneans. Elijah is a prophet, whose mission is to mend the ways of a generation mired in the grave sin of idolatry. He acts as God's emissary to cause the nation to repent. It is a complex task and the process is characterized by extreme shifts in the relationship between the prophet and the nation.

Ḥoni is not a prophet. He is a pious individual whose status before God in some ways resembles that of Elijah. He is not God's emissary to His people, but the people's emissary toward God. He "exploits" his special relationship with God in a one-sided manner – solely for the overt benefit of Israel.

Ḥoni's generation, too, despite all its problems, is not like the generation of Elijah. It is not a generation of idolaters, and there is no need to cause them suffering, as was the case in the generation of Elijah. Ḥoni's generation follows the instruction of Shimon ben Shetaḥ, and there are Sages who convene in the Chamber of Hewn Stone.

Despite these differences between Elijah and Ḥoni, and between the respective periods in which they live, the midrash draws a direct comparison between them. The Sages comment on the verse "For the Lord had not caused it to rain upon the earth, and there was no man to till the ground" (Gen. 2:5) as follows: "There was no man [leader] to cause people to serve the Holy One, blessed be He, like Elijah and like Ḥoni HaMe'agel" (Genesis Rabba 13:6).

What the midrash seems to be saying is that when there is no "man" of the stature of Elijah or Ḥoni – the type of leader who leads people to the service of God – then God does not bring rain upon the earth. The mention of these two characters together in this context would appear to be based on the comparison set forth above between the biblical story of the rain in the days of Elijah, and the similar story of rabbinical origin about Ḥoni. Thus, Ḥoni is viewed in this midrash as someone who may not be a prophet but nevertheless "causes people to serve the Holy One, blessed be He."

Horeb

לֹא בָרוּחַ... לֹא בָרַעַשׁ... לֹא בָאֵשׁ ה׳

Not in the wind... not in the earthquake... not in the fire was God.

I Kings 19:11–12

Chapter 22

Structure of the Story (I Kings 19:1–21)

F rom the beginning of this narrative to its end, Elijah undertakes a long journey, leaving the Land of Israel and returning, traveling in an almost-complete geographical circle. He departs from the city of Jezreel, which is to the west of Beit She'an (where he arrived at the end of I Kings, ch. 18), goes southward, and via the city of Beer Sheba he sets off for the depths of the wilderness of Sinai and reaches his ultimate destination at the mountain of Horeb. From there he returns along the same route, arriving, by the end of chapter 19, in Abel Meholah, the city of Elisha, which is southeast of Beit She'an.[1]

---

1. An introduction to this section is to be found in the appendix to the chapters on the Drought – "The Complete Narrative of I Kings Chapters 17–19 and Its Components."
   Our discussion of the story of Horeb is based on Midrash from various sources, and the commentators who develop the midrashic approach. The midrashim are consolidated into a systematic view of the narrative by Rabbi Yehoshua Bachrach in *Yona ben Amitai VeEliyahu* (Jerusalem, 5727), 131–42.
   Our discussion here is inspired by an article by Y. Zakovitch, "Kol Demama Daka – Tzura VeTokhen BeMelakhim I, 19," *Tarbitz* 51 (5742), 329–46. The central innovative contribution of his article is cited in his name and in his words, in chapter 28 below.

Most of the action of this story (19:8–18), and the events that are also central to the narrative take place at Mount Horeb. The real heart of the story is the revelation at Mount Horeb, in verses 11–12. This revelation is at the very center of the story, with ten verses preceding it (vv. 1–10) and nine following (vv. 13–21); thus, it serves as a central axis. The various events of the story form a symmetrical structure around the revelation:

A: Elijah leaves Jezreel for the wilderness of Beer Sheba, to be alone there, at the outskirts of habitation. "He left his attendant." (vv. 1–4)

  B: The revelation of the angel who commands Elijah to eat, "For *the way* is too far for you" to Mount Horeb. (vv. 5–8)

    C: God speaks to Elijah at the cave, "What do you seek here, Elijah?" Elijah answers, "I have been exceedingly zealous… and they seek my life, to take it." (vv. 9–10)

      D: The revelation: the wind, the earthquake, and the fire, and after these – the still small voice. (vv. 11–12)

    C': God's word to Elijah at the entrance to the cave: "What do you seek here, Elijah?" and his answer – "I have been exceedingly zealous… and they seek my life, to take it." (vv. 13–14)

  B': God's word commanding Elijah, "Go, return on *your way*" from Mount Horeb back to the Land of Israel. (vv. 15–18)

A': Elijah's return from the wilderness to Abel Meholah, where Elisha joins him as his servant. (vv. 19–21)

Clearly, this structure, built around the revelation in verses 11–12, testifies to the great importance of this revelation. Both style and content here reflect its exalted atmosphere and the fact that it is the culmination of all that has preceded it and the reason for all that follows.

The parallels between the corresponding parts of the story in its symmetrical structure are varied in nature: C' is a perfect, word-for-word repetition of C (God's question as to what Elijah is doing there, and his reply); there is a thematic parallel between B and B' (command by God or by His angel to Elijah to set off on a journey), with a contrasting parallel in geographical terms (the direction of B is southward, to Mount Horeb, while B' directs the prophet northward, from Mount Horeb back to the Land of Israel); a completely contrasting parallel exists between A and A', both geographically and in terms of Elijah's actions (he departs habitation for the wilderness, leaving his attendant in Beer Sheba, and then returns from the wilderness to habitation and takes another attendant, Elisha, to serve him).

It is of great importance to uncover the structure of the story. The parallels between the various parts of the story help us understand the significance of various events that take place along the way, as well as clarify the significance of the story as a whole. The structure also helps to define the exact boundaries of the story and refutes various claims that have been made contesting its integrity.[2]

---

2. Lack of attention to the structure of our story (which is typical of many biblical narratives), along with other factors, have led certain critics to discard various elements of the overall narrative. Parts of the story have been discounted on the basis of weak arguments, with no concern for the grave damage to its clear, harmonious structure. E. Würthwein, in his article "Elijah at Horeb," in *Proclamation and Presence – Old-Testament Essays in Honour of G. H. Davies* (London, 1970), quoted by Zakovitch in "Kol Demama Daka," p. 339, n. 20, uproots the very heart of the story, verses 11–12, following which his discarding of other parts pales into insignificance. J. Wellhausen, *Die Composition des Hexateuchs* (Berlin, 1899), likewise cited by Zakovitch in the same article, p. 335, n. 11, discards verses 9–10 ("What are you doing here" – "I have been exceedingly zealous"), arguing that they represent a repetition of verses 13–14. Zakovitch himself (p. 330), following in the footsteps of J. J. Stamm, in "Elia am Horeb," in *Studia Biblica et Semitica* (Wageningen, 1966), to whom he refers in notes 1–2, proposes omitting verses 19–21 (the encounter between Elijah and Elisha). Each of these proposals deals a mortal blow to the texture of the story – before we even approach the question of the legitimacy of such textual revision in principle.

Chapter 23

Elijah's Flight
(I Kings 19:1–4)

JEZEBEL'S THREAT

Ahab recounted to Jezebel all that Elijah had done, and that he had put all the prophets to death by the sword. (19:1)

Ahab's recounting to Jezebel, his wife, "all that Elijah had done," is both the point of departure for our story and the connecting link between the present narrative and the previous one. The character of Ahab, and his motives in telling Jezebel what happened, are given no further treatment in our story[1] (and no unequivocal conclusion can be drawn from the indirect reporting of the verse itself); hence, we shall move on to

---

1. Based on verse 1 it is difficult to make any unequivocal assertion concerning Ahab's motives in this story, since his words are reported indirectly and, it would seem, only partially. Perhaps he tells his story from a neutral perspective, as an objective report. Some commentators (Abrabanel and Malbim) maintain that Ahab's purpose in recounting the events is "to extol Elijah." However, we might also suggest the opposite: that he seeks to incite Jezebel and cause her to act against Elijah. If this is indeed the case, we must conclude that there is a new turning point in Ahab's stance, from the moment he returns to Jezebel's sphere of influence. Her uncompromising threat of execution, issued to Elijah immediately upon hearing Ahab's account, would seem to support this view. If Ahab had tried to extol Elijah, how could Jezebel think that she could realize her threat?

address the results of his report: "Jezebel sent a messenger to Elijah, saying: So shall the gods do to me, and more, if I do not end your life like the life of one of those by this time tomorrow" (v. 2).

Why does Jezebel postpone the death sentence for Elijah by a whole day, and why does she inform him of it in advance? By doing so, she leaves open the possibility of his escape!

In *Midrash Shemuel* (*parasha* 22), R. Yehuda, in the name of R. Shimon, draws a parallel between this act of Jezebel and a somewhat similar act by Saul, who does not inform David in advance of his plan to kill him: "Saul sent messengers to the house of David, to guard him and to kill him in the morning" (I Sam. 19:11). While disapproving of Saul's act, R. Yehuda in the name of R. Shimon expresses praise for Jezebel:

> Concerning that which is written, "Because you have been more tumultuous than the nations surrounding you … and have not acted [even] in accordance with the practices of the nations that are around you" (Ezek. 5:7), R. Yehuda said in the name of R. Shimon: You have not acted even as the worst [among the nations]. Jezebel was the daughter of pagan priests, but she sent to Elijah and told him, "…if I do not end your life like the life of one of those by this time tomorrow," *thereby leaving him an opportunity to escape.* But here, "Saul sent messengers.…" Thus, you [the nation of Israel] have not acted even as the worst of the nations.

This view that Jezebel wants to leave Elijah an opportunity to escape seems difficult to accept as an accurate interpretation of the literal text. Along with the threat, Jezebel attaches an oath to her gods: "So shall the gods do to me, and more." If she really means to allow Elijah to escape, her oath is meaningless.

A different possibility as to Jezebel's motives may arise from the narrative of the vineyard of Naboth, in I Kings, chapter 21. A question that is somewhat similar to ours arises in relation to the complicated plot that Jezebel weaves around Naboth, to put him to death by means of a false, staged verdict with the hidden cooperation of the elders of his city. Radak comments as follows (21:10):

We must ask: Since the princes and nobles knew that this matter was false, why did they need all of this [procedure of a court case]? They could simply put him to death at Jezebel's command, with no need for testimony or anything else!

The answer is ... [that] *if Jezebel wanted to kill him without any judgment, she would not be able to do it.... If [Ahab and Jezebel] were to kill and seize without judgment, the nation would rebel against them,* for they would not allow a king to reign over them who did not rule by justice.... Therefore Jezebel sought some ruse whereby Naboth could legally be put to death.

In light of the above explanation by Radak, we may similarly explain in our chapter that Jezebel was obligated to "organize" Elijah's death in a legal manner, by presenting official, open accusations. Jezebel is aware of the limitations of her power; she cannot kill Elijah through an act of royal despotism. Masses of subjects would object to such an act and would rebel. Therefore, she must prepare Elijah's execution in an apparently legal way, in order to silence the claims that Elijah's supporters might raise. For this purpose, she needs the cooperation of Ahab, her husband, and the legal authorities, and all of this will take some time. (Malbim suggests that Ahab's account of Elijah's actions had been sympathetic toward the prophet, and Jezebel wanted time to convince him that Elijah was indeed deserving of death.)

This, then, is the reason for the delay, and for the messengers. In other words, this is a declaration of Jezebel's intentions. She will not kill Elijah in secret, by means of covert executioners. She intends to put him to death openly, in an official, open court case. She wants his death to repay, measure for measure, his execution of "her" prophets of Baal. She expresses this explicitly: "I shall end your life *like the life of one of those.*" Just as they were killed openly, so Elijah will be killed openly. And since the Kingdom of Israel, with its legal and executive institutions, is the plaintiff, as it were, and consolidated against him, Jezebel has no fear that he will escape. It is possible that Jezebel even took the trouble to post guards around the area where Elijah was located. However, as we know, Jezebel's plan fails, and Elijah escapes: "He [Elijah] saw this, and he arose, and went for his life" (v. 3).

THE JOURNEY TO BEER SHEBA AND THE WILDERNESS

> When he saw [this] he arose and went for his life, and he came
> to Beer Sheba which is in Judah, and he left his attendant there.
> And he went a day's journey into the wilderness, and he came
> and sat under a certain broom tree, and asked for himself that
> he might die, and he said: Enough now, God; take my life, for I
> am no better than my fathers. And he lay down and slept under
> a certain broom tree. (19:3–5)

Elijah wastes no time: "When he saw [this] he arose and went..." (*vayaar,*
vayakom, vayelekh) (v. 3). The three successive verbs give the impression
of intensive activity. "He saw"[2] – this indicates that he assessed the situation and reached his conclusion: "He arose and went...."

What is the meaning of the expression "He went for his life"?
Ralbag explains: "He went *to escape* for his life" Why, then, did he go
specifically to Beer Sheba? It seems that the verse itself may be pointing
to the answer: "which is in Judah." Radak comments as follows: "Meaning, he left the jurisdiction of Ahab and his land, and went to the land
of Judah, out of fear of Jezebel."

But Elijah's next actions do not fit our interpretation thus far. If
Elijah's intention is simply to flee from Jezebel and save his life, why
does he leave his attendant in Beer Sheba and go a day's journey into
the wilderness, apparently with neither food nor drink? What is his
intention in this journey?

It seems that Elijah means to meditate alone in the middle of the
wilderness, under a certain broom tree (v. 4). But for what purpose? The
continuation of the verse answers the question: "And asked for himself
that he might die, and he said: Enough now, God; take my life, for I am
no better than my fathers."

Till now we have interpreted Elijah's actions as flight or escape.
A person who flees for his life is trying to stay alive. How, then, are we
to reconcile his intensive activity to save himself with the contradictory

---

2. Thus the text reads in our version *vayaar,* "he saw." However, in some Hebrew
   manuscripts, as well as in the ancient translations (with the exception of the Aramaic
   translation), the word is rendered *vayira,* "he feared."

action of going out alone into the wilderness, with no possibility of survival, for the purpose of explicitly asking God to take his life?

Let us review the answers proposed by some of the commentators. The first approach is presented by Radak (representing several other similar opinions), who restricts himself to the literal level:

> "And he went … into the wilderness" – even in the land of Judah he was not safe, for perhaps Jezebel would send messengers to kill him there. Therefore, he left inhabited areas and went into the wilderness, a place where he would find no means of subsistence and would die, for he had chosen death over life, *or so that God would appear to him and tell him what to do.* "And he said: Enough …" – in other words, I have had enough of this world, *I am in danger daily.*

Ralbag presents a similar view:

> He chose to go into the wilderness so that no one would see him and be able to report to Jezebel. "And he asked for himself that he might die" – *he was so hungry* that he would prefer to die.

In other words, according to these commentators the transition from Elijah's determined flight to save himself to his despairing request that God take his life arises from the hopelessness of his situation – the constant danger that cannot be avoided, or from the hunger that threatens his life in the only place where he is not in danger of being caught. Radak adds a positive alternative to our interpretation of Elijah's request to die: *"or that God would appear to him and tell him what to do."* This possibility does admittedly remove the contradiction between his two states of mind, but it has no support whatsoever in the text.

It is difficult to accept the view proposed by Radak and Ralbag, simply because if we assume their psychological explanation, Elijah's transition to wanting to die is too sudden. He has just embarked on his flight and already complains that he is in danger "daily" (Radak); he is already so overcome with starvation (Ralbag) that he prefers to die?

Let us turn to Malbim and his interpretation:

"He went for his life" – for Elijah secluded himself most of the
time, working on perfecting himself; only when it was necessary
was he a prophet sent to the nation. After seeing that all the wonders that he had brought about had not had the intended effect,
he saw that he had no business trying to perfect the nation, and
therefore he arose *and returned to the occupation of perfecting himself.* … "He left his attendant there" – so as to separate himself from
human company, to go out into the wilderness to be alone, for
this is what he now sought to do, as it is written, "If only I could
be in the wilderness, a lodge for wayfarers" (Jer. 9:1). He walked
alone a day's journey into the wilderness, "and came" – i.e., then
he came to the place that he had sought. Having distanced himself a day's journey from habitation, he was where he wanted to
be, for there he could be alone with God.

What the other commentators interpreted simply as a flight from Jezebel,
Malbim regards as a *quest to perfect himself* – isolation and meditation
for the positive purpose of spiritual perfection. How, then, does Malbim
explain Elijah's request to die?

"And he asked for himself" – for he saw that he had already
achieved, on the individual level, that which he was supposed
to achieve in his mortal life, and therefore it was proper that his
soul should return to the source of life and leave the material
garb separating it from the radiant light. This is the meaning of
the expression "He asked for himself" (literally, "for his soul") –
namely, for the benefit of his soul. Not dying would mean … that
he had not yet achieved all that he was supposed to in his life,
and it was concerning this that he said, "Enough now, God" – he
had already perfected himself and performed more than enough.

According to this understanding, even Elijah's request to die is to be
interpreted in a positive light, without bitterness or despair, but simply
as a well-thought-out spiritual conclusion with a positive aim.

Let us now try to explain Elijah's flight to the wilderness of
Beer Sheba and his request to die there, in a way that departs from

both perspectives that have been presented thus far. We shall start by borrowing from Malbim the element of his explanation with which we must agree: Elijah went off into the wilderness "after seeing that all the wonders that he had brought about had not had the intended effect." Relative to the exalted sensation and great success at Mount Carmel, described in the previous chapter, the current events represent, for Elijah, a descent from great heights to abysmal depths. Elijah's words to God at Mount Horeb, uttered twice (v. 10 and v. 14), testify to his overwhelming sense of failure and defeat with regard to all of his efforts to bring the nation to repentance. In retrospect, his request that God take his life must be understood as an expression of despair over his prophetic role and the path that he has taken thus far. What does it mean when a prophet despairs of his role? It can only mean that he despairs of the nation. The prophet's role is to be God's emissary to the nation, and the failure of his mission is in fact the failure of Israel to engage in repentance and return to God. Malbim wisely quotes the verse from Jeremiah ("If only I could be in the desert, a lodge for wayfarers") to explain that the wilderness is an appropriate place for the prophet to isolate himself and meditate. However, Malbim quotes only the first part of the verse and writes "etc.," instead of explicitly including the rest of the verse, which is the essence of the parallel to Elijah: "I would abandon my people and go from them, for they are all adulterers, a gathering of treacherous people … they do not fight for the truth in the land." Indeed, this verse sheds much light on Elijah's quest to be alone in the desert, out of despair over the people.[3]

Now we must find a different explanation for the reason for Elijah heading specifically to Beer Sheba. "The end of the act" – going off into the desert in despair and asking to die – has been thought out from the beginning. That is exactly why Elijah chooses to go to Beer Sheba,

---

3. The citation of the verse from Jeremiah above requires that we also emphasize in what ways the situation here is different. Jeremiah expresses a theoretical wish, as part of his sermon of rebuke to the nation. Thus, he describes a situation of solitude in the desert merely as a rhetorical prophetic device. Elijah, on the other hand, actually goes to the desert, in order to physically distance himself from the nation. In addition, Jeremiah, in contrast to Elijah, makes no mention of death; he describes only the solitude.

bordering on the wilderness and representing the outskirts of the inhabited area of the country (as referred to in many places in Tanakh in the expression "from Dan to Beer Sheba").

Many of the commentators question the essence of this despair. Are all yesterday's achievements at Mount Carmel eradicated just because of Jezebel's decree? Did Elijah expect that even she would be included among those who would return to God? Why does Elijah despair of his mission and of the entire nation just because of the predictable behavior of the gentile queen, daughter of the king of Sidon?

The answer must be sought on two levels. On the objective level, we need an explanation that makes Elijah's response compatible with what is going on – Jezebel's threat. On the subjective level, his response has to make sense in light of his personality as depicted in the previous chapters (and in the events to follow).

On the objective level, it would seem that if the situation allows Jezebel to act exactly as she would have done previously and to threaten Elijah's life so openly and brazenly, then the practical and national significance of the events at Mount Carmel has indeed, to some extent, been nullified. Seemingly, a huge spiritual revolution has taken place: The people recognized God as the only true God worthy of worship and even expressed readiness to translate this religious consciousness into action, by taking part in the slaughter of the 450 false prophets who ate at Jezebel's table. They were prepared to confront Jezebel, the powerful wife of the king.

But such revolutions are not complete if they are not given immediate political expression. Elijah, it seems, hoped that one of the following developments would ensue: Either the gathering at Carmel would not disperse, but would collectively head for Ahab's palace with the demand that Jezebel be banished; or, at least, Ahab, who cooperated with Elijah and was shown a gesture of reconciliation by the prophet, who ran before his chariot, would decide to limit his wife's scope of activity so that her power would be lessened and she would no longer be an active incitement to idolatry in Israel (and, obviously, would no longer pursue the prophets of God).

However, none of this happened. Jezebel continues to act as she always has, and no one objects. Ahab has not only taken no steps against

Jezebel, but in returning to the sphere of her influence, has returned to his old ways. It is he who causes her (whether intentionally or not) to act against Elijah by telling her of the slaughter of her prophets. How disappointed Elijah must be in the behavior of this fickle king, to whom he had awarded honor by running before his chariot in the pouring rain just the day before. We noted above that Jezebel's threat demonstrates her intention to have Elijah sentenced to death by an open, public court. But where are all the masses who were gathered at Carmel? Why have they all now deserted the prophet? Why are they not preventing the queen from carrying out her plan? Only yesterday they witnessed the fire descending from heaven at Elijah's command, and the rain that came down in his merit. Now this great prophet, who brought them back to the God of their forefathers, is forced to flee from their midst like a criminal. Clearly, everything that was achieved at Carmel was external and temporary.

Aside from this objective perspective, relating to Jezebel's threat, attention must also be paid to Elijah's path as a prophet thus far. He has acted (and, to some extent, will continue to act) in drastic ways, expecting immediate results. We see this in his decree of absolute drought, in his encounter with the widow at the gates of Zarephath, and in several aspects of the episode at Carmel. This path, involving harsh punishment of the people, fails to meet with divine approval; on the contrary, God gradually urges Elijah away from it. But when the prophet's strict and demanding path turns into one that involves not punishment but rather a drastic awakening, as at Carmel, he seems to be granted divine approbation. However, now Elijah experiences profound personal disappointment: His path is not bearing the fruit that he anticipated. Any words of comfort that we may imagine ourselves offering to him – that the seed sown at Carmel might eventually ripen at a later time, etc. – would not console Elijah, who expects full and immediate success.

What Elijah sees now is what Moses saw as he descended Mount Sinai: The nation that just weeks ago declared, as one man with one heart, "All that God has spoken we shall do and we shall hear" (Ex. 19:8), and that merited a divine revelation and the gift of God's holy commandments, is now prancing around the Golden Calf.

The power of revelation and miracles is only temporary, for they are essentially a form of external coercion, forcing man to attain the special spiritual level that their occurrence brings about. Hence the expression of *Ḥazal* concerning the experience at Sinai: "He held the mountain over them like a bucket" (Shabbat 88a). The experience of fire descending from heaven before the eyes of Israel gathered at Carmel brought about a great elevation of spirit and a realization that "the Lord – He is God." But a profound, thorough, long-term change in consciousness was not achieved. Elijah realized this the very next day, and it caused him great despair.

It would seem that the narrative of Elijah going off to isolate himself in the wilderness of Beer Sheba and seeking to die is, like the continuation of this chapter, meant as a criticism of the prophet. This moment, in which the lonely, despairing prophet sits under the broom tree, asking God to relieve him of his mission and of his life, in which he sees no further purpose, is the nadir of Elijah's prophetic career.

ELIJAH'S FEAR OF JEZEBEL

As we read of Elijah's hurried flight in the face of Jezebel's threat – "He saw this, and arose and went for his life and came to Beer Sheba" (19:3) – we cannot but echo the question posed by the Zohar (I, 209a):

> But Elijah, who would decree and the Holy One would fulfill his decree – who decreed concerning the heavens that they would not give rain and dew – how could he fear Jezebel who sent to him, as it is written: "At this time tomorrow I shall make your life like the life of one of them"? And immediately he was afraid and fled for his life.

The Zohar answers the question as follows:

> It may be established that righteous people do not seek to trouble God [to provide them with special protection] in cases of common, obvious danger. Like Samuel, who protested (I Sam. 16:2), "How can I go? Saul will hear of it and will kill me!" and God told him, "You shall take a heifer with you...." Likewise here,

Elijah, seeing that danger was clear and immediate, did not wish to trouble his Lord.

However, this answer, seeking to explain the behavior of these two great prophets in situations of danger, raises a real difficulty. The threat facing each of these prophets was not an incidental danger that happened to arise in the course of their mission as divine agents. Were this the case, we could indeed argue that since this was a common sort of danger, they would be obligated to take the appropriate precautions. But the danger involved in each of the instances in question arose from opposition to the prophetic mission itself, and the opponents who represented the "common and obvious danger" were the very people against whom the prophetic mission was directed, and they therefore sought to sabotage it! How is it possible that a prophet should be forced to fulfill his mission in a roundabout manner, or to flee from it, rather than being able to stand squarely against his opponents? Should a request of God that He protect His emissaries against those seeking to destroy them and to silence the word of God at the very time that they are trying to fulfill their mission, be considered as "troubling" God?

There are many instances in Tanakh that would seem to contradict this theory. The prophets are not afraid to carry out their missions, even when the danger to their lives is clear and predictable. Elijah himself appears before Ahab and before his son, Ahaziah, with stern messages that may put him at risk. We understand the readiness of the prophets to take these risks on the assumption that the very imposition of the mission upon the prophet includes a divine promise to protect him from those plotting against him and his message. Indeed, God tells Jeremiah explicitly, at the outset of his prophetic endeavor:

> As for you, gird your loins and arise and speak to them all that I shall command you; do not be dismayed at them, lest I dismay you before them. Behold, I have made you this day a fortified city and a pillar of iron and walls of brass against the whole land, against the kings of Judah and its princes, its priests, and the people of the land. They shall fight against you but shall not prevail against you, for I am with you, says God, to deliver you. (Jer. 1:17–19)

Jeremiah was, in fact, in danger of his life on several occasions, but he did not desist from prophesying.

The Netziv[4] provides insight as to a proper understanding of Samuel's fear of fulfilling his prophecy by noting the context in which the dialogue between God and the prophet takes place:

> A person who is utterly devoted to God, with no will of his own at all, should not fear anything, even common and obvious danger.... But Samuel sensed in himself some sadness concerning Saul, as we know,[5] and could not muster joy at the fulfillment of the divine command, bringing him to love of God and closeness to Him. For this reason he asked, justifiably ["How shall I go?"], and the Holy One answered him, appropriately ["Take a heifer..."].

Thus, it is only when the prophet performs his mission without identifying with it, that it is appropriate that he fear any common danger. And then God allows for this (even though He does not thereby justify the reason for the prophet's need for precautionary measures).

Let us now return to the Zohar's question concerning Elijah. Here, too, we may say that were Elijah completely agreeable to his prophetic mission, and were he prepared to continue in his efforts to bring Israel back to serving God, then even in the face of Jezebel's threat to his life and with no support from the nation, he would be able to muster the strength to face her without fear, and he would merit divine protection from this danger. Then the promise made to Jeremiah would be fulfilled in him, too: "Behold, I have made you this day a fortified city and a pillar of iron and walls of brass against the whole land ... for I am with you, says God, to deliver you."

However, Elijah does not wish to continue his prophetic mission. Without the joy of fulfilling God's command, with no sense of identification with his endeavor, he does not feel safe against Jezebel's threats.

---

4. *Haamek Davar* and *Harḥev Davar* on Exodus 32:26.
5. In other words, Samuel wanted Saul's reign to continue, and therefore it was difficult for him to identify with the mission of anointing Saul's successor.

Therefore, he justifiably senses the obvious, immediate danger, and flees for his life to Beer Sheba.

We may now conclude that it is not the flight from Jezebel that gives rise to Elijah's despair and his wish to die; in fact, the reverse is the case. Elijah's despair of his role and of the nation, to whom his mission is addressed, comes first; it is this despair that causes him to fear and to flee from Jezebel.

SUPPLEMENT: "A MAN AND NOT GOD"

As we noted above, the moment when Elijah sits alone under the broom tree and asks to die represents the lowest point in his prophetic career. But even here, where it seems that the text is making no attempt to speak in the prophet's favor, describing him instead as wallowing in the depths of despair, the Midrash finds something good to say about him.

Midrash Tanḥuma (*Bereishit* 7) presents a lengthy indictment of great rulers who considered themselves gods: Hadrian, the Roman caesar; the king of Tyre – to whom an entire chapter (28) in the book of Ezekiel is devoted in light of his declaration there (v. 2), "*I am God; I sit in God's seat in the heart of the seas,*" while in truth: "*You are a man, not God, although you have set your heart as the heart of God.*" The midrash continues this rebuke by quoting, as the shining example of the opposite of the king of Tyre, the quintessential Israelite character who is the most elevated above humans and the closest to God – Elijah the prophet:

> "You are a man, not God," the Holy One said:
>
> | I revive the dead | and Elijah revived the dead, |
> | | *but he did not say, "I am God."* |
> | I bring rain | and Elijah brought rain; |
> | I withhold rain | and Elijah did too, |
>
> as it is written: "There shall be no dew or rain during these years, except by my word" (I Kings 17:1).
>
> I brought down fire and sulfur upon Sodom,
> and Elijah did too,

as it is written; "If I am a man of God, let fire descend from the heaven" (II Kings 1:12),

> *but he did not say, "I am God,"*
> *yet you say, "I am God; I sit in God's seat"?*

If you say that it is because you lived long.[6] He [Elijah] lives and continues to live until the resurrection of the dead.

Concerning God it is written, "His throne is sparks of fire" (Dan. 7:9).

Concerning Elijah it is written, "Behold, a chariot of fire and horses of fire" (II Kings 2:11).

Concerning God it is written, "God's way is in the tempest and the storm" (Nahum 1:3).

Concerning Elijah it is written, "Elijah ascended in a storm to the heavens" (II Kings 2:11).

Finally: He asked for himself to die – yet you declare, "I am God"?

The midrash draws six parallels between Elijah and God. Four are related to miracles that Elijah performed, and these are quoted to prove that despite the prophet's immense power to carry out deeds that can generally be performed only by God, Elijah never claimed to be divine. The midrash places special emphasis on the fact that Elijah did not die a normal mortal death, but rather "lives and continues to live until the resurrection of the dead." His passing from the mortal world – to which the midrash devotes another two comparisons to God – was in a wondrous ascent in a storm to the heavens, in a chariot of fire with horses of fire. But all of these proofs are only meant to emphasize the

---

6. According to the Midrash, this king of Tyre concerning whom Ezekiel prophesied at the time of the destruction of the Temple was the same king who reigned in the days of David.

negative assertion: *But Elijah did not say,* "I am God." Finally, the midrash seeks out a final and decisive positive proof that Elijah saw himself as a mortal and not as God. What is this proof? It is the most human situation in which Elijah is described: The scene in which he sits, alone and despairing beneath the broom tree in the wilderness, asking to die. (The midrash may also be alluding to the continuation of the verse – "For I am no better than my forefathers.")

This is the highest praise of the great figures of Tanakh; this is what makes them our moral guides and shining examples for all of humanity: For all of their elevated greatness, far above our understanding, they never cease to be human. And for this reason, they are susceptible to human mistakes and weaknesses. Examples of this in Tanakh are meant not only to teach us a lesson but also to lend the characters in question a human dimension, and thereby to imbue them with the power to serve as our models.

Chapter 24

God's Angel's Two Revelations to Elijah (I Kings 19:5–8)

A COMPARISON

God's angel is revealed twice to Elijah, and the descriptions of the revelations and their content are almost identical in both cases:

	First revelation	Second revelation
Elijah's state	v. 5: *He lay down* and he slept under a certain broom tree,	v. 6: And he *lay down* again.
Description of angel's revelation	and behold, an *angel touched him,*	v. 7: Then God's *angel* came back again a second time *and touched him,*
Substance of angel's message	*and he said* to him: *Arise, eat.*	*and he said: Arise, eat,* for the way is too far for you.
Elijah's response	v. 6: He looked, and behold, by his head ... *so he ate and he drank.*	v. 8: So he arose *and ate and drank,* and he went on the strength of that eating.

If we compare the wording in each case, we see that most of the differences arise from the fact that the second revelation is a repetition of the first; hence the expressions "again" and "came back." The place where Elijah lies ("under a certain broom tree") is omitted in the second revelation because it is superfluous. Likewise, the element of surprise on seeing the angel ("Behold, an angel") and discovering the cake and the cruse of water ("Behold, there was a cake") is also absent the second time.

There is only one substantial difference between the two revelations. In the second one, the angel adds that which was omitted the first time: the purpose of the eating which he commands Elijah, "Arise, eat, for the way is too far for you." As a result, Elijah's response to the second command relates to this new element, as we shall presently explain.

There are two differences between Elijah's first response and his second. The first thing that strikes us in his response to the second command is that "he arose." This was not mentioned in his response to the first command, since there the command, "arise," was meant in the sense of "wake up," to eat. Elijah could continue to lie (or lounge, or sit) while eating.[1] There is, therefore, no need for the text to note explicitly that he "arose," since the very fact that we read, "He looked … and he ate and drank" tells us that he awoke from his sleep. However, in the second command, the instruction "arise" means "to stand up." We understand this because we are not told that Elijah slept in between the two revelations, only that he lay down. In addition, he needed to get up on his feet in preparation for the journey.

The second, striking difference between Elijah's two responses is that after Elijah eats and drinks for the second time (apparently partaking of the same cake and water, and this time finishing them), we are told, "He went on the strength of that eating for forty days and forty nights." This is consistent with the angel's warning that "the way is too far for you."

---

1. This is how the word *kima* (arising) should be understood in most instances in Tanakh where it appears in the context of sleeping – as waking from sleep, not necessarily standing up. Admittedly, in the angel's first command, the command "arise" is not linguistically connected to Elijah's sleep (the angel does not say, "Arise from your sleep"), and therefore we might understand it in the literal sense, as "get up." However, Elijah seems to follow the first interpretation.

The obvious question is: Why could the angel not tell Elijah immediately, in his first revelation, that he must eat and drink in preparation for a lengthy journey, thereby sparing the need for a completely separate revelation?

Our assumption here is that Elijah's eating had one, single purpose – preparing him for a long walk in the desert – but this purpose becomes apparent retroactively, only after the angel's second appearance. However, this assumption is not necessarily accurate. Perhaps each revelation has its own individual purpose.

Clearly, if we seek to discover the purpose of the angel's first revelation, we must connect it to the last thing that we learned about Elijah in the previous unit: The fact that Elijah wanted to die and asked God to take his soul. Earlier, we explained Elijah's request of God as an expression of despair over his mission, and as an appeal to be relieved of prophecy. How is this request related to the first appearance of the angel?

The answer would appear to be simple. The angel who appears to Elijah and commands him, "Arise, eat," is expressing God's refusal of Elijah's plea to be relieved of his role as prophet and die. The angel answers him, as it were: "You will not die; you will live!" In other words, Elijah is required to continue in his mission as prophet. For this purpose, he must return to the norms of life: He must awaken, eat and drink, and stand up with renewed vigor, ready to serve his God, as in the past. Perhaps the angel touching him also expresses the transmission of renewed divine strength.[2]

Prophecy is not a privilege granted to the prophet – one that he may take on of his own free will or reject. It is a commandment to the prophet like any other commandment addressed to any other Jew. The prophet has no right to dismiss it. Indeed, God has never accepted a "resignation" from any prophet, nor any request to be relieved of a prophetic mission. This was the case from the time of Moses, the father of all prophets, until the time of Jeremiah, both of whom would have been happy to have been relieved of their role. Elijah, even in our chapter, does not succeed in becoming an exception to this rule. His profound

---

2. Compare the angel's touch that purifies Isaiah and readies him for prophecy (Is. 6:6–7).

despair, under the broom tree, and his request to die, are countered by the command of the angel, who touches him and instructs him quite unequivocally, "Arise, eat!" If Elijah were to acquiesce to this demand and its implications, he would depart right then, on the strength of *this* meal, heading back north toward his people and his land, to continue his task of bringing his people back to God. However, this is not what he does.

Elijah, indeed, obeys the command, but only on the literal level, and even then, only in the narrowest sense. He fulfills the demand, "Arise, eat!" – as we read afterward, "He ate and drank" – but he does not get up on his feet. He appears to partake of his meal under the tree, either sitting or lounging. Above, we explained that Elijah interpreted the instruction to "arise" in its narrow sense – to wake up. In this sense, Elijah did indeed fulfill the command. But did he accept the implications of the angel's command concerning the continuation of his prophetic role and his return to his country?

If we understand the significance of the angel's command correctly, the answer to the question is clear: Elijah does not respond to the implications of the command. Not only does he not actually "arise," but after eating and drinking a little – in order to just obey the command and no more – he lies down again. What is the meaning of this behavior? Elijah maintains his refusal to return; he wants to remain in his isolation under the broom tree in the desert. This being the case, the argument between the prophet and God has only just begun. If the prophet is not ready to return northward to continue his prophetic service, he will not be granted a reprieve allowing him to languish and die in the burning desert heat. He will be sent southward, with the explicit information that "the way is still far for you." He will face new arguments and instructions that he cannot begin to imagine.

Therefore, the angel appears to Elijah, still lying in the same spot under the tree, a second time. Corresponding to "He lay down *again*," we read: "God's angel came back *again, a second time*, and touched him." The divine demand does not let up on Elijah; the prophet's insistence is met with insistence on the part of the angel, who even adds a new demand: "For the way is too far for you." In other words, "If you are not ready to set off northward, as the first command suggested, prepare yourself for a long and surprising journey in the opposite direction."

Thus, the second revelation is not a clarification of the first (as we originally assumed); on the other hand, it is also not a substantially different revelation. Both turn on the same axis: The dispute between a despairing prophet seeking to end his mission and his life, and his Sender, who wants him to continue serving as a prophet and to return to his land and his people. The first revelation is the first stage of the argument: The angel's announcement that his "resignation" has been refused. The second revelation, the result of Elijah's stubborn stance, is a preparation for the continuation of the argument on a different level: the confrontation at Mount Horeb.

The deliberate echoing of the first revelation in the wording of the second may now be understood in terms of the common goal that they share. Both are aimed at turning the prophet back from the path that he is pursuing, and they represent two stages of the same dispute.

TO MOUNT HOREB

The angel who commands Elijah for the second time, "Arise, eat, for the way is too far for you," does not explain the purpose of the journey. How, then, does Elijah know which direction to choose and which destination he must reach? The text keeps all of this concealed, describing only the bare facts: "He went on the strength of that eating for forty days and forty nights until the mountain of God, at Horeb" (19:8).

Commenting on verse 7, Radak explains:

> He did not know where he would be going; he simply walked, unquestioningly, for forty days and forty nights until Mount Horeb. And the path there was made straight for him, as it was for the Ark, as it is written (I Sam. 6:12), "The cows walked a straight road." And when he got there he stopped, for he thought that God's word would be revealed to him there, since at that same mountain He had first revealed himself to Moses, and there His glory had been revealed when He gave the Torah to Israel.

Radak's explanation seems to be correct; otherwise we must posit that the angel told Elijah the purpose of his journey in advance. But then the text would not have hidden that conversation. It would be recorded, at least in some brief form: instead of telling Elijah only that "the journey is still far off for you," the angel might just add the words, "to Mount Horeb." Besides this, the concealment of this information from Elijah corresponds to the purpose of the journey, as Radak explains, and which we shall now clarify.

Why is Elijah led to Mount Horeb? Mount Horeb symbolizes the covenant forged between God and the nation at that place, and the divine revelation to Israel at the giving of the Torah. The historical roots of the people of Israel as God's nation are to be found at Mount Horeb. The irony of the situation should not be ignored. Elijah had fled from his people and headed for the wilderness in order to be alone there: "If only I was in the wilderness, in a lodge for wayfarers, that I might leave my people and go from them" (Jer. 9:1). But against his will, his legs carry him to the heart of that wilderness, to the exact spot where the historical foundations of Israel lie. Thus, Elijah, who is fleeing from his mission and from his nation, finds himself suddenly face-to-face with the most powerful symbol of the beginnings of Israelite existence and identity: Mount Horeb. The desert, the place of flight and isolation from his nation, is suddenly the place recalled by the prophet:

> So says the Lord: I remember in your favor the kindness of your youth, your love as a new bride, *when you walked after Me in the desert, in a land that was not sown.*" (Jer. 2:2)

> So says the Lord: The nation of survivors of the sword *found grace in the desert*, when Israel sought rest. (31:1)

The role of Mount Horeb, in light of these verses, is to remind Elijah of Israel's merit before God, for having accepted His Torah at this mountain and having entered into a covenant with Him. Does Elijah accept this lesson, hinted at in the fact that he is led to Mount Horeb?

Midrash Eliyahu Zuta (ch. 8) views the situation as follows:

> When the Holy One said to Elijah, "What do you seek here, Elijah?" Elijah should have answered: "Master of the universe, they are Your children, the children of Your faithful ones, Abraham,

Isaac, and Jacob, who performed Your will in the world." Not only did he not say this, but he said: "I have been zealous for the Lord God of Hosts, for the children of Israel have abandoned Your covenant."

Thus, the midrash emphasizes, the significance hinted to Elijah in the fact that he is led to Mount Horeb is not sufficient; he needs to be told explicitly what this mountain symbolizes. According to this midrash, the function of the revelation that follows is to state that which has so far only been implied:

> The Holy One immediately began speaking words of comfort to Elijah. He said to him: When I revealed Myself to give Torah to Israel, only the ministering angels were revealed with Me, for they seek the welfare of Israel. As it is written, "He said: Go out and stand at the mountain before God; and behold, God passed over, and a great and mighty wind broke apart the mountains and shattered the rocks before God – but not in the wind was God. And after the wind, an earthquake – but not in the earthquake was God. And after the earthquake, a fire – but not in the fire was God. And after the fire, a still, small voice" (19:11–12).

The midrash is interpreted as follows by Rabbi Shmuel Haida of Prague, author of *Zikukin deNura* (a commentary on *Midrash Tanna deVei Eliyahu*):

> All that is mentioned in this verse concerning the strong wind, the earthquake, the fire, and the still, small voice, which occurred at this mountain for Elijah, all of it also happened at that same mountain at the time of the giving of the Torah.[3] Thus, the Holy One reminded Elijah of the merit of the giving of the Torah to

---

3. There are verses proving the presence of an earthquake and fire at Sinai: "And Mount Sinai smoked in every part, because the Lord descended upon it in fire; and the smoke of it ascended like the smoke of a furnace, and the whole mountain quaked greatly. And then the voice of the shofar sounded louder and louder" (Ex. 19:18–19). With regard to the wind, however, there is no parallel mention at Mount Sinai.

Israel, in order that Elijah would plead for mercy and stand up in defense of Israel.

As the midrash sees it, the revelation to Elijah was meant to be a sort of reminder of the experience at Sinai and God's revelation to Israel there. The wind, the earthquake and the fire, which preceded the divine revelation upon the mountain, are God's messengers, announcing His arrival. Although they usually signify forces of destruction in the world, in this context of their appearance at Mount Sinai at the time of the giving of Torah, they are "ministering angels" that "seek the welfare of Israel" by preparing the people for God's revelation. This is undoubtedly a hint to Elijah as to the proper use of these powers and how they should be turned into angels who seek Israel's welfare, rather than angels of destruction sent to punish them.

This is one perspective on the purpose of Elijah being led to Mount Horeb. By depicting the revelation to Elijah at Mount Horeb in the context of the divine revelation to Israel at the time of the giving of the Torah, the midrash attempts to solve the great mystery of our chapter – the significance of the wind, the earthquake and the fire, and the still, small voice, in a way that connects them with the central theme of the story as a whole: the dispute between Elijah and God.

In the following chapters, we shall explore other possibilities as to the significance of bringing Elijah to Mount Horeb and the revelation that he experiences there.

ELIJAH IN MOSES'S FOOTSTEPS

We cannot ignore the deliberate manner in which our narrative draws a clear parallel between Elijah and Moses. Let us examine the similarities, in the order in which they appear in our chapter:

1. Even before we find out Elijah's ultimate destination in the wilderness, we already sense the parallel between the two prophets: "And he went on the strength of that eating for forty days and forty nights" (I Kings 19:8).

    Concerning Moses we read: "He was there with God for forty days and forty nights; he ate no bread nor did he drink water" (Ex. 34:28).

2. The actual arrival at Mount Horeb is also recorded in language reminiscent of Moses, but this time the parallel recalls Moses's first visit to the mountain, while he was shepherding the flock of Jethro, his father-in-law:

   Moses: "He came to the mountain of God, to Horeb." (Ex. 3:1)

   Elijah: "He went…until the mountain of God at Horeb." (I Kings 19:8)

   The name of this mountain, Horeb, appears seventeen times in Tanakh, but only in the above two instances is the additional appellation, "the mountain of God," attached.

3. Immediately thereafter, we are told concerning Elijah: "He came there to the cave, and he slept over there" (I Kings 19:9). This verse is reminiscent of verses 4–5 in our chapter, where the text describes Elijah's stay in the wilderness of Beer Sheba: "He came and dwelled under a certain broom tree…and he lay down and he slept under a certain broom tree."

It is specifically the similarity between the two sources that serves to emphasize the difference between them. At Mount Horeb we are not told, "He came there to *a certain cave* and he slept over there," but rather, "He came there to *the cave*" – the text uses the definite article. Which cave is this that should be so familiar to Elijah and to us, the readers? *Ḥazal*, in the midrashim, as well as the Aramaic translation and classical as well as modern commentators, identify this cave as the cleft in the rock that is mentioned in the context of Moses's ascent of Mount Sinai following the sin of the Golden Calf:

   God said: Behold, there is place by Me; you can stand upon the rock. And it shall be, when My glory passes over, that I shall place you in a cleft of the rock, and I shall cover you with My hand until I have passed over. And I shall remove My hand and you shall see the back of Me; but My face shall not be seen. (Ex. 33:21–23)

There, in the cleft of the rock, God was revealed to Moses in His goodness, with the thirteen traits of mercy. Indeed, the word *nikra* (which we translate here as "cleft") is synonymous to *me'ara* – cave, as Onkelos translates it, and as is apparent from the comparison of two verses in chapter 2 of Isaiah:

> They shall come into the caves (*me'arot*) of rocks and into the tunnels of the earth for fear of God and for the glory of His majesty, when He arises to shake the earth. (v. 19)

> To come into the clefts (*nikrot*) of rocks and into the crevices of boulders for fear of God and for the glory of His majesty when He arises to shake the earth. (v. 21)

4. Adopting this identification, we find further comparisons between the two sources, pertaining to the revelations experienced by these two prophets at this cave.

    i.   Moses is told, "Stand upon the rock" (Ex. 33:21), and further on we read, "You shall stand with Me there, at the top of the mountain" (34:2); Elijah is told, "Go out and stand at the mountain before God" (I Kings 19:11).
    ii. Moses is told, "And it shall be, when My glory passes over" (Ex. 33:22), while Elijah is told, "Behold, God is passing over" (I Kings 19:11).
    iii. Moses is told, "I shall place My hand upon you until I have passed over" (Ex. 33:22), and the first time he comes to Horeb we are told, "Moses hid his face for he feared to look at the Lord" (Ex. 3:6); while concerning Elijah we read; "And it was, when Elijah heard it, that he wrapped his face in his mantle" (I Kings 19:13).

It appears, then, that each of Moses's ascents to Mount Horeb serve as the precedent for Elijah being led there. Moses is the shepherd of Jethro's flocks when he first comes upon the burning bush, then he ascends later for the giving of the Torah, and again to ask forgiveness following the sin of the Golden Calf, and to receive the second set of tablets. But what is the significance of Elijah walking in the footsteps of Moses? What is this meant to teach us, or him?

In *Midrash Eliyahu Zuta* (ch. 8), quoted above, we find a sharp expression describing Elijah being led to Mount Horeb, hinting back to the dispute between God and Elijah concerning the drought – an argument which, according to the midrash, continues into our chapter:

> Not only that [God sent Elijah to Ahab to end the drought], but God then *pushed Elijah* to the place where the forefathers of Israel asked for mercy for their descendants.

Despite the use of the term "forefathers" (*avot*), the midrash would appear to be referring to Moses's request for mercy for the nation at Mount Sinai following the sin of the Golden Calf. Indeed, most of the parallels that we noted above between Elijah and Moses involve chapters 33–34 of Exodus, in which Moses tries to renew the covenant between God and Israel after it has been violated with the Golden Calf. Moses pleads that the covenant should be renewed and that Israel be granted complete forgiveness at the end of the first forty days of his stay atop Mount Sinai, after God notified him of Israel's sin, and after Moses prayed to God not to annihilate them, and was answered (Ex. 32:11–14).

Now the purpose of bringing Elijah to Mount Horeb, in the footsteps of Moses, is clear: Elijah is being asked to examine the ways of Moses, the teacher of all prophets of Israel – for his ways are the proper ways of prophecy. Even when the prophet comes to convey stern reproof, when he is with God his task is to be a spokesperson for Israel's defense. When Moses was atop Mount Horeb, he prayed for Israel and succeeded in canceling the decree of annihilation that hung over them (32:14). When he descended from the mountain to the camp, he cast the tablets from his hands and shattered them, and was ruthless in punishing the sinners. But afterward, when he ascended the mountain once again, he retained nothing of his anger; he expressed only supplication on behalf of the nation, and even spoke brazenly to God: "And now, if You will forgive their sin – and it not, please erase me from Your book which You have written" (Ex. 32:32).

All of this is reminiscent of Elijah's request, "Take my life" – but in the opposite direction: Moses speaks as he does out of devotion to Israel, while Elijah asks to die out of despair at the nation. The *Mekhilta* (introduction to *Parashat Bo*) notes this difference between Moses and Elijah. As to the former, the *Mekhilta* teaches:

> This we find: the forefathers and the prophets were devoted to Israel. Moses declares: "And now, if You will forgive their sin – and if not, please erase me from Your book which You have written."

Elijah, by contrast, is noted by the *Mekhilta* as having the opposite intention:

> Elijah stood up for the honor of the Father (God), rather than for the honor of the son (Israel), as it is written, "I have been greatly zealous for God, the Lord of Hosts."

Chapter 25

"He Announced Rebuke at Sinai, and Judgments of Vengeance at Horeb" (*Sefer Ben Sira*)

GOD'S QUESTION

> And behold, God's word came to him, and He said to him: What do you seek here, Elijah? (I Kings 19:9)

Radak interprets this question as follows:

> The reason for the question is that God starts talking to him in order to hear his response, as is customary in human speech.... even though He knows man's heart. Similarly, "He said to him, Where are you?" (Gen. 3:9); "What is that in your hand?" (Ex. 4:2). Likewise, the meaning of "What do you seek here?" is "Why did you leave your place; what are you looking for here?"

The Baal HaMetzudot adopts a similar interpretation:

> The question comes in the manner of a person's speech, asking *in order to enter into conversation with him*. Likewise we find (Gen. 4:9), "Where is Abel, your brother?"

However, we must still seek – not only here, but in every instance where God asks a person something "in order to enter into conversation with him" – the hidden meaning behind the specific question that is chosen to introduce the dialogue. The question is always connected to the essence of the conversation that it serves to introduce, and it hints to the direction that the dialogue will take.[1] If the person to whom the question is addressed is able to sense its intention, he can know in advance what God is going to ask of him.[2]

What, then, hides behind the question that God asks Elijah here? In light of all that we have discussed concerning Elijah's journey into the desert and the significance of him being led to Mount Horeb, it is clear that this question is meant as a covert rebuke and a gentle attempt to lead him to change his path. Indeed, this is what arises from *Midrash Eliyahu Zuta* (ch. 8) which we quoted above:

> When the Holy One said to Elijah, "What do you seek here, Elijah?" Elijah should have answered: "Master of the universe, they are Your children, the children of Your faithful ones – Abraham, Isaac, and Jacob, who performed Your will in the world."

It would seem that the emphasis, in God's question, is on the word "here." However, while some commentators view it as a negative emphasis (namely, "here" as opposed to some other place), others view the

---

1. It seems that in characterizing this sort of question as being asked "in order to enter into conversation" (*lehikanes imo bidevarim*) Ḥazal do not mean initiating a general conversation (*bidevarim*) but rather initiating a conversation on the topic that the dialogue actually addresses (*badevarim*).
2. Zakovitch suggests a similar idea in his article "Kol Demama Daka," 355, concerning this sort of question that God (or His angel) poses to a person: "In all these situations God seeks to hear man's side; to offer him an opportunity to have his say before speaking to him sharply."

emphasis in the positive sense ("here" – specifically here). Malbim, for example, takes the first view:

> Is a prophet not meant to be among the people, to reprove and to prophesize, rather than isolating himself in the desert and in the mountains?

The question, then, is: "Why are you here – and not among the nation?" Thus, the question refers to Elijah's journey into the desert and its deepest cause: "If only I could be in the wilderness, a lodge for wayfarers, that I may abandon my nation" (Jer. 9:1). The question, clearly, is meant as a rebuke.

The problem with Malbim's interpretation is that the word "here," in his view, does not refer specifically to Mount Horeb, but rather to the entire desert, as the place of Elijah's flight and isolation. However, as we noted in the previous chapter, there is special significance in Elijah being led specifically to Mount Horeb, and God's question would appear to hint to that special meaning. This question appears to be aimed at clarifying whether Elijah has understood the hint of his being led to Horeb. What it means is, "Have you understood why you were brought here, Elijah? Has this hint had any effect on you and changed your position?"

Therefore, to supplement Malbim's view we may quote the commentary of Rabbi Moses Alsheikh, who explains most eloquently the importance of the emphasis on Mount Horeb in God's question:

> "And behold, God's word came to him.… What do you seek here, Elijah?" As though to say, "Behold, this place – that which took place here is the opposite of your intention." For there Moses entered, by God's command (Ex. 33:22), "I shall place you in the cleft of the rock, and I shall place My hand over you until I have passed over," and there (Ex. 34:6), "God passed over his face," listing the thirteen attributes of divine mercy.… For it was in that cave that God was revealed to Moses as He passed over before him, and He told him the thirteen attributes of mercy by which He shows compassion to Israel. And therefore God said to Elijah, "What do you seek here, Elijah" – for your intention is the opposite of what once took place here. *In other words: Have you repented of that trait;*

will you now ask for mercy and long-suffering patience toward My children? What God sought was that Elijah would reverse his intention, such that God could commit Himself to do the same, and exercise long-suffering patience and have mercy upon His people.

ELIJAH'S RESPONSE

How does Elijah respond to God's question? His answer is set out in a lengthy declaration composed of six brief clauses:

> He said: I have been zealous for the Lord God of Hosts,
> For the children of Israel have abandoned Your covenant,
> They have destroyed Your altars
> And put Your prophets to death by the sword
> And I alone remain
> And they seek my life, to take it. (19:10)

Clearly, in order to match Elijah's answer here with God's preceding question, such that his answer will indeed be a response to what he was asked, we must return to our discussion from the previous section as to the intention of the question. Any commentator who proposes a certain meaning for God's question must go on to explain Elijah's answer as addressing that meaning.

Those who regarded Elijah's journey to the desert as a flight from his prophetic mission and a sign of despair over the nation of Israel, and his being led to Mount Horeb as a hint to Elijah to change his view toward the nation, and who then go on to explain God's question as a concealed rebuke to the prophet and an invitation to present his stand in the argument, will have no difficulty revealing, within Elijah's response, a harsh condemnation of Israel, consisting of a list of four accusations. The entire nation here bears responsibility for the guilt of Queen Jezebel, since they do not protest her policies. Elijah attributes even the threat to his life to the nation as a whole: "They seek my life, to take it." The plural form here refers to "the children of Israel," against whom three other accusations have already been presented.

The seamless juxtaposition of this final clause with the preceding ones shows that what happened between the events of the previous clauses and those of the final one (the climactic mass repentance at Mount Carmel, and the slaughter of the prophets of Baal) has been forgotten as though it never happened, and is not even given consideration as a reason for calming Elijah's zealousness for God. The renewed threat to Elijah's life resurrects the previous sins, creating a continuum with them that nullifies any transient achievement that may have been attained in the interim. We explained this perspective of Elijah above.

In what way does this litany of accusations serve as a response to God's question, "What do you seek here, Elijah"?

Malbim, according to whom God's question was why Elijah was not now among the nation as his mission as a prophet requires, explains Elijah's response as follows: "Behold, I cannot be a prophet, instructing and rebuking this nation, for I am oppressed by my zealousness over their evil deeds." Thus, Elijah explains his flight to the desert as being prompted by despair at the state of the nation, and his lack of will and ability to continue in his role among them.

Alsheikh, who regards God's question as a call to Elijah to cleave to Moses's trait of mercy, interprets Elijah's answer accordingly:

> But he [Elijah] maintained his view and said, "I have been exceedingly zealous – I have been zealous for Your glory...I shall not turn back from it...." He did not recant his view.

In other words, it is a refusal to accept the instruction implied in being led to Horeb, in the footsteps of Moses. Mount Horeb, for Elijah, is not a place of prayer on behalf of Israel, as it was for Moses, but rather a place to accuse them for "abandoning Your covenant" – the very covenant that was forged at that place.

In any event, whether we adopt the interpretation of Malbim or that of Alsheikh, the repeated verb "I have been exceedingly zealous" (*kano kineiti*) should not be interpreted as referring only to the past. Rather, it describes an action that began in the past and continues in the present: "I was zealous, and I continue to be zealous now, too." The reason for the continued zealousness is that which was revealed to Elijah when "they seek my life, to take it." The slaughter of prophets continues; Jezebel is still free to act, with the approval of Ahab, her husband, and the silent acquiescence of the entire nation.

It would seem that we have not yet altogether clarified the far-reaching ramifications of Elijah's answer. Does his answer contain merely a description of his mood ("I have been exceedingly zealous") or is there more? Ralbag interprets his answer as follows:

> Behold, Elijah answers that he is zealous for God [in the present!] because the Israelites have abandoned the covenant of the Torah and have destroyed God's altars, for they wanted to worship only foreign gods, and they have put God's prophets to death by the sword – because Jezebel is slaughtering them as before; Elijah alone remains of all the prophets known to her, and she seeks to kill him, too. *It is as though he asks God to exact his vengeance for these evils that Israel has committed.* But this has happened to Elijah because of his great anger over Israel's sins.

According to this view, not only is Elijah consumed with "anger over Israel's sins," but this very anger gives rise to a plea for revenge on Israel in the present! It is this request for revenge that is the practical essence of what Elijah is saying.

Long before Ralbag, the same idea was expressed in *Sefer Ben Sira*, in the expression that we have borrowed as the title of this chapter: "He [Elijah] announced rebuke at Sinai, and *judgments of vengeance at Horeb*."[3]

What is the source of this idea?

Zealousness, in Tanakh, is never just a mood. It is always an impulse for drastic action that accompanies it and which it requires. Let us examine a few verses that speak of God's jealousy and express its practical result:

> "For the Lord your God *is a consuming fire*, a jealous God." (Deut. 4:24)

---

3. This quote is from chapter 48 in a series of chapters at the end of *Sefer Ben Sira*, entitled "Praise for the Forefathers of the World" (Segal edition, p. 330 [Hebrew]), the first part of which is devoted to Elijah.

"For then God's anger and jealousy shall smolder against that person... *and God will erase His name from beneath the heavens."* (Deut. 29:19)

"I have been jealous for Jerusalem and for Zion, with a great zealousness. *And I am greatly angry at the nations that are at ease."* (Zech. 1:14–15)

The same applies to human jealousy, or zealousness – whether for the sake of God or for other things that are dear. In the case of a husband over whom "a spirit of jealousy has passed, and he is jealous for his wife," he brings her to the priest to clarify the matter and to cause the wife to swear: "A man over whom a spirit of jealousy passes, and he is jealous for his wife – *he shall present the wife before God"* (Num. 5:30).

The following verse includes both divine jealousy and human zealousness for God:

"Pinhas, son of Eleazar, son of Aaron the priest, has turned back My anger from upon the children of Israel, in his zealous zeal in their midst, *such that I did not annihilate the children of Israel* in My jealousy." (Num. 25:11)

Pinhas's zealousness was that "he took a spear in his hand... and pierced both of them... and the plague was stopped from upon the children of Israel" (Num. 25:8–9).

From the above examples, and others which we have not quoted here, we see how correct Ben Sira and Ralbag were in their interpretations, attributing to Elijah's cry – "I am exceedingly zealous for God" – the sense of asking for revenge on Israel for the evil that they have committed.

Now the argument between Elijah and God assumes even sharper significance. The argument concerns not only the past, the fact that Elijah has abandoned his role and his people, but also God's policy toward Israel now and in the future. Elijah demands punishment and revenge, the exact opposite of the stance adopted by Moses, who – standing at this very spot – succeeded in turning back God's anger from against Israel.

This interpretation of Elijah's words also explains, retroactively, his journey to the desert and his request to die there. These actions reflect not only despair over Israel, and not only the wish to be relieved of his mission, but more. Elijah's actions reflect his protest against God's policy toward the nation of Israel in that generation, a policy that Elijah regards as excessively merciful and forgiving. When his request to die is not accepted, and he is led to Mount Horeb and asked to clarify his position, Elijah gives vent to his innermost feelings and explains his argument with his Creator in clear and fiery terms:

"I am exceedingly zealous for the Lord God of Hosts."

Chapter 26

Revelation in a "Small, Silent Voice" (I Kings 19:11–14)

He said: Go out and stand at the mountain before God. And behold, God passes over, and a great and mighty wind breaks apart the mountains and shatters the rocks before God; but not in the wind is God. And after the wind, an earthquake; but not in the earthquake is God. And after the earthquake, a fire; but not in the fire is God. And after the fire, a small, silent voice. And it was, when Elijah heard, that he wrapped his face in his mantle, and went out and stood at the entrance to the cave. (19:11–14)

Anyone who reads this chapter senses that its climax is the description of God's revelation to Elijah in the "small, silent voice," which comes after the wind, the earthquake, and the fire. This climax, in verses 11–12, also stands at the center of the story: There are ten verses that precede it, and nine that follow. But the event itself, for all of its powerful impact, is shrouded in mystery. This is the most obscure part of the story. What is the meaning of this revelation, and how does it fit in with the story's broader message? What is the meaning of the repetition of the question,

307

"What do you seek here, Elijah?" following this revelation? What new significance does this question assume in light of the revelation, and what is the significance of Elijah repeating the same answer afterward?

Before addressing these questions, we must first clarify the primary, literal meaning of this excerpt. The beginning of verse 11 records God's words to Elijah: "Go out and stand at the mountain, before God." Where does the quotation of this direct speech end? Are the following words – "And behold, God passes (in the present tense) over" – still part of the direct speech, or are they part of the narrative? And what of the words "A great wind ... before God" – are they part of the narrative, or still part of God's speech? If they are part of the narrative, who is it that says, "God is not in the wind"? The latter two questions apply to the earthquake and the fire, as well.

In verse 13 we read, "And it was, when Elijah heard, he wrapped his face in his mantle." What did he hear? If we postulate that all of verses 11–12 are God's direct speech, we may explain that what Elijah heard was all of this speech, informing him of what awaits him when he emerges from the cave; Elijah listened until the end and then covered his face and went to stand at the entrance to the cave, as commanded. There, in the middle of verse 13, as Elijah stands with his face covered, all that God told him while he was still in the cave indeed occurs. Pursuing this hypothesis, we may suggest that, for the sake of brevity, the text does not repeat the description of the event itself. After the stage of the small, silent voice, Elijah hears a voice asking him, "What do you seek here, Elijah?"

But if, on the other hand, we explain the description of the wind, the earthquake, the fire, and the voice as part of the narrative, rather than as a quotation of God's direct speech, then what is it that Elijah heard? Was it the "small, silent voice"? How can that be? We may further ask: Why did Elijah wait until the stage of the silent voice before emerging from the cave, rather than doing so immediately upon being commanded, at the beginning of verse 11, even before the wind came?

It is admittedly easier to explain verse 13 if we adopt the view that verses 11–12 record a continuous monologue by God, but this interpretation seems inappropriate to the literal meaning of those verses. Why would the text choose to present us with a description of this dramatic revelation in the form of God's advance notice, rather than as a description of the event itself? Therefore it would seem more logical to suggest that God's speech to Elijah concludes with the words, "And behold, God passes over" – meaning, "Go and stand at the mountain before God *when God passes over, not right away*" (which also explains the words *"before God"* – namely, in the sight of God as He passes over). Elijah therefore waits *in the cave* for a sign that God is indeed passing over. Then he hears "a great, strong wind…before God" (this time "before" is meant in the sense of time – i.e., before God comes), and the description of its arrival is in the reported narrative of the text. The words "not in the wind is God," may be the voice of prophecy that Elijah hears (as a continuation of God's previous words, "Go and stand…and behold, God passes over," as though telling him, "Do not be mistaken; God is not yet passing over"). However, it is also possible that these words are part of the narrative, representing a projection of Elijah's consciousness as he tells himself, "God is not in the wind." This combination between the narrative description of each of the natural phenomena and the reaction to it – "God is not in the …," continues up until the description of the small, silent voice. Here the reaction (whether external or internal), "God is not in the small, silent voice," is absent; Elijah understands that the small, silent voice announces God passing over.

The words "When Elijah heard" may be understood, in light of the above, as a description of an inner sense of hearing. Following the series of sounds that preceded it, Elijah "hears" the "voice" that emerges from the silence. But the Aramaic translation offers a different interpretation, which is adopted by Rashi and other commentators; it suggests that this was a "voice of quiet praise," understanding the word *demama* as praise, and the adjective *daka* as a low voice.[1]

In any event, when he hears this voice, Elijah understands that the time has come to emerge from the cave and present himself before God who is passing over. Therefore he covers his face with his mantle (as we read concerning Moses, in Exodus 3:6 – "Moses hid his face for he feared to gaze at God"), and goes to stand at the entrance to the cave.

---

1. For an explanation of this interpretation of *demama*, see Moshe Seidel, *Ḥikrei Lashon* (Jerusalem, 1986), 16–17.

Then, from the midst of the silence, God's voice suddenly emerges: "And behold, a voice came to him and said, 'What do you seek here, Elijah?'"

We must also clarify a further question. From the description of the revelation here it would seem that the wind, the earthquake, and the fire are not expressions of God's revelation; on the contrary, they are portrayed as being devoid of God's Presence: "God is not in the ...." However, in several places in Tanakh the opposite would appear to be the case; God's reveals Himself specifically through (or even in the form of) wind, earthquakes, and fire.[2]

Even in our chapter we do not read that there is no connection between the wind, the earthquake and the fire, and God. On the contrary, these phenomena serve as an introduction and preparation for God's appearance. This is stated explicitly in relation to the wind: "A great and strong wind... *before God*." Even though it is not stated explicitly concerning the other phenomena, it applies to them as well; it is noted in the case of the wind because that is the first of the list of natural forces that manifests itself here.[3]

What, then, is the meaning of the three fold repetition, "God is not in the ..."? It would seem that the text seeks to distinguish between God's emissaries – the means at His disposal, testifying to His rule over

---

2. Concerning wind and fire as accompanying divine revelation, see Psalms 114:4.

    The *raash* in this context is an earthquake, as the early commentators explain, based on the context, and this word has the same meaning in other places in Tanakh, too (Ezek. 38:19; Amos 1:1; Zech. 14:5). Concerning this term see Psalms 104:32 and Exodus 19:18, which also includes a description of fire.

    At the beginning of the book of Nahum (one of the twelve minor prophets) we find a description of God's appearance that is accompanied by all three forces mentioned in our chapter (along with additional destructive phenomena), in the same order:

    The Lord, His way is **in the tempest and in the storm** (*besufa uvise'ara*), and the clouds are the dust of his feet. (Nahum 1:3)

    The mountains **quake** (*raashu*) at Him, and the hills melt. (v. 5)

    His fury is poured out **like fire** (*ke'esh*), and the rocks are broken up by Him. (v. 6)

3. For the same reason, the wind is described in greater detail than the other two forces. First, we are told that the wind is "mighty and strong"; second, its action is to "break apart the mountains and shatter the rocks." From the description of the wind, we infer the power of the quaking and the fire, understood here as forces of destruction, and their role as preceding the appearance of God.

the world – and God Himself, who is infinitely above all the natural forces that He controls, and who must not be identified with any of them.

Thus, although the description of the revelation here does not contradict the other sources, it is nevertheless different from them in that it emphasizes specifically the *distinction* between the destructive natural forces and God Himself. This perspective is not reflected in any of the other instances where these natural phenomena occur in the context of divine revelation.

Now we can explore the meaning of God's revelation in the context of our narrative.

In chapter 24, "God's Angel's Two Revelations to Elijah (I Kings 19:5–8)," we quoted the midrash that understands this revelation to Elijah as a reminder of the revelation at Sinai and the receiving of the Torah. This perspective serves to connect this revelation with the main subject of our narrative – the ongoing debate between God and His prophet (the purpose of the revelation being to remind Elijah of the merit of Israel for having forged a covenant with God at this mountain and accepting the Torah). However, according to this approach, the wind, the earthquake, and the fire (and the negation of their identification with God) serve no independent function that is connected to the plot. Their role is merely to introduce the association with the revelation at the time of the giving of the Torah.

We may raise two difficulties in relation to this approach. First, the revelation at Sinai (Ex. 19) lacks the sharp distinction between the noises and the fire, on the one hand, and the actual revelation of God, on the other, that we find in our chapter. Second, the above approach connects the revelation to the plot of the story in a secondary way, but we have the sense that this revelation contains a direct and central argument in the ongoing debate between God and Elijah.

Let us now examine the approaches of two commentators in order to explain the first dialogue between God and Elijah (vv. 9–10), and we will see how each of them molds his interpretation of the present revelation in such a way as to adapt it to the interpretation of the previous dialogue.

Malbim, we recall, interprets God's question, "What do you seek here, Elijah?" as a rebuke to the prophet for being "here," in the desert, rather than among the people, guiding them and prophesying for them.

He also interprets Elijah's response to mean, "I cannot be a prophet guiding and rebuking this nation, because I am consumed with zealousness in light of their evil deeds." Malbim pursues the same idea further, interpreting the prophetic revelation here as a rebuke to Elijah, instructing him as to how to act as a prophet among the people. Malbim explains:

> He showed him that God is not to be found in the camp of wind, earthquake, and fire; [He is to be found] only in a small, silent voice. God's emissaries and prophets are to learn from this that they should not "raise a storm," nor cause the earth to quake, nor cause fire to burn (as Elijah did in his zealousness for the Lord of Hosts – by shutting up the heavens and by slaughtering the prophets of Baal). God sends His prophets to go to [the people] with a silent voice – to draw the nation close with bonds of love and with soft words.

Ralbag, on the other hand, interpreted Elijah's words "I have been exceedingly zealous…" as a quest for revenge upon Israel for their evil deeds. He, too, continues with the same approach and regards the revelation as a response to this demand on Elijah's part:

> So the blessed God told him to go out and stand at the mountain, before God.… And it would appear that God did this so that Elijah would ask for mercy upon Israel, and not pray that they be destroyed for their evil deeds. For it was the will of the blessed God to be patient with them, so that they would return to Him. It was for this reason that He showed him the destructive phenomena, such as the great and strong wind that broke apart mountains and shattered rocks, but God was not in the wind – *because God does not bring about evil unless there is some positive result that will emerge from it*. And since it was clear to the blessed God that they would not accept rebuke (after all, we see that the withholding of dew and rain for three years did not lead them to submit themselves to God), He did not wish to punish them for their sins as they deserved, but rather waited for them so they might repent their evil way.

And after the wind came an earthquake; this was destructive, being a phenomenon that overturns countries; and once again we are told that God was not in the earthquake, just as we read concerning the wind. And following the earthquake – a fire, which is even more destructive. There, too, we read that God was not in the fire, for the same reason that we discussed above.

The Baal HaMetzudot, who interprets Elijah's words, "I have been exceedingly zealous for God," in the same way as Ralbag does – as a demand for revenge on Israel – also goes on to understand the revelation in a similar way:

He was shown the divine glory, which did not pass over in a wind or in the earthquake or in a fire, but rather in a small, silent voice, *for He desires kindness and does not arouse all of His anger,* to come in [the form of] wind or an earthquake or fire.

According to Malbim, the wind, the earthquake, and the fire – and, in contrast to them, the small, silent voice – are a *metaphor* as to the improper and proper attitudes toward Israel. They represent God's approach and that of His prophet. The revelation as a whole is a rebuke and guidance to Elijah as to how he should go about his role as prophet among the nation. According to Ralbag and the Baal HaMetzudot, on the other hand, the wind, earthquake, and fire are to be understood literally. They are the forces of destruction that God unleashes in order to punish His creations – both individuals and entire nations. The purpose of the revelation is to make God's ways in managing the world known, and to provide a response to Elijah's demand for revenge: "It is not God's way to bring about evil unless there is some good that will emerge from it." Therefore, it is not proper that the prophet pray for their destruction; rather, "Elijah should plead for mercy upon Israel."

In a chapter 28 we will return to the discussion of the significance of God's revelation to Elijah, and discover a new facet to it.

Chapter 27

"They Seek My Life, to Take It" (I Kings 19:14)

Following God's revelation in a "small, silent voice," God repeats His question to Elijah: "What do you seek here, Elijah?" This time the question comes against the background of the insight afforded by the revelation; hence, its meaning now is, "Have you understood the lesson of the revelation? Do you still maintain your position?" And Elijah, whose response here is a word-for-word repetition of the previous one, means to say: "I have not changed my view in any way; I maintain my position."

How are we to regard this prophet, who clings to his opinion with such tenacity, not agreeing to relinquish it even after such a sharp and prolonged argument with God? Should we not admire such uncompromising loyalty to his principles? *Ḥazal* take a more critical view, questioning the authenticity of Elijah's zealousness for God, for which God has no desire. In Midrash Song of Songs Rabba (1:39), they analyze very closely the arguments that he repeats again and again:

> He said: "I have been exceedingly zealous for the Lord God of Hosts, for the children of Israel have abandoned Your covenant."

The Holy One, blessed be He, said to him: "My covenant – is it then your covenant?"

"They have destroyed Your altars." [God said,] "My altars – are they then your altars?"

"And they have put Your prophets to death by the sword." God said, "My prophets – of what concern is it to you?"

"And he said: I alone remain, and they seek my life, to take it!"

In this sharp dialogue, God breaks down Elijah's fundamental accusations against the nation, one after the other. Each of his claims to zealousness for the sake of God's name is rejected by the "interested party" Himself: The covenant is His covenant, the altars are His altars; why should any mortal need to show greater concern for these than God Himself does? But when Elijah raises the accusation, "They have put Your prophets to death by the sword," the style of God's questions changes: He does not ask, "My prophets – are they then your prophets?" following the pattern of the previous questions, because this accusation by Elijah is already touching on his real issue. Therefore the question "Of what concern is it to you?" is posed in order to draw out Elijah's answer. In other words, perhaps this is what concerns you more than all of the previous accusations? And Elijah's response indeed confirms this: "Of course it concerns me; they seek to take my life, too!" Thus the cause of Elijah's zealousness is uncovered: It arises from his fear for his own life, and his indignation at the fact that it is in danger. The *mussar* masters call this the "point of contact" that exists in the deepest recesses of a person's psyche, even while he declares all kinds of idealistic and important motives for his actions.

Does the above analysis of Elijah's claims arise from the claims themselves, or do they reflect the perspective of Ḥazal in their interpretation – a perspective in which they garb Elijah's words, using an imaginary dialogue between the prophet and God as the exegetical device through which they convey their view?

At first, it would seem that Elijah's accusations against the nation would all seem to give voice to the same protestation of zealousness of his own part. Even the last three clauses, describing the fate of God's prophets, and Elijah among them, would seem to bemoan not Elijah's own problem, but rather God's situation in a world that will, seemingly, soon be bereft of all prophets: "They have put Your prophets to death by the sword!" Lest anyone protest, "There are plenty of prophets; the loss is not so terrible," Elijah adds, "I alone remain" – and even this represents no surety as to the future of God's message, since "They seek my life, to take it!" If they succeed, God's world will be left with no prophets. It is possible that this represents the significance of Elijah's words on the overt level (ignoring, for the moment, the strangeness of his argument). But, as we shall see, a close syntactical analysis of his argument leads us to a justification of Ḥazal's view in the midrash.

Elijah's response is comprised of six short clauses. The first four mention God – either explicitly or by using the second person possessive form – "Your covenant," etc. Only the last two clauses, which address Elijah's fate, lack any reference to God. The first of them places Elijah's own "I" as the subject and focus of the sentence – "I alone remain"; the second, while admittedly presenting Israel as the subject and Elijah's life as the object, now lacks the possessive form that characterized the previous clauses. Elijah does not say, "They seek the life of *Your servant*, to take it." The people of Israel are being accused only for their attitude toward Elijah's life. There is no reference to God here. "I" and "my life" are at the center of Elijah's concern, at the end of his speech, and this reveals the "point of contact" – the personal interest – that lurks behind the previous clauses, too. Thus, the syntactical analysis of Elijah's words, the straightforward reading (*peshat*), serves to support the exegesis (*derash*) of Ḥazal.

We may bring further support for Ḥazal's view that it is Elijah's concern for his own life that underlies his actions and speech in our chapter. A sensitive reading of our narrative (until 19:18) easily reveals one word that repeats itself throughout: That word is "*nefesh*" (soul, life); it is a key word that appears seven times in the story. Let us list its appearances:

1. By this time tomorrow I shall end *your life* (v. 2)
2. like *the life* of one of them (v. 2)
3. He went (fled) for *his life* (v. 3)

4. and asked (lit. "pleaded for *his life*") to die (v. 4)
5. It is enough, God; take *my life* (my soul) (v. 4)
6. They seek *my life*, to take it (v. 10)
7. They seek *my life*, to take it (v. 14)

Every one of the appearances of the word "life" or "soul" refers to Elijah. Even in number 2, where the subject is the slaughtered prophets of Baal, it is meant to equate his life with theirs. We may therefore say that "Elijah's life" is what stands at the center of the story. In the first two appearances of the key word, Jezebel uses it, expressing her wish to take Elijah's life. Corresponding to these two expressions of Jezebel, we find the word repeated twice at the end of the list (6, 7), this time by Elijah, in his complaint over Jezebel's attempt to take his life. The three appearances in the middle of the list (3, 4, and 5) testify to Elijah's intensive occupation with his own life: he "flees (goes) for his life" – *vayelekh el nafsho* (while the unusual expression indicates an act of escape, it may also hint here that Elijah takes himself off to occupy himself with matters of his own life). His soul asks to die (*vayishal et nafsho lamut*), and he asks of God to take his life (*kaḥ nafshi*).

The expression "to take a/the life," voiced in Elijah's request of God – "take my life" – appears twice more afterward, in his complaint: "They seek my life *to take it.*" Thus we conclude that Elijah attaches great value to his life. It is the source of his "going for his life" to the desert; it is also the root of his zealousness for God and his request that God take revenge upon Israel. The desire of his soul to die and his request of God, "Take my life," are simply an inverted expression of the great value that he attaches to his life – to the extent that when his life is endangered and he has no protection, he reacts with the vehemence that we witness here.

In chapter 25 above we concluded that it was despair over his role as prophet that led Elijah to flee to the desert. Now we may modify this statement and formulate it as follows: It is Elijah's preoccupation with his "soul," his life, his personal fate, that leads to both his despair over his role and his flight to the desert.

Chapter 28

The Mission
(I Kings 19:15–18)

THE DIFFICULT QUESTION

> God said to him: "Go, return on your way to the wilderness of
> Damascus, and you shall come and anoint Hazael as king over
> Aram. And Jehu son of Nimshi, you shall anoint as king of Israel,
> and Elisha son of Shafat, of Abel Mehola, you shall anoint as
> prophet in your stead." (I Kings 19:15–16)

The mission that God entrusts to Elijah, following the indecisive conclusion of their protracted debate, appears at first to have no connection with what preceded it: What does the appointment of new kings
(for Aram and for Israel) and a new prophet (Elijah's successor) have
to do with the question of divine policy toward the sinful nation of
Israel? And what do these personalities have to do with the argument
over Elijah's approach?

However, as we continue reading, and discover the purpose of
these appointments, the connection becomes more apparent:

> And it shall be that whoever escapes from the sword of Hazael
> will be put to death by Jehu, and whoever escapes from the sword

of Jehu will be put to death by Elisha. But I shall leave among
Israel seven thousand: All the knees that did not bow to Baal, and
every mouth that did not kiss it. (vv. 17–18)

These three figures will assume positions that will enable them to punish
Israel terribly. It seems that Elijah's view has prevailed in the argument.
His call for revenge on Israel is being answered, and his aspiration to
operate among the nation "in a strong wind, in an earthquake, and in
fire" is about to be fulfilled. How is this possible?

RELATIONSHIP BETWEEN REVELATION AND MISSION

To answer this question we must reexamine our discussion of the significance of God's revelation in verses 11–12, and the connection between it
and the mission that is now being entrusted to Elijah. Let us consider
the interpretation proposed by Professor Y. Zakovitch, in his commentary on this chapter:

> Let us take note of the striking connection between the description
> of the revelation ... (vv. 11–12) and the mission that is given to Elijah
> (vv. 15–18), both of which express God's response to the prophet's
> complaint and to his call for revenge. The two answers – the sym-
> bolic one, presenting the revelation that is perceived through the
> senses of sight and hearing (vv. 11–12), and the one clarifying to
> the prophet what he needs to do – are related to one another like
> a riddle and its solution. The identical response by the prophet
> to God's repeated question ("What do you seek here?") testifies
> that the prophet did not solve the riddle the first time around;[1] he
> needs further clarification.... This relationship between the rev-
> elation and its interpretation is not unusual in Tanakh. M. Weiss
> writes:[2] "There are a few instances of revelations in which that

---

1. Perhaps it would be more accurate to say (in the spirit of our preceding chapter) that
   Elijah understands what is hinted at in the riddle, but still does not change course
   as a result.
2. M. Weiss, "Temuna VeKol BePirkei Marot HaNevua," in *Proceedings of the Sixth
   World Congress of Jewish Studies I* (Jerusalem, 5737), 91ff. Reprinted in Weiss's book,
   Mikraot KeKavanatam (Jerusalem, 5748), 99ff.

which becomes known to the prophet by [divine] voice seems to be nothing but a chronological succession, with no thematic connection to what was previously revealed to him in a vision – as though the vision was no more than a stage prop, and after that screen is in place the [divine] word comes.... I intend to demonstrate a structural regularity that is created, and the consistent relationship between that which is seen and that which is heard.... The vision and the voice explain one another, and the mutual contact between them creates the message of that unit."[3]

Malbim, in his commentary on verse 14, notes this correspondence between the revelation and the mission that follows:

> He told him that ... He would punish the nation through Hazael and Jehu and Elisha; these [three personalities] would correspond to the three symbols of punishment that he had seen – wind, earthquake, and fire.

We may elaborate upon Malbim's commentary as follows: The order of the forces that Elijah sees in the revelation moves from the furthest to the nearest. The wind comes from afar and destroys everything in its path; the earthquake emerges from the depths of the earth, but only destroys that which is directly above it; while the fire devours – in its place – whatever it takes hold of. The order of the personalities who will bring punishment upon Israel follows the same pattern: Hazael will come upon Israel from afar; he is king of Aram. The rebellion of Jehu will arise from the midst of the nation of Israel, revealing the profound popular dissatisfaction with the reign of the House of Ahab. Elisha will act at the most overt and immediate layer: among the nation itself.

Professor Zakovitch broadens this parallel, giving it deeper significance. Before returning to his article, let us first briefly address a literary model that is quite common in Tanakh – the "three and four" model.

---

3. Zakovitch, "Kol Demama Daka," 341–42.

Zakovitch devotes an entire book[4] to the discovery of this model and a clarification of its significance. At the beginning of his book he writes the following:

> There are literary units in Tanakh that consist of four layers: The first three echo one another; the transition from one element to the next does not usually entail any change or progress. The fourth element represents a sharp turning point, a change that is the central point and climax of the literary unit. This literary model ... is extremely common in Tanakh. It appears in various literary genres and plays a role in the molding of many and varied topics.

We will now return to our chapter and to Zakovitch's article.[5] The description of the revelation (vv. 11–12) is arranged according to the literary model of "three and four." Three destructive natural forces appear in the beginning, and the "small, silent voice" following them is a contrast.

Let us set out the description of the revelation in such a way as to highlight this model:

(1) A great and mighty wind, broke apart mountains and shattered rocks before God,   but not in the wind was God;

(2) And after the wind, an earthquake;   but not in the earthquake was God;

(3) And after the earthquake, a fire;   but not in the fire was God;

(4) And after the fire, a small, silent voice.

Returning to the article:

> Despite the similarity between the elements comprising the description – the anaphora[6] "And after the ... ," then a repeat of

---

4. Y. Zakovitch, *Al Shelosha ... VeAl Arbaa* (Jerusalem, 5739).
5. "Kol Demama Daka," 339.
6. A rhetorical device in which a sequence of words is repeated at the beginnings of

the words "Not in the …," and then the epiphora[7] "God" – we see a deliberate variation. The narrator elaborates in the description of the first destructive power, the wind, noting its manifestation in, and effect on, nature. No such elaboration characterizes the descriptions of the earthquake or the fire, so as not to interfere with the rapid and intense rhythm leading us to the appearance of God Himself. Furthermore, in order to emphasize the connection between these destructive forces and God, the narrator links "Behold, God passed over" and the description of the wind, by explaining that the wind precedes God's appearance: "Before God.…"

The final element, the small, silent voice – the climax of this unit and its turning point – is different. Its title is longer than any of the destructive forces ("a small, silent voice" as opposed to "earthquake" or "fire"), and it also lacks the concluding phrase that characterizes the three preceding elements.… It is specifically the absence of this conclusion that serves to highlight the contrast, since the lack of the negative assertion implies the positive corollary: While God had not yet appeared in the preceding destructive forces, He was present in the small silence.

Let us now move on to Zakovitch's analysis of the verses describing Elijah's mission (vv. 15–18):

> Hazael, Jehu and Elisha will bring destruction and death upon Israel; of the nation there will remain only those who are faithful to God and did not go after the Baal gods. The three people who will sow death are mentioned twice in this unit: First Elijah is commanded to anoint the two kings and the prophet, and the reader is left wondering what connection could exist between this mission and the prophet's harsh accusations. Then the three are mentioned again – and now the purpose of the mission and its connection with Elijah's com-

---

neighboring clauses.

7. Repetition of the same word or words at the end of successive phrases.

plaints becomes clearer. The three personalities – Hazael, Jehu, and Elisha – parallel the three destructive forces that succeed one another in the description of the revelation: the wind, the earthquake, and the fire. And just as the narrator introduces some variation in the presentation of the destructive forces, here too is variation despite the almost word-for-word rhythmic repetition – to the point of creating the rather unusual expression of "anointing" a prophet (v. 16). For the purposes of variation, the narrator gradually lengthens the titles of the three people whom Elijah must anoint: First, simply "Hazael," then "Jehu son of Nimshi" (including his father's name), and finally "Elisha son of Shafat, of Abel Meholah" (including his father's name and his city of origin).[8]

Now Zakovitch goes on to note the connection between the structure of the revelation verses and the structure of the mission verses:

Here we are witness to the final aspect of the correlation between verses 11–12 and verses 15–18. The mission is also built along the lines of the "three and four" model: Here too, the fourth element is a contrast to the first three. There, God appeared after the forces of destruction, in the small, silent voice. Here, God appears after the revenge, after the slaughter; He has mercy and leaves a remnant of His people.… The remnant is a sign of God's mercy and His positive relationship toward Israel.[9]

In his final words above, Zakovitch is referring to the concluding verses of God's mission for Elijah:

And it shall be that whoever escapes from the sword of *Hazael* will be put to death by *Jehu*, and whoever escapes from the sword of *Jehu* will be put to death by *Elisha*. *And I shall leave* of Israel

---

8. Zakovitch, "Kol Demama Daka," 343.
9. Ibid., 344.

seven thousand; all the knees that did not bow to Baal, and every mouth that did not kiss it. (vv. 17–18)

Here the author refers us to several examples – principally from the book of Isaiah (see, for example, Is. 37:31–32), demonstrating that "leaving a remnant" is an expression of God's mercy toward Israel. As further support for this idea, we may add that the number "seven thousand" is not meant here in its exact, mathematical sense. Rabbi Y. Kaspi notes this and comments: "'Seven thousand' – not necessarily [this exact number]. What it means is – few in number." Elaborating slightly, Abrabanel writes:

> The intention here is not that no more than seven thousand souls will remain throughout the Land of Israel. Rather, [the idea is that] he should not think that after permission has been given to the Destroyer to wreak destruction…that he will make no distinction between the righteous and the wicked, for this will not be the case. For at all times "an angel of God rests around those who fear Him, and saves them" (Ps. 34:8).

Why, then, does the narrator choose specifically the number seven thousand? It would seem that the number is chosen for the symbolic significance of the number seven. What the text appears to be saying is that there will always be a *sanctified core* among the nation of Israel that will not become defiled through idolatry, and therefore there will always be a group of people upon whom God's mercy may extend.

What have we gained from this clear parallel between God's revelation to Elijah and the mission entrusted to him thereafter, in terms of our understanding of the significance of the mission? How does the parallel help us to answer our original question? Zakovitch answers:

> From the description of the actions of the anointed ones (v. 17) it would seem that God is acquiescing to Elijah's bitter accusation… Hazael, Jehu and Elisha will "put to death by the sword" to avenge Elijah's claim, "They have put Your prophets to death by the sword"… It is Elijah who has asked for revenge, and it

is therefore necessary that he himself go and exert effort and anoint those who will perform the revenge. His will is going to be fulfilled, but it is his own hands that will end up having spilled this blood.[10] And what thereafter?… "I shall leave of Israel seven thousand" – the attribute of mercy, "I shall leave," is the attribute of God.[11]

The picture that arises from the parallel is therefore one that depicts Elijah's mission not as a comforting response on God's part to Elijah's demands, but rather as a *punishment to Elijah himself*: He will now serve as an instrument in God's hand to carry out a policy that God Himself does not identify with. Not in these was God.[12]

The instruction of the mission to Elijah serves to move the prophet from the theoretical argument, in which a person may demand of God the exaction of the attribute of strict justice toward Israel, to the practical level, in which that same person is required to realize the same demand that he made of God, through his own terrible actions. Will Elijah be capable of carrying out such actions against his people? Will his hands not tremble at the appointment

---

10. Of course, Elijah's hands do not actually spill blood, but his call for revenge becomes a mission in which he will have to be personally involved; it will not remain a theoretical rallying cry.

11. Zakovitch, "Kol Demama Daka," 343–44.

12. The mission with which Elijah is entrusted, according to this explanation, raises a question of principle: Is it possible that Israel be punished simply on the basis of Elijah's claims? However, it seems that the dialogue in this chapter between God and Elijah concerns not the question of whether or not Israel are deserving of punishment, but rather what the role of the prophet is as he stands before God: Is he meant to criticize the nation's faults and call for their chastisement, or the opposite – to defend them and advocate on their behalf? Thus, it may be that Israel's punishment at the hand of Hazael and the other anointed leaders is something that God planned long before, but it is realized at this time, with Elijah's participation. However, Ralbag, commenting on v. 15, writes: "Elijah's desire that Israel be punished – as indicated by his finding fault with them before God – is the reason for the anointing of Hazael as king of Aram, and the anointing of Jehu as king of Israel…". See our discussion of a similar question in the section "The Drought," chapter 4.

of a gentile king so that the latter may wave his sword over Israel and slaughter many of them?[13]

"I DO NOT DESIRE YOUR PROPHECY"

This approach of viewing the mission given to Elijah as a punishment for his ongoing campaign of accusation against Israel (and as a test of his ability to act against his own nation on the basis of these accusations), was based principally on the parallel between this mission (vv. 15–18) and the revelation that preceded it (vv. 11–12). We shall now continue with the same approach and demonstrate that the words of the verses describing the mission serve to support it.

We shall focus on two precise linguistic analyses and one stylistic-thematic clarification.

1. At the start of the mission we read: "God said to him: Go, return on your way to the wilderness of Damascus" (v. 15).

   This raises the obvious question: Did Elijah come from the wilderness of Damascus that he is now commanded to "return"? Surely he came from Jezreel. The commentators offer various explanations; Abrabanel appears to propose the most accurate answer:

   In accordance with the view of the Sages and the accepted view among the commentators, that Elijah sought revenge upon Israel for their evil deeds, we might interpret the words "Go, return on your way" as a way of God telling him: Since your way is to be

---

13. In this section, the revelation to Elijah in vv. 11–12 is interpreted as notification in advance of the mission that he will be given, and as an explanation of the meaning of this mission, which is a test and a punishment for Elijah.

   In chapter 26, by contrast, following in the footsteps of some of the commentators, we explained the revelation as part of the argument with Elijah over his approach as a prophet who criticizes Israel. According to these commentators, the revelation represents a rebuke to Elijah, and an explanation of that which came before: drawing Elijah to Mount Horeb, and that which is hinted to him there.

   Obviously, there is no contradiction between these two understandings of God's revelation in vv. 11–12; on the contrary, they complement one another.

"vengeful and unforgiving as a snake" (see Yoma 23a), your wish and request being that I should punish Israel and "heap evils upon them" (Deut. 32:23), [therefore] *go from here and return to your custom and your way* of seeking to punish Israel. *therefore,* go to the wilderness of Damascus … and they [Hazael, Jehu and Elisha] will exact your revenge.

Abrabanel interprets the command "Go, return on your way, not in the literal, geographical sense, but rather in the borrowed sense of "returning" to one's way of thinking and behaving.

2. The specification of Elijah's destination, "The *wilderness* of Damascus," is no less unusual. A prophet is sent to act in inhabited places; why does the divine command make mention of the wilderness? If we recall Elijah's journey to the wilderness of Beer Sheba, and the significance of that journey, this command arouses an association with "Elijah's way" – his personal preference for isolation in the wilderness, away from his people.

3. The list of appointments that Elijah is commanded to carry out ends as follows: "And Elisha son of Shafat, of Abel Meholah, you shall anoint as prophet in your stead" (v. 16).

What is the purpose of this appointment? At first glance its purpose seems identical to that of the two preceding appointments; namely, to punish Israel, as we read in the following verse: "And he who escapes from the sword of Jehu shall be put to death by Elisha." But if this is the case, we are faced with two difficulties – one stylistic, the other thematic.

If we compare the style of the three commands in verses 15–16, we immediately note the difference between the command to anoint Elisha and the preceding commands to anoint the two kings. Hazael is to become king of Aram; Jehu is to become king of Israel; while Elisha is to be anointed as "prophet in your stead."

The similarity between the three commands in the instruction to anoint all three figures (although a prophet is not anointed at all), would seem to require that in Elisha's case, as in the case of the two kings, there should be a definition of the "target population" among whom he will be active: "a prophet in Israel" (corresponding to "king of Aram/Israel"). Alternatively, the two preceding appointments should include mention of the kings that they will be replacing: "Hazael as king of Aram in place of Ben Hadad."

The thematic difficulty concerns the purpose of the command. Why should Elijah himself not be the prophet who continues the work of Hazael and Jehu in killing Israelites?

For the above reasons, Ḥazal's teaching in the *Mekhilta* (beginning of *Parashat Bo*) would seem to be directed, in this case, toward the literal sense of the text:

> Elijah sought the honor of the Father [God] and not the honor of the son [Israel], as it is written: "I have been zealous for the Lord God of Hosts." Hence what the text means in saying, "God said to him: Go, return on your way to the wilderness of Damascus…and Jehu son of Nimshi, you shall anoint as king of Israel, and Elisha son of Shafat…you shall anoint as prophet in your stead," *is not "he will succeed you as prophet," but rather "I do not desire your prophecy."*

We have already mentioned that prophecy is a command that is given to a person; the prophet is not free to absolve himself of it. It is for this reason that God does not accept Elijah's request to die under the broom tree (just as He does not accept Jonah's attempt to flee from his prophetic mission). But if the prophet maintains his stand and is not convinced by God's words that are aimed at educating him and bringing him closer to God's attribute of mercy, then that mission, which is forced upon him, is his last in his capacity as prophet. While God will not retract the mission of a prophet who disagrees with it and seeks to be relieved of it, He also has no desire for a prophet to continue standing before Him angrily without any sense of identification with his mission.

ELIJAH'S WAY AND GOD'S WAY

With God's command to Elijah, "Go, return on your way," Elijah's journey is about to be completed: From Mount Horeb he will return to the Land of Israel, and the only stop along the route mentioned in the text is Abel Meholah, where Elisha lives. This completes an almost perfect geographical circle. Elijah left the city of Jezreel, situated to the west of Beit She'an (18:46); he journeys via the city of Beer Sheba into the heart of the wilderness and arrives, after a very long walk, at his destination – Mount Horeb. From there he retraces his footsteps, ending up in Abel Meholah, which is to the east of Beit She'an.

Although most of the action (vv. 8–18) takes place at Mount Horeb, and the events there also represent the essence of the story in every sense, it would not be fair to call our story "Elijah's journey to and from Mount Horeb." After all, it was not to Mount Horeb that Elijah directed himself when he set out, and his arrival there, as well as his return from there, are unexpected developments in the story. Elijah's journey may be divided into three stages: Three times he sets off (heading, respectively, for Beer Sheba, Mount Horeb, and Abel Meholah), but only the first time does he set off at his own initiative, to achieve an objective that he has set for himself. The other two journeys are undertaken at God's command, and their respective purposes are dictated to him either directly (in God's words at Horeb) or through indirect divine instruction (after the angel's revelation to him).

The Journey to Beer Sheba, and from There to Mount Horeb

The first two stages of the journey – to Beer Sheba and to Mount Horeb – are on the same geographical continuum; therefore, they may be viewed as a single journey whose second stage is simply a completion of the first stage. Elijah's stay in Beer Sheba is, as it were, no more than a stop on the way to his main destination: Mount Horeb.

However, there is a linguistic symmetry between these two journeys, indicating that the road from Jezreel to Horeb should not be viewed as a single, continuous journey (with a stopover in Beer Sheba), but rather as two parallel journeys. A comparison of the two reveals its significance:

From Jezreel to the wilderness of Beer Sheba	From the wilderness of Beer Sheba to Mount Horeb
When he saw it *he arose and went* for his life, and he came to Beer Sheba which is in Judah (v. 3)	*He arose* and he ate and drank, and *he went* ... until the mountain of God at Horeb (v. 8)
and he came and sat beneath a certain broom tree (v. 4)	And he came there to a cave (v. 9)
and he lay down and slept under a broom tree (v. 5)	and he stayed the night there (v. 9)
and behold, an angel touched him and said to him: Arise, eat (v. 5)	*and behold, God's word came to him, and He said to him*: What do you seek here, Elijah? (v. 9)
God's angel came back a second time, and touched him, and said: Arise, eat (v. 7)	*and behold, a voice came to him and it said*: What do you seek here, Elijah? (v. 13)
for *the way is far for you*	God said to him: *go, return on your way* (v. 15)

What was the purpose of going to the wilderness of Beer Sheba? Elijah determined the purpose himself. He set off on this journey of his own initiative, in order to flee from his people to the wilderness, where he could seclude himself, with a view to removing the yoke of prophecy – as well as the yoke of life itself – from his shoulders: "If only I could be in the wilderness, a lodge for wayfarers, that I may leave my people ..." (Jer. 9:1).

The trek toward the unknown at the beginning of the second part of the journey is a continuation of the first part of the journey only in the geographical sense (extending even further southward). But after forty days and forty nights, Elijah discovers that his feet have led him to Mount Horeb, recalling the root of the existence of Israel as God's covenantal nation. In fleeing from the nation of Israel, Elijah finds himself connecting, against his will, with the roots of his nation's existence. Thus, the *geographical continuation* of the path that Elijah walks is, in fact, the very *opposite of the purpose* of his journey – a reversal that happens through divine guidance. Therefore, the broom tree in the wilderness of Beer Sheba is not a halfway station on a single, continuous journey, but rather a clear point of separation between two paths with opposing purposes.

The conflict that we are discussing here is the conflict between *Elijah's purpose* in heading for the wilderness of Beer Sheba and *God's purpose* in leading him from the wilderness of Beer Sheba to Mount Horeb. This conflict is expressed in the first parallel demonstrated above – a contrasting parallel:

"He arose and went *for his life* and he came to Beer Sheba" (v. 3)

"He arose … and went … *until the mountain of God* at Horeb" (v. 8)

However, from God's perspective, there is one single intention that operates in relation to Elijah, both during his first journey and during his second. The revelation of the angel, taking Elijah by surprise under the broom tree and commanding him, "Arise, eat," and the revelation of God that takes him by surprise at the cave at Mount Horeb, asking him, "What do you seek here, Elijah" – the fourth parallel above – share the same purpose: They aim to dissuade Elijah from forsaking his nation and accusing them, and to return him to his place. Because Elijah fails to respond to what is hinted to him in Beer Sheba by the angel, and does not return to his place and to his role, the divine message must be made clearer by means of the journey to Mount Horeb, in the footsteps of Moses.

From Elijah's point of view, too, there is little change in intention between the two parts of his journey. He treats the cave at Mount Horeb – the cleft in the rock – in the same way as he treated the broom tree in the wilderness of Beer Sheba: as a hideout. We learn this from the second parallel set out above, as well as from the third parallel, in which we discover that Elijah lodged at the cave just as he slept under the tree. As becomes clear from Elijah's response to God's question, "What do you seek here?" Elijah has not absorbed the message that he should have learned from being led to Mount Horeb and to this cave. This is why God commands him to leave the cave in preparation for a revelation that will communicate the divine message even more clearly, as well as prepare Elijah for what awaits him if he persists in maintaining his stand.

Nevertheless, there is something of a contrast between Elijah's words under the tree in the wilderness of Beer Sheba and his words at the cave at Horeb. Under the broom tree he asks to die, telling God, *"Take my life."* At the cave, he complains repeatedly about Israel, who seek *"my life, to take it."* This contrast is only external. It is his complaint at the cave that reveals what is troubling Elijah: It is the threat to his life that troubles him; this is the root of his flight from his nation, just as this is the basis of his argument with God.

From Mount Horeb Northward

What is the meaning of God's command to Elijah, "Go, return on your way" from Horeb northward? Geographically speaking, it would seem to indicate a return to his point of departure, a *nullification of the flight* from the nation and from his role as prophet in their midst. "Returning on the same way" is an expression used in some places in Tanakh to mean a nullification of the meaning of what has happened, or what has been achieved, during the first journey.[14]

Elijah is commanded to retract having turned his back on his people and to return to them and to his land, bearing a mission that renews his role as prophet. But all of this is only on the surface. In fact, his return to his land is a sort of punishment for Elijah, who has maintained his view and his zealousness that is undesirable in God's eyes. The return that he is commanded to undertake is "to your way" – Elijah's way, not God's way. Therefore, he is given the prophetic mission of bringing punishment upon Israel. This mission will be the final chord in his performance as prophet; his final task is to appoint Elisha "as prophet in his stead," for God no longer desires Elijah's prophecy. The mention of Elijah's destination, the wilderness of Damascus, is likewise reminiscent of the wilderness of Beer Sheba to which he fled.

---

14. Thus, the Torah's prohibition on returning to Egypt by the same route that the Israelites left there (Deut. 17:16, 28:68) may be understood as a prohibition on reversing (even on the merely symbolic level) the process of leaving Egypt from slavery to freedom. On the other hand, Abraham, on his return from Egypt to the land of Canaan, takes care to follow the same route he traveled on his way there (compare Gen. 12:8 with 13:1; and 12:9 with 13:1), with a view to "erasing" the effects and significance of having left the land of Canaan.

Thus, it is specifically in God's command that Elijah return to his nation and to his land that the prophet is granted his wish to be absolved of the burden of prophecy, and to see Israel punished for their sins. However, this happens not out of divine approval of his view; rather, out of rebuke for the prophet who insists on maintaining his stubborn stance. *Once again, it turns out that the geographical direction of Elijah's path, returning to the Land of Israel, is the opposite of the intention that it conceals* – to conclude his role as prophet in Israel. The final comparison set out above presents a clearly contrasting parallel between "*the way* – to *Mount Horeb* – is too far for you," and "Go, return *to your way*" – from *Mount Horeb to the Land of Israel*.

Thus we discover that God's way, leading Elijah to different places, should not be understood at face value, and its purpose should not be analyzed in geographical terms. For God's way is the opposite of Elijah's way, even where, on the surface, they would seem to be in harmony.

> For your thoughts are not My thoughts, nor your ways – My ways, says God. For just as the heavens are high above the earth, so are My ways elevated above your ways, and My thoughts, above Your thoughts. (Is. 55:8)

Chapter 29

Was the Mission Fulfilled?

T he mission entrusted to Elijah at Mount Horeb, in I Kings 19:15–18, has thus far been addressed in terms of its significance in relation to the preceding narrative. We saw how this mission represents a continuation and practical summary of the ongoing polemics between the prophet and God. We shall now examine the mission in terms of its relationship to what follows in our chapter, in verses 19–21.

The attempt to match what Elijah is told, within the framework of this mission, with what actually happens afterward, gives rise to serious difficulties – first and foremost in the comparison between the command and its fulfillment. Elijah is commanded to perform three actions:

Go, return on your way to the wilderness of Damascus,

1. and you shall come and anoint Hazael as king over Aram; (v. 15)
2. and Jehu son of Nimshi you shall anoint as king over Israel,
3. and Elisha son of Shafat, from Abel Meholah, you shall anoint as prophet in your stead. (v. 16)

Further on in our chapter we are told that Elijah starts to fulfill this command, but in inverse order: "He went from there and found Elisha, son of Shafat, and he was plowing with twelve pairs of oxen in front of him" (v. 19). Why was Elijah's first stop in Abel Meholah?

This is not the only difficulty with which we have to grapple: Nowhere do we find Elijah fulfilling the other two parts of the divine command! We are not aware of Elijah ever reaching Damascus. Hazael is appointed by Elisha in Damascus (II Kings 8:7–15) long after Elijah is taken heavenward in a storm. And Jehu son of Nimshi is anointed at Elisha's command by one of his disciples (II Kings 9:1–10). This happens even later than Hazael's ascent to the throne in Aram.

Even that which Elijah does appear to fulfill – the appointment of Elisha – he performs differently from how he was commanded. He is told to appoint Elisha as a prophet *in his stead*, but in practice this is not what he does. We are told only that "[Elisha] arose and went after Elijah, and *he served him*" (v. 21).

Indeed, we encounter no prophetic activity on the part of Elisha until after his master is gathered up to the heavens, at which point the sons of the prophets declare, "Elijah's spirit rests upon Elisha." Until then, Elisha operated only as Elijah's attendant. Elijah's departure is itself the occasion of Elisha's appointment as prophet in place of his master (see II Kings 2:9–15).

From the above it also becomes clear that Elijah did not cease serving as a prophet following his return from Mount Horeb. The essence of God's message to him, "You shall anoint as prophet in your stead" – as interpreted by Ḥazal, "I do not desire your prophecy"[1] – was not fulfilled. Not only does Elijah continue to act as a prophet for a long time, but God Himself even sends him to fulfill various prophetic missions in the conflict against the House of Ahab. Thus, in chapter 21, in the story of the vineyard of Naboth, God sends him to rebuke Ahab, who is taking possession of the vineyard (21:17–29); likewise, in II Kings 1, Elijah is sent by God's angel to halt the emissaries of Ahaziah on their way (1:3–4) and to appear before Ahaziah himself (1:15).

In summary, we may ask: Why does Elijah not fulfill the command given at Mount Horeb?

---

1. See chapter 28, p. 326.

This question is addressed by various commentators. Let us review some of their explanations:

Radak and Ralbag divest the expressions, "You shall come and you shall anoint" and "You shall anoint," of their primary meaning as absolute commands, regarding them rather as a command enabling him to convey these responsibilities to Elisha, who will replace him. Since Elisha's acts will be carried out by virtue of having been instructed by Elijah, his teacher, it will be "as though Elijah anointed them." Because this is a forced and improbable explanation. the two commentators endeavor to explain how Elijah deduced that this was how he was meant to interpret the divine command. They conclude that Elijah derived this from the fact that when he went to fulfill the command to appoint Hazael, he happened upon Elisha on the way. He viewed this as a sign that he should first appoint Elisha, and then make Elisha the executor of the first two tasks – the anointment of Hazael and the anointment of Jehu.

Abrabanel offers a completely different approach to the above question (commenting on v. 17):

> What appears to me to be the case, in this matter, is that the blessed God told Elijah that he would soon anoint Hazael and Jehu, for it was God's will to punish Israel in the days of Ahab and in the days of Elijah. When Ahab yielded and turned to God in repentance [after Elijah rebukes him at the vineyard of Naboth, 21:27–29], God saw fit to withhold His anger. As He tells Elijah, "Have you seen how Ahab has humbled himself before Me… I shall not bring the evil in his days; in the days of his son I shall bring the evil upon his house" (21:29). It was for this reason that Elijah anointed neither Hazael nor Jehu, as God had commanded him, for God had retracted the evil and withheld His anger toward them; therefore Elisha anointed them after the death of Ahab. There is no doubt that Elijah instructed him to anoint them by God's word, for [although] you will not find any divine command or utterance to Elisha concerning the anointment of either of them, he himself told Hazael that he would be king over Aram after the death of Ben Hadad (II Kings 8:13), and

he likewise commanded the prophet Jonah (according to the Midrash),[2] of his own initiative, to go and anoint Jehu (II Kings 9:1–3), for he did this since Elijah had commanded him, by God's word. Hence, that which Elijah could not do because the blessed God withheld His anger from Ahab, was done by Elisha in the days of [Ahab's] son.

But Abrabanel's solution does not really answer the question. Ahab's repentance happens a considerable time after Elijah's return from Mount Horeb.[3] How, then, does Elijah know to first head for Elisha, and refrain from anointing Hazael and Jehu? If one were to suggest that this was revealed to him in prophecy by God, to whom everything is revealed and known in advance (even though Ahab still had free choice as to whether to yield to God or not), then what was the point of giving Elijah this mission in the first place?

Let us try to propose a different solution. In the previous chapter, we chose to view Elijah's mission as a test for the prophet, and as a punishment for his accusations against Israel and his call for revenge on them. His call is answered, but he himself is the one who will have to bring the punishment upon his nation, and this mission will be his last. We speculated there as to whether Elijah would be capable of carrying out these actions: Whether his hands would not tremble as he anointed the enemy of his people as king, to wave his terrible sword over Israel.

But actually we do not find Elijah carrying out his mission. Even that which he does fulfill, out of all that he is commanded – the appointment of Elisha – is not fulfilled in the spirit of the command, nor in

---

2. The name of the individual from among the "sons of the prophets" whom Elisha sends to anoint Jehu is not named in the text. Abrabanel identifies him as Jonah, based on a midrash.

3. According to the order of events as set out in the text (and we have no reason to assume that the chronological order is different): Elijah's return to the Kingdom of Israel (end of ch. 19) and the story of Naboth's vineyard (ch. 21) are separated by Ahab's two wars against Ben Hadad (ch. 20), with a year in between the first war and the second (see 20:26). In fact, the time lapse between chapter 19 and chapter 21 may be even longer.

accordance with its intention, as noted above. He does not appoint Elisha as prophet in his stead, but rather takes him along as his attendant, while Elijah himself continues to act as prophet for a not insignificant period of time. How, then, can Elijah's actions be reconciled with *Hazal's* teaching that God's words to Elijah: "Anoint as prophet in your stead" represent his dismissal by God – "I do not desire your prophecy"?

It must be that Elijah, returning from Mount Horeb to the Kingdom of Israel, has finally changed his mind and his attitude toward his nation; he no longer desires the termination of his prophetic mission. If this is so, it is no longer appropriate that he be dismissed from his job, and his encounter with Elisha no longer requires that he transfer the prophetic mission to Elisha. Instead, Elijah takes Elisha along with him, to serve him and to be apprenticed to him in the ways of prophecy.

This change that takes place in Elijah is admittedly absent from the text, but it is depicted in the brief concluding scene in our chapter. In this scene (19:19–21), two highly powerful personalities meet. We discern a desire on the part of the teacher to draw the disciple along with him, just as the disciple is drawn to the teacher by a magnetic force. Even though this scene is meant to describe the beginning of the new era of Elisha's prophecy, it in no way testifies to an end of the previous era of Elijah. On the contrary, Elijah stands out in this picture with the full force of his personality, and there is no sign of any cessation of his prophetic activity in the near future.

The integration of the concluding scene within the overall structure of the narrative, points to the far-reaching significance of its content. In chapter 22 of this book, we noted that I Kings 19 is built as a symmetrical framework around the central axis of the Revelation at Horeb in verses 11–12. Each pair of units arranged around this axis, we noted, represents a parallel that is sometimes inverse. The unit corresponding to the concluding scene (vv. 19–21) is the description of Elijah walking off to the desert of Beer Sheba, in verses 1–4.

These two scenes are clearly the inverse of one another. In the opening scene Elijah is fleeing from the center of the kingdom, from the city of Jezreel, toward the wilderness, with the intention of abandoning his nation and his mission. He makes his way to Beer Sheba – the furthest outskirts of habitation in the southern part of land, accompanied by his attendant. But at Beer Sheba he leaves his attendant behind while he goes to isolate himself in the wilderness. Consumed with despair, Elijah lies down under a certain broom tree and asks to die.

In the concluding scene, Elijah returns from the wilderness, where he has spent considerable time alone, and travels toward the eastern side of the same valley that lies at the heart of the Kingdom of Israel, to the city of Abel Meholah. He does this despite the danger still lurking over him, as a result of Jezebel's threat, to which he now pays no attention. He appears to make his return journey to his land, to habitation, alone. But at Abel Meholah he takes up Elisha, who goes after him and attends to him. This is the inverse of Elijah leaving his attendant in Beer Sheba in order to go and isolate himself in the wilderness.

The significance of this inverse parallel between the beginning of the story and its end is that Elijah, in the act of taking Elisha with him, returns to human society, returns to his nation, and nullifies the implications of his isolation in the wilderness and his will to die there. If the image of Elijah under the broom tree symbolizes his will to cease serving as a prophet in Israel, out of despair at his nation, then the concluding image symbolizes exactly the opposite: a nullification of his previous desire, and an expression of his reborn will to serve in the role of prophet of Israel.[4]

Thus, in light of the story's structure, several contrasts between the beginning of the story and its conclusion are brought together to show that in the end, there is a change in Elijah's position. God's word has ultimately achieved its aim: At the end of their long debate, Elijah is convinced. The angel that appears to him twice; the journey in the footsteps of Moses to Mount Horeb; God's repeated rebuke, "What do you seek here, Elijah?"; the wondrous revelation in the form of a small, silent voice following God's absence from the wind, the earthquake, and the fire; and the mission of punishment entrusted to the prophet who

---

4. At the end of the previous chapter we noted that the direction in which Elijah is commanded to travel – returning to the Land of Israel – does not necessarily indicate any intention on his part to return to his role; in fact, it may indicate the opposite. However, this was in relation to the intention of the divine command to punish Elijah and terminate his role. What happened in reality was that Elijah's repentance reversed the meaning of God's command, and his return to the Land of Israel became a return to his role as prophet.

stubbornly maintains his view – the compound effect of all of these factors finally softens Elijah and convinces him to return to his nation and to his role in their midst. But it would seem that of all of these "arguments," the final one was the most decisive. Giving Elijah the terrible responsibility of appointing a cruel king, who would be the enemy of his nation, and who would slay with his sword many thousands of Israelites, was the test of the limit of Elijah's criticism. Elijah does not agree to this mission, and thereby withdraws from the position that he has maintained throughout the argument.

> As the rain and the snow fall from the heavens but do not return there, but rather water the earth and cause it to bring forth and grow, and give seed to the sower and bread to the eater, so My word that emerges from My mouth shall not return to Me empty; it shall accomplish that which I please, and shall succeed in that for which I sent it. (Is. 55:10–11)

Sometimes God's word is "absorbed" in the heart like rain that waters the ground, and immediately it begins to have its effect inside. But sometimes God's word remains "frozen" at the entrance to a person's heart, like snow that builds up upon the ground. Even then, the delay in God's word having its effect is only temporary. Ultimately the snow will melt and penetrate the ground, watering it and causing it to bring forth vegetation.

Now we must ask: If it is indeed true that at the end of our story, in the final three verses, there is a turnaround and Elijah retracts the stand that he has maintained since the beginning of the story, why does the text not state this explicitly? How can such a significant conclusion to the story be left to the reader's sensitivity, to his ability to discern the meaning of the final scene and the message arising from its comparison with the introductory scene?

Before attempting to answer this question, it must be emphasized that unlike certain other personalities in Tanakh who are depicted as God's enemies, and whose ultimate submission the text therefore takes pains to describe in very clear language (Pharaoh, Jeroboam, Ahab), Elijah is not – heaven forefend – opposed to God's word. He represents a position that has some truth to it, but it is a one-sided position that God does not want upheld by His prophet. The dispute in our chapter is an internal, delicate matter between God and His prophet, and there is no point in presenting Elijah's withdrawal from his position as submission, or as a victory for God's word. Nevertheless, we must still answer the question we posed above. Even if Elijah's turnaround is not presented as submission, it could still be noted explicitly, in such a way as to preserve the prophet's dignity.

The answer would seem to be that wherever the text hides a person's reaction and the change that takes place within him – as we believe to be the case concerning Elijah – there is a reason for this. It comes to depict the nature of the change, and we are able to appreciate its extent. In our instance, in stating that Elijah retracts his position, we do not mean that he underwent a comprehensive change in his approach, nor that some fundamental change occurred in his personality. The essence of the change in Elijah concerns his attitude toward his prophetic role: He is ready for a change in policy. He will no longer demand punishment for the nation, nor will he abandon his position in protest. He is now ready to go back to acting as God's emissary, attempting to promote repentance among Israel, particularly through criticism of the royal house.

The fact that Elijah has not fundamentally changed, and that he remains just as severe a prophet as he always was, is reflected in the concluding image of the story. Even though Elijah is described as returning to his people and to his role, a careful examination of the verses leads us to the conclusion that he reacts sternly to Elisha and to his request, "Let me kiss my father and my mother, and I shall go after you."[5] Likewise, throughout the remainder of his prophetic activity, until he is carried up to the heavens, we are aware of his sternness. In chapter 21 he rebukes Ahab for killing Naboth and inheriting his vineyard, and declares a terrible verdict; in II Kings 1, he rebukes Ahaziah son of Ahab for seeking out Baal-Zebub, the god of Ekron, during his illness, and sentences him to die of that same illness. In chapter 2, when God "carries Elijah up in a storm toward the heavens," we still sense Elijah's stern attitude toward Elisha; this cold treatment thaws only toward his dramatic departure.

---

5. As discussed in detail in the next chapter.

However, there is a noticeable change in Elijah's manner. In both appearances in which he acts as a prophet in Israel, he acts only by explicit divine command:

Vineyard of Naboth (I Kings, ch. 21)	To the messengers of Ahaziah (II Kings, ch. 1)
(v. 17): God's word came to Elijah the Tishbite, saying:	(v. 3): An angel of God spoke to Elijah the Tishbite:
(v. 18): Arise, go down to meet Ahab, king of Israel	Arise, go up to meet the messengers of the king of Samaria
(v. 19): and you shall speak to him, saying:	and speak to them.
So says the Lord: Have you murdered and also inherited?!	Is it for lack of any God in Israel
	that you go to seek out Baal-Zebub, god of Ekron?

Elijah's behavior until now has been characterized by actions undertaken without any explicit divine command, but rather on his own initiative and at his discretion. This was the case when he vowed that there would be no rain, and again in the test that he arranged at Mount Carmel. But now, following his return from Mount Horeb, Elijah is no longer zealous on his own initiative; but rather acts only when he is sent by God with an explicit instruction.

How does all of this solve the question that we posed at the very start of this chapter? In a manner that is essentially similar to the approach of Abrabanel, but with one important difference: It is not the future repentance of Ahab, as yet unbeknownst to Elijah (and to us, the readers), that cancels Elijah's appointment of Hazael and Jehu, but rather the present repentance of Elijah himself. The perception of the mission entrusted to him as a test and a punishment turns it into a conditional mission: As long as Elijah maintains his position and his accusations, "I have been exceedingly zealous for God," he must fulfill the mission. But when Elijah returns to his nation and to his role, thereby implicitly nullifying his previous accusations against Israel, this reproachful mission is silently removed from his shoulders.[6]

OUR NARRATIVE'S PROPHECY OF PUNISHMENT VS. ITS REALIZATION IN THE DAYS OF ELISHA

We now understand that the decree that Hazael, Jehu, and Elisha will serve as God's agents in punishing Israel is not dependent on Elijah's criticism. The nation has sealed its fate by its own actions. Indeed, although Elijah has been relieved of the heavy burden of appointing these personalities to their respective stations for the reasons addressed at length above, the nation of Israel has not been exempted from the punishment that it deserves. Hazael and Jehu are eventually appointed by a prophet, so that they can wield their sword over Israel. Nevertheless, a comparison between God's words to Elijah concerning the destruction that these kings will inflict, and what actually happens, as described further on in the book of Kings, raises several questions.

First of all, let us examine how God's words to Elijah filter down through the words of Elisha and of his disciple to the kings whom they appoint. Elijah is told:

> It shall be that those who escape from the sword of Hazael shall be put to death by Jehu, and those who escape from the sword of Jehu shall be put to death by Elisha. And I shall leave of Israel seven thousand – all the knees that did not bow to Baal, and every mouth that did not kiss it. (I Kings 19:17–18)

However, when Elisha notifies Hazael that he is going to reign over Aram, he tells him:

---

6. Thus we learn that the fact that Elijah began to fulfill God's command backwards, by first taking Elisha with him, as well as the character of this act – deviating from the instruction to appoint Elisha as prophet in his stead – are the key to the question of why Elijah did not fulfill the first two instructions and anoint Hazael and Jehu.

   Elijah's failure to fulfill the instructions that he was given reinforces our perception of these instructions as having been given as a test and as a punishment. Upon his return from Mount Horeb, there is a change in the position of the prophet who has been zealous for God, and he is therefore exempted from the heavy task of fulfilling these instructions.

> For I know the evil that you are going to do to the children of Israel; you will set their strong places on fire, and kill their young men with the sword, and dash their infants, and rip up their pregnant women. (II Kings 8:12)

Then, when one of the "sons of the prophets," Elisha's disciple, anoints Jehu at Elisha's order, he tells him:

> You shall smite the House of Ahab, your master, and I shall avenge the blood of My servants, the prophets, and the blood of all of God's servants, at the hand of Jezebel. And the whole of Ahab's house shall die…and Jezebel shall be consumed by dogs in the portion of Jezreel, with none to bury her. (II Kings 9:7–10)

When we compare God's words to Elijah with the reality that is supposed to occur, we encounter several difficulties:

1. The punishment that Jehu brings upon the House of Ahab and all the worshippers of Baal in Israel is described at length in II Kings chapters 9–10. But this precedes the punishment inflicted by Hazael. Why, then, does God initially describe it as the completion of the punishment brought about by Hazael?
2. The punishment inflicted on Israel by Hazael is described for the first time in the days of Jehu:

> In those days God began to cut off parts of Israel, and Hazael smote them throughout the borders of Israel. From the Jordan eastward, all the land of Gilead, of Gad and Reuben and Manasseh, from Aro'er which is by Wadi Arnon, and the Gilead, and the Bashan. (II Kings 10:32–33)

Here the text is speaking of the smiting (and perhaps even the conquest) of the eastern side of the Jordan. Far more grave is the punishment that Hazael is described as inflicting in the days of Jehoahaz son of Jehu:

> God's anger burned against Israel, and He gave them into the hand
> of Hazael, king of Aram, and into the hand of Ben Hadad, all their
> days … for the king of Aram oppressed them. … Nor did He leave for
> Jehoahaz any followers except for fifty horsemen and ten chariots
> and ten thousand footmen, for the king of Aram had destroyed them
> and had made them like the dust from threshing. (II Kings 13:3–4, 7)

This punishment occurs a long time after Jehu's actions against
Israel (in the days of Jehu's son, and some of it is inflicted by Hazael's son). It is difficult to match this with the punishment foretold
in the days of Elijah while Ahab and Jezebel ruled over Israel. More
than a generation has passed since then, Ahab's dynasty has been
annihilated, and the worshippers of Baal have already been put to
death by Jehu.

Likewise Elisha's words to Hazael, which we quoted above,
do not appear to be fulfilled. Hazael admittedly destroys most of
the army of Jehoahaz, king of Israel ("followers" here means those
who followed him into war), but there is no textual evidence of him
annihilating a civilian population (women and children) with great
cruelty, as described by Elisha.

3. The most puzzling problem is that Elisha is described, in God's words
   to Elijah, as a prophet who will bring death upon Israel, completing
   the punishment inflicted on them from without by Hazael, and
   from within by Jehu. How distant is this image from Elisha, whose
   activities are described at length in the text. All his acts are of help
   to various individuals and to the nation of Israel as a whole. The text
   portrays Elisha's actions as the exact opposite of the role destined
   for him in Elijah's prophecy!

In order to explain the matter, let us return to the hypothesis that we
proposed above that the lack of fulfillment of the mission by Elijah
reflects his retraction of the demand for revenge against Israel, "I have
been exceedingly zealous for God."

However, the mission is not altogether canceled (for the punishment that Israel deserves is not because of Elijah); rather, it is

simply transferred from Elijah to Elisha, and it is for this reason that we find Elisha appointing Hazael and Jehu, after Elijah is taken up to heaven. What, then, is the significance of Elijah removing this mission from his own shoulders and transferring it to his disciple? After all, the punishment will ultimately be carried out. Moreover, is it fair of Elijah to transfer this mission, which he himself no longer desires, to his disciple?

In order to answer this question we must first clarify a more fundamental issue: Is there any connection between the content of a prophecy and its fulfillment in reality, and the personality of the prophet who receives that prophecy? Is the prophet merely a vessel for conveying God's word, or is he to some extent a partner in molding the process by which God's words are applied in reality? It would seem that the principle set down by Ḥazal, that "no two prophets prophesy in the same style" (Sanhedrin 89a), applies not only to their monologues, but also to their style of action. Each prophet's unique style of action reflects his personality and his influence on the prophecy's fulfillment.[7]

A clear expression of this is to be found in the Talmud (Megilla 14b). When the Torah scroll was found in the Temple precinct in the days of Josiah, the king sent his messengers to Huldah the prophetess, rather than to Jeremiah, the major prophet of the generation:

> Go, seek out God on my behalf and on behalf of the nation, and on behalf of all of Judah, concerning the words of this book that has been found, for great is the wrath of God that has been kindled against us.… So Hilkiah the priest went…to Huldah the prophetess. (II Kings 22:13–14).

The Talmud asks: "How could Josiah put aside Jeremiah, and send to her?" Several answers are proposed. The first of them is: "R. Shila said: Because women are merciful."

Thus, there is significance in the identity of the prophet who speaks God's words (which, in the case of Josiah, would certainly be

---

7. See the introduction, p. xxi.

words of rebuke and punishment), and the fact that the prophecy comes through a woman can have a softening effect.[8]

In light of this, we can understand the significance of the appointment of Hazael being transferred from Elijah to Elisha. Elisha, while a loyal disciple of Elijah and his attendant, pouring water over his hands, is a prophet whose personality and manner of action are completely different from those of his master. Almost all of his actions are acts of salvation extended toward individuals and toward the nation as a whole. The transfer of responsibility for appointing Hazael to him therefore symbolizes an attempt to soften the punishment. This is no mere theoretical consideration, but rather an effect that is clearly illustrated in the manner in which Elisha goes on to act. In his encounter with Hazael, where he appoints him king over Aram and tells him of the imminent death of his master, Ben Hadad, Elisha adopts a peculiar manner:

> He maintained his countenance as long as he could, and then the man of God wept. And Hazael said: Why does my master weep? And he said: For I know the evil that you are going to do to the children of Israel; you will set their strong places on fire, and kill their young men with the sword, and dash their infants, and rip up their pregnant women. And Hazael said: But what is your servant, who is a dog, that he should do this mighty thing? And Elisha said: God has shown me that you will be king over Aram." (II Kings 8:11–13)

If later on we find no evidence of Hazael acting with such cruelty (although he succeeds in conquering parts of the land on the eastern side of the Jordan, and later on also wipes out a large portion of the

---

8. Maharsha, in his *Ḥiddushei Aggadot* (ad loc.) explains the words of the Talmud: "It does not seem that R. Shila means that Josiah sent word to Hulda because 'women are merciful' – and therefore she would utter a positive prophecy. Could she then change her prophecy from strict to beneficent just because women are merciful? And if he feared that Jeremiah would issue a prophecy of doom, she would certainly say the same. Therefore we must conclude that what R. Shila meant was that 'women are merciful,' and therefore Hulda would plead for divine mercy on their behalf, to change [their fate] from negative to positive."

Israelite army), this may be explained by Elisha's weeping at the dramatic moment when he tells Hazael that he will soon be king. The news of his imminent new status, conveyed to Hazael by God's prophet, thereby granting legitimacy to his reign, must have accompanied him for the rest of his life, along with the memory of the prophet who bore these tidings weeping bitterly. Perhaps this influenced him, moderating his actions against Israel.

Here we are witness to the prophet's influence over the realization of the prophecy that is conveyed through him, in ways that are clearly discernible: Not through the formulation of the prophecy, nor through prayer or supplication for mercy, but rather through overt psychological influence over the king who serves as God's agent in bringing punishment upon Israel. Could we possibly imagine Elijah weeping as he appoints Hazael?

What stems from all of the above is that the transfer of the task of appointing Hazael from Elijah to Elisha is itself a testimony to Elijah's abandonment of his critical, prosecuting approach toward Israel, and represents part of his "repentance." By handing his mission over to Elisha, Elijah reveals his wish to soften the punishment. He knows that if he himself were to carry out the mission it would not only be a punishment to himself, but would also not be for the benefit of the nation. Handing over the mission to Elisha is not only the removal of an unpleasant task from his own shoulders, but also represents a gesture that will, to some extent, ease the punishment that Hazael is destined to inflict on the nation.

Chapter 30

Elijah and Elisha's First Encounter (I Kings 19:19–21)

He went from there and found Elisha son of Shafat who was plowing – twelve yoke of oxen in front of him, and he with the twelfth. Elijah passed by him and cast his mantle toward him. Then he abandoned the cattle and ran after Elijah, and said: "Let me kiss my father and mother, and I shall follow you." And he said to him: "Go and [then] return, for what have I done to you?" So he returned back from him and took a yoke of oxen and slaughtered them, and boiled the meat with the equipment of the oxen, and gave it to the people, and they ate. Then he arose and went after Elijah, and attended him. (vv. 19–21)

There are two aspects to the first encounter between Elijah and Elisha. On one hand, this description concludes the story in I Kings, chapter 19, about Elijah at Mount Horeb, such that the circle is closed with Elijah returning to his land and to his people, and taking Elisha as his attendant instead of the servant whom he left in Beer Sheba.

On the other hand, this first meeting between the prophet who is about to complete his task and the person who is destined to succeed him as the major prophet of Israel, is one that signifies the beginning of a new era: the era of Elisha's prophecy. The description of this meeting is instructive not only as to itself, but also concerning the root of the profound contrasts between these two radically different prophets. The scene of their meeting brings together, like a mirror, Elijah's past and Elisha's future. Therefore, every detail in this brief description is of great value in understanding the relationship between the two men and their respective eras.

The direct thematic continuation of the three verses above is to be found in the description of the final meeting between Elijah and Elisha, their parting encounter (II Kings 2:1–12). Despite what we read in verse 21, "He arose and went after Elijah and attended him," we do not encounter both of them together again, until their final meeting.[1]

STRUCTURE OF THE UNIT

Although the meeting between Elijah and Elisha is not an independent narrative, but rather part of the story of Elijah at Mount Horeb, the description has its own special character, differing from that of the preceding narrative. This arises from the fact that only in this unit does Elijah maintain a mutual connection with another person, and this connection is the focus of the text. Thus the three verses above turn into a miniature story that is part of a greater narrative, and we are therefore justified in attempting to analyze the structure of this brief and semi-independent unit.

Like many other biblical narratives, our tiny unit may be divided into two more or less equal halves that correspond to one another. This is true in terms of content, style, and the composition characterizing the unit. Let us first examine the two halves in relation to each other, and then we shall explicate them.

---

1. There is no evidence of Elisha's presence over the course of Elijah's activities from this point onward – neither in the story of Naboth's vineyard (21:17–29), nor in Elijah's appearance before Ahaziah and his emissaries (II Kings, ch. 1). On the contrary, to all appearances, Elijah acts alone. Of course, this in no way negates the idea that in between their first and last encounter, Elisha serves as Elijah's attendant, and was routinely in his presence. We shall discuss this question further later in this chapter. Their parting encounter, to be addressed in the last section of this book, "The Storm," obviously serves as a summary and conclusion of Elijah's activity and an introduction to the period of Elisha's activity as a prophet of Israel.

First half	Second half
1. [Elijah] went from there, and he found Elisha son of Shafat	i. [Elisha] said: Let me kiss my father and my mother, and I shall follow you
2. [Elisha] plowing with twelve yoke of oxen in front of him, and he was with the twelfth	ii. [Elijah] said to him: Go and return, for what have I done to you? (v. 20)
3. [Elijah] passed by him and cast his mantle toward him. (v. 19)	iii. [Elisha] returned from after him and he took a yoke of oxen and slaughtered it, and boiled the meat with the equipment of the oxen, and he gave it to the people and they ate
4. [Elisha] left the oxen and *ran after Elijah*	iv. [Elisha] arose *and went after Elijah,* and attended him. (v. 21)

The unit is characterized by rapid exchanges between Elijah and Elisha as the subjects of the brief, succinct sentences that make up the story. These successive alternations create a great deal of dynamic. We have divided the unit into eight "lines" (more or less corresponding to the syntactical division into sentences), each devoted to the description of an action with a defined purpose by one of the two characters. This style highlights the alternation of the subject in most of the pairs of "lines," and the transition back and forth, from Elijah to Elisha and from Elisha to Elijah.

But in the middle of the unit there is a turning point. While the first four "lines" follow the order Elijah-Elisha-Elijah-Elisha, the fifth line reverses the pattern and starts a new one: Elisha-Elijah-Elisha-Elisha. This reversal of the order of the subject supports the division into two halves that we proposed, each half comprising four "lines." (No difficulty lies in the fact that the turning point occurs in the middle of verse 20.)

The inversion is not a mere technical, extraneous matter; rather, it indicates a change in the nature of the story and in the mutual relationship between its two main characters. In the first half, the initiative lies with Elijah: It is he who comes to where Elisha is, while the latter is busy with routine activity, quite unprepared for what is to happen (lines 1–2).

It is Elijah who all at once disturbs Elisha's routine by casting his mantle toward him (line 3). Elisha reacts as expected, taking off after his master who has just been revealed to him, and abandoning his work (line 4).

Attention should be paid to the nature of this half, which records only actions – no speech at all. The interaction that is created between the two characters requires no words, only powerful, highly symbolic actions. The verbs that the text uses in connection with each of them express the development of the plot toward the dramatic turning point at the end of the first half – Elisha abandoning his plowing and running after Elijah.

Elijah: "went," "found," "passed by," "cast."

Elisha: "plowing," "left," "ran."

At the end of the first half of this unit it seems that everything is proceeding as it should: Elisha reacts as Elijah expects him to, and with the energy appropriate to the power of the message that Elijah gives him.

The beginning of the second half brings a surprise: The initiative passes from Elijah to Elisha. Unlike the previous order, Elisha is now the subject of the first line. Moreover, a first utterance breaks the silent, intensive activity of the first half.

The change in the atmosphere of the story, at the beginning of the second half, expresses the change in reality: Everything is not proceeding as smoothly as we had thought (and as Elijah must certainly have believed). Elisha, who is running after Elijah, suddenly stops and addresses his new master. The content of the speech that Elisha initiates carries the plot a step backward: Elisha is unwilling to join Elijah immediately, as we thought at the end of the first half ("he ran after Elijah"); rather, he wants to visit his father and mother (symbolizing normal routine) in order to take leave of them. This slight delay that Elisha intends to create causes Elijah, in turn, to speak (line ii). Elijah, who has initiated the action so far, now reacts to the initiative of the other. As we shall see below, Elijah's reaction is not an expression of agreement, but rather of reservation – to the extent that the connection between them seems to be in danger of being severed. This, then, is a complete reversal in the direction of the plot.

According to the established order (and taking into consideration the point of departure of the second half) it is now Elisha's turn to serve as the subject of the next line (line iii), and this is indeed the case. Elisha appears in the midst of a long list of actions which he performs in silence: "He returned ... took ... slaughtered ... boiled ... gave." The relationship between this line and its predecessor is interesting. Linguistically, Elisha's activity looks like a positive reaction to Elijah's preceding words: Elijah said, "Go [and then] return," and Elisha's actions start with "He returned from after him." The nature of Elisha's actions, executed in silence, likewise seems like a return to the mute activity of the first half of the unit. However, as we shall discover, this is not so. Quite the contrary, Elijah's words, "Go and return, for what have I done to you," seem to be spoken with sharp criticism, and the (partial) linguistic parallel between Elisha's actions ("Elisha returned") and Elijah's preceding words ("Go return") expresses the fact that Elisha ignores this criticism. Moreover, the string of actions that appear in this line do not match Elisha's previous words – "Let me kiss my father and my mother," and Radak is correct in explaining that Elisha performs all of these actions *after* taking leave of his parents. In contrast to the verbs that characterize the first half, those that appear here are of a quieter, less dramatic nature. In this line Elisha's delay of the plot reaches its climax, and the tension increases. Does Elisha still intend to join Elijah, or has he changed his mind, and therefore adopts delaying tactics? Will Elijah tolerate the growing delay in Elisha's cooperation, or will he give up and leave?

The fourth line of the second half (iv) resolves the tension with a single stroke. While we expect (in accordance with the fixed order) some action or utterance on the part of Elijah, and we fear for the tone of his reaction, there appears another line with Elisha as its subject. This deviation from the pattern of alternation from one line to the next – the only such instance in this unit, other than the change in order between the first half and the second – demonstrates that in the second half of the story Elisha is the main character (in contrast to the first half, where Elijah played this role). Elisha is the subject of three out of the four lines; he initiates, he speaks, and he acts, while Elijah merely waits. Elijah's contribution to the second half of the story is limited to an expression of bitter annoyance at Elisha's delay in following him.[2]

---

2. The deviation of line iv from the order of the story has an additional purpose: this line, in terms of both language and content, parallels line 4 in the first half: there, Elisha "runs after Elijah," now he "goes after Elijah." This similarity serves to

We may depict the structure of our story by presenting its two halves as paralleling one another in chiastic form:

A: [Elijah] went from there, and he found Elisha son of Shafat

> B: [Elisha] plowing with twelve yoke of oxen in front of him, and he was with the twelfth

>> C: [Elijah] passed by him and cast his mantle toward him

>>> D: [Elisha] left the oxen and *ran after Elijah*

>>> D': [Elisha] said: Let me kiss my father and my mother, and I shall follow you

>> C': [Elijah] said to him: Go and return, for what have I done to you?

> B': [Elisha] returned from after him and he took a yoke of oxen and slaughtered it… and he gave it to the people and they ate

A': [Elisha] *went after Elijah,* and attended him.

The outer framework of the story (A-A') comprises its two decisive facts, which complement one another: Elijah goes and finds Elisha, and Elisha goes after Elijah to attend to him. All the other parallels within the unit describe the process that lead to this outcome, such that it develops from the original intention. The process itself is full of contrasts and inner tension, as expressed in the relationship between

---

neutralize the tension that has accumulated over the course of the second half, as well as retroactively imbuing the previous line in this half (line iii) with new meaning: Elisha's silent actions are not a delaying tactic, but rather an expression of his severance from his previous life in order to follow Elijah (see later sections of this chapter: "Elijah vs. Elisha" and "The Parting Feast").

each pair of corresponding lines. Only in the introduction and conclusion to the story are the subjects of the corresponding lines exchanged, from Elijah (A) to Elisha (A'), with Elijah's action in line A finding its appropriate response on the part of Elisha in line A'. All the other corresponding lines describe the same subject, with a clear contrast between the two halves.

The most important contrast concerns lines D and D', with Elisha as their subject. In D, Elisha offers an immediate response to Elijah casting his mantle toward him; he abandons his oxen right away and runs after Elijah. But in D' he halts and delays following Elijah for a final embrace of normal life, which he has just abandoned: "Let me kiss my father and my mother," only then "I shall go after you." These words spoken by Elisha are the first spoken words in this short incident. They constitute a dramatic turning point in the plot, completely changing the atmosphere of the occasion. As in many other cases in biblical narratives, it represents the touchstone for the beginning of the second half of the story. This sudden delay, and what it expresses, is the reason for the contrast in the outer pair, C and C'.

The subject of C and C' is Elijah. While in C he casts his mantle toward Elisha, in C' he negates his action: "What have I done to you?" As Radak comments: "In other words, just because I lowered my mantle in your direction, therefore you run after me?" This contradiction in Elijah's behavior toward Elisha arises from the preceding contradiction in Elisha's own behavior. Just as Elisha's words at the beginning of the second half seem as though he is reconsidering his action of running after Elijah at the end of the first half, so Elijah's words in the second half express almost denial of, and regret over his action in the first half.

The subject of lines B and B' is Elisha. In B he is absorbed in the routine work of plowing behind a yoke of oxen, in B' he negates this activity by slaughtering the very oxen that he has just been following, using the equipment of the oxen to make a fire upon which to boil the meat. This contrast hails Elisha's parting with his previous way of life, as preparation for going after Elijah; it serves as a bridging stage between the previous contrasts (D-D'; C-C') and the complete solution to all of these contrasts and tensions (both in the behavior of each character alone, and with regard to the mutual relationship between them) – a solution that is achieved only in the closing sentence of the unit, completing its outer framework (A-A'). As noted, the pair A and A' not only contains no tension, but expresses mutual completion between Elijah's aim and Elisha's full cooperation.

But here we must ask: Is the point of conclusion of the story not somewhat lower than the corresponding point of conclusion of the first half? There we find, "He *ran* after Elijah," while the unit ends by stating simply that he "*went* after Elijah." Is this meant to imply that Elisha's delays in joining Elijah express some cooling of his original enthusiasm, thus justifying Elijah's criticism?

This is not the case. We learn this from the words of the prophet: "Those who wait upon the Lord shall renew their strength; they shall rise up with wings like eagles; they shall run and not tire; they shall walk and not faint" (Is. 40:31).

Commenting on this verse, Nechama Leibowitz writes:[3]

This verse raises a question: As we know, the model of biblical poetry is for the two corresponding parts of the verse to move from the simple to the more intensive. Seemingly, the verse here should read: "They shall walk and not faint, [and] they shall [even] run and [nevertheless] not tire."[4] Why is the verse formulated in the reverse order? I have found the following in the commentary on the *haftarot*:[5] "Under a wave of enthusiasm, we are all capable of an isolated act of heroism, i.e., to 'soar' or 'to run' for a time. It is far harder to follow the monotonous round of everyday duty when vision has faded and splendor seems gone, undeterred by trials and hindrances, meeting them in the spirit of faith and conquering them by steadfastness. This is the achievement of those who 'wait for

---

3. N. Leibowitz, "Daf LeTarbut Yehudit," 11 (Tevet 5734).
4. Cf. Proverbs 4:12, "*When you go,* your steps shall not be confined, and *when you run,* you shall not stumble."
5. The reference here is to Rabbi Hertz's commentary on the *haftara* of *Parashat Lekh Lekha* found at the end of the book of Genesis, in Rabbi Dr. J. H. Hertz, ed., *The Pentateuch and Haftorahs* (London: Soncino Press, 1971).

the Lord.'" Therefore the verse is correct: "They shall run [with the energy of enthusiasm] and not faint" – but even when they have to walk, to continue without racing, "They shall not grow weary." Thus – [the verse moves] from the simple to the more intensive!

The first half of the unit, then, presents Elisha overcome with initial, uncontrolled enthusiasm. The second half of the unit is meant to move the plot forward by having Elisha undergo a process that readies him for his role: He stops himself in the midst of his enthusiasm to think about whom and what he is leaving behind, and where he is headed. Only after this necessary delay can there be serious, committed meaning behind his decision: To *go* after Elijah and attend him.

CASTING OF THE MANTLE

> Elijah passed him by and cast his mantle toward him … and he ran after Elijah. (vv. 19–20)

Elijah's casting of his mantle toward Elisha unquestionably signals his intention to take Elisha with him. Radak comments:

> He made a sign for him that he should follow him. He did not tell him so explicitly, for he knew that [Elisha] would understand, for it is God who makes a person a prophet, and he knew that God had put into Elisha's heart to follow him and serve him; therefore he merely gave the sign.

But why does Elijah choose this specific sign? Is it an arbitrary sign? Ralbag (commenting on v. 15 – a different explanation is provided in v. 19) writes as follows:

> He cast his mantle upon him so as to give him a sign that he would be a prophet, and would be garbed in the prophecy of Elijah, since the wearing of the mantle was the sign of a prophet. This is the meaning of the verse (Zech. 13:4) "[And it shall be on that day that the prophets shall be ashamed, each one of his

visions that he prophesies]; and they shall not wear the hairy mantle in order to deceive."[6]

A mantle of animal hair was the typical dress of a prophet in Israel. In casting his mantle toward Elisha, Elijah is not only signaling that Elisha is going to become a prophet (as the Baal HaMetzudot, for example, suggests), but also implies that Elisha is destined to inherit Elijah's own role as the prophet of the generation – in Ralbag's words, "And would be garbed in the prophecy of Elijah." The wearing of Elijah's mantle signifies the "garb of his prophecy."

Malbim regards this act of Elijah's as having even more profound significance, serving to connect Elisha, by means of the mantle, not only to Elijah the Prophet, but also to his past and future actions:

> After Elijah cast his mantle toward him, his soul cleaved to Elijah's mantles for he sensed within it the spirituality that had radiated upon it since the time that [Elijah] spent in the cave,[7] like the veil upon Moses's face, and as we read further on (II Kings 2:2), that he split the Jordan with this mantle. The casting of the mantle was a sign that he would replace him and take his mantle; therefore he abandoned his work and ran after him.

Thus these verses serve as an introduction to verses that we encounter later on:

> He lifted Elijah's mantle which had fallen from him, and he returned and stood on the bank of the Jordan. And he took Elijah's mantle

---

6. This verse is from a prophecy about the false prophets who masqueraded as true prophets. We deduce from here that wearing a hairy mantle was the custom of prophets in Israel. Likewise, the description that Ahaziah's messengers provide of Elijah: "He was a hairy man, and with a girdle of leather about his loins" (Kings II 2:8), is understood by some commentators as meaning "a man with a hairy mantle." Indeed, based on this description, Ahaziah identifies him: "And he said, 'It is Elijah, the Tishbite.'"

7. The reference here, obviously, is to verse 13 in our chapter: "And it was, when Elijah heard it, that *he covered his face with his mantle*, and he went out and stood at the entrance to the cave."

which had fallen from him, and he struck the water, and he said: Where is the Lord God of Elijah? And when he had struck the water, they parted to the one side and the other, and Elisha passed through." (II Kings 2:13–14)

Indeed, Abrabanel elaborates as follows, commenting on II Kings 2:

> There is no doubt that it [Elijah's mantle] did not fall from him [as he went up in a storm to heaven] by accident; rather, he cast it upon Elisha deliberately, for it was a vessel that could carry the divine blessing and prophecy that had rested upon Elijah, such that Elisha would wear his mantle and his prophecy, and stand in [Elijah's] place. This was already hinted to him when Elijah found him plowing with twelve pairs of oxen, and he cast his mantle toward him – hinting that when he would be taken from this world, he would cast his mantle upon him, and [Elisha] would be garbed in his prophecy and take his place.

This connection between Elijah and Elisha, symbolized in the casting of the mantle, expresses just one aspect of their relationship: the aspect of the continuity between teacher and disciple.

"GO, RETURN, FOR WHAT HAVE I DONE TO YOU?"

The casting of the mantle toward Elisha produces its immediate and powerful effect: "He left the oxen and ran after Elijah, and he said: Let me kiss my father and my mother, and then I shall follow you" (v. 20). But what is the meaning of Elijah's reaction, "Go, return, for what have I done to you"?

Rashi explains the literal meaning of the words as follows: "'Go, return' – from after me, 'for what have I done to you' – that you should follow me." However, this fails to clarify the intention behind this incomprehensible utterance. Was it not Elijah's intention, in casting the mantle toward Elisha, that Elisha should follow him? Elisha understood this signal, so why is Elijah rejecting him and pretending that he has done nothing?

Rashi's explanation, while not providing any insight into Elijah's intention, is still of great value: It is apparently intended to bar other interpretations that might seek to turn Elijah's words around.[8]

Radak, who apparently accepts Rashi's comment, attempts to explain Elijah's intention:

> What he means by the words, "Go, return, for what have I done to you" is to test him, to see whether he spoke wholeheartedly. And the meaning of the words, "What have I done to you" is: If I dropped my mantle over you, therefore you go after me?

This interpretation indeed suits the tone of rejection that we detect in Elijah's words. This rejection, explains Radak, is simply a test that Elijah presents for Elisha. Still, we must ask: Why does Elijah see fit to test Elisha, who is already running after him, and who has just announced his readiness to leave his parents and his birthplace to follow Elijah? What reason does Elijah have for suspecting his motives or integrity? Furthermore, we may ask: If Elijah's intention, in these words, is to test Elisha, then Elisha's response should serve to clear up Elijah's doubt and to prove that what he said was said in good faith. But in reality, he offers no response at all. He merely performs actions that follow his plan; in addition, he also offers the yoke of oxen as a sacrifice and feeds the people. How does Elijah deduce, while Elisha is doing all of this, that Elisha's previous words were spoken in good faith? Why does he not demand a clear answer?

ELIJAH VS. ELISHA

Before proposing a different explanation for Elijah's words, we must first examine briefly the main character traits of each of these two prophets.

Of course, the fact that the most dominant element in the personality and prophetic activity of Elijah is his zealousness for God needs no elaboration. This is abundantly clear throughout the chapters describing his activity, and we have discussed this matter at length in previous chapters. This trait reaches its climax here in chapter 19, when

---

8. See, for example, Ralbag's interpretation.

as a result of Elijah refusing to rethink his position and repeating his words, "I have been exceedingly zealous...," God commands him: "Go, return on your way... and you shall anoint Elisha ben Shafat as prophet in your stead" (vv. 15–16).

Hazal regard this command as a "dismissal notice," as it were: "Elijah fought for the honor of the Father (God), but not for the honor of the son (Israel)... for the words 'as prophet in your stead' mean, 'I have no desire for your prophecy.'"[9]

This divine command already indicates that God has chosen, as Elijah's successor, a prophet whose attitude toward the "honor of the son," the nation, is different from that of Elijah. The selection of a successor for Elijah, who is zealous for God and who finds fault with His children, must certainly be meant to correct this "deficiency" in Elijah's approach. It is not enough that "I have no desire for your prophecy" because of your harsh criticism of Israel; there must be a corresponding "I desire" that applies to the prophecy of a different prophet, who is unlike you. This prophet is Elisha, whose actions are almost without exception acts of salvation and redemption for the nation as a whole or for its individuals.

In truth, it is difficult to find so stark a contrast as that between the prophetic activity of Elijah, whose path is storm and wind,[10] and the prophetic activity of Elisha – "by still waters." The juxtaposition of the Elijah narratives to the Elisha narratives and the closeness between these two personalities of master and disciple serve to highlight this contrast. Moreover, it is specifically in those places where there is some similarity between Elisha's actions and those of Elijah, and it starts to look as though the disciple is indeed walking in the footsteps of his teacher – and such instances are not few in number – that we discern Elisha's independent approach, which is different, even opposite, to that of Elijah.

The difference between them, in nature and in attitude toward their surroundings, is clear from their very first encounter. Let us recall for a moment Elijah's first appearance as he bursts into the narrative: "Elijah the Tishbite, of the inhabitants of Gilead, said to Ahab: As the

---

9. See chapter 28, p. 326.
10. See "The Drought," end of chapter 1.

Lord God of Israel lives, before whom I stand, there shall be no rain or dew during these years, but by my word" (17:1).

Who is this prophet? What is the background to his appearance? The omission of this information is not an oversight in the text. The blurring of Elijah's background, all that preceded his sudden appearance as a prophet, is meant to express the defining element of his personality: his absolute dedication to his task, his identification with his prophetic role to the point of nullification of any personal aspect. Nowhere is there any mention of Elijah's father, nor any other detail pertaining to his personal life.

By contrast, Elisha son of Shafat makes his first appearance even before he becomes a prophet, and he is named along with the name of his father. We see him for the first time in the fields of his city of birth, Abel Meholah: "He was plowing, with twelve yokes of oxen in front of him, and he with the twelfth" (v. 19).

Beyond the symbolic significance of the number of yokes of oxen, the most literal level of the text presents us with the description of a young man living in a very wealthy home. As Ralbag comments: "It seems that this is mentioned in order to point out that Elisha's father was exceedingly wealthy."

And with what is his son, Elisha, occupied? With plowing his father's vast field, and watching over his father's workers as they plow in front of him. Could we imagine a scene in which Elijah is busy plowing a field?

The casting of Elijah's mantle toward Elisha causes the latter immediately to abandon his work, as an inexplicable, magnetic pull draws him after Elijah. No economic or professional consideration can stand in his way. He does not even wait to complete the furrow that he is busy plowing; he spares no thought for the pair of oxen that he was leading, nor for the other eleven yokes that his father's servants are leading in front of him.

"He left the oxen and ran after Elijah."

It immediately becomes apparent, however, that this magnetic pull is an attraction of opposites, between two people of utterly contrasting character. Is there really no consideration that stands in the path of Elisha, postponing his pursuit of Elijah? Does he really run after him with no hesitation or restraint? Not necessarily, for, as we read at the beginning of the second half of this brief unit: "He said: 'let me kiss my father and my mother;'" only afterward "'I shall follow you.'" It is not the economic consideration that gives Elisha pause, but rather something far more important: his love and reverence for his parents.

Thus the text provides a very clear character sketch, pointing to the warm, human personality of Elisha. Not only is his father's name provided, but also concrete evidence of his relationship with his parents: He is a beloved son who "goes to receive permission from his father and his mother" (as Radak explains) and to share a parting embrace.

Elijah, zealous for God, would appear to have a different way about him:

> Who said of his father and of his mother, "I have not seen him," and who did not recognize his brothers, nor did he know his children; for they observed Your utterance and preserved Your covenant. (Deut. 33:9)

The preservers of the covenant, who are called upon to stand guard and protect it while Israel violates this covenant, require absolute devotion to their job, to the extent of nullifying any family loyalties or sentimentality. Who, more than Elijah, is a defender of the covenant ("angel of the covenant")? Who is more pained than he is over the fact that "the children of Israel have abandoned Your covenant"? Here, neither time nor position allows for family ties. The person who is destined to serve Elijah and to be his disciple, later on inheriting his role as prophet, should be someone who follows his master with no hesitation, not tarrying even to kiss his father and mother.

Tradition records the following about the Ari and his disciples:[11]

> Once, on the Sabbath eve, close to the time of welcoming the Sabbath bride, he went with his disciples out of the city of Safed … to

---

11. This version of the account is from *Emek HaMelekh* by Rabbi Naftali Hertz Bachrach of Frankfurt (Amsterdam, 5413), in the third introduction, chapter 5. Different versions exist in other works.

receive the Sabbath, starting with "A psalm of David. Give to God, you sons of the mighty" (Ps. 29) ... and the established song for welcoming the Sabbath[12] and "A psalm, a song for the Sabbath day" (ibid. 92) and "God reigns" (ibid. 93) ... with a pleasant tune. While they were singing, the rabbi said to his disciples: "Friends, would you like us to go to Jerusalem before Sabbath, and we shall spend Sabbath in Jerusalem?" (Jerusalem is more than twenty-five *parsa'ot* from Safed!) Some of the disciples answered: "We shall do as you say." *Some others answered: "Let us first go and tell our wives."* When they said, "Let us first go home," *the rabbi was greatly distressed*; he clapped his hands together and said: "Woe to us, that we did not have the merit to be redeemed. If all of you had answered unanimously that you wanted to go, with great joy, all of Israel would immediately have been redeemed, for that moment was the appointed time for redemption. However, since you rejected it, the exile returned to its full strength, for our many sins."

With a note of disappointment and with bitter irony, Elijah reacts to Elisha's words ("Let me kiss my father and my mother"), telling him: "Go, return, for what have I done to you?"

In other words: if your father and mother are more important to you than following me immediately, here and now, then "Go, return" from following me. Perhaps you are not suited to the task; perhaps you are not worthy of being my disciple and my successor. If so, remain here, in the bosom of your family. Go on plowing, "for what have I done to you," that you should come after me? Does the casting of my mantle oblige you to run after me?[13]

---

12. The reference, of course, is to the liturgical poem *"Lekha Dodi,"* which was widely known in varied versions. The last, compiled by Rabbi Shlomo Alkabetz, who was a contemporary of the Ari, was starting to become popular at the time.

13. Dov Kimḥi, *BiShevilei HaTanakh* (Tel Aviv, 5712), 161, offers the following explanation of Elijah's words in a brief fragment entitled "Sanctity of the Role":

Elisha understands the sanctity of the role, and abandons the work he is busy doing in the field ... and runs to his master. Up to this point, all is as it should be. However, immediately thereafter, the prophet suffers great disappointment and is deeply saddened.... What is this singular young man talking about? "Let

Elisha gives no verbal answer to this implied criticism. He neither agrees nor argues with his newfound master. His answer is expressed in actions. What will he do now? Will he go back on his request and follow Elijah without taking leave of his parents, as Elijah's veiled criticism would seem to require, or will he follow his heart and act in accordance with his personality, and go to them? Here, again, we find a clear depiction of Elisha's personality: He does not go back on his plan. Without words he does what he believes to be right, while his great master stands and waits for him.

Radak comments: "'He turned back from after him' – to kiss his father and mother, even though this is not noted in the text."

We ought to consider the reason for this omission. Why does the text omit the description of Elisha taking leave of his parents in verse 21, replacing it with a series of other actions which Elisha did not tell Elijah about in advance, in verse 20?

There is something that is common to the kissing and to the feast that Elisha holds. Both are acts of taking leave of those around him in his birthplace and in the various spheres of his life. The kissing is meant for taking leave of his parents, who are the closest to him; the feast, for taking leave of his father's laborers, with whom he has worked, and perhaps also for taking leave of the other people of his city. This being so, we may say that Elisha's announcement to Elijah in verse 20, and the

---

me kiss my father and my mother, and I shall follow you"… What? How is he capable of thinking of his father and mother at such a moment, a moment of acceptance of this sanctified role? In other words, this individual, who is destined to serve as a lofty symbol for all of the living, is still connected to the living, to the reality of relatives and parents, even if they are his father and mother. The prophet lowers his head to the ground, for this young man has seemingly not yet understood what [Elijah] meant by casting his mantle, and so he responds, as if in anger, "Go, return, for what have I done to you?" Meaning: Go back to your work – your plowing; and then to the house of your father and mother, for you have not understood me. You have not yet understood in depth the sanctity of the role that I meant to confer upon you at this sacred time.

Kimchi clearly identifies with Elijah's response and views the narrative itself as critical of Elisha. We, however, take the opposite view, as discussed below: The point of the story is to highlight the positive nature of Elisha's personality. There is no contradiction between the "sanctity of the role" and kissing one's father and mother.

description of his actions in verse 21, serve to complement one another. His announcement to Elijah should be interpreted with elaboration: "Let me take leave of those who are close to me, and then I shall go after you." However, Elisha does not wish to list all of the acts of farewell that he is planning; quite the opposite, he wants to minimize the impression of the delay that he is about to cause, referring to it as a brief act (a kiss) and one that is necessary from a human, family perspective. When Elijah understands and agrees to this, so Elisha believes, he will be able to broaden his farewell gestures to other spheres too.

But this attempt by Elisha to earn Elijah's approval fails, and his words only arouse Elijah's bitterness. Nevertheless, Elisha is not deterred from his plan. He carries it out – not in its minimalist form, but in full, as he had apparently planned from the outset.

But how was Elisha not fearful of exacerbating Elijah's impatience toward him by lengthening his delay even further with actions that he had not even mentioned in advance? The reason lies in the additional significance of Elisha's actions: They are not merely polite gestures of farewell, but actions symbolizing his taking final and absolute leave of his former life as a farmer, in order to assume the new life of a prophet (we shall discuss this idea further below). Therefore, Elisha believed that these actions would not anger Elijah; on the contrary, they express the wholeheartedness of his going after him; they show his decision to be irreversible.

Thus, Elisha's actions express two opposing ideas. On one hand, his delay speaks of his perception of prophecy not as severance from the cycle of life surrounding him, as Elijah viewed it, but rather as a connection to that cycle. On the other hand, his delay allows him to express in action the transition that he experiences from being a tiller of the soil on his father's estate, to being a prophet of Israel.

Finally, attention should be paid to the use of the verbs *heh-lamed-khaf* (to go, walk) and *shin-vav-bet* (to turn back, return) by Elijah, by Elisha and by the narrator. The interplay of these verbs hints at the essence of the polemic between the two characters, without expressing it explicitly. Elisha makes his request of Elijah, "Let me kiss my father and my mother, and I shall go (*elekha*) after you." Elijah answers him, "Go (*lekh*), return (*shuv*), for what have I done to you?" meaning: why are you going after me; go, turn back from after me. Thus Elijah, in his criticism, inverts the direction of Elisha's act of "going."

But Elisha remains firm in his perception: "He turned back (*vayashav*) from after him." The text does not say: he went (*vayelekh*) and turned from after him; this is because the concept of "going" (*heh-lamed-khaf*) is reserved, in Elisha's consciousness, for going after Elijah. His turning back from after Elijah is not done with the intention sarcastically proposed by Elijah, that he should turn back and not return, but rather in accordance with his own intention: First "'Let me turn back from after you'" to kiss my father and mother; after that I shall once again "'go after you.'" Indeed, after Elisha completes his parting gestures, "He arose and went after Elijah, and attended him." He did as he had intended to do.

The young disciple vanquishes his great master in their first encounter. He establishes his view and his approach, and immediately thereafter, he becomes Elijah's attendant. There is no clearer illustration of Elisha's attitude toward Elijah, his master: He is powerfully attracted to the personality of his master and has unbounded admiration for him; he runs after him, pours water over his hands and serves him. However, all of this is done while maintaining his own independent personality and unique way, since it is for this reason that he was chosen.

Rabbi Ḥayyim of Volozhin, disciple of the Vilna Gaon and founder of the famed Volozhin Yeshiva, writes as follows in his commentary *Ruaḥ Ḥayyim* on Mishna Avot:

> Yosei ben Yo'ezer, a man of Tzereda, used to say: Let your house be a gathering place for the wise; cover yourself (*mitabek*; also related to the word *maavak*, struggle, hence wrestle) with the dust of their feet…'" (*Avot* 1:4)
>
> Torah study is called "struggle," for it is written, "The war of Torah"; if so, then Torah scholars must be called "fighters." As our Sages taught (Kiddushin 30b), "'They shall not be ashamed when they speak openly with their enemies' (Ps. 127:5): even a father and his son, a teacher and his disciple, who are engaged in a debate over a matter of Torah, become like enemies, but they do not end their debate until they are friends again." A disciple dare

not accept his master's teaching if he finds flaws in it. Sometimes, the truth will lie with the disciple, just as a match may kindle a large log. This is as it is written, "Let your house be a gathering place for the wise, and wrestle...," in the sense of the expression, "A man wrestled (*vaye'avek*) with him" (Gen. 32:25), meaning the wrestling of battle, for it is a worthy battle. Likewise we, against our holy teachers in the world... we are exhorted in this regard, and we are permitted to wrestle and do battle with their words, to defend our position and not to retreat in deference to their status, but simply to love the truth.

But at the same time, a person should take care not to speak with pride or arrogance.... Therefore it should be [done] only with great humility, with the sense that "Although I am not worthy, this is Torah and I must [do my best to] study it." This is what is meant by the expression *hevei mitabek* ("wrestle" [with their words]), as we have explained above, but on condition that it is "with the dust of their feet." In other words, one must do so with humility and submission, presenting one's case from a position of inferiority.

THE PARTING FEAST

We should not ignore another aspect of Elisha's personality that is revealed here. Before going after Elijah to serve him, Elisha does something else, which takes much longer than it took him to kiss his father and his mother: "He took the yoke of oxen and slaughtered it, and boiled the meat with the equipment of the oxen, and he gave it to the people to eat" (v. 21)

We have already seen that this act has two meanings, one of which is suited to Elijah's difficult demand of him: It symbolizes his parting from his previous way of life and the beginning of a new one. It should be noted that for the purpose of this feast he slaughters the very pair of oxen with which he has just plowed, and to cook the meat he uses the wooden plowing implements. Radak explains his actions as follows:

> In his great haste to follow Elijah, he does not tarry to hew wood for making a fire; he breaks apart the "instruments of the oxen," meaning, the plow, and cooks the meat upon them.

However, it seems that we may go further and suggest that by slaughtering the oxen with which he has just plowed, and cooking their meat upon the instruments that he has likewise just used for plowing, Elisha is showing himself, as well as those who partake of the feast, and even Elijah, that the period of his plowing at his father's house is over. His parting from his birthplace and from his way of life is final and absolute; it is irreversible.[14] He turns toward the role of the prophet; a person who fulfills this role can no longer concern himself with everyday tasks, with production and making a living, as he has done until now.

The commentators address this extra significance to Elisha's actions:

Rashi: "Out of great joy, he made a feast."

Radak: "He slaughtered the oxen and made a feast in that same field for those engaged in the plowing and for the people who came with him, to escort him … for he was parting from them."

Going after Elijah, as preparation for his new role as prophet, does not, in Elisha's view, require that he separate himself from the people; it does not require the sort of severance that characterizes the approach of his

---

14. Elisha's act here has an interesting parallel: Saul, despite having been anointed in secret by Samuel and then in public, at Mizpah, does not abandon his previous lifestyle as a farmer in his father's house in Gibea, thus continuing his flight from power. It is the siege of Jabesh Gilead, imposed by the Ammonites (I Sam. 11), that brings about Saul's inner transformation from farmer to king: "And, behold, Saul came after the cattle, from the field, and Saul said, 'What troubles the people that they weep?' And they told him the news of the men of Jabesh." This triggers the desired change: "And the spirit of God came upon Saul when he heard this news, and his anger burned greatly" (v. 6). His first act, then, as king of Israel is: "And he took a yoke of oxen, and cut them up in pieces, and sent them with messengers throughout all the borders of Israel, saying: Whoever does not come forth after Saul and after Samuel – so shall be done to his oxen" (v. 7). The episode ends in victory. The cutting up of the oxen, despite being accompanied by a threat ("So shall be done…"), marks Saul's parting with his previous life. The live oxen that had served him in plowing the field as a private citizen are now cut up in an act symbolizing the resolute and mighty leadership of the king, who will no longer be walking "after the cattle."

master. Moreover, his going off to his new role should be a source of joy: his own personal happiness – "out of great joy he made a feast" – and rejoicing with his family, his father's laborers and all of people of his city, whose leave he takes with a festive feast. It is for their sake and for their benefit that he is going to be a prophet of God.

Already in this act we discern Elisha's essence; asking, as it were: "'Now, let a musician be found for me.' It was when the musician would play, that God's hand would be upon him" (II Kings 2:15). We see, too, his path as a prophet who cares for the people around him, for the sons of the prophets, and for everyone. The expression, "He gave it to the people and let them eat" (v. 21) is echoed several times with reference to Elisha: "He poured for the people and they ate"; twice the phrase "Give to the people, that they may eat"; "He set it before them and they ate, and left some over, according to God's word" (II Kings 4:41–44).

Our analysis of the encounter between these two such different personalities shows that it was not without tension: Elisha's instant magnetic attraction to Elijah gives off sparks. Is this tension the reason that in Elijah's next appearances, at the vineyard of Naboth (ch. 21) and in the clash with Ahaziah and his messengers (II Kings 1), he acts alone? May we assume that Elisha's job of attending his master did not last long, and they met up again only when Elijah is gathered up to the heavens (II Kings 2)? This would seem to be a mistaken impression. The sons of the prophets in Beit El and in Jericho regard Elisha as Elijah's main disciple, as evidenced in their words to him: "Did you know that today God will take your master from over your head?" (II Kings 2:3, 5). This implies that up until this time Elijah was Elisha's master and his crown. Later on, one of the king's servants describes Elisha thus: "Here is Elisha son of Shafat, who poured water over the hands of Elijah" (II Kings 3:11). This implies that Elisha attended Elijah constantly, from the moment that he went after him to serve him (in our narrative) onward.

Nevertheless, we cannot ignore the fact that Elijah, even when accompanied by his attendant (as we saw previously, at the end of chapter 18, and as we see at the end of our chapter here), tends to engage in his prophetic activity alone (I Kings 18:46, 19:3, 21; II Kings 1). Elisha, by contrast, often appears with his attendant, or in the company of the sons of the prophets; it is rare to find him alone. This is yet another aspect of the contrast between the two figures.

Thus we see how, in three verses that describe a few actions and a few words that are exchanged in the first encounter between the two prophets, the text presents us with two different worlds. The contrast between them, and the attraction that exists despite the differences (or perhaps because of them) between the disciple and his teacher – all of this is illustrated here quite clearly, as if in a sketch, representing the basis for what will come later, in the description of Elisha's career.

Appendix I – Horeb

Comparison Between Elijah's and Jonah's Flight and Move East of Nineveh

There are many obvious similarities between our narrative and the story of Jonah. In both instances we read about a prophet who sought a place to be alone outside the city and there asked God to take his life. The connection between the two situations is highlighted by means of similar, even identical, linguistic expressions. Let us consider some aspects of this comparison:

1. Both stories start with the prophet fleeing:

    Elijah: "And when he saw it, he *arose*, and went for his life..." (I Kings 19:3)

    Jonah: "But Jonah *arose* to flee to Tarshish from the presence of the Lord..." (Jonah 1:3)

At first glance, this comparison seems baseless: Elijah is fleeing in the wake of Jezebel's threat to his life, and in flight he turns *toward* God, and asks to die. Jonah, by contrast, wishes to flee to Tarshish *from* the presence of God. Thus, the two situations would seem to be the opposite of one another. As we progress through the respective narratives, however, we see that they are similar in many respects. Jonah's flight is understood by *Ḥazal* as an attempt to flee from his task as a prophet, as we find in the *Mekhilta DeRabbi Yishmael* (*Petiḥta* to *Parashat Bo*):

> Was it then from God's Presence that he was fleeing? Is it not written (Ps. 139:7), "Where shall I go from Your spirit? Or where shall I flee from Your Presence?" Rather, Jonah said to himself, "I shall go out of the Land of Israel, to a place where the Divine Presence does not make itself manifest."

Elijah's journey to the desert is likewise a flight from his role as prophet. While Elijah admittedly does not flee "from God's Presence," as in the case of Jonah, his journey might be described in the words of the poet Rabbi Solomon ibn Gabirol in his song "Keter Malkhut": "I shall flee from You, toward You; and take cover from Your wrath, in Your shadow."

There is another element of similarity between the two fleeing prophets. As we find in the midrash: "R. Natan said: Jonah's intention was to end his life in the sea, as it is written (Jonah 1:12), 'And he said to them: Take me up and cast me into the sea'" (*Mekhilta DeRabbi Yishmael, Petiḥta* to *Parashat Bo*). Elijah, too, headed for the wilderness of Beer Sheba seeking to die.

Along with the similarities we must also note the differences. The motive for Jonah's departure is his direct opposition to the prophecy that he has received from God. In attempting to flee he becomes a "prophet who suppresses his prophecy" (see Sanhedrin 89a). By contrast, Elijah's immediate motive for leaving is Jezebel's threat to his life (although he also has some deeper motives), and his supplication that God take his life is not intended as a suppression of his prophecy.

2. In both narratives we find the prophet sleeping in a strange place and in strange circumstances: Elijah sleeps under the broom tree

in the wilderness, and in the cave at Horeb. Concerning Jonah, we read (1:5) "And Jonah went down into the recesses of the ship, and he lay down, and was fast asleep."

In both instances, agents of God awaken the sleeping prophets and make demands of them:

> **Elijah:** "And as he lay and slept under a broom tree, behold, then an angel touched him *and said to him, 'Arise* and eat…for the journey is too great for you.'" (I Kings 19:5–7)

> **Jonah:** "So the shipmaster came to him *and said to him,* 'What do you mean, O sleeper? *Arise,* call upon your God.'" (Jonah 1:6)[1]

There is no question that sleep plays the same role in both instances: It serves as an escape from the reality that is created by the conflict between the prophet and God. Since both prophets are ready to die, sleep for them is literally "a sixtieth part of death," as Ḥazal define it.[2] The awakening, at the hand of God's agent, is meant in each case to prevent this escape into sleep and to force the prophet into deeper contemplation of his protest.

3. The greatest similarity between the two narratives is expressed in the wish to die:

> **Elijah:** "And he asked for himself *that he might die,* and said, 'It is enough, now, O Lord, *take my life,* for I am not better than my fathers.'" (I Kings 19:4)

> **Jonah** (not in order): "And he asked for himself *that he might die.*" (Jonah 4:8)

---

1. The shipmaster is an unknowing agent of God when he addresses Jonah. His words convey veiled criticism for his sleeping at such a time, and he uses similar expressions to those found in God's original command to him: God had told him, "Arise…and cry against it," while the shipmaster says, "Arise, cry to…."
2. Berakhot 57b.

> "Therefore now, O Lord, *take my life* from me, I pray You, for it is better for me to die than to live." (Jonah 4:3)

The reasons that Jonah explicitly states his request to die the first time, shed light on the somewhat opaque reasons for the same request on the part of Elijah. Jonah's request that God take his life stems from the prophet's frustration at being forced to act against his principles and his view of justice, in fulfilling a mission that he does not agree with and accepting God's forgiveness of Nineveh (4:1–3). Elijah, too, asks to die, not out of physical discomfort or some other existential anguish (for example, Jezebel's persecution), but rather because of his disagreement with God's way, showing patience and mercy toward Israel. Perhaps Elijah, too, feels that he has become the executor of a policy that he does not agree with. Asking for death is the drastic expression of someone whose principles are more dear to him than his very life. Thus, Elijah's despair is in some way an expression of his desire to resign from his prophetic role and his lack of identification with the path that is being forced on him.

4. Both Elijah and Jonah resign themselves to the harsh natural conditions:

> **Elijah**: "But he himself went a day's journey into the wilderness, and came and *sat down under* a broom tree..." (I Kings 19:4)

> **Jonah**: "So Jonah went out of the city, and sat on the east side of the city, and there he made himself a shelter and *sat under it* in the shade..." (Jonah 4:5)

The departure from the city out to the wilderness, or to the east side of the city, and just sitting in the shade of a broom tree or a shelter, is an act of protest against the prophetic mission.

In both stories, God ensures that the prophet does not die of heatstroke or of thirst, even though the prophet is not taking proper care of himself and is even expressing his readiness to die. God appoints a castor-oil plant "and made it come up over Jonah, that it might be a shade over his head, to deliver him from his distress" (Jonah 4:6), while Elijah looks and sees "a cake baked on the coals and a cruse of water at his head" (I Kings 19:6).

5. In both stories, the prophet demands that the divine attribute of justice be applied to those who have sinned (in different circumstances, of course), while God applies His attribute of mercy. The dispute or dialogue that God maintains with His prophet is conducted in a similar manner in each case: He provides experiences that offer the prophet an opportunity to understand God's ways.

In both stories the argument is conducted in two stages. After Jonah asks to die, God asks him, "Are you so greatly vexed?" (Jonah 4:4), and then causes the castor-oil plant to sprout miraculously over his head. After the plant withers, God asks him again, "Are you so greatly vexed on account of the plant?"

Elijah, too, is asked the same question twice: "What do you seek here, Elijah?" with the divine revelation in the small, silent voice separating the two iterations.

Since neither prophet accedes to God's veiled rebuke after either the first or the second question (nor, of course, does he take to heart the lesson of the event that he experiences in between them), there comes a more explicit message from God, although even at this stage one has to look deeper to expose the rebuke.

In Elijah's case, the rebuke emphasizes the contrast between the prophet's way and the way of God. The words, "Go, return on your way... and when you come there, anoint..." (I Kings 19:15) hint to Elijah's zealousness, which will lead him to appoint and anoint the enemies who will attack Israel with the sword. The rebuke concludes with God's path of mercy: "Yet I will leave seven thousand in Israel" (v. 18).

In the rebuke to Jonah, too, God emphasizes the contrast between the prophet's thoughts: "You are concerned for the castor-oil plant," and God's merciful approach: "Shall I not be concerned for Nineveh, the great city?" (Jonah 4:10–11).

The principle that recurs in all the aspects of the comparison that we have discussed above serves to highlight the comparison between the book of Jonah and our narrative: In both cases, the prophet is locked in a dispute with God and a struggle against his prophetic mission. The nature of the argument is the same in each case: The prophet demands the full implementation of the divine attribute of justice, while God, in a complex process comprising several stages, shows the prophet His way – that of compassion.

Haftara of *Parashat Pinḥas*

C

hapter 19 of I Kings is read as the *haftara* for *Parashat Pinḥas*, when this *parasha* is not read during the period between the 17th of Tammuz and the 9th of Av. Pinhas and Elijah are the two great biblical zealots for God. The Sages go so far as to assert that "Pinhas is Elijah."[1] However, there is a great difference between the attitude toward the zealousness of Pinhas and the attitude toward the zealousness of Elijah.

God's response to Pinhas's actions expresses unreserved praise, and a promise of a double reward:

> And the Lord spoke to Moses, saying, Pinhas, son of Eleazar, son of Aaron the priest, has turned My wrath away from the children of Israel, in that he was zealous for My sake among them, so I did not consume the children of Israel in My jealousy. Therefore say, Behold, I give him My covenant of peace. And he shall have it, and his seed after him – the covenant of an everlasting priesthood, because he was zealous for his God, and made atonement for the children of Israel. (Num. 25:10–13)

---

1. *Yalkut Shimoni* I:771, from *Midrash Yelamdenu* and several parallel sources.

The Sages, too, offer many homilies and statements in praise of Pinḥas.

The zealousness of Elijah, in contrast, is viewed in a critical light, both by God, in His "dispute" with the prophet, and in *Ḥazal*'s teachings (some of which we have cited above). What is the difference between these two personalities, and in what way is the zealousness of Pinḥas preferable to that of Elijah?

The difference is clear: Elijah is zealous for God, and to this end he directs his criticism toward Israel, the nation of God. As *Ḥazal* teach in the *Mekhilta* (*Petiḥta* to *Parashat Bo*), "Elijah upheld the honor of the father, but not the honor of the son." The one-sided zealousness that he maintained leads to separation and distance between Israel and God.

The zealousness of Pinḥas, on the other hand, is whole: He is zealous for the honor of God and, at the same time, for the honor and survival of His children. Pinḥas's act of zealousness is recorded at the end of *Parashat Balak*. When Zimri takes the Midianite woman, in the presence of Moses and the entire congregation of Israel, and Moses and Aaron weep at the entrance to the Tent of Meeting, a plague starts to spread among the nation, as a punishment for their consorting with the daughters of Moab and with their idolatry:

> … and the people began to commit harlotry with the daughters of Moab. And they called the people to the sacrifices of their gods, and the people ate, and bowed down to their gods. And Israel joined themselves to Baal Pe'or, and the anger of the Lord was kindled against Israel. (Num. 25:1–3)

> And when Pinḥas, son of Eleazar, son of Aaron the priest, saw it, he rose up from among the congregation and took a spear in his hand. And he went after the man of Israel into the chamber and thrust both of them through, the man of Israel, and the woman, through her belly, so the plague was stayed from the children of Israel. (25:7–8)

Pinḥas acts not only to defend God's honor in the face of desecration, but also to stop the plague that is decimating the people. The combination of these two goals is the proper expression of a complete, positive zealousness that seeks both the honor of the Father and the honor of the son.

For this reason God says that Pinhas "has turned My wrath away from the children of Israel." Pinhas acts out of zealousness for God ("in that he was zealous for My sake among them"), but through his action he spares the nation the full brunt of God's zealousness and wrath ("so I did not consume the children of Israel in My jealousy"). The zealousness of Pinhas might be compared to the prayer that Moses offers after the debacle of the Golden Calf: It has the effect of halting the devastation of God's anger, and restores peace between God and His people. For this reason, Pinhas is rewarded measure for measure:

"Behold, I give him My covenant of peace."

Naboth

הֲרָצַחְתָּ וְגַם יָרָשְׁתָּ?

Have you murdered and also taken possession?

I Kings 21:19

Chapter 31

The Episode of Naboth and the King's Rights

T he story of the killing of Naboth is one of the most shocking episodes in all of Tanakh. The chain of events leading to this abominable act is described from the beginning of chapter 21 until verse 16; from verse 17 onward the text describes the dramatic confrontation between Elijah and Ahab, which takes place in Naboth's vineyard.

> Ahab spoke to Naboth, saying: "Give me your vineyard that it may be for me for a vegetable garden, for it is near to my house; I shall give you in its stead a better vineyard [or,] if it is good in your eyes, I shall give you its worth in money." (I Kings 21:2)

Naboth responds with a categorical refusal; Ahab is inconsolable in his disappointment, and Jezebel intervenes – all leading to the killing of Naboth and the appropriation of his vineyard.

In order to be able to judge the characters and their actions, in a balanced light, and in order to understand the actions themselves, we must first address the question: Did Ahab, king of Israel, not have the legal right to take over the vineyard of Naboth, which bordered on his palatial estate, and annex it to his own garden? If this was indeed his right, as king, why did he, or Jezebel, simply not do so, instead of resorting to such base machinations in order to have Naboth removed from the scene? This question is also important for our understanding of Naboth's refusal. If Ahab's request is anchored in his legal rights as king, then Naboth's response is unjustified. Hence, some of the responsibility for what happens must lie with Naboth himself!

To clarify this issue, which is just one detail out of an entire system of rules determining the status of the king of Israel, let us recall Samuel's enumeration of the king's rights. When the elders of Israel approach Samuel asking for a king, God tells him: "And now, listen to what they say, but you shall surely testify before them and tell them the rights of the king who will rule over them" (I Sam. 8:9). Samuel goes on to warn the people as to what the king is able to do:

> He said: This shall be the custom of the king who will rule over you. He will take your sons and commandeer them for his chariot, and as his horsemen, and they shall run before his chariot. And he shall appoint himself officers of a thousand and officers of fifty, to carry out his plowing and his reaping, and to fashion his instruments of war and the instruments of his chariot. And he shall take your daughters as perfumers and cooks and bakers. And he shall take the best of your fields and your vineyards and your olive yards, and give them to his servants.... (I Sam. 8:11–14)

Samuel goes on for another three verses, describing what the king is liable to do, and then concludes as follows: "And you shall cry out on that day because of your king whom you have chosen for yourselves, but God will not answer you on that day" (v. 18).

The list of despotic norms set out in these verses is referred to by Samuel as *mishpat hamelekh*, the king's custom (or right). Is the king indeed permitted to do all of this?

The *Tanna'im* and *Amora'im* are divided in this regard, as recorded in Sanhedrin 20b:

> R. Yehuda said in the name of Shmuel: "All that is mentioned in the 'king's custom' [Rashi: in the book of Samuel – 'Your sons … and your daughters he shall take …' etc.] is permitted to the king." Rav [Abba Arikha] said: "This was only told to them in order to threaten them."

Rav's view, that the king is actually forbidden to act in this way, seems the most compatible with the literal text in the book of Samuel. The impression arising from reading these verses is one of a cruel, despotic regime; hence, the description seems to be meant not to render all of this permissible, but rather to show the people to what level a monarchy may descend, so as to deter them and dissuade them from asking for a king. The term *mishpat hamelekh*, according to this view, means "custom" (or perhaps it is meant ironically, as Abrabanel suggests, since the word *mishpat* is usually used in the sense of justice), rather than legitimate legal right. Clearly, according to this view, Ahab had no right at all to demand Naboth's vineyard.[1]

From the narrative in our chapter, too, it is clear that neither Ahab nor even Jezebel, nor the elders and the people, nor even Naboth himself, believed that the king had any legal right to arbitrarily take possession of the estate of one of his subjects, not even with fair compensation.

Indeed, this is spelled out explicitly in the book of Ezekiel: "The prince shall not take of the people's inheritance, to relieve them deceitfully of their possession; he shall give his sons an inheritance from his own possessions, in order that My people not be scattered each man from his possession" (Ezek. 46:18).

Our chapter sheds light on the status of royalty in Israel in those times. Radak explains Jezebel's plotting to stage a false trial (I Kings 21:9–10) as follows:

> We must ask: Since the officers and nobles knew that the matter was false, why was all of this necessary? They could have simply killed him at Jezebel's orders, with no need for testimony or anything else!

---

1. Even according to Samuel's view in the Talmud, as explained by Maimonides (*Laws of Kings* 4:6), Ahab's demand to take possession of Naboth's vineyard was clearly illegal.

The answer: The elders of the city and the officers were few in number, and they collaborated with Jezebel. For if the elders had revealed the matter to the people, they, and certainly those who were close to Naboth, in the city, would not have allowed [Naboth] to be killed for no reason. And if Jezebel had tried to kill him with no trial, she would not have been able to do so, for even seizing the vineyard was beyond her strength. For Ahab and Jezebel, although they were wicked in the eyes of heaven, worshipping idolatry, if they had killed and robbed without trial, Israel would have rebelled against them, for they would not have tolerated a king over them who did not impose justice in the land.... Therefore Jezebel sought some pretext by which Naboth could be killed lawfully, since the property of those put to death by royal command becomes the property of the crown.

Jezebel, daughter of the king of Sidon, unquestionably bridles against these "limitations" in her mocking words to Ahab: "Will you now assert sovereignty over Israel?" (v. 7).

But even she, the daughter of a foreign king and undoubtedly familiar with other concepts of royalty, is forced against her will to act within the framework of those limitations imposed upon the Israelite institution of royalty. She is not empowered to seize the field, nor is she able to order the summary execution of a citizen. Such actions would cause the nation to rise up and rebel against the royalty.

The reign of Ahab and Jezebel is certainly corrupt, religiously, morally, and socially. The elders and nobles of the city of Jezreel, that aristocratic stratum close to the king, were faithfully obedient to Jezebel and were her secret accomplices to this crime. However, this moral corruption had to be hidden from the eyes of the common people, for if the matter became known, there would be revolution. Hence the need for a staged trial, held ostensibly in accordance with Torah law.

Paradoxically, our chapter proves how the law of the Torah concerning the status of royalty in Israel was indeed enrooted among the nation. In ancient society (as in our times under certain despotic regimes), it would have been inconceivable that a king should be so limited in his rights in deference to the rights of his subjects, as arises from our chapter.

The intention of the Torah with regard to the status of the king in Israel is set out in detail in the commandment concerning the king, in Deuteronomy, concluding with the following words of summary: "Lest his heart be held higher than his brothers, and lest he deviate from the commandment to the right or the left" (Deut. 17:20). The king of Israel does not stand above the law; he and his subjects must obey the same divine laws and statutes.

Our chapter also illuminates quite clearly the limitation of the absolute status of the king by means of the prophet who confronts him. This was the case ever since the first king, Saul, who was confronted by Samuel.[2] In many cases the prophets warn of *religious* corruption in the king's rule over the nation. This is also Elijah's principal task with regard to Ahab and his household. But in our chapter, Elijah's mission focuses on rebuke for the social, moral aberration. This rounds out the picture of Elijah as a prophet who is zealous for God not only in relation to commandments between man and God, but also in relation to the commandment governing interpersonal relationships.

---

2. See I Samuel, chs. 13, 15.

Chapter 32

"Have You Murdered and Also Inherited?" – Ahab's Responsibility

Elijah's words, quoted in the title, are his introduction to the prophetic rebuke that stands at the center of the second half of our chapter (21:17–29), where the final dramatic confrontation between Elijah and Ahab takes place.

In order to fully understand this rebuke we must consider the following: It is not Ahab who orchestrates Naboth's murder; rather, it is Jezebel. Ahab never considered such an idea in the beginning (v. 4), after Naboth refused to sell him the vineyard, and when Jezebel promised to "give" the vineyard to him, she gave no indication of how she intended to do this.

Admittedly, on the last point, Abrabanel disagrees:

> "Arise, eat bread, and let your heart be merry; I shall give you the vineyard of Naboth the Jezreelite" (v. 7). Undoubtedly, she immediately told him what she intended to do, for she wrote letters in Ahab's name to the elders.

But if this is so, why does the text conceal this vital link in the plot, which clarifies Elijah's rebuke, "Have you murdered and also inherited"?

Even as the narrative develops, and Jezebel brings about the murder of Naboth, there is no indication that she shares what is going on with Ahab. She receives the news of Naboth's death alone, and when she tells Ahab, "Arise, take possession of Naboth's vineyard...for Naboth is not alive, but dead" (v. 15), she does not divulge the circumstances of his death, and Ahab asks no questions.

Obviously, we should not go out of our way to protest Ahab's innocence: He should have asked, at the various stages of the episode, what Jezebel was intending to do, or what she had done. Nevertheless, can lack of clarity and ignorance, grave negligence as they may be, be equated with murder? Would it not be more accurate to accuse Ahab with the words, "Have you inherited him who your wife Jezebel murdered"? Why is Ahab the main culprit, while Jezebel is only second on the list: "Also to Jezebel God spoke..." (v. 23)?

Let us analyze the structure of the first half of our chapter (vv. 1–16). It presents five scenes, each defined by (1) the characters who are active in it, and (2) the place where it happens:

1. Ahab's request	vv. 2–3	Ahab – Naboth	Jezreel
2. Jezebel's promise	vv. 4–7	Ahab – Jezebel	Samaria
3. The "trial"	vv. 8–14	Jezebel – the elders	Samaria/Jezreel
4. Fulfillment of Jezebel's promise	v. 15	Ahab – Jezebel	Samaria
5. Realization of Ahab's desire	v. 15	Ahab – Naboth's vineyard	Jezreel

Clearly, this structure serves to emphasize the importance of scene 3, which is the heart of the narrative and the point of reference for all that precedes and follows it.

In other words, Ahab's desire for Naboth's field is what leads to Jezebel's promise. This promise necessarily leads to the false trial. It is the false trial and the murder that then allow Jezebel to fulfill her promise, and which allow Ahab to realize his desire.

In between the second and fourth scenes, in which Jezebel is the main actor, we find the third, the "trial," which is her initiative and her doing. But these three scenes are included in a wider sphere – the sphere of Ahab as the main character, in scenes 1 and 5. In other words, everything that happens in the internal part of the story takes place for the sake of the realization of Ahab's desire, and it is therefore Ahab who is responsible for the entire episode.

But does his responsibility extend to actual guilt for the murder of Naboth, or is it merely overall responsibility?

From the scheme of the structure as presented above we see that the character who appears in four of the five scenes, Ahab, is absent from the central one, the "trial." Not only is he not active in this scene, but also in the preceding scene there is no indication that he knows what is going to happen; likewise, in the following verse, he is not told about what happened.

This might seemingly lead us to conclude that Ahab is innocent of direct collaboration in the murder of Naboth. However, the matter is not as simple as that. In light of the fact that Ahab is a central figure in all of the four outer scenes (1, 2, 4, 5), and in light of his surprising "disappearance" from scene 3, the heart of the narrative, we discern a deliberate attempt on the part of the active characters (Ahab, Jezebel, the elders) to leave Ahab "out of the picture" of Naboth's murder, to keep his hands clean. He is to enjoy the final achievement without being involved in the process that leads to it.

Their intention, of course, is conscious, although it is not formulated explicitly (indeed, how could such a thing be stated explicitly?). It arises from that which is not said in the second and fourth image, although the reader expects to hear it: Jezebel's presentation of her plan to Ahab, and her report following its execution. Likewise, from the fact that the elders report to Jezebel after carrying out her instructions, even though she had stamped these instructions with Ahab's seal, we discern a purposeful attempt to leave Ahab out of the picture.

This being the case, Ahab's lack of active cooperation and his ignorance of Naboth's murder do not testify to good faith; rather, they are the result of a conscious and deliberate strategy among all those involved, not to include him and not to inform him.

Still, we must ask: After all of this, did Ahab really not know – could he not have guessed – what was going to happen, or was he able to guess Jezebel's intentions, such that the fact of his lack of active cooperation and his ignorance are nothing more than an attempt to relieve him of formal responsibility for the murder?

To answer this question, we must first clarify an important detail in the plot: How does the murder of Naboth enable Ahab to take possession of his vineyard? This matter is discussed in a *baraita* quoted in Sanhedrin 48b:

> Our Rabbis taught: Those sentenced to death by the king [Rashi: such as those who rebel against the king], their assets belong to the king. Those sentenced to death by the court, their assets belong to their heirs.

Further on in the *baraita*, proof for this law is brought from our chapter, where Naboth is accused of blaspheming God and the king, and therefore Ahab goes and takes possession of his vineyard, in accordance with the law concerning one who rebels against the sovereignty of the king. This clarifies for us how Jezebel intended to carry out her promise: "I shall give you the vineyard of Naboth the Jezreelite" – by exploiting the Israelite legal system.

But what was Ahab thinking when he heard this promise? How did he think that Jezebel was going to bring this about? It was obviously clear to him that whatever he could not legally do, Jezebel was likewise unable to do. Therefore he must have known that her intention was to act in an illegal way in order to obtain the vineyard. But such means still have to be ostensibly legitimate and anchored in law.

Within these limitations, it appears that there really was only one way of obtaining the vineyard, and that was the way that Jezebel chose. And Ahab could have made this same calculation himself. Further on we shall see that Ahab did indeed understand Jezebel's unspoken intentions. But he asks no questions and shows no interest; he is silent.

His silence continues even when Jezebel tells him: "Arise, take possession of Naboth's vineyard...for Naboth is not alive, but dead" (v. 15). He does not ask why or how Naboth died. But there can be no doubt here that he understands the circumstances of his death, for the possession of the vineyard is now possible only by virtue of the fact that Naboth died as a rebel against the crown. There is no other possible explanation for Jezebel's words!

Indeed, this is what Ahab has been waiting for – Naboth's death as a rebel – paving the way for him to take possession of the vineyard. The text gives us an inkling of his expectation, with the words: "And it was, when Ahab heard that Naboth had died, that Ahab arose to go down to the vineyard of Naboth the Jezreelite, to take possession of it" (v. 16).

The moment he hears of Naboth's death, he immediately goes off to the vineyard. He acts silently, but surely. This is what he has been waiting for; things have turned out as planned. This behavior represents proof that from the outset Ahab knew what was going to happen, and silently acquiesced.

Now, let us add additional weight to Ahab's responsibility: "She wrote letters in Ahab's name, and stamped them with his seal" (v. 8).

From this verse we see that it is Ahab's authority that lends support to Jezebel's base plan. Admittedly, she does not consult him, nor does she receive his approval to do what she does. Even the elders understand who is really behind what is written in the letters. But all of this is part of the conspiracy of silence in which they all participate with the intention of distancing Ahab from formal responsibility for the murder.

Thus Ahab becomes a hidden but necessary partner, even in that scene from which he is absent as an active figure. Only in body is he absent from that scene, but his name hovers in the air, in the form of his silent agreement, representing the formal source of authority for the entire horrible scene.

Following this description of the chain of events in our chapter, we have a better understanding of why Elijah is sent to bring God's word to Ahab only when he goes down to take possession of Naboth's vineyard. Ahab's responsibility for the murder is revealed there in all its clarity. So long as Ahab does not take possession of the vineyard, he could evade responsibility for the act of murder, and attribute it to Jezebel. He could claim that he did not know, that he could not have known, what Jezebel was planning. But now that he is there, in person, his partnership in the crime is revealed retroactively; it is now clear that it is he who was really behind the murder.

What is the lesson of our chapter, in light of the analysis of Ahab's responsibility?

Ahab is not just accused of an act of murder committed by his wife Jezebel without his knowledge, on the basis of his overall responsibility, as a superficial reading might initially suggest. He is also not charged with active responsibility, with advising and giving the order, as Abrabanel maintains. He is charged with a despicable attempt to evade real responsibility, pretending instead a less onerous overall responsibility.

The attempt to enjoy the fruits of wickedness without dirtying one's hands with the actual deed, thereby evading responsibility and punishment, is common practice among people, and especially among kings and heads of state. While it may work in relation to other people, who can judge only what they can see, it cannot work in the real reckoning between man and God. Before God nothing is hidden. He knows a person's innermost thoughts and emotions, understands his silences and inferences. Before God, the sinner's true measure of responsibility is clear, as is his attempt to hide himself and escape punishment.

> The heart is most deceitful of all and terribly weak – who can know it? I am the Lord, who searches hearts and examines innermost parts, to give to every man in according with his ways and the fruits of his actions. (Jer. 17:9–10)

Despite all that we have said above concerning Ahab's responsibility for the murder of Naboth, we must take the following reservation into account: Ahab was not the one to think of the idea of killing Naboth in order to take possession of his vineyard. In fact, at first the idea did not occur to him at all. Ahab, lying on his bed, refusing to eat, helpless in the face of Naboth's refusal to sell him the field, seems far removed from any murder plot. The plot is devised by Jezebel. Ahab's partnership and responsibility arise from his silent acquiescence, born of convenience. If we look closely, we see that his level of responsibility for the crime gradually increases during the course of the chapter.

At the beginning of scene 1, he lacks any intention or plan. Thereafter, in scene 2, he receives an unexplained promise from Jezebel, a promise whose process of realization he could have foreseen. In scene 3, the trial and murder are already being carried out in Ahab's name and with his seal; namely, they are inspired by him, even though he is still unaware that this is actually taking place. In scene 4, Ahab already knows about Naboth's murder, and he offers no objection, implying that he agrees. And in scene 5, his responsibility (retroactively!) reaches its climax, when Ahab goes to take possession of the vineyard of murdered Naboth.

Here we must ask, how is it that Ahab degenerates to such behavior? How does he make the transition from a situation in which he never dreamed of murder, to partnership through acquiescence, and ultimately even in deed, in an actual murder that is carried out?

Maimonides, in *Laws Pertaining to Theft and Loss* 1:11, writes as follows:

> Desire brings a person to coveting, and coveting leads to theft. For if the owner (of the object that one desires) is not willing to sell, even though one offers a hefty sum and pleads with them, then he will come to steal, as it is written: "They have coveted fields and stolen" (Mic. 2:2). And if the owner confronts him, so as to save his property, or to prevent him from stealing, then he will come to shed blood. This we learn from the story of Ahab and Naboth.

Chapter 33

Naboth's Refusal and His Motives

WHO WILL "GIVE" THE VINEYARD TO AHAB?

The great dilemma that is presented in the first half of chapter 21 (vv. 1–16) is: Will Naboth agree to give his vineyard to Ahab, or won't he? This dilemma is crafted through repeated use of the verb root *nun-tav-nun* (to give) in relation to Naboth and to the vineyard. It appears a total of seven times, thus representing a key word in this narrative. Let us examine each of its appearances:

1. *Give me* your vineyard, that it may be a vegetable garden for me (v. 2)
2. *God forbid that I should give* the inheritance of my fathers to you (v. 3)
3. Sullen and angry over the matter that he had spoken to him.... *I shall not give you* the inheritance of my fathers (v. 4)
4. And I said to him: *Give me* your vineyard for money (v. 6)
5. And he said: *I shall not give you* my vineyard (v. 6)
6. *I shall give you* the vineyard of Naboth the Jezreelite (v. 7)
7. Arise, take possession of the vineyard of Naboth the Jezreelite, *who refused to give it to you* for money (v. 15)

Ahab's request to give the vineyard appears twice (1, 4), while Naboth's refusal is repeated four times (2, 3, 5, 7). This creates a tension between Ahab's desire that the vineyard be given to him and Naboth's firm refusal, with the refusal prevailing.

The sixth appearance of the root *nun-tav-nun*, in Jezebel's words to Ahab, is strange: "*I shall give you* the vineyard of Naboth the Jezreelite" (v. 7).

This is not a request from someone to whom the vineyard does not belong (as in 1 and 4), nor is it a refusal on the part of the owner to give it (as in the other appearances of the verb). Rather, it is a promise to give the vineyard made by someone who does not own it at all!

The ironic tragedy of this chapter lies in the last pair of appearances of the verb (6–7): Ahab asks that the vineyard be given to him, Naboth refuses to give it and stands by his refusal, but ultimately the vineyard is in fact "given" to Ahab. It is not Naboth who gives it, nor is it given in return for money, as Ahab proposes – for Naboth "refused to give it to you for money" (v. 15) until the bitter end. Rather, it is Jezebel who "gives" the vineyard as the one who promised it, and for free, too (she hints at the advantage of her "giving" in verse 15). Clearly, the "giving" in verse 7 is merely Jezebel's ironic use of the verb that stands at the heart of the plot. From this point onward the text is careful to note that Ahab *takes possession* of the vineyard, which he had so wanted to *have given* to him (see vv. 15 [Jezebel's words], 16, 18, 19).

NABOTH'S REFUSAL: HIS REASONS

What is the meaning of Naboth's categorical refusal to give his vineyard to Ahab – the refusal that ultimately prevails over the request, but ultimately becomes a "giving" without a giver?

In chapter 31 of this book, we discussed Naboth's legal right to refuse Ahab's request. We clarified there that the "king's rights" have nothing to do with the subject at hand, and do not give Ahab any right to Naboth's field. Still, is Naboth's stubborn refusal not spiteful for its own sake? After all, he is promised fair conditions, and he is given a choice of two possibilities for payment: "I shall give you in its stead a better vineyard, or…its worth in money" (v. 2). Ahab's request is also supported by good, logical reasoning: "Give me your vineyard, that it may be a vegetable garden for me, for it is close to my home" (v. 2).

It seems eminently reasonable for a king to want to extend the area surrounding his palace (and Naboth's vineyard is located "near the palace of Ahab," as we read in verse 1); Ahab even has in mind some orderly and well-defined development plans. Despite all of this, Naboth refuses. Is he not responsible, in some measure, for the developments that follow? Would it not behoove him to concede to the logic of Ahab (who, as king of Israel, is surely deserving of some honor and even sacrifice on the part of his subjects), rather than insisting on his legal rights, when none of his rights is being violated?

Let us look closely at the manner in which Naboth's refusal is recorded. Our chapter records his refusal four times, and a comparison between them is most instructive:

1. The original refusal: "God forbid that I should give the inheritance of my fathers to you" (v. 3)
2. As it sounds in Ahab's thoughts: "I shall not give you the inheritance of my fathers" (v. 4)
3. As related by Ahab to Jezebel: "I shall not give you my vineyard" (v. 6)
4. Jezebel's version (inversion of word order): "Who refused to give you the vineyard of Naboth the Jezreelite for money" (v. 15)

From this comparison it arises that the further we move from the original refusal, the more it loses of its moral, religious validity, becoming petty instead. The original refusal is substantiated by the claim that this would be a religious transgression, and therefore it is formulated as an oath in God's name: "God forbid that I should. . . ." The reason for this solemn refusal is that it is "the inheritance of my fathers"; only at the very end does the refusal contain the words "to you." In the first repetition of the refusal, in Ahab's thoughts, the oath in God's name disappears, becoming a simple "I shall not." The relational "to you" now precedes "the inheritance of my fathers," and thus the impression is created that Naboth's objection is a personal matter directed specifically toward Ahab.

In the second repetition, in Ahab's report to Jezebel, in addition to all of the above, the highly significant expression "the inheritance of my fathers" becomes "my vineyard," expressing mere economic value. Thus, nothing remains of the original justification for Naboth's refusal; his position now seems altogether spiteful.

Ahab seems to want to forget the real justification. Moreover, he seems to want to hide it from Jezebel – to the point where in Jezebel's version there is an emphasis on Naboth's refusal to give "his vineyard" (as in the second repetition), despite the offer of monetary payment. Above, the term "for money" was interpreted as an expression of Jezebel's self-satisfaction on having "organized" the vineyard for Ahab for free. But her words may convey a different, or additional meaning: Jezebel hints that Naboth's refusal stems from his appetite for profit; he wants to be offered a higher price. Thus the entire situation is turned upside down. In fact, what Ahab actually offered was a vineyard better than Naboth's, and the offer was rejected by Naboth for religious reasons!

Why, time after time, does Ahab change the formulation of Naboth's refusal? It seems that in his heart of hearts, Ahab understands the justness of Naboth's refusal, not only in terms of the law, which awards him the right to refuse, but also from the perspective of religious law and custom, which obligate him to refuse. But since Ahab's desire for Naboth's vineyard is very strong, he tries to silence this voice of truth that echoes in his mind, and to turn it into an inexplicable, mean stubbornness.

PRESERVING THE PATRIARCHAL INHERITANCE

Let us now return to Naboth's original refusal and try to draw from there the answer to our question as to the meaning of his point-blank refusal. We have already noted that his refusal carries the validity of a religious obligation, "God forbid," and it arises from the fact that this vineyard is, for Naboth, "the inheritance of my fathers." But this requires further clarification.

The piece of land upon which an Israelite dwelled, in ancient times, and which had been bequeathed by his ancestors, was not regarded merely as an asset with monetary value, nor even as a mere "means of production," as modern man tends to regard it. The Torah tries to create a fixed and permanent relationship between a person and his inheritance in the land (his "possession"), as part of a social structure in which the individual is connected to his family, his tribe, and the inherited land that belongs exclusively to them. At the end of the book of Numbers, we read the following concerning the daughters of Zelophehad:

> An inheritance shall not be transferred from one tribe to another, for each person of the children of Israel shall cleave to the inheritance of the tribe of his fathers, in order that the children of Israel may inherit, each individual the inheritance of his fathers. (Num. 36:7–8)

It is for this purpose (*inter alia*), that the Torah institutes the law of the Jubilee year: "You shall return, each man to his inheritance, and you shall be restored, each man to his family" (Lev. 25:10). Between one Jubilee year and the next, "The land shall not be sold in perpetuity, for the land is Mine, and you are sojourners and residents with Me. And throughout the land of your possession, you shall give redemption to the land" (25:23–24).

When the sons dwell on the land of their fathers and continue to work it, they carry the connection of their fathers' lives to their children, from generation to generation. The cleaving of successive generations to the family inheritance of land, which serves as a force that binds the generations together, grants the transient individual a foothold in eternity. Thus, the individual's hold on the inheritance of his fathers represents an act of kindness toward previous generations. An interruption of the order of inheritance and settlement of the inheritance of the fathers is therefore a deviation from the intention of the Torah, and a violation of its commandments.

The very sale of land, even only until the Jubilee year, which is really a kind of rental, "For what he sells you is the number of its harvests" (Lev. 25:16), is permissible only in dire circumstances. Even then, the seller, or his relatives, are entitled to redeem the field, if they are able to, as explained in *Parashat Behar*. But the sale of an inheritance in perpetuity is forbidden under any circumstances, both to the seller and to the buyer.

The sale of the field to Ahab is therefore not halakhically proper, especially since Ahab certainly had no intention of permitting the redemption of the field or its return in the Jubilee year. His intention is to buy it in perpetuity. Indeed, it is in this light that Abrabanel understands Naboth's refusal:

> Naboth answers him, "God forbid that I should give the inheritance of my fathers to you." It seems to me that his intention was that since the Torah commands that the land should not be sold in perpetuity, and that every part of the land should always remain in the hands of its inheritors, as it was divided among their father's households, therefore it would be a transgression for [Naboth] to give him the vineyard. He could neither sell it for money nor give it in exchange for another vineyard, since it was the inheritance of his fathers from the time of the division of the land. Therefore he says, "*God* forbid" – because Naboth believes that God prohibits this and that it would be evil in His eyes, since [the vineyard] was the inheritance of his forefathers.

Naboth's refusal to give his vineyard to Ahab therefore testifies to the independence of the individual in Israel, and the preference given to the laws of the Torah over the request of a sinful king. It also demonstrates the extent of inculcation of the Torah laws pertaining to inheritance of land among the nation.

Chapter 34

Ahab's Punishment and That of His Household

ELIJAH'S MISSION

In the second half of our narrative (I Kings 21:17–22:1) Elijah appears in the vineyard of Naboth when Ahab goes down to take possession of the vineyard, and conveys God's word to him. This section may be divided into six units, each with its own subject:

1. God's command to Elijah to meet Ahab at the vineyard of Naboth and to convey God's word to him (vv. 17–19)
2. Brief dialogue between Ahab and Elijah (v. 20a)
3. Elijah's words to Ahab: the cutting off of Ahab's house, and Jezebel's punishment (vv. 20b–24)
4. Parenthetical narrative: negative summary of Ahab's reign (vv. 25–26)
5. Ahab's sorrowful reaction (v. 27)
6. God's word to Elijah – postponement of the punishment of Ahab's house to the next generation (vv. 28–22:1)

In this chapter we shall address the first four units, up to verse 26. Each of these units presents some difficulty. Let us address each in turn.

Unit 1

> You shall speak to him, saying: So says the Lord, Have you murdered and also taken possession? And you shall speak to him, saying: So says the Lord: At the place where the dogs licked the blood of Naboth, the dogs shall lick your blood, too. (v. 19)

These words, which Elijah is commanded to convey to Naboth, do not appear later on in the chapter.

Unit 2

Ahab said to Elijah: "Have you found me, my enemy?" And he said: "I have found you." (v. 20a)

The dialogue between the king and the prophet in this verse is sudden; we are given no background. There is no description of their actual meeting, prior to Ahab's question.

Unit 3

> Since you have given yourself over to do evil in the eyes of God, behold, I will bring evil upon you and will sweep you away; I shall cut off from Ahab every male, and him that is shut up and him that is left free in Israel. And I shall make your house like the House of Jeroboam son of Nebat, and like the House of Baasa son of Ahijah, for the anger that you have provoked in Me, and for causing Israel to sin. And God spoke of Jezebel, too, saying: The dogs shall eat Jezebel by the wall of Jezreel. He who dies of Ahab in the city – the dogs shall eat him, and he who dies in the field – the birds of the sky shall eat him. (vv. 20b–24)

What Elijah says in this unit is not what he was originally commanded to say, in unit 1. The accusation of Ahab is all encompassing, and does not address his specific sin with regard to Naboth (v. 22, "for causing Israel to sin," refers to the sin of idolatry). The punishment, too, is general; it is not related to the sin of killing Naboth. It speaks of Ahab's house being cut off, like the prophecy of Ahijah the Shilonite concerning the House of Jeroboam (I Kings 14:9–11), and that of Jehu son of Hanani concerning the House of Baasa (I Kings 16:1–4); indeed, these two kings are even mentioned by Elijah. He is not talking about Ahab's personal fate, with a punishment that corresponds measure for measure with what he did to Naboth, as God commanded him in verse 19. Jezebel's punishment (v. 23) is also something new; it is not mentioned in God's words to Elijah.

Unit 4

> There was none like Ahab, who gave himself over to do evil in the eyes of God, to which he was incited by Jezebel, his wife. And he acted most abominably in going after idols, like all that the Amorites did – whom God cast out before the children of Israel. (vv. 25–26)

This summary of Ahab's evil interrupts the continuity of the narrative. Its proper place would logically be at the end of the next chapter (22:39), after the description of Ahab's death.

As we shall discover from the resolution of these difficulties, they are connected to one another.

UNITS 1–3: SEVERAL PROBLEMS – A SINGLE SOLUTION

When, in a biblical narrative, God commands His prophet to convey a message to an individual or to the public, the content of the message is sometimes recorded twice in the text: once in God's words to the prophet, and again when the prophet delivers the message. In many cases, though, the text is economical in style, and the message is not repeated. Nahmanides, in his commentary on the Torah (Num. 16:5), presents this phenomenon:

> I have already demonstrated that in many places we find that the text will either elaborate in [recording] God's words to Moses and be brief in Moses's speech, or the opposite; and *sometimes one of these [speeches] is not mentioned at all.*

The words that we have emphasized include two possibilities. One is that God's word to Moses is recorded in the text, while what Moses actually says when conveying God's message, is not recorded. The second possibility is that that text mentions only Moses's speech, and from this we are meant to deduce that God had previously commanded him to say this, even though God's words do not appear in the text. The same principle obviously applies to understanding the books of the prophets.

According to this rule, we may posit that the solution to our questions on units 1 and 3 is one and the same: The text is brief in unit 1, recording only God's words to Elijah, while omitting the repetition of the same exact words when Elijah conveys them to Ahab. At the same time, in unit 3 the text suffices with Elijah's words, and it is clear that Elijah is speaking in God's name, even though the initial divine message is omitted. This manner of presentation serves to save a considerable volume of text, and the two units shed light on one another: Just as the message in unit 1 is conveyed by God to Elijah, so is the message in unit 3; and just as the message in unit 3 is conveyed by Elijah to Ahab, so is the message in unit 1

But we must still ask: Why does the text choose this particular manner of presentation, rather than one of the other devices that are usually employed for the sake of brevity? For instance, the text could have conveyed God's message to Elijah in its entirety, and then given us to understand that it was passed on faithfully to Ahab. Alternatively, this section could have started immediately with Elijah's encounter with Ahab and the speech that Elijah delivers in God's name, in such a way that it would be clear to the reader from Elijah's words ("So says the Lord...") that he had been commanded by God to convey this message. Furthermore, concerning the complex technique that the text employs here, with one part of God's message recorded only when God speaks to Elijah, while the other part of the message only when Elijah speaks to Ahab, we may ask: Why is God's message cut off at just that place?

Let us start with the last question: The speech is cut off in the middle for two reasons. One reason is related to the content of the parts of his speech: As noted in the question we posed on unit 3, the content of unit 3 is not directly related to Ahab's sin with Naboth. The same is not true of unit 1, in which the two parts of the divine message – the part containing the accusation and the part containing the punishment – both clearly relate to the sin that preceded them.

The other reason is connected to Ahab's reactions upon hearing God's word. The first message (which is not explicitly recorded as having been conveyed to Ahab, but the reader is expected to deduce that this did happen), leads to the reaction, "Have you found me, my enemy?" and to Elijah's response, "I have found you." This creates a division between the two parts of Elijah's speech. Clearly, this dialogue could not be put off until the end of his speech, since its second part (unit 3) leads to an altogether different response on Ahab's part: "He tore his garments" (v. 27).

In light of the above, there is clearly no possibility of conveying God's entire message to Elijah as a single unit, since it would be impossible to incorporate Ahab's reaction in the middle of God's speech to Elijah. The incorporation of his reaction is possible only when the text narrates Elijah's actual appearance before Ahab.

What remains is to clarify the reason for avoiding the one other possibility: For the text to start this section by immediately describing Elijah's appearance in the vineyard of Naboth and his words to Ahab there, in God's name. This would have facilitated the incorporation of Ahab's words at the proper juncture, and the division of the two halves of Elijah's speech. The advantage of this presentation would have been the cohesiveness of the description and a natural flow that would not have required complex interpretation.

The reason for the text not adopting this approach would seem to be as follows: When the reader arrives at the result of the sin of Ahab and Jezebel, when Ahab comes to take possession of the vineyard of the murdered Naboth, he expects to read, first and foremost, God's reaction to this crime. And an immediate reaction indeed appears: "God's word came to Elijah…" (v. 17). If, instead of this verse, we were to read, as proposed above, "Elijah went down to meet Ahab, and he found him in the vineyard of Naboth, and he said to him: So says the Lord…," not only would there be some delay in the reader's hearing God's immediate response, but more importantly we would hear God's response only indirectly, from Elijah's mouth, and by deducing that he had been told by God to say this. This would weaken the impact of the divine response, while the text is trying to do the opposite: to strengthen and amplify its impact. This effect is achieved by conveying God's word to Elijah in direct speech.

The advantage of the approach adopted by the text here could also have been a disadvantage, since the proximity of God's word to the criminal deed on one hand, may have distanced it from Ahab's reaction to it, on the other. This would have diminished the drama of Elijah's encounter with Ahab. This would have been the case if the text had gone back and spelled out Elijah's going to the vineyard of Naboth, and recorded the encounter with Ahab there, and Elijah's conveying of God's word. But the text describes the rebuke in such a way as to maintain and heighten the drama. It is specifically by refraining from describing the actual encounter between them, and the recording of Ahab's rhetorical question, "Have you found me, my enemy?" immediately after God's preceding words, that the text deliberately creates the impression that this is Ahab's reaction to God's words which have just been conveyed to him by Elijah. God's words to Elijah thus become, in the text, Elijah's words to Ahab.

AHAB'S SIN OF IDOLATRY: WHY IS IT RECALLED HERE?

Thus, we arrived at an answer to questions 1, 2 and 3. However, we have not yet explored the content of unit 3. Having established that Elijah's message to Ahab in this unit was given by God, as a continuation of the message in unit 1, let us now try to understand why this general message, seemingly extraneous to the sin of killing Naboth, appears here, in the encounter between Elijah and Ahab in Naboth's vineyard.

Elijah's words here are indeed a sweeping indictment of Ahab's sins as king, with the inference that he also led Israel as ray to practice idolatry (v. 22). In keeping with the accusation, the punishment is also a collective one for Ahab's entire household. This message belongs right here and nowhere else. The killing of Naboth was not a sin of merely local significance, requiring a personal punishment for Ahab and Jezebel. This was the "last straw," which brought about God's final decision concerning Ahab's royal dynasty, which was no longer worthy of continuing. This reflects on the severity of this sin, which not only led to the punishment of Ahab personally (as suggested in God's initial message, in verse 19), but also, together with all of his other sins, brought about the end of his dynasty.

Maimonides presents the relationship between this sin of Ahab and all of his previous sins as follows:

Although there are sins that are more serious than bloodshed, they do not lead to destruction of civilization in the way that bloodshed does. Even idolatry or, needless to say, prohibited sexual relations, or desecration of Shabbat, are not like bloodshed [in this respect]. For these belong to the category of transgressions between man and God, while bloodshed belongs to the category of sins between man and his fellow. And anyone who commits such a sin is a completely wicked person, and all the commandments that he may have performed throughout his life are not equal in weight to this sin, nor will they save him from judgment. As it is written, "A man who is burdened with the blood of a person, let him flee to a pit; let none support him" (Prov. 28:17). We learn this from the example of Ahab, who was an idolater, as it is said of him, "But there was none like Ahab, who gave himself over to do evil in the eyes of God … and acted most abominably in going after idols' (I Kings 21:25–26). However, when his sins and merits were set out before God, there was no sin that made him deserving of being wiped out, nor any other matter that stood against him, like the blood of Naboth." (*Laws Pertaining to a Murderer* 4:9)

We may point out another aspect of the relationship between the murder of Naboth, which is the subject of our chapter, and the sin of idolatry that is also mentioned here in relation to Ahab. The common denominator underlying both of these abominations is, of course, his wife, Jezebel, "who incited him." These words in verse 25, in the summary of his reign, unquestionably refer to the idolatry that is mentioned in the following verse. But in the episode of Naboth's murder, too, Jezebel's central role is so obvious as to require no comment.

Having noted above that the murder of Naboth was the deciding factor, coming after all of Ahab's previous sins of idolatry and thereby sealing the fate of his household, we may now add that the root of Ahab's sin in our chapter, the sin of murder, which is the most serious of all sins between man and his fellow man, lies in the idolatry that preceded it. The foreign, pagan culture that entered Israel together with Jezebel, introduced new concepts into Israelite society and into the Israelite royalty with regard to the status of the king and the norms of the monarchy.

Religious corruption is the source of the moral and social corruption that ultimately characterizes Ahab's household. But it is specifically the social corruption, epitomized by the story of Naboth, that seals their fate.

In light of the above, it now becomes clear why specifically here, in verses 25–26, the text presents its summary of Ahab's reign. This summary, which speaks mainly of his idolatry, is necessary because of the sin of killing Naboth and the punishment decreed as a result. This negative summary would be out of place at the end of chapter 22, since there we read of Ahab's heroic death in battle against Israel's enemies, an episode that certainly stands in his favor. For this very reason, the summary is presented in the midst of our narrative rather than at its conclusion, since Ahab ultimately demonstrates subservience to God's word, thereby earning an easing of his verdict.

Chapter 35

"Have You Found Me, My Enemy?" (I Kings 21:20)

Ahab reacts twice to Elijah's words – the first time following the first part of Elijah's speech, and then again after the end of the speech. Both reactions demand some clarification, as does the obvious development between the two reactions. In this chapter we shall focus on Ahab's first reaction, which follows God's double message to him as conveyed by Elijah:

> So says the Lord: Have you then murdered and also taken possession?... So says the Lord: In the place where the dogs licked the blood of Naboth, the dogs shall lick your blood, too. And Ahab said to Elijah: "Have you found me, my enemy?" And he said: "I have found [you]." (vv. 19–20)

What is the meaning of Ahab's question, and what does it tell us about his spiritual stance in the face of Elijah's rebuke?

The literal meaning of Ahab's question may lead us to view it as an affront to the prophet, suggesting that he is a persona non grata, that the king has no desire to encounter him. It gives the impression that the king regularly evades such encounters, but is now suddenly forced to confront Elijah face-to-face. But this simplistic interpretation disregards the context of this tense dialogue. It fails to clarify how the dialogue arises from what preceded it, and how it contributes to a significant deepening of our understanding of the situation as a whole.

Abrabanel (as well as the Baal HaMetzudot and Malbim, who adopt his approach) interprets Ahab's words as an attempt to evade responsibility for Naboth's murder:

> "Have you found me, my enemy?" – Have you found me guilty as a murderer in this regard, my enemy? Claiming, as it were, that he had not been present at Naboth's murder, and that he knew nothing about it; rather, it was Jezebel who was responsible. He [Elijah], as [Ahab's] enemy, is suspecting him of something that he did not do. Therefore Elijah says, "I have found [you]" – I know the truth – that she committed the act at your instigation and with your knowledge.

The Baal HaMetzudot briefly cites Abrabanel's view, and then adds an extra sentence describing Ahab's stance: "And he thought of denying what the prophet said, as though it had not been committed on his initiative."

But this interpretation cannot be regarded as the plain meaning of the text. Firstly, linguistically: These commentators project onto Ahab's two words, and Elijah's single word of response, a notion that appears nowhere in the verse. Ahab does not say, "Have you found me guilty"; nor does Elijah respond, "I have found you guilty." The debate that these commentators seek to create between Ahab and Elijah, as to whether the murder of Naboth was Jezebel's act or one that could be attributed to Ahab, is not even hinted at.

Secondly, the nature of the situation described in this dialogue is full of dramatic tension; it is not suited to legal debate, whether explicit or implicit. Hence it is clear that Ahab's question, "Have you found me, my enemy," must be understood as a rhetorical question; Elijah's response is likewise to be understood in that context, and the dialogue can therefore not be a legal debate, as the above commentators suggest.

Earlier in this book,[1] we compared the encounter between the king and the prophet in our chapter with that recorded at the beginning of chapter 18, when Ahab and Obadiah go off together in search of some feed for the animals. We noted that there, Ahab felt that Elijah was responsible for the difficult situation of the nation, and therefore when he meets Elijah he assumes, with some degree of justification, the role of accuser, addressing Elijah with the rhetorical question: "Is that you, o troubler of Israel?" The title that Ahab uses shows that he regards himself as a king who cares about his nation and views Elijah as the people's enemy because of the drought that he has decreed.

In our chapter, the roles are reversed. Here it is Elijah who accuses Ahab, who understands that he has been caught in his disgrace. Ahab's response here is not an expression of accusation, as in chapter 18. His rhetorical question, "Have you found me, my enemy," means: "Have you finally managed to catch me in my disgrace – you, the prophet who has been lying in wait for me, awaiting my downfall?" Elijah's unequivocal answer, "I have found you," is to be understood accordingly: "Indeed, you have been discovered in your disgrace, at the peak of your crime, and at the very site of the crime!" There is no attempt at evasion here. On the contrary: Ahab recognizes that he has been caught in the most compromising of situations, and expresses an implied admission to the accusation: "Have you then murdered and taken possession?"

On the other hand, we should obviously not get carried away in interpreting Ahab's words here as a manifestation of repentance and regret. His words are uttered in anger, as someone who is pained at having his crime exposed. We may say that there is acknowledgment of sin here, but the next stage of repentance, regret, is absent, and without it there can be no process of repentance.[2] This situation is preferable, in some ways, to the usual scenario in which the accused tends to deny his sin outright (sometimes even claiming that what he did was a worthy deed), or to claim that he is in no way responsible for the sin. In dealing with a sinner

---

1. See chapter 8, "The Second Encounter between Elijah and Ahab," section "Supplement: The Confrontations between King and Prophet in Chapters 17 and 21 – a Comparison."
2. See Maimonides, *Laws of Repentance* 2:2, for the stages of repentance.

of this more common type, the prophet must first and foremost disprove his claims and bring him to recognition of the truth and an admission, before specifying his punishment.[3] In our chapter, by contrast, Ahab's position, which is at least honest, allows the legal argument to be omitted, and moves right on to his punishment.

It appears, then, that Ahab's response here may be a first stage leading to his submission, which we shall discuss below.

---

3. Compare the lengthy, stage-by-stage dialogue between Samuel and Saul following the war against Amalek, I Samuel 16:13–31.

Chapter 36

The Significance of Ahab's Submission (I Kings 21:27–29)

After Elijah finishes the second part of his speech (I Kings 21:20b–24), in which Ahab is told that his household is going to be cut off, Ahab responds a second time. This time, he does not react with words, but with actions: "And it was, when Ahab heard these words, that he rent his garments and placed sackcloth upon his flesh, and he fasted, and lay upon sackcloth, and he went about softly" (v. 27).

What is this behavior meant to express? Is this genuine and complete repentance, with heartfelt regret for his whole life's work, or is it simply brokenheartedness in the face of the terrible punishment of which he has just been informed by God's prophet? The absence of any verbal reaction makes it difficult for us to decide. Clearly, however, Ahab's behavior in some way reflects submission before God. As God Himself tells Elijah:

Have you seen how Ahab has humbled himself before Me (*milefa-nai*)? Since he has humbled himself before Me (*mipanai*), I shall not bring the evil in his days; in the days of his son I shall bring the evil upon his household. (v. 29)

Once again we ask, using the terminology of Malbim: Was this a sub-mission "in the face of the greatness and exaltedness" of God, or was it "out of fear of punishment"?

The commentators are divided in this regard. In Abrabanel's view, "He did not repent out of fear of punishment, but rather from the great-ness of the Lord God of Hosts." Abrabanel bases his view on God's words of testimony, quoted above, as well as on the actual postponement of Ahab's punishment until the days of his son.

However, based on the very same source, God's words in verse 29, Malbim draws precisely the opposite conclusion. He notes the change in God's formulation, from "how Ahab has humbled himself before Me (*milefanai*)" to the continuation of His words where he uses the word *mipanai*:

There is a difference between *milefanai* and *mipanai*. *Milefanai* means because of His greatness and His exaltedness, while *mipa-nai* means out of fear of punishment. One who humbles himself *milefanav* will try to draw close to God and to serve Him; he will submit himself to God's grandeur. One who humbles himself *mipanav* will hide himself and flee from God, so as to save himself from punishment. In other words [God is saying to Elijah]: Even if he appears to you to have submitted himself *milefanai* ("Have you seen how Ahab has humbled himself before Me?"), this is not the case; he merely humbles himself out of [fear of] Me – out of fear of punishment. Therefore, "Since he has humbled himself out of [fear of] Me," I shall not bring the evil in his days. However, because he has not humbled himself before Me, I shall bring the evil in the days of his son; the decree shall not be nullified completely.

Malbim's explanation for this exchange of wording in our verse does not appear to represent the plain meaning of the text, especially as regards his interpretation of God's question, "Have you seen how Ahab has humbled himself before Me?" which, according to his thesis, is not meant to praise Ahab, but rather to castigate him. Nevertheless, let us consider his position.

Firstly, Malbim proves his explanation from the conclusion of verse 29: The verdict is not canceled altogether, but rather postponed, for a period that is not very long. Moreover, only the punishment of having his household "cut off" is postponed till his son's lifetime. "The decree that the dogs would lick his blood cannot occur during his son's lifetime; it can only be [at the end of] his own life," as Rashi points out.

Secondly, the absence of a verbal response in verse 27 is not a trivial matter: The confession of the sinner is central to the process of repentance. As Maimonides teaches in *Laws of Repentance* (2:2): "He must confess verbally and utter these matters that he has resolved in his heart." We also learn (2:4), "It is the way of repentance for the penitent always to cry out before God in weeping and supplication." Ahab's silent behavior therefore does not testify to ideal, complete repentance.

Thirdly, it would seem that the use of the verb *khaf-nun-ayin* (humbling, submission) in relation to Ahab testifies to an inferior level of repentance. This root does appear several times in Tanakh in the sense of repentance (particularly in the book of Chronicles), but when the repentance in question is genuine and deep, there are usually other verbs that accompany it, expressing a higher level of repentance. For example:

> My nation, upon whom My name is called, shall humble themselves and pray and seek My countenance and return from their evil ways, and I shall hear.... (II Chr. 7:14)

> [Manasseh:] And when he was afflicted he sought out the countenance of the Lord his God, and humbled himself greatly before the God of his fathers. And he prayed to Him and beseeched him, and He heard his supplication. (II Chr. 33:12–13)

> [Josiah:] Since your heart was submissive, and you humbled yourself...and you tore your garments and wept before Me, I too have heard you. (II Chr. 34:27)

Furthermore, God's response to the penitents in the verses above is described in terms of "hearing." In our verse, by contrast, God asks Elijah: "Have you *seen* how Ahab has humbled himself?" – since Ahab's repentance is truly just a matter of appearances.

The matter of Ahab's repentance and its evaluation is treated in various midrashim, but the opinions of the Sages is not always expressed directly. There is one midrash that does formulate a direct and unequivocal judgment of Ahab (*Pirkei DeRabbi Eliezer*, ch. 43):

> Take note of the power of charity and repentance. Learn from Ahab, king of Israel, who seriously repented. He stole and oppressed and murdered, as it is written, "Have you murdered and also taken possession?" but he sent for Jehoshaphat, king of Judah, and [the latter] would administer forty lashes to him three times every day, and with fasting and prayer he would arise and go to bed before God, and he occupied himself with Torah all of his days and never again returned to his evil deeds, and his repentance found favor, as it is written, "Have you seen how Ahab has humbled himself before Me?"

However, this view is not the prevailing one in the midrashim. From most of the sources we deduce that the Sages regard Ahab's repentance as having been less than perfect. Rabbi David Luria cites some of these midrashim in his commentary on *Pirkei DeRabbi Eliezer* (ad loc., Warsaw, 5612). We shall merely add that in Mishna Sanhedrin (10:2) we read:

> Three kings … have no portion in the World to Come … Jeroboam, Ahab, and Manasseh. R. Yehuda says: Manasseh does have a portion in the World to Come, as it is written, "He prayed to Him and He heard his supplication" (II Chr. 33:13).

Here we must ask: Why does R. Yehuda not extend his exclusion of Manasseh from the list to Ahab as well, on the basis of the verses in our chapter describing his submission? The answer must surely be that he does not believe that Manasseh's repentance, and God's acceptance of it, as described in the book of Chronicles, can be compared to the repentance of Ahab and God's acceptance of it as described in our chapter.

From the continuation of the text's description of Ahab in the next narrative (ch. 22), which records the last episode in which he is active, it is likewise difficult to accept a depiction of Ahab as being wholeheartedly repentant and qualitatively different from how we have known him until now. We refer here to the episode of Micaiah son of Imlah. Ahab himself testifies to his attitude toward this prophet: "I hate him, for he prophesizes about me not good, but evil" (I Kings 22:8).

Further on in the narrative, before he sets off for his final battle – upon which he embarks despite what the prophet Micaiah appears to be telling him – he commands: "Place this person in prison, and feed him scant bread and scant water, until I return in peace" (22:27).

Are these words, and Ahab's optimism that he will return in peace from the battlefield, appropriate to a true penitent?

> The way of penitents is to be downcast and extremely humble ... for to the extent that they are ashamed of the deeds that they have done and are mortified over them, so their merit is great and they attain greater levels. (Maimonides, *Laws of Repentance*, 7:8)

How far Ahab is from this description of "the way of penitents"!

Hence, we may conclude that the description of Ahab that arises from *Pirkei DeRabbi Eliezer* should not be regarded as reflecting the plain meaning of the text. Ahab, in humbling himself before God, certainly showed that he believed Elijah's words and was fearful, and even took pains to act as though, in his great anguish, he was in mourning. But nothing more than that. Still, even this demonstration of humility is worthy of consideration and, indeed, God responds immediately, with His attribute of mercy speaking out in inverse parallel to the attribute of justice that previously decreed Ahab's fate:

God's original decree	God's amended decree:
I Kings 21:17: "God's word came to Elijah the Tishbite, saying:"	I Kings 21:28: "God's word came to Elijah the Tishbite, saying:"
v. 19 "Have you murdered and also taken possession?... In the place where the dogs licked...the dogs will lick your blood, too."	v. 29: Have you seen how Ahab has humbled himself before Me? Since he has humbled himself out of [fear of] Me, I shall not bring the evil in his days."

The stylistic similarity here is meant to highlight the contrast of content. Both utterances are introduced with identical words. Then comes a rhetorical question, followed by a verdict that arises from the implicit answer to the question. However, the intention behind these three components (introduction, rhetorical question, and verdict) in the one case is the opposite of the intention in the other case.

This parallel must still be treated with some reservation. Firstly, the easing of the punishment in God's amended decree does not apply to the punishment set out in the original decree: The "evil" that is postponed from Ahab's lifetime until the lifetime of his son is not the licking of Ahab's blood, but rather the cutting off of his household. Secondly, while God's first speech to Elijah is meant to be conveyed to Ahab, and is addressed to Ahab in the second person, the second speech is addressed to Elijah himself, with no intention of its being conveyed to Ahab. The significance of this is that Ahab is not worthy of this prophetic revelation of the divine attribute of mercy (even if Elijah later makes it known to him). The whole point of this divine message is to teach Elijah himself about God's acceptance of repentance, even where it is only partial and defective.

We have not yet exhausted the lesson to be learned from God's message. What is the purpose of the rhetorical question that God addresses to Elijah – "Have you seen how Ahab has humbled himself before Me"? What would be lacking were the text simply to begin with the words that follow: "Since he has humbled himself..."?

It seems that God's question here expresses the great wonder at the fact that a person with the status of the king of Israel, who is mired in the depths of terrible sin, can break down and humble himself before God. Even if this is not complete repentance, Ahab's submission demonstrates a person's ability to melt his own heart of stone and thereby to attain some measure of divine pardon.

Indeed, this is the lesson to be learned from this narrative: The great power that a person possesses to turn back from the depths of sin, and the power of repentance which, even if not complete, is accepted before God and has an effect.

The lesson is formulated as follows in *Pesikta DeRabbi Kahana Shuva, piska* 24:11:

> Israel said before God: Master of the universe, if we engage in repentance, will You accept us?
>
> He said to them: I accepted the repentance of Cain; shall I not then accept your repentance?
>
> *I accepted the repentance of Ahab; shall I not then accept your repentance?*
>
> He had a terrible verdict decreed upon him. As it is written, "Have you murdered and also taken possession? And you shall speak to him, saying: So says the Lord, in the place where the dogs licked the blood of Naboth, the dogs will lick your blood, too."
>
> "And it was, when Ahab heard these words, that he rent his garments and he placed sackcloth upon his flesh, and he fasted, and he lay upon sackcloth, and he went about softly." To what extent did he fast? If he was used to eating every three hours, he now ate only after six hours. If he usually ate every six hours, he would now eat only after nine hours… What is written there? "God's word came to Elijah the Tishbite, saying: Have you seen how Ahab has humbled himself before Me?" God said to Elijah: Do you see, Ahab has repented. "Have you seen how Ahab has humbled himself?" – *Shall I not then accept your repentance?*

Chapter 37

Ahab's Two Responses: A Comparison

I
t remains for us to clarify the reason for the change in Ahab's reaction, from his response to the first part of Elijah's speech – "Have you found me, my enemy?" – to his manifestation of submission to God when he hears the second part.

In the previous chapters we arrived at a partial answer to the question: The transition between Ahab's two reactions is, in fact, not as sharp as it might appear at first glance. The first response is not meant as an evasion of responsibility as much as an implied acknowledgment of his sin (see above, ch. 35), and as such it represents an appropriate prelude to his second reaction. Likewise, the second reaction does not tell us that Ahab has undergone complete, profound repentance. It is submission before God in view of the threat of the terrible punishment that Elijah describes (see above, ch. 6). The psychological transition between these two reactions is gradual and well within the bounds of rational, normative behavior. Thus the question is less acute.

Nevertheless, the discrepancy between the two reactions remains, and it changes Ahab from a complete criminal into a partial penitent, who is granted some degree of divine pardon. What causes this development? Is this the accumulated effect of Elijah's words, where his first speech (21:19) was not sufficient to break Ahab's stubborn, unrepentant attitude, but his following words (vv. 21–24) finally achieved this aim?

Perhaps this is indeed the answer. However, it seems that the distinction between what Ahab says following Elijah's first words and his reaction after the rest of what Elijah has to say (see above, ch. 34), may hint at a deeper explanation for the change.

Elijah's first prophecy concerns Ahab's personal punishment, measure for measure, for the murder of Naboth. The second prophecy, on the other hand, concerns Ahab's royal household, his dynasty. Specifically in this context, Ahab is not judged personally (unlike Jezebel). Usually, what affects a person most is his personal punishment and suffering, and indeed, Ahab is told that he will die an unnatural death, followed by a desecration of his remains. Punishment of those around one, and even of one's own family, usually has less of an immediate effect. This is the very claim that Satan has when Job passes the first test in maintaining his faith after losing all his children and property:

> Skin covers skin; a person will give all that he has for the sake of his life. But put forth Your hand now and touch his bone and his flesh; (see) if he will not then curse You to Your face. (Job 2:4–5)

Ahab's reactions, however, are the opposite. To explain this phenomenon, let us broaden our perspective to survey Ahab's kingdom against the background of its history. If we review the history of the Kingdom of Israel, from the time of its establishment by Jeroboam son of Nebat until the ascent of the House of Omri, its most outstanding feature is the acute deterioration in its political stability, with a dizzying turnover of royal houses at its head. While the Kingdom of Judah is governed exclusively by descendants of the Davidic dynasty, as a fact that is accepted without question, and only three kings have reigned during this period (Rehoboam, Abijam, and Asa), the

Kingdom of Israel has witnessed a series of political assassinations where each new king has eliminated his predecessor together with his entire dynasty. Ahab was the seventh king to rule over Israel, and a member of the third dynasty to have risen to power, following four murders of kings or personalities aspiring to the crown, all within a period of a little over sixty years!

Following all of this, it is the House of Omri, and especially King Ahab himself, that has restored national and political stability to the kingdom. In terms of politics, the military, and settlement of the land, there is no comparison between the House of Omri and any of the previous kings. This conclusion may be drawn from the biblical text, from Midrash, and from archaeological evidence.

We may unquestionably assert that the restoration of national order in all spheres, with the establishment of a stable royal house for future generations, in order to prevent the sort of upheavals that had characterized the kingdom in the past, was a vision and aspiration shared by Omri and Ahab, one to which much of their effort and action was directed.

Indeed, Omri and Ahab are given credit for this aspiration, both elsewhere in the Tanakh itself (see below), and in the teachings of the Sages, when they explain why this royal dynasty merited to produce four kings who ruled for some fifty years – twice as long as any other royal house had lasted until then.

Now Elijah appears in Naboth's vineyard, and employs the language of two previous prophets – Ahijah the Shilonite, who had prophesied the downfall of the House of Jeroboam, and Jehu son of Hanani, who had foretold the end of the House of Baasa. Elijah adds his voice to theirs in vilifying the House of Ahab and prophesying its destruction, using exactly the same words with which the previous prophets had berated the two dynasties that had preceded the House of Omri. Moreover, these two dynasties are portrayed in his words as a precedent and basis for comparison with what is destined for the House of Ahab (v. 22). Let us compare the three prophecies:

Prophecy of Elijah concerning the House of Ahab (I Kings 21:20–24)	Prophecy of Jehu son of Hanani concerning the House of Baasa (I Kings 16:2–7, not in the order of the text)	Prophecy of Ahijah the Shilonite concerning the House of Jeroboam (I Kings 14:7–16, not in the order of the text)
Since you have devoted yourself to doing evil in the eyes of God	Since I have lifted you up.... You have gone in the way of Jeroboam	Since I have lifted you up...you have done worse than all who came before you
Behold, I shall bring evil upon you I shall sweep you away I shall cut off for Ahab all males, and any that is shut up or abandoned in Israel	I shall sweep away Baasa and his household	Therefore, behold, I shall bring evil upon the House of Jeroboam, and I shall sweep away the House of Jeroboam I shall cut of all males, and any that is shut up or abandoned in Israel
I shall make your house **like the House of Jeroboam son of Nebat, and like the House of Baasa ben Ahijah**, for the anger to which you have provoked Me, in having caused Israel to sin	I shall make your house **like the House of Jeroboam son of Nebat**... In provoking Him to anger with the work of his hands You have caused My people, Israel, to sin	Who sinned and caused Israel to sin
He who dies of Ahab in the city shall be consumed by the dogs, and he who dies in the field shall be consumed by the birds of the sky.	He who dies of Baasa in the city shall be consumed by the dogs, and he who dies of him in the field shall be consumed by the birds of the sky.	He who dies of Jeroboam in the city shall be consumed by the dogs, and he who dies in the field shall be consumed by the birds of the sky.

This comparison is specifically what hurts Ahab, since it implies that the House of Ahab will be nothing but a brief episode, devoid of influence, in the stormy history of the Kingdom of Israel, just like the House of Jeroboam and the House of Baasa. All of the enormous efforts at which Omri and Ahab had excelled – the creation of the new capital city, Samaria (16:24); the building of other cities and of the royal palace (22:39); forging of courageous political ties with the former enemy Kingdom of Judah (ch. 22) and with the kingdom of Sidon, the old ally from the days of David and Solomon (16:31); the reinforcement of Israel's army and leading it to victory against the principal enemy in that generation, the Kingdom of Aram (ch. 20) – all of this will be counted for nothing, and the royal house that has achieved all of this will be cut off! All of Ahab's aspirations and plans, all of his positive qualities as the king of Israel, seeking the welfare of his nation as he saw it (even if at times his view was distorted), is dealt a mortal blow with Elijah's message that his royal line is about to end.

Therefore, it is when Ahab hears of the imminent collapse of his life's work that he breaks down and mourns. Verse 27 is very precise in its wording: "And it was, *when Ahab heard these words*" – this speech that prophesied the same fate for the glorious House of Ahab as that which the Houses of Baasa and Jeroboam had suffered – then "he rent his garments, and he placed sackcloth upon his flesh, and he fasted and lay upon sackcloth, and he went about softly."

What emerges is that it is not only the actual submission of Ahab that is credited to him in God's speech to Elijah. The reason for it (the content of Elijah's second speech), too, is counted in his favor, lending depth to the significance of his mourning and his submission, and endowing it with a more elevated nature than simple fear of his own death.

The easing of the divine verdict is likewise suited to the punishment that had led to Ahab's submission: The cutting off of the House of Ahab is postponed until the days of his son (a period of seventeen years). But Ahab's personal punishment, for the murder of Naboth and the inheritance of his vineyard – the punishment that did not lead Ahab to submission – is not eased, since there is no repentance that can shield him from it.

Rashi summarizes by commenting on verse 29, on the words, "I shall not bring the evil in his days":

> I shall not bring the evil *on his household* in his days, but the decree of "the dogs will lick his blood" cannot come in the days of his son; it can only be at the end of his own life.

The story of Naboth's vineyard is a shocking one, but it does not end with the harsh words "I shall bring evil upon his household" (as the later division into chapters would have it), but rather, in accordance with the traditional division into *parashot*, with the words, "They dwelled three years with no war between Aram and Israel" (22:1).

These three years of quiet, with even Ahab's personal verdict being postponed, represent a further easing of the decree in addition to the postponement of the punishment to his household until the next generation. This is how Ḥazal and several of the commentators understand it. Ḥazal derive from this verse (Y. Sota, 3:1, 18): "There is some merit that serves to postpone Ahab's punishment for three years: 'They dwelled three years with no war between Aram and Israel.'"

Thus, with a spirit of submission in the face of the verdict, on one hand, and God's postponement of the punishment, on the other, the prophecy ends the secret encounter between the king and the prophet having achieved at least something partially positive.

Chapter 38

Conclusion: Structure of the Narrative

We have chosen to discuss the structure of the narrative specifically in this concluding chapter, since most of the elements that will guide us here are based on our analysis of the narrative in the preceding chapters.

We have mentioned on several occasions that this narrative is composed of two parts, of more or less equal length: The first covers sixteen verses (I Kings 21:1–16), while the second covers fourteen verses (21:17–22:1). Indeed, according to the traditional division of the text, too, the first half of the story is all included as one *parasha*, while the second half (v. 17) introduces a new *parasha*.

Another clear sign of this division is the particular title used to refer to Ahab at the beginning of each half. Ahab is mentioned fifteen times in this narrative by name, but only twice is his royal title added. At the beginning of the story we read:

> A vineyard belonged to Naboth the Jezreelite, which was in Jezreel, close to the palace of Ahab, king of Samaria. (v. 1)

Then, at the beginning of the second half, we find:

> And God's word came to Elijah the Tishbite, saying: Arise, go
> down to meet Ahab, king of Israel who is in Samaria; behold, he
> is in the vineyard of Naboth, where he has gone down, to take
> possession of it. (vv. 17–18)

The most striking difference between the two halves is that in the second, we encounter two characters who were absent from the first: God, and His emissary, Elijah. The second half begins (vv. 17–20) and also ends (vv. 28–29) with God's word to Elijah. As a result of God's first words to Elijah, the prophet appears before Ahab and conveys a harsh message in God's name, concerning Ahab's future and that of his dynasty (vv. 21–24). This message generates Ahab's submission (v. 27), which in turn gives rise to another divine message to Elijah.

What is the difference between the first and second half in terms of subject? The answer appears simple and clear: The first half describes Ahab's sin, while the second records God's response to that sin – the announcement of his punishment. It is for this reason that God, and Elijah, His prophet, are the central "characters" in this half.

But this answer fails to address fully the substance of either the first or the second half. Does the first half describe the murder of Naboth by Ahab? Actually – no. We have already seen that Ahab was not actively involved in either the murder or even its planning. Moreover, we have seen that the degree of Ahab's responsibility for the murder is gradually clarified over the course of the first half of the story; only at the end of that half does it reach its climax, when he is told of Naboth's death and he reacts with silence and, especially, when he goes to actualize the purpose of the murder, to take possession of Naboth's vineyard. Hence, the first half of the story is not a description of Ahab's sin in murdering Naboth, but rather a description of Ahab's descent from coveting someone else's possession, to silent acquiescence to the murder of that person, to actualizing the benefits of that act. Ahab is depicted in this half as a person undergoing a process of moral deterioration. In his original proposal to Naboth he commits a "light" sin, an almost imperceptible transgression of the command "You shall not covet" (Deut. 5:18). His next sin is his failure to come to terms with Naboth's refusal, followed by his acceptance of Jezebel's tempting promise, and concluding with the act of going down to take possession of the vineyard, which, as we have pointed out, demonstrates retroactively his complicity in the murder that was committed.

Nor is the second half of the story adequately summed up by the title proposed above – the announcement of Ahab's punishment. This title suits the first (main) part of this half – verses 17–24, and seemingly also 25–26. However, the final four verses deal with Ahab's reaction of submission before God upon hearing the announcement of his punishment, and God's message to Elijah concerning the postponement of that punishment until the days of Ahab's son. The "announcement of the punishment" is a title suited to a static issue that is external to Ahab, the main character of the narrative, whereas the second half of the story, like the first, actually describes a dynamic process. This process is expressed first and foremost in Ahab himself: The message concerning his punishment breaks him emotionally, and brings about his submission before God. However, it is expressed also in the announcement itself, which softens in light of Ahab's submission. Hence, it is not the announcement of punishment itself that is the subject of the second half, but rather the process of positive change that Ahab undergoes in the wake of his encounter with Elijah and the prophet's stern message, and the consequent easing of his punishment.

This dual transformation that takes place in the second half – a change both in Ahab and in his punishment – is not absolute. In a previous chapter we discussed the fact that Ahab's repentance is only partial; it lacks some central characteristics of complete repentance (such as confession). For this reason the punishment is not canceled outright, but rather is postponed until the days of his son.

Hence, it would be simplistic to sum up the relationship between the two halves of the story as sin and punishment; a relationship of cause and effect. Rather, the halves reflect two inverse processes that Ahab undergoes: His deterioration from transgressing a "light" prohibition to complicity in the most terrible of sins, murder, and his ascent from the depths of his sin to the level of a penitent (albeit not a wholehearted, complete one). These inverse processes represent the essence of our narrative.

The above description of the narrative would seem to call for a structure that molds these two opposing processes; with the two halves of our story placed in inverse symmetrical parallel. We have already encountered this common type of structure on several occasions in previous chapters.

The symmetrical structure of a biblical narrative often turns on a central axis, which serves as the focus of the plot. Where, in our narrative, do the two inverse processes cross one another? Where is the lowest point in Ahab's descent, representing the beginning of his ascent? This point would appear to be located in verse 16: "And it was, when Ahab heard that Naboth had died, that Ahab arose to go down to the vineyard of Naboth the Jezreelite to take possession of it."

From the point of view of the plot, this verse still belongs to the first half (indeed, it is the concluding verse of the traditional *parasha* that covers this half). However, if we try to expose the structure of the narrative as a whole, this verse should be regarded as the central axis. In this case, the central axis represents the lowest point in the story. It is located almost exactly in the middle of the narrative (this, too, characterizing many narratives of similar structure): There are fifteen verses that precede it, and fourteen that follow. We addressed the importance of this verse, as evidence of Ahab's hidden complicity in the act of murder, in chapter 32. There we discussed why Elijah is sent to bring God's word to Ahab specifically at that place – in Naboth's vineyard, and specifically at the time when Ahab goes there in order to take possession of it.

Can the two halves of the story be set in inverse symmetrical form around verse 16? The answer is yes, but with some reservation. We are able to point to some clear parallels between the two halves, but this is not the precise symmetrical structure that we see, for example, in chapter 19. The reason for this is that the literary nature of each of the two halves is very different. The first half has a narrative, descriptive nature, while the second is mostly a prophetic monologue.

Let us note the parallels, with a view to sketching the structure of the narrative as a whole.

1. Surrounding verse 16 (the central axis) and adjacent to it, we find two monologues: There is Jezebel's message to Ahab in verse 15, and

the beginning of God's message to Elijah in verses 17–18. We may summarize this schematically as follows:

> And it was, when Jezebel heard that Naboth had been stoned and had died, that Jezebel said to Ahab: *Arise, take possession of the vineyard of Naboth the Jezreelite…* for Naboth is not alive, but dead. (v. 15)

> (*Central Axis*) And it was, when Ahab heard that Naboth was dead, that Ahab *arose to go down* to the *vineyard of Naboth the Jezreelite, to take possession of it.* (v. 16)

> And God's word came to Elijah the Tishbite, saying: *Arise, go down* to meet Ahab, king of Israel who is in Samaria; behold, he is in *the vineyard of Naboth, where he has gone down to take possession of it.* (vv. 17–18)

The linguistic and substantial parallel between Jezebel's message to Ahab and God's message to Elijah is clear. Both speakers send the person to whom they are talking to the same place, and using the same command: Jezebel tells Ahab, "Arise, take possession," while God tells Elijah, "Arise, go down." Both utterances are linguistically and also substantially linked to the verse that stands in between them – the description of Ahab's act: Ahab, having been commanded by Jezebel, his wife, "*Arise, take possession* of the vineyard of Naboth the Jezreelite," executes the mission: "Ahab *arose* to go down to the vineyard of Naboth the Jezreelite *to take possession of it.*" Only one word (in the Hebrew) is added to the description of Ahab's act: *laredet* (to go down). This addition prepares us for the next parallel – between the description of Ahab's actions and God's word to Elijah. Corresponding to the description, "Ahab arose *to go down* to the vineyard of Naboth the Jezreelite, *to take possession of it,*" God tells Elijah, "Behold, [he is] in the vineyard of Naboth, to where he has *gone down, to take possession of it.*"

This dual connection between the description of Ahab's actions in the central axis and the respective utterances on each side of it, is not uniform in nature. The linguistic connection between Jezebel's words to Ahab and the description of Ahab's actions arises from the fact that Jezebel issues a command and Ahab dutifully carries it out; hence, it is altogether logical that the language of the execution echoes that of the command.

The connection between God's word to Elijah and the preceding description of Ahab's actions is seemingly technical: it arises from the need to indicate Ahab's location, so that Elijah will be able to find him. However, this is not sufficient reason for the parallel; if this were God's sole intention, it would suffice for Him to say, "Behold, he is in the vineyard of Naboth." What is the purpose of the words, "To where he has gone down, to take possession of it"? (Since it is these words that create the parallel to the description of Ahab's actions.) Not only Ahab's location, but also the timing, is important and worthy of noting in God's message. This is the exact time and place to catch Ahab absolutely red-handed, as it were, and thereby to expose his complicity and shared responsibility for the murder. Only at this specific time and place is it appropriate to address him with the question, "Have you murdered and also taken possession?" Hence the connection between the description of the criminal act and the command that Elijah receives to be present when and where the crime is being committed.

Now, let us return to the echoing parallel between Jezebel's words to Ahab, "Arise, take possession (*kum resh*)," and God's words to Elijah, "Arise, go down (*kum reid*)," and consider its significance. Clearly, the intention behind the inverse parallel here is to emphasize the sin and the response to it: The terrible instruction by Jezebel, and its acceptance by Ahab, are met with a divine response. Just as Jezebel's instruction is meant to pave the way for the completion of the act of murder by Ahab taking possession of the vineyard, so God's command to Elijah is meant to pave the way for the message of the punishment that will come later. This echoing similarity between the two commands heightens our awareness of "the eye that sees and the ear that hears" – the divine providence from which nothing is hidden, not even a secret conversation between a man and his wife.

2. As we move away from the central axis of the story, we encounter two units of different lengths, facing each other in the symmetrical structure that we have proposed:

False trial of Naboth and his stoning (Jezebel's instructions, their execution, and her report of this) (vv. 8–14)

(*Central Axis*)

Ahab's indictment for Naboth's murder and the announcement of his punishment; Ahab's reaction (vv. 19–20a)

Aside from the obvious difference in length between these two units (seven verses vs. two verses), they are also very different in terms of the characters active in each of them; in fact, they do not share a single common character. In the "trial" scene the characters involved are Jezebel, the elders of the city of Jezreel and its inhabitants, the two false witnesses, and Naboth. In the corresponding unit in the second half, the "characters" are God, Elijah, and Ahab, none of whom is mentioned in the "trial" scene. Even from a linguistic point of view, there is no indication of any link between these two units. Nevertheless, it is proper that they be placed facing one another. The parallel between them represents a continuation of the parallel that we saw in parallel 1.

Ahab's absence from the "trial" scene has been treated in chapter 32 above. We explained it as a deliberate absence that is not innocent. It is the result of an intentional association between Ahab, Jezebel, and the elders of Jezreel, allowing Ahab not to be party to the despicable deed and not to be informed of it. Ahab will merely benefit from the final result, without having to dirty his hands with this crime. However, as we noted, Ahab could have guessed how Jezebel would go about realizing her promise – and this he did. This becomes clear retroactively, when he goes down to take possession of Naboth's vineyard, having heard from Jezebel that Naboth is dead. His act can only be interpreted as the realization of a plan set out in advance to take possession of the assets of a man deliberately and wrongfully murdered as a traitor, such that his property goes to the king.

God's words to Elijah, conveyed to Ahab at the vineyard of Naboth when he goes there to take possession of it – "Have you then murdered and also taken possession?" – expose Ahab's true complicity in Naboth's trial and his death. The web of silence that all those involved wove in order to keep Ahab out of the "trial" and to keep his hands clean has achieved nothing in relation to God, who knows even that which has not been said. Just as God's command to Elijah, "Arise, go down," hints at the divine providence that listens to a conversation between a husband and wife that takes place in a closed room (as Jezebel tells Ahab, "Arise, take possession…"), so God's words to Ahab, "Have you then murdered and also taken possession?" are meant to expose the identity of the person who was truly responsible for the murder of Naboth, and to show that a person's schemes are of no value in the face of God who knows everything.

Thus far we have examined the parallel that indicates a connection between the concealment of the sinner in the first half of the story and his exposure in the corresponding scene in the second half. But God's words in verse 19 are clearly divided into two parts: "You shall speak to him, saying… And you shall speak to him, saying…" The first utterance exposes Ahab's guilt and his responsibility for the murder; the second declares his punishment: "So says the Lord: In the place where the dogs licked the blood of Naboth, the dogs will lick your blood, too."

The parallel between this utterance of God and the act of stoning Naboth requires no elaboration. The relationship between the sin and its punishment, measure for measure, is obvious.

3. Moving another step away from the central axis of the story, we find the following:

> The dialogue between Jezebel and Ahab, and Jezebel's promise to give Naboth's vineyard to Ahab (vv. 5–7)

> (*Central Axis*)

> Punishment of Ahab's house being cut off, and the punishment of Jezebel. Summary of Ahab's sins as an idolater (vv. 20b–26)

Here, too, the units are of different lengths (three verses vs. more than six), and once again it would appear, at first glance, that there is no connection between them. In the first half we read of a conversation between a husband and wife, which in itself seems unimportant. In the corresponding unit in the second half, we find the second part of God's message to Ahab, with a final accounting of all of his sins – especially the idolatry that he has spread throughout Israel (v. 22: "The anger to which you have provoked Me, by leading Israel to sin"), and the final verdict concerning the cutting off of Ahab's house from Israel. What is common to these two such different units, in terms of both subject and literary character?

The answer to this question is clear: Jezebel, wife of Ahab, is the link between these two corresponding units. Jezebel is introduced into our narrative for the first time in this narrative in verses 5–7. She appears for the first time in an innocent dialogue between a concerned wife and her husband, who lies dejected upon his bed. But as this conversation progresses, Jezebel is revealed in her familiar role as the person who incites Ahab to sin. Ahab, lying upon his bed, is far removed from the murderous plot against Naboth. He is tempted to agree to Jezebel's opaque suggestion, "I shall give you the vineyard of Naboth the Jezreelite," partly as a result of the scornful words that precede it: "Are you now ruler over Israel?"

While Jezebel's principal sin is described in the next scene, the "trial," in which she operates in an independent fashion, without any direct involvement by Ahab, it is her role as Ahab's wife, who incites him to commit terrible sins, that is addressed in the present scene.

The corresponding unit in the second half is the only one in this half that mentions Jezebel. It starts with the verdict against her: "To Jezebel, too, God spoke, saying: The dogs will devour Jezebel by the wall of Jezreel" (v. 23). She is mentioned once again, in the summary of Ahab's sins: "But there was none like Ahab who gave himself over to perform evil in the eyes of God, *to which he was incited by Jezebel, his wife*" (v. 25).

From the context it is clear that the text refers to Jezebel's incitement of Ahab to idolatry (in keeping with the rest of Elijah's second speech, which addresses this sin on the part of Ahab). The focus on the sin of idolatry stems from the fact that it is the murder of Naboth that finally seals the fate of Ahab and his household, and when this sin is addressed, Ahab's principal sin, that of idolatry, is considered at the same time. Jezebel is the link between the two abominations committed by Ahab – idolatry and murder. It is she who causes her husband to commit both of them.

There are two aspects to this parallel. One concerns Jezebel herself: Her incitement of Ahab, and her various endeavors leading to the murder of Naboth, although undertaken in secret, are revealed before God, and therefore even Jezebel herself will not escape the punishment that awaits the House of Ahab. Her end will be like that of her husband: Just as "the dogs will lick his blood," so they will consume her flesh. This is measure for measure, a punishment for her role in the murder of Naboth.

The other aspect concerns Ahab, and here the significance of the parallel is reversed. The unit that we are now addressing in the first half, describes Jezebel's decisive role in the process that brought about the murder of Naboth. This serves to lessen some of Ahab's guilt, since at the beginning of this stage Ahab is indeed innocent of any thoughts of murder; not for a moment does he entertain such a possibility. It is only after Jezebel incites him (with her scorn: "Are you then king of Israel?") that he finds himself acquiescing to her veiled plans ("I shall give you the vineyard of Naboth the Jezreelite"). This, then, is a mitigating factor for Ahab, who is not the instigator of the crime.

This point is highlighted, in an unusual way, in the concluding verses that sum up Ahab's rule: "But there was none like Ahab who gave himself over to perform evil in the eyes of God, *to which he was incited by Jezebel, his wife*" (v. 25).

The Jerusalem Talmud (Sanhedrin 10:1, 28b) records the following teaching of R. Levi, who addresses this verse:

> For six months, R. Levi interpreted this verse – "But there was none like Ahab who gave himself over to perform evil in the eyes of God" – to Ahab's discredit. Then Ahab came to him in a dream, and said: How have I sinned toward you? What wrong have I caused you? You are looking only at the beginning of the verse, and not at the end – "To which he was incited by Jezebel, his wife." Then for six months R. Levi took a more charitable view toward Ahab: "But there was none like Ahab... to which he was incited by Jezebel, his wife."

The significance of this parallel is the first sign, within the structure of the narrative, of the two opposite processes that Ahab undergoes, and which we have addressed above. The symmetrical structure of the story is what creates the parallel between similar stages of inverse processes. In the next two corresponding pairs, this phenomenon continues.

4. The next pair of corresponding units comprises the descriptions of Ahab's two reactions. In the first half, there is his reaction to Naboth's refusal to sell his vineyard; in the second half, his reaction to hearing God's dual message from Elijah:

> Ahab came to his house sullen and angry *for the thing that Naboth had spoken to him....* And *he lay* upon his bed and turned away his face, *and would not eat bread.* (v. 4)

> (*Central Axis*)

> And it was, *when Ahab heard these words,* that he rent his garments and placed sackcloth upon his flesh, *and he fasted, and he lay* upon sackcloth, and he went about softly. (v. 27)

Here the parallel is clear: both units describe similar behavior on the part of Ahab as a result of "bad news" that he has heard.

However, this parallel also serves to illustrate the inversion that takes place between the first half and the second in terms of the description of Ahab. In the first half, Ahab's tortured reaction to Naboth's refusal to part with his vineyard represents a stage in Ahab's moral descent, which deteriorates from transgressing the command "You shall not covet" to complicity in the sin of "You shall not murder." It is his original pining that leads Jezebel to intervene "for his benefit." By contrast, in the second half, Ahab's fasting and his other customs of mourning represent an ascent from the depths of his sin, to become a penitent who submits before God.

Attention should be paid to the fact that Ahab's expressions of sorrow are more intensive at the end of the story than they are in the beginning: Upon hearing God's word from Elijah he casts himself into real mourning; tearing his clothes and wearing sackcloth on his flesh. The point of similarity between the two reactions – refraining from eating – is also described in more extreme terms in the second half: as opposed to "and did not eat bread," we are told that after hearing Elijah's message he actually fasted. This tells us that committing the sin did not ultimately ease Ahab's psychological state, his depression; on the contrary, it exacerbated it. The sin had missed its aim. The illusion that once he attained the vineyard that he had so coveted all would be well, burst in the face of the bitter reality: Here he was, at the moment when he should have been full of joy, sunk in even greater mourning and depression.

5. What remains is to compare the three verses at the beginning of the story (1–3), describing Ahab's request of Naboth to give him his vineyard for a fair price, and Naboth's categorical refusal, with the three verses at the end of the story (21:28–22:1) in which God tells Elijah that the punishment of the House of Ahab will be delayed until the days of Ahab's son, and in which the text records three years of quiet that prevail between Aram and Israel.

It is difficult to detect any linguistic or thematic connection between these two units. Nevertheless, we may say that a reading of the first verses of the chapter give rise to a mental image of Ahab as a generous man, who offers his neighbor a substantiated and fair offer, not in any way exploiting his status as king to coerce Naboth. It is difficult for the reader to imagine, at this stage of the story, the way in which Ahab is going to descend from this innocent request to what actually happens in the end. In truth, had it not been for the intervention of Jezebel ("who incited him"), it would not have happened.

A reading of the closing verses likewise depicts a positive character who, having understood the significance of his actions and the punishment to which they have led him, breaks down and submits to his God, and is indeed granted something of a reprieve. In this sense the beginning of the story and its conclusion are similar. Between the beginning and the end, both of which are at the same level of morality, Ahab undergoes two opposite processes: One of descent to the lowest possible level; the other, of ascent from that lowest point to the positive position that he attains at the end.

THE STRUCTURE OF THE NARRATIVE

First Half: Ahab's Descent **Second Half: Ahab's Ascent**

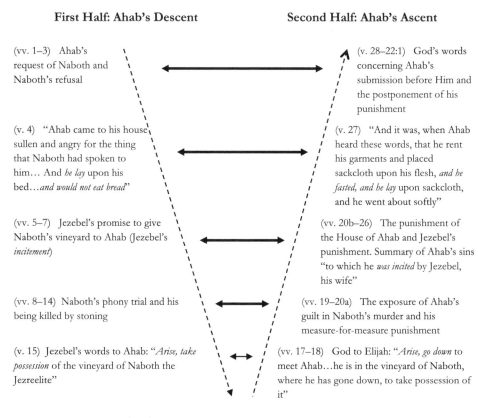

(vv. 1–3) Ahab's request of Naboth and Naboth's refusal

(v. 28–22:1) God's words concerning Ahab's submission before Him and the postponement of his punishment

(v. 4) "Ahab came to his house, sullen and angry for the thing that Naboth had spoken to him… And *he lay* upon his bed…*and would not eat bread*"

(v. 27) "And it was, when Ahab heard these words, that he rent his garments and placed sackcloth upon his flesh, *and he fasted, and he lay* upon sackcloth, and he went about softly"

(vv. 5–7) Jezebel's promise to give Naboth's vineyard to Ahab (Jezebel's *incitement*)

(vv. 20b–26) The punishment of the House of Ahab and Jezebel's punishment. Summary of Ahab's sins "to which he *was incited* by Jezebel, his wife"

(vv. 8–14) Naboth's phony trial and his being killed by stoning

(vv. 19–20a) The exposure of Ahab's guilt in Naboth's murder and his measure-for-measure punishment

(v. 15) Jezebel's words to Ahab: "*Arise, take possession* of the vineyard of Naboth the Jezreelite"

(vv. 17–18) God to Elijah: "*Arise, go down* to meet Ahab…he is in the vineyard of Naboth, where he has gone down, to take possession of it"

(v. 16) "And it was, when Ahab heard that Naboth was dead, that Ahab arose to go down to the vineyard of Naboth the Jezreelite, to take possession of it"

Ahaziah

הַמִבְּלִי אֵין אֱלֹהִים בְּיִשְׂרָאֵל?

Is it because there is no God in Israel?

II Kings 1:3

Chapter 39

Ahaziah Son of Ahab: Overview

T he reign of Ahaziah son of Ahab is described in the text over the course of twenty-one verses, from I Kings 22:52 until II Kings 1:18. The first four verses of this description (I Kings 22:52 – II Kings 1:1), as well as the last verse (II Kings 1:18) present a general evaluation of his reign, while the intermediate verses (II Kings 1:2–27) represent the boundaries of the sixteen-verse narrative that will be the subject of the next few chapters. The story starts with Ahaziah's fall, leading to his illness, and it ends with his death from this illness "according to God's word that Elijah spoke."

There are two aspects to this narrative: On one hand, it is another chapter in the history of Ahab's household and its decline; on the other hand, this is one of the Elijah narratives, including the last record of Elijah's prophetic activities prior to his ascent in a storm to the heavens (in the following chapter). The history of Ahab's household is not the focus of the next chapters, and therefore we shall present here a brief overview of Ahaziah son of Ahab.

Ahaziah's reign was a short and bitter one: He reigned for less than two years (see I Kings 22:52 and II Kings 3:1), and this period was characterized by a rapid decline of the House of Ahab. Ahaziah rose to power after Ahab, his father, was killed in the war of Ramot Gilead, a battle that was altogether futile (I Kings 22:35–40).

Although most of what the Tanakh has to say about Ahaziah is to be found within our narrative, a few additional details about him, as well as a general evaluation of him, lie outside its boundaries.

The decline of the House of Ahab during the days of Ahaziah is apparent on two levels. Firstly, there are the sins of Ahaziah, which are more serious than the sins of his fathers; and secondly, there are the punishments that befall him and the Kingdom of Israel, which show signs of the disintegration of Ahab's royal dynasty.

Ahaziah is described as a loyal successor of both of his parents:

> He performed evil in the eyes of God and walked in the way of his father and in the way of his mother.... And he served Baal and worshipped it, and angered the Lord God of Israel, like all that his father had done. (I Kings 22:53–54)

Our narrative begins with a stark illustration of Ahaziah's idolatry:

> And Ahaziah fell through the lattice in his upper chamber that was in Samaria, and he fell ill, and he sent messengers and said to them: Go, inquire of Baal-Zebub, the god of Ekron, whether I will live through this illness. (II Kings 1:2)

Ahab, Ahaziah's father, is accused more than once of leading Israel astray after idolatry, but never is he mentioned as personally serving idols. This grave sin of Ahaziah, which also represents a terrible desecration of the name of God – "Is it because there is no God in Israel...?" (II Kings 1:3, 6, 16) – is what seals Ahaziah's fate to die of his illness such a short time after assuming the throne.

Even prior to his illness, Ahaziah fails in other areas of royal leadership. His partnership with Jehoshaphat, king of Judah, in building a fleet of merchant ships in Etzion Geber does not work out as he had hoped (I Kings 22:49–50; II Chr. 20:37); and Moab, which was under Israelite rule, rebels against Israel after the death of Ahab (II Kings 1:1).

Ahaziah's fall through the lattice in the upper chamber of his palace, and his ensuing illness, are perceived by the commentators as a punishment. However, not only does this punishment not cause him to repent; he goes on to sin even more gravely – both by sending messengers to inquire of Baal-Zebub, the god of Ekron, and in his violent confrontation with Elijah, as recounted in the first chapter of II Kings.

Ahaziah's death represents the speedy realization of God's word to Elijah: "He died according to God's word that Elijah spoke" (II Kings 1:17).

One further detail in this verse associated with his death awards his punishment even more serious significance: "And Jehoram [Ahaziah's brother] reigned in his stead ... for he had no son."

Chapter 40

Ahaziah's Messengers: King vs. Prophet

Elijah is the main character in our narrative, appearing throughout II Kings 1:1–18. Elijah already has experience in standing before a king of Israel and conveying harsh messages. This is what he has done since his very first appearance in Tanakh, when he swore before Ahab that there would be no rain (I Kings 17:1), as well as in his meeting with him close to Samaria in the third year of the drought (18:18), and in his encounter with him at the vineyard of Naboth (21:17–24). Still, in our narrative the hostility between Elijah and the king of Israel reaches its climax. Not only does God's word, which Elijah bears, not succeed in softening the sinful king (as happened in the case of Ahaziah's father, Ahab, in the vineyard of Naboth); it even brings the king to attempt violence against the prophet. This time, Elijah does not withdraw from the imminent hostility against the king, as he did twice in the past (following his oath in front of Ahab, 17:3ff., and after Jezebel's threat against him, 19:4). He is ready to do battle against the king and his messengers, until God's word prevails.

The clash between Ahaziah and Elijah in our chapter is unique in that it takes place through Ahaziah's various messengers, who have the misfortune to find themselves on the battlefield between the king and the prophet. A description of the negotiations between Ahaziah's messengers and Elijah takes up most of the narrative in our chapter, both quantitatively (vv. 3–14, twelve verses out of a total of sixteen), and in terms of dramatic quality. On the other hand, the description of the meeting between Elijah and Ahaziah, at the end of the story, occupies only one verse, adding nothing new.

Two types of messengers sent by Ahaziah are active during the course of the narrative in relation to Elijah. In verses 2–8 there are Ahaziah's messengers who are sent to inquire of Baal-Zebub, the god of Ekron; Elijah stops them along the way and sends them back to Ahaziah. In verses 9–17 we find the captains of fifty with their fifty men, who are sent to Elijah himself. We may divide the narrative into two parts based on this division.

The centrality of the concept of "sending" in our narrative is highlighted by means of a key word that is repeated throughout. The root *shin-lamed-ḥet* (to send, dispatch) appears a total of seven times in this story (never as *shelihim*, a noun; the messengers sent by Ahaziah are referred to as *malakhim* in the first part of the story, and "captains of fifty" in the second part):

1. Ahaziah fell…and he fell ill; and he *sent* messengers and said to them. (v. 2)
2. And he said to us: Go, return to the king who *sent* you…
3. Is it because there is no God in Israel that you *send* to inquire of Baal-Zebub? (v. 6)
4. He *sent* to him a captain of fifty, and his fifty. (v. 9)
5. And again he *sent* to him another captain of fifty, and his fifty. (v. 11)
6. And again he *sent* a third captain of fifty, and his fifty. (v. 13)
7. Since you *sent* messengers to inquire of Baal-Zebub. (v. 16)

In all seven cases, Ahaziah is the "sender," and in each instance the act of sending is a sin. In the first three instances, as well as in the seventh, the "sending" in question involves sending messengers to inquire of Baal-Zebub: There is the sinful act itself (no. 1); and the rebuke and promise of punishment (nos. 2, 3, 7). After Elijah manages to halt this delegation and send the messengers back to Ahaziah, along with his prophecy of punishment, the king tries three times to send soldiers to attack the prophet (nos. 4, 5, 6). Following the failure of these attempts, Elijah once again conveys to Ahaziah – this time directly, with no intermediary – the prophecy of punishment for his first "sending" (no. 7).

Ahaziah's various messengers react in different ways to the challenge that faces them, requiring them to choose between the mortal, formal authority of their king and the authority of the man sent by God. The decisions of the messengers, and the reactions of Elijah to their decisions, represent the essence of the story, and these will be the focus of the coming chapters.

Chapter 41

Ahaziah's Messengers: "Go, Inquire" vs. "Go, Return" (II Kings 1:2–6)

Ahaziah fell through the lattice in his upper chamber that was in Samaria, and became sick. And he sent messengers, and said to them: Go, inquire of Baal-Zebub, the god of Ekron, whether I shall live through this illness. Then an angel of God said to Elijah, the Tishbite: Arise, go up to meet the messengers of the king of Samaria, and speak to them: Is it because there is no God in Israel, that you go to inquire of Baal-Zebub, god of Ekron? Therefore, so says the Lord: The bed to which you have gone up – you shall not come down from it, but you shall surely die. And Elijah departed. (vv. 2–4)

Why was Elijah not sent directly to Ahaziah? Why does God's angel command him to speak only with Ahaziah's messengers? We may suggest several possible reasons:

1. Perhaps God does not want Elijah to appear before Ahaziah himself because he is such a wicked king, and because there is no hope of him repenting in the wake of such an encounter.

2. A venture into Samaria could well endanger Elijah's life. Ahaziah, who is even more wicked than Ahab and, more significantly, his mother, Jezebel, may kill him. Jezebel's threat (I Kings 19:2) is still valid, and she still holds power in her son's kingdom. Since God's word can be conveyed via Ahaziah's messengers, there is no need to create a situation in which Elijah will later require a miraculous rescue.

3. The king's sin is expressed in practice by the journeying of his messengers to the Philistine city of Ekron. Elijah's confrontation with them along the way therefore represents catching Ahaziah "in the act" of sinning. It is reminiscent of Elijah's encounter with Ahab in Naboth's vineyard when Ahab went down to take possession of it.

4. Were Elijah to be sent to Ahaziah himself, the messengers would continue on their mission, eventually arriving in the foreign city. The resulting desecration of God's name would be public knowledge: "Is it because there is no God in Israel?"

5. The mission entrusted to Elijah concerns not only the notice of punishment that will be conveyed to Ahaziah, but also the rebuke that he delivers to the messengers, leading them to repent for having served as "messengers for a sinful matter."

The final reason listed above relates to a central theme of the narrative: Elijah presents Ahaziah's messengers with the need to choose between obeying the king's demand that they carry out his sinful mission, and their obligation to obey God's word, which is revealed to them via Elijah. God's word is not only an exposure of the severity of the act to which they are lending their hand, by going to Ekron, and a demand that they desist, but also much more: God demands of them that they become Elijah's messengers to Ahaziah, conveying to their king Elijah's announcement of his punishment, in the name of the Lord God of Israel.

When Elijah addresses them, Ahaziah's messengers represent the fulfillment of the prophetic words:

I answered those who did not ask Me; I was found by those who did not seek Me. I said, "Here I am, here I am" to a nation that was not called by My name. I have spread My hands all day toward a wayward nation that walks in a way that is not good, after their own thoughts. (Is. 65:1–2)

> So the messengers returned to him, and he said to them: Why have you returned? Then they said to him: A man came up to meet us, and he said to us: Go, return to the king who sent you, and say to him: So says the Lord: Is it because there is no king in Israel, that you send to inquire of Baal-Zebub, god of Ekron?! Therefore, the bed to which you have gone up – you shall not come down from it, but you shall surely die. (II Kings 1: 5–6)

In acceding to Elijah's demand that they convey his own message to the king, the messengers transfer their allegiance from one side of the conflict to the other. By doing so, they clearly endanger themselves, since Ahaziah could punish them for "betraying" him. In the next chapter, we shall see how the messengers managed to fulfill Elijah's mission without arousing the king's anger at them.

Let us now compare the words of God's angel to Elijah (vv. 3–4), which are also the words that Elijah conveys to the messengers, with how the messengers convey them to Ahaziah upon their return. This comparison serves to support our contention that one of Elijah's aims is to cause the messengers themselves to engage in repentance and to make them into his own emissaries, who place themselves at the disposal of God's word.

Angel's message to Elijah (vv. 3–4)	Messengers' words to Ahaziah (v. 6)
Arise, go up to meet the messengers of the king of Samaria, and speak to them:	Go, return to the king who sent you, and say to him:
	So says the Lord:
Is it because there is no God in Israel *that you go* to inquire of Baal-Zebub, god of Ekron?	Is it because there is no king in Israel *that you send* to inquire of Baal-Zebub, god of Ekron?
Therefore,	Therefore,
so says the Lord:	
You shall not come down…but you shall surely die.	You shall not come down…but you shall surely die.

449

Aside from the command to the messengers, "Go, return to the king..." (which is not found in the angel's words to Elijah, but which is implied in them) there are two changes in the message which the messengers pass on to Ahaziah, in relation to Elijah's words. The first is that they include the formula, "So says the Lord," before the rebuke, while in Elijah's words they come later, preceding the punishment. The second is that instead of Elijah's, "That you go," they say, "That you send." These two changes are interrelated, and their reason will be discussed below.

Elijah's message to the messengers (in accordance with the angel's words to him) may be divided into two parts. At first, Elijah addresses the messengers themselves: "Is it because there is no God in Israel that you go to inquire of Baal-Zebub, god of Ekron?" (v. 3). Thereafter, he addresses Ahaziah, in the second person (through the messengers): "Therefore, so says the Lord: The bed to which *you* have gone up – *you* shall not come down from it, but you shall surely die" (v. 4).

Clearly, then, the first part of Elijah's speech is meant as a rebuke to the messengers, aimed at causing them to desist from their journey. As Malbim comments on verse 3:

> "Arise, go up to meet the messengers of the king of Samaria": He commanded him, firstly, that he should not go to the king, but only to meet the messengers; and also that he should rebuke them for their journey.

Obviously, the significance of the messengers' return to Ahaziah is, as Malbim comments: "They listened to the prophet's rebuke."

In the conflict between the order of their king, "Go, inquire of Baal-Zebub, god of Ekron," and the contradictory order of the prophet, "Go, return to the king who sent you," the prophet's order prevails. By returning, they not only violate the king's order, but actually serve as messengers of the prophet – an enemy of the royal house and loathed by Ahaziah and by Jezebel, his mother – to announce to the king that he will die as punishment for sending them to inquire of Baal-Zebub.

The prophet achieves this through his harsh criticism of the messengers: "Is it because there is no God in Israel that *you go to inquire*?"

However, they, in speaking to Ahaziah, replace the words, "you go" with "you send," thereby making the king the object of the rebuke: "Is it because … that *you send to inquire* of Baal-Zebub?"

The messengers altered the message because, with regard to Ahaziah, there was no significance to the sin of his messengers in agreeing to carry out his mission. On the contrary, they were obliged to emphasize the king's responsibility for having sent them.

Are the messengers entitled to alter the message in this way? The answer would appear to be yes, since the change is assumed and hinted at already in Elijah's words to them. Had Elijah's intention, in his first words, been merely to rebuke the messengers for their sinful expedition, it would be difficult to understand the connection between the rebuke to them at the beginning of his speech and the message to Ahaziah at its end: "Therefore, so says the Lord: You shall not come down. …" This link, created by means of the word "therefore," turns the first clause into the cause, and the second into the result. This can be understood only by explaining the rebuke in the first clause as being directed toward Ahaziah, too, and not only toward the messengers. In other words, "Is it because there is no God that you go, *at the behest of your king*, to inquire of Baal-Zebub? Therefore, since you, Ahaziah, sent them, you shall not come down. …"

This amendment by the messengers (which they appear to have made at their own initiative) leads in turn to another change. In Elijah's words we find the formula, "So says the Lord," prior to the result: "Therefore, so says the Lord: you shall not descend. …" The messengers, however, bring it forward, such that it rings out as an introduction to the rebuke: "So says the Lord: Is it because there is no God. …" The reason for this change is that the messengers seek to emphasize that their whole speech, both the rebuke and the punishment, is a prophetic message, delivered in God's name. This is in contrast to Elijah's words, "So says the Lord," which appear in the middle, so as to separate between the rebuke to the messengers and the message to Ahaziah himself. But when the entire prophecy becomes one intended for Ahaziah, there is no reason to postpone these words; it is altogether fitting to introduce the prophecy with them.

Confirmation that the changes made by the messengers are appropriate is to be found further on in the narrative, in Elijah's own words to Ahaziah, in which the same changes are repeated for the same reason:

> He said to him: *So says the Lord* – Since *you sent* messengers to inquire of Baal-Zebub, god of Ekron (is there then no God in Israel of whom to inquire?), therefore the bed to which you have gone up – you shall not come down from it, but you shall surely die. (v. 16)

We conclude that Ahaziah's messengers not only listened to the prophet's rebuke, by refraining from fulfilling the mission entrusted to them by their king, but also undertook a new and opposing mission, given to them by Elijah, which they carried out faithfully and with insight. The sign of a faithful and conscientious messenger is that he does not suffice with a mechanical fulfillment of his mission, but executes it throughout the changing circumstances in accordance with the aim of his dispatcher. This ideal is reflected in the messengers and the changes that they introduce into Elijah's words. In fact, their message anticipates the prophecy that Elijah is destined to declare before Ahaziah.

The transformation that takes place in the messengers of Ahaziah, whereby they become messengers of Elijah, is expressed in the story by means of the opposing roots *heh-lamed-khaf* (to go) and *shin-vav-bet* (to return), which function in verses 2–6 as a key inverse pair. These two opposite roots occur in close succession, a total of seven times, and then do not appear again in the story:

1. Go (*lekhu*), inquire of Baal-Zebub (v. 2)
2. Is it because there is no God…that you go (*holkhim*) to inquire (v. 3)
3. and Elijah departed (*vayelekh*) (v. 4)
4. The messengers returned (*vayashuvu*) to him
5. and he said to them: Why have you returned (*shavtem*)? (v. 5)
6–7. A man came up to meet us and he said to us, "Go, return (*lekhu shuvu*) to the king" (v. 6)

The verses speak of three "goings": Ahaziah's messengers "go" to inquire of Baal-Zebub (no. 1 – at the king's order, no. 2 – in Elijah's rebuke); then Elijah "goes" at the command of God's angel, aimed at halting the messengers' "going" and at sending them back to the king (no. 3); and finally, the messengers' "going" in the opposite direction at Elijah's command, so as to fulfill the mission entrusted to them by the prophet (no. 6). The messengers' "return" to Ahaziah and his surprise at their "return" (nos. 4–5) ultimately represents their acquiescence to the prophet's command, "Go, return" (no. 7). Thus, a sinful "going" is transformed into a journey of "return" – *teshuva*, repentance.

Chapter 42

"A Hairy Man with a Girdle of Leather About His Loins" (II Kings 1:7–8)

> And he said to them: What sort of man was he who came up to meet you and told you these things? So they said to him: A hairy man with a girdle of leather about his loins. And he said: He is Elijah the Tishbite. (vv. 7–8)

This dialogue, conducted between Ahaziah and his messengers, has dual significance: It guides us toward a proper understanding of the messengers' act in deciding to return to the king and fulfill Elijah's mission, and it also helps us understand Ahaziah's motives in questioning his messengers.

In the previous chapter we addressed the praiseworthy decision of the messengers, who became emissaries of Elijah and conveyed his message to their sinful king. But one could argue with this positive view of the messengers by asking whether they had any idea that it was Elijah who was rebuking them for their journey, and that it was he who was demanding that they become his emissaries on their return journey to their king. It is clear that they were not familiar with him at all! In verse 6 they report back to Ahaziah saying, "A man came up to meet us." Then they give a description of his external appearance: "A hairy man with a girdle of leather about his loins." When Ahaziah immediately identifies him, on the basis of this description – "He is Elijah the Tishbite," we understand that the messengers did not recognize him.

In truth, even if they did not know him, it was clear to them that this "man" was a prophet of God, both because of the content of his message (a prophecy in God's name) and because of his external appearance, which apparently was typical of prophets. (Some commentators understand the expression "a hairy man" as meaning that he wore a mantle of hair, which was characteristic of prophets, as explained in Zechariah 13:4. Alternatively, the expression may be understood as meaning that he had long hair, which would certainly hint to the fact that Elijah was a *nazir*, as many other prophets probably were; see Amos 2:11). But the fact that they failed to recognize him is most surprising, as Radak notes (commenting on v. 8): "This is surprising: How could the messengers of the king of Israel not recognize him? Did he not regularly appear before Ahab, and in Samaria?"

This question leads us to conclude that the messengers certainly did recognize the man in front of them as Elijah the prophet. Even if they had never met him or seen him in person, they would certainly have heard about him and could have identified him by his powerful presence and by the prominent signs which they used to describe him to Ahaziah. However, they also knew that mentioning the name of Elijah would arouse their king's anger, since he was the prophet's archenemy, and they might be endangering their lives by revealing that they had obeyed Elijah and become his emissaries vis-à-vis Ahaziah. Therefore, they pretend ignorance and report to the king as though they have no idea who Elijah is. They have returned speedily, as it were, since there is no longer any need for them to continue all the way to Ekron. Their king's question – "Will I live through this illness?" – has already received an answer: "You will surely die." What difference does it make to the king whether he receives this answer from a "local man of God" or from the Philistine oracle? After all, Elijah did demand of Ahaziah's messengers that they fulfill his mission, but he did not require of them to give up their lives or to endanger themselves unnecessarily. Hence, they had the sense to convey God's message to the king without arousing his anger against themselves. But in this play of innocence, they take care to ensure that Ahaziah himself concludes that the man who spoke to them – and through them, to him – "He is Elijah the Tishbite."

Let us now clarify the significance of this dialogue from the point of view of Ahaziah's intentions in questioning his messengers. Why is it so important to Ahaziah to know "What sort of man was he" who sent him a message via his own messengers? What does he gain from a description of the man, and why does he think that he will be able to identify him based on his messengers' description?

It seems likely that Ahaziah was not familiar with all of the prophets who were active in Israel at the time. However, he certainly knew the most prominent among them, the main prophet of the generation, Elijah. His heart told him that this prophet, who had hounded his father, Ahab, on several occasions, and who had been persecuted by Jezebel, his mother, was the same one who had revealed himself to the messengers and sent the prophecy of destruction. This prophet was already known for his manner of catching the king "red-handed," as it were, rebuking him with a piercing rhetorical question, and ending off his rebuke with a prediction of terrible punishment. This is what Elijah had done to his father, Ahab, at Naboth's vineyard, at the exact time when Ahab had gone down to take possession of it: "Have you then murdered and also taken possession? In the place where the dogs licked the blood of Naboth, the dogs will lick your blood, too" (I Kings 21:19).

Here, too, the same man of God appears to meet Ahaziah's messengers just as they make their way to inquire of Baal-Zebub. He sends, through them, his rebuke in the form of a rhetorical question ("Is it for lack of…that you send to inquire…?") and the imminent punishment ("Therefore…").

It is with great and barely concealed anxiety, then, that Ahaziah directs his question toward his messengers: "What sort of man was it?" In response he hears an exact description of the characteristic signs of Elijah. What he suspected has turned out to be the truth: "He is Elijah the Tishbite!"

It is with these dramatic words that the first part of the narrative ends. This dialogue between Ahaziah and his messengers lays the foundation for the second part of the story, where it becomes clear that Ahaziah's questioning is intended not only to confirm his suspicions, but also for a practical purpose: To try to lay his hand on the prophet in hiding, who so embitters the lives of the royal family.

Chapter 43

The Consumption by Fire of the Two Captains of Fifty and Their Fifty Men (II Kings 1:9–12)

In his commentary, *Marot HaTzovot*, Rabbi Moses Alsheikh raises the principal question in relation to the second part of our narrative with the following words:

> Attention should be paid: What was the sin of these two captains of fifty, and their respective companies of fifty men, whom Elijah consumed with fire? They were merely emissaries, having been commanded by their king to declare their message!

In the chapters devoted to "The Drought" and "Horeb," we noted that the Sages, in the Talmud and in the midrashim, do not hesitate to express criticism of Elijah and his actions. In our chapter, however, we do not find among their comments any hint of such criticism. This is explained by the fact that the Sages do not criticize Elijah based on their subjective feelings, but rather on veiled criticism concealed in the text itself. In other words, they regard part of the Elijah narratives as having been recorded with the intention of criticizing his actions, and they decode these textual hints in their midrashim.

Such criticism, both on the level of the text itself and in its interpretation by the Sages, is possible only in a case where Elijah operates on his own initiative, as in his oath concerning the cessation of rain, in chapter 17, or his journey to the desert in chapter 19. But wherever Elijah acts in accordance with a divine command as, for example, in the story of the vineyard of Naboth, there is clearly no room for any criticism.

What is the nature of Elijah's actions in our narrative? Elijah is guided by an angel of God both at the beginning of the story, when he is instructed to interfere with Ahaziah's delegation dispatched to inquire of Baal-Zebub, god of Ekron, and also at its end, where he is commanded to descend from the mountain together with Ahaziah's third captain of fifty. In the two middle units, the burning of the two captains of fifty together with their men, representing the subject of our present discussion, Elijah acts on his own. He himself decrees the descent of fire from the heavens, and God immediately responds, with no hint of any tension or criticism. We return, then, to the question of the commentators, formulated this time in the words of Rabbi Yitzḥak Arama in his commentary *Akeidat Yitzḥak*:

> What capital offense did these first (two) captains of fifty and their respective fifty men do to him...such that he cast the fire of his anger among them, to consume them?

MISSION OF THE TWO CAPTAINS OF FIFTY WITH THEIR MEN: RATIONALE

After Ahaziah correctly identifies the "hairy man with a girdle of leather about his loins," we are told: "He sent to him a captain of fifty with his fifty" (v. 9).

Why does he send them? This question is of great significance for a clarification of the main problem set forth above. Ralbag proposes a surprising explanation as to the purpose of this dispatch: "This means to say that he sent to Elijah, to honor him and summon him, an important captain who would have fifty men walking before him, and those fifty men went with him."

In his opinion, the king sent an honorary delegation to ask Elijah to come to the king. Elijah's honor is expressed in the status of the captain who is sent to him. This is a captain of such importance that fifty men usually walk before him, and they do so now, too.

But this is a very problematic interpretation. Our text speaks of a "captain of fifty, with his fifty" – meaning, a captain who commands a unit of soldiers numbering fifty men. Thus, the captain is not of such important rank after all, and the purpose of sending him to Elijah cannot be to honor the prophet. We therefore return to our question: Why is a commander sent together with a platoon of soldiers to Elijah?

Clearly, the platoon of soldiers, with their commander, is dispatched with a view to violent "military" action. These fifty men are apparently entrusted with the task of seizing Elijah at any price. Such a great number of soldiers sent to confront a single man must be meant to prevent any possibility of disappearance on the part of the prophet, who is known for his ability to disappear and elude his pursuers.

The approach that views the captains of fifty and their men as being sent in order to force Elijah to come down to them is accepted among certain commentators. But why would Ahaziah want to capture Elijah? We may suggest three possible reasons:

1. Ahaziah wants to force Elijah to appear before him and to declare his prophecy directly, rather than through the agency of messengers.
2. Ahaziah wants to punish Elijah for the prophecy of punishment that he has conveyed to him, and for preventing his messengers from carrying out their mission.
3. Ahaziah wants to kill Elijah for the above reasons, and perhaps also as a continuation of the policy of Jezebel, his mother, who swore to have him put to death (I Kings 19:2) and who was still capable of doing so (see II Kings 9:30–31).

We shall now attempt to decide which of these possibilities seems the most likely.

THE "INNOCENT" POSSIBILITY AND ITS DIFFICULTIES

Of the three possible reasons why Ahaziah would want to seize Elijah, as enumerated above, there are some commentators who appear to support the first reason, even if they do not state this explicitly. This unquestionably represents the view of Ralbag, who maintains that Ahaziah "sent to Elijah, to honor him and summon him, an important captain." Why was he "sending" for Elijah? It could not have been to punish him, as if that had been the case, he would not have given such honor to the prophet. Apparently, what Ralbag means is that Ahaziah called for Elijah to clarify the prophecy that had been conveyed to him secondhand. Abrabanel elaborates in the same direction:

> Ahaziah sent a captain of fifty to Elijah, and commanded them to bring him forcibly, if he would not be willing to come to Samaria, for the king knew that on account of Jezebel, his mother, he had not been there for a long time.
>
> Then the captain of the fifty says to him, "Man of God – the king has spoken; come down!" He does not say, "The king has said that you should go to see him, for he is ill and bedridden," but rather, "The king has spoken; come down"; come down from the top of the mountain, for he does not wish for you to sit there in isolation.
>
> When Elijah saw that the captain of the fifty was preparing his men to bring him down by force, with wrath and anger, he said: "And if I am a man of God – as you have said – then I am not subordinate to the king, nor am I under his control, for I am a servant of God. But if the matter is as I say, a fire of God will emerge from the heavens and consume you and your fifty, so that you will know that there is a God who judges the earth."
>
> When yet another captain of fifty comes, adding insult to injury by ordering, "So says the king: Come down quickly!" with malice and arrogance, he replies as he replied to the first, and they are all burned there.
>
> Elijah chooses to bring fire down upon them and to burn them, just as he brought down fire from the heavens at Mount Carmel before the eyes of Ahab and all of his servants. And now

that they had seen this divine miracle with their own eyes and still did not fear him, but instead came to him with malice and arrogance, their punishment was to be burnt with fire, for "Anyone who approaches the Sanctuary of God will be put to death," and the prophet was God's Sanctuary.

However, this explanation raises several difficulties:

1. Why would Ahaziah want Elijah to appear before him? Was it not enough that he had received the message in Elijah's name via the messengers?
2. Why did they decide to act violently against Elijah, rather than bring him with honor and dignity? Even if he could be brought with force, they would not be able to force him to speak!
3. The captains of fifty give no hint that the purpose of their mission is to bring Elijah to Ahaziah in order to state his prophecy in front of the king.
4. From the perspective of this interpretation, the grave punishment of burning which Elijah decrees for the captains of fifty and for their men, makes no sense. If their sin was merely committing an affront to Elijah's dignity, the prophet could forgo his honor, go along with them, and convey God's word to Ahaziah, as he eventually does anyway.
5. Abrabanel adds the following to his words above:

> There is no doubt that Elijah thought that Ahaziah meant to kill him, and therefore he sought to avenge his own death and to burn the captains of the forces so that Ahaziah would fear him and not harm him. It was his intention to do this to anyone who would come to him.

Abrabanel seems to be saying that while Elijah "thought" that Ahaziah meant to kill him, this was not really the case. According to this interpretation, some one hundred men are burnt to death by mistake, owing to a misunderstanding! Why would Elijah not clarify the reason for the order to bring him to Ahaziah before meting out such a punishment to the king's emissaries?

"THEY SCHEMED TO TAKE HIS LIFE"

Having examined the many difficulties that arise from the first possible explanation of Ahaziah's motives, we see that there is no choice but to accept one of the two more "sinister" explanations. This was not a misunderstanding on Elijah's part, but rather an accurate understanding of Ahaziah's intention to harm him. The aggressive nature of the delegations sent to seize him – each consisting of a captain of fifty, and his fifty men – and the brazen orders that the captains issue, leave no other possibility as to Ahaziah's intention in sending them.

It must be remembered that the "first lady" of the Kingdom of Israel at the time was Ahaziah's mother, Jezebel, who had long ago sworn to avenge the deaths of the prophets of Baal, whom Elijah had slain: "So shall the gods do to me, and more, if I do not end your life like the life of one of those by this time tomorrow" (I Kings 19:2).

All that time, Elijah had succeeded in eluding her, but since then there is no record of him having been active in Samaria. Ahaziah himself walks "in the way of his father and in the way of his mother" (I Kings 22:53), and therefore it can be assumed that he is also hostile to Elijah.

Therefore, it is reasonable to assume that of the two remaining possibilities – that the delegations are sent either to punish Elijah or to kill him – the latter is more likely. We must conclude that Elijah's appearance close to the city of Samaria following years of absence, in a manner that Ahaziah would perceive as a taunt to the royal family, would have led the wicked king to try and realize his mother's old dream of killing the prophet.

Indeed, this is the conclusion reached by Rabbi Moses Alsheikh:

> Why did he send a captain of fifty and his fifty men? To give him honor, he could have sent one, two, or three men of valor. Moreover, why did [the captains of fifty] not say, "The king has spoken: Come down to him," but rather, "The king has spoken: Come down"? ... The intention was not that he come down to the king, to speak with him, but rather to speak with them. He should come down to them, to the foot of the mountain, since they had schemed to take his life because of the message that he had sent to the king in God's name, that he would not arise

from his sickbed. Therefore they said: "You, the man of God who sends messages in His name – the king has spoken: Come down."... They do not say, "Come down to the king," but rather "come down" – to us, their intention being to take his life.

Support for Rabbi Alsheikh's view – not only as to the general intention that he attributes to Ahaziah (to take Elijah's life) but also as to the novel idea that it was the captains of the fifty themselves who were to carry this out, is to be found in verse 15, which refers to the third captain and his fifty: "An angel of God spoke to Elijah: Go down to him; do not fear him."

Why is Elijah commanded not to fear? Some commentators understand the verse as referring to Ahaziah, but syntactically this is problematic, since the king has not been mentioned here, and only appears at the end of the verse in a different sentence: "So he arose and went down with (to) him, to the king." The flow of the verse would suggest that "do not fear him" refers to this third captain of fifty. From the angel's message we understand that Elijah need not fear this captain of fifty, since he will do him no harm; he will simply bring him to the king. The two previous captains, however, did give Elijah good reason to fear, since they themselves had been ordered to harm him.

AHAZIAH'S MAIN MOTIVE IN HARMING ELIJAH

It seems that Ahaziah's desire to kill Elijah includes more than we have said thus far. There is an element within it that may well have been his main intention, and it is important that we discern its identity in order to understand the story properly. According to the prevailing perception in Tanakh, there is a close connection between the personality of the prophet and the prophecy that he utters. The significance of this is that the personal and family life of the prophet are subjugated to God's message, turning the prophet himself into a prophetic sign. As a result, those who oppose his prophecy believe that by causing the prophet bodily harm, they are also harming his prophecy, causing it to be nullified. This explains the attempts on the part of several kings in Tanakh to harm or even kill prophets who had uttered prophecies of punishment against them. It is not merely an attempt to silence the opposition, as the modern reader may interpret the move. Rather, it is a "metaphysical" intention to nullify the prophet's undesirable message.

It seems that for Ahaziah, lying in his sickbed and surely terrified that the prophecy conveyed to him from Elijah would be realized, an assault on Elijah would nullify the validity of his prophecy. He sends his soldiers to harm Elijah in order to bring about his own recovery. The opposition to the "man of God" is therefore, in essence, opposition to the "word of God." Harming the prophet is an attempt to thwart the realization of his prophecy.

This analysis of Ahaziah's motives, shedding new light on the second half of the story, brings all the elements of the story together around a single theme: The victory of God's words over His opponents, until they are realized in full.

In the first part of the story, God's word is revealed via Elijah, and wins over Ahaziah's messengers. They abandon the mission entrusted to them by their king and become Elijah's messengers instead, bearing his message to Ahaziah. This is the first victory of God's word, and it is a double victory: First, Ahaziah's act of desecration of God's name (inquiring of Baal-Zebub) is halted. Second, God's word is brought to Ahaziah against his will and by his own messengers. This dual victory is facilitated thanks to the repentance of the messengers and their subjugation to God's word as conveyed by Elijah.

The second part of the story addresses Ahaziah's response to this first victory of God's word. He tries to thwart the fulfillment of God's decree by sending soldiers to kill Elijah. The struggle to preserve the life and independence of the man of God is a "secondary struggle" that is part of a larger struggle for the realization and victory of God's word. God's word is indeed bound up with the prophet, but not in the sense understood by Ahaziah. (Were the prophet to disappear from the scene, for whatever reason, God's word would not be dependent upon him; it would still be realized.) Rather, it is bound up with him in the opposite sense: The immunity of God's word in the face of His opponents renders the prophet, who bears God's word with selfless devotion, similarly immune to any attack. Thus, the victory of the man of God over his opponents becomes a prophetic sign, foretelling the imminent victory of the word of God that he conveys. As discussed above, the prophet in person, through his very existence and the events of his life, serves as a sign and symbol of the prophecy that he utters.

Elijah's immunity in our chapter arises not only from the divine protection afforded him by virtue of his bearing God's word for the practical end of allowing him to fulfill his mission. Elijah's victory over his opponents is also his own victory: "If I am a man of God, let fire descend from the heavens and consume you and your fifty!" And indeed, Elijah's decree is fulfilled: "A fire descended from the heavens and consumed him and his fifty." This shows us that Elijah's immunity is the product of his being a man of God, and his victory over his opponents anticipates the victory of God's word. The similarity between the victory of God's emissary over the emissaries of the king, and the victory of God's word concerning the king himself, finds expression in the fact that both involve a decree of death and destruction.

God's word, once it has descended to the world, needs no further protection by God. From the moment it comes into the world, it is subject to the principle: "So shall be My word that emerges from My mouth; it shall not return to Me empty unless it has performed that which I desired, and has succeeded in that for which I sent it" (Is. 55:11). Similarly, the bearer of God's word, the prophet, is independent in his struggle: It is he who decrees how he will prevail over his opponents, and God fulfills his word.

In two instances, there is conflict between the word of the king – a word borne by his emissaries, the captains of the fifty ("The king has spoken…") and meant to lead to the prophet being trapped and killed – and the opposing word of the man of God. In both cases, the word of the prophet prevails. There is a third time when the man of God prevails over the king who seeks to harm him, but this time it is not achieved by means of his own words. Rather, the words of the third captain of fifty, who recognizes the superiority of the man of God over the king, and pleads with Elijah for his life, represent the victory of the man of God. Here there is no longer any need for Elijah to speak; indeed, the prophet is silent.

Elijah's third "secondary" victory in his struggle against the king who seeks his life generates – necessarily, in the context of the events – a renewed appearance of God's original message. It is also a new victory of this word of God in the primary struggle, which takes place in the outer sphere of the story. The victory of God's word near the end of the second half resembles, to some extent, the victory in the first half: Here too, an angel of God is revealed to Elijah and commands him to convey God's word once again, as revealed to him in the first half. But the nature of the victory of God's word this time is related to the previous victory of the man of God, who bears it, in the course of the second half of the story. After Elijah overcomes, time after time, the king's attempts to harm him by means of his messengers, he appears before the king himself, immune from any harm in the very "lion's den," and he declares God's word to the king once again. Once again, the king is forced to hear the prophecy that sentences him to die on his sickbed. Now the king knows that he does not have the power to oppose God's word. He can neither silence it nor thwart it by harming the prophet.

The text does not tell us how Elijah is saved from harm when he fulfills his mission and appears before the king, and various hypotheses may be offered to fill in this gap. However, we must question the reason for the text's silence on this matter. It would seem that at this stage we return to the victory of God's word that is proudly uttered before the king. If the text were to start describing how Elijah eludes assault by the king or his servants, we would be back in the minor struggle of the previous scene, conducted between the king (and his emissaries) and the man of God. Thus the impression of the resounding victory of God's word would be lost.

The last verse of the story (II Kings 1: 17) brings us to its purpose, from the prior victory of the prophet in bearing God's word, to its actual fulfillment in reality. The continuity between God's word as borne by Elijah and its realization is underlined by the threefold repetition of the root *mem-vav-tav*, twice in God's message and a third time in its realization: "The bed to which you have gone up, you shall not come down from it, but you shall surely die (*mot tamut*). And he died (*vayamot*), according to God's word. ..."

With the fulfillment of God's word in the death of Ahaziah, the text reminds us that this word of God is not merely a heavenly decree of whose existence only we, the readers, are aware. Rather, it is "according to the word of God *which Elijah had spoken.*" It is the same word of God that has been identified throughout the story with its speaker. The ultimate victory of God's word is, at the same time, the victory of the prophet who bears it.

"DO NOT RENDER EVIL TO MY PROPHETS"

Let us now return to the question with which we started: Elijah acts out of self-defense in the face of those who seek his life, but at the same time his actions also bring a well-deserved punishment to the two captains of fifty and their men. They find themselves on the battleground between the king and the prophet. Admittedly, they are acting by order of their king, who has instructed them to kill the prophet. However, what is this order worth, the order of a mortal, miserable king, a sinner and transgressor, in comparison with the command of God, the King of kings? The attempt to kill Elijah is not just an act of murder; it is an attempt to kill the prophet of God because he is a prophet of God, while he is fulfilling his mission. For lesser offenses the psalmist declares,: "He allowed no man to oppress them, and reproved kings for their sakes. Do not harm My appointed ones, nor render evil to My prophets" (Ps. 105:14–15).

The argument that they are carrying out orders is not an excuse; on the contrary, this itself is the indictment. The order to kill the man of God for fulfilling his prophetic mission stands in contradiction to a person's subservience to Him to whom all are subservient, from the king to the lowliest of his servants. The two captains of fifty and their men (even though the latter may have been of low rank) are faced with a conflict between the order of their king and the command of the King of the world, and they choose the former.

It is not through misunderstanding or lack of knowledge that they make their choice. Elijah is not an unknown, anonymous prophet whose authenticity and credentials may be questioned. Likewise, no one suggested that he is a false prophet and therefore deserving of death. On the contrary, the order to kill him comes specifically because he is a well-known prophet whose words have always been fulfilled. Here, the intention behind killing him is to thwart his prophecy and nullify it; the attempt therefore arises from the knowledge that he speaks the truth, in the name of God.

The clear awareness of the two captains of fifty, who knowingly choose to prefer the order of their king over that which was represented by the man of God, is expressed explicitly in their words to Elijah:

The first captain of fifty: "He spoke to him: Man of God, the king has spoken: Come down." (v. 9)

The second captain of fifty: "He answered and spoke to him: 'Man of God, so says the king: Come down quickly.'" (v. 11)

Their words reveal their acknowledgment of Elijah as a man of God and their preference, notwithstanding, for the order of their king.

These captains of fifty are not the first characters in our narrative to be placed on the battlefield between the king and the prophet. They are preceded by Ahaziah's messengers, who were sent to inquire of Baal-Zebub, god of Ekron. Elijah met these messengers and challenged them to choose between loyalty to God's word as conveyed by His prophet, and blind obedience to the orders of their sinful king. Those messengers "believed in the word of God, and returned to Ahaziah" (Abrabanel). Not only did they desist from continuing on the mission of their king in the wake of Elijah's rebuke, but they also became Elijah's messengers to Ahaziah.

The captains of fifty are introduced into the conflict between the king and the prophet at Ahaziah's initiative. It is he who presents them with the challenge, by ordering them to seize the man of God and kill him. The two captains of fifty should have learned a lesson from Ahaziah's earlier messengers; they should have had the proper respect for Elijah and shown preference for him over their sinful king. They ignore the lesson, and are duly punished.

ELIJAH'S VICTORY: PROPHETIC SIGN OF VICTORY OF GOD'S WORD

We concluded above that Ahaziah's intention in killing Elijah is to thwart God's word as conveyed by Elijah, concerning his imminent death. Does this justify the burning of the two captains of fifty together with their men?

The answer to this question is certainly in the affirmative. Thus far we have seen, in Elijah's actions against the two delegations, self-defense along with punishment for their sin. These two explanations leave his actions within the realm of his own initiative, contrasting them with the two other actions of Elijah, at the beginning of the story and at its conclusion, where he acts according to the instructions of an angel of God. As actions undertaken at his own discretion, they are open to criticism: Perhaps there is some personal animosity or revenge here, or even excessive zealousness. It is precisely the fact that at the beginning of the story, Elijah is guided in his actions by an angel of God, while further on he acts without such guidance, that gives rise to the possibility that God may not wholeheartedly endorse his choices. (The fact that God responds to him by bringing down fire from heaven does not necessarily imply God's full agreement with his decree.)

However, based on our explanation of the narrative as a whole, we find that all the parts of the story converge around one single subject: The victory of God's word over His opponents. The events of the second half are not a side issue; rather, they are part of the battle for the victory of God's word. We referred above to Elijah's battle in this half as a "secondary struggle." The victory of the man of God in this instance is a prelude to the victory of God's word that follows: The victory of the man of God over his opponents is a prophetic sign, foretelling the imminent victory of the word of God that he bears.

It is specifically because the victory of the prophet must precede and mold the victory of God's word that comes later, that the prophet must prevail over his opponents in an independent manner, just as God's word prevails over His opponents as an independent entity. Only after the immunity and independence of the bearer of God's word has been proven, and the attempt to assault him has failed, does God's word reappear in the story (again, at the command of God's angel), and is ultimately realized in full.

We may conclude that the transition that Elijah makes from prophetic action guided by the angel to independent action undertaken at his own discretion and by his own decree (as well as in the later transition back to action guided by the angel) is necessary for the purposes of the battle between God's word and its bearer, and those opposed to them. It is not out of personal motives or inclinations that Elijah decrees concerning the captains of fifty and their men, but rather within the framework of his activity as a prophet, to bring about the realization of God's word and its victory over all of its opponents.

Chapter 44

The First Captain of Fifty vs. the Second (II Kings 1:9–12)

T he fate of the first delegation sent by Ahaziah to seize Elijah –
being burnt by fire from heaven – is repeated almost exactly in the case
of the second delegation. However, in most places in Tanakh where this
sort of almost identical repetition occurs, small changes can be detected,
and our case is no exception. Many scholars ignore these differences, but
some commentators, especially the later ones, note every tiny discrepancy and attempt to explain their significance.

Let us compare the descriptions of the two delegations. This will
serve to highlight the difference between them. (Words that appear in
one instance but not the other are indicated in bold; words that occur
in both cases but in a different way are italicized.)

First delegation (vv. 9–10)	Second delegation (vv. 11–12)
He sent to him a captain of fifty	He **repeated this** and sent to him **another** captain of fifty
and his fifty	and his fifty
and he went up to him and behold, he was sitting at the top of the mountain.	

First delegation (vv. 9–10)	Second delegation (vv. 11–12)
	And he answered
And he spoke to him:	and spoke to him:
Man of God, *the king has spoken,*	Man of God, *so says the king,*
come down.	come down **quickly.**
And Elijah answered and spoke *to the captain of fifty*:	And Elijah answered and spoke *to them*:
And if I am a man of God,	If I am a man of God,
let a fire descend from heaven	let a fire descend from heaven
and consume you and your fifty.	and consume you and your fifty.
So a fire descended from heaven	So a fire **of God** descended from heaven
and consumed him and his fifty.	and consumed him and his fifty.

The differences that arise from the above comparison may be analyzed on three levels:

Distance

Concerning the first captain of fifty, the text says, "He went up to him"; this is omitted with regard to the second. Commenting on this, Malbim writes: "The first captain had no fear of him; he simply went up to him, to the top of the mountain … [but] the second captain was afraid to go up to Elijah."

Despite the "bravery" of the second captain and his complete loyalty to his king, he adopts some cautionary measures in order to guard himself from the fate met by his predecessor. The highlighting of this act serves to explain how the second captain could have dared to undertake this mission, after what had happened before: He did not go up to Elijah at the top of the mountain. He kept a good distance from Elijah, believing that the power of this man of God to bring down fire from heaven was limited to his close environs.

This brings in its wake another difference. Elijah's response to the first captain is prefaced with the words, "He spoke to the captain of fifty," while his response to the second starts, "He said to them" – meaning, to the captain of the fifty as well as all of the fifty men.

Once again, Malbim addresses this difference. With regard to the first captain he writes, "'Elijah answered and spoke to the captain of the fifty' – His fifty men were standing at a distance; only he was close by, therefore Elijah answered him alone."

With regard to the second captain, he comments: "'Elijah answered and spoke to them' – He spoke to all of them, for now the captain of fifty was standing below [at the foot of the mountain]."

Style

When comparing how the two captains address Elijah, we find two differences:

1. The first captain says, "The king has spoken" (i.e., commanded), while the second says, "So says the king." The second captain awards the king's message greater authority and power by introducing it with a formula that is usually associated with kings (as *Daat Mikra* comments here). Thus, the second captain compares the words of his king to Elijah's words in God's name, "So says the Lord" (v. 6).

2. The first captain says, "Come down," while the second commands Elijah to "Come down quickly." Alsheikh offers the following insight:

> The second captain is doubly guilty. He should have learned a lesson [from the fate of the first captain] and acted as the third did. Instead, he was even more disrespectful, adding "Come down quickly," as if to say – it is not as it was at first, when you could have [permitted yourself to] come down slowly, since you were unwilling; now the decree has been decided decisively. This is the meaning of, "Come down quickly."

Clearly, there is no contradiction between the differences arising from distance and those related to style; on the contrary, they share the same root. The assumption of the second captain, that if he stood far enough from Elijah then he would not be harmed, and his brazenness arise from the same source.

The Punishment

Having considered the disrespectful behavior of the second captain, we now come to the third point: the severity of the punishment. In relation to the first captain, we read, "A fire descended from heaven"; the second time, we read, "A fire of God descended from heaven." Obviously, the first fire was also from God, and its descent was no less miraculous; the text notes explicitly that it came "from heaven." What, then, is the significance of the emphasis, in the second instance, that this was a "fire of God"?

Radak offers an explanation that appears for the first time in connection with the second verse of Genesis: "The spirit of God hovered upon the surface of the water," and then reappears in several other places in his commentary on Tanakh: "This is a figure of speech; when the Torah wants to amplify something, it juxtaposes it with God, as in, 'A great city to God' (Jonah 3:3); 'cedars of God' (Ps. 80:11)."

Clearly, this is the intention in our instance too, meaning that the fire that descended the second time was greater than the previous one. Alsheikh concludes as follows: "Therefore [since the second captain was even more brazen than the first], this fire [that descended] to the second [captain] was higher and burned faster."

Malbim, having already drawn our attention to the distancing of the second captain from Elijah, writes:

> Since [the second captain] thought that if he stood far from Elijah then the latter could not harm him, therefore [Elijah] said to him: If I am indeed a man of God, I shall do this, too. Therefore it is written, "A fire of God descended," indicating a great fire that burns even from a distance.

Finally, we may comment that the punishment meted out to the second captain of fifty also fulfills a certain linguistic measure for measure. Since he sinned in saying, "Man of God … come down," he is punished by "a fire of God."

If we consider the accumulated significance of all of these differences, we arrive at their common denominator: The confrontation between the second captain of fifty and Elijah is more acute than the first, both in terms of the behavior and speech of the captain and in terms of the punishment that emerges from heaven at Elijah's decree.

This conclusion arises not only from the details of the descriptions of the two episodes, which we have discussed above, but also – first and foremost – from the very fact that the second delegation is what it is: A commander and his men who arrive after the burning of the first delegation (as noted by Alsheikh in the commentary that we cited above, concerning the "style" of the second captain). The fact that this is already a second delegation is underlined in the text in the first and most obvious of the differences arising from our comparison: "He repeated this and sent to him another captain of fifty and his fifty."

Both Ahaziah and the second captain of fifty (along with his men) have failed to learn their lesson from the burning of the first delegation: The attempt to sabotage God's word by assaulting the man of God who bears it will not succeed. The second captain of fifty would have had an excellent excuse, had he sought one, for not obeying his king's order and endangering his life and the lives of his soldiers. However, not only does he not seek to evade his mission; he sharpens his words to Elijah with even greater brazenness and disrespect. This disgrace, against the backdrop of the burning of the first delegation, shows that he is a full partner, in heart and mind, of the king and his views.

Chapter 45

The Third Captain of Fifty (II Kings 1:13–14)

So he sent again, a third captain of fifty and his fifty. And the third captain of fifty went up and came and fell on his knees before Elijah, and he beseeched him and said to him: Man of God, let my life and the life of your servants, these fifty, be dear in your eyes. Behold, fire came down from heaven and consumed the first two captains of fifty, and their fifties; Now, let my life be dear in your eyes. (vv. 13–14)

The story of the third delegation that Ahaziah sends to Elijah is placed in the same external framework as its predecessors. It is specifically the repetition of the fixed patterns that are familiar to us from the previous incidents that illustrates the contrast so clearly.

The opening verse, "He sent again, a third captain of fifty and his fifty," is an almost verbatim repetition of the introduction to the previous delegation ("He sent again to him another captain of fifty and his fifty").

The way the third captain of fifty starts out ("The third captain of fifty went up and came") is similar to that of the first captain ("He went up to him, and behold, he was sitting at the top of the mountain").

Even the third captain's appeal to Elijah contains elements that echo his predecessors: "He said to him: Man of God. ...." These exact words, juxtaposed in this way, are to be found in connection with all three of the captains of fifty.

The almost exact repetition of the description of Ahaziah's action in dispatching the third captain of fifty testifies to his fixed, unchanged intentions. The king awards no weight to the disappearance of his two previous delegations and the loss of life involved. He is quite determined. No price is too high to pay for the capture of the prophet whom he hates so bitterly. It is in contrast to Ahaziah's stubborn stance that the change in the behavior of the third captain of fifty stands out so prominently.

The difference here consists of more than simply what is added to or omitted from the fixed pattern of his predecessors. More importantly, there is a huge difference in the intention that is concealed in the formulaic expressions themselves as we hear them repeated once again.

This third captain of fifty does not desert his mission together with his men, nor does he refuse the order that he receives from his king. On the contrary, like his predecessors, he goes about carrying out his task. However, while the first captain ascended to the man of God sitting atop the mountain since he was unaware of the punishment awaiting him, and while the second refrained from ascending the mountain since he believed that he would thereby save himself from destruction, the third captain adopts the same policy as the first – specifically because he understands the extent of the danger. Although he fears the fate of his predecessors, he understands that distance will not save him (as it did not save the second captain). Instead, he tries a different approach: Talking to the prophet directly, so that the prophet will understand his terrible situation. Therefore, "The third captain of fifty went up and came."

Even before he opens his mouth to utter his plea, the third captain starts with an action, which symbolizes perfectly the difference between him and the other captains: "He fell on his knees before Elijah."

This falling expresses clearly his acceptance of the prophet's authority and his preference for the man of God over the king.

The words that are repeated in all three missions, "He spoke to him: Man of God," are preceded this third time by words that change the significance of his address entirely: "He pleaded before him and he spoke to him: Man of God…."

Even before we hear what he has to say, we already know that the words of this man, uttered with bent knee and in supplication before the prophet, will also be different in terms of content. The words, "He spoke to him," with reference to the first two captains of fifty, meant, "He commanded him" (as the Sages interpret elsewhere – "words as harsh as arrows"). When spoken by the third captain, however, these words assume the opposite meaning. The exclamation repeated by all three of them, "Man of God," expresses the awareness shared by all of them that Elijah is a prophet and emissary of God. However, in the case of the first two, this awareness only increases their guilt since, for them, this address means, "Although you are a man of God, that fact neither adds nor detracts anything in relation to fulfilling the king's order. Come down." When it comes to the third captain, the recognition that Elijah is a "man of God" translates into submission to his authority, and the supplications that follow. Let us examine these:

Let my life and the life of your servants, these fifty, be dear in your eyes. (v. 13)

Behold, fire came down from heaven and consumed the first two captains of fifty, and their fifties;

Now, let my life be dear in your eyes. (v. 14)

This short speech comprises three parts: an opening plea, an explanation of the background to the plea, and an abbreviated repetition of the opening plea, using the same language.

What is it that this captain wants? If it is to prevent the descent of fire that will kill him and his men, there is no need for him to ascend the mountain and plead before Elijah; he could have simply remained at his place in Samaria. Clearly, then, he too is coming to demand something of Elijah, and he fears that his demand will bring down fire from heaven, as has happened already twice. But what is his demand, and why does he not express it?

Malbim asks why in verses 13–14 the captain repeats the words "Let my life be dear in your eyes." While we may have regarded this repetition as a purely rhetorical device, to conclude the speech with extra emphasis using the same language as in its introduction, Malbim adds a further insight:

> The first time [these words are mentioned] he was asking that [Elijah] not burn him and the others; therefore he says, "My life and the life of your servants." The second time, he was asking that [Elijah] *go with him*, for if he did not, the king would kill him for not having brought [the prophet] by force. Therefore, he says, "Let *my* life be dear."

In Malbim's opinion, these are not two identical requests. In the second request Elijah is asked in a clearer manner to do that which is only hinted at in the first request: to go with him and appear before the king.

Two differences between the opening and closing requests serve to support Malbim's interpretation. The first is the introduction to the second request with the words, "and now," meaning, "Now, I am coming to the practical point of my words." However, an exact repetition of words spoken previously, with no new significance, cannot be regarded as the point.

The second difference concerns that which is omitted from the second request in comparison to the first. Here the captain does not plead for the life of his fifty men, but only for his own life. Seemingly, this omission is merely for the sake of brevity. However, the essence of his request's morality lies in the fact that he is concerned for the safety of his men, and not only for his own life. He should not be omitting this important element from his second request! Malbim's interpretation explains the omission: The danger posed by Elijah, who may bring down fire upon the third delegation in light of the veiled request that he accompany them, is a danger to all of them – the captain as well as his men, as the previous incidents have demonstrated. However, if Elijah were to answer this captain of fifty that he does not intend to punish him, but also refuses to come down with him, then the danger posed by the king affects the captain alone, since as the commander only he will be held responsible for the command not being fulfilled. Therefore, in this context of his request that Elijah come with him, he asks for himself, "Let my life be dear in your eyes" – namely, "Do not give me into the hand of my king, to be killed by him."

Thus, the third captain of fifty makes exactly the same request of Elijah as did his two predecessors: To come down from the top of the mountain, as per the king's order. How, then, is he better than them? In at least three respects:

1. He falls on his knees before Elijah, pleads with him, and does not command him.
2. The actual request that Elijah come down with him is only hinted at; it is not stated explicitly.
3. He explains his request on the basis of his own life being in danger, not on the fact that this is the king's command.

In his distress the third captain of fifty appeals to the only figure of the two who threaten his life, who is likely to listen, to understand, and to have mercy on him: the man of God. Now, it is no longer he, the captain, who will have to deal with the conflict between these opposing authorities, but rather Elijah who will have to find a solution to the situation that has transpired.

The dilemma that Elijah faces is a difficult one: If he goes down with the captain of the fifty, he will be submitting to the king's authority, by fulfilling his order. This will represent an acknowledgment of the king's superiority over the man of God – and it is precisely over this acknowledgment that the struggle has been conducted thus far. On the other hand, if he refuses to go down with the captain of fifty, evil will befall this innocent man who deserves no such punishment. Elijah's deliberation is expressed by his silence. Unlike the two previous incidents, this time he offers no verbal reaction to the words of the captain of fifty. He waits for God to guide him as to what he should do.

To save Elijah from the dilemma in which the third captain of fifty has placed him, God's angel is once again revealed to him: "An angel of God spoke to Elijah: Go down with him; do not fear him" (v. 15).

In the angel's first appearance to Elijah in this narrative (1:3), Elijah was commanded to go up to meet the messengers of Ahaziah and to present them with a test: a choice between proceeding, out of loyalty to their king, or accepting the rebuke of the prophet and returning home. Now, in the angel's second appearance, Elijah is commanded to go down to Ahaziah's messengers, thereby saving the captain from the difficult predicament in which the king has set him.

Elijah acts as the angel commands him: "He arose and went down with him to the king." On the surface, Elijah's descent from his seat at the top of the mountain, together with the captain of fifty, looks like capitulation. However, we soon discover that this is simply a prelude to the final victory in the battle between the king and the prophet:

> He spoke to him: So says the Lord: Since you sent messengers to inquire of Baal-Zebub, god of Ekron – is it for lack of any God in Israel that you seek his word? Therefore, the bed to which you have gone up – you shall not come down from it, but you shall surely die. (v. 16)

Elijah's victory at this moment, as he appears confidently before Ahaziah and conveys his terrible prophecy with no fear of any harm, is greater than the victory he experienced in transforming Ahaziah's messengers into his own messengers, and greater than his victory in punishing Ahaziah's messengers who came seeking his harm.

SUPPLEMENT: THE THIRD CAPTAIN OF FIFTY AND OBADIAH, GOVERNOR OF THE HOUSE

In our study of the Elijah narratives we have encountered two officers of two different kings who seemingly have dual loyalties. Both officers fear God and respect His prophet, Elijah, and find themselves embroiled in the deep conflict between king and prophet, resulting in a real threat to their lives. The first is in the narrative of the drought: Obadiah, the governor of Ahab's house (I Kings 18:3–16). The second is in our narrative: the third captain of fifty, the captain of Ahab's son, Ahaziah.

Both these officers bow down on meeting Elijah:

> Obadiah: "behold, Elijah met him; and he knew him, and he **fell on his face**." (I Kings 18:7)

> The captain of fifty: "and the third captain of fifty went up and came and **fell on his knees** before Elijah." (II Kings 1:13)

They both speak emotionally to the prophet, explaining their distress: their submission to the king and his earthly power, on the one hand, and their loyalty to God's prophet and their wish to respect him, on the other, are likely to cost them their lives. It is therefore incumbent on the prophet to extricate them from their adverse situation.

There are even similarities between the two speeches. They both open and end with an impassioned plea to the prophet to have pity on their lives, and in between they describe the circumstances that led to their fears.

	Obadiah	The third captain of fifty
Opening	How have I sinned, that you are giving your servant into the hand of Ahab, to put me to death? (18:9)	Let my life and the life of your servants, these fifty, be dear in your eyes. (v. 13)
End	*And now* you say, "Go tell your master, Elijah is here," and he will kill me. (18:14)	*And now*, let my life be dear in your eyes. (v. 14)

As a result of the different circumstances and his need to clarify them, Obadiah's speech is clearly longer and far more complex than that of the captain of fifty,[1] yet the basic similarity is striking.

At the same time, we must nevertheless note the difference between them. In chapter 18 it is Elijah's command, "Go, tell your master: Elijah is here!" (v. 8), that causes Obadiah to be involved in the confrontation between his two masters, Elijah and Ahab. Elijah's command puts Obadiah to a test: Obeying the prophet might cost him his life at the hands of Ahab his king. He therefore demands the prophet to waive his dangerous command.

Regarding the captain of fifty, it is King Ahaziah's command that causes his predicament. Obeying the king's command would endanger his life, which he would lose as the captains who preceded him did.

Therefore, each one of the officers emphasizes the threat that is unique to him. Obadiah repeats three times his fear that *Ahab* is likely

---

1. See above, "The Drought," chapter 7.

to kill him if he obeys Elijah's commands, while the captain of fifty explains that he fears the fire that *Elijah* has already twice brought down from heaven, which consumed the two previous captains and each of their fifty men.

The tone in which they speak to Elijah corresponds to this difference as to who is the cause of the danger in each narrative. Obadiah blames Elijah, berating him for issuing such a dangerous command. By contrast, the third captain of fifty cannot blame Elijah for his plight. Ahaziah his king has endangered him by ordering him to capture the man of God. He can only plead to Elijah to spare his life and the lives of his men.

The common denominator in these two stories is that both officers know that the address for their claims is the prophet. Only he will be able to help them out of their predicament. The king, who is undoubtedly responsible for their situation is unapproachable, and they expect nothing from him. Both officers were right in turning to the prophet, who did not disappoint them.

However, the prophet's response was stronger in the second case than in the first. In chapter 18, Elijah assuages Obadiah's exaggerated fear that the prophet has come to mock Ahab and disappear. He swears, "As the Lord of Hosts, before whom I stand, lives – today I shall appear before him" (v. 15). In those circumstances, the oath is sufficient to calm Obadiah, and Elijah has no need to change or retract his command: "And Obadiah went to meet Ahab, and he told him" (v. 16).

In our chapter, the pleas of the third captain of fifty cause Elijah to change his plan at the angel's instructions. He now acts in accordance with the captain's request to come down and accompany him to the king.

From both stories we learn to what extent Elijah the prophet, who was secluded from his people, was actually close to them and sensitive to their feelings, and to what extent the people realize that "God's word in his mouth is truth."[2]

.

---

2. Based on the words of the widow of Zarephath (I Kings 17:24). See "The Drought," chapter 6, for our interpretation thereof.

Chapter 46

"Who Has Ascended to Heaven and Descended Again?" (Proverbs 30:4)

DESCENT FOR THE SAKE OF ASCENT

In the previous chapter we saw that, in order to spare Elijah the compromising position imposed on him by the third captain of fifty, God's angel appears to him once again. It is instructive to compare this revelation to the first one (II Kings 1:3–4):

First revelation	Second revelation
v. 3: An angel of God spoke to Elijah the Tishbite: Arise, *go up* to meet the messengers of the king of Samaria.	v. 15: The angel of God spoke to Elijah: *Go down* to him; do not fear him.

In the first revelation, Elijah is commanded to go up to meet the messengers of Ahaziah and put them to the test. They will have to either remain loyal to their king, or accept the prophet's rebuke and turn back. In the second revelation he is commanded to go down with Ahaziah's emissaries, thereby saving the captain of fifty from his fearful mission.

This inversion ("going up" as opposed to "going down") is no mere topographical issue. Rather, the metaphoric significance of "ascent" and "descent" hint that the proper path for a prophet is one of flexibility and consideration for changing circumstances. There is a time to go up, and there is a time to come down.

A midrash which appears in several different places (*Pesikta DeRabbi Kahana*; *Pesikta Rabbati* 5; Numbers Rabba 12:11; *Midrash Mishlei*, ch. 30) expresses this idea specifically in relation to Elijah, addressing this very scene:

> "Who has ascended to heaven and descended again" (Prov. 30:4): "Who has ascended to heaven" – this refers to Elijah, as it is written concerning him (II Kings 2:12), "Elijah ascended heavenward in a storm"; "And descended again" – (this refers to II Kings 1:15) "Go down to him; do not fear."

In the angel's first revelation to Elijah, the prophet is commanded to act in a manner of "going up." Presenting Ahaziah's messengers with a challenge will be a real "ascent" for them, an "ascent" in Elijah's status, and, most significantly, an "ascent" in terms of sanctification of God's name, and avoidance of its desecration. Now, however, in the second revelation, Elijah is commanded to act in a manner of "going down." From his lofty position at the top of the mountain, he must temporarily forgo his honor and, out of consideration for mortal weakness and distress, go down with the captain of fifty and face the king.

However, at the same time, this "descent" is, in truth, "for the sake of ascent." Firstly, Elijah is revealed, in this descent, in a new light. The prophet who has projected power and authority from his very first appearance, bringing punishment to those around him and bringing down fire from heaven, is exposed in his "descent" as considerate and merciful toward those who are deserving of it, even at the price of a temporary loss of status in his clash with the king.

Secondly, we have already seen how it becomes retroactively clear that even this surrender is simply a prelude to the final victory in the struggle between the king and the prophet. Elijah's victory as he stands fearlessly before Ahaziah and conveys his terrible prophecy, with no fear of any harm, is greater than his victory in punishing the emissaries of Ahaziah who come seeking to harm him. The same words that Elijah told to Ahaziah's first messengers, when he *went up* to them, are now repeated before the king himself, directly and openly, after Elijah *comes down* with the king's messengers.

THE ROOTS *AYIN-LAMED-HEH* AND *YOD-RESH-DALET*: KEY OPPOSITES IN THE NARRATIVE

From a broader perspective we note that the roots *ayin-lamed-heh* and *yod-resh-dalet* are "key opposites" throughout our narrative. We refer here to a pair of opposite words which together serve as a two-part key word in a literary unit in Tanakh. The existence of key words in Tanakh is well known. There are also literary units in Tanakh in which pairs of opposite words serve this function. One of the signs of them being meaningful is that both words appear a significant number of times – usually seven or a multiple of seven. An example that we have already met (above, ch. 41 of this narrative) is the pair *heh-lamed-khaf* and *shin-vav-bet* which appear a total of seven times in verses 2–6.

The roots *ayin-lamed-heh* and *yod-resh-dalet* appear a total of twenty-one times as verbs: There are seven appearances in the first half of the story (vv. 2–8), and fourteen appearances in the second half (vv. 9–17). It is not only the convenient total (3x7) or the division between the two halves of the story (7:14) that support the view of these roots as being "key opposites." We shall see below that the story as a whole is forged around this pair of verbs, following a fixed pattern.

Let us start by reviewing all the appearances of these verbs:

First half

1. An angel of God spoke…. Arise, *go up to meet* the messengers of the king of Samaria and speak to them… (v. 3)
2–3. The bed to which you have *gone up* – you shall not *come down* from it, but you shall surely die. (v. 4)
4. They said to him: A man *came up to meet* us and he said to us…
5–6. Therefore the bed to which you have *gone up* – you shall not *come down* from it, but shall surely die. (v. 6)

7. He spoke to them: What was the description of the man who *came up to meet* you and who spoke to you...? (v. 7)

Second half

8. He sent to him a captain of fifty with his fifty men, and he *went up* to him... and he spoke to him:
9. Man of God, the king has spoken: *Come down!* (v. 9)
10. And if I am a man of God, let fire *come down* from the heaven...
11. And fire *came down* from the heaven and consumed... (v. 10)
12. He sent him another captain of fifty with his fifty men, and he *answered* (*vayaan*) and spoke to him:
13. Man of God, so says the king: *Come down* quickly! (v. 11)
14. If I am a man of God, let fire *come down* from the heaven...
15. And a fire of God *came down* from the heaven, and consumed... (v. 12)
16. And again he sent a third captain of fifty and his fifty men, and he *went up* and he came... and he spoke to him... (v. 13)
17. Behold, fire has *come down* from the heaven... (v. 14)
18. And the angel of God spoke to Elijah: *Go down* to him...
19. And he arose and he *went down* to him, to the king. (v. 15)
20–21. The bed to which you have *gone up* – you will not *come down* from it, but you shall surely die. (v. 16)

The obvious question arising from our schematic presentation above concerns appearance number 12 (v. 11): The root of the word *vayaan* is *ayin-nun-heh*, meaning to lift one's voice. Nevertheless, we propose that this word be read as *vayaal*, by exchanging the *nun* for a *lamed* in accordance with the rule of the interchangeability of the letters *lamed, mem, nun,* and *resh*.[1] We are prompted to suggest this interpretation by the clear structural pattern of the story, with the roots *ayin-lamed-heh* and

---

1. It should be noted that in most of the early manuscripts of the Septuagint, the word is indeed translated as "went up."

    The tendency of these letters to interchange with one another stems from their phonetic relationship. Both early and later commentators and linguists point out several words both in Tanakh in which these letters are interchanged. In the book of Nehemiah the words *lishkha* and *nishkha* are interchanged several times. Early commentators brought this as proof of the interchangeability of *lamed* and *nun* in Tanakh.

yod-resh-dalet at its foundation. Let us consider the pattern followed in the first half of the story:

1. Elijah *goes up* to meet the messengers of Ahaziah (v. 3 – command by God's angel)

   2–3. Ahaziah *goes up* to his sickbed and *does not come down* (v. 4 – command by God's angel)

      4. Elijah *goes up* to meet Ahaziah's messengers (v. 6 – report by the messengers)

   5–6. Ahaziah *goes up* to his sickbed and *does not come down* (v. 6 – report by the messengers)

   7. Elijah *goes up* to meet Ahaziah's messengers (v. 7 – Ahaziah's question)

The second half follows a pattern that groups appearances of our "key opposites" into pairs of appearances:

v. 9:	v. 11:	vv. 13–14:
1. First captain of fifty *goes up* to Elijah	5. Second captain of fifty *goes up* to Elijah	9. Third captain of fifty *goes up* to Elijah
2. He demands that Elijah *come down*	6. He demands that Elijah *come down*	10. He asks of Elijah that fire not *come down* upon him and his fifty men
v. 10:	**v. 12:**	**v. 15:**
3. Elijah calls for fire to *come down*	7. Elijah calls for fire to *come down*	11. God's command to Elijah to *go down* with him
4. Fire does in fact *come down*	8. Fire does in fact *come down*	12. Elijah in fact *goes down* with him
v. 16:		
13–14. Ahaziah *goes up* to his sickbed and *does not come down*		

A fixed pattern is repeated for all three captains of fifty: First, the roots *ayin-lamed-heh* and *yod-resh-dalet* appear in connection with the captain of fifty and his demand of Elijah, then we find the root *yod-resh-dalet* twice in connection with Elijah's response. The pattern is repeated in identical form for the first two captains of fifty, while in the case of the third captain only the outer framework remains the same, while the inner elements are inverted: The first two appearances of *ayin-lamed-heh* and *yod-resh-dalet* are still attributed to the captain, but although he goes up to Elijah and speaks to him, like his two predecessors, he does not command him – as they did – to "come down"; rather, he recalls the "coming down" of the fire, which consumed the previous companies, and he begs not to suffer the same fate. The next two appearances of the verb *yod-resh-dalet* occur within the framework of Elijah's response, as in the two previous episodes, but this time Elijah does not bring down fire; this time, he himself comes down with the captain of fifty.

A slight change in one of the linguistic components of *ayin-lamed-heh* and *yod-resh-dalet*, such as the omission of the "going up" of the second captain of fifty, would destroy the entire pattern of the description of these three delegations around the *ayin-lamed-heh* and *yod-resh-dalet* pair.

A linguistic comparison of the verses describing the arrival of the three captains of fifty serves to reinforce our interpretation of verse 11, according to which *vayaan* should be read as *vayaal*:

> He sent to him a captain of fifty and his fifty men, and he *went up* (*vayaal*) to him, and behold he was sitting…and he spoke to him. (v. 9)

> And again he sent to him another captain of fifty and his fifty men, and he *answered* (*vayaan*) and he spoke to him. (v. 11)

> And again he sent a third captain of fifty and his fifty men, and he *went up* (*vayaal*) and he came…and begged him and he spoke to him. (v. 13)

The linguistic element that is common to all three delegations therefore boils down to the phrases:

> He sent a captain of fifty and his fifty men
> And he went up…and spoke to him.

The first phrase ("He sent…and his fifty men") undergoes slight changes, in the case of the second and the third captains, owing to the fact that they follow after the first captain. As to the second phrase ("And he went up…and spoke to him"), it is specifically its appearance in connection with the second captain of fifty that preserves the minimal common basis (on condition, of course, that we read *vayaan* as *vayaal*). In connection with the first captain there is an addition ("and behold, he was sitting…") that arises from the need to indicate the place to which this captain went up, while in the case of the third captain there is a lengthy addition that describes the captain's different actions before Elijah ("He fell on his knees"), and the change in the content of his words ("he beseeched him").

The linguistic comparison, then, serves to strengthen the case for reading *vayaan*, in the case of the second captain, as *vayaal*.

However, we must ask why it is that specifically in verse 11, *vayaal* became *vayaan*. One possible answer is that the exchange is influenced by the beginning of the next verse, verse 12: *Vayaan Eliya* – "And Elijah answered.…" Thus the following parallel is created:

And he answered and he spoke to him: Man of God… (v. 11)

And Elijah answered and he spoke to them: If I am a man of God… (v. 12)

Another possible explanation is that *vayaan* implies a lifting of the voice – as Rashi and other commentators usually understand the root *ayin-nun-heh* wherever it introduces speech (e.g., Ex. 15:21, 20:13; Deut. 26:5; Job 3:2, etc.). This would hint to us that although the second captain of fifty also "goes up" to Elijah (since *vayaan* = *vayaal*), he does not come close to him, as the first captain did, but rather stands at a "safe distance," and therefore has to lift his voice in order to say what he wants to say to Elijah. Malbim adopts this interpretation of our verse.

To this latter possibility, which awards a deliberate dual significance to the *vayaan* which stems from *vayaal*, we may add that the two roots *ayin-lamed-heh* and *ayin-nun-heh* may actually be connected. Both express "lifting": the one designates a lifting of the body, the other a lifting of the voice. The exchange between them is therefore not merely a phonetic issue (i.e., the exchange of *lamed* and *nun*, which belong to the same consonantal group) but also an exchange of actions that share a similarity.

WHO "ASCENDS" BUT DOES NOT "DESCEND"? WHO "ASCENDS" AND ALSO "DESCENDS"?

How does the "key pair of opposites" (*ayin-lamed-heh* and *yod-resh-dalet*), discussed above, contribute to our understanding of this story? We may say that this pair of roots serves to mold the confrontation that is at the center of the narrative, between the king and his emissaries, on one hand, and Elijah, on the other, with the eventual victory of the prophet. The narrative employs this pair of opposite verbs in relation to all of the main characters: Elijah, Ahaziah, and the captains of fifty. However, we need to define the precise meaning of each of these verbs as they appear in the context of each of the characters.

Who, in the story, "ascends"? Everyone does:

- Elijah "goes up" to meet the messengers of Ahaziah, and this appears three times (vv. 3, 6, 7).
- Ahaziah "goes up" to his sickbed, and this too is mentioned three times (vv. 4, 6, 16).
- The captains of fifty "go up" to Elijah, and once again, this happens three times (vv. 9, 11, 13).

However, the significance of the "going up" and its purpose is different in each instance:

- Elijah goes up to meet the messengers of Ahaziah with a view to causing them to repent and become his own messengers to the king. While his ascent is also a literal, topographical one, it is principally meant in the metaphoric sense: He "ascends" to perform his prophetic mission.
- Ahaziah "goes up" to his sickbed, and this too is a literal description, in that the bed is a raised surface onto which a person must "ascend."

However, in the present context, the reason for his "ascent" is his illness, and the significance of the ascent here is therefore a negative one. It is an ascent that expresses weakness and helplessness. The linguistic and numerical balance among the three "ascents" of Elijah and the three "ascents" of Ahaziah represents an ironic device meant to hint at the victory of the prophet, who succeeds in fulfilling his mission, over the king who is trying to sabotage him.

- The three captains of fifty also "ascend" to Elijah who is sitting at the top of the mountain. Their ascent is meant to serve as a tool in the hand of the king, who has "gone up" to his sickbed and is therefore incapacitated, in order to negate Elijah's "ascent" in the first part of the story. Their ascent is therefore Ahaziah's counterstrike in response to the success of the prophet in his own ascent. Their ascent is meant to cause Elijah's "descent" at the king's command – namely, to nullify the success of the prophet's ascent in the first half of the story. However, in this section of the story, covering the ascents by the captains of fifty, the unity that characterized the ascent in the previous sections starts to disintegrate. The ascent of the first two captains of fifty is indeed carried out in accordance with the king's wishes, and they demand that the prophet "come down" by order of the king. The third captain of fifty does "ascend" to Elijah, but it is an ascent that leads him to join Elijah: "The third captain of fifty went up and he came and he fell upon his knees before Elijah, and beseeched him" (v. 13).

He does not relay the king's order – "Come down," but rather expresses the opposite idea: an awareness of the prophet's ability to prevail over his opponents: "Behold, fire *came down* from the heavens" (v. 14).

Thus, Ahaziah's "counterstrike" fails twice because of Elijah's actions, and the third time because of the submission demonstrated by the third captain of fifty, which changes the meaning of his "ascent" into the opposite of what it had been in the case of his predecessors. He even uses the verb *yod-resh-dalet* in the opposite sense to they way they meant it.

Let us now review the various uses of the root *yod-resh-dalet*.

- The root *yod-resh-dalet* appears three times in relation to Ahaziah (vv. 4, 6, 16), always accompanied with the negative prefix: "The sickbed to which you have gone up – you *will not come down* from it." The fact that Ahaziah will not descend from his sickbed (as a continuation of the negative implication of his "ascent" in the first place) does not mean that his situation will remain static, but rather that he will die – as we learn from the end of the sentence in each case: "You will surely die."

- We have already noted above that on three occasions the captains of fifty use the root *yod-resh-dalet* in their words to Elijah, but the aim of the first two captains (vv. 9, 11) is the opposite of that of the third captain (v. 14). The "descent" that is being demanded of Elijah by the first two, by order of the king, means coming down to his death (as discussed above), and it is not realized. Elijah persists in his "ascent" at the top of the mountain; namely, in his prophetic victory over Ahaziah and his two emissaries.

- The root *yod-resh-dalet* appears four times in relation to the fire that comes down from heaven, consuming the first two captains of fifty and their men. Twice it occurs in Elijah's prior warning (vv. 10, 12), and twice more in the description of the event actually taking place in these same two verses. In other words, Elijah does not "come down," as the king demands, but instead "brings down" fire, thereby preventing the captains from taking him down forcibly. At the same time, it prevents the return "descent" of the captains and their men. Thus, the first two delegations resemble the king who has sent them. Like him, they too have "gone up" (a negative ascent) but never "come down," and for the same reason: They are dead. The "descent" of the fire is what prevents their own descent.

- In the case of the third captain, the situation is different. Concerning him we are told explicitly that he "went up" to Elijah, and in his case Elijah is commanded explicitly to "go down to him." This he does: "And he arose and went down to him" (v. 15). Thus, this third captain who goes up and demonstrates submission to Elijah, merits to come down with him.

Twice the root *yod-resh-dalet* is used in relation to Elijah in this verse: First in the angel's command, "Go down to him," and then in his fulfillment of this command: "He went down to him, to the king." The prophet, then, is the only character in the story who is said to go up and also to come down from the place of his ascent. (The third captain and his men do come down, but the verb is used in relation to Elijah, not to them.)

In summary we may say that the question that is asked in this story, in which everyone "goes up," is: Who goes up and also comes down? Those whose ascent was positive merit also to come down. They are then able to continue their lives and to complete their missions. Those whose ascent was bound up with sin (the ascent of Ahaziah because of the sin of idolatry; the ascent of the first two captains of fifty because of their intention to assault the prophet) do not merit to come down from the place of their ascent, for they die.

The victory of Elijah, as bearer of God's word, is expressed not only in his "ascent" at the beginning of the story – for the act of ascent is not limited in the story to him: Ahaziah "goes up" before him, and the captains of fifty "go up" after him. Rather, his victory is expressed in the fact that he later "comes down." His descent is to life and safety, and he completes his mission by standing before the wicked king and fearlessly declaring God's message to him.

This analysis of our narrative on the basis of the "key pair of opposites" serves to strengthen our thesis set out earlier, that Elijah's "descent" at the end of the story is a "descent for the purposes of ascent." It expresses the duty of a prophet in Israel to "come down" after every spiritual "ascent."

In this regard, it is interesting to note the next narrative, which likewise speaks of an "ascent" by Elijah: "And it was, when God caused Elijah to go up (*behaalot*) in a storm to heaven…and Elijah went up (*vayaal*) in a storm to heaven." This ascent is not followed by any descent, but at the same time there is no statement of his "not descending," as in our story with regard to Ahaziah and the first two captains of fifty. Indeed, this ascent by Elijah is not perceived as an image of death and destruction, but rather the opposite, the preface to his renewed revelation at the End of Days [Mal. 3:23]: "Behold, I send to you Elijah the prophet, before the great and terrible day of God."

Chapter 47

Structure of the Narrative

Wₑ have already noted that our narrative (II Kings 1) is
clearly divided into two halves of fairly similar length: verses 2–8
(7 verses), and verses 9–17 (9 verses). The distinction between the
two halves stems, first and foremost, from their content: The first
half discusses the messengers of Ahaziah, whom Elijah succeeds in
transforming into his own messengers to Ahaziah. The second half
covers the story of messengers of a different type. The captains of
fifty, and their men, are soldiers whose mission is to capture Elijah,
with a view to harming him. Although Elijah has to deal with messengers sent by Ahaziah in both instances, the nature of these emissaries and their objectives, along with the biblical terminology for
them and the way in which Elijah handles them, are entirely different.

The conclusion of the first half is left dramatically open-ended.
Ahaziah discovers that the man who has stopped his messengers and
sent them back to him, bearing an ill-boding prophecy for him, is none
other than Elijah, the enemy of the royal house. All of the bad feeling
from the past, along with the fear that the prophet's present message
will indeed be realized, are condensed into Ahaziah's emotional exclamation after hearing the prophet's identifying characteristics: "He is
Elijah the Tishbite!"

This name for Elijah – "Elijah the Tishbite" – concludes the first half. The same title appears at the beginning of this half: "And God's angel spoke to Elijah the Tishbite" (v. 3). It occurs nowhere else in our narrative, and is quite rare in all the Elijah narratives.

The second half begins with a dramatic turning point: Ahaziah responds to Elijah's victory and to the message that he conveys in the first half. He attempts to sabotage the prophecy of his impending death by doing away with the prophet. However, in the second half, too, Elijah prevails over Ahaziah's scheme. The emissaries who do not submit willingly to Elijah (as Ahaziah's messengers had done in the first half) are burnt with a fire that comes down from heaven, and the last captain is therefore ready and willing to submit. It would appear, therefore, that Ahaziah fails in his attempt to have Elijah brought down from his elevated seat by the king's messengers. However, it then turns out that it is specifically those messengers who submit to Elijah, who succeed in getting the prophet to descend and accompany them to the king. In this way Elijah ends up prevailing not only over Ahaziah's messengers, but over the king himself. Ahaziah is forced to hear God's word directly from Elijah's mouth, without being able to harm him in any way.

As in many other biblical stories, including most of the Elijah narratives, the two parts of our story parallel one another in inverse symmetrical form (a chiastic parallel). This symmetrical structure is especially prominent in the beginning and ending of the story, with increasingly close examination required as we approach the center. The relationship between the corresponding elements of the two halves is not a fixed one. Sometimes it is a relationship of cause and effect, while at other times there is a comparison, with some degree of development in the second half. Aside from the two innermost elements which are not equal in length (and which in turn cause the two halves of the story to be of unequal length), all the other corresponding elements occupy exactly the same number of verses.

The following presentation of the story highlights the parallel between the two halves. Thereafter we shall discuss each pair of parallel elements independently.

A: Ahaziah fell through the lattice…and he became sick; and he sent messengers: …Go, inquire of Baal-Zebub…*whether I will live* through this illness. (II Kings 1:2)

B: And *an angel of God spoke to Elijah* the Tishbite: Arise, go up to meet the messengers of the king of Samaria, and speak to them: *Is it because there is no king in Israel that you go to inquire of Baal-Zebub, god of Ekron?* (v. 3)

Therefore, so says the Lord: You shall not come down from the bed to which you have gone up, but you shall surely die. And Elijah departed. (v. 4)

C: And the messengers returned to him and he said to them: Why have you returned? (v. 5)

And they said to him: A man came up to meet us, and he said to us: Go, return to the king who sent you, and speak to him. So says the Lord: Is it because there is no king in Israel that you send to inquire of Baal-Zebub, god of Ekron? Therefore you shall not come down from the bed to which you have gone up, but you shall surely die. (v. 6)

D: And he said to them: What was the manner of the man who came up to meet you and who spoke these things to you? (v. 7)

And they said to him: He was a hairy man, and with a leather girdle around his loins. And he said: He is Elijah the Tishbite! (v. 8)

(*Central Axis*)

D': And he sent to him a captain of fifty and his fifty men…. And he said to him: Man of God, the king has spoken: Come down. (v. 9)

And Elijah answered and he spoke... Let a fire come down from the heavens.... And a fire came down from the heavens and consumed him and his fifty men. (v. 10)

And he again sent to him another captain of fifty and his men.... So says the king: Come down quickly. (v. 11)

And Elijah answered and spoke to them.... And a fire came down from the heavens and consumed him and his fifty men. (v. 12)

C': And again he sent a third captain of fifty and his fifty men, and he went up and he came... and he fell upon his knees before Elijah and beseeched him and said to him: "Man of God, Let my life, and the life of your servants, these fifty, be dear in your eyes. (v. 13)

Behold, fire came down from the heavens and consumed the two captains of fifty.... And now, let my life be dear in your eyes. (v. 14)

B': And *an angel of God spoke to Elijah*: Go down to him, do not fear him. So he arose and went down to him, to the king. (v. 15)

And he said to him: *So says the Lord: Since you sent messengers to inquire of Baal-Zebub*, god of Ekron – is it because there is no God in Israel that you inquire of him? *Therefore the bed to which you have gone up – you shall not come down from it, but you shall surely die.* (v. 16)

A': *And he died*, according to God's word which He spoke to Elijah. (v. 17)

A-A': This pair of elements represents the framework of the story. Verse A recounts Ahaziah's fall, his illness, and his inquiry as to whether he will live, while A' records his death from that illness. His death is not merely the natural outcome, but an event that happens "according to God's word which He spoke to Elijah." Ahaziah has made no attempt to inquire of God, and God's word decrees that he is to die as a punishment for having inquired of Baal-Zebub. In other words, A' arises out of the two facts that pave the way for it in A: The actual fall and illness, and the fact that the king chooses to inquire of Baal-Zebub as to his fate. God's announcement of his imminent death is uttered by Elijah, and everything that leads from the announcement to the result is covered in all the sections in between A and A'.

B-B': An angel of God is revealed to Elijah in each of these units, and the purpose of the revelation is to send Elijah to convey God's word to Ahaziah. In B the angel instructs Elijah, "Arise, *go up*," and he places God's word in Elijah's mouth so that the prophet will pass it on, via Ahaziah's messengers, to the king. In B' the angel commands him, "*Go down* to him." He does not repeat God's message, since it is already known to Elijah. Instead of hearing God's word uttered by the angel (as in B), we now hear it from Elijah as he addresses Ahaziah. (On the other hand, in B we do not hear Elijah's words to the messengers of Ahaziah, and thus the two units maintain equal length.) Corresponding to, "Elijah departed," at the end of B, we find in B' – "He arose and went down to him." The second unit represents a development in that this time the message is conveyed to the king by Elijah himself, rather than through the agency of any messengers. This is as a result of the confrontation that is played out in the second half of the story. (The parallel between the two revelations was discussed above.)

C-C': There are two sets of emissaries from the king, each of which submits to Elijah: In C the messengers return to the king, at Elijah's command, becoming the prophet's messengers to Ahaziah to convey God's word concerning his imminent death. The messengers in C' likewise fail to prevail over Elijah and to fulfill their king's command to bring him down by force. They are reduced, eventually (in the person of the third captain), to beseeching him for their lives. This pair of parallel elements reflects an interesting reversal: Elijah's success in C results in the messengers going against the king's instructions, and instead of going to Ekron, they go back to Ahaziah. By contrast, the prophet's success in C' leads to a situation in which the messengers themselves (unlike their predecessors in the first half) actually do fulfill Ahaziah's command to bring Elijah down from his seat, and to present him before the king. Elijah performs the wish of the third captain of fifty (at the command of the angel of God) because the captain is submissive and pleads for his life. This reversal heralds the development that follows: Now Elijah's word will prevail over Ahaziah's rejection of it, even within the framework of the king's desire (that Elijah be brought to him) being fulfilled.

D-D': This pair reflects a relationship of cause and effect. In the dialogue between Ahaziah and his messengers upon their return from the encounter with Elijah, the king seeks to discover the identity of the prophet who has uttered such a terrible prophecy about him. When he realizes that he is "Elijah the Tishbite," he is driven to dispatch captains of fifty with their men to capture and do away with him. Thus, D represents a psychological and practical stage of preparation for the actions that Ahaziah undertakes in D'. The quantitative imbalance between the two units arises from the fact that Ahaziah's efforts to have Elijah captured by his soldiers are repeated over and over. Furthermore, in D' the text describes not only Ahaziah's efforts, but also their subversion by Elijah. Therefore this unit is twice as long as D (such that the overall equality between the two halves of the story is also affected).

The subject of our story is the victory of God's word and its bearer over the king who has sinned and then seeks to disrupt God's word by injuring its bearer, the man of God. The victory of God's word is in its ultimate fulfillment, and it is this that serves as the framework of the story (A-A'). However, the real message of the story is the failure of the attempts to harm Elijah, and his ability to declare God's word to the king unimpeded, whether through the agency of the king's own messengers, or directly, in person. Those who attempt to sabotage the fulfillment of God's word by harming its bearer are punished. By contrast, those who submit to the prophet are not harmed, even though the act of submission would seem to endanger them. This is true of Ahaziah's first set of messengers, as well as of the third captain of fifty and his men.

Chapter 48

God and His Prophet's Word vs. the King's Word: Summary

A**s in many other biblical narratives where God's word stands the test of prevailing over its opponents, here too, in II Kings 1, the root *dalet-bet-resh* appears often, either as a verb or as a noun, serving as a key word in the story. The repetition of this root is conspicuous (seventeen appearances within sixteen verses) since sometimes it seems to be superfluous, or selected deliberately instead of the more commonly used *alef-mem-resh*. The following are two examples:

> And he spoke (*vayedaber*) to them: What was the appearance of the man who came up to meet you and spoke (*vayedaber*) these things (*hadevarim ha'eleh*) to you? (v. 7)

> And he spoke (*vayedaber*) to him: Man of God, the king has spoken (*dibber*): Come down. And Elijah answered him and he spoke (*vayedaber*).... (vv. 9–10)

The key word appears in our narrative in groups, usually with one *dalet-bet-resh* paired against another. There is *devar Hashem* (the word of God) as opposed to the *devar hamelekh* (the word of the king), or *devar hamelekh* contrasting with the word of Elijah, the man of God. A review of the appearances of this key word throughout the story will serve to clarify its messages.

Group A – First Half of the Narrative (vv. 2–8)

> *God's word:*
> 1. An angel of God spoke (*dibber*) to Elijah the Tishbite:
> 2. Arise, go up to meet the messengers of the king of Samaria, and speak (*dabber*) to them… (v. 3)
> 3. Go, return to the king who sent you, and speak (*vedibartem*) to him… (v. 6)

Thus God's word is conveyed from the angel to Elijah (1), from Elijah to Ahaziah's messengers (2), and from them to Ahaziah (3).

> *The king's word:*
> 4. And he spoke (*vayedaber*) to them: What was the appearance of the man who came up to meet you
> 5. and spoke (*vayedaber*) to you
> 6. these things (*hadevarim ha'eleh*)? (v. 7)

Three appearances of God's word correspond to three appearances of the king's word. The king's word (4) comes to oppose the word of the prophet (5), which contains the word of God (6). The question that the king asks of his messengers is meant as preparation for his own "word" which will be revealed in the second half of the story.

Group B – First Captain of Fifty (vv. 9–10)

> *The king's word:*
> 7. And he spoke (*vayedaber*) to him:
> 8. Man of God, the king has spoken (*dibber*): Come down! (v. 9)

The word of the man of God:
9. And Elijah answered and he spoke (*vayedaber*) ... and if I am a man of God.... (v. 10)

In the second half of the story, the initiative passes over to the king. His "word" precedes the "word" of Elijah, unlike the situation in the first half.

Group C – Second Captain of Fifty (vv. 11–12)

The king's word:
10. And he answered and he spoke (*vayedaber*) to him: Man of God, so says the king.... (v. 11)

The word of the man of God:
11. And Elijah answered and he spoke (*vayedaber*) to them: If I am a man of God.... (v. 12)

While in the previous group (B) the "word" of the king (two appearances) prevailed over the "word" of Elijah (one appearance), in this group, following the descent of the fire onto the first delegation, the two parties are balanced out.

Group D – Third Captain of Fifty (vv. 13–15)

12. He fell on his knees before Elijah and beseeched him, and he spoke (*vayedaber*) to him.... (v. 13)
13. And an angel of God spoke (*vayedaber*) to Elijah: Go to him.... (v. 15)

In this group the two *dibburim* (instances of speech) do not contrast with one another, as in the previous groups, but rather form a relationship of cause and effect.

In groups B and C, the subject under discussion is not "God's word" concerning Ahaziah, as it was in the first half of the story, and as it becomes once again at the end (in group E – see below). Rather, the issue is whose word is going to prevail. Will it be that of the king to his messengers, commanding them to seize Elijah, such that he will be forced to come down from the mountain, or will it be the word of the man of God, punishing the messengers of the king and thwarting his plan?

Group D brings a surprising reversal: The "word" of the captain of fifty no longer reflects the "word of the king," as it did in the previous groups. Rather, it now represents the opposite: complete submission to the prophet. Similarly, the "word" of the angel of God no longer reflects the word of the man of God, as we have seen it thus far. Rather, it too now carries the opposite message: It contains consideration for and mercy toward the captain of fifty, and it prepares us for the renewed appearance of the "word of God" in the next group.

Group E – Ultimate Victory of the Word of God (vv. 16–17)

14. And he spoke (*vayedaber*) to him: So says the Lord…
15. Is it because there is no God in Israel of whom you can ask His word (*bidvaro*)? Therefore…but you shall surely die. (v. 16)
16. And he died, according to God's word (*kidvar Hashem*)
17. which He had spoken (*dibber*) to Elijah. (v. 17)

These four appearances of "the word of God" join the three appearances in group A. In group E, the key word *dalet-bet-resh* is related to sin (appearance no. 15 – Ahaziah's failure to inquire of God, and his quest to inquire of Baal-Zebub, the god of Ekron); punishment (appearance no. 14 – "He *spoke* to him: So says the Lord…therefore…you shall surely die"); and its fulfillment (appearances 16–17 – which is "according to God's word which He spoke to Elijah").

Let us now attempt to outline the progression of the narrative on the basis of the appearances of the key word, *dalet-bet-resh*, in its various contexts. Ahaziah's sin in sending messengers, in his illness, to inquire of Baal-Zebub brings God's word into the world, with a dual purpose: To stop the messengers of Ahaziah from continuing on their way, and to inform the king, by means of those same messengers, of his imminent death. The conveying of God's word from God's angel to Elijah, from Elijah to the messengers of Ahaziah, and from them to the king, causes the key word *dalet-bet-resh* (in the sense of "God's word") to appear three times. God's word is successful, and its dual objective is attained in full. However, already in the first half of the story it becomes clear that the king is not going to sit by idly in the face of this prophecy. He "speaks" to his messengers in an attempt to discover the identity of the man who "spoke" such harsh *dibburim* (words) to them concerning him. The three appearances of the key word in the king's speech hint at the impending confrontation between the king and God's word and its bearer. The equilibrium – three appearances versus three appearances – hints that at this stage, the question of who will prevail is still an open one.

In the second half of the story, the initiative shifts to Ahaziah. His attempt to sabotage the fulfillment of the prophecy against him is aimed at the bearer of the prophecy, the man of God. This is based on his belief that the fulfillment of the prophecy is dependent on the survival of its bearer. The king's "word," as revealed through the "words" of the first captain of fifty (two appearances) is meant to harm the prophet, who is ordered to descend from the mountain.

However, this is immediately followed by the contrasting "word" of the prophet, and despite the king's numerical advantage (echoed in the doubling of the appearances of the key word in relation to the sole appearance in Elijah's response), the prophet's "word" prevails, and his decree is fulfilled in the miracle of fire that descends from the heavens.

The arrogance of the second captain of fifty grows to compensate for the weakness of his appearance before the man of God. The "word" of this captain and the "word" of the prophet are placed here in equilibrium. The second delegation meets the same fate as the first. The "word" of the prophet has prevailed once again.

The victory of Elijah in the battle that the king wages against him reaches its climax in the arrival of the third captain of fifty: The "word" of this captain is nothing but an expression of submission before the prophet. Now there appears the "word" of the angel of God, commanding Elijah to accede to the captain's pleas and to go down with him to the king.

Following the victory of the man of God over those who seek his harm (the king and his messengers) through his "word," the "word of God" reappears, at the end of the story. The ultimate victory of the word of God comes in the wake of the victory of its bearer, the prophet, over his opponents. Elijah announces God's word to Ahaziah himself, and this word of God is soon fulfilled, as the prophet had "spoken" it.[1]

---

1. For a comparison between this story and that in I Samuel 19, and the "three and four" literary model that exists in both, see the Hebrew edition of this book, pp. 473–79.

The Storm

בְּהַעֲלוֹת ה׳ אֶת אֵלִיָּהוּ בַּסְעָרָה הַשָּׁמָיִם.

When God took up Elijah in a storm to the heavens.

II Kings 2:1

Chapter 49

Preface

BOUNDARIES OF THE STORY

The narrative of the storm starts with the first verse of II Kings, chapter 2: "And it was, when God took up Elijah in a storm to the heavens," and ostensibly ends with the echo of these words in verse 11: "And Elijah went up in a storm to the heavens." However, verse 12, describing Elisha's immediate reaction to Elijah's ascent, should certainly be included within the boundaries of the narrative. Moreover, on closer study, it would seem correct to include the whole of the chapter in the narrative, even though as of verse 13 Elisha acts alone.

There are many points to support this hypothesis. First, verse 13 – "He lifted Elijah's mantle ... and went back and stood at the bank of the Jordan" – does not seem to introduce a new subject. From the point of view of its content and vocabulary, this verse is a direct continuation of the previous one, to the extent that the name of Elisha, who is the subject of the sentence, is not even mentioned. Likewise, in terms of the topic of this verse and those that follow, Elijah's ascent continues to pervade the action. Although Elijah has left Elisha, the events of the first half of the chapter continue to occupy us: Elijah's mantle serves Elisha, and his name is mentioned by Elisha (v. 14) and the sons of the prophets (v. 15) alike; afterward (vv. 16–18) the text describes the search undertaken by the sons of the prophets to find Elijah.

Let us now examine why it is justified to include the continuation of the chapter within the narrative of Elijah's ascent.

At the beginning of the unit comprising verses 19–22 (the subject of which is the healing of the waters of the Jordan River), we read: "The people of the city said to Elisha …," with no mention of the name of the city. Obviously, the city in question is Jericho, but the reader knows this only because in the previous unit, we are told that Elisha stays in Jericho. Thus, the episode described in verses 19–22 must follow on from the preceding unit.

In the same way, the next episode, described in verses 23–25 (the taunting boys and the bears emerging from the woods), must be connected to the unit that precedes it. It starts with the words, "He went up from there to Beit El. …" "There" clearly refers to Jericho, the city of the previous unit, which is alluded to again later on in verse 23: "And some small boys came out from the city. …" Once again, this unit rests upon the previous one, and both are dependent on the name of the city, Jericho, which appears in verse 18.

The missing name of the city is not the only reason to connect the two short units at the end of our chapter with the story of Elijah's ascent at its start. Although these episodes make no mention of Elijah's name, Jericho and Beit El – the cities mentioned in these two units – are two of the stations along Elijah's route to the place where he is taken up in a storm. Elisha, who goes back to the place where Elijah ascended, crosses the Jordan River at the same place where his teacher did so previously, continues on his way toward Jericho, where Elijah had previously passed through, and then goes up to Beit El, where Elijah is mentioned as having also passed on his way. Thus, Elisha is retracing Elijah's footsteps, in the opposite direction.

Thus we can say that II Kings, chapter 2, is a single narrative, with the route of journeying and returning serving to shape its boundaries, its structure, and its internal unity.

The geographical turning point in the story is in verse 13: "And he *went back* and stood on the bank of the Jordan." It is from here that Elisha sets off on his own journey, alone and bereft of his master, but retracing his master's steps in the opposite direction. Thus the story is divided into two equal halves: In verses 1–12 Elijah and Elisha proceed toward the place from which Elijah ascends, while in verses 13–25 Elisha returns alone along the same route. Verses 13–18, describing the various reactions to Elijah's ascent, therefore belong to the second half of the story, but the chapter in its entirety should be regarded as a single narrative.

Elisha's intention in retracing Elijah's route is manifest in the scene of him crossing the Jordan. Elisha crosses over the river at the same point where he did so previously, together with his master, using the same mantle, and even invoking Elijah's name. It is therefore no wonder that the sons of the prophets, who had previously accompanied Elijah and Elisha on their way to the Jordan and had waited on the banks for Elisha to return, regard the disciple's retracing of his steps as proof that "the spirit of Elijah rests upon Elisha."

Elisha cannot continue his path as Elijah's successor until it is clear to him that his master's ascent is irreversible (at least, at that stage of history). Therefore he stops at Jericho and stays there until the sons of the prophets, who are stationed there, report that their search for Elijah has yielded nothing (v. 18).

Elisha's presence in Jericho is what gives rise to the appeal by the people of the city for Elisha to solve the water problem. Following this, Elisha resumes his retracing of Elijah's journey, and goes from Jericho to Beit El. It is here that the episode of the boys who jeer at him takes place, along with the bears' attack on the children.

These two events are less clearly associated with Elisha's desire to retrace his master's steps than the previous units were, and they require some explanation. For the moment, suffice it to say that the key to understanding these events lies in recognizing that this is a continuation of the story of Elisha retracing the steps of Elijah, with the figure of the master and the fact that he has just been taken up in a storm to the heavens serving as the foundation for the events that are described here.

The fact that the story as a whole ends with Elisha going to Mount Carmel (and from there to Samaria), rather than returning to Gilgal, which is the story's point of departure, in no way contradicts our hypothesis above; rather, it is the obvious result of the idea that we have asserted.

Had Elisha retraced his previous journey with Elijah to the same place from which they had departed, Gilgal, he would be expressing the exact opposite of his true intention. "Retracing steps" is a concept that is usually perceived, in the biblical context, as a negation of the significance of the original journey. When a person retraces his steps to the place from whence he set out, it is as though he never left there; it is as though he re-establishes the original situation. Clearly, this is not Elisha's intention in retracing Elijah's steps. Rather, he means almost the opposite: He wants to show that he is Elijah's successor. In the same places where Elisha had so recently appeared as the disciple and servant of his great master, he now appears alone, as the prophet who takes the place of the master who is gone.

Therefore, instead of ending his journey in the footsteps of Elijah at their point of departure, which would have characterized Elisha's state prior to inheriting Elijah's role, he continues in his master's footsteps – those that go back to an earlier time. He goes back to the most important arena of his master's national activity, to Mount Carmel. It was there that Elijah achieved his greatest victory in the fight for the nation's soul. By this act, Elisha is demonstrating unequivocally that he has inherited Elijah's role.

STRUCTURE OF THE NARRATIVE

After defining the boundaries of the story, we find that we can divide it into two halves of almost identical length. II Kings 2 occupies twenty-five verses in total. The first half extends from verse 1 to verse 12, and its subject is Elijah's ascent to heaven in a storm. This is explicit in the introductory words and is repeated in similar language near the end of the first half:

> And it was, when God took up Elijah in a storm to heaven ... (v. 1)
> ... And Elijah went up in a storm to heaven (v. 11)

Verse 12 describes Elisha's reaction of mourning to Elijah's disappearance. While this is the first verse in the story where Elisha remains alone, it should nevertheless be regarded as concluding the first half, because Elijah's presence is still felt at the beginning of the verse: "And Elisha saw (him)...and he saw him no more." The second part of the verse, "He took hold of his clothes and he tore them ...," also describes Elisha's reaction to Elijah's ascent in the previous verse, and therefore it is still connected to the same subject.

The second half of the story includes thirteen verses, from verse 13 to verse 25. The subject of this half is the beginning of Elisha's independent path as the prophet who inherits the role of Elijah, his master, and the measure of recognition that he receives as such. The words of the sons of the prophets, as they see Elisha crossing the Jordan just as Elijah had done so previously, are an appropriate summary of this half: "The spirit of Elijah rests upon Elisha."

It should be emphasized that even in the first part of the story, which deals with Elijah's ascent, the subject of the second half – Elisha's succession – is given extensive treatment. Elisha is mentioned in every verse of the first half, not only as the disciple and loyal attendant of his master, but principally as the one who is destined to inherit him. This idea is addressed in different ways throughout the first half of the story. Both Elisha's accompaniment of Elijah on his way to the place of his ascent and the distinction in this regard between him and the other sons of the prophets hint to this idea. There is also an explicit reference to the question of succession in the dialogue between Elijah and Elisha in verses 9–10. Elisha sees Elijah's ascent, thereby fulfilling the condition, "If you see …," and its result, "then you will have it," namely, a double measure of Elijah's spirit that will rest upon him.

The second half of the story comes not only to tell us that Elisha did indeed inherit Elijah's role, but also thereby to clarify two matters that this new situation necessarily entails: (1) What is the measure of recognition awarded to Elisha among the various social groups that he comes into contact with at the beginning of his new path, as the successor of Elijah and as the prophet of the generation, and what is done to strengthen this recognition and to overcome the opposition? (2) Does Elisha, as a prophet, set off in the path of his predecessor, or does he have his own, independent, different path?

Each of the two halves of the narrative may be divided into four units. The main consideration for this internal division is the geographical location of the events. This consideration aside, the two halves of the story differ from one another in terms of their internal structure.

The first half of the story is built on the very common biblical literary model of "three and four." Three times in this half the same dialogue between Elijah and Elisha is repeated, but the reader has no sense of progression or development over these three occurrences. However, these three lead to the fourth, which represents the focus and climax of all that has happened up until now. This fourth unit is the dialogue between Elijah and Elisha on the other side of the Jordan, just prior to Elijah's ascent.

The four units comprising the first part of the story may therefore be set forth as follows:

1. From Gilgal to Beit El – first dialogue (vv. 1–3)
2. From Beit El to Jericho – second dialogue (vv. 4–5)
3. From Jericho to the other side of the Jordan – third dialogue (vv. 6–8)
4. On the other side of the Jordan (Elisha's request, Elijah's reply, Elijah's ascent, Elisha's response, vv. 9–12)

In the next chapter we shall present a detailed analysis of this structure, and its relationship with the structure of the second half of the preceding narrative (Elijah and Ahaziah's captains of fifty – II Kings 1:9–17), which follows the same literary model.

Unlike the first half, in which the use of the "three and four" literary model guides and directs the action toward the climax at the end of that half, the second half of the story has a complex structure that is full of contrasts.

Its four parts may be defined as follows:

1. Crossing of the Jordan – the sons of the prophets recognize Elisha as the successor of Elijah (vv. 13–15)
2. In Jericho – failed attempt by the sons of the prophets to find Elijah (vv. 16–18)
3. In Jericho – the miracle of healing the spring water (vv. 19–22)
4. On the way from Jericho to Beit El – the bears maul forty-two children (vv. 23–25)

These four units may be grouped in two different ways. One way is based on geographical location; the other is based on the people who are involved, vis-à-vis Elisha. Each approach serves to highlight the contrast between its corresponding pair of units in terms of the main subject of the story: The attitude toward Elisha and the level of recognition of him as the prophet of the generation.

Division on the Basis of Geographical Location

The four sections are arranged in chiastic parallels, with unit 1 corresponding to unit 4 (in each case Elisha is in motion, on his return trip in the footsteps of his master), while units 2 and 3 find Elisha in a temporary stopover in Jericho.

In unit 1 Elisha is given recognition and honor by the sons of the prophets who had previously emerged from Jericho to accompany Elijah and Elisha to the Jordan. They now prostrate themselves before him and compare him (favorably) to Elijah: "The spirit of Elijah rests upon Elisha." In contrast, in unit 4 Elisha suffers the scorn of "young boys" who come out after him from Jericho, as he makes his ascent to Beit El. They curse him, comparing him (unfavorably) to Elijah: "Go up, bald one; go up, bald one."

Units 2 and 3 correspond to one another not only in that Elisha is in Jericho in both cases, but also because in each case the people of the city request something of him. However, there is a difference between the implication of the first request and that of the second, and this contrast is the inverse of the contrast reflected in the pair of units 1 and 4. Those who make the request, in unit 2, are the sons of the prophets of Jericho, and here their request expresses a lack of reconcilement to the finality of Elijah's disappearance, implying also a lack of acceptance of Elisha as his successor. They thereby reverse their reaction of acceptance of Elisha in the previous unit. Their request is met with opposition by Elisha ("You shall not send"); even his eventual reluctant agreement, after they beseech him, is meant solely to bring them to a recognition of the failure of their efforts and the mistake underlying their request in the first place. In unit 3, those who make their request of Elisha are the (regular) "people of the city." Their request specifically proves their full recognition of Elisha as a prophet who is able to solve their critical problem. To them Elisha responds willingly, with no reservations, and their request is successful.

Division on the Basis of Characters

On the basis of the characters that have dealings with Elisha, the four units comprising the second half of the story may be divided into two pairs. In units 1–2 the characters are the sons of the prophets of the city of Jericho, while units 3–4 introduce the "simple" people of the city – first the adults, in unit 3, and then their young children who emerge from the city, in unit 4.

This division likewise highlights a contrast between each corresponding pair of units in terms of attitude toward Elisha. Unit 1 contrasts with unit 2 in its depiction of the view that the sons of the prophets have regarding Elisha. The contrast here involves the same people – the sons of the prophets. Unit 3 contrasts with unit 4 in terms of the attitude of the "simple" inhabitants of the city toward Elisha, as the prophet of the generation who has taken over his master's role. Here, the contrast is between the adults and their young children.

This tumultuous structure of the second half of our story relates to the complexity of the mission facing Elisha as he sets out on his independent path. He needs general recognition as the prophet of the generation, among all sectors and levels of the population, from the sons of the prophets to the unruly youth. This is no easy task and it is not easily accomplished. The second half of the story comes to tell us of the socio-spiritual reality with its many contrasts that Elisha encounters, and the measures that he adopts in his various interactions.

The second half of the chapter lies outside the realm of the Elijah narratives, and therefore we shall only address that which is necessary for a discussion of the first half.

CHARACTERIZING THE STORY OF ELIJAH'S ASCENT

A spirit of mystery and secrecy surrounds the part of our story that directly describes Elijah's ascent in a storm to heaven (vv. 1–18). There can be no doubt that the text means to convey a powerful event of which more is left unsaid than that which is stated. Even the characters who are party to this event, whether directly (Elijah and Elisha) or indirectly (the sons of the prophets) do not speak of it openly and give no explicit expression to its essence.

The following details create the atmosphere of mystery:

1. The very introduction (v. 1), "And it was, when God took up Elijah in a storm to the heavens," arouses tension in the reader. He expects to find an elaboration of this unexpected introduction: How and why does God take up Elijah in a storm, and what does this mean? At the end of the first half of the story (vv. 11–12), an answer of sorts is given, but it is only a partial one.

2. The appearance of Elijah and Elisha together on their way from Gilgal (after previous stories in which Elijah appears alone) is shrouded in questions: How did they meet? Where did each of them come from? And what is the purpose of their common journey? Also, what is the meaning of Elijah's missions to Beit El and to Jericho?

3. Elijah, who is on his way to the place where he will be taken up to heaven, does not tell Elisha this. On the contrary, he tries to take leave of him so as to continue alone to the place of his ascent.

4. Elisha, who repeatedly swears that he will not abandon his master, likewise makes no attempt to justify his stubbornness in light of his knowledge that "this day God would take his master from over his head," even though it becomes clear that he is aware of this.

5. The children of the prophets, who encounter Elisha in Beit El and in Jericho, turn to *Elisha* with their question, "Do you know…?" From their question we discern the emotion accompanying their knowledge of what is going on. They do not dare to approach Elijah.

6. Elisha answers them, "Be silent!" This implies that the matter of Elijah being taken up is a secret one that should not be spoken about openly.

7. The sons of the prophets, who accompany Elijah and Elisha from Jericho to the Jordan, stand "facing them, from a distance"; they do not dare approach them, much less make any attempt to cross over the Jordan in the footsteps of the master and his disciple. Their awe of the auspiciousness of the event holds them back.

8. When, eventually, Elijah reveals to Elisha that he is about to be taken from him (v. 9), and the place and time are right for this to happen, he is not certain that Elisha will merit to see him being taken up: "If you see me being taken from you…" (v. 10). In other words, Elijah

knows that the manner in which he will depart from Elisha is not the manner in which people usually die, and he believes that it will be so mysterious that Elisha, although he is standing right by him, may not "see" it.

9. The description of Elijah's ascent (vv. 11–12) gives an impression of breathtaking wonder, but it is opaque.

10. The sons of the prophets, who knew that "today God will take your master from over your head," do not for a moment imagine how this has actually happened, and therefore they beg Elisha to allow them to search for Elijah, "lest God's spirit has carried him and cast him upon one of the mountains, or in one of the valleys" (v. 16).

11. Elisha does not correct them; he does not tell them explicitly that Elijah was carried up in a storm to heaven. Only after their three-day search yields no results does he allow them to conclude on their own that Elijah departed in a wondrous, miraculous manner, unlike the death of regular people. In other words, the matter of Elijah's ascent is not for public discussion – not even among the children of the prophets.

Chapter 50

Elijah's Journey to His Place of Ascent

THE ROUTE

At the beginning of his commentary on our chapter, Abrabanel asks the following question, his third:

> For what reason does Elijah, prior to being taken up, decide to go to Gilgal and to Beit El and to Jericho? If we propose that he was commanded to do so by God, then we must ask further: What need is there for this command and for his going there?

To this question we may add that the purpose of Elijah's journey would appear to be to reach the eastern side of the Jordan, the plains of Moab. Why, then, is this particular place chosen as the point of his ascent to heaven? To quote further from Abrabanel (fifth question), "Why is he not taken while on the way or at one of the places that he visits?"

Before discussing the purpose of Elijah's journey, let us first define its route.

The journey begins with Elijah and Elisha departing from Gilgal (v. 1). Where is this place called Gilgal? Gilgal is a name that occurs many times in Tanakh, with reference to a few different places in the Land of Israel:[1]

1. It is the name given to the place "at the eastern edge of Jericho" where Israel encamped after crossing over the Jordan (Josh. 4:19).
2. In Deuteronomy 11:30, the Torah mentions, in describing the location of Mount Gerizim and Mount Eival, a place called Gilgal that is close to Shekhem: "Are these not on the other side of the Jordan ... facing Gilgal, by the terebinths of Moreh?"
3. In Joshua 15:7, in the description of the boundaries of the inheritance of Judah, we are told: "And the border goes up ... to Gilgal which is opposite the ascent of Adumim." This refers to a third Gilgal, east of Jerusalem.
4. In Joshua 12:23, in the list of the thirty-one kings, mention is made of "the king of Goi'im at Gilgal." From the geographical context there, it would appear that this Gilgal is located in the northern part of the country.

The Gilgal in our narrative would appear to occupy a place of relatively high altitude; one descends from there to Beit El, as in verse 2: "They went down to Beit El." Clearly, then, this cannot be the famous Gilgal, the one close to Jericho, since the journey from there to Beit El involves a steep and difficult ascent. Likewise, the geographical route taken by Elijah and Elisha would make no sense if we identify the Gilgal here as being close to Jericho, since they return to Jericho afterwards.

Hence we must conclude that the Gilgal mentioned here is not one of the places listed above. Many commentators and scholars seek to identify the place as being somewhere in the region of the Arab village of Jiljilya (close to present-day Ma'aleh Levona, fourteen kilometers north of Ramalla and twelve kilometers north of the biblical Beit El, where the Arab village of Bittin is now located).

---

1. In fact, the Arabic names of several sites preserve the biblical name "Gilgal," a phenomenon which has led some scholars to propose that the name indicates some recurring phenomenon in the landscape of the country, such as a large mound (*gal*) of rocks; see H. Gevaryahu, *Biblical Encyclopedia* [Heb.], vol. 2, "Gilgal," 487.

If we assume that Gilgal is north of Beit El and fairly close to it, it seems easier to answer Abrabanel's question above. Elijah's purpose appears to be to reach the place where he will be taken up, on the eastern side of the Jordan (the reason for the choice of this site remains to be discussed). A person who is in Gilgal, north of Beit El, would indeed follow the route set out in our chapter in order to reach that destination. He would head south toward Beit El, then turn eastward, on the ancient road that goes down to Jericho, and then he would head toward the Jordan River, in order to cross over it.

However, this conclusion fails to answer the question. Elijah tells Elisha (v. 2), "For God has sent me up to Beit El," and then says (v. 4), "For God has sent me to Jericho." The simplest meaning of his words is that his appearance in both of these cities is at God's command, as an objective in its own right, rather than just as way stations on the road to the eastern side of the Jordan. Furthermore, we must ask: What have Elijah and Elisha been doing in Gilgal, so that this place became the point of departure for their journey?

REASON FOR ELIJAH'S APPEARANCE IN GILGAL

Gilgal appears again later on in the narratives of Elisha. Following the episode of his revival of the Shunammite woman's son, we read: "And Elisha returned to Gilgal, and there was famine in the land, and the sons of the prophets sat before him" (II Kings 4:38).

From where does Elisha "return," and why is his arrival in Gilgal considered a "return" at all?

In the story of Elisha and the Shunammite woman, we find Elisha (and his attendant) "passing through" Shunem and being based at Mount Carmel. However, it is only in Gilgal that we find him in the company of the sons of the prophets, who sit before him, and further on in chapter 4 (v. 43) it turns out that they now number a hundred followers. Elisha is depicted, in this narrative, as the person who is responsible for their sustenance.

Like Samuel, Elisha is a prophet who is constantly on the move among the cities and towns of Israel. Just as we read of Samuel, "He would cover a circuit of Beit El and Gilgal and Mitzpeh … and would then return to Rama, for there was his home, and there he judged Israel, and he built an altar there to God" (I Sam. 7:16–17), it seems that the same applies to Elisha. He covers a circuit of Samaria, Shunem, and Mount Carmel, and then returns to Gilgal, his home. "His home" means, first and foremost, his family – his wife and children. In addition, however, this is his "professional headquarters" as a prophet: It is here that the sons of the prophets whom he teaches, and for whose sustenance he is responsible, gather. Therefore, after describing Elisha's various activities in Shunem and at Mount Carmel, as part of his "circuit" through the cities of Israel, the text tells us, "And Elisha *returned* to Gilgal…and the sons of the prophets sat before him…" (II Kings 4:38).

Let us return to our discussion of chapter 2. At this stage, the sons of the prophets are not yet sitting before Elisha; in fact, it would seem that at this point there are no "sons of prophets" in Gilgal at all. This is not surprising: Elisha is not yet a prophet; he is simply Elijah's attendant. Nevertheless, we may assume that even at this early stage, Elisha has established his home in Gilgal. It is there that his family resides, and when he is not accompanying Elijah, his teacher, that is where he is to be found.

If our assumption (based mainly on the narrative in II Kings 4:38–44) is correct, we can now understand the meaning of Elijah's appearance in Gilgal and Elisha's journey with him from there. Elijah comes to Gilgal on the day that he is going to be taken up to heaven in a storm, in order to bid farewell to his disciple and attendant, who is at his home in Gilgal. Elisha readies himself to leave his home in order to accompany his master, while Elijah tries to persuade him to stay there: "Please remain here [in your city, in your home], for God has sent me as far as Beit El" (II Kings 2:2). However, Elisha, who understands the meaning and purpose of Elijah's appearance in Gilgal, is determined to go on with his master to the place where he will be taken up.

When Elisha later consolidates his position as Elijah's prophetic successor, the sons of the prophets flock to his city, and then the number of them sitting before Elisha in Gilgal are double the number of the sons of prophets who were previously in Jericho. (Compare 4:43 to vv. 7 and 16 of our chapter.)

REASON FOR ELIJAH VISITING BEIT EL AND JERICHO

The clarification of Elijah's point of departure, Gilgal, may guide us in seeking the reason for the continuation of the journey via Beit El and

Jericho. Apparently, the purpose of Elijah entering these cities is connected to the only event that the text describes as happening when he gets there. Both of these cities house "sons of the prophets," and they approach Elisha and conduct identical conversations with him: "They said to him: Did you know that today God will take your master from over your head? And he said: I do know it; be silent" (vv. 3 and 5).

Apparently, Elijah's passage through these cities, at God's command, is meant as a gesture of farewell to the apprentice prophets. As we know from the narratives about Samuel (I Sam. 19) and Elisha (II Kings 4), the prophet of the generation is regarded as the teacher of the apprentice prophets of his generation. While Elijah does not seem to have served as the head of a group of apprentice prophets, as Samuel and Elisha did (perhaps because he was not based in one place), all the "sons of the prophets" of the generation are considered his disciples, and he must therefore take leave of them before he is taken from them.

Here we must ask: Where is there any hint of Elijah taking leave of Elisha in Gilgal, or of the apprentice prophets in Beit El and in Jericho? The apprentice prophets do not say a word to Elijah in either place, nor does Elijah say anything to them!

Addressing the rather surprising dialogue that the apprentice prophets have with Elisha both in Beit El and in Jericho, and its implications, Abrabanel asks:

> Who told all of the apprentice prophets, those in Beit El and those in Jericho, that Elijah was going to be taken on that day? If it came to them in the form of a prophecy, how is it that all of them experienced it? … And what was the purpose of and the need for this revelation to them?

Seemingly, the answer to Abrabanel's questions is connected to our discussion concerning the purpose of Elijah's stopover in Beit El and in Jericho.

The knowledge that Elijah is going to be taken up to the heavens in a storm is known to us, the readers, already in the first verse of the narrative. However, as discussed above, it remains a secret that is not discussed before it happens, nor are its details made clear afterward. In this situation, Elijah's farewell to Elisha and to the apprentice prophets could end up being one-sided and hence meaningless: Elijah knows that he has come to give honor to Elisha and to the apprentice prophets by taking leave of them before he is taken from them, but since they are unaware of what is going to happen (and of course Elijah will not reveal his secret), Elijah's passage through Gilgal, Beit El, and Jericho will be strange and unintelligible in the eyes of those to whom Elijah is meant to be bidding farewell.

In order to avoid such a situation, there is a prophecy that comes in advance to tell both Elisha ("I do know it") and the apprentice prophets in the two cities where Elijah will be stopping over, that on this day God will be taking Elijah from them. It is possible that the prophecy is experienced by all of them; however, it may be revealed to only one, or to a few. In any event, the news is spread throughout the entire company.

Nevertheless, this prophetic revelation remains a secret, and the apprentice prophets do not dare to mention it to Elijah himself – the subject of the secret – out of their immense awe and respect for him, and especially on this auspicious and awesome day. Hence, we are left with a peculiar farewell: Elijah's act of farewell lies in his mere appearance in those cities where the apprentice prophets are to be found, while the act of farewell on their part is realized in their emotionally charged dialogue with Elisha, in which they reveal their awareness that this encounter with Elijah is their last.

Thus, everyone – Elijah himself, Elisha, and the apprentice prophets – is fully aware of why Elijah visits these stations on his journey, but the atmosphere of secrecy prevents this knowledge from being raised in open conversation with Elijah. Even Elisha, Elijah's faithful disciple and attendant, does not express his knowledge of what is going to happen in his words to Elijah.

REASON FOR ELIJAH BEING TAKEN UP ON THE PLAINS OF MOAB

Now that we understand the reason for Elijah's appearance in Gilgal, and the significance of his passing through Beit El and Jericho before being taken from his disciple, we are in a better position to explore the meaning of his journey as a whole, and its objective – to reach the eastern side of the Jordan, the "plains of Moab opposite Jericho," where he is destined to be taken up.

Some of the commentators explain the reason for Elijah being taken up specifically at this place as a continuation of the parallel between Elijah and Moses that we discussed in the story of the revelation at Mount Horeb (I Kings 19; see details above in ch. 24). Radak, commenting on II Kings 2:1, formulates the idea as follows:

> The reason for them going to the other side of the Jordan would appear to be that Elijah had been told, through prophecy, that he would be taken there. Perhaps he was taken up at the same place where Moses was gathered up, to honor him, since his greatness was close to that of Moses. God appeared to him at Mount Horeb just as He had appeared there to Moses; he fasted for forty days and forty nights just as Moses had.

Indeed, like chapter 19 of I Kings, in our narrative too there are clear similarities between Moses and Elijah in several areas.[2] However, behind

---

2. 1. Just as Moses stretches out his staff over the sea and Israel passes through on dry land (Ex. 14:15–21), so Elijah hits the waters of the Jordan with his mantle (the symbol of his being a prophet), and the waters divide, enabling him and Elisha to pass through on dry land. This deed resembles Moses's deed more than it resembles the description of the Israelites crossing of the Jordan in Joshua's days.

    2. Just as Moses ends his life in a mysterious way: "And Moses went up from the plains of Moab to mount Nebo, to the top of Pisgah, that is opposite Jericho" (Deut. 34:1), so Elijah goes up to heaven in a mysterious way from that very place – the plains of Moab opposite Jericho.

    3. Just as Moses is taken when he still has all his faculties and strength: "His eye was not dim, nor his natural force abated" (ibid., v. 7), so is Elijah taken in a storm without any sign of weakness. His journey from Gilgal to the plains of Jericho on that day testifies to this.

    4. Just as no one knows Moses's burial place "until this day" (ibid., v. 6), so no one knows how Elijah was taken or where he is. Even the apprentices of the prophets could not find him after searching for three days.

    5. Just as Moses merits having a disciple, Joshua, who is filled with his spirit (ibid., v. 9) and continues to lead Israel, so Elijah merits having a disciple who inherits two-thirds of his spirit and continues Elijah's role as Israel's prophet.

these similarities there lies a fundamental distinction between the two prophets, and perhaps this is the purpose of the comparison between them. Concerning Moses we are told explicitly that after he completed his life's mission, he died and was buried. In Elijah's case, there is no mention of either death or burial. Thus, these two leaders do not end their lives in the same way; it is only the geographical location and the mystery surrounding the manner of their departure that serve to create the parallel.

Let us now turn our attention to the question of the place where Elijah is taken up, and the reason for him having to undertake the lengthy journey described in our narrative. Perhaps the parallel to Moses can be of assistance here – but in inverse fashion. Moses led the children of Israel on their journey to the land of their destiny up to the plains of Moab, at the Jordan, opposite Jericho – the place from which they would soon depart in order to cross over the Jordan and conquer the land. Elijah, by contrast, reaches the same point from the opposite direction – from the very heart of the now well-populated Land of Israel, from Mount Ephraim, from the land of Benjamin and from Jericho. He crosses over the Jordan in an easterly direction, to the place where the children of Israel encamped before entering the land.

Thus, Elijah's journey is the inverse of the journey of conquest of the land in the days of Joshua. At the same place where Israel readied themselves for the conquest of the land, on the plains of Jericho – right there Elijah departs from the people of Israel and from the Land of Israel.

We suggested above that Elijah's intention, in this journey of farewell, was to take leave of his disciple, Elisha, who was in Gilgal, and of the apprentice prophets (also his disciples) who were in Beit El and in Jericho. Now we may broaden this hypothesis to include the entire journey up until its ultimate destination. Elijah undertakes a journey of farewell from his generation, from the land in which he has been active, and from the historical process whose realization is described in Tanakh – the process of conquest and settlement of the land.

What is the meaning of this journey of farewell, signifying Elijah's taking leave of the nation and of the land?

In the world of Tanakh, a Jew who dies in the bosom of his family would be "gathered unto his fathers" in their burial ground, such that his presence would still somehow be felt – even after his death – at the place where his children and grandchildren would continue their lives, on the family estate. Thus, while the deceased person would have departed from the living, he (or his tangible memory) would not be cut off from the human process that continued after his death. His "name" and the place of his burial would remain a part of the lives of his descendants.

Elijah is taken up in a storm to the heavens, leaving no tangible memory and no link with the living. Therefore, in his case, the opposite process takes place.

In the last chapter of this narrative, we shall discuss the significance of Elijah ascending to the heavens while still alive. It would seem that this ascent does not signify an act of separation between death and life, but rather a separation from the reality that continues in this world. Therefore, Elijah's journey prior to his ascent – a journey of taking leave of the people and the land – is a journey of only temporary separation. A person who departs in this way means to return to the object of his farewell at a later time in the future.

THE "THREE AND FOUR" MODEL IN OUR NARRATIVE AND ITS SIGNIFICANCE

The description of Elijah's journey to the place where he is to be taken up and the description of what happens thereafter are built on a doubled literary model of "three and four." (As we have pointed out in the past, there are also other parts of the Elijah narratives that follow the same model.)

An examination of the description in II Kings 2:1–8 shows that it is composed of three units that repeat themselves, and these serve as a preparation for the appearance of the fourth unit, which is the climax of the next literary unit, starting in verse 9.

The following schematic presentation shows the parallels between the first three units and the fourth:

I	II	III	IV
From Gilgal to Beit El	**From Beit El to Jericho**	**From Jericho to the Jordan**	**From the Jordan to the other side**
v. 1: Elijah and Elisha went from Gilgal. v. 2: And Elijah said to Elisha: Remain here, I pray you, for God has sent me as far as Beit El. And Elisha said: As God lives, and by your life, I shall not forsake you. And they went down to Beit El.	v. 4: And Elijah said to him: Elisha – remain here, I pray you, for God has sent me to Jericho. And he said: As God lives, and by your life, I shall not forsake you. And they came to Jericho.	v. 6: And Elijah said to him: Remain here, I pray you, for God has sent me to the Jordan. And he said: As God lives, and by your life, I shall not forsake you. And they went, both of them.	v. 9: And it was, as they were passing over, that Elijah said to Elisha: Ask what I shall do for you before I am taken away from you. And Elisha said: I pray you, let a double portion of your spirit be upon me... v. 11: And it was, as they were walking along and talking, that behold – there was a chariot of fire and horses of fire, and separated them from one another, and Elijah ascended in a storm to heaven. v. 12: And Elisha saw it...
In Beit El	**In Jericho**	**At the Jordan**	**Back at the Jordan**
v. 3: And the sons of the prophets who were in Beit El came out to Elisha and said to him: Did you know that today God will take your master from over your head? And he said: Yes, I know it; be silent.	v. 5: And the sons of the prophets who were in Jericho approached Elisha and said to him: Did you know that today God will take your master from over your head? And he said: Yes, I know it; be silent.	v. 7: And fifty men of the apprentice prophets went and stood facing them, at a distance, and both of them stood at the Jordan. v. 8: And Elijah took his mantle and rolled it up, and struck the waters, and they	v. 14: ... And he went back and he stood at the bank of the Jordan, And he took the mantle of Elijah... and he struck the waters, and they were parted to one side and to the other, and Elisha passed over. v. 15: And the sons of the prophets who were in Jericho, facing them saw him, and they said: The spirit of Elijah rests

In Beit El	In Jericho	At the Jordan	Back at the Jordan
		were parted to one side and to the other, and both of them passed through on dry ground.	upon Elisha. And they came toward him and they bowed themselves to the ground before him.

From the schematic presentation above it is clear that the "three and four" model is doubled in our narrative – namely, each of the three units (I, II, III) comprises two parts: The first records a fixed dialogue between Elijah and Elisha ("Remain here, I pray you, for God has sent me... As God lives, and by your life, I shall not forsake you"). In all three instances, the dialogue concludes with Elijah and Elisha proceeding together to the next station on their journey.

The second part of each of the three units describes the activity of the apprentice prophets, who are aware of the secret of Elijah's journey on this day. In contrast to the corresponding first part of each unit, where the dialogue between Elijah and Elisha is described as they make their way from one station to the next, the activity of the apprentice prophets is fixed, in each case, in one place – in Beit El, in Jericho, and at the Jordan. In the first two units, the same emotional dialogue between the apprentice prophets and Elisha is repeated in exactly the same words: "Did you know that today God will take your master from over your head? And he said: Yes, I know it; be silent." In the third unit, this dialogue is not repeated. Its absence arises from the circumstances of the plot. The station that follows Jericho is the Jordan, which is not a place of habitation; apprentice prophets do not normally dwell there, as they do in Beit El and Jericho. Nevertheless, right now there are apprentice prophets even at the Jordan, and they are most interested in Elijah's imminent departure (v. 7): "And fifty men of the apprentice prophets went and stood facing them, at a distance." From where did they go? Obviously, from Jericho. These fifty apprentice prophets are the same ones who were described in Jericho previously, in the second unit. Clearly, there is no point in repeating the same conversation that has already been held between the apprentice prophets and Elisha in Jericho.

The fifty "sons of prophets" have obviously come to the Jordan in order to be present at the nearest spot that they dare approach to where Elijah will be taken up, on the other side of the Jordan, "facing them, at a distance." From their observation point they view Elijah parting the Jordan using his mantle, and they see him crossing over on dry land together with Elisha. At this point, it seems, the two characters disappear from view.

Thus, the description of the activity of the apprentice prophets in the third unit differs from the description of their activity in the previous two units. There, they held a dialogue with Elisha, while here they watch in silence as Elijah and Elisha pass over the Jordan, after it has been parted in a miraculous manner. What is common to all three units is that the apprentice prophets, who are moved at the knowledge that on this day God will take Elijah from them, attempt to draw close to this mysterious event in different ways, but remain limited in their success. In Beit El and in Jericho their desire to be part of what is going on is manifest in their dialogue with Elisha, who commands them, "Be silent." At the Jordan the same desire is reflected in their silent vigil "facing them, at a distance" from the place where Elijah and Elisha crossed over, and their continued observation of the two characters as they move further into the distance. Moreover, the apprentice prophets are aware in all three units that Elisha not only knows, as they do, the secret of Elijah's journey on this day, but he is the only one who is permitted to accompany Elijah on his journey to the final station. In the third unit this knowledge is further reinforced: They view Elisha proceeding together with Elijah to the place – hidden from their eyes – where he will be taken up.

Let us now discuss the fourth unit of the story, representing the climax of the three preceding ones.

Just as the first three units are divided into two separate parts (the dialogue between Elijah and Elisha, and the description of the activity of the apprentice prophets), so the fourth unit, which complements them, is likewise composed of two parts. The complement to the first part of each of the three units (the repeated dialogue between Elijah and Elisha) is to be found in the description of the fourth and final dialogue between them, in verses 9–12. This dialogue too, like its predecessors, occurs as the two characters are on the move: "*And it was, as they were passing over,* that Elijah said to Elisha ..." (v. 9); "And it was, *as they were walking along and talking,* that behold – there was a chariot of fire ..." (v. 11).

Unlike the preceding three units, in the fourth unit Elijah does not protest Elisha's accompaniment, and the content of their dialogue is the opposite of what it has been until now. Elijah rewards Elisha for accompanying him, and asks him: "What shall I do for you before I am taken from you?" Elisha's response, "I pray you, let a double portion of your spirit be upon me," is granted when Elijah's condition is fulfilled: "If you see me being taken from you, then it shall be so for you."

The description of Elijah's ascent in a storm to heaven, and the dialogue between him and Elisha that preceded it, are not connected to the apprentice prophets (to the second part of the preceding three units). It takes place out of their sight, and their presence at the Jordan in the third unit makes no contribution to what happens between Elijah and Elisha at the place where Elijah is taken up.

What, then, is the complement to the description of the activity of the apprentice prophets in the preceding three units? It would seem that the section we are looking for is the description of Elisha's return to the western side of the Jordan, where the apprentice prophets are waiting, and where they welcome him, as described in verses 13–15.

The presence of the apprentice prophets at the Jordan and their observation of Elijah and Elisha crossing over, as described in the third unit, represent the necessary background and buildup to this fourth unit. The description of Elisha crossing back over the Jordan, alone, in the fourth unit, clearly parallels the description of Elijah's crossing in the previous unit. What is important to note, however, is that just as in Elijah's case the miraculous act is performed before the eyes of the apprentice prophets, so likewise in the fourth unit, Elisha's crossing of the Jordan is witnessed by them (v. 15): "And the apprentice prophets, who were in Jericho facing them, saw him."

This parallel between the fourth unit and the third, with regard to the observation by the apprentice prophets, is completed through the parallel between the fourth unit and the first two. Just as in the first two units the words of the apprentice prophets concern the bond between

Elijah and Elisha – "Did you know that today God will take your master from over your head?" – so in the fourth unit the subject of their speech remains the same: "Elijah's spirit rests upon Elisha." And just as in the first two units we read, "The apprentice prophets who were in Beit El/Jericho came out to/approached Elisha," so in the fourth unit we read, "They came to meet him." However, in the first two units they approach Elisha with a view to talking with him, while in the fourth unit, as in the third, there is no dialogue between them. "They came to meet him, and they prostrated themselves to the ground before him" – in silence.

APPEARANCE OF THE "DOUBLE" MODEL: SIGNIFICANCE

Wherever we encounter the literary model of "three and four" in Tanakh, we must ask in what way it contributes to the subject of the unit in which it appears. In our case, where the model is doubled, we must ask whether this doubling serves a single purpose or two purposes.

The recurrence of some event in a biblical narrative three times in succession creates a *ḥazaka* (an established precedent) and negates the possibility of the characters perceiving it as coincidence. A three-fold repetition affects a change in their consciousness and prepares them for the event that constitutes the fourth link in the chain. At the same time, the repetition of an event over and over again creates a delay in the progression of the plot, facilitating the ripening of some process or development, as an escalation to the climax that comes in the fourth link.

Let us examine each part of the "double model" in our narrative. The difference in the subject of the two parts of the model is clear. The first part focuses on the relationship between Elijah and Elisha, while the second part describes the relationship between the apprentice prophets and Elisha.

In the first part of the model, then, it would seem that the three-fold repetition of the dialogue between Elijah and Elisha is meant to establish Elisha's decisiveness and his stoic withstanding of the test with which Elijah repeatedly presents him. It is this that makes Elisha worthy of Elijah's change in attitude toward him in the fourth link; it is this that causes Elijah to view him as his successor in the role of the prophet of the generation. (We shall elaborate on this point below.)

This change in Elijah's attitude toward Elisha begins to make itself felt already in the third unit. After Elisha repeats his oath for the third time, we are not told that he and Elijah "came to the Jordan," in keeping with the model of the two preceding units. Rather, we read: "They proceeded; *both of them*" (v. 6), meaning "in mutual agreement." The same impression arises from the subsequent verses: "*They both* stood at the Jordan" (v. 7); "*They both* passed through on dry ground" (v. 8). This implied accord, born of Elisha's stubborn insistence on accompanying his master, bears fruit in the dialogue between them in the fourth unit. The nature of this dialogue is the opposite of the substance of their conversations in the preceding units, and it is this that ultimately leads to Elisha's succession with "double the spirit" of his master.

Let us now turn our attention to the second part of the "three and four" model. In the first two links, the apprentice prophets in Beit El and in Jericho approach Elisha and ask him: "Do you know that today God will take your master from over your head?" Apparently, this question is meant as a way of engaging Elisha in discussion, and showing him, with great emotion, that they are aware of the meaning of Elijah's appearance in their cities. Elisha's response, "Yes, I know it; be silent," like the entire encounter between them, testifies to his superiority in relation to the apprentice prophets. It is he who arrives with Elijah in the cities of these apprentice prophets, and he is the only one who leaves the cities as Elijah's escort.

In the third link, the apprentice prophets in Jericho dare to emerge from their city in the footsteps of Elijah and Elisha, and to follow them to the Jordan, at an appropriate distance. This link therefore brings the apprentice prophets closer to the secret event where Elijah will be taken up. Is Elisha's status further elevated in their eyes at this stage? It would seem that the answer is in the affirmative. On the bank of the Jordan, the apprentice prophets see that Elisha's accompaniment of Elijah does not end there; he proceeds with him to the other side of the Jordan, to the place where Elijah will be taken up. That which actually happens there – Elijah being taken up to heaven in a storm, and Elisha receiving a double portion of his spirit – they cannot see.

The presence of the apprentice prophets at the Jordan, in the third link, prepares the ground for the events of the fourth link, which affect a fundamental change in their attitude toward Elisha. Up until now, Elisha has been shown to be superior to them, since he is Elijah's chosen attendant, accompanying him on his final journey. Now, however, as they see him returning alone toward the Jordan, and repeating the same miracle that Elijah had recently performed there, holding Elijah's mantle in his hands, the apprentice prophets understand that the attendant has become the prophet of the generation. They understand that now that Elijah has been taken from them, his spirit rests upon Elisha.

It is therefore the fourth link that changes the attitude of the apprentice prophets toward Elisha. Even though they did not directly hear Elisha's request of Elijah ("I pray you, let a double portion of your spirit be upon me"), nor Elijah's conditional agreement ("If you see me being taken from you, it will be so for you"), and even though they do not witness the fulfillment of this condition ("And Elijah went up in a storm to heaven, and Elisha saw it"), they deduce on the basis of what they can see, that "Elijah's spirit rests upon Elisha."

As in the first two links, they once again approach Elisha. Now, however, they no longer regard him as the attendant who may be drawn into conversation on matters that are meaningful to them. Now they silently bow to the ground before him, thereby wordlessly expressing their recognition of him as the new prophet of the generation.

Thus, the second part of the "three and four" model serves as a framework for a description of the change in the attitude of the apprentice prophets toward Elisha, until their acceptance of him as the prophet who has taken the place of his master. At the beginning of the process, in the first two links, they clearly regard him as Elijah's chosen attendant. In the third link, his status is further elevated in their eyes, in terms of his connection with Elijah, and the ground is readied for the revolution in their view of him as Elijah's successor. The progression is completed with his appearance before them in the fourth link, as the next prophet of the generation.

COMPARISON OF OUR NARRATIVE AND THE PREVIOUS NARRATIVE

The second half of the previous narrative of Elijah and Ahaziah's messengers is also built according to the "three and four" literary model. Three captains of the fifty are sent by Ahaziah to forcefully bring Elijah down from the mountain. These efforts are unsuccessful, and only finally, after meeting the fourth squad does Elijah confront Ahaziah himself and convey God's word to him.

Besides the actual use of this literary model in two consecutive narratives, there is also similarity in how it appears in both of them. The third link in each narrative is intrinsically different from the first two, constituting an essential bridge to the unit's climax, the fourth link, which is completely unlike the previous ones. This point has been discussed above in our discussion of both narratives.

There are, however, more similarities between the two narratives:

- The number fifty is repeated in both. In the previous narrative, this is the number of soldiers in each of the squads sent by Ahaziah to bring Elijah down from the mountain. In our narrative, the number of apprentice prophets who stand on the bank of the Jordan opposite the place where Elijah and Elisha cross the river is fifty. From the continuation of the story (v. 15 and vv. 16–18) it seems that this is the total number of apprentice prophets in Jericho. This number can be attributed retroactively to the second link of those in Jericho and even to the first, of those in Beit El. If this is indeed the case, Elijah finds himself opposite fifty men in all three links in both narratives.

- In both narratives we read of miraculous fire. In the previous narrative it is the fire that Elijah brings down to consume the two captains of fifty with their soldiers, whereas in our narrative we are talking of the chariot and horses of fire sent to carry Elijah in a storm to heaven. The fire appears in the previous narrative in the first three links (actively in the first two, and in the third in the words of the captain of fifty: "Behold, fire came down from heaven and consumed"), but is missing in the fourth. In our narrative the chariot and horses of fire only appear in the fourth link.

These connections between the two adjacent narratives, both in structure and in central details that appear in both, cannot be accidental. In order to understand the significance of the similarities we must pay attention to the differences between them, especially the differences that exist in the parts we have compared.

Let us look at the relationship between Elijah and the groups of fifty men in the first links of each of the narratives.

In the previous narrative Elijah is static. He is alone on top of the mountain, while the captains with their fifty men come to him time after time to bring him down and to prevent his being there alone. The opposite is the case in our story. The apprentice prophets are in their cities (at least in the first two links), and it is Elijah who travels from place to place together with Elijah, and enters their confines.

This difference stems from the different motives of those who are traveling in each narrative. These motives determine the nature of the interpersonal relationships in the stories. The motives of the captains of fifty were to fulfill the orders of their king and to bring Elijah down from the mountain with the intention of harming him. A violent confrontation develops between them and the prophet, with the prophet having the upper hand, and his pursuers being consumed by fire. The prophet remains alone at the top of the mountain.

In our chapter the situation is completely different. We claimed above that he was sent by God to Beit El and Jericho, on the way to where he is to be taken up, in order to take leave of the apprentice prophets. On this special day Elijah avoids being alone and his appearance in the different cities is to pay respect to the apprentice prophets. There is no confrontation here, only mutual respect. The apprentice prophets are so full of awe of Elijah that they do not express any parting words directly to him, but rather speak impassionately to Elisha.

Elijah's wish to be alone at the top of the mountain in the previous story, although successful at first, does not materialize at the end. God's angel orders him to descend and go to King Ahaziah, and this he does. In our story, Elijah does not wish to be alone on his journey (he visits the apprentice prophets); however his ultimate aim is to come to the place of his being taken up alone, and to ascend heavenward alone. In our story too, Elijah's wish does not fully materialize with his accepting Elisha's company at the final stage of his journey.

In the fourth link of both narratives we find Elijah detaching himself from the person he is with. But the difference between the two cases is vast. Elijah's detachment from Ahaziah is a result of punishment and death coming to the king. His separation from Elisha in our narrative occurs with a sense of exaltation and is accompanied by expressions of sorrow. The tidings of continuity emanated from the event: Elijah's prophetic spirit and his role as prophet of the generation are transferred to Elisha.

Thus the contrast between the interpersonal relationships described in the first links of each story continues into the fourth link.

The role of fire in our narrative also stands in contrast to its role in the previous one. There the fire wreaks punishment and death on those who plot against Elijah. Here the chariot and horses of fire appear in honor of Elijah – to carry him heavenward in a way that will prevent his body from decomposing. There fire descends to burn and destroy; here fire ascends from the earth heavenward to preserve and sustain.

"God made this corresponding to that" (Eccl. 7:14). Two adjacent stories, similar in structure and in some of their details, but in essence the absolute opposite of each other. What is the significance of the contrast including similar elements?

Elijah, a zealous prophet, satiated with confrontations, concludes his prophetic activity in the previous narrative by castigating the royal house. This is one of his harshest confrontations with a king and his men.

In our narrative, "when God took up Elijah in a storm to the heavens," Elijah merits one day of human tenderness, of mutual respect between him and his followers. His departure from his generation and followers is accomplished in a contrasting fashion to his life full of harsh encounters. His last day, as described in the text, constitutes a small compensation for a prophet whose words are as fire.

This time the fire did not appear at his word, but rather to honor him and to detach him from his generation: "And it was, as they proceeded – walking and talking – that there appeared a chariot of fire, with horses of fire, and separated them from one another" (II Kings 2:11).

Chapter 51

Elijah and Elisha on Their Way to the Jordan

T here are two occasions on which Elijah and Elisha journey together. First, after their initial meeting, in the fields of Abel Meholah, when Elijah takes Elisha from his father's house and Elisha follows him, to minister to him (I Kings 19:19–21). The second time is in our chapter (II Kings 2), in their last encounter, when Elisha accompanies his master to the place from where he ascends in a storm to the heavens. These are the only two instances where the text speaks about Elijah and Elisha together. During the period between these episodes, Elijah acts alone (in the vineyard of Naboth [I Kings 21], and in confrontation with Ahaziah and his messengers [II Kings 1]). We should not conclude from this that Elisha spent no time with his master between the first and the final meetings. At the end of the initial meeting we read (19:21), "He went after Elijah and ministered to him," and after Elisha is already serving as a prophet, following Elijah's ascent, he is described by one of the servants of the king of Israel as "Elisha son of Shafat, who would pour water over the hands of Elijah" (II Kings 3:11). Quite simply, Elijah likes to carry out his prophetic missions alone, and perhaps even when not engaged in some particular act he may tend to seclude himself at times.

The descriptions of the two encounters (and especially the one in our chapter) should be viewed as junctures of special significance, indicating a transition from the period of Elijah's prophecy to the period of Elisha's prophecy. These encounters give clear expression to the dialectical relationship between the master and his disciple, with great admiration on the part of the disciple toward his teacher and a strong desire to continue his path, on one hand, along with the disciple's insistence on maintaining and expressing his own personality, so different from that of his master, on the other. It is this dynamic that fills these fascinating encounters with tension. They hold the key to understanding not only the relationship between the two prophets, but also the relationship between the two periods: the era of Elijah as prophet of his generation, and the era of Elisha as prophet of his generation.

"REMAIN HERE, I PRAY YOU"

In chapter 30 of this book, devoted to the initial meeting between Elijah and Elisha in the fields of Abel Meholah, we saw that despite the magnetic attraction that drew Elisha after Elijah, the encounter between them was characterized by the tension generated by two such different personalities. Elisha, who delays following Elijah until he has had a chance to bid his parents farewell and to arrange a parting feast for the people of his city, receives an ironic, offhand rejection on Elijah's part: "Go, return, for what have I done to you?" (I Kings 19:20).

Is the final encounter between them characterized by greater harmony? Not necessarily. Here, too, we find a sort of rejection on Elijah's part after he comes to Gilgal, the place where Elisha resides, in order to bid him farewell. Three times – first in Gilgal (II Kings 2:2), then in Beit El (v. 4), and in Jericho (v. 6) – Elijah tries to cut himself off from his loyal disciple by telling him, "Remain here, I pray you, for God has sent me...." What is the meaning of this request? Both the master and his disciple know the secret of Elijah's journey to the place where he will be taken up; hence, as Abrabanel questions:

> Why does Elijah coax Elisha to remain in Gilgal, or in Beit El, or in Jericho, such that he would not see him being taken up? Elisha has been his attendant and his disciple, and knows that he will

achieve completion through his witnessing [of the event]; thus, he would be "withholding good from his owner" [namely, from one who deserves it, Elisha].

We discussed this journey as being a farewell tour for Elijah, where he takes leave of the land and of the apprentice prophets stationed at the various places along his route. Elijah apparently meant to take his leave of Elisha, too. It is doubtful whether they were in the same place before our narrative begins. Elisha seems to have been permanently stationed in Gilgal, while Elijah comes to Elisha's place in order to bid him farewell. When he departs, with Elisha accompanying him, he tries to convince Elisha to remain in Gilgal, with the intention of continuing alone to bid farewell to the apprentice prophets until he reaches the Jordan. His plan is that when he reaches there, alone – as he was for most of his life – he will be taken up by God.

In repeating his exhortation, "Remain, I pray you…" in Beit El and again in Jericho, it is as though Elijah is trying to take leave of Elisha like any one of the apprentice prophets there. As Abrabanel comments, "He tried to get Elisha to remain, like one of them." Indeed, at each of these stations Elisha functions as a sort of link between Elijah and the apprentice prophets, for they, having become aware that Elijah is going to be taken that day, and thus having an understanding of Elijah's visit to their city as a parting gesture, do not dare to address the great prophet himself. Abrabanel explains:

> They did not speak to Elijah, owing to their awe of him, and lest he reply by rebuking them, "Do not inquire into that which is too wondrous for you." However, *to Elisha, who was an apprentice like them*, they said. …

In terms of joining him for the journey, it appears that Elijah regards Elisha as one of the apprentice prophets. Although he has been his attendant and disciple, he does not wish Elisha to accompany him, to see him being taken up. Why does he behave in this manner? It is surely clear to him that Elisha is not merely one of the apprentice prophets, but rather his successor, as he is told at Mount Horeb (I Kings 19:16): "And you shall anoint Elisha son of Shafat, of Abel Meholah, as prophet in your stead."

It seems that Elijah believes that he fulfilled this part of the divine command when he cast his mantle toward Elisha and then took him under his patronage as a disciple and attendant. This constituted Elisha's preparation for his future role. As Ralbag comments on 19:21:

> "And he arose and went after Elijah and ministered to him" – in order that he [Elisha] could learn more of his wisdom than his other disciples learned. For an attendant is always with his master, and observes his behavior and hears his words at all times, such that he could learn more than a disciple who was not an attendant.

However, it is not within Elijah's power to make Elisha the next prophet of the generation. Only God can decide this. "As prophet in your stead" is not enough to define fully the nature of the relationship between Elijah's prophecy and that of Elisha. Will Elisha be the prophet who *succeeds* and *replaces* Elijah, or will he also *continue* the prophecy of his teacher, standing in his stead not only in chronological terms but also in substance?

It seems that the contrast of personality that is revealed at their very first encounter (and which becomes much clearer after Elisha starts to act as an independent prophet) leads Elijah to assume the first possibility. Elisha will succeed him, but only in terms of chronology; he will not be his heir who continues his way. Therefore Elijah believes that when he leaves the world, his way will also come to an end. He knows that God has appointed another prophet to bear His word, and he knows that it will be Elisha. In keeping with his characteristic prophetic style, tending to isolate himself even from the attendant who accompanies him (see I Kings 18:43–44; 19:3), Elijah wants to take leave of everyone and stand alone even at the auspicious moment of being taken up by God. This will be a moment of mystery that will be shared only by the prophet and his God, and then the way of the great prophet, who has no spiritual heir, will come to an end.

Like Abraham, who conceals the reason for his journey to Mount Moriah with Isaac from his attendants, telling them, "Remain here (*shevu lakhem po*) with the donkey, while I and the boy proceed further" (Gen. 22:5), Elijah tells Elisha: "Remain here (*shev na po*), for God has sent me to Beit El" (II Kings 2:2).

Thus, Elijah's recurring "rejection" of Elisha in our chapter carries the distant echo of his rejection of him in chapter 19: "Go, return, for what have I done to you?" There, the words were uttered with irony (expressing personal criticism), with no practical intention, while in our chapter the opposite is true: The words "Remain here…" are addressed to Elisha with no hint of criticism and with no personal misgiving; at the same time, they have practical meaning in that they convey a rejection of Elisha as Elijah's spiritual prophetic heir.

"AS GOD LIVES, AND BY YOUR LIFE, I SHALL NOT LEAVE YOU"

Elisha thinks differently. On each of the three occasions when Elijah tries to turn him away (vv. 2, 4, and 6) Elisha utters a solemn vow: "As God lives, and by your life, I shall not leave you." This commits him, by oath, to continue with his master on his special journey. As in the fields of Abel Meholah, here too the disciple prevails over his master and forces him to accept his escort.

Why does Elijah submit to Elisha time after time? After Elisha swears the first time, in Gilgal, Elijah could have spoken up more forcefully in Beit El, and thereby prevented Elisha from continuing with him. Not only does he accede to Elisha again, but after Elisha utters his oath for the third time in Jericho, it seems that Elijah comes to terms with the idea of Elisha escorting him to the place on the other side of the Jordan River, from where he will be taken up: "And they both journeyed" (v. 6).

Had this journey resembled their previous stations, the text would have stated, "They went to the Jordan," in keeping with the model: "They went down to Beit El" (v. 2); "They came to Jericho" (v. 4). The omission of any destination this time indicates that this is not another temporary "accession" on Elijah's part, until they reach the next stop. He is now ready to accept Elisha's company for the entire journey.

The expression "they both journeyed" is again reminiscent of the story of *Akedat Yitzḥak* in the repeated expression referring to Abraham and Isaac: "Both of them journeyed together" (Gen. 22:6, 8). Thus Elisha is transformed from the status of Abraham's attendants, who are told, "Remain here," to the status of Isaac, who accompanies his father.

Here, though, we read only that "they both journeyed," as yet without the decisive "together."

Proof of our assertion as to the change in Elijah's attitude toward Elisha is the fact that when they reach the Jordan (concerning which Elijah had previously said that "God has sent me there," as in the case of Beit El and Jericho) he does not tell him, "Remain here, I pray you, for God has sent me to the other side of the Jordan." On the contrary, he takes Elisha with him over the Jordan: "And they both passed over on dry land" (v. 8).

Has Elijah then gone back on his original intention of isolating himself before being taken up? To a large extent, we must answer in the affirmative. What has caused this? It must be the firmness of Elisha's intention to accompany him, reflecting his desire to be Elijah's successor and prophetic heir from the moment his "master is taken from over his head." Elisha's presence at the mysterious occasion of Elijah's ascent to heaven serves to indicate that he is his great master's heir. His threefold "stubbornness" in making his oaths is proof that he may be worthy of this, and therefore Elijah softens and agrees that he accompany him.

It would seem that from the outset Elijah's mind was not firmly made up with respect to Elisha, and therefore he makes his request rather feebly, with an unconvincing explanation ("Remain here, I pray you, for God has sent me..."), so as to invite a stronger response on Elisha's part. We may perhaps suggest that Elijah wishes to test Elisha, to see whether he will leave him alone or accompany him further. Elisha's threefold rise to the challenge gains him Elijah's agreement that he continue with him.

Chapter 52

The Dialogue on the Other Side of the Jordan (II Kings 2:9–10)

"ASK WHAT I SHALL DO FOR YOU BEFORE I AM TAKEN FROM YOU"

The change in Elijah's attitude toward Elisha, following the latter's thrice-repeated oath before they pass over the Jordan, finds even clearer expression once they have passed over: "And it was, when they passed over, that Elijah said to Elisha: Ask what I shall do for you *before I am taken from you*" (II Kings 2:9).

It is important to note that this is the first time that Elijah explicitly voices his "secret." The purpose of Elijah's journey had been clear to Elisha, as it had been to the apprentice prophets, but it had remained a secret which was not discussed openly – and certainly not mentioned in front of Elijah himself. It is for this reason that Elisha does not formulate any reason for his firm oath not to abandon Elijah on the way, even though both of them are quite well aware of his motive. For the same reason, the apprentice prophets, full of emotion aroused by the knowledge of what is going to happen, approach Elisha rather than Elijah, and for the same reason he tells them, "Be silent." Here, however, in this final dialogue between the master and his disciple, close to the place where Elijah will be taken up, the veil of secrecy is lifted and he talks openly with Elisha.

Even more significant than the open conversation is its content: "Ask what I shall do for you." A gentle, fatherly attitude is manifest here in the master's words to his disciple before they part. It seems that Elijah is inwardly pleased by Elisha's display of loyalty, and seeks to provide him with some reward that he can take back with him on his return journey. Had Elisha acceded to Elijah's pleas – "Remain here, I pray you" – he would not have deserved this largesse on Elijah's part.

What sort of request is Elijah expecting from Elisha? It is difficult to know, because it immediately becomes apparent that Elisha's answer does not match what Elijah intended. Nevertheless, a close analysis of his offer, "What shall I do for you?" tells us that he had some specific action in mind, perhaps the granting of a blessing or giving Elisha some object.

"LET A DOUBLE PORTION (*PI SHENAYIM*) OF YOUR SPIRIT BE UPON ME"

In his answer, Elisha is once again revealed to his master (and to us, the readers) as having his own, different view of things. He requests something that Elijah would never have imagined to offer: "And Elisha said: Then, I pray you, let a double portion of your spirit be upon me" (v. 9).

What is the meaning of this request? The commentators offer various interpretations.

Some understand the term *pi shenayim* as meaning "double" (as in contemporary usage, and as we have translated thus far), such that Elisha's request is, as formulated by the Baal HaMetzudot, "Let the spirit of prophecy rest upon me at twice the level that it rested upon you."

It would seem that Rashi, too, understands the request thus. Although he writes nothing on this verse, he comments on Elijah's words, "You have asked something difficult," as follows: "It is impossible to give you more than what I myself have."

This interpretation raises some difficult problems. The Zohar questions (*Vayeshev* I, 191b):

What is the meaning of the expression, "a double portion of your spirit upon me"? Could he possibly have thought to ask two (double) from someone who had only one? How could he ask Elijah for something that Elijah himself did not possess?

Abrabanel poses the same question at the beginning of his commentary on our chapter (eighth question), adding a more critical dimension:

> This is a grave and most inappropriate request – both toward Elijah, who would not be able to give double of what he had, and in terms of Elisha himself – for having the great arrogance to ask of his master that he [the disciple] be greater and more elevated than him. And although our Sages teach that a person does not feel jealousy toward either his own son or his disciple, it seems strange that Elisha would ask not only to be like Elijah, his teacher, but that he should have double of what he had.

In some places, Ḥazal interpret Elisha's request as asking for the power to perform twice as many wonders as his master had performed. The earliest formulation of this view is to be found (in rhyming verse) in *Sefer Ben Sira*, in the section entitled, "Praise for the Forefathers of the World":

> Elijah was concealed in a storm
> And Elisha was filled with his spirit
> *He increased signs twofold*
> And all that his mouth spoke were wonders.

The same view is expressed very concisely in the *Baraita of the Thirty-Two Middot, midda* 1: "'Then, I pray you, let a double portion of spirit be upon me' – thus we find eight wonders performed by Elijah, and sixteen performed by Elisha."

In several places Ḥazal assert that Elijah revived one person who had died, while Elisha, as a result of the "double portion," revived two:

the son of the Shunammite woman (4:34–35) and the dead man who got up when he touched Elisha's bones (13:21), or alternatively, Naaman, whose recovery from leprosy is comparable to revival from death (biblical leprosy was considered like death).

However, it seems difficult to accept either variation of this view as a satisfactory interpretation of the literal level of Elisha's request. Firstly, is the number of miracles performed by the prophet any indication of his prophetic spirit? After all, what Elisha asks for is a double portion of Elijah's spirit. Secondly, is Elisha a collector of miracles? The miracles performed by Elijah and by Elisha were not for their own sakes; rather, they were needed for the generation as a whole, necessitated by the times and by the prophetic role that they fulfilled. It is difficult to imagine that what Elisha asks of Elijah is a multiplication of the number of miracles that he performed! Thirdly, as Abrabanel comments on this interpretation: "Based on these views, I cannot understand why Elijah would answer him, 'You have asked something difficult.' Did it seem unlikely that Elisha would perform more miracles than Elijah?"

Without changing our understanding of the expression *pi shenayim* as meaning "double," Ralbag nevertheless manages to arrive at a different interpretation of the verse as a whole. To his view, Elisha requests double that portion of Elijah's spirit that is bestowed on each of the apprentice prophets. He writes:

> This means: Out of what you bestow of your spirit upon all of the apprentice prophets, let that which is bestowed upon me be double that of all the others. This is reminiscent of what is written: "Rather, he shall acknowledge the son of the less-loved [wife], to give him double of all that he has" (Deut. 21:17).

The difficulty inherent in Ralbag's explanation is that he introduces into our verse an element that is not hinted anywhere: the apprentice prophets and their status as inheritors of Elijah's spirit. The example that he brings from the inheritance of the firstborn is not the same as our case. There, the text explicitly compares the son of the most-loved wife to that of the less-loved wife for the purposes of inheritance: "And it shall be, on the day he bequeaths to his sons that which he has, he cannot show preference to the son of the most-loved wife over the son of the less-loved wife if [the latter] is the firstborn." In that event, the basis for calculating the double inheritance to be received by the eldest son is that which is received by the son of the most-loved wife. In our case, however, there is no mention at all of the apprentice prophets in relation to Elisha.

The earliest proposal of a different interpretation of our verse, based on the understanding that the expression *pi shenayim* cannot mean double, was the grammarian Rabbi Yona Ibn Janach, in his *Sefer HaShorashim*. His view is adopted by Ibn Ezra in his commentary on the Torah as well as by Rabbi Yosef Kimhi, whose explanation is cited by his son, Radak, on our verse.

Before examining how these commentators explain the matter, let us review the only three places in Tanakh where the expression *pi shenayim* occurs. Aside from our verse and the aforementioned discussion of the inheritance of the firstborn in Deuteronomy, it appears once in the book of Zechariah: "And it shall be throughout the land, promises God, that two parts (*pi shenayim*) of it shall be cut off and shall perish, while the third part (*hashelishit*) of it shall remain" (Zech. 13:8).

It is clear from the context here that *pi shenayim* does not mean "double," but rather "two-thirds." This conclusion is deduced from the end of the verse, "while the third part of it shall remain." This interpretation would also make sense in the context of the inheritance of a firstborn who receives a double portion in relation to an (only) brother: "To give him *pi shenayim* of all that he has," namely, to give him two-thirds of the entire inheritance.

Now let us return to the commentators, starting with Rabbi Yona Ibn Janach, in his discussion of the root *peh-heh* (*Sefer HaShorashim*, Bakhar Edition, 395):

> "*Pi shenayim* of all that he has ...," similar to "two parts of it will be cut off and perish"; "let two parts of your spirit be upon me." The meaning of *pi shenayim* is two parts. Sometimes it means

two-thirds of the total, as in "two parts of it will be cut off and perish, while the third part shall remain," and likewise, "I pray you, let two parts of your spirit be upon me." Then there are another two-thirds of the total, when it says, "Two parts of all that he has," when he divides between only two, in other words, between the elder son and one other son. But when he divides among more than two, then it refers not to two-thirds of the total, but rather double of what each of the other inheritors receives.

Pi shenayim, then, means two parts of the total, whether the total is divided among three (in which case the expression means "two-thirds") or more than three equal parts. Rabbi Yona Ibn Janach understands our verse, "I pray you, let a double portion of your spirit rest upon me," specifically in the sense of two-thirds. Thus, Elisha requests "two-thirds" (obviously meaning the greater part) of the spirit of Elijah. That which, according to the first interpretation of his request, would have been "arrogant," in the words of Abrabanel, now become an expression of the true humility of a disciple who makes no pretense of being even as great as his master, but rather aspires to have only "most" of his spirit.

Let us now look at Ibn Ezra's commentary on Deuteronomy 21:17:

> To give him *pi shenayim* – that he should take two parts. If there were three (sons), they should calculate as though they were four, and he takes two parts. If there were two sons, they should calculate as though they were three, and so on. As I understand it, this is also the meaning of, "let two parts of your spirit be upon me," as I have explained.

Ibn Ezra's commentary on the book of Kings is no longer extant, but another commentator who offers a similar interpretation of our verse is Radak, citing his father:

> My father, of blessed memory, interpreted *pi shenayim* as meaning that he asked for two parts of Elijah's spirit. Similarly, the Torah says, "two parts of all he has," two parts of his estate, for

the firstborn takes two portions of the estate, while the other
brother takes the third part.

The comparison drawn by these three commentators between what
Elisha is asking and the law of inheritance by the firstborn can help
us understand what lies behind Elisha's request. Abrabanel poses the
following challenge to all of the views that we have examined thus far:

> It seems to me that Elisha did not ask Elijah for a double portion
> of his spirit, neither in miracles nor in prophecy (as Ḥazal, Rashi,
> and the Baal HaMetzudot would have it), neither from him nor
> from the other prophets (as Ralbag suggests), for this would be in
> the hands of God, who "grants wisdom to the wise" (Dan. 2:21);
> Elijah could not have granted this even if Elisha had asked it of him.

The double inheritance of the firstborn son is a positive commandment:
"He shall acknowledge the firstborn son … to give him a double portion."
However, this does not mean that if the father refuses to acknowledge
his firstborn son and regards him as equal to his other children, the firstborn son loses out. The commandment is to recognize and acknowledge
that which the Torah states: That the firstborn has a preferential status
in relation to his brothers, and receives a double portion. The father's
bequeathing of a double portion of the inheritance to the firstborn may
be defined as a formal act of recognizing him as the firstborn. The law
itself is set down by the Torah, and the father is powerless to change it.
The significance of this law is a recognition of the fact that the firstborn
is the "primary" son, who continues his father's personality and leads
the family after his father's death.

On the basis of the parallel between the law of the firstborn in
Deuteronomy and Elisha's request we may say that the same applies
in our case. The measure of the prophetic spirit that will rest upon
Elisha, as inheritor of Elijah's role, is indeed up to God; it is not in Elijah's hands – as Abrabanel correctly argues. What Elisha is asking of
his master is that Elijah acknowledge him as his main successor, as the
prophet who continues after him. In this respect Elisha does answer
Elijah's question, "Ask what I shall *do* for you."

The attitude that Elijah displays toward Elisha, during their joint journey as far as Jericho, is, as we have seen, similar to his attitude toward the other apprentice prophets: "He tried to get him [Elisha] to remain [in Beit El and in Jericho], like one of them," as Abrabanel defines it. Of course, Elijah has not forgotten God's words – "and Elisha…you shall anoint as prophet in your stead." Both of them are well aware that Elisha will inherit Elijah's role as the prophet of the generation. The question that remains to be clarified is whether Elijah will acknowledge and recognize Elisha as his successor, or whether Elisha's rise to the status of the prophet of the generation will be the result of an independent process that will take place after Elijah's death. Will Elisha be a prophet who starts a new path, or will his path be an unbroken continuation of that of Elijah? This is the essence of the covert conflict between Elijah and Elisha with regard to Elisha's accompaniment of his master on his journey to the place where he will be taken up.

It is this, then, that Elisha now openly requests: He wants Elijah's recognition of him as his successor and the one who will continue his path among the nation, in precisely the same way as a father acknowledges and recognizes his firstborn son as his successor in leading the family, expressed through the act of giving him a double portion of the inheritance. "Of all that he has," in the case of Elijah, means neither silver nor gold nor a piece of land; it means his prophetic spirit. When Elijah's spirit rests upon Elisha then everyone will recognize that Elisha is to succeed and continue the path of his great master, who is also his spiritual father.

"YOU HAVE ASKED A DIFFICULT THING"

Elijah's reply to the request that he recognize Elisha as his successor and heir is, "You have asked a difficult thing." This tells us that Elijah's doubts whether Elisha would continue in his path are still nagging at him. Although Elijah has agreed to Elisha accompanying him, he is not yet convinced that Elisha's physical presence at the scene of his ascent necessarily indicates that he is Elijah's spiritual heir. Elijah has certainly brought Elisha close to that status by allowing him to accompany his master to the very end of his journey, but Elisha's status is not yet final. Now Elisha asks that Elijah assert and declare it, openly. However, his request is a difficult one. Is it possible for a person with qualities so different and opposed to those of Elijah to inherit his role and his prophetic path?

Malbim offers an interpretation that is different from those we discussed above concerning Elisha's request for a "double portion" of Elijah's spirit:

> He asked … that Elijah's spirit rest upon him, as it is written, "Elijah's spirit rested upon Elisha" (v. 15), and that at the same time he would still retain his own thoughts, such that he would have "double" – his own spirit, and the spirit of Elijah that would be added to him. And this is what is meant by the words, "I pray you, let double …," by having your spirit added to me.

Although this explanation does not sit well with the literal meaning of the words (*pi shenayim* not meaning "double," but rather two portions out of the whole), Malbim's interpretation reflects the situation wonderfully. Elisha requests Elijah's recognition of him as his successor, although it is clear to both of them that Elisha has "thoughts" that are different from those of his master, and he is not prepared to negate them. What he wants is for Elijah's spirit to rest upon him in addition to his own, independent and different spirit.

"You have asked a difficult thing": Is such a merging of Elijah's spirit with the spirit of Elisha possible? Can a person who maintains his independent thoughts, so different from those of his master, become his master's heir and successor to the extent that his master would recognize him as such?

"IF YOU SEE ME WHEN I AM TAKEN FROM YOU, THEN IT SHALL BE SO FOR YOU; IF NOT, IT SHALL NOT BE SO"

Elijah directs his doubts heavenward. It is not he who will rule on this complex question. He who chose Elisha as "prophet in your stead" will decide what the nature of the continuity between these two prophets will be. Will "in your stead" mean merely "who comes after you" chronologically, or will it mean as successor and spiritual heir? Elijah tells Elisha, "If you see me when I am taken from you, then it shall be so for you; and if not, it shall not be so."

This is not just an external sign testifying to God's decision concerning Elisha, but rather an internal test as to the degree of Elisha's involvement in this event and all of its implications. This, we recall, was the essence of the question at the beginning of our narrative: Would this auspicious occasion of Elijah's ascent to heaven in a storm represent the end of his path? Would this be a mysterious occasion that would be shared only by the prophet and his God – as Elijah perceived it – or would it be an occasion of great national significance, expressing the "changing of the guard" between the prophet who was taking leave of his generation and ascending to heaven, and the new prophet who was ascending the stage, as his heir – as Elisha saw it? This was the purpose of Elisha's repeated oaths; the purpose of his stubborn accompaniment of his master on his final journey: To be present at this great occasion, in order to be considered the one who continues his master's path and his prophecy. Elijah allows Elisha to accompany him, but when it comes to the possibility that Elisha will be present not only in body, but also in "seeing" – in prophetic vision – this is not for Elijah to decide. Only God, who is about to take Elijah up to heaven, and who long ago chose Elisha as prophet in Elijah's stead, can decide this.

What is there in seeing Elijah's ascent that would turn Elisha into his spiritual heir and successor? What is the secret of Elijah's ascent, and how is this secret connected to Elisha's status?

In chapter 55 below, we shall discuss the assumption that Elijah's bodily ascent to heaven implies that Elijah did not die. The deeper implication of this is that Elijah did not complete his mission. He must return to this world, to his people, in the generations to come, and soften his zealousness.

This "softening" that is destined for Elijah's reappearance in the future, has its origins in the Tanakh, in the generation immediately after Elijah, in the form of Elisha. As Elijah's attendant and as his spiritual "son," continuing his path, as someone upon whom Elijah's spirit rests and who, by virtue of this, carries out his prophetic activity, Elisha repairs and softens Elijah's impact, specifically through his independent way of thinking, so different from that of his master. However, he does this because he is Elijah's disciple and continues his path. In this sense he may be compared to a son who brings credit to his father through his actions.

"If you see me when I am taken from you, then it shall be so for you."

If God opens Elisha's eyes and shows him the wondrous vision of Elijah's ascent to heaven, alive, and also the meaning of this vision – that Elijah's mission is not yet complete, and that his path in this world must be continued, with a change of direction, with a softening of the way – then "it shall be so" for him, as he has asked: He will be Elijah's heir and successor. He will be his spiritual "firstborn," assuming a double portion of his prophetic spirit, and everyone will recognize him as the heir of the prophet who is elevated above the nation.

"And if not, then it shall not be so."

If Elisha does not merit this, and the vision of Elijah ascending, live, to heaven escapes him (as it escapes the apprentice prophets, who are aware only that Elijah is no more, without having any knowledge of how he disappeared), then it will be clear that God does not desire Elisha to be Elijah's successor. It will then be clear that the special attributes of this disciple – quite different from the attributes of his master – are his own, and their independent existence is not a continuation of those of his master.

Will the different path chosen by Elisha, prophet of the next generation, represent a revolution against the path of his master, or will it be the continuation of his master specifically by virtue of its being different? This is the question that is put to the test on the other side of the Jordan.

Chapter 53

Elijah's Ascent
(II Kings 2:11–12)

THE PARTING

> And it was, as they proceeded – walking and talking[1] – that there
> appeared a chariot of fire, with horses of fire, and separated them
> from one another, and Elijah went up in a storm to heaven. And
> Elisha saw it.... (vv. 11–12)

The condition, "If you see me taken from you," is fulfilled. This was not a
physical, external observation, but rather a prophetic vision. The "chariot of fire with horses of fire" appear to Elisha later on (6:14–17), when
they come to protect him in Dothan from the real horses and chariots,
the mighty army, of the king of Aram, when these come to encircle and
capture him by night. His attendant, awakening early in the morning to
find the host of Aram surrounding the city, calls to Elisha:

> Alas, my master! What shall we do? And he said to him: Do not
> fear, for those who are with us are more numerous than they.

---

1. Rabbinic midrash depicts Elijah and Elisha engaged in deep discussion of weighty
   topics. See Y. Berakhot 5:1.

> And Elisha prayed and he said, Lord, I pray You, open his eyes that he may see. And God opened the eyes of the youth and he saw, behold, the mountain was full of *horses and chariots of fire* around Elisha. (6:15–17)

In our instance too, it would seem that there is a need for "opening of the eyes" to see the hidden, supernal reality that is far removed from the tangible scene that is perceived through regular vision. The ascent of Elijah, alive, in a storm to heaven, in that "chariot of fire with horses of fire" that are sent to honor him and carry him heavenward, is a vision that would not be perceived by a regular person standing at the scene.

The emphasis in the text that Elisha "sees" his master's ascent is meant to establish that Elisha is worthy of being Elijah's loyal successor. His request of Elijah, "I pray you, let a double portion of your spirit be upon me," has been fulfilled. Elijah told him, "If you see me being taken from you, then it shall be so for you" – "And Elisha saw."

Elisha, who is going to return alone from the place of Elijah's ascent, succeeds and continues his master's path, but also repairs and sweetens it, by virtue of the fact that he is the heir to the prophet "who never tasted the flavor of death and burial" (as the poem "Eliyahu HaNavi," recited after the close of the Sabbath, describes Elijah), and whose path needs to be continued and amended.

"AND ELISHA SAW, AND HE CRIED OUT: MY FATHER, MY FATHER!"

Elisha voices two cries of sorrow when Elijah is taken from him to the heavens, each expressing a different relationship with his great master. The first is his repeated cry, "My father, my father," expressing the personal, intimate relationship that Elisha feels toward Elijah, as a son toward his father. We are reminded here of their first encounter, when Elisha says to Elijah, "Let me kiss my father and my mother, and I shall follow you" (19:20). At that time, Elisha left his biological father and mother, "and he went after Elijah and attended him." His revered master became a new father figure for him.

This "fatherly" relationship between a teacher and his disciple is regarded by *Ḥazal* as the proper relationship between every teacher and his disciples (see *Sifrei* on Deut. 6:7), and not as something unique to Elijah and Elisha. Nevertheless, Elisha's cry, "My father, my father!" expresses a most personal pain, for the loss of someone who was as close to him as a real father. By contrast, when the apprentice prophets speak to Elisha about Elijah, both prior to Elijah's ascent (vv. 3, 5) and afterwards (v. 16), they call him "your master." Although they are "disciples" and therefore "sons" in the pedagogic sense, the degree of closeness that they feel toward their great master does not allow them to relate to him as a father. Even when they are talking about Elisha's relationship with Elijah, they do not dare to refer to Elijah in any other way than what they themselves call him – "master."

Indeed, what the apprentice prophets feel toward the prophet of the generation is different from the relationship between Elijah and Elisha, who has "poured water on his hands" (II Kings 3:11), accompanying him and attending him. Elisha has earned an unmediated closeness with Elijah, as *Ḥazal* teach: "The practice (practical ministering) is greater than the study." It is on the basis of this relationship that Elisha's request of Elijah, "I pray you, let a double portion of your spirit be upon me," is understood as the request of a firstborn son of his father, asking that he acknowledge his status and award him two-thirds of his inheritance. Even before we hear Elisha's cry – "My father, my father!" – the bond with Elijah as his spiritual father has already found expression in his request and its specific formulation.

"THE CHARIOT OF ISRAEL AND ITS HORSEMEN!"

In the second part of his cry of sorrow, Elisha calls Elijah "the chariot of Israel and its horsemen." This is meant to express Elijah's value for the whole Jewish nation.

What is the meaning of this title?

Targum Yonatan provides the following interpretation: "That his prayer is better for Israel than a chariot and horsemen." Rashi and Radak cite this *Targum* in its Aramaic original, while other commentators offer their own formulations, approximating the *Targum*'s idea more or less accurately. The Baal HaMetzudot notes the similarity between a chariot with horsemen and a prophet: "For he was of assistance to Israel before the enemy like a chariot with horsemen, as *Targum Yonatan* explains."

Ralbag identifies the chariot and horsemen with Elijah:

> He calls him, "the chariot of Israel and its horsemen" as if to say
> that he (Elijah) is the spine and strength of Israel in war. In this
> sense he is the "chariot and the horsemen" by means of which
> they are victorious in battle.

Abrabanel perceives the advantage of the prophet in the midst of Israel
over the earthly chariot and horsemen, and his interpretation is closer
to the intention of the *Targum*:

> He says "the chariot of Israel and its horsemen" as if to say that
> it was [Elijah] who protected the people of his nation, deliver-
> ing them from their enemies *to a greater extent* than the chariot
> and horsemen did.

How does Elisha arrive at this unique appellation for Elijah, describing him as protecting the nation in its wars? Nowhere do we find any
connection between Elijah and any of Israel's wars! In the chapters that
describe battles that took place during the period of Elijah's activity
(I Kings, chs. 20 and 22, describing Israel's wars against Aram), Elijah
is nowhere to be seen. Instead we meet another prophet, Micaiah the
son of Imlah. Is this description of Elijah as "the chariot of Israel and
its horsemen" really suited to the nature of his activity, as described
in the previous chapters?

Firstly, it is necessary that we consider the source for this specific
image in the previous verse: "And behold, a chariot of fire and horses
of fire appeared, and they separated the two of them" (II Kings 2:11).

Radak, in his commentary on verse 1, points to the connection
between Elisha's cry and the vision that preceded it:

> The chariot of fire and horses of fire appeared to Elisha, to tell
> him that when [Elijah] was taken up, Israel lost its chariot and
> horsemen, as Elisha then says: "My father, my father; the chariot
> of Israel and its horsemen!"

Chariots and horsemen are associated with war; therefore, the "chariot of fire with horses of fire" is a symbol connected to war. The meaning of this symbol is clarified later in the text (6:14–18) when the king of Aram sends his forces to Dothan, where Elisha dwells, with the mission of capturing him:

> He sent horses to there, and chariots, and a great host, and they came at night and surrounded the city. And the attendant of the man of God arose early, and he went out, and behold – there was a host around the city, with horses and chariots. And his attendant said to him: Alas, my master! What shall we do? And he said to him: Do not fear, for those who are with us are more numerous than they. And Elisha prayed and he said: Lord, I pray You, open his eyes that he may see. And God opened the eyes of the youth and he saw, behold, the mountain was full of *horses and chariots of fire* around Elisha. And they came down to him. (II Kings 6:14–18)

This tells us that "horses and chariots of fire" is a prophetic image of God's hidden power, protecting Israel (or, in ch. 6, protecting Elisha and his attendant), and superior to the physical power of actual "horses and chariots" (II Kings 6:15). In the words of a different prophet – "Their horses are flesh but not spirit" (Is. 31:3), and therefore "those who are with us are more numerous than they" (II Kings 6:16). The chariots of fire and horses of fire, as an expression of divine protection, are connected to the prophet and are granted in his merit. Thus they are revealed to Elisha's attendant: "Behold – the mountain was full of horses and chariots of fire, *around Elisha. And they came down to him.*" In our chapter, too, the chariots of fire and horses of fire come down to receive Elijah and to take him up to the heavens. Hence the image of Elijah as formulated by Elisha – "the chariot of Israel and its horsemen." As the *Targum* explains, this means that Elijah was, for Israel, a chariot of fire with horsemen of fire, preferable to (stronger than) real chariots and horsemen.

Here we must ask once again: Is this image truly appropriate, given the nature of Elijah's activity as we have witnessed it in the preceding chapters? Is Elijah depicted as being connected to the wars waged by Israel and the victories attained?

It may be specifically because Elijah is *not* connected to the great political and military events of his generation that Elisha seeks to expose the hidden truth. Elijah, who has chastised his generation and at times brought suffering upon them, is the one in whose merit they have enjoyed victory and success. Merely by his existence as part of this generation, he represents a source of inner spiritual empowerment for the children of Israel, and this is worth more than any sort of material, military empowerment.

According to our discussion in the previous chapter, concerning Elisha's role as Elijah's heir and successor specifically through his own adaptation of this role, this cry by Elisha may be understood as his first step on the way to softening and "sweetening" his master's path. This is something that he undertakes not only from this point onward, in his actions as an independent prophet who has inherited his master's role, but also retroactively: Through this cry, Elisha reveals the hidden dimension of Elijah as someone who, by his very existence, protected Israel from their enemies. This dimension will be revealed in the continuation of Elisha's path as Elijah's heir, just as it is destined to be revealed in the distant future, in Elijah's own appearance in Jewish history.

Elisha, starting from his very first steps as a prophet, while still not fully recognized (II Kings 3:11), and until the end of his life, in his final illness, is openly and energetically involved in the deliverance of Israel and the furthering of their victories over their enemies. It is to this end that much of his activity is directed. Therefore, when he reaches the end of his life, he is mourned by Joash, king of Israel, with the same words that Elisha uses in farewell to Elijah:

> And Elisha fell ill with the illness that he would die from, and Joash king of Israel came down to him, and wept over his face, and said: "My father, my father; the chariot of Israel and its horsemen." (II Kings 13:14)

The expression coined by Elisha, the disciple, when describing the aspect of Elijah that has been hidden from his generation, is used to refer to him on the day of his own death, as open acknowledgment of him by the representative of the entire nation, the king of Israel.

Chapter 54

After Elijah's Ascent

RENT PIECES THAT CAN NEVER BE REPAIRED

> Elisha saw it, and he cried out… and he saw him no more. And
> he took hold of his clothes and he rent them into two pieces.
> (II Kings 2:12)

Elisha has merited witnessing his master's ascent in a storm to heaven,
and has thereby been shown to have inherited two-thirds of Elijah's
spirit. As Elijah is transported heavenward he cries out, "My father; my
father, the chariot of Israel and its horsemen!" Now comes the final bitter moment, the watershed defining the new reality: "And he saw him
no more." This is the clear line of demarcation in Elisha's life, separating his former role as a disciple serving his master and accompanying
him, thereby meriting his guidance and patronage, and his new role as
a prophet in his own right, orphaned, facing his responsibility alone. At
this difficult moment, before he starts to return – this time alone, Elisha
performs the customary rite of mourning: "He took hold of his clothes
and he rent them into two pieces."

What a mighty emotional load weighs down on this simple
action! Here is the mourning of a son for his father, "My father, my
father"; the mourning of a disciple for his most revered teacher, to whom
he had been drawn – "And he ran after Elijah" (I Kings 19:20) and whom

he served – "And he followed Elijah and he attended him" (v. 21), "who poured water over the hands of Elijah" (II Kings 3:11). And here is the mourning for the prophet and protector of the generation: "the chariot of Israel and its horsemen."

Indeed, the halakha deduces from Elisha's act the relative levels of mourning with regard to the tearing of garments. The *Baraita* (*Semaḥot* 9; Mo'ed Katan 26a) teaches:

> In the following instances the rent pieces are not sewn together: In the case of one who tears for his father, for his mother, for his teacher who taught him Torah, and for the *nasi* [of the Sanhedrin], and for the head of the court.

The Talmud, in Mo'ed Katan (ad loc.) seeks to clarify the source for the above law:

> "For his father, for his mother, for his teacher who taught him Torah" – from where [do we learn these]? As it is written: "Elisha saw it and he cried out, My father, my father; the chariot of Israel and its horsemen." "My father, my father": [from here we deduce] for his father and his mother; "chariot of Israel and its horsemen": this refers to his teacher who taught him Torah.... "Are not sewn together" – from where [do we learn this]? As it is written, "And he took hold of his clothes and he rent them into two pieces." From the fact that it says "he rent them," is it not clear that it was "into two pieces"? The text is teaching that they remain rent in two pieces forever.

What is the significance of rending into pieces that are never sewn together? The act of rending in mourning is an outward manifestation of the mourner's sense that something of himself has been rent; part of his own personality has been lost. For most of the close relatives for whom one is obliged to rend clothes and to mourn, this inner "rending" is healed after thirty days. After all, there is "a time for rending and a time for sewing" (Eccl. 3:7), and "the dead are destined to be forgotten from the heart" (as Rashi explains on Gen. 38:35, based on Pesaḥim 54b).

If the rending is an outward expression of the sense of loss over someone who has been part of the mourner's self, then the sewing together of the pieces reflects the consolation; the rehabilitation of his life which must go on.

A rending that is never sewn together expresses mourning that has an element of permanence to it. The other customs of mourning gradually cease at the various stages of rehabilitation: Some cease after burial, others after three days, after the seven days of shiva, after thirty days, and after the year of mourning. The rent garment, on the other hand, in those cases where halakha teaches that it is never sewn together, remains in that state for the rest of the mourner's life, reminding him of his mourning for the person who is gone, or for the act because of which the garment was rent.

A person's father and mother and his primary Torah teacher live on in his heart forever. Even after they leave his earthly world, they appear in his dreams and speak to him, and their guidance continues throughout his life. It is precisely because their image is a continuous part of his life even after they have died that he will experience moments, at various junctions in his life, in which he feels alone and bereft of those who brought him into the world and guided his early steps in it. The "rent pieces that are never sewn together" express this. They are an expression of continuous memory, of the eternal presence and vitality, in a person's consciousness, of those who are most precious to him.

The *baraita* quoted above, teaching us when the garment that is rent is not to be repaired, goes on to list eleven such instances. Only the first three, one's father, mother, and Torah teacher, are private rendings over personal loss. The other eight involve public, national, and spiritual sorrows: "The death of the *nasi* [of the Sanhedrin] or of the head of the court; hearing bad news [such as the nation's defeat in battle]; hearing blasphemy; a Torah scroll that is burnt; the [destruction of the] cities of Judah; the [ruins of the] Temple and Jerusalem." In these cases, as stated, the "rending that is not sewn together," as an expression of unceasing mourning, is clear to all. Here it is not a matter of a private loss, destined to be "forgotten from the heart," but rather the sorrow of a living nation, the sorrow of the land bereft of its children and waiting to be redeemed by them, the sorrow of the Divine Presence. From these eight instances where rending expresses mourning over some living thing, and where the pieces may therefore not be sewn together, we learn something about the three instances of private loss: Here, too, there is an expression of mourning that does not cease, because the memory of a person's father, mother, and Torah teacher, lives on throughout his life.

All of this is especially true in the case of Elisha's mourning for Elijah, who has not died, but rather was carried up in a storm to heaven. This manner of Elijah's "passing" expresses his continued existence and hints to his revelation in the future. Therefore, the mourning for the loss of Elijah joins the mourning over all the other living, eternal values listed in the *baraita*, like the mourning over a Torah scroll that is burnt (concerning which R. Ḥanina b. Teradion testifies that "the scroll is burnt, but the letters fly up in the air" – Avoda Zara 18a), or the mourning for the cities of Judah, the Temple, or Jerusalem. Therefore, "he rent them into two pieces," and "they remain rent into two pieces forever." The image of Elijah will continue to accompany Elisha, his heir and successor, throughout his prophetic career. Even now that he is an independent prophet, Elisha will always be the one "who poured water over Elijah's hands" (II Kings 3:11). In all of his future actions, he will have Elijah in mind, and his whole aspiration will be to follow in the footsteps of his master and to realize his legacy, revealed to him as he witnessed him being carried up in a storm to heaven.

The fact that Elijah does not die the same death as other people who leave the world, departing in a manner that is unlike the death of "one's father, and mother, and Torah teacher," leads Reish Lakish to raise a question regarding the Talmud's extrapolation from Elisha's rending to the other rendings of mourning. The Talmud records the following:

> Reish Lakish said to R. Yochanan: [But] Elijah still lives! [Hence, how can we learn laws of mourning from his example?] He said to him: Since it is written, "And he saw him no more." For him, it was as though he were dead.

"ELIJAH'S MANTLE, WHICH HAD FALLEN FROM HIM"

And he took hold of his clothes and he rent them into two pieces. And he lifted Elijah's mantle which had fallen from him, and he went back and stood at the bank of the Jordan. And he took Elijah's mantle which had fallen from him, and he struck the water. (II Kings 2:12–14)

Here we close the circle that began with our discussion of the original encounter between Elijah and Elisha, and we find ourselves returning to Elijah's mantle. This mantle is the tangible artifact that connects Elijah and Elisha from the very beginning of their acquaintance until after their final encounter. In chapter 30, we discussed the role of the mantle in these two appearances. Here we shall complete the discussion by clarifying the significance of its appearance here, at the beginning of the second half of our story, which follows Elisha as he takes his first steps as Elijah's heir and successor.

There are two phenomena that stand out clearly in the verses cited above:

1. The contrast between Elisha's two actions – in verse 12 and in verse 13, each involving a garment.
2. The seemingly superfluous word-for-word repetition in verse 14 of the description of the mantle: "Elijah's mantle, which had fallen from him."

The first part of our narrative (recounting Elijah's ascent to heaven) concludes with Elisha's mourning in response to his master's passing: "He took hold of his garments and he tore them into two pieces." The second half of our chapter, covering the beginning of Elisha's journey as an independent prophet who has inherited his master's role, begins with the opposite action: lifting and taking Elijah's mantle. Corresponding to "he took hold of" for the purposes of tearing, we now find "he lifted" – for the purposes of using. Instead of Elisha grasping "his (own) garments," we now read that he lifts "Elijah's mantle." Replacing the act of tearing his clothes into two pieces, he now takes up Elijah's mantle in its wholeness.

What is the meaning of this contrast? It seems to be an expression of the ambivalent nature of the situation. On one hand there is sorrow and mourning over the parting, the pain of loss now that the master has left his disciple alone and orphaned. Elisha's sense of abandonment is expressed in his act of tearing his own clothes.

At the same time, Elisha feels joy at the privilege of being Elijah's heir and successor as prophet in Israel. (This status could not be taken for granted, as discussed in previous chapters.) Elisha expresses this feeling by lifting up Elijah's mantle and then making use of it.

However, these two contradictory emotions are not intermingled, at least with regard to their external manifestation. First, Elisha reacts with a gesture of mourning; only thereafter does he take up Elijah's mantle.

In a *baraita* in Tractate Berakhot (59b) we find a halakhic formulation of this ambivalent emotional state:

> If a person's father dies and he is his heir, first he says, "Blessed is the true Judge," and thereafter he says, "Blessed is He who is good and who does good."

This halakha seems strange: Is a financial windfall that comes to a person through such tragic circumstances sufficient reason to mix joy with his mourning? Surely if the person were given the choice, he would happily forgo the money; he would far rather his father remain alive! The answer is that the Talmud is not talking about a mere monetary bonus. The very possibility of a person who leaves this world being able to bequeath to his own children the assets that he toiled to accumulate during his lifetime, the products of his conscientious efforts, is a privilege, both for the person who bequeaths, and for his heirs. (This is especially the case if the inheritance includes assets passed down through several generations.) An inheritance is not merely a technical, monetary arrangement for the transfer of rights to property whose owner has passed away. There is far more involved. The inheritance is a link connecting generations, allowing children to continue their parents' endeavors in the world. The blessing of "who is good and who does good," recited by the children, refers not only to their financial good fortune, but also to the fact that it represents the inheritance of their father. This creates a continuity that is "good" both for them and for their father who left it to them. For this reason, the possibility of passing on an inheritance represents a drop of consolation within the bitter cup of mourning.

This is even truer in our case, when it comes to the spirit of the person who has passed on and the continuity of his role as prophet in Israel. However, attention should be paid to the fact that even Elisha's inheritance of his master, although mainly centered around the inheritance of Elijah's spirit, is also expressed in the inheritance of a tangible object – Elijah's mantle. And although this object is full of symbolic and spiritual significance, both as the prophet's typical garb and as the mantle associated with several of Elijah's miraculous deeds, it is ultimately a physical object, which may be taken up and worn. It is specifically in the lifting of this object, and the use of it, that we find the contrast to the preceding mourning. It is these acts that express the joy of inheritance and continuity.

Why, in verse 14, does the text repeat the fact that the mantle that Elisha uses to strike the water is "Elijah's mantle which had fallen from him," after this has just been stated, in verse 13? It would appear that each time this description of the mantle occurs, it fills a special role. In its first appearance, it comes to explain that which preceded it – Elisha's act of lifting it – and to answer the question of where the mantle comes from. In its second appearance, the description of the mantle is meant to explain the purpose of the mantle falling, and to clarify the significance of what comes next: "And he struck the water." In other words, had the text simply read, "And he took the mantle and he struck the water," we would have understood it as a sort of "improvisation" on Elisha's part; an idea that occurred to him right there and then – to use Elijah's mantle in order to cross the Jordan. However, the seemingly superfluous elaboration causes Abrabanel to comment:

> There is no doubt that [the mantle] did not fall by chance; rather, Elijah deliberately cast it toward Elisha, because it was a tool with which to effect the [divine] blessing and prophecy that had rested upon Elijah. Elisha was meant to clothe himself in [Elijah's] mantle and in his prophecy, and to remain in his stead.

The language of the text seems to suggest that Elisha's act of striking the water, upon his return, with Elijah's mantle, as Elijah himself had done when they were walking together, is perceived by Elisha as a command implied by the falling of Elijah's mantle. It is for this reason that the mantle fell.

The apprentice prophets see Elijah's mantle, with all that it implies, in Elisha's hand, and they see what Elisha does with it, repeating the miracle of crossing the Jordan River as performed previously by Elijah. This leads these fifty apprentice prophets, waiting upon the western bank of the Jordan River, to recognize Elisha as Elijah's heir and successor: "And the apprentice prophets who were in Jericho, on the opposite side, saw him" (v. 15).

This "seeing" implies "understanding": they saw all of these things, and understood their significance. "And they said: The spirit of Elijah rests upon Elisha. And they came toward him, and bowed down before him to the ground."

Thus it becomes clear that Elisha's request to be Elijah's heir, inheriting "a double portion (two-thirds) of his spirit," as the firstborn, has been answered. The very fact that he sees his master ascending in the storm to heaven in a chariot of fire and horses of fire is sufficient for Elisha to know that his request has been fulfilled: "If you see me taken from you, it shall be so for you"; "And Elisha saw." Yet, while this "seeing" is a sign from heaven that Elisha is the heir of his master, Elisha is the only one who knows this. However, the commandment to bequeath a double portion to the eldest son involves a formal, public acknowledgment of the eldest son's status by the father: "He shall *acknowledge*... [the firstborn], to give him double" (Deut. 21:17). Apparently, Elisha's request of his master included the element of this formal recognition. How does Elisha achieve open, public recognition as Elijah's successor? Through the falling of Elijah's mantle, and the implied signal as to how Elisha should use it, Elisha is given a tangible sign, full of symbolic significance, which will allow him to be acknowledged by the apprentice prophets, and perhaps even by all of Israel, as Elijah's successor. Since the apprentice prophets were not witness to the lofty, secret "changing of the guard," some alternative evidence is required. Elijah's mantle, in Elisha's hand, serves this purpose.

Let us examine the place of the mantle in each of the two encounters between Elijah and Elisha. In the first narrative, in I Kings 19, the mantle introduces the encounter, immediately creating the attraction between the master and disciple: "And he cast his mantle to him. And he left the cattle, and ran after Elijah" (vv. 19–20). Immediately thereafter, we already discover the tension between them and we detect a note of rejection: "Go, return, for what have I done to you?" The rest of the story highlights their differences in personality and nature.

Our chapter follows the reverse order. From the beginning of the story we note a suppressed tension between Elijah and Elisha, and there is a hint of Elijah rejecting his disciple: "Remain here, I pray you ..."; "As God lives, and by your life, I shall not leave you." However, as the story progresses, this tension dissipates, and Elijah grows increasing accepting of Elisha's accompaniment of him. The mantle of Elijah falling to Elisha is the symbolic climax of the rapprochement; it is a closeness that becomes a continuation. Ultimately, the rapprochement prevails. Thus the circle is closed. Despite the tension that prevailed between Elijah and Elisha after the mantle was cast for the first time, and before it falls for the second time, the transfer of the mantle from master to disciple is what ultimately defines the nature of the bond between them.

Chapter 55

Elijah Lives On

And it was, when God *took up* Elijah in a storm to heaven… (II Kings 2:1)

Did you know that today God will *take* your master from over your head? (v. 3, 5)

What shall I do for you, before I *am taken* from you? (v. 9)

If you see me *taken* from you, it shall be so for you. (v. 10)

And behold, a chariot of fire and horses of fire, and they separated the two of them, and Elijah *ascended* in a storm to heaven. (v. 11)

DID ELIJAH DIE?

What is the purpose of the description of Elijah's ascent to heaven – a description so radically different from any other account of death recorded in Tanakh? Are his "ascent" (mentioned twice) and his being "taken" (mentioned four times) meant as euphemistic expressions of his death, or are they telling us that Elijah did not die?

If we are to remain loyal to the literal text, it must be acknowledged that it describes Elijah's bodily ascent. Elisha watches his ascent until he disappears from sight – "and he saw him no more" (v. 12). The only tangible evidence that remains after Elijah's ascent is his mantle, which has fallen from him. This tells us that Elijah ascends bodily, dressed in his clothes – except for his mantle. Indeed, the apprentice prophets, who comb the area for Elijah for three days, do not find him (vv. 16–17).

However, if this is so, and Elijah's ascent to heaven is meant to signify his transition from this world to that which lies beyond, to the divine realm, then we are faced with a difficult theological problem. The *Baraita* (Sukka 5a) teaches:

> R. Yosei said: The Divine Presence never descended, nor did Moses or Elijah ascend on high, as it is written, "The heaven is God's heaven, and the earth He has given to mankind" (Ps. 115:16).

R. Yosei draws an absolute and unequivocal distinction between the human realm and the divine. (His categorical denial of any possibility of blurring the boundaries is doubtless directed toward the various pagan mythologies, until and including Christianity.) The Talmud questions this assertion, citing instances that would appear to contradict it. The same response is used to counter each verse:

> Did the Divine Presence not come down? It is written, "God descended upon Mount Sinai" (Ex. 19:20) –
> but higher than ten handbreadths.

> It is written, "His legs will stand that day upon the Mount of Olives" (Zech. 14:4) –
> but higher than ten handbreadths.

> And did Moses and Elijah not ascend on high? It is written, "Moses ascended to God" (Ex. 19:3) –
> but lower than ten [handbreadths].

It is written, "Elijah ascended in a storm to heaven" –
but lower than ten [handbreadths].

Ten handbreadths represents the boundaries of man's domain, while
whatever exists above ten handbreadths belongs to God's domain. While
there does exist some mutual relationship between God and man, as evidenced in the verses cited by the Talmud as well as many other sources,
this connection never represents any blurring of the sharp distinction
between the two realms.

The limitation of man, in his human, bodily state, from crossing
this barrier is conveyed to Moses, master of all the prophets, during the
Revelation at Horeb: "And He said: You shall not be able to see My face,
for no man shall see Me and live" (Ex. 33:20).

Only when a person's soul is separated from his body, when it
departs from the world that is "under the sun" (Eccl. 1:3, among others) and
"below ten handbreadths" – only then can the soul rise up: "The dust settles
back upon the earth, as it was, while the spirit returns to God, who gave it"
(Eccl. 12:7). How, then, are we to reconcile Elijah's ascent to heaven with
his human, material state? Furthermore, what is the meaning of the talmudic solution to the question – that he went "lower than ten handbreadths"?

Let us compare the approaches of two commentators, Radak
and Ralbag. Both introduce their discussion of our question in verse
1 of our chapter: "And it was, when God took up Elijah in a storm to
heaven." Radak comments as follows:

> The storm wind took him up from the ground into the air. As one
> lifts things that are light, so [the wind] lifted him, by God's will,
> to the fiery [chariot] wheel, which burned his clothes, except for
> the mantle. His flesh and his life were consumed, while the spirit
> returned to God, who had given it.

Radak returns to this image in his comment on verse 11, "And Elijah
ascended in a storm to heaven":

> As I have explained … Elijah became a spiritual entity, with
> his body consumed in the divine fire, such that each element

returned to its source. Elisha witnessed his ascent from the earth, and when he became air, he saw the image of a fiery chariot, with horses of fire, which separated them from each other.

In Radak's view, Elijah dies. It is only his spirit that "returns to God, who had given it." What is special about the description of his death is the manner in which he died, which is different from any other death recorded in Tanakh. In Elijah's ascent in a storm to heaven there is a process whereby the body is separated from the soul. The soul (spirit) ascends to heaven, while the body and its garments are consumed, such that there remains nothing for burial. This is Radak's solution to the fundamental problem of whether Elijah died or not.

Is Radak's explanation compatible with the language and spirit of the text? Abrabanel is skeptical:

> Whether Elijah died or not, and where he is – we have no way of ascertaining these things through rational logic; we can only go by the tradition of our forebears and the Sages, and by their interpretations of the verses. Nowhere does the text actually mention "death" in connection with Elijah, as it does concerning Moses and all of the other prophets. This indicates that his body was not separated from his soul, in the manner of all people who pass away naturally. Although the commentators have asserted that it is impossible that human bodies dwell among the heavenly bodies and not upon them ... still, we need not accept their view that his body and his clothes were burnt in that heated air or in the element of fire that was upon it, while the soul of the prophet is bound up with the bundle of life, with God, like the souls of the other prophets and the righteous men of God [as Radak explains]. For if this were so, the text would not elaborate on this matter when Elijah was taken up, nor that he was taken up in a storm. Why is there no mention of death? Can we suggest that people who are burnt do not die like those who are buried in the ground?

Ralbag takes a different approach. After presenting the problem: "It is impossible to understand that he was taken up to heaven, for mortal bodies do not ascend there," he explains:

What it means is, to midair. As it is written, "Great cities, fortified to the heaven" (Deut. 9:1); "A tower with its top in the heaven" (Gen. 11:4). God's wind lifted him to an as-yet-unknown place, and he remains alive there, as we have explained.

Ralbag again proves that Elijah did not die in his commentary on verse 3:

"Today God will take your master from over your head" – this explains that [Elijah] was taken only from over his head. Likewise, Elijah tells Elisha (v. 9), "before I am taken from you." This shows that God did not take him altogether, He only took him from Elisha.

According to Ralbag, Elijah lives on, bodily, in some unknown place, where he waits for the day when he will be manifest again. Where is this place? Is it "in midair" (somewhere in the sky), or is it here on earth? This is "as yet unknown."

The exegetical innovation, by means of which Ralbag solves the question with which he introduces the discussion, is his interpretation of the word "heaven," indicating the place to which Elijah ascends. In his view, this does not refer to the divine realm, that which extends "above ten handbreadths" (as referred to in several verses speaking of "heaven," including the verse cited by R. Yosei in the *Baraita* – "the heaven is God's heaven"), but rather to a high place in our world, "in midair," but still within the human realm – "lower than ten handbreadths." He then cites verses in which the Torah uses the word "heaven" to indicate a great height, attained by humans, within the human realm.

Ralbag's interpretation fits in well with the Sages' teaching in several places. It would seem that this is what the Talmud means when it explains the verse, "Elijah ascended in a storm to heaven," with the words, "lower than ten handbreadths." *Targum Yonatan* on this verse, as well as on verse 11, seems to tend toward the same idea. He translates, "Elijah ascended in a storm toward heaven." Likewise, Ralbag's interpretation helps to resolve a debate between Reish Lakish and R. Yoḥanan, recorded in Tractate Mo'ed Katan (26a). Reish Lakish asks how the laws of rending clothes (for mourners) may be deduced from the actions of

Elisha, who tears his garments when Elijah disappears from his view: "Reish Lakish said to R. Yoḥanan: Elijah lives on! He replied: Since it is written, 'he saw him no more,' we deduce that, *for him*, Elijah was considered dead."

Both agree that "Elijah lives on," but R. Yoḥanan's response points in the direction of Ralbag's distinction: Based on verses 3, 5, and 8, we say that "God did not take him altogether, He only took him from Elisha."

A sort of compromise between the approaches of Radak and Ralbag is proposed in the Ḥatam Sofer's *Responsa* (part 6, ch. 98):

> Elijah never ascended bodily more than ten handbreadths, but his soul was separated from his body there [in accordance with Radak's view], and the soul rose up and still serves on high, among the ministering angels, while his body became fine-pressed and lies in the lower Garden of Eden, in this world. On the day of God's redemption, may it be speedily in our days, his soul will be clothed in this holy body, and then he will be like any other of the sages and prophets of Israel.... Likewise, every time he is revealed and perceived in this world, he is garbed in his pure body; but when he is revealed [only] spiritually, as on the day of a circumcision [when he occupies the "seat of Elijah"], then he is not obligated by the commandments, as it is written, "The dead are free" (Ps. 88:6).... When he is revealed in this way, he is an angel. [Hence,] even though he studies Torah and reveals laws, the law is not determined in accordance with his words, since he is like a dream or a prophetic spirit, and "We do not take heavenly voices into account" (Berakhot 52a). However, when he is revealed in the garb of his body, he is like one of the great sages of Israel, and (*Tosefot Yom Tov*, Eduyot 8:7) "[Elijah] the Tishbite will resolve questions and puzzles."

Here the Ḥatam Sofer addresses a crucial question pertaining to Elijah. The image of this great prophet continues to manifest itself, in a most wondrous way, throughout the history of Israel and its literature. In most places where Elijah is mentioned in rabbinical literature, Elijah's character is completely different from the way he is depicted in Tanakh. He is described as conversing and debating with the Sages, or as being destined to appear in the future with the solutions to all unresolved halakhic questions. However, not only during the period of the Sages, but also afterward, Elijah continues to appear in our tradition, in our customs, in legends that tell of his appearances, and even in his revelations to several Jewish sages and leaders. We shall discuss this subject below.

APPEARANCES OF ELIJAH IN TANAKH AFTER HIS ASCENT

Explicit accounts of Elijah's appearances after the time of his ascent to heaven appear already in Tanakh, in two different sources, concerning two periods that are very distant from each other.

The Letter from Elijah

Chapter 21 of II Chronicles records the period of the reign of King Jehoram of Judah, son of Jehoshaphat and grandson of Asa. (He should not be confused with his contemporary and kinsman, Jehoram of the Kingdom of Israel, who ascended to the throne upon the death of his older brother, Ahaziah; both Jehoram and Ahaziah were sons of Ahab.) Jehoram of Judah is of Davidic stock, but he marries into the House of Ahab and follows their ways: "He went in the way of the kings of Israel, as the House of Ahab had done, for Ahab's daughter was his wife, and he did evil in the eyes of God" (II Chr. 21:6).

The beginning of his reign is marked with a killing spree, as recorded there: "And Jehoram took over his father's kingdom, and he grew strong, and he killed all of his brethren by the sword, and also some of the princes of Israel" (v. 4).

Jehoram receives a letter of prophetic rebuke:

A letter came to him from Elijah the Prophet, saying: "So says the Lord, God of David, your father: Since you have followed neither the ways of Jehoshaphat, your father, nor the ways of Asa, king of Judah; and you have followed the ways of the kings of Israel, and have caused Judah and the inhabitants of Jerusalem to become unfaithful, like the unfaithfulness of the House of Ahab; and you have also killed your paternal brothers, who were better than you; behold – God will strike your people and your children and your wives and all of your property with a great plague, and you will be greatly ill with an illness of the bowels, until your bowels fall out because of the illness." (vv. 12–15)

Later on in the same chapter, the text describes the complete fulfillment of this prophecy.

Many commentators note the fact that Jehoram's ascent to the throne of his father, Jehoshaphat, came several years after Elijah had already ascended to heaven. The earliest source to address this question is a midrash in *Seder Olam Rabba*, ch. 17:

> Ahaziah son of Ahab reigned two years, and in the second year of Ahaziah's reign, Elijah was taken up.… Then, when Jehoshaphat died, Jehoram took the throne… "a letter came to him from Elijah" – it had already been *seven years* since Elijah's passing.

The early commentators do not note an exact number of years, but they prove, from the chronology of the events, that in the time of Jehoshaphat, Jehoram's father, Elisha was already the generation's prophet, having succeeded Elijah. Clearly, then, the reign of Jehoram came after Elijah had ascended to heaven. The Ibn Ezra comments as follows, on the concluding verse of Malachi (3:24):

> I now conclude the commentary on this book with the matter of Elijah [mentioned in the previous verse]. We find that he lived during the time of Ahaziah son Ahab, and it is written that Jehoram ben Ahab, as well as Jehoshaphat, inquired of Elisha the Prophet. It is written there (in II Kings 3:11), "Here is Elisha, son of Shafat, who poured water over the hands of Elijah." This indicates that [Elijah] had already ascended in a storm to heaven, for the text does not say: pours water [in the present tense]; furthermore, Elisha did not part from Elijah, after attending him, until Elijah's ascent. Here we find written, after the death of Jehoshaphat, in the days of his son Jehoram: "A letter came to him from Elijah the Prophet." This tells us that *then* [after his ascent], Elijah wrote to him and sent to him. Had the letter been written

prior to his ascent, the text would have said: He found [a letter], or: a letter came to him that Elijah had left behind. There is also no doubt that in the days of our holy Sages he was seen. May God in His mercy speed his prophecy and soon bring about his coming.

Radak summarizes the Ibn Ezra's words in his own commentary on Chronicles, and Ralbag adopts a similar logical argument, elaborating on two elements that are necessary to prove this point:

1. Elijah's spirit rested on Elisha, making him prophet in his stead, only after he was taken from him, as becomes clear from an examination of what is written in the book of Kings. Then, Elisha was anointed as prophet in place of Elijah, as God had told Elijah (I Kings 19:16). That verse also tells us that he would become a prophet only when Elijah ceased to be a prophet.
2. If we do not accept this assumption [that Elijah's letter was written after his ascent] then we are forced to posit that Elijah prophesied, before this death, that this would be the case [that Jehoram would kill his brothers] and that this would already make him liable for the punishment noted (II Chr. 21:14–15). However, we cannot propose this, for were it so, the punishment for the sin would have been decreed before the person had sinned, and he would have no choice but to sin. This contradicts all the roots of the Torah.

What can we conclude from all this?

Ralbag uses this as proof for his exegetical approach to Elijah's ascent in the book of Kings:

It should be clear from this that Elijah did not die when he was taken from over Elisha's head.... It is clear that this letter, which came from Elijah to Jehoram son of Jehoshaphat after the death of Jehoshaphat, was after Elijah had been taken from over Elisha's head. Once this matter is clear, it turns out that Elijah was, of necessity, alive at the time when Jehoram killed his brothers, which was after he had been taken from over Elisha's head.... Thus we find no indication that Elijah died ... and his life was wondrously extended, in a miraculous way, as we noted in the book of Kings.

According to the Ḥatam Sofer, too, Elijah's letter presents no problem: The angel Elijah was sent to write the letter of rebuke to Jehoram son of Jehoshaphat, and for this purpose he was revealed in "this world."

But how does Radak explain the matter? To his view, we recall, Elijah's "ascent" was simply a special manner of death. How, then, could Elijah have written this letter after his own death? Radak explains:

> "A letter came to him from Elijah the Prophet" – this was after he had ascended. What this means is that Elijah was revealed in a prophetic vision to one of the prophets, and he put in his mouth the words of this letter and told him to write them in a letter and to bring the letter to Jehoram. Then [the prophet] told [Jehoram] that this letter had been sent to him by Elijah, in order that Jehoram would think that the letter had come to him from the heavens; he would feel remorse knowing that he had performed great evil.

This is difficult to understand. Where do we find any instance of the spirit of a dead prophet appearing to a living prophet, placing words of prophecy in his mouth, and even going so far as to command him to perform certain actions? Prophecy is supposed to be a connection between God and the prophet, with no one else involved.

It seems, then, that the book of Chronicles presents the earliest instance of Elijah's revelation which occurs not very long after his ascent. This also serves to strengthen the impression created by the literal text in the book of Kings, that Elijah does not die. However we interpret the details of his ascent, what the text appears to be telling us is that Elijah continues to exist even afterward, and obviously his existence has a purpose: He is entrusted to continue his role as an active force in the reality of human history. Here, in Chronicles, his role seems to complement his mission throughout the book of Kings: He is the prophet who rebukes the House of Ahab and foretells its end. Indeed, in his commentary on Chronicles, Malbim writes:

"A letter from Elijah" – this was after he had been taken, and it appears that he is still alive, appearing in this world from time to time, as accepted in the traditions of the Sages. Since Elijah foretold the end of the House of Ahab, and since [Jehoram son of Jehoshaphat] was Ahab's son-in-law, his prophecy applied to him too, such that he would be included in the death of the House of Ahab.

Elijah's Mission in the Book of Malachi

In Elijah's next appearance in Tanakh, he is given an entirely different mission:

> Remember the Torah of Moses, My servant, whom I commanded at Horeb for all of Israel, statutes and judgments. Behold, I shall send to you Elijah the Prophet before the coming of the great and awesome Day of God. He shall restore the heart of fathers to their children, and the heart of children to their fathers – lest I come and strike the land with a curse. (Mal. 3:22–24)

These are the last words of prophecy recorded in Tanakh, concluding the period of prophecy both in the sense of being uttered by Malachi, the last of the prophets chronologically, and in the sense of their location at the end of the book of Twelve Prophets, the final volume of the division of Tanakh known as "Prophets."

The Malbim offers the following explanation as to the connection between the exhortation in verse 22, "Remember the Torah of Moses, My servant," and the two verses that follow:

> By concluding his prophecy with these words – representing the last prophecy, following which no prophet or seer will prophesy until the End Times – he tells them that from now on they should not expect to attain God's word through prophecy; they should only remember Moses's Torah, to do all that is written in it, and it will instruct them as to what to do. "Behold I shall send…": [Meaning, that the above applies] until just prior to the coming of the great Day of God, when prophecy will return to [the Jewish

nation] through the greatest of the prophets, Elijah the Prophet, who will then be revealed.

This is not the only place in Tanakh where a person who has lived and died reappears at a later time. Jeremiah utters the following prophecy:

> So says the Lord: A voice is heard in Rama, wailing and bitter weeping – Rachel is crying for her children; she refuses to be comforted for her children, for they are gone. So says the Lord: Keep your voice from weeping and your eyes from tears, for there is a reward for your actions, says God, and they shall return from the land of the enemy. And there is hope for your end, says God, and the children will return to their border. (Jer. 31:14–16)

Here, however, at least on the literal level, we must concur with Rabbi Yosef Kara, that "this is not said to Rachel, the wife of Jacob, in the literal sense." Malbim comments, "The text depicts Rachel as the matriarch of the children, crying out over her two sons who are exiled."

Similarly, we find King David mentioned in some prophecies about the redemption:

> "Thereafter, the Israelites will repent and seek the Lord, their God, and David, their king." (Hos. 3:5)
> "And My servant, David, will be king over them, and there will be a single shepherd for them all." (Ezek. 37:24)

These prophets are clearly not referring to David himself, but rather to one of his descendants, whose name is as yet unknown to us; therefore, he is referred to by the name of his ancestor, founder of the Davidic dynasty.

In the verse in the book of Malachi, by contrast, Elijah is invoked not in the metaphorical sense; nor as a literary depiction; nor as the founder of a dynasty, such that his name could be used with reference to one of the prophets that come later. Here, Malachi is talking about an actual appearance of Elijah, and a specific, defined mission that he must fulfill. Admittedly, this mission will be carried out toward the End of Days, but still within human and historical reality, and the mission is clear: He must "restore the heart of the fathers to the sons, and the heart of the sons to their fathers." What is the meaning of this appearance of Elijah before the coming of God's great Day? Was he not taken up in a storm to the heavens?

Once again, the text provides support for our understanding of the narrative in Kings as indicating that Elijah did not die. He still has tasks to fulfill, both in his own generation (as recorded in II Chr. 21:12–15) and at the End of Days (as prophesied by Malachi).

In the interval between these two missions, Elijah appears frequently to the Sages, as recorded at length in talmudic and midrashic literature as well as later works.

Once again we ask: How does Radak explain these verses in Malachi? We recall that according to his understanding of the book of Kings, Elijah died. How, then, can he appear in the future as a prophet sent before the great Day of God? Radak explains:

> "Behold, I shall send you": For your benefit I shall send you Elijah the Prophet. What this means is that God will restore his soul, which has ascended to heaven, to a body, created like his original body. For his original body had returned to the ground, with his ascent, each element returning to its place. After reviving him in a body, God will send him to Israel before the Day of Judgment, which is the "great and awesome Day of God," and he will adjure fathers and children alike to repent and return to God with all their hearts.

Thus, according to Radak, there will be a "revival of the dead" for Elijah alone. He will arise and carry out the mission of restoring the hearts of the fathers to the children. But here we must ask, why could God not appoint a prophet of that future generation to carry out the task? And if, for whatever reason, there is a specific need for a prophet from the early generations, why is it Elijah who is miraculously revived, rather than some other prophet – Moses, perhaps, or Isaiah?

Is it coincidental that only Elijah appears and is active after leaving this world – in dispatching a letter to Jehoram son of Jehoshaphat, and in coming to Israel before the coming of the great Day of God? Can we deny the clear connection between that which is written in the books of Chronicles and Malachi, and the description of Elijah being taken up *live* to the heavens? Sometimes, the meaning of a source cannot be clarified from its own context alone. The two opaque sources in question, in Chronicles and in Malachi, are examples. It would be difficult to understand these sources, discussing a prophet who has already left this world, without going back to the nature of that prophet, and especially the manner in which he left the world. There lies the key to understanding his reappearance later on. One prophecy connects to the other, each sheds light on the other, and they lead to a single conclusion: Elijah did not die.

It would seem that this connection between the description of Elijah's ascent to heaven in the book of Kings and his future appearance prior to the Day of God in Malachi, as well as the perception of the whole as a deliberate divine plan, is noted already in the Apocryphal *Sefer Ben Sira* (48:9–10): "He was taken on high in a storm, and with the heavenly troops of fire. Written as ready for the time to cut off fury before anger, to restore the heart of fathers to children and to prepare the tribes of Israel."

Moses Tzvi Segal explains in his edition of *Ben Sira*: "The subject of the word 'written' is Elijah...in other words, the one about whom it is written that he is ready for the End Times, which is the Day of God." Where is it written concerning Elijah that he is ready and waiting for the End Times? The answer to this lies in the connection drawn by Ben Sira between the fact that Elijah is taken up in a storm and troops of fire to heaven, and his appearance in the book of Malachi at the End of Days. It shows that he is taken in this manner precisely so that he will be ready, from that time until the time of the Redemption, to prepare the tribes of Israel for the End of Days, and this intention is as clear as though it had been explicitly written in the text.

Concerning Elijah's appearance in book of Malachi, too, it is not necessary to accept Ralbag's literal explanation, contending that Elijah lives on and is hidden from sight until the time of his revelation. Rather, we may return to the more complex view of the Ḥatam Sofer, who maintains that Elijah did not die like any normal person, but rather turned into an angel. Since then, he stands ready to perform missions entrusted to him at various times. Sometimes he executes these missions in a "spiritual" manner; at other times, in his bodily garb.

This interpretation, viewing Elijah after his ascent as an "angel," is given further support from book of Malachi itself. At the beginning of that same prophecy (Mal. 3:1–3), we find a description that bears several parallels to this conclusion:

v. 1: *Behold, I shall send*	v. 23: *Behold, I shall send* to you
My angel (malakhi),	*Elijah the Prophet,*
and he shall clear a path *before Me,*	*before the coming*
and suddenly God whom you seek will come to His Temple. And the angel of the covenant (*malakh habrit*) in whom you delight – behold, he shall come, says the God of Hosts.	of the great and awesome Day of God.
v. 2: But who can bear the day of his coming, and who shall be standing when he appears? For he is like a refiner's fire and like the washers' soap.	
v. 3: And he shall sit (*veyashav*) like a refiner and purifier of silver, and shall purify the sons of Levi, and purge them like gold and like silver, and they shall offer to God an offering in righteousness.	v. 24: He shall restore (*veheshiv*) the heart of fathers to their children, and the heart of children to their fathers – lest I come and strike the land with a curse.

On the basis of this parallel, some commentators have identified Elijah, who is sent before the Day of God, as the angel of God who is sent to clear a path for God, before He suddenly comes to His Temple. Elijah, then, is "the angel of the covenant."

Rabbi Yosef Kara offers the following commentary on verse 23 at the end of Malachi: "This explains what is written before, 'Behold, I shall send My angel, and he shall clear a path before Me.'" Radak, too, raises this as a possible explanation: "He says 'angel of the covenant' with reference to Elijah."

Admittedly, in the above presentation of the two prophecies, we note a vast difference between the purpose of the appearance of the angel of the covenant (to purify and purge the children of Levi with fire) and the purpose of Elijah's appearance (to restore the hearts of fathers to children). Possibly, the tension between the implications of the beginning of the chapter and the implications of its conclusion (assuming that both are speaking about Elijah) is what gives rise to the tannaitic discussion recorded in the final mishna (8:7) of Tractate Eduyot. The nature of the coming of the "angel of the covenant" at the beginning of the prophecy presents a difficulty: He comes in order to purge people, the children of Levi (the priests), with fire, to reveal the purity of their lineage, and it will be difficult to withstand the day of his coming. Elijah, at the end of the same prophecy, comes to make peace between fathers and children, thereby preventing God's curse from striking the land. The Mishna teaches:

> R. Yehoshua said: I learned from Rabban Yoḥanan ben Zakkai, who in turn heard it from his teacher, and his teacher from the teacher before him, all the way back to Moses at Sinai, that Elijah does not come to declare people impure or pure, nor to distance people or bring them close, but rather to distance those who have come close by force, and to draw near those who have been distanced by force.
>
> R. Yehuda said: To bring close, but not to distance.
>
> R. Shimon says: To solve (halakhic) disputes.
>
> The Sages said: Neither to distance nor to bring close, but rather to make peace in the world. As it is written, "Behold, I shall send to you Elijah the Prophet … and he will restore the heart of fathers to children, and the heart of children to their fathers."

REVELATIONS OF ELIJAH IN LEGEND: THE TRANSFORMATION

Thus far, we have seen that the description of Elijah's ascent in a storm to heaven is meant to tell us that Elijah did not die as all people do, but rather is destined to continue his mission in various ways. The prophecy of his future appearance before the coming of the Day of God, therefore, rests upon the description of his ascent.

It seems that Elijah's appearances in talmudic times – a unique and unparalleled phenomenon – similarly rests on the description of his ascent in the book of Kings. His revelation to the Sages fills in the void that stretches from his revelation in the letter to Jehoram son of Jehoshaphat, just a few years after his ascent, to his revelation in the future, before the coming of the great Day of God. However, his revelations to the Sages are more than just a timely "fill-in" between two distant eras. They are also a fill-in in terms of the nature of his appearance. The nature of his message in the letter to Jehoram matches his biblical image as molded in all of the narratives in earlier chapters: The prophet rebuking the House of Ahab. His future revelation, by contrast, depicts him as a prophet foretelling the great redemption and "making peace in the world." His revelation in rabbinical literature is a contrast to each of these images. Elijah's role in talmudic and midrashic literature (and even later sources) is to save individuals from various states of distress, to clear up misunderstandings and quarrels between people, and to be Israel's great advocate before their Father in heaven.

The scope of this chapter does not allow for a comprehensive or even general review of the huge quantity of material concerning Elijah's appearances in rabbinical literature, from the time of the Sages until our own era. We shall therefore suffice with a few characteristic examples, drawn from A. Margaliyot's work.[1] We have divided the sources cited there into three spheres in which Elijah's great transformation is manifest in aggadic literature, in contrast with his biblical prophetic image.

1. First, let us see how Elijah is perceived in Aggada after his ascent, when he is *not* manifest in our world. What is he doing in heaven? What is he engaged in?

Seder Olam Rabba (ch. 17) offers the following answer: "And in the second year of Ahaziah, Elijah passed away…and now he inscribes the doings (*maaseh*) of all generations." Does this mean to say that Elijah engages in the occupation of the author of *Seder Olam Rabba* himself, chronicling Jewish history? Perhaps this is indeed the intention. However, it seems

---

1. *Elijah the Prophet in Jewish Literature, Faith, and Spiritual Life* [Hebrew] (Jerusalem, 5720).

more likely that it is referring to the good deeds (*maasim tovim*) of generations of Jews, as reflected in a different aggada:

> Previously, a person would perform a mitzva and the prophet would inscribe it; now, a person performs a mitzva – and who inscribes it? Elijah and King Messiah; and the Holy One, blessed be He, signs it for them. (Leviticus Rabba 34:8)

The same idea is echoed by Maharil, at the end of his Laws of Shabbat, in the name of Maharash (Rabbi Shalom of Ostreich):

> The reason for the custom to recite the verses about Elijah and songs about him on Saturday night is because it is written in the Torah[2] that on Saturday night, Elijah sits beneath the Tree of Life and inscribes the merits of those who observe Shabbat.

On special occasions too, according to the Midrash, Elijah serves as Israel's advocate in heaven: "When the Holy One, blessed be He, shakes His world, Elijah recalls the merit of the patriarchs… and the Holy One, blessed be He, is filled with compassion for His world" (Genesis Rabba 71:9).

In Midrash Esther Rabba 7, Elijah is described as calling upon the patriarchs and Moses to save the Jews from Haman's decree, and as the one who notifies Mordekhai of "all that was done (*naasa*)" (Est. 4:1).

2. Let us now turn our attention from Elijah's activities in heaven to some of his revelations in the world, most of which describe his kindness for the needy or for the nation as a whole. For the sake of brevity we shall merely hint at some of the most famous of his revelations, noting sources for further study:

- Elijah appears as Harbona and tells Ahasuerus (Est. 7:9), "Here also are the gallows which Haman made for Mordekhai" (Esther Rabba 10:9).

---

2. Margaliyot notes in his book (p. 19, n. 68), that he finds no source for this in either the Tosefta or in the *Tosafot*.

- Elijah is revealed to R. Eliezer ben Horkanus, weeping and afflicted, and advises him to go up to Jerusalem to study Torah with Rabban Yoḥanan ben Zakkai (*Pirkei DeRabbi Eliezer*, ch. 1).
- Elijah comes to the rescue of Naḥum Ish Gam Zu, in his mission to the caesar (Taanit 21a).
- Elijah comforts R. Akiva and his wife, daughter of Kalba Savua, when he is revealed to them as a destitute old man, requesting that they give him straw for his wife, who has just given birth (Nedarim 50a).
- Elijah stands at the entrance to the cave where R. Shimon bar Yochai is hiding and notifies him of the caesar's death and the annulment of his decree (Shabbat 33b).
- Elijah heals R. Yehuda HaNasi's toothache, thereby restoring peace between him and R. Ḥiyya (Y. Kilayim 9:3, 32b, and parallel versions).
- In several later sources there are stories of Elijah appearing to anonymous individuals in distress and coming to their aid.[3]

3. A separate category includes all of Elijah's debates with various Sages in matters of Torah, halakha, and *mussar*. In the famous story of the oven of Akhnai (Bava Metzia 59b), Elijah reveals to the Sages what goes on in heaven. After the heavenly voice emerges, declaring that R. Eliezer's interpretation of the law is correct, the rest of the Sages refuse to accept this verdict, since the law is not decided on the basis of heavenly voices. R. Natan then encounters Elijah:

> He said to him: "What did the Holy One, blessed be He, do at that moment [when they overruled the heavenly voice]?" [Elijah] said to him: "He smiled and said, 'My children have prevailed over Me; My children have prevailed over Me.'"

One of the Sages who converses regularly – daily, even – with Elijah is R. Yehoshua b. Levi. The Jerusalem Talmud (Terumot 8:4, 46b) recounts

---

3. Two such stories are to be found in Midrash Ruth Zuta (1:20, 4:11).

how the Romans sentence to death a man named Ulla bar Kushav, and he flees to Lod, the city of R. Yehoshua b. Levi. The Romans threaten to destroy the entire city if Ulla bar Kushav is not handed over to them. R. Yehoshua b. Levi convinces Ulla to surrender and hands him over, and Elijah stops appearing to him. R. Yehoshua b. Levi then takes upon himself a number of fasts, until Elijah reappears:

> [Elijah] said to him: "Am I then revealing myself to one who hands Jews over to non-Jewish rulers?" He answered: "Did I not act in accordance with the law?" He replied: "Is this how pious people behave?"

This story is a typical example of Elijah chiding the Sages when they do not act charitably toward common people. In these stories, Elijah is depicted as sternly admonishing, but his severity is expressed in criticism for those Sages who do not pass the test of complete love of the Jewish people, as he demands of them.

This may shed light on the following account, recorded in Sanhedrin 113a–b:

> R. Yosei taught, in Tzippori: "Father Elijah is strict." Elijah used to come to him, but he then disappeared for three days and did not come. When he came, he said to him: "Why did my lord not come?" He said: "You called me strict." He replied: "This itself is proof that my lord is strict!"

R. Yosei's evaluation of Elijah is correct – but not completely, for it fails to take into account the change in his character since the days of Ahab. It is not the same strictness that characterizes him in the Tanakh, directed toward the Israelites. His sternness is now expressed on their behalf, and it is always directed against the sages and leaders of Israel. Elijah is no longer strict toward the simple people at all! Therefore, Elijah chides R. Yosei this time too, for his failure to discern this. While his response does indeed represent further proof of his strictness, it also clarifies whom the reproach is directed against, as well as the reason for the reproach: R. Yosei's failure to note the great transformation that Elijah has undergone since the days of the Tanakh.

It should further be noted that Elijah continues to appear to great Torah scholars long after the talmudic period, and legends abound describing his appearances during the period of the *Geonim, Rishonim* and even *Aḥaronim*, to masters of Torah, Kabbala, and Ḥasidut.

Accounts of Elijah's appearance to help people in distress or to be present at moments of spiritual upliftment have been passed down orally and in writing to the present day. In this connection, we may note the relatively new custom in some communities of placing a "cup for Elijah" on the Seder table, in honor of Elijah the Prophet, who visits Jewish houses on that night.

We conclude this discussion by referring the reader back to A. Margaliyot who, in his brief introduction (pp. 8–11), summarizes the main characteristics of Elijah's appearances over the generations.

The point of the above review is to arrive at the great question that is formulated quite clearly by the scholar A. Kaminka:

> These are two seemingly different faces, far removed from one another and with no relationship between them: the Elijah of the Tanakh, and the Elijah of Aggada. Elijah of the Tanakh is the angry prophet, the great zealot…: "I have been very zealous for Lord, God of Hosts, for the Israelites have forsaken Your covenant" (I Kings 19:10, 14). However, by the end of the books of the Prophets, what seems to be an entirely new tradition grows around him. The image of Elijah in later Aggada starts to become manifest (Mal. 3:23): "Behold, I send you Elijah the Prophet." This Elijah who, at first glance, appears to have a fundamentally different character from, and no connection to, the great prophet zealous for God and for justice in the world, is already, by the time of the ancient Mishna, at the end of the Second Temple Period…a sort of angel of God…ready to make peace throughout the world.[4]

---

4. Kaminka, "Elijah the Prophet in the Bible and in Aggada," in *Kitvei Bikoret Historit* (New York, 5704), 12–13.

After citing various examples from Aggada, presenting Elijah in sharp contrast to the biblical description, he again asks:

> Are these truly different faces – the zealous prophet of the Bible…
> and the Elijah of Aggada, who is merciful, good and beneficent,
> recalling only the merits of Israel? We cannot assert this, since
> already at the end of Malachi we find the connection between
> the two faces, with the promise that Elijah will come to "restore
> the heart of fathers to their children, and the heart of children
> to their fathers" (Mal. 3:24). There can be no doubt that this is
> one single historical and aggadic personality.

We shall address this important question further in the next section.

UNIQUENESS OF ELIJAH'S ASCENT AND CONTINUED APPEARANCES

The commentators – and we, too, in their wake – are so deeply immersed in the question of *what* happens when Elijah is taken up in a storm to heaven, that the more important question of *why* he is taken in a manner so different from the deaths of other people is pushed to the sidelines.

Abrabanel formulates the question as follows:

> Still, why is Elijah taken in this surprising way, remaining alive
> in body and soul in the Garden of Eden? Why does he not die
> like Moses, "the dust returning to the earth, as it had been" (Eccl.
> 12:7); why was he not buried in the dust like the other prophets?
> Among our early and later sages alike I find no attention, either
> extensive or brief, in connection with this matter.

Abrabanel goes on to offer three explanations; we cite here only the third:

> The third reason comes from the *purpose*…. Elijah is going to
> appear many times in the future, to prophets, esteemed pious
> people, or the Sages of Israel in their study halls, as well as in the
> time of our Messiah, as it is written (Mal. 3:23–24), "Behold, I
> shall send to you Elijah the Prophet before the coming of the great

and awesome Day of God. He shall restore the heart of fathers to their children. ..." Since he is destined to show himself among people and to appear many times, he is taken in body and soul; he remains alive constantly, in his [full] constitution, to indicate that *he is still needed in this world.*

What Abrabanel says here is unquestionably true, and we have noted this above, by pointing out the connection between the description of Elijah's ascent to the heavens and his appearances later on, in Tanakh and elsewhere. However, the *theoretical* question that Abrabanel raises does not find its solution in his explanation. We may formulate the question thus: Why is Elijah taken in this surprising manner, remaining alive in order to reappear many times throughout Jewish history, up until his coming as the harbinger of the redemption? This happens to no other prophet, nor to any other personality in the Tanakh (or afterward); why does it happen to Elijah? Why is it necessary for Elijah to keep reappearing throughout history, until the redemption? Abrabanel's answer only adds to the question surrounding this unique phenomenon – a question that includes both the manner of Elijah's ascent and the fact of his reappearance later on.

The key to answering this puzzle lies, to our view, in a difficulty, which we have already addressed: The striking contrast between the image of Elijah that arises from the book of Kings and his alternative image, which begins to be formed already at the end of Tanakh (in the final verses of Malachi) and continues to develop over the course of Elijah's many appearances during the times of the Sages and later on. We noted the sharp contrast between the strict prophet waging a battle against Israel out of his zealousness for God, and the compassionate sage who loves Israel and defends them before their Father in heaven, directing his criticism toward those who are not sufficiently merciful toward the nation.

What is the connection between these two questions, and how does the one resolve the other?

It appears that Elijah's virulent, one-sided zealousness, as expressed in his first and most important appearance in the book of Kings (in the series of episodes in chapters 17–19 of I Kings: "I have been exceedingly zealous for the Lord God of Hosts," 19:10, 14), arouses criticism which finds expression in the biblical narrative itself, as well as in the teachings of the Sages, who interpret the verses in such a way as to highlight God's dissatisfaction. All of this was addressed at length in our discussions of those chapters, and we shall not repeat it here. We note only the *Mekhilta* (from the beginning of *Parashat Bo*), with its negative view of Elijah's one-sidedness, in comparison to another prophet, who fulfills his mission in a more complete way:

> We find that there are three prophets: one upholds the honor of the Father (God) and the honor of the son (Israel); one upholds the honor of the Father, but not the honor of the son; and one upholds the honor of the son, but not the honor of the Father.
>
> Jeremiah upholds the honor of the Father as well as the honor of the son...therefore his prophecy is doubled, as it says, "And there were added besides them many like words" (Jer. 36:32).
>
> Elijah upholds the honor of the Father, but not the honor of the son, as it is written, "I have been exceedingly zealous for Lord, God of Hosts" – and what is written there? "God said to him: 'Go, return to your way, to the wilderness of Damascus.... And Elisha son of Shafat...shall you anoint as prophet in your stead'" (19:15–16); this does not mean: as a prophet under you, but rather: ["in your stead," namely,] "I do not want your prophecy."
>
> Jonah upholds the honor of the son, but not the honor of the Father.... What is written? "And God's word came to Jonah a second time, saying..." (Jonah 3:1) – He speaks to him a second time, [but] not a third.

The prophet's task in Israel is a dual one: He must defend the honor of the Father, in his mission to His sons as God's prophet, but, no less important, he must also defend the honor and welfare of Israel, as their representative before God. The first time that the word *navi* (prophet) appears in the Torah, with reference to Abraham, it is used in this latter sense: "And now, restore the man's wife, for *he is a prophet; and he will pray for you, that you may live*" (Gen. 20:7).

The ultimate test of a prophet comes specifically in a sinful generation, where there is acute crisis in the relations between Israel and God. At such a time, there is a contradiction, as it were, between the two roles of the prophet, who is called upon to heal the rift and to serve as a go-between, giving alternate representation to the seemingly opposing sides. It is for this reason that the *Mekhilta* cites the example of Jeremiah, the prophet who is tragically torn between loyalty to his divine mission and his total love and dedication toward his people. Jeremiah (unlike Moses) does not succeed in his mission of bringing the nation back to God and restoring peace between the Father and His children, but this is not his fault. From the perspective of his own actions, Jeremiah acts properly; therefore God approves and "his prophecy is doubled."

However, when a prophet takes a one-sided view of his role, as though he identifies with only one side of the encounter, God has no desire for his prophetic mission to continue. "I do not want your prophecy," God tells Elijah, who is zealous for God and critical of Israel, God's nation; God sends him from before Him, in order to appoint a prophet in his stead. Likewise, Jonah – who, according to the midrash, defends the honor of the son (Israel) to the point where he refuses to undertake the divine mission to Nineveh – is punished with a termination of his prophecy after he completes his mission: "He spoke to him a second time, but not a third."

Like Jeremiah, Elijah lives in a generation of spiritual crisis. Israel is ruled by a powerful king who has given his foreign, pagan queen power over himself and his kingdom. Elijah chooses to approach his prophetic mission in this generation with complete zealousness for his Sender, while ignoring the other aspect of his role: showing compassion for his generation and defending them. When he stands before God at Mount Horeb, it becomes clear that Elijah's zealous approach is more than just a drastic prophetic tactic aimed at bringing the nation to repentance (as one may have argued in ch. 17). It reflects a one-sided identification of his role as God's messenger, to the point where he actually condemns Israel before God. It is not for this purpose that God has appointed him as a prophet, and since he is not fulfilling his role properly, his prophetic mission is brought to a premature conclusion.

Indeed, just as Elijah's first appearance is sudden and dramatic, in the midst of his activity, as it were, so his departure is surprising, inexplicable, and without any prior signs of failing strength: "And it was, when God took up Elijah in a storm to the heavens" (II Kings 2:1). Elijah does not complete his mission; he is taken in the midst of it. The story of his prophecy is one that ends in the middle.

Should Elijah's abrupt ascent be regarded as some sort of punishment for this zealous prophet? This seems unlikely, since Elijah's departure is not through death. Rather, Elijah will continue to be active throughout the reality of Jewish history in the generations to come, allowing him to amend the zealous prophetic approach that characterizes his activity as described in the book of Kings. This amendment will become possible when Elijah returns to his people and becomes aware of the great change that has taken place: This is no longer a nation "straddling the two options" (18:21) alternating between worshipping Baal and worshipping God; Ahab and Jezebel (and their like) are no longer the leaders. Instead of a strong nation dwelling securely in its land and exposing itself to pagan influences, Elijah encounters an abused people, suffering persecution and fighting to survive – precisely because of their stubborn loyalty to God. Then Elijah gathers his supernatural strength to help this persecuted nation and its individual members to withstand their struggle for survival. Instead of being zealous for God, as has been his way throughout the book of Kings, Elijah will now be zealous for the welfare of Israel, and he will act to that end. His arguments in heaven will also be reversed, and he will become Israel's defender before God. Thus he corrects and heals his path. His zealousness will now be whole and perfect, insofar as it will be directed to the welfare of Israel.

It is impossible for the image of this great prophet to remain as incomplete and one-sided as depicted in the book of Kings. That which Moses and Jeremiah merit to realize and fulfill during their lifetimes is completed by Elijah after his ascent to heaven, in his reappearances among Israel.[5]

---

5. Indeed, there are many people who do not complete their lifework during their lives, or whose achievements need rectification, yet these individuals have not been granted the chance to return to the world as Elijah was. However, one may not

Elijah's criticism of Israel reflects the perspective of a prophet living in a very specific generation. However, the prophet in his lifetime views only a very small portion of the historical reality. The truth about the nation is revealed to Elijah only over the course of all of the generations until the final redemption, as he encounters the nation in its future states. Elijah then acknowledges the unfairness of his criticism, and this acknowledgment is expressed in the very actions that he is destined to perform; namely, in his own turnaround.

It is not only the *tikkun* (rectification) of Elijah's way that is expressed in his reappearance after his ascent; the manner of his reappearance represents something of a retroactive cleansing of his image in Tanakh, amending the impression of him and of his motives that arises from the book of Kings. Thus we find in the midrash:

> It is said of Hosea and of Elijah that they were cruel. Heaven forbid! They were not cruel, for would a cruel person save [his victims]?...
>
> When Elijah saw the children of Israel straying after Ahab, he said: "It is better that they have three years of famine than fall into the bottomless pit." In other words, Elijah did this to them out of love. (*Pesikta Rabbati* 44, "*Shuva Yisrael*")

Admittedly, "Elijah did this [decreeing famine] to them out of love," but his love for them in the book of Kings is hidden, while his rebuke is overt and painful. He causes them real suffering, even if he does this out of caring and concern, and therefore people err and think that Elijah is cruel.

Elijah's reappearance shows that his heart burns with passion for Israel. His hidden love rises to the surface and is manifest to all; thus, his image is cleansed and his motives clarified – retroactively.

---

compare them to Elijah. First, we are talking of one of the greatest personalities in Tanakh, a prophet closely connected to Moses, the master of all prophets. Second, stopping his prophetic activity prior to its completion, and returning to Israel later, was designed to teach a lesson not only to Elijah himself, but also to his followers and the whole nation. This lesson relates to the shaping of a fitting attitude toward Israel even when the nation is in an abject state. The lesson is primarily meant for Israel's prophets and leaders.

Thus, it turns out that the contrast between Elijah's portrayal in the Aggada and his portrayal in the book of Kings reflects necessary correction and repair. It is the key and the solution to the question of his wondrous ascent, live, to the heavens, as well as to the question of his reappearance over the course of all generations.

ELIJAH'S *TIKKUN*

We conclude this series with an illustration of the idea (set forth explicitly in the Aggada) of the *tikkun* (rectification) expressed in Elijah's appearance in later generations,

In Elijah's criticism of the nation at Mount Horeb – "I have been exceedingly zealous for the Lord God of Hosts, for Israel has forsaken Your covenant... and I alone remain, and they seek my life, to take it" (I Kings 19:10, 14) – the prophet gives voice to his sense of doom: The Israelites have forsaken God's covenant, and there is no other prophet who can bring them back to the proper path. Even Elijah himself is no longer able to do this! The situation is hopeless; it cannot be fixed.

The midrashic literature reveals the *tikkun* for this pessimism: Elijah's continued activity and his frequent appearances on earth after his ascent to heaven. In *Seder Olam Rabba*, chapter 17, Elijah is depicted as follows, after his ascent: "He inscribes the doings of all the generations (*maaseh hadorot kullam*)."

Elijah testifies to the continuity of the generations of Israel. The chain of the generations is not broken, and Elijah himself is responsible for documenting this fact. Of course, the source of this concept (of Elijah's responsibility for the connection between the generations) is to be found in the prophecy of Malachi (3:23–24): "Behold, I shall send to you Elijah the Prophet.... He shall restore the hearts of fathers to children, and the hearts of children to their fathers."

Thus, Elijah – who formerly accuses Israel of forsaking the covenant with God, causing a rift in the course of the generations – is responsible for the healing of this very rift. It is he who connects the generations together and unifies them, with a single heart, to return to God.

Elijah's criticism of Israel is given clear expression in *Pirkei DeRabbi Eliezer*, at the end of chapter 28:

And this is how Israel would practice circumcision, until they split into two kingdoms, and the rulers of Ephraim (the Northern Kingdom) prevented them from performing the covenant of circumcision. Elijah, of blessed memory, arose and was exceedingly zealous, swearing that the heavens would not drop "dew or rain" upon the earth (I Kings 17:1).... The Holy One, blessed be He, appeared to him and said (19:9): "What are you doing here, Elijah?" He answered (19:10) "I have been exceedingly zealous..." The Holy One, blessed be He, said: "Will you be zealous forever.... By your life, Israel will (henceforth) perform no circumcision without you seeing it with your own eyes." On this basis, the Sages ruled that a place of honor should be set aside for the "messenger of the covenant (*brit*)," as it is written (Mal. 3:1), "And the messenger of the covenant, in whom you delight – behold, he shall come...." May the God of Israel bring the Messiah speedily in our days to comfort us, and may he renew our hearts, as it is written, "He shall restore the hearts of fathers to children."

A similar theme is echoed in the Zohar (*Lekh Lekha* 93a):

Behold – first it is written, "What are you doing here, Elijah?" and it is written, "I have been exceedingly zealous... for Israel has forsaken Your covenant." The Holy One, blessed be He, said to Elijah: "By your life, wherever My children will engrave this holy impression, the covenant of circumcision, upon their flesh, you will be there. And the mouth that testified that Israel had forsaken the covenant will testify in the future that Israel observes this covenant. As we have learned: "Why was Elijah punished by God? For having slandered His children." (Zohar, *Lekh Lekha* 93a)

All that we have said is included in the above words, which are also the source for the customs of having a "chair for Elijah" at a circumcision and of addressing Elijah as a participant in the ceremony. God rebukes Elijah, "Will you remain zealous forever?" – and the *tikkun*, rectification, of this attribute of the prophet is his future constant appearance at every circumcision. On the one hand, his personal witnessing of the event is a negation of his accusation (and thus a continuation of God's "dispute" with him). On the other hand, Elijah is a guest of honor; he certainly "will recall this merit before God," and this will be a "rectification of his accusation" (quoting the language of Rabbi David Luria, a commentator on *Pirkei DeRabbi Eliezer*). As the Zohar asserts, "The mouth that testified that Israel had forsaken the covenant will testify in the future that Israel observes this covenant." Elijah's accusation of "they have forsaken Your covenant (*brit*)" is interpreted here in relation to circumcision (*brit mila*), which connects fathers to their sons; therefore, it is Elijah who must be present and testify that the covenant is alive and healthy and being maintained from generation to generation. His presence at every circumcision (as well as at every Seder table, where fathers fulfill the commandment to recount the events of the Exodus to their children, Ex. 13:8) is in preparation for and anticipation of his great mission of restoring the hearts of fathers to children, and the hearts of children to their fathers.

Other Books in the *Maggid Tanakh Companions* Series

To This Very Day:
Fundamental Questions in Bible Study
Amnon Bazak

Textual Tapestries:
Explorations of the Five Megillot
Gabriel Cohn

Places in the Parasha:
Biblical Geography and Its Meaning
Yoel Elitzur

Creation: The Story of Beginnings
Jonathan Grossman

Abraham: The Story of a Journey (forthcoming)
Jonathan Grossman

Subversive Sequels in the Bible:
How Biblical Stories Mine and Undermine Each Other
Judy Klitsner

Tribal Blueprints:
Twelve Brothers and the Destiny of Israel
Nechama Price

The fonts used in this book are from the Arno family

Maggid Books
The best of contemporary Jewish thought from
Koren Publishers Jerusalem Ltd.